SHAREHOLDER ACTIVISM IN BELGIUM

strada lex

How to active a book online
Identification code

02822-INTERS702822-78233-0055

If you have a subscription to our database Strada lex **www.stradalex.com**, Strada lex Luxembourg **www.stradalex.lu**, or Strada lex Europe **www.stradalex.eu** you could activate the digital version of this book* for free by entering the identification code mentioned above.

When a problem occurs during the activation, you could contact our helpdesk: tel. : **+32(0)2 548 07 20** · fax : **+32(0)2 548 07 22** · **info**@**stradalex.com**. You will be asked for a proof of purchase.

The identification code can only be used once by one user subscribed to Strada lex. Once activated the book can only be consulted in Strada lex, keeping into account the terms of the subscription.

You have not yet a subscription to our databases and you would like some more information or a presentation by on of our representatives? Please contact us at the following e-mail address: info@stradalex.com.

*If the book is included in one of the mentioned databases.

SHAREHOLDER ACTIVISM IN BELGIUM

Boon or curse for sustainable value creation?

Arie Van Hoe
Tom Vos

Cambridge – Antwerp – Chicago

Intersentia Ltd
8 Wellington Mews | Wellington Street
Cambridge | CB1 1HW | United Kingdom
Tel.: +44 1223 736 170
Email: mail@intersentia.co.uk
www.intersentia.com | www.intersentia.co.uk

Distribution for the UK and the rest of the world (incl. Eastern Europe):
NBN International
1 Deltic Avenue, Rooksley
Milton Keynes MK13 8LD
United Kingdom
Tel.: +44 1752 202 301 | Fax: +44 1752 202 331
Email: orders@nbninternational.com

Distribution for Europe:
Lefebvre Sarrut Belgium NV
Hoogstraat 139/6
1000 Brussels
Belgium
Tel.: +32 3 680 15 50 | Fax: +32 3 658 71 21
Email: mail@intersentia.be

Distribution for the USA and Canada:
Independent Publishers Group
Order Department
814 North Franklin Street
Chicago, IL60610
USA
Tel.: +1 800 888 4741 (toll free) | Fax: +1312 337 5985
Email: orders@ipgbook.com

Shareholder Activism in Belgium. Boon or curse for sustainable value creation?
© Arie Van Hoe and Tom Vos 2023

The author has asserted the right under the Copyright, Designs and Patents Act 1988, to be identified as author of this work.

No part of this book may be reproduced, stored in a retrieval system, or transmitted, in any form, or by any means, without prior written permission from Intersentia, or as expressly permitted by law or under the terms agreed with the appropriate reprographic rights organisation. Enquiries concerning reproduction which may not be covered by the above should be addressed to Intersentia at the address above.

Cover image: © Danny Juchtmans / www.dsigngraphics.be

ISBN 978-1-83970-282-2
D/2023/7849/157
NUR 827

British Library Cataloguing in Publication Data. A catalogue record for this book is available from the British Library.

CONTENTS

Introduction xiii

Setting the Scene: The Characteristics, Causes and Consequences of Shareholder Activism
      Tom Vos 1

1. Introduction 1
2. Defining shareholder activism 2
   - 2.1. Traditional shareholder activism versus ESG shareholder activism 3
   - 2.2. The type of activist: hedge fund, other institutional investors, retail investors and NGOs 4
   - 2.3. No shareholder activism: short-seller activism and external stakeholder activism 9
3. The characteristics of shareholder activism 10
   - 3.1. The characteristics of hedge fund activism 11
   - 3.2. The characteristics of other types of shareholder activism ... 15
4. Explaining different levels of shareholder activism across countries 19
   - 4.1. Differences in the size of the stock market 20
   - 4.2. Differences in shareholder rights 21
   - 4.3. Differences in shareholder structures 24
   - 4.4. Differences in securities laws 26
   - 4.5. Difference in the market capitalization of corporations ... 32
   - 4.6. Differences in stock market liquidity 34
   - 4.7. Differences in culture 34
   - 4.8. Differences in the number of shareholder proposals ... 35
5. The economic consequences of shareholder activism 38
   - 5.1. The economic consequences of hedge fund activism for shareholder value 38
   - 5.2. The economic consequences of hedge fund activism for other stakeholders 42
   - 5.3. The economic consequences of other types of shareholder activism 44
6. Conclusion 46

ESG-Focused Hedge Fund Activism
Anna CHRISTIE 49

1. Introduction 49
2. ESG Hedge Fund Activism. 50
   2.1. Origins of ESG Hedge Fund Activism 50
   2.2. A Pivotal Moment for ESG Hedge Fund Activism 52
3. A Framework of ESG Hedge Fund Activism. 55
   3.1. Types of ESG Hedge Fund Campaigns 55
   3.2. ESG Activist Hedge Fund Players 62
   3.3. The Promise and Limitations of ESG Hedge Fund Activism 63
4. The Role of Global Asset Managers and Other Institutional
   Investors in ESG-Focused Activism. 65
   4.1. Collaboration and Voting 65
   4.2. Portfolio-wide Campaigns and Engagement 67
5. Conclusion 69

Shareholder Stewardship and Sustainability – The Current European Legal Framework and Possible Ways Ahead
Marleen OCH 71

1. Introduction 71
2. Conceptualising Stewardship 73
   2.1. Shareholder Stewardship in Contrast to Shareholder Activism . . . 73
   2.2. Origins and Varieties. 75
3. Legal Framework 78
   3.1. SRD II. 78
       3.1.1. Overview 78
       3.1.2. Scope and objective 79
       3.1.3. Engagement and Investment Policy 80
       3.1.4. Enforcement and Application in Practice 81
   3.2. Stewardship Codes. 81
4. Analysis. 84
   4.1. Controlling Shareholders 84
   4.2. Incentives for Institutional Investors 87
   4.3. Investor Cooperation. 91
   4.4. Disclosure and Monitoring. 94
5. Conclusion 96

Towards a political corporation? NGOs as ESG shareholder activists and litigators influencing corporate strategies in continental Europe
Hans DE WULF 99

I. Introducing the main themes of this Chapter: There is a tension resulting from contradictory regulatory choices in company law in the EU 99
II. Three court cases to illustrate current trends 108
    1. ClientEarth v. Shell directors 108
    2. NGO due diligence litigation against TotalEnergies 110
    3. Boskalis/Fugro: the Dutch don't like shareholder proposals 113
III. From shareholders pursuing ESG goals to NGOs becoming shareholder activists 115
    1. Traditional and ESG shareholder activism 115
    2. NGOs using shareholder activism tactics to press for ESG change at corporations 117
    3. Halo activism 122
IV. Empirical research on NGO-sponsored ESG shareholder proposals in Europe, 2020–2022 125
    1. Tallarita's study on US E&S shareholder proposals 126
    2. Michael Bakker's research on E&S shareholder proposals in Europe between 2020 and 2022 127
        a. Bakker's research on worldwide activity in the 2021 AGM season 127
        b. Bakker's research on E&S shareholder proposals in Europe in 2020–22 128
V. The Netherlands and Germany (and France?): no shareholder proposals concerning the board's strategy development 133
    1. The Netherlands: a board-centric stakeholder system 133
    2. Germany: doubts about shareholder proposals on climate strategy 135
    3. France: greater legal uncertainty, but a conservative approach dominates 138
VI. Enforced stakeholder dialogue and strategic stakeholder litigation 140
    1. Sustainability due diligence legislation creates leverage for stakeholders 140
        a. European law: from internal to external stakeholders 140
        b. The draft CSDDD imposes stakeholder dialogue 143
        c. Stakeholders in the French due diligence legislation 144
        d. The more reluctant German attitude 145
        e. External stakeholders are not investors 146
    2. NGO litigation in order to change corporate (climate) strategies .. 147

		a.	Strategic litigation in general, or why climate litigation is different	147
		b.	French due diligence litigation	150
VII.	The politicized corporation – or why Europe is too restrictive for shareholder proposals and too accommodating for stakeholder litigation			153
	1.	boards are under pressure to weigh incommensurable conflicting stakeholder interests and values		153
	2.	The distinction between desirable and undesirable shareholder proposals – and why Germany and the Netherlands should become more tolerant of proposals that touch upon corporate strategy...		155
		a.	Shareholder proposals should be allowed to touch upon corporate strategy......................................	155
		b.	But prescriptive divestment and climate proposals are unwarranted	156
		c.	The link with the debate on stakeholderist directors' duties...	158
		d.	Illustrations of the right approach	160
	3.	ESG is even more politicized in the US........................		164
VIII.	Board effectiveness and board structure: sustainability committees and ESG lead directors			166
	1.	Sustainability committees and ESG lead directors...............		167
	2.	Balkanized one-tier boards struggle with strategy-making		169
		a.	Boards as oversight bureaucracies	169
		b.	The oversight-strategy trade-off..........................	172
	3.	A switch to a dual board structure as part of the solution?........		174
IX.	Conclusion			177

Securities Lending as a Barrier to (or an Instrument for) Shareholder Activism and the Role of Intermediaries as Lending Agents
Louise VAN MARCKE... 179

1.	Introduction' ··	180
2.	Securities Lending Agreements and the Role of Intermediaries	185
3.	The Effect of Securities Lending Agreements on the Exercise of Shareholders' Voting Rights..	190
4.	The Entitlement to Vote	190
5.	The Right to Recall Shares on Loan	191
6.	Obstacles For Shareholders to Recalling Shares on Loan in the US Compared to the EU	193
7.	Empirical Findings and Input from the Industry....................	197
8.	Activists as Stock Borrowers: Stock Lending as an Instrument for Shareholder Activism	198

9.	Short selling and Negative Voting by Short Shareholder Activists		200
10.	Negative Risk-decoupling.		203
11.	Formal Shareholder for Governance purposes (Other Than Voting Entitlement)		203
12.	Formal Shareholder to Exercise Voting Rights: 'Empty Voting'		205
13.	Empty Voting and Record Date Capture in Practice		208
14.	Mediobanca/Generali		208
15.	Laxey Partners/British Land		210
16.	Other Empirical Findings Related to Activism: The Emergence of a Trend?		210
17.	Regulatory Concerns		212
18.	Conclusion		215

The Company's Rights, Challenges and Obligations when Faced with Shareholder Activism
Deborah JANSSENS and Sigrid VERVERKEN 219

1.	Activist Funds and Recurring Themes			220
2.	Tools of Activist Campaigns			226
3.	How to Anticipate and Prepare for Activism			230
	3.1.	Introduction: What to expect if an activist fund emerges		230
	3.2.	Stakeholder engagement plan		232
	3.3.	Early Signals Monitoring		233
		3.3.1.	Signals during Shareholder Engagement	233
		3.3.2.	Legal levers for identifying activist funds	233
			3.3.2.1. Mandatory disclosure by activist fund of significant shareholding	233
			3.3.2.2. Mandatory disclosure by certain "wolf packs"	236
			3.3.2.3. SRD II	238
			3.3.2.4. Short Positions	240
			3.3.2.5. Mandatory Disclosure during Takeover Bid Period	241
		3.3.3.	Spotting an Activist: Impact under MAR	243
	3.4.	Organise Core Team and Escalation Chart		244
	3.5.	Regularly Review Vulnerability from an Activist Fund Perspective		244
	3.6.	Governance		245
	3.7.	Activism Manual		246
	3.8.	Mock Exercise		247
4.	Rights and Obligations of Activist Funds			247
	4.1.	Company Law rights and obligations		247
		4.1.1.	Rights	247

		4.1.2. Limits to company law rights 250
	4.2.	Right to Make Public Statements and Limits under MAR 252
		4.2.1. Rights 252
		4.2.2. Limits under MAR and other Legislation 253
	4.3.	Potential civil liability of activist funds 255
	4.4.	Criminal liability under Belgian law 256
5.	Rights and obligations of companies 257
	5.1.	Role of the board of directors and corporate interest 257
	5.2.	Disclosure Requirements in Case of Activist Approach 260
		5.2.1. Inside Information 260
		5.2.2. Permitted Delay of Disclosure of Inside Information 261
		5.2.3. Disclosure of Activist Approach 262
		5.2.4. Insider List and Selective Disclosure 262
	5.3.	Shareholders' Information Rights and Activist Information Requests 264
	5.4.	Conclusion: How to Engage with an Activist Fund 266

The Securities Law Framework: A Fly in the Ointment of Activists?
Marijke SPOOREN, Ruben FORIERS and Jean-Sébastien ROMBOUTS 269

1.	Introduction 269
2.	Transparency rules 270
	2.1. The Transparency Directive 271
	2.2. The Transparency Law 272
	2.2.1. Reporting thresholds 273
	2.2.2. "Equivalent" financial instruments 274
	2.2.3. Persons acting in concert 277
	2.2.4. Filing and publication deadlines 278
	2.2.5. No mandatory disclosure of intent 278
	2.2.6. Enforcement and sanctions 279
3.	The right to identify shareholders 280
	3.1. SRD II 281
	3.2. SRD II Law 281
	3.2.1. No minimum threshold 282
	3.2.2. Limited to "shareholders" 282
	3.2.3. Type of information 283
4.	Disclosure of net short positions 283
5.	MAR 285
	5.1. General framework 285
	5.1.1. What is MAR? 285
	5.1.2. Scope of application 287
	5.1.3. The four main prohibitions and obligations under MAR . 288
	5.2. The core concept of "inside information" 288

		5.2.1. Precise 289
		5.2.2. Price sensitive 291
		5.2.3. Not public 292
		5.2.4. Relating to an issuer or financial instruments. 293
	5.3.	Interplay between MAR and shareholder activism from the issuer's perspective 294
		5.3.1. Disclosure obligations 294
		5.3.2. Insider dealing 296
		5.3.3. Unlawful disclosure. 297
	5.4.	Interplay between MAR and shareholder activism from the activist's perspective. 298
		5.4.1. Disclosure obligations 298
		5.4.2. Insider dealing 299
		5.4.3. Unlawful disclosure. 302
	5.5.	Market manipulation. 303
	5.6.	Investment recommendations 306
6.	Acting in concert 307
6.1.	Transparency rules 309
		6.1.1. Background. 309
		6.1.2. Definition 309
		6.1.3. Analysis of the definition 311
		(i) An "agreement" 311
		(ii) Regarding a "concerted exercise of their voting rights". 313
		(iii) With a view to adopting a "lasting common policy towards [the management of] the issuer". . . . 313
		6.1.4. Transparency notifications. 314
	6.2.	Takeover Bids Law 315
		6.2.1. Background and definition. 315
		6.2.2. Analysis of the definition 316
		(i) An "agreement" 316
		(ii) Aimed either at "acquiring control", "frustrating the successful outcome of a bid" or "maintaining control" 317
		6.2.3. ESMA public statement. 317
		6.2.4. Mandatory takeover bid 319
	6.3.	General corporate law 321
		6.3.1. Standalone squeeze-outs. 321
		6.3.2. Capital increases. 322
	6.4.	Assessment. 322
7.	Conclusion 323

Shareholder Activism in the Belgian Courtroom
    Karel Schulpen 325

1. Introduction 325
2. Investigative measures: the expert report 326
    §1. Introduction and legal basis 326
    §2. Application criteria 326
    §3. Claimants and procedure 328
    §4. The expert and his mission 329
3. actions interfering with the management of the company and/or the administration of its assets 330
    §1. Introduction 330
    §2. Provisional administrator 330
        A. Basis and definition 330
        B. Conditions for the appointment 331
        C. Claimants and procedure 332
    §3. *Ad Hoc* Trustee 333
        A. Basis and definition 333
        B. Conditions of appointment 334
        C. Claimants and procedure 334
    §4. Judicial Sequester 334
        A. Basis and definition 334
        B. Material conditions 335
        C. Claimants and procedure 335
4. ACTIONS against majority decisions or votes 336
    §1. Basis and definition 336
    §2. Conditions of implementation 336
    §3. Claimants and procedure 339
5. Liability claims – the derivative action 340
    §1. Basis and definition 340
    §2. Application criteria 341
    §3. claimants and procedure 342
6. Judicial dissolution 343
    §1. Introduction and legal basis 343
    §2. Application criteria 344
    §3. Claimants and procedure 344
7. Conclusion 344

Shareholder Activism in Belgium: What is Awaiting Us?
    Marieke Wyckaert 347

INTRODUCTION

Shareholder activism has long been an established phenomenon in the US. In Europe, including Belgium, shareholder activism is on the rise and expected to become more and more important. Investors increasingly voice their discontent instead of opting for the exit. This new attitude will change the dynamic between investors and boards.

In addition, the days where shareholders exclusively focused on their financial return are gone. Today, financial objectives are complemented with the realization of ESG (environmental, social and governance) objectives. This push toward sustainability creates new battlefields between investors and boards.

Notwithstanding its importance, the topic of shareholder activism has not yet been explored in Belgium legal scholarship. This book aims to fill this gap. The book explores the present and future of shareholder activism in Belgium. This will help readers understand whether shareholder activism can be a boon or a curse for sustainable value creation.

Many of the contributions of this book are based on presentations at a conference on 9 June 2022 on "shareholder activism in Belgium: boon or curse for sustainable value creation?", co-organized by the Jean-Pierre Blumberg Chair at the University of Antwerp and the Federation of Enterprises in Belgium (FEB-VBO). In addition, several other authors have been invited to contribute to this book. We believe that this has resulted in a very interesting collection of contributions, which will greatly add to the debate on shareholder activism in Belgium. Several contributions will also be relevant for readers outside of Belgium, who will undoubtedly recognize many features of Belgian corporate law and corporate governance in their own legal systems.

The first chapters of the book (chapter 1–5) are more general in nature and are not limited to Belgium. They provide the theoretical foundations upon which the rest of the book builds. The subsequent chapters (chapters 6–8) take a closer look at the different aspects of Belgian law that are relevant for shareholder activists. Even those chapters will be relevant for readers outside of Belgium, to the extent that the law in other countries is relatively similar. The final chapter (chapter 9) offers a general assessment of shareholder activism in Belgium, and some reflections on its future.

Introduction

The first chapter of the book, by Tom Vos (University of Antwerp), "sets the scene" by discussing "the characteristics, causes and consequences of shareholder activism". He defines shareholder activism, discusses the various types of shareholder activism, and describes the typical characteristics of hedge fund activism and other types of shareholder activism. In addition, he discusses several reasons why shareholder activism is generally more common in the US than in other jurisdictions (including Belgium), such as differences in corporate law, securities laws, shareholder structures, the size of the stock market, the size of the corporations, stock market liquidity, and culture. Finally, he reviews the empirical evidence on the impact of shareholder activism on a firm's performance, both toward shareholders and toward other stakeholders. He concludes that most of the different types of shareholder activism have a positive and complementary role to play in the corporate governance landscape, even though some types of activists may also behave opportunistically in certain situations.

In chapter 2, Anna Christie (Edinburgh Law School and University of Cambridge) discusses the growing trend of "ESG-focused hedge fund activism". She analyzes several interesting case studies of ESG-focused hedge fund activism, such as the campaign of Engine No. 1 against ExxonMobil and the campaign of Bluebell against Solvay. She distinguishes different types of ESG-focused hedge fund activism: "pure ESG" campaigns, which focus on ESG goals at the expense of shareholder value, versus "win-win" campaigns, which focus on ESG goals while also increasing shareholder value. She also argues that these different types of activism are driven by different incentives of hedge funds. Pure ESG hedge fund campaigns are likely driven by the personal values and reputational concerns of fund managers, making them less likely to win support from other investors and therefore less likely to be successful than "win-win" campaigns. Win-win campaigns could be motivated by a strategy of improving ESG performance to improve financial performance, but Anna Christie warns that ESG arguments can also be used to make a purely financially focused activist campaign more acceptable to ESG-oriented investors, even though the campaign does not genuinely increase ESG performance ("greenwashing").

Chapter 3, written by Marleen Och (KU Leuven), continues on the theme of sustainability, with a contribution on "Shareholder stewardship and sustainability – the current European legal framework and possible ways ahead". She explains how shareholder stewardship (a less aggressive form of shareholder activism) could have a positive impact on corporations' sustainability, due to the large and growing share ownership of institutional investors and asset managers. However, she also identifies several obstacles for effective stewardship in continental Europe (including Belgium): controlling shareholders are prevalent, making stewardship by institutional investors and asset managers less effective; institutional investors have only limited incentives to genuinely engage with their portfolio corporations; and the provisions in the Shareholder Rights Directive II that aim to promote stewardship are vague and therefore only partially effective. Nevertheless, she concludes that shareholder stewardship can play an important role in making corporations more sustainable, although more work needs to be done by legislators.

Closely related to the previous two chapters, chapter 4, written by Hans De Wulf (Ghent University), is titled "Towards a political corporation? NGOs as ESG shareholder activists and litigators influencing corporate strategies in continental Europe". In this chapter, Hans De Wulf discusses how NGOs have increasingly tried to influence the corporation's strategy through "E&S" (environmental and social) shareholder activism without a profit goal, which he calls "halo activism" (Anna Christie called this "pure ESG activism"). However, such shareholder activism faces important obstacles in corporate law (especially in Germany and the Netherlands, but to a lesser extent also in other countries), which generally allocates the competence to set a strategy to the board. Therefore, NGOs have taken to an alternative tool to influence corporation's strategy, strategic litigation, which is (and will be even more in the future) facilitated by national and European corporate sustainability due diligence legislation. Hans De Wulf argues that this has politicized boards and suggests that two-tier boards may be better suited in this new climate, in order to insulate managers from stakeholder pressures. He also argues that shareholder proposals are a better way of involving stakeholders than strategic litigation, as long as such shareholder proposals are not overly prescriptive.

In chapter 5, Louise Van Marcke (Ghent University) discusses "Securities lending as a barrier to (or an instrument for) shareholder activism and the role of intermediaries as lending agents". She argues that securities lending can be a barrier to shareholder activism, because shareholders must recall the shares that they lent out in a timely manner if they want to exercise their voting rights. While several authors have considered securities lending an obstacle to shareholder activism, she takes a more nuanced view, noting that recalling shares has become more common, although some obstacles remain, particularly in the US. In addition, she argues that securities lending can be used as a tool by shareholder activists to increase their voting power. Even though such "risk decoupling" through securities lending is controversial, she argues that it is generally legal in the EU (but not in the UK). She ends with some recommendations and guidelines for future regulation of securities lending.

Chapter 6 contains a contribution by Deborah Janssens and Sigrid Ververken (Freshfields) on "The company's rights, challenges and obligations when faced with shareholder activism". They discuss the tools that shareholder activists typically use and provide guidance on how Belgian companies can prepare for shareholder activism "in peacetime" (before being targeted by a shareholder activist), how companies can spot shareholder activist threats early, and how companies should respond to an actual shareholder activist, taking into account the legal framework. The key point is that the board's response should be a calm, efficient, carefully planned, and thoughtful process.

Marijke Spooren, Ruben Foriers and Jean-Sébastien Rombouts (Cleary Gottlieb Steen & Hamilton) discuss in chapter 7 how securities laws can be an obstacle for shareholder activists. More specifically, they discuss in great depth the relevance for shareholder activism of the rules relating to transparency of participations, the right for the company to identify its shareholders, the Market Abuse Regulation (including the rules on disclosure of inside information, insider dealing and market manipulation), and the rules on acting in concert. They conclude that because most securities laws have not been designed with shareholder activism in mind, they often lead to legal uncertainty and may in some cases even be overly broadly formulated (for example with regards to the definition of acting in concert).

In chapter 8, Karel Schulpen (Arcas Law) discusses shareholder activism in the Belgian courtroom. In particular, he discusses the different judicial proceedings that can be used by shareholder activists to achieve their aims, such as an expert report, a provisional administrator, an ad hoc trustee, a judicial sequester, the suspension or nullity of decisions of the board of directors or the general meeting, a derivative action for directors' liability, or the judicial dissolution of the corporation. He concludes that, even though many tools are available to shareholder activists, there is little case law on the application of these tools to listed companies. One explanation for this is that minority shareholders have to advance the costs for judicial proceedings, which poses an obstacle to shareholder activism in the Belgian courtroom. He argues that this problem is exacerbated by the fact that the case law generally frowns upon "speculative" behavior, such as activists increasing their participation after the alleged harm to the corporation has arisen.

Finally, in chapter 9, Marieke Wyckaert (KU Leuven) offers some concluding reflections on the future of shareholder activism in Belgium. She argues that shareholder activism is not novel in Belgium – it has existed for a long time. However, shareholder activism has changed a lot over time, becoming more and more professionalized. According to Marieke Wyckaert, shareholder activism will probably remain relatively rare in Belgium, as Belgium is a relatively small market with many controlling shareholders, which makes the investment in learning about local corporate law and culture not worth the costs for many foreign funds. She also argues that, despite the global surge of ESG-focused shareholder activism, the main focus of activists will remain financial, although NGOs also have a role to play (albeit one that is quite different from other activists). Finally, she argues that shareholder activism is neither generally bad nor generally good and that a reasonable balance should be found between the rights of all stakeholders.

We believe that this book offers a wide range of perspective on shareholder activism in Belgium, which will be useful for practice and academia, both in Belgium and in other countries. We hope that you enjoy reading it.

Arie Van Hoe, *Head Legal Service FEB-VBO*
Tom Vos, *Visiting professor (full-time) at the Jean-Pierre Blumberg Chair (University of Antwerp); voluntary scientific collaborator at the Jan Ronse Institute for Company and Financial Law (KU Leuven); lawyer (part-time) at Linklaters LLP*

SETTING THE SCENE: THE CHARACTERISTICS, CAUSES AND CONSEQUENCES OF SHAREHOLDER ACTIVISM

Tom Vos[*]
Visiting professor (full-time) at the Jean-Pierre Blumberg Chair (University of Antwerp); voluntary scientific collaborator at the Jan Ronse Institute for Company and Financial Law (KU Leuven); lawyer (part-time) at Linklaters LLP

1. INTRODUCTION

Shareholder activism used to be rare in Belgium. Recently, however, there seems to be a rising trend of shareholder activism in Europe.[1] High-profile shareholder activism campaigns have been making headlines in the Belgian financial press too, targeting companies like Euronav, Solvay, Orange, Ontex, Telenet and Agfa Gevaert.[2] This

---

[*] I wish to thank Sofie Cools, the anonymous peer reviewers, and the participants in the conference organized by the University of Antwerp and the Federation of Belgian Enterprises (FEB-VBO) on "shareholder activism in Belgium" for their valuable comments. Disclosure statement: the Jean-Pierre Blumberg Chair is funded by donations from several private partners, including listed corporations (the topic of this chapter) and lawyers that typically advise such corporations. See this link for an overview of these partners: <www.uantwerpen.be/en/chairs/jean-pierre-blumberg/partners/>.

[1] A. Quinio and H. Agnew, 'Investor activism in Europe to enter 'golden age'', *Financial Times* (London, 6 December 2021) <www.ft.com/content/34e08494-e8a1-4ca1-91eb-0c3ccf5d9206>.

[2] J. Portala and D. Mandia, 'Euronav shareholders signal support for Frontline merger', *Reuters* (20 May 2022), <www.reuters.com/business/energy/euronav-says-shareholder-cmb-fails-get-directors-onto-board-2022-05-19/>; V. Za and S. Jessop, 'Activist Bluebell urges Solvay's board to oust CEO over sea discharge' (15 September 2021) <www.reuters.com/business/sustainable-business/exclusive-activist-bluebell-urges-solvays-board-oust-ceo-over-sea-discharge-2021-09-15/>; C. Donkin, 'Orange falls short in full Belgium takeover bid', *Mobile World Live* (6 May 2021) <www.mobileworldlive.com/featured-content/home-banner/orange-falls-short-in-full-belgium-takeover-bid/>; 'L'actionnaire activiste d'Ontex décroche trois sièges au conseil', *L'Echo* (19 April 2021) <www.lecho.be/entreprises/produits-de-consommation/l-actionnaire-activiste-d-ontex-decroche-trois-sieges-au-conseil/10299048.html>; N. Fildes and L. Abboud, 'Activist takes aim at Liberty-controlled Belgian telecoms

illustrates that the European trend may have spilled over to Belgium. In addition, there seems to be a global trend of "ESG activism", where the tools of shareholder activism are used to pursue environmental, social and governance objectives.[3] Such ESG activism can be pursued because the activist believes that it could contribute to long-term shareholder value, but it can also be pursued with a non-profit objective. An example of the latter is the "one share ESG activism" campaign against the Belgian company Solvay by the hedge fund Bluebell, which has urged Solvay to stop the discharge into the sea of waste from a soda ash production plant in Italy.[4]

Shareholder activism, and especially the recent trend of ESG activism, has not received much attention in Belgian legal scholarship, which this book on "shareholder activism in Belgium" aims to address. This chapter sets the scene for the rest of the book. I first define shareholder activism, discuss the various types of shareholder activism, and delineate shareholder activism from other types of activism (Part 2). Next, I describe the typical characteristics of hedge fund activism and compare it with other types of shareholder activism (Part 3). Part 4 then compares the different levels of shareholder activism across countries and investigates what could explain these differences. Finally, part 5 gives an overview of the economic evidence on the impact of shareholder activism on a firm's performance toward shareholders and other stakeholders. Part 6 concludes.

2. DEFINING SHAREHOLDER ACTIVISM

The first question that a book on shareholder activism needs to answer is: what *is* shareholder activism? Brav, Jiang and Li give a simple definition in their excellent review of the literature: shareholder activism is *"shareholders' attempt to pressure management for changes in corporate policies and governance with the aim to improve firm performance"*.[5] Christie adds that it is typical for shareholder activists that they try to initiate change without acquiring control

---

group', *Financial Times* (28 February 2020) <www.ft.com/content/f2253130–5a2c-11ea-abe5–8e03987b7b20>; W. DE PRETER, 'Duitse activist koopt zich in bij Agfa-Gevaert', *De Tijd* (6 July 2018) <www.tijd.be/ondernemen/technologie/duitse-activist-koopt-zich-in-bij-agfa-gevaert/10029294.html?fbclid=IwAR07rquCQULJ3Q6ukMZysO7ZpFTk8cZs7KRic_1wV7bQ 0jy_q_SeIBSviZps>.

[3] See, for example: K. Liekefett, H. Gregroy and L. Wood, 'Shareholder Activism and ESG: What Comes Next, and How to Prepare' (29 May 2021) *Harvard Law School Forum on Corporate Governance* <https://corpgov.law.harvard.edu/2021/05/29/shareholder-activism-and-esg-what-comes-next-and-how-to-prepare/>.

[4] V. Za and S. Jessop, 'Activist Bluebell urges Solvay's board to oust CEO over sea discharge' (15 September 2021) <www.reuters.com/business/sustainable-business/exclusive-activist-bluebell-urges-solvays-board-oust-ceo-over-sea-discharge-2021–09–15/>.

[5] A. Brav, W. Jiang and R. Li, 'Governance by Persuasion: Hedge Fund Activism and the Market for Corporate Influence' (November 2021) *ECGI Working Paper Series in Finance* <https://papers.ssrn.com/sol3/papers.cfm?abstract_id=3955116>, 6.

over the corporation, but rather by influencing the corporation in other ways.[6] Katelouzou brings these elements together in her definition, stating that shareholder activism consists of *"first, an equity stake as a starting point and, secondly, the exercise of "voice", this being the use of influence to effect value-enhancing changes in a company's management or policies without a change in the company's control".*[7] Such broad definitions of shareholder activism cover several different types of shareholder activism, including shareholders who would not describe themselves as "activists", but simply as shareholders conducting "active engagement". Nevertheless, I believe that such broad definitions are useful, because the analysis below will show that the same tools of shareholder activism can be used for different purposes and by different actors.

2.1. TRADITIONAL SHAREHOLDER ACTIVISM VERSUS ESG SHAREHOLDER ACTIVISM

A first distinction in the type of shareholder activism is based on how the objective of improving "firm performance" is understood. First, in the case of "traditional" shareholder activism, increasing firm performance can be understood as increasing value for shareholders, or even narrower, as increasing short-term profits.[8] Alternatively (and more recently), the objective of shareholder activism can also be understood in a broader sense, for example as improving the firm's performance with regards to various aspects of "sustainability" or "ESG", which could be called "sustainability shareholder activism" or "ESG (shareholder) activism".[9] ESG activists can be further subdivided into two types of activism: on the one hand, activism that tries to improve ESG performance because they believe that this will lead to more shareholder value in the long term, and on the other hand activism that tries to improve ESG performance without any profit motive, because the activist sees good ESG performance as valuable per se.[10] The distinction is sometimes hard to make, and activists may sometimes be intentionally vague about which of the two objectives they pursue in order to try to convince as large an audience as possible.

---

[6] A. Christie, 'The new hedge fund activism: activist directors and the market for corporate quasi-control' [2019] *Journal of Corporate Law Studies* 1, 13.

[7] D. Katelouzou, 'Myths and realities of hedge fund activism: some empirical evidence' [2013] *Virginia Law & Business Review* 459, 466.

[8] D. Katelouzou, 'Myths and realities of hedge fund activism: some empirical evidence' [2013] *Virginia Law & Business Review* 459, 466.

[9] See on this topic: A. Christie, 'The Agency Costs of Sustainable Capitalism' [2021] *UC Davis Law Review* 875. See also the chapter of Anna Christie in this book.

[10] In his chapter in this book, Hans De Wulf refers to this type of activism as "halo activism".

2.2. THE TYPE OF ACTIVIST: HEDGE FUND, OTHER INSTITUTIONAL INVESTORS, RETAIL INVESTORS AND NGOS

Shareholder activism can also be distinguished based on the type of activist. First, the most well-known type of shareholder activist is the hedge fund activist.[11] Hedge fund activism is typically what people think of when they think of shareholder activism. In fact, shareholder activism by other institutional investors, such as pension funds, index funds and insurance companies, is often called "shareholder engagement" or "stewardship"[12] instead of shareholder activism. Hedge fund activism differs from engagement by other shareholders by the fact that hedge funds often take a position in corporations that they identify to be underperforming, while engagement by other institutional investors often occurs "ex post" to protect a pre-existing investment in the target corporation.[13] Cheffins and Armour call this offensive versus defensive shareholder activism.[14] Shareholder engagement is often also less confrontational than the "activism" by hedge funds. Institutional investors rarely launch shareholder proposals or proxy fights but prefer expressing their discontent in private meetings or in shareholder votes.[15] This has led two different narratives, with hedge fund activism often regarded as "bad" and "engagement" by institutional investors as "good".[16]

However, such a simplified narrative is arguably misguided, as hedge funds generally have more powerful financial incentives than other institutional

---

[11] Hedge funds can be loosely defined as: *"i) pooled, privately organized investment vehicles, ii) administered by professional investment managers with performance-based compensation and significant investments in the fund, iii) not widely available to the public, and can only be placed to "accredited investors" who are institutional investors and qualified high net worth individuals, and iv) operate outside of securities regulation and registration requirements"*. See: A. Brav, W. Jiang and R. Li, 'Governance by Persuasion: Hedge Fund Activism and the Market for Corporate Influence' (November 2021) ECGI Working Paper Series in Finance <https://papers.ssrn.com/sol3/papers.cfm?abstract_id=3955116>, 8.

[12] However, stewardship can also be considered a broader concept. See for example the UK Stewardship Code 2020: *"Stewardship is the responsible allocation, management and oversight of capital to create long-term value for clients and beneficiaries leading to sustainable benefits for the economy, the environment and society"* (p. 4). In this view, engagement is just one aspect of stewardship, in addition to investment decisions.

[13] A. Brav, W. Jiang and R. Li, 'Governance by Persuasion: Hedge Fund Activism and the Market for Corporate Influence' (November 2021) ECGI Working Paper Series in Finance <https://papers.ssrn.com/sol3/papers.cfm?abstract_id=3955116>, 9; M. Kahan and E. Rock, 'Hedge funds in corporate governance and corporate control' [2007] University of Pennsylvania Law Review 1021, 1069.

[14] B. Cheffins and J. Armour, 'The Past, Present, and Future of Shareholder Activism by Hedge Funds' [2011] Journal of Corporation Law 51, 56.

[15] L.A. Bebchuk, A. Cohen and S. Hirst, 'The Agency Problems of Institutional Investors' [2017] *Journal of Economic Perspectives* 89, 105. See also further in part 3.

[16] See about the competing narratives of good and bad activists: J. Hill, 'Good Activist/Bad Activist: The Rise of International Stewardship Codes' [2018] *Seattle University Law Review* 497.

investors to increase the value of the corporation that they target. Bebchuk, Cohen and Hirst have argued that index funds and "closet indexers"[17] do not have strong incentives to monitor their portfolio corporations, even though they hold large participations.[18] Such funds are paid only a small asset management fee (typically around 0.12%), so that they capture only a small part of the value that they could add through engagements with their portfolio corporations. In addition, a free rider problem exists: institutional investors have to bear the costs of monitoring portfolio corporations themselves, even though the benefits are shared with other shareholders. This problem is even stronger for index funds and closet indexers, as competing funds track the same index and therefore benefit to the same extent from any value increase that the index fund could generate through its engagement, while the competing funds can offer lower fees to their clients because they do not have to bear the costs of engagement. The incentives of managers of actively managed funds are not much better: because these managers are compensated on the basis of their fund's relative performance to other funds, they only have incentives to spend resources on engagement with a corporation to the extent that the corporation is overweighted in the fund's portfolio compared to the benchmark index.[19] Finally, many institutional investors may suffer from conflicts of interest that induce them to be less activist than optimal. For example, fund managers could hope to attract investment management business from corporations, including managing corporations' cash, short-term investments and employee pension plans.[20] There is some empirical evidence that such business ties distort the fund managers' votes.[21] In

---

[17] These are actively managed funds *"whose holdings substantially overlap with their benchmark index, deviating only by underweighting and overweighting certain stocks"*. See: L.A. Bebchuk, A. Cohen and S. Hirst, 'The Agency Problems of Institutional Investors' [2017] Journal of Economic Perspectives 89, 98.

[18] L.A. Bebchuk, A. Cohen and S. Hirst, 'The Agency Problems of Institutional Investors' [2017] Journal of Economic Perspectives 89. For empirical evidence on the low level of shareholder engagement and excessive deference to management by index funds, see: L.A. Bebchuk and S. Hirst, 'Index funds and the future of corporate governance: theory, evidence, and policy' [2019] Columbia Law Review 2029. Other authors have made similar arguments. See for example: E.B. Rock, 'Institutional Investors in Corporate Governance' in J.N. Gordon and W.-G. Ringe (eds.), The Oxford Handbook of Corporate Law and Governance, Oxford University Press, Oxford 2018, pp. 373–374; D.S. Lund, 'The Case Against Passive Shareholder Voting' [2018] Journal of Corporation Law 493.

[19] L.A. Bebchuk, A. Cohen and S. Hirst, 'The Agency Problems of Institutional Investors' [2017] Journal of Economic Perspectives 89, 98–99.

[20] L.A. Bebchuk, A. Cohen and S. Hirst, 'The Agency Problems of Institutional Investors' [2017] *Journal of Economic Perspectives* 89, 102–103; L.A. Bebchuk and S. Hirst, 'Index funds and the future of corporate governance: theory, evidence, and policy' [2019] *Columbia Law Review* 2029, 2062–2065.

[21] See, for example: D. Cvijanovi, A. Dasgupta and K.E. Zachariadis, 'Ties That Bind: How Business Connections Affect Mutual Fund Activism' [2016] *Journal of Finance* 2933 (mutual fund families with business ties to the corporation (through the management of pension plans) vote more often with management on shareholder proposals in closely contested votes); R. Ashraf, N. Jayaraman and H.E. Ryan, Jr., 'Do Pension-Related Business Ties Influence Mutual Fund Proxy Voting? Evidence from Shareholder Proposals on Executive

addition, institutions who also provide underwriting services to corporations may be more likely to support management to avoid antagonizing potential future clients.[22] These incentive problems make it less likely that institutional investors will engage in effective shareholder activism.

While hedge funds also suffer from a free rider problem, this problem is generally less pronounced for them. The looser regulation and the lock-up of their investors for longer time periods allows hedge funds to take more concentrated positions in their targets.[23] In addition, hedge funds' fee structure usually includes a performance fee (in addition to a fixed fee as a percentage of assets under management), giving them stronger incentives to create value in their target corporations.[24] Finally, hedge funds rarely have business ties to their portfolio corporations, in contrast to many other asset managers.[25] That is why Gilson and Gordon have argued that hedge fund activists can function as "governance arbitrageurs", proposing governance changes to other institutional investors, who are generally "rationally reticent", as they have few incentives to actively engage with corporations themselves.[26] Of course, many authors have argued that the disadvantage of hedge fund activists is that they are excessively focused on short-term value increases, after which they sell their participation and the stock price goes down again.[27] Further in part 5.1 of this chapter, I will

---

Compensation' [2012] *Journal of Financial and Quantitative Analysis* 567 (similar study with regard to votes on executive compensation); G.F. Davis and E.H. Kim, 'Business Ties and Proxy Voting by Mutual Funds' [2007] *Journal of Financial Economics* 552 (similar study with regard to shareholder proposals in general).

[22] There is also empirical evidence for this: A. Hamdani and Y. Yafeh, 'Institutional Investors as Minority Shareholders' [2013] *Review of Finance* 691 (with regards to votes on compensation-related proposals that required approval by a majority of the minority shareholders).

[23] A. Brav, W. Jiang and R. Li, 'Governance by Persuasion: Hedge Fund Activism and the Market for Corporate Influence' (November 2021) *ECGI Working Paper Series in Finance* <https://papers.ssrn.com/sol3/papers.cfm?abstract_id=3955116>, 8 and 17–19.

[24] L.A. Bebchuk, A. Cohen and S. Hirst, 'The Agency Problems of Institutional Investors' [2017] *Journal of Economic Perspectives* 89, 104; A. Brav, W. Jiang and R. Li, 'Governance by Persuasion: Hedge Fund Activism and the Market for Corporate Influence' (November 2021) *ECGI Working Paper Series in Finance* <https://papers.ssrn.com/sol3/papers.cfm?abstract_id=3955116>, 16.

[25] L.A. Bebchuk, A. Cohen and S. Hirst, 'The Agency Problems of Institutional Investors' [2017] *Journal of Economic Perspectives* 89, 104–105; A. Brav, W. Jiang and R. Li, 'Governance by Persuasion: Hedge Fund Activism and the Market for Corporate Influence' (November 2021) *ECGI Working Paper Series in Finance* <https://papers.ssrn.com/sol3/papers.cfm?abstract_id=3955116>, 16–17.

[26] R. Gilson and J. Gordon, 'The agency costs of agency capitalism: activist investors and the revaluation of governance rights' [2013] *Columbia Law Review* 863.

[27] See for this view, for example: M. Lipton, 'Do Activist Hedge Funds Really Create Long-Term Value' (22 July 2014) *Harvard Law School Forum on Corporate Governance* <https://corpgov.law.harvard.edu/2014/07/22/do-activist-hedge-funds-really-create-long-term-value/>; L. STRINE, 'One Fundamental Corporate Governance Question We Face: Can Corporations Be Managed for the Long Term Unless Their Powerful Electorates Also Act and Think Long Term?' [2010] *Business Lawyer* 1.

review the evidence on whether hedge funds are effective in improving the long-term performance of corporations.

Institutional investors are not the only shareholders who can engage in activism, as retail investors can also take an activist role. For example, in the US, the thresholds for bringing a shareholder proposal are relatively low[28], which means that even many retail investors can bring them. Activist retail investors that repeatedly file such shareholder proposals are sometimes called "gadflies", because they are supposed to be annoying, but not harmful for corporations. However, empirical evidence shows that these gadflies are responsible for 41% of shareholder proposals, of which 26% passed.[29] This illustrates that activism by retail investors plays an important role in the corporate governance of US corporations. In contrast, in Belgium, retail investors rarely meet the threshold of 3% of legal capital to bring a shareholder proposal.[30] Nevertheless, all shareholders can ask questions at the general meeting about the items on the agenda[31], which activists can also use to pressure a corporation to change its policies. For example, Eric Geenen, a Belgian activist famous for the green caps that he and his supporters wear, has used the right to ask questions to attract media attention to general meetings and pressure listed corporations such as Electrabel, Belgacom (now Proximus), Fortis (now BNP Paribas Fortis), AB InBev, and the National Bank of Belgium, to name a few.[32] However, evidence from the Netherlands shows that such shareholder questions are rarely effective in changing corporate behavior, except if the questions are part of a campaign coordinated by an investor association.[33]

A final type of shareholder activist is the NGO, which can use the tools of shareholder activism to further their non-profit objectives.[34] For example, peace activists who owned a few shares in the Belgian corporation Barco have used their right to ask questions at the general meeting to criticize the corporation's alleged

---

[28] For example, to bring a proposal, shareholders need to hold only $2,000 in securities with voting rights for three years, $15,000 for two years or $25,000 for one year. See: 17 CFR §240.14a-8(b)(i).

[29] K. Kastiel and Y. Nili, 'The Giant Shadow of Corporate Gadflies' [2021] *Southern California Law Review* 569, 591–593.

[30] See article 7:130 Belgian Code on Companies and Associations ("BCCA"). See also the chapter of Deborah Janssens and Sigrid Ververken in this book for a more detailed discussion of shareholder rights in Belgium.

[31] See article 7:138 BCCA.

[32] See for a profile of Eric Geenen: P. Den Dooven, 'Erik Geenen, de Tijl Uilenspiegel van de haute finance' (30 April 2010) *De Standaard*.

[33] A. Lafarre and C. Van Der Elst, 'Shareholder sustainability engagement in AGMs' (21 May 2022) Presentation at the *Law & Business Conference Vanderbilt-Ghent*, slides available here: <www.ugent.be/re/mpor/nl/onderzoeksgroepen/instituut-financieel-recht/lbc2022/papers.htm>.

[34] See for a discussion: A. Hoepner and Q. Li, 'The Impact of NGO Activism' in C. Mayer and B. Roche (eds.), *Putting Purpose Into Practice: The Economics of Mutuality*, Oxford University Press, Oxford 2021, pp. 250–251. This type of shareholder activism is also discussed by Hans De Wulf in his chapter in this book.

arms exports to Israel.[35] Alternatively, NGOs may coordinate investors to vote in favor of against a certain resolution at a general meeting, or speak up at a general meeting. For example, ShareAction coordinates several activist campaigns relating to responsible investment.[36] In addition, 13 climate NGOs wrote a letter that asked investors to vote against TotalEnergies' allegedly inadequate climate strategy.[37] Such campaigns in general do not receive substantial shareholder support, potentially because the activists' message is typically targeted at public opinion rather than shareholder interests.[38] Nevertheless, pressure by the public may prove effective as well in changing corporate behavior.

All these types of investors can in principle engage in either traditional shareholder activism or ESG shareholder activism. For example, empirical evidence shows that institutional investors and retail investors both launch shareholder-focused and ESG-focused shareholder proposals.[39] Even hedge funds, which are most well known for their traditional shareholder-focused activism, may engage in ESG activism. For example, Bluebell Capital Partners launched a "pro bono campaign" against the Belgian chemicals corporation Solvay because of alleged harmful waste discharge in the sea at a soda ash plant in Rosignano (Italy).[40] Despite owning only one share, Bluebell succeeded in convincing Solvay to commit to the reduction of the release of limestone waste.[41] Another example of a hedge fund engaging in ESG activism is the

---

[35] For a discussion of the Barco case, see: P. Baert, 'En hoe gaat het met uw wapenproductie? Bedenkingen bij het vraagrecht van de aandeelhouder naar aanleiding van de Barco-zaak' [2002] *TRV* 397.

[36] See their website for a description of their activities: <www.shareaction.org>.

[37] Green Peace et al., 'Call on TotalEnergies' financiers and shareholders to push for a 1.5°C-aligned climate plan and the end of oil and gas expansion' (4 May 2022) <https://reclaimfinance.org/site/wp-content/uploads/2022/05/Inter-NGO-letter-to-TotalEnergies-investors.pdf>.

[38] See in this sense: A. Hoepner and Q. Li, 'The Impact of NGO Activism' in C. Mayer and B. Roche (eds.), *Putting Purpose Into Practice: The Economics of Mutuality*, Oxford University Press, Oxford 2021, p. 251 ("*While such shareholder activism is unlikely to win majority support, it can increase public awareness and may lead to self-reflection among corporate executives, as shareholder meetings and results are often covered by the media*").

[39] S. Gillan and L. Starks, 'The Evolution of Shareholder Activism in the United States' [2007] *Journal of Applied Corporate Finance* 55 (describing the type of shareholder proposals filed by institutional investors and retail investors); G. Michelon and M. Rodrigue, 'Demand for CSR: Insights from Shareholder Proposals' [2015] *Social and Environmental Accountability Journal* 157 (showing that institutional investors, especially dedicated socially responsible investing funds and pension funds, file a significant number of shareholder proposals relating to corporate social responsibility); K. Kastiel and Y. Nili, 'The Giant Shadow of Corporate Gadflies' [2021] *Southern California Law Review* 569, 595 (showing that retail investors bring a mix of traditional governance-focused and ESG-focused shareholder proposals).

[40] V. Za and S. Jessop, 'Activist Bluebell urges Solvay's board to oust CEO over sea discharge' (15 September 2021) <www.reuters.com/business/sustainable-business/exclusive-activist-bluebell-urges-solvays-board-oust-ceo-over-sea-discharge-2021-09-15/>.

[41] Solvay, 'Solvay and Bluebell Capital Partners reach a settlement and issue joint statement' (6 September 2022) <www.solvay.com/en/press-release/solvay-and-bluebell-capital-partners-reach-settlement-and-issue-joint-statement>.

proxy fight in the US against ExxonMobil by Engine No. 1, a hedge fund and 0.02% shareholder.[42] Engine No. 1 proposed four alternative directors, alleging that ExxonMobil was underperforming because of the lack of an adequate climate change transition plan. Engine No. 1 also emphasized that better ESG performance would increase long-term shareholder value, making this an example of the other type of ESG activism. This may have helped to convince several major pension funds and index funds to support the campaign, resulting in the election of three of the directors proposed by Engine No. 1.[43]

2.3. NO SHAREHOLDER ACTIVISM: SHORT-SELLER ACTIVISM AND EXTERNAL STAKEHOLDER ACTIVISM

Although the definition of shareholder activism mentioned above is very broad, we can still distinguish shareholder activism from two other types of activism, which I call "short-seller activism" and "external stakeholder activism". Short-seller activism consists of an investor taking a "short" position (selling shares that it borrowed), after which the investor launches a public campaign with the goal of driving down the stock price, so that the investor can buy back the shares that it needs to return to the lender at a lower price.[44] Typically, the short-seller alleges some kind of fraud that the corporation has hidden from its investors, which justifies a lower stock price once the fraud becomes public. A prominent recent example are the fraud allegations against Wirecard by short-sellers.[45] Short-seller activism should be distinguished from shareholder activism, because the incentives of the investors are fundamentally different: a short-seller is no shareholder and benefits from the stock price going down, while shareholder activists benefit from an increase in the stock price. That is why short-seller activism is not covered in this book.

Secondly, "external stakeholder activism" should also be distinguished from shareholder activism. I use the term "external stakeholder activism" for activism against companies that is not brought by shareholders and does not rely on the tools available to shareholders. Think of an NGO campaign to boycott a corporation's products, a labor union strike, or environmental litigation by concerned citizens

---

[42] See for a description of this campaign: M. Philips, *'Exxon's Board Defeat Signals the Rise of Social-Good Activists'* (9 June 2021) <www.nytimes.com/2021/06/09/business/exxon-mobil-engine-no1-activist.html>.

[43] M. Philips, *'Exxon's Board Defeat Signals the Rise of Social-Good Activists'* (9 June 2021) <www.nytimes.com/2021/06/09/business/exxon-mobil-engine-no1-activist.html>.

[44] See for a description of short seller activism: Z. Bach, A. Fink and R. Leithauser, 'Short Selling Activism in Europe – A Strategic Communications Perspective' (10 July 2022) *Harvard Law School Forum on Corporate Governance* <https://corpgov.law.harvard.edu/2022/07/10/short-selling-activism-in-europe-a-strategic-communications-perspective/>.

[45] 'Wirecard's scandal shows the benefits of short-sellers', *The Economist* (24 June 2020 <www.economist.com/leaders/2020/06/24/wirecards-scandal-shows-the-benefits-of-short-sellers>.

or an NGO against a polluting corporation.[46] A famous recent example of the latter is the climate change litigation case, *Milieudefensie v. Shell*.[47] Such external stakeholder activism is not the focus of this book, as it has in principle little to do with shareholder activism, as both the means and the end are different. Sometimes, it may be hard to draw the line, however, as NGOs may also use the tools available to shareholders to achieve their objectives (see above in part 2.2). In his contribution for this book, Hans De Wulf critically discusses such external stakeholder activism, and contrasts it with shareholder proposals by NGOs.

Figure 1 below summarizes all the different types of shareholder activism, although not all real-life activist campaigns will neatly fit into a category.

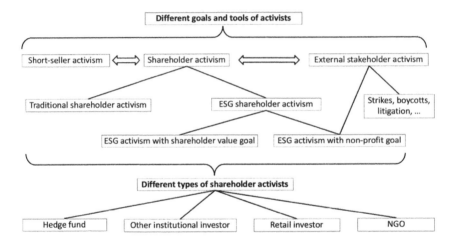

Figure 1. The different goals, tools and types of shareholder activists.

3. THE CHARACTERISTICS OF SHAREHOLDER ACTIVISM

This part describes the typical characteristics of shareholder activist campaigns. I start with an overview of the evidence on characteristics of hedge fund activist campaigns (part 3.1), because this is the archetypical model of shareholder activism that is being exported around the world. Nevertheless, I also discuss what shareholder activism by other institutional investors and by retail investors typically looks like (part 3.2).

---

[46] See about this type of activism: T. Lin, *The Capitalist and the Activist: Corporate Social Activism and the New Business of Change*, Berreth-Koehler, Oakland 2022.

[47] Hague District Court, 26 May 2021, ECLI:NL:RBDHA:2021:5337, English version available here: <https://uitspraken.rechtspraak.nl/inziendocument?id=ECLI:NL:RBDHA:2021:5339>.

3.1. THE CHARACTERISTICS OF HEDGE FUND ACTIVISM

In a typical hedge fund activist campaign, the hedge fund is a substantial minority shareholder. The average share ownership of a hedge fund activist is around 10% across the world, although the median is a bit lower, around 6.6% in the US, probably because the average is skewed upwards by a few hedge funds with a very large ownership percentage.[48] This implies that hedge fund activists need the support of other (institutional) investors, who may not have sufficient incentives to vote with hedge funds against management (as discussed above in part 2.2)[49], to be successful in their campaigns. In ESG shareholder activism, smaller ownership stakes seem to be the norm (as illustrated by the Engine No. 1/ExxonMobil case mentioned above), and even one-share activism exists (as illustrated by the Bluebell/Solvay case mentioned above). In such cases, support by other investors may also be necessary to be successful, although it is also possible that the real audience consists of other stakeholders of the corporation.

It is often said that hedge funds only hold their participation for a short period of time. This depends on what one considers a short holding period. US hedge fund activists hold their participations on average for 532 days (median: 262).[50] In a sample of shareholder activism in 17 non-US countries, 73.6% of activists held their shares in the target corporation for more than a year, and 39.1% of activists even for more than three years.[51] These holding periods are not that short, although they are probably shorter than the critics of hedge fund activism would like to see.[52]

What factors explain which corporations are targeted by hedge fund activists? The empirical evidence suggests that hedge fund activists are more likely to target corporations with a small market capitalization in the US, although the largest corporations are by no means safe from activism.[53] However, in

---

[48] A. Brav, W. Jiang and R. Li, 'Governance by Persuasion: Hedge Fund Activism and the Market for Corporate Influence' (November 2021) *ECGI Working Paper Series in Finance* <https://papers.ssrn.com/sol3/papers.cfm?abstract_id=3955116>, 112 (average share ownership of hedge fund activists in the US is 9.5% and the median is 6.6%); M. Becht, J. Franks, J. Grant and H. Wagner, 'Returns to Hedge Fund Activism: An International Study' [2017] *Review of Financial Studies* 2933, 2939 (average share ownership of hedge fund activists is 12% in Asia, 11% in the US and 10% in Europe).

[49] L.A. Bebchuk, A. Cohen and S. Hirst, 'The Agency Problems of Institutional Investors' [2017] *Journal of Economic Perspectives* 89, 106–107.

[50] A. Brav, W. Jiang and R. Li, 'Governance by Persuasion: Hedge Fund Activism and the Market for Corporate Influence' (November 2021) *ECGI Working Paper Series in Finance* <https://papers.ssrn.com/sol3/papers.cfm?abstract_id=3955116>, 112.

[51] D. Katelouzou, 'Myths and realities of hedge fund activism: some empirical evidence' [2013] *Virginia Law & Business Review* 459, 479.

[52] See for an argument that the average holding periods of hedge fund activists are relatively long: D. Katelouzou, 'Myths and realities of hedge fund activism: some empirical evidence' [2013] *Virginia Law & Business Review* 459, 478–480.

[53] A. Brav, W. Jiang and R. Li, 'Governance by Persuasion: Hedge Fund Activism and the Market for Corporate Influence' (November 2021) *ECGI Working Paper Series in Finance* <https://papers.ssrn.com/sol3/papers.cfm?abstract_id=3955116>, 30–31 and 112.

an international sample of hedge fund activism, there seems to be a much smaller effect of size on the likelihood of being targeted.[54] Hedge fund activists also seem to target underperforming corporations, because firm value and past stock returns are negatively correlated with the likelihood of being targeted.[55] Hedge fund activists are more likely to target firms with a low dividend yield (i.e. the ratio between the dividend and the stock price), consistent with the typical strategy of shareholder activists of increasing shareholder pay-outs.[56] However, targeted firms also have higher leverage on average, which is inconsistent with the idea that hedge fund activists target firms with low leverage and load them up with debt to increase shareholder pay-outs.[57] Institutional ownership, and especially ownership by US institutional investors, is positively associated with the likelihood of being targeted, consistent with the idea that shareholder activists need the support of institutional investors to succeed in their campaigns (see also further in part 4.3).[58] Finally, liquidity of the shares is positively associated with hedge fund activist campaigns.[59] This can be explained by the fact that higher liquidity facilitates stakebuilding by an activist (see also further in part 4.6).

---

[54] M. Becht, J. Franks, J. Grant and H. Wagner, 'Returns to Hedge Fund Activism: An International Study' [2017] *Review of Financial Studies* 2933, 2948.

[55] A. Brav, W. Jiang and R. Li, 'Governance by Persuasion: Hedge Fund Activism and the Market for Corporate Influence' (November 2021) ECGI Working Paper Series in Finance <https://papers.ssrn.com/sol3/papers.cfm?abstract_id=3955116>, 31–32 and 112 (using a sample of US hedge fund activist campaigns, with "Tobin's Q", i.e. the ratio between the market capitalization and the book value of assets, as a proxy for firm value, and the abnormal stock returns over the last 12 months as a proxy for stock returns); M. Becht, J. Franks, J. Grant and H. Wagner, 'Returns to Hedge Fund Activism: An International Study' [2017] *Review of Financial Studies* 2933, 2946–2947 (using a sample of international hedge fund activist campaigns, with market-to-book ratio, i.e. total assets minus book value of equity plus market value of equity over total assets, as a proxy for firm value).

[56] A. Brav, W. Jiang and R. Li, 'Governance by Persuasion: Hedge Fund Activism and the Market for Corporate Influence' (November 2021) ECGI Working Paper Series in Finance <https://papers.ssrn.com/sol3/papers.cfm?abstract_id=3955116>, 32 and 112 (US sample); M. Becht, J. Franks, J. Grant and H. Wagner, 'Returns to Hedge Fund Activism: An International Study' [2017] *Review of Financial Studies* 2933, 2947 (international sample).

[57] A. Brav, W. Jiang and R. Li, 'Governance by Persuasion: Hedge Fund Activism and the Market for Corporate Influence' (November 2021) ECGI Working Paper Series in Finance <https://papers.ssrn.com/sol3/papers.cfm?abstract_id=3955116>, 32 and 112 (US sample); M. Becht, J. Franks, J. Grant and H. Wagner, 'Returns to Hedge Fund Activism: An International Study' [2017] *Review of Financial Studies* 2933, 2947 (international sample).

[58] A. Brav, W. Jiang and R. Li, 'Governance by Persuasion: Hedge Fund Activism and the Market for Corporate Influence' (November 2021) ECGI Working Paper Series in Finance <https://papers.ssrn.com/sol3/papers.cfm?abstract_id=3955116>, 33 and 112 (US sample); M. Becht, J. Franks, J. Grant and H. Wagner, 'Returns to Hedge Fund Activism: An International Study' [2017] *Review of Financial Studies* 2933, 2946 (international sample).

[59] A. Brav, W. Jiang and R. Li, 'Governance by Persuasion: Hedge Fund Activism and the Market for Corporate Influence' (November 2021) ECGI Working Paper Series in Finance <https://papers.ssrn.com/sol3/papers.cfm?abstract_id=3955116>, 34 and 112 (US sample); M. Becht, J. Franks, J. Grant and H. Wagner, 'Returns to Hedge Fund Activism: An International Study' [2017] *Review of Financial Studies* 2933, 2947 (international sample).

Although hedge fund activists have a reputation for engaging in hostile tactics, this is not always the case. In around 49.3% of hedge fund activist campaigns in the US, the hedge fund only holds its participation for investment purposes or to communicate privately with management about increasing firm value.[60] More hostile tactics, such as a proxy fight or litigation, are also used, but more rarely (11.6% and 3.6% of campaigns, respectively), although publicly criticizing the target corporation (including through shareholder proposals) occurs in 35.6% of cases. Typical objectives of a US hedge fund activist are forcing a sale of the target corporation (18.5% of campaigns), changing the capital structure (for example by demanding dividends or blocking debt or equity issuances – 13.1%), changing the business strategy (for example to increase operational efficiency or restructure the business – 18.5%), or changing the corporate governance (for example to fire the CEO or remove takeover defenses – 35.5%).[61] In 47% of cases the hedge fund does not want to change the corporation's policy but just holds the stake because the corporation is undervalued.

Panel A: Hedge funds' stated objectives (US)	
General undervaluation	47.0%
Capital structure	13.1%
Business strategy	18.5%
Sale of target corporation	18.5%
Governance	35.5%
Panel B: Hedge funds' tactics (US)	
The stake is for investment purposes. Alternatively, the intent is to communicate with the board/management to enhance shareholder value.	49.3%
The hedge fund seeks board representation without a proxy contest or confrontation with the existing management/board.	23.4%
The hedge fund makes formal shareholder proposals, or publicly criticizes the company and demands change.	35.6%
The hedge fund threatens to wage a proxy fight in order to gain board representation, or to sue the company for breach of fiduciary duty etc.	8.0%
The hedge fund launches a proxy contest in order to replace the board.	11.6%
The hedge fund sues the company.	3.6%
The hedge fund intends to take control of the company, for example, with a takeover bid.	3.2%

Table 1. Summary of activists' stated objectives and tactics in a sample of 4657 hedge fund activist campaigns in the US. Based on: A. Brav, W. Jiang and R. Li, 'Governance by Persuasion: Hedge Fund Activism and the Market for Corporate Influence' (November 2021) *ECGI Working Paper Series in Finance* <https://papers.ssrn.com/sol3/papers.cfm?abstract_id=3955116>, 111.

---

[60] A. Brav, W. Jiang and R. Li, 'Governance by Persuasion: Hedge Fund Activism and the Market for Corporate Influence' (November 2021) *ECGI Working Paper Series in Finance* <https://papers.ssrn.com/sol3/papers.cfm?abstract_id=3955116>, 111.

[61] A. Brav, W. Jiang and R. Li, 'Governance by Persuasion: Hedge Fund Activism and the Market for Corporate Influence' (November 2021) *ECGI Working Paper Series in Finance* <https://papers.ssrn.com/sol3/papers.cfm?abstract_id=3955116>, 111.

Similar to the US, the most hostile tactics are only used in a minority of the hedge fund activist campaigns outside the US. Table 2 summarizes the tactics used by hedge fund activists in an international sample, based on empirical evidence by Katelouzou.[62]

Hedge funds' tactics (international)	Number of activist campaigns
Gentle activism	263
1. Quiet Persuasion (behind the scenes)	84
2. Communication (letter/meetings)	123
3. Informal Proposals/Business Plans	56
Soft activism	349
4. Public Criticism/Change Demand	241
5. Board Representation (no reported management confrontation)	44
6. Formal Shareholder Proposal	64
Aggressive activism	271
7. Against Management Resolution / Proxy Fight for Reasons Other than Board Replacement	47
8. Board Representation Against Management \Will	32
9. Against re-election or removal of key executives (via an extraordinary general meeting)	21
10. Threat: Removal of Director(s) or Litigation or Takeover Bid	42
11. Litigation	38
12. Board control seeking campaign	54
13. Takeover bid	37
All activist events	883

Table 2. Summary of activists' stated objectives and tactics in an international sample of 883 hedge fund activist campaigns. Based on: D. Katelouzou, 'Myths and realities of hedge fund activism: some empirical evidence' [2013] *Virginia Law & Business Review* 459, 485–486.

On average, hedge funds are fairly successful in achieving their objectives. Brav and co-authors report that hedge fund activists achieve all or most of their stated objectives in around two-thirds of all campaigns.[63] In an international sample,

---

[62] D. Katelouzou, 'Myths and realities of hedge fund activism: some empirical evidence' [2013] *Virginia Law & Business Review* 459, 485–486. The sample consists of 883 hedge fund activist campaigns between 1 January 2000 and 31 December 2010 in Australia, Brazil, Canada, China, France, Germany, India, Italy, Japan, Netherlands, Russia, South Africa, Spain, Sweden, Switzerland, Turkey and the UK.

[63] A. Brav, W. Jiang and R. Li, 'Governance by Persuasion: Hedge Fund Activism and the Market for Corporate Influence' (November 2021) ECGI Working Paper Series in Finance <https://papers.ssrn.com/sol3/papers.cfm?abstract_id=3955116>, 27 (US sample).

Becht and co-authors report a 53% chance of success on at least one stated objective, although the chance of success differs strongly between regions: 61% in North America, 50% in Europe and only 18% in Asia.[64] Becht and co-authors also find that the hedge fund activist obtains a change in the management or the board in 32% of cases, a change in pay-out policy (increasing dividends or share buybacks) in 16% of cases, a sale of the target in 14% of cases, a restructuring (a divestiture or spin-off of non-core assets, or the cancellation of a diversifying acquisition) in 22% of cases, and a mix of these outcomes in 16% of cases.[65]

Hedge fund activists not only obtain their successes through winning proxy contests, but also through "settlement agreements", where the corporation agrees with the activist to implement certain changes in return for the activist dropping the campaign.[66] Bebchuk and co-authors study these settlements and find that they have become more common over time: from 3% of campaigns in 2000 to 21% of campaigns in 2013.[67] They also find that such settlements are more likely when the activist has a higher chance to win board seats in a contested vote and when the reputational costs for the incumbent management are higher. Settlements typically focus on the allocation of board seats, but they are often followed by other operational changes at the corporation, such as replacing the CEO, increasing shareholder pay-outs, and improving operating performance. This suggests that activists can accomplish their objectives through their representation on the board, while allowing the incumbent management to avoid losing face.

3.2. THE CHARACTERISTICS OF OTHER TYPES OF SHAREHOLDER ACTIVISM

Shareholder activism by other types of activists than hedge funds looks quite different: other activists are generally less confrontational and rely more on shareholder proposals and less on proxy contests. For example, Fos provides evidence that 57% of US proxy contests between 1994 and 2012 were conducted by hedge fund activists, with this figure growing toward 70% in later years of the sample.[68] In contrast, pension funds only launched two proxy contests in this period and index funds zero.

---

[64] M. Becht, J. Franks, J. Grant and H. Wagner, 'Returns to Hedge Fund Activism: An International Study' [2017] *Review of Financial Studies* 2933, 2934 (international sample).
[65] M. Becht, J. Franks, J. Grant and H. Wagner, 'Returns to Hedge Fund Activism: An International Study' [2017] *Review of Financial Studies* 2933, 2955 (international sample).
[66] Settlement agreements are discussed as well in the chapter in this book by Deborah Janssens and Sigrid Ververken.
[67] L. Bebchuk, A. Brav, W. Jiang and T. Keusch, 'Dancing with activists' [2020] *Journal of Financial Economics* 1.
[68] V. Fos, 'The disciplinary effects of proxy contests' [2017] *Management Science* 655, 660.

An empirical study by Bebchuk and Hirst confirmed that the "Big Three" index funds (BlackRock, Vanguard and State Street) typically refrain from the more confrontational tactics that are typical for hedge fund activists: they did not launch any proxy contests, shareholder proposals or litigation against their portfolio corporations in the US.[69] Instead, the Big Three index funds try to influence corporate policy by "behind the scenes" private engagements. Bebchuk and Hirst show that the Big Three index funds on average engage at least one time with 7.5% of their portfolio corporations in a given year, which Bebchuk and Hirst consider a low figure.[70] Index funds focus in their engagements on systemic portfolio-wide issues, such as promoting good governance and climate risk management, rather than on firm-specific issues, such as replacing underperforming directors.[71] The reason is that idiosyncratic, firm-specific risks are minimized by index funds' diversified portfolio, while systemic risks are not.

Public pension funds and labor union funds tend to be a bit more confrontational in their activism than index funds. For example, out of 6827 shareholder proposals filed between 2005 and 2018 in S&P 1500 companies, 9% were filed by public pension funds and 10% by labor union funds.[72] Of the shareholder proposals filed by public pension funds, 30.9% receive majority support in the general meeting, while this is the case for 19.1% for shareholder proposals filed by labor union funds.[73]

Individual investors play an even more important role in the filing of shareholder proposals in the US, filing 48% of all shareholder proposals.[74] This is driven by six (families of) individuals, the so-called "gadflies", who are responsible for 41% of all shareholder proposals.[75] Of the proposals filed by the "gadflies", 26% pass with majority support, only slightly lower than the rate for public pension funds.[76] Most of the shareholder proposals filed by gadflies, public pension

---

[69] L. Bebchuk and S. Hirst, 'Index funds and the future of corporate governance: theory, evidence, and policy' [2019] *Columbia Law Review* 2029, 2098, 2104 and 2114.

[70] L. Bebchuk and S. Hirst, 'Index funds and the future of corporate governance: theory, evidence, and policy' [2019] *Columbia Law Review* 2029, 2087.

[71] J. Gordon, 'Systematic stewardship' [2022] *Journal of Corporation Law* 627. See also the empirical evidence by: J. Azar, M. Duro, I. Kadach and G. Ormazabal, 'The Big Three and corporate carbon emissions around the world' [2021] *Journal of Financial Economics* 674 (finding that the big three index funds focus their engagement effort on large firms with high emissions).

[72] K. Kastiel and Y. Nili, 'The Giant Shadow of Corporate Gadflies' [2021] *Southern California Law Review* 569, 591.

[73] K. Kastiel and Y. Nili, 'The Giant Shadow of Corporate Gadflies' [2021] *Southern California Law Review* 569, 594.

[74] K. Kastiel and Y. Nili, 'The Giant Shadow of Corporate Gadflies' [2021] *Southern California Law Review* 569, 591.

[75] K. Kastiel and Y. Nili, 'The Giant Shadow of Corporate Gadflies' [2021] *Southern California Law Review* 569, 590–591.

[76] K. Kastiel and Y. Nili, 'The Giant Shadow of Corporate Gadflies' [2021] *Southern California Law Review* 569, 593.

funds and labor union funds are corporate governance proposals that aim to increase shareholders' rights to hold management accountable.[77] Because shareholder proposals are non-binding in the US, not all shareholder proposals are implemented. From the gadfly shareholder proposals that passed, 64.5% were followed by a management proposal to implement the shareholder proposal, while this figure was only 49% for pension funds.[78]

It can be concluded from this data that gadflies and (to a lesser extent) public pension funds play an important role in setting the agenda for general meetings. Index funds, in contrast, do not initiate shareholder proposals, but often support shareholder proposals launched by other shareholders, similar to their role in supporting hedge fund activist campaigns.[79]

Shareholder proposals in the UK and continental Europe are rarer than in the US, even when taking into account the difference in the size of the stock market (see further in part 4.8 for potential explanations of this difference).[80] Nevertheless, shareholder proposals in Europe potentially have a higher impact as in the US, because they are in general binding and can also be used to elect or remove directors, in contrast to the US.[81] In the UK, around two-thirds of the shareholder proposals concerned the election of removal of directors, while in continental Europe, this constituted only 10% of shareholder proposals and most proposals related to strengthening shareholders' role in corporate governance.[82] Most shareholder proposals did not obtain a majority of the votes: shareholders proposals received an average of 30.3% of the votes in the UK and 21.1% of votes cast in continental Europe.[83]

---

[77] K. Kastiel and Y. Nili, 'The Giant Shadow of Corporate Gadflies' [2021] *Southern California Law Review* 569, 595–596 (regarding gadflies); S. Gillan and L. Starks, 'The Evolution of Shareholder Activism in the United States' [2007] *Journal of Applied Corporate Finance* 55, 57 and 63 (regarding public pension fund and labor union funds).

[78] K. Kastiel and Y. Nili, 'The Giant Shadow of Corporate Gadflies' [2021] *Southern California Law Review* 569, 598.

[79] See for this point: K. Kastiel and Y. Nili, 'The Giant Shadow of Corporate Gadflies' [2021] *Southern California Law Review* 569, 605. Kastiel and Nili refer to Gilson and Gordon, who made this point earlier for hedge funds: R. Gilson AND J. Gordon, 'The agency costs of agency capitalism: activist investors and the revaluation of governance rights' [2013] *Columbia Law Review* 863, 864–865. As discussed above in part 2.2, index funds may also suffer from conflicts of interest, however.

[80] P. Cziraki, L. Renneboog and P. Szilagyi, 'Shareholder Activism through Proxy Proposals: The European Perspective' [2010] *European Financial Management* 738, 750.

[81] P. Cziraki, L. Renneboog and P. Szilagyi, 'Shareholder Activism through Proxy Proposals: The European Perspective' [2010] *European Financial Management* 738, 744 and 750–751.

[82] P. Cziraki, L. Renneboog and P. Szilagyi, 'Shareholder Activism through Proxy Proposals: The European Perspective' [2010] *European Financial Management* 738, 751.

[83] P. Cziraki, L. Renneboog and P. Szilagyi, 'Shareholder Activism through Proxy Proposals: The European Perspective' [2010] *European Financial Management* 738, 752.

A more recent empirical study investigated a sample of 261 shareholder proposals between 2012 and 2018 in Belgium, France, the Netherlands and Luxembourg.[84] Of the shareholder proposals not supported by the board, most occurred in France (77%), although Belgium (19%) and Luxembourg (3%) also saw a few proposals, while the Netherlands had none. The study found that most shareholder proposals that were not supported by the board concerned the election (41%) or the removal (25%) of directors. These proposals were also the only ones that received majority support in the sample, in 18% and 6% of shareholder proposals, respectively. Of the successful proposals, 6 occurred in Belgium and 11 in France. The sponsors of the proposals that were not supported by the board include a mix of activist investment funds (27%), other investment funds (24%), family holding vehicles (25%), corporations (3%), employee funds (9%), governments (2%), investor associations (10%), and other shareholders.

Finally, it is worth investigating how the characteristics of ESG shareholder activism differ from traditional shareholder activism. One study used a proprietary dataset of 847 interventions by a single responsible investment fund at 660 different portfolio corporations throughout the world between 2005 and 2014 to study the characteristics of ESG shareholder activism.[85] These interventions concerned social (43.3%), environmental (42.3%) and governance (14.4%) matters, which shows the difference with traditional activism, which focuses on director elections and other governance matters. The average share ownership of the responsible investment fund in a targeted corporation was 0.2% – much lower than what is typical for activist hedge funds engaging in traditional shareholder activism (see above in part 3.1) The evidence suggests that the responsible investment fund is more likely to target firms with low ESG ratings – similar to how hedge funds target corporations that are underperforming on traditional metrics, such as share price and return on assets (see above in part 3.1). Firms in industries that are likely to have a large impact on ESG matters, such as financial firms and oil and petroleum firms, are the most common target. The most common tactic of the responsible investment fund is private engagement with the firm's management, either through a letter (18.5%), an e-mail (33%), a conference call (11.4%), or an in-person meeting (10.9%). Public engagements, such as press releases or engagements at a general meeting, are significantly less common (5.6% of interventions), another significant difference with traditional hedge fund activism (see above in part 3.1). 60% of the engagements by the activist are considered successful by the activist, and firms with low ESG ratings see their ratings improve on average. This suggests

---

[84] V. Verheyden, 'When shareholders use their rights to convene meetings and to submit proposals. A comparative and empirical analysis of activism in four EU Member States' [2020] *TRV-RPS* 975.

[85] T. Barko, M. Cremers and L. Renneboog, 'Shareholder Engagement on Environmental, Social, and Governance Performance' [2021] *Journal of Business Ethics* 777.

that ESG shareholder activism can be effective in increasing ESG performance, despite the different focus, the different tactics and the lower share ownership than in hedge fund activism.

The analysis above illustrates the diversity in the characteristics of shareholder activism. The hedge fund activism playbook, with relatively high ownership stakes, a focus on replacing directors to increase shareholder value, and the (threat of) aggressive tactics, differs substantially from the playbook of other activists. Other activists rely more often on private engagement and shareholder proposals, and often own smaller stakes in the target corporation (with the exception of index funds, who also own significant ownership stakes). Nevertheless, the evidence shows that each of these types of activism has a chance of success that cannot be ignored by corporations. These different types of shareholder activism could therefore play a complementary role. Whether this role is positive for target corporations is discussed further in part 5. However, I will first discuss why shareholder activism may be more common in some countries than in others.

4. EXPLAINING DIFFERENT LEVELS OF SHAREHOLDER ACTIVISM ACROSS COUNTRIES

The levels of shareholder activism differ substantially across the world. Table 3 contains the number of hedge fund activist campaigns for a select number of countries around the world: the US, the UK, Germany, Italy, France, the Netherlands and Belgium. Two conclusions are clear from this table.

First, shareholder activism seems to be on the rise: in almost all of the countries, the number of shareholder activist campaigns is much larger in the period 2010–2018 than in the period 2000–2010. This is consistent with statements by commentators, who have spoken of "record years" for shareholder activism in the US and of the "golden age" for shareholder activism in Europe.[86] The only exception among the countries included in the table is Belgium, where the number is smaller in the period 2010–2018. Nevertheless, more recently, shareholder activism also seems to be on the rise in Belgium.[87]

---

[86] Lazard, '2018 Review of Shareholder Activism' (January 2019) <www.lazard.com/media/450805/lazards-2018-review-of-shareholder-activism.pdf>; A. Quinio and H. Agnew, 'Investor activism in Europe to enter 'golden age'', *Financial Times* (London, 6 December 2021) <www.ft.com/content/34e08494-e8a1-4ca1-91eb-0c3ccf5d9206>.

[87] For example, in his presentation at the conference "Shareholder activism in Belgium: boon or curse for sustainable value creation?" on 9 June 2022, Wouter Gabriëls showed that 7 hedge fund activist campaigns occurred in the period 2018–2021, as much as in the period 2010–2018. See for the slides of this presentation: <www.vbo-feb.be/events/20220609---activisme/Program/>. See also on this evolution: B. Haeck, 'De opmars van de activistische

The second conclusion from table 3 is that the number of activist campaigns is still much larger in the US than in the UK and continental Europe. Below, I examine several potential explanations for this difference, including the differences in the size of the stock market, shareholders' rights, securities laws, shareholder structures, the size of corporations, differences stock market liquidity, and culture.

	Becht et al., 2017 (2000–2010)		Maffett et al., 2021 (2010–2018)
Country	Frequency	Frequency per 1000 listed firms	Frequency (per year)
US	1125	19.6	4105
UK	165	6	343
Germany	53	7.3	124
Italy	42	13.3	69
France	27	3	68
The Netherlands	22	11.6	27
Belgium	9	4.6	7

Table 3. Number of activist campaigns for a select number of countries. Based on: M Maffett, A. Nakhmurina and D. Skinner, 'Importing Activists: Determinants and Consequences of Increased Cross-border Shareholder Activism' [2022] *Journal of Accounting and Economics*, 6; M. Becht, J. Franks, J. Grant and H. Wagner, 'Returns to Hedge Fund Activism: An International Study' [2017] *Review of Financial Studies* 2933, 2939 and 2941.

4.1. DIFFERENCES IN THE SIZE OF THE STOCK MARKET

A first and obvious explanation for the much higher level of shareholder activism in the US and (to a lesser extent) the UK than in continental Europe is the difference in the size of the stock market: stock markets in the US and the UK contain many more corporations than stock markets in continental Europe, especially with regards to the Belgian stock market. Unsurprisingly, an empirical study by Maffett and co-authors confirms that the number of corporations listed on a stock market is a strong predictor for the number of activist campaigns.[88]

It is also insightful to look at the number of hedge fund activist campaigns in relation to the number of listed firms. Table 3 shows that the US still has the

---

[88] aandeelhouder', *De Tijd* (Brussels, 6 June 2022) <www.tijd.be/dossiers/de-verdieping/de-opmars-van-de-activistische-aandeelhouder/10393863.html>.
M. Maffett, A. Nakhmurina and D. Skinner, 'Importing Activists: Determinants and Consequences of Increased Cross-border Shareholder Activism' [2022] *Journal of Accounting and Economics*, 11.

largest number of activist campaigns, even as a ratio of the number of listed firms. The UK, on the other hand, actually has a relatively low number of activist campaigns, relative to the number of listed corporations, despite the high absolute number of activist campaigns. Table 3 also shows that Belgium and France have a very low number of hedge fund activist campaigns, even when taking into account the number of listed firms. The question therefore remains why European countries, and especially countries like Belgium and France, have fewer activist campaigns.

4.2. DIFFERENCES IN SHAREHOLDER RIGHTS

A second explanation could be that stronger rights for shareholders encourage shareholder activism by making it easier to influence the corporation's management. This seems intuitively plausible. The empirical study by Maffett and co-authors also finds an association between the activist-friendliness of corporate laws and the number of activist campaigns.[89] In addition, the study finds that a change in corporate law to make it more activist-friendly leads to an increase in the number of activist campaigns, relative to a control group. This effect is concentrated in those countries that had weak shareholder rights before the change. Maffett and co-authors measure the activist-friendliness of corporate laws through an index of shareholder rights, including shareholder rights relating to the notification of general meetings, the disclosure of executive compensation, the right to request the board to convene a general meeting, the right to add items to the agenda of the general meeting, the right to vote on executive compensation, whether independent directors are legally required (and if so, how many), and whether term limits are legally required (and if so, the duration of the term limits).

This empirical study should be nuanced and interpreted with caution, however, because of two problems with the index of the activist-friendliness of corporate laws. First, the authors of the paper coded the index for each country themselves without the help of local lawyers, even though the latter is generally recommended by the comparative law and finance literature.[90] This seems to have led to certain coding errors and some coding choices that fail to capture the nuances of the legal framework. For example, the paper codes Belgian corporate law as "0" on the variable that measures whether a shareholder vote is required for executive compensation and "0" on the variable relating to the general meeting notice period, because the notice period in Belgium used to be shorter than the median. However, the legal situation has changed in 2010: the law of 6 April

---

[89] M. Maffett, A. Nakhmurina and D. Skinner, 'Importing Activists: Determinants and Consequences of Increased Cross-border Shareholder Activism' [2022] *Journal of Accounting and Economics*, 12.

[90] H. Spamann, 'The "Antidirector Rights Index" Revisited' [2010] *Review of Financial Studies* 467, 483.

2010[91] required a vote on the remuneration report and the law of 20 December 2010[92] lengthened the notice period to 30 days for listed corporations, which would normally lead to coding these variables as 1. These legal changes are not listed in the overview provided by the authors, which suggests that they have missed this. In addition, some variables are also coded without sufficient nuance. For example, while it is true that shareholders in the Netherlands can add items to the agenda of the general meeting at a relatively low share ownership threshold, the case law in the Netherlands makes it clear that the board of directors is competent for setting the strategy of the corporation and can refuse to add shareholder proposals to the agenda of the general meeting when the proposals of the activist infringe on the board's competence to set the corporation's strategy.[93] This undermines to a large extent the effectiveness of shareholder proposals as a tool for shareholder activism, but the index is still coded as 1 on this variable for the Netherlands. Of course, it is possible that these coding issues do not have a material impact on the results. However, the problems identified above raise the question for which other countries the index may be miscoded. It also illustrates that the law is often complex, and that without the help of specialized local lawyers, quantifying shareholder protection is hard.

A second, more fundamental issue with the index of Maffett and co-authors is that it is unclear why several shareholder rights would matter in practice for hedge fund activists. For example, the index is coded as 1 in the US for the ability to add items to the agenda of the general meeting at a low threshold of share ownership.[94] The problem, however, is that shareholder proposals in the US must be non-binding and cannot be used to elect or remove directors.[95] That is why shareholder proposals are not the main tools used by activist hedge funds in the US, as activists can gain more leverage from (threatening to launch) a proxy fight.[96] In contrast, in Europe, shareholder proposals can also be binding and can be used to

---

[91] Law of 6 April 2010 on the reinforcement of corporate governance in listed corporations, *Belgian Official Journal* 23 April 2010.

[92] Law of 20 December 2010 on the exercise of certain shareholders' rights in listed corporations, *Belgian Official Journal* 18 April 2011.

[93] See for example: Tribunal of The Hague, 17 March 2015, *Boskalis Holding B.V. v. Fugro N.V.*, ECLI:NL:RBDHA:2015:3452; Tribunal of Amsterdam, 10 August 2017, *Elliott International, L.P. v. Akzo Nobel N.V.*, ECLI:NL:RBAMS:2017:5845. See for a discussion of these cases: T. Vos, 'The AkzoNobel Case: An Activist Shareholder's Battle against the Backdrop of the Shareholder Rights Directive' [2017] *European Company Law Journal* 238.

[94] To bring a proposal, shareholders need to hold only $2,000 in securities with voting rights for three years, $15,000 for two years or $25,000 for one year. See: 17 CFR §240.14a-8(b)(i). See for this coding decision: M. Maffett, A. Nakhmurina and D. Skinner, 'Importing Activists: Determinants and Consequences of Increased Cross-border Shareholder Activism' [2022] *Journal of Accounting and Economics*, 29.

[95] 17 CFR §240.14a-8(i)(1) and (8).

[96] A. Brav, W. Jiang and R. Li, 'Governance by Persuasion: Hedge Fund Activism and the Market for Corporate Influence' (November 2021) *ECGI Working Paper Series in Finance* <https://papers.ssrn.com/sol3/papers.cfm?abstract_id=3955116>, 14.

elect and remove directors.[97] For example, in Belgium, (groups of) shareholders owning shares amounting to at least 3% of legal have the right to add items to the agenda of the general meeting, with the agenda and proxies distributed by the corporation.[98] In the US, hedge fund activists that want to get their director nominees elected need to launch a costly proxy fight to reach the same goal[99], an important nuance that is not reflected in the coding by Maffett and co-authors. In addition, it is unclear why the term limits for directors that are coded by Maffett and co-authors should matter for hedge fund activists targeting European countries, because in most European countries, directors can be removed at any time by the general meeting if the proposal is included in the agenda, regardless of their term limit.[100] In contrast, many corporations in the US have staggered boards, where shareholders can only replace one-third of the directors each year, although the number of corporations with a staggered board has been declining recently.[101] Therefore, the variables coded by Maffett and co-authors do not necessarily reflect the ease with which hedge fund activists can replace incumbent directors with their own nominees.

Nevertheless, Maffett and co-authors do find an association between (changes in) their index and the number of activist campaigns, so the question remains what could explain this association. One possibility is that other country-level differences have an impact on this association (the so-called "omitted variable bias"), for example the securities laws, the typical shareholder structure of corporations, the stock market liquidity, the market capitalization of corporations, or the cultural differences. Maffett and co-authors do not control for these factors explicitly in their model (except for market capitalization), although they do try

---

[97] S. Cools, 'Shareholder proposals shaking up shareholder say: a critical comparison of the United States and Europe' in A. Afsharipour and M. Gelter (eds.), *Comparative Corporate Governance*, Edward Elgar, Cheltenham 2021, pp. 308–311; P. Cziraki, L. Renneboog and P. Szilagyi, 'Shareholder Activism through Proxy Proposals: The European Perspective' [2010] *European Financial Management* 738, 744 and 750–751.

[98] Article 7:130 BCCA.

[99] The average costs of a proxy fight are estimated by one paper at $10.71 million: N. Gantchev, 'The Costs of Shareholder Activism: Evidence from a Sequential Decision Model' [2013] Journal of Financial Economics 610.

[100] S. Cools, 'Europe's Ius Commune on Director Revocability' [2011] European Company and Financial Law Review 199 (*"a mandatory rule of at will revocability of company directors is typical of European civil law"*). See also: S. Cools, 'Shareholder proposals shaking up shareholder say: a critical comparison of the United States and Europe' in A. Afsharipour and M. Gelter (eds.), Comparative Corporate Governance, Edward Elgar, Cheltenham 2021, pp. 316.

[101] M. Tonnello, 'Corporate Board Practices in the Russell 3000 and S&P 500' (18 October 2020) Harvard Law School Forum on Corporate Governance <https://corpgov.law.harvard.edu/2020/10/18/corporate-board-practices-in-the-russell-3000-and-sp-500/> (*"a majority of companies in both indexes now elect members of their boards of directors annually, having abandoned the staggered-years structure of the past. However, classified boards are still found at 41.2 percent of Russell 3000 companies (down from 43.2 percent in 2016) and 10.9 percent of S&P 500 companies (down from 15.4 percent in 2016)"*). Outside their terms, directors in a staggered board can only be replaced for cause in Delaware. See: §141(k) DGCL.

to address the omitted variable bias through country fixed effects in their panel regressions and through the difference-in-difference design in their analysis of corporate law changes. Both methods cannot completely solve the potential omitted variable bias, however.[102] That is why it remains unclear whether differences in shareholder rights are truly important for explaining the different levels of shareholder activism, and which other explanations are also important.

4.3. DIFFERENCES IN SHAREHOLDER STRUCTURES

Another difference between countries that could explain the different levels of shareholder activism is the different shareholder structures that are typical in each country. Countries with high levels of shareholder activism, such as the US and to a lesser extent the UK, generally have more dispersed shareholder structures than continental European countries, where shareholder activism is less common and shareholder structures are typically more concentrated. Table 4 summarizes the degree of insider ownership in a select number of countries.

	Average voting rights held by		Percentage of listed corporations with		
Country	Largest shareholder	5 largest shareholders	Controlling shareholder	Non-controlling blockholder	Dispersed share ownership
FR	46.4%	63.3%	68%	29.8%	2.2%
IT	44%	63.1%	68,5%	26.6%	4.9%
DE	45.3%	59.1%	68.7%	28.5%	2.8%
BE	38.6%	55.6%	63.4%	31.7%	5%
NL	34.6%	54.4%	46.6%	51.9%	1.5%
US	21.4%	33.9%	28.4%	57%	14.6%
UK	19.5%	37.1%	20.6%	66.3%	13.1%

Table 4. Ownership concentration in certain selected countries. Corporations are considered as being controlled if the voting rights held by a shareholder (or group of shareholders controlled by the same ultimate owner) exceed 20%; and as having a blockholder if the voting rights exceed 5%. Based on: G. Aminadav and E. Papaioannou, 'Corporate Control around the World', *Journal of Finance* 2020, (1191) 1205.

---

[102] Fixed effects control for omitted variables that are constant over time, but it is possible that some of the omitted variables mentioned vary over time. A difference-in-difference design assumes that the control group would follow a parallel trend to the treatment group in absence of the treatment. Maffett and co-authors create a control group by matching the treated country (i.e. the country with the corporate law change) to a country with the same score on the index of shareholder-friendliness of corporate laws. See: M. Maffett, A. Nakhmurina and D. Skinner, 'Importing Activists: Determinants and Consequences of Increased Cross-border Shareholder Activism' [2022] *Journal of Accounting and Economics*, 13. However, it is possible that other factors than the relevant corporate law also change at the moment of treatment in the treatment group, but not in the control group.

Intuitively, activism is more difficult in corporations with significant insider ownership, as insiders are probably less likely to support an activist that challenges their own position. An empirical study by Barko and co-authors also confirms that the presence of a controlling shareholder is associated with a lower chance of success for shareholder activists, although they only study ESG engagements by a socially responsible investment fund.[103] Unfortunately, the paper by Maffett and co-authors on the determinants of shareholder activism does not explicitly control for shareholder structure.[104]

This does not mean that shareholder activism is impossible in controlled corporations. Kastiel provides empirical evidence that shareholder activism exists even in US corporations with a controlling shareholder with more than 30% of the voting rights, finding 209 activist campaigns between 2005 and 2014.[105] Kastiel shows that these activists often used hostile tactics, but different ones than other hedge fund activists, often relying on minority shareholder rights, such as director nomination rights for minority shareholders, veto rights for minority shareholders in going-private transactions, and shareholder litigation. In addition, some activist campaigns occur "against all odds", when the sole possibility to influence corporate strategy is through reputational effects on the controlling shareholders. Some of these campaigns were even successful, although the chance of success is higher when activists have bargaining power through formal legal mechanisms.

Activism against controlled corporations also exists in Belgium. For example, activists launched campaigns against Solvay, which has a 30,81% controlling shareholder.[106] As discussed above in part 2.2, they were even successful in reaching a settlement.

Another aspect of the shareholder structure that may determine the number of activist campaigns is the percentage of shares held by institutional investors. Hedge fund activists typically own only a small stake in their target, so they need

---

[103] T. Barko, M. Cremers and L. Renneboog, 'Shareholder Engagement on Environmental, Social, and Governance Performance' [2021] *Journal of Business Ethics* 777, 779.
[104] M Maffett, A. Nakhmurina and D. Skinner, 'Importing Activists: Determinants and Consequences of Increased Cross-border Shareholder Activism' [2022] *Journal of Accounting and Economics*, 6. The country fixed effects in their panel regressions and their difference-in-difference design do control for factors that are constant over time, so to the extent that the shareholder structure of countries is relatively stable, this is controlled for in their analysis.
[105] K. Kastiel, 'Against all odds: hedge fund activism in controlled corporations' [2016] *Columbia Business Law Review* 60.
[106] See for information on the activist campaigns: V. Za and S. Jessop, 'Activist Bluebell urges Solvay's board to oust CEO over sea discharge' (15 September 2021) <www.reuters.com/business/sustainable-business/exclusive-activist-bluebell-urges-solvays-board-oust-ceo-over-sea-discharge-2021-09-15/>. See for information on the shareholder structure: <www.solvay.com/en/investors/share-information/major-shareholders> (last checked on 20 June 2023).

support from other shareholders. Institutional investors are generally more likely to vote in a general meeting than retail investors, which means that activists may be more likely to be successful in corporations where institutional ownership is high. The empirical evidence confirms that firms with high institutional ownership are more likely to be targeted by hedge fund activists.[107]

In general, institutional ownership is higher in the US and the UK than in continental European countries, as is illustrated by table 5.[108] Therefore, differences in institutional ownership could offer another explanation for why shareholder activism is less common in continental European countries than in the US.

Country	Private corporations	Public sector	Strategic individuals	Institutional investors	Other free float
FR	18%	7%	11%	28%	36%
IT	10%	12%	15%	29%	34%
DE	15%	6%	7%	34%	39%
BE	26%	5%	5%	37%	28%
NL	18%	4%	6%	46%	27%
UK	7%	7%	2%	63%	22%
US	2%	3%	4%	72%	19%

Table 5. Average ownership by category of investor at the end of 2017, weighted by market capitalization. Based on: A. De La Cruz, A. Medina and Y. Tang, 'Owners of the world's listed companies', *OECD Capital Markets Series*, 17 October 2019, <www.oecd.org/corporate/Owners-of-the-Worlds-Listed-Companies.htm>, 37.

4.4. DIFFERENCES IN SECURITIES LAWS

Another potential explanation for the difference in the levels of shareholder activism across countries is that the securities laws in countries with a lot of shareholder activism are more activist-friendly.[109] Indeed, securities laws in

---

[107] A. Brav, W. Jiang and R. Li, 'Governance by Persuasion: Hedge Fund Activism and the Market for Corporate Influence' (November 2021) ECGI Working Paper Series in Finance <https://papers.ssrn.com/sol3/papers.cfm?abstract_id=3955116>, 33 and 112 (US sample); M. Becht, J. Franks, J. Grant and H. Wagner, 'Returns to Hedge Fund Activism: An International Study' [2017] *Review of Financial Studies* 2933, 2946 (international sample).

[108] However, it should be noted that some of these differences could be related to the fact that there is more data available on institutional ownership in the US. See on this issue: S. STEUER, 'Common Ownership and the (Non-)Transparency of Institutional Shareholdings: An EU-US Comparison' (July 2022) SAFE Working Paper No. 354 <https://papers.ssrn.com/sol3/papers.cfm?abstract_id=4171508>.

[109] The Belgian and European securities laws relating to shareholder activism are discussed in more depth in the chapter in this book written by Marijke Spooren, Ruben Foriers and Jean-Sébastien Rombouts.

the US seem to be relatively favorable to activists with regards to the disclosure of share ownership and with regards to the formation of "wolf packs" among investors.

A first element of securities laws that is important to activists is the size of the stake that they can buy in their target before being required to disclose the stake. The reason is that as soon as the activist announces that it owns a stake in a corporation, the stock price will typically go up.[110] This makes it more expensive for the activist to acquire more shares. Laxer ownership disclosure requirements therefore allow activists to acquire larger stakes at a lower price, boosting activists' returns.[111] If activists can more easily require larger stakes, they will also have more voting rights and hence more influence in the general meeting. Therefore, the threshold at which investors must disclose their ownership participation matters. In the US, the ownership disclosure threshold is set at 5% of a class of shares.[112] In the EU, the Transparency Directive sets the minimum threshold at 5% of voting rights[113], but EU member states can set lower thresholds. Several EU member states, including Belgium and France, have set the mandatory minimum threshold at 5%, while the Netherlands, Germany, the UK and Italy have set the threshold at 3%.[114] In addition, in some EU member states, such as Belgium and France, the minimum threshold can be set at a lower percentage by corporations in their articles of association, with the possibility to go as low as 1% in Belgium and 0,5% in France, for example.[115] This shows that the potential for stakebuilding by an activist may be higher for US corporations than for European corporations.

Another factor that impacts the potential for activist stakebuilding is the number of days that an activist has after passing the ownership threshold before

---

[110] A. Brav, W. Jiang and R. Li, 'Governance by Persuasion: Hedge Fund Activism and the Market for Corporate Influence' (November 2021) *ECGI Working Paper Series in Finance* <https://papers.ssrn.com/sol3/papers.cfm?abstract_id=3955116>, 36–37.

[111] See for this argument: D. Katelouzou, 'Worldwide hedge fund activism: dimensions and legal determinants' [2015] *University of Pennsylvania Journal of Business Law* 789, 810.

[112] 17 CFR §240.13d-1(a).

[113] Directive European Parliament and Council 2004/109/EC of 15 December 2004 on the harmonisation of transparency requirements in relation to information about issuers whose securities are admitted to trading on a regulated market and amending Directive 2001/34/EC [2004] OJ L390/38.

[114] ESMA, *Practical Guide. National rules on notifications of major holdings under the Transparency Directive*, 1 July 2022, <www.esma.europa.eu/sites/default/files/library/practical_guide_major_holdings_notifications_under_transparency_directive.pdf>, 78–79. Note, however, that in Italy, the 3% threshold is not applicable to SMEs. In addition, in Germany, the 3% threshold only applies to the percentage of voting rights, not for positions in other financial instruments, such as derivatives. See for the UK: DTR 5.1.2.

[115] Article 18 Law of 2 May 2007 on the transparency of important participation in corporations listed on a regulated market, *Belgian Official Journal* 12 June 2007; article L233-7, III French Commercial Code.

being required to disclose their stake. In the US, the crossing of the threshold must be disclosed within ten calendar days[116], while in the EU, the disclosure must be made within four trading days.[117] The shorter deadline in the EU may give the activist less time to continue buying shares after the threshold has been crosses but before the participation is disclosed, therefore making stakebuilding harder.[118]

Which participations count toward the threshold also differs significantly between the US and the EU. In the US, derivatives that give investors economic exposure to the shares without giving them physical ownership of the shares or the voting rights, such as cash-settled total return equity swaps, do not count toward the threshold.[119] In the EU, on the other hand, such derivatives would count toward the threshold, regardless of whether they are physically settled or not.[120] If such derivatives must not be disclosed, activists can use this "hidden ownership" to increase their economic exposure to the target corporation, and therefore their profits if the activist campaign is successful.[121] In addition, the financial institutions concluding the derivative contract with the activist may hedge their own economic exposure by buying the target's shares. Some authors have suggested that these banks may be inclined to vote these shares in accordance with the activists' interests (or even instructions), which could give the activist more voting control than would normally be expected.[122]

Securities laws can also impose limits on activists' abilities to partner with a so-called "wolf pack", i.e., a group of loosely affiliated but supportive investors

---

[116] 17 CFR §240.13d-1(a).
[117] Article 12(2) Transparency Directive. See also: ESMA, *Practical Guide. National rules on notifications of major holdings under the Transparency Directive*, 1 July 2022, <www.esma.europa.eu/sites/default/files/library/practical_guide_major_holdings_notifications_under_transparency_directive.pdf>, 83.
[118] J. Coffee and D. Palia, 'The Wolf at the Door: The Impact of Hedge Fund Activism on Corporate Governance' [2016] *Journal of Corporation Law* 545, 594; D. Katelouzou, 'Worldwide hedge fund activism: dimensions and legal determinants' [2015] *University of Pennsylvania Journal of Business Law* 789, 813.
[119] D. Katelouzou, 'Worldwide hedge fund activism: dimensions and legal determinants' [2015] *University of Pennsylvania Journal of Business Law* 789, 812.
[120] Article 13(1)(b) Transparency Directive.
[121] D. Katelouzou, 'Worldwide hedge fund activism: dimensions and legal determinants' [2015] *University of Pennsylvania Journal of Business Law* 789, 811; L. Bebchuk, 'The Law and Economics of Equity Swap Disclosure' (March 2022) *Harvard Law School Program on Corporate Governance Working Paper* <https://papers.ssrn.com/sol3/papers.cfm?abstract_id=4063000>.
[122] J. Gordon, 'Why the SEC's Proposal for "Modernization of Beneficial Ownership Reporting" Is Flawed' (28 June 2022), *CLS Blue Sky Blog* <https://clsbluesky.law.columbia.edu/2022/06/28/why-the-secs-proposal-for-modernization-of-beneficial-ownership-reporting-is-flawed/> (noting, however, that *"industry participants have vociferously challenged these contentions as a factual matter"*).

that aim to avoid disclosure as a group under securities laws.[123] Because the members of the wolf pack are not subject to the disclosure requirements, they can build up a larger stake and therefore increase their influence and the potential benefits from the campaign.[124] In the US, wolf pack members must avoid being qualified as a "group" under the securities laws, as otherwise their ownership will have to be aggregated and disclosed.[125] Although the definition of group is not very clear, it is generally agreed that mere parallel actions and communications between hedge funds does not suffice to constitute a group, and that some kind of agreement is required.[126] Activists can interpret the concept of a group in a broad manner, because the main sanction is corrective disclosure, which will not deter many activists.[127] In the EU, to escape disclosure requirements, members of a wolf pack should refrain from concluding an agreement regarding the concerted exercise of voting rights.[128] Member states can impose broader definitions of acting in concert, as France and Germany have done, for example.[129] The definition of acting in concert is therefore not necessary broader in the EU than in the US, although this may be the case in certain EU member states under their national laws. In addition, in the EU, the members of the wolf pack may be subject to the mandatory bid rule if they are acting in concert[130], which further constrains the formation of (large) wolf packs.[131]

---

[123] See about the wolf pack strategy: J. Coffee and D. Palia, 'The Wolf at the Door: The Impact of Hedge Fund Activism on Corporate Governance' [2016] *Journal of Corporation Law* 545, 561–562.

[124] D. Katelouzou, 'Worldwide hedge fund activism: dimensions and legal determinants' [2015] *University of Pennsylvania Journal of Business Law* 789, 816; J. Coffee and D. Palia, 'The Wolf at the Door: The Impact of Hedge Fund Activism on Corporate Governance' [2016] *Journal of Corporation Law* 545, 562.

[125] 17 CFR §240.13d-5(b)(1): *"When two or more persons agree to act together for the purpose of acquiring, holding, voting or disposing of equity securities of an issuer, the group formed thereby shall be deemed to have acquired beneficial ownership, for purposes of sections 13(d)"*.

[126] J. Coffee and D. Palia, 'The Wolf at the Door: The Impact of Hedge Fund Activism on Corporate Governance' [2016] *Journal of Corporation Law* 545, 568.

[127] J. Coffee and D. Palia, 'The Wolf at the Door: The Impact of Hedge Fund Activism on Corporate Governance' [2016] *Journal of Corporation Law* 545, 569.

[128] Article 10(a) Transparency Directive (stipulating that the disclosure requirements also apply to *"voting rights held by a third party with whom that person or entity has concluded an agreement, which obliges them to adopt, by concerted exercise of the voting rights they hold, a lasting common policy towards the management of the issuer in question"*).

[129] Mentioning France and Germany: D. Katelouzou, 'Worldwide hedge fund activism: dimensions and legal determinants' [2015] *University of Pennsylvania Journal of Business Law* 789, 816. See also the chapter in this book written by Marijke Spooren, Ruben Foriers and Jean-Sébastien Rombouts for an analysis of Belgian law in this regard.

[130] See article 5 of the Directive European Parliament and Council nr. 2004/25/EC of 21 April 2004 on takeover bids, OJ L142/12.

[131] D. Katelouzou, 'Worldwide hedge fund activism: dimensions and legal determinants' [2015] *University of Pennsylvania Journal of Business Law* 789, 817.

Another important factor in the formation of wolf packs is the ability for hedge fund activists to tip prospective members of the wolf pack that they intend to launch an activist campaign. Such a tip allows the wolf pack members to buy shares before the share price has risen, while the hedge fund activist is able to secure additional supporters and therefore influence.[132] In the US, such tipping is not considered illegal insider tipping, because there is no duty of the activist toward the company to keep the information confidential.[133] In contrast, in the EU, such tipping would probably be illegal, as the prohibition for insider trading and tipping applies to everyone who knew or ought to have known they are in possession of material non-public information.[134] The underlying idea of the European approach is that traders should have equal access to information (the "parity of information theory"), but this idea can be criticized, as it does not reward the activist for the value that it creates (the "property rights theory").[135] Again, securities laws in the EU seem to be less activist-friendly than in the US.

The analysis above shows that US securities laws is in general more activist-friendly than EU securities laws, with a higher ownership threshold (at least in comparison to some EU member states), shorter deadlines for disclosure after crossing the threshold, more limited application to activists' hidden ownership through derivatives, and a more lenient approach to insider tipping to members of the wolf pack. These factors could therefore help to explain why hedge fund activism is generally more common in the US than in the EU.

However, the empirical evidence to support this hypothesis is mixed. Becht and co-authors find an average ownership of hedge fund activists of 11% in the US and of 10% in Europe, which is not economically significant.[136] Nevertheless, it is possible that hedge fund activism campaigns at lower ownership thresholds

---

[132] J. Coffee and D. Palia, 'The Wolf at the Door: The Impact of Hedge Fund Activism on Corporate Governance' [2016] *Journal of Corporation Law* 545, 565; J. Gordon, 'Why the SEC's Proposal for "Modernization of Beneficial Ownership Reporting" Is Flawed' (28 June 2022), *CLS Blue Sky Blog* <https://clsbluesky.law.columbia.edu/2022/06/28/why-the-secs-proposal-for-modernization-of-beneficial-ownership-reporting-is-flawed/>.

[133] J. Coffee and D. Palia, 'The Wolf at the Door: The Impact of Hedge Fund Activism on Corporate Governance' [2016] *Journal of Corporation Law* 545, 566. It would be considered illegal if the aim of the activist was to launch a tender offer for the target, however.

[134] Article 8(2) Regulation European Parliament and Council 596/2014 of 16 April 2014 on market abuse (market abuse regulation) and repealing Directive 2003/6/EC of the European Parliament and of the Council and Commission Directives 2003/124/EC, 2003/125/EC and 2004/72/EC, OJ L173/1.

[135] A. Taleska, 'European Insider Trading Theory Revisited: The Limits of the Parity-of-Information Theory and the Application of the Property Rights in Information Theory to Activist Investment Strategies' [2020] *European Company and Financial Law Review* 558.

[136] M. Becht, J. Franks, J. Grant and H. Wagner, 'Returns to Hedge Fund Activism: An International Study' [2017] *Review of Financial Studies* 2933, 2939.

are simply not undertaken and are therefore not visible in the sample, which would still explain the relatively low number of activist campaigns in Europe. Katelouzou also finds evidence that activists in countries with a lower disclosure threshold have smaller ownership stakes, consistent with the idea that securities laws matter.[137] Finally, Becht and co-authors do find evidence that wolf packs are more common in US activist campaigns (26%) than in European activist campaigns (17%)[138], consistent with the idea that the US takes a more lenient approach to wolf packs.

Two additional caveats need to be made. First, some US corporations have recently tried to fill in the "gaps" in securities laws by adopting anti-activist poison pills that impose shorter deadlines and broader definitions of the concept beneficial ownership (including hidden ownership) and of the concept of group (including members of a wolf pack).[139] To what extent these anti-activist poison pills will be accepted by the US courts remains to be seen.[140] Second, the SEC has recently formulated certain proposals that could make US securities laws less activist-friendly, including by shortening the deadline for disclosures to five calendar days instead of ten, extending the scope of application of the disclosure requirements to hidden ownership through derivatives, and extending the definition of group to investors who have been tipped by an activist of a campaign (regardless of whether an agreement has been concluded).[141] Whether these proposals will be adopted again remains to be seen, especially given the vehement criticism offered by some authors.[142]

---

[137] D. Katelouzou, 'Worldwide hedge fund activism: dimensions and legal determinants' [2015] *University of Pennsylvania Journal of Business Law* 789, 843.

[138] M. Becht, J. Franks, J. Grant and H. Wagner, 'Returns to Hedge Fund Activism: An International Study' [2017] *Review of Financial Studies* 2933, 2939.

[139] See for a discussion: J. Gordon, 'Corporate Vote Suppression: The Anti-Activist Pill in The Williams Companies Stockholder Litigation' (19 August 2021) *CLS Blue Sky Blog* <https://clsbluesky.law.columbia.edu/2021/08/19/corporate-vote-suppression-the-anti-activist-pill-in-the-williams-companies-stockholder-litigation/>.

[140] See, for example: In re Williams Cos. Stockholder Litig., 2021 Del. Ch. LEXIS 34 (February 26, 2021), *aff'd* (Del., November 3 2021) (invalidating a poison pill with a 5% ownership threshold, an expansive definition of "acting in concert", and a definition of ownership that encompassed derivatives, because no specific threat, other than the pandemic, was invoked for such an extreme poison pill).

[141] SEC, *Modernization of Beneficial Ownership Reporting. Proposed rule*, 10 February 2022 <www.sec.gov/rules/proposed/2022/33-11030.pdf>.

[142] See, for example: L. Bebchuk, 'The Law and Economics of Equity Swap Disclosure' (March 2022) *Harvard Law School Program on Corporate Governance Working Paper* < https://papers.ssrn.com/sol3/papers.cfm?abstract_id=4063000>; J. Gordon, 'Why the SEC's Proposal for "Modernization of Beneficial Ownership Reporting" Is Flawed' (28 June 2022), *CLS Blue Sky Blog* <https://clsbluesky.law.columbia.edu/2022/06/28/why-the-secs-proposal-for-modernization-of-beneficial-ownership-reporting-is-flawed/>.

4.5. DIFFERENCE IN THE MARKET CAPITALIZATION OF CORPORATIONS

In part 4.4, I have already argued that the possibility for hedge fund activists to engage in stakebuilding is an important factor in explaining levels of shareholder activism. The typical market capitalization of corporations listed in a country also has a large impact on stakebuilding.

First, the size of a corporation matters, because it determines whether launching an activist campaign is economically interesting for an activist. As discussed in part 4.4, transparency requirements limit the size of the ownership stake that an activist can acquire before being forced to go public, resulting in ownership stakes of on average 10%. Of course, owning 10% of a large corporation gives the activist a larger potential upside than owning 10% of a small corporation. This is especially true because the costs of launching an activist campaign (and especially those of launching a proxy contest) are to some extent fixed, or at least do not continue to increase proportionally as the market capitalization of the target corporation grows.[143]

For example, assume that a corporation is worth € 10 billion, but an activist can increase the value of the corporation by 10%, i.e. € 1 billion, by launching a proxy fight that will cost the activist € 10 million. Therefore, if the activist owns 10% of the corporation, he will gain € 100 million (10% of € 1 billion) minus the costs of € 10 million, resulting in a net gain of € 90 million. However, if the corporation is only worth € 100 million, and the activist can again increase the value of the corporation by 10%, i.e., € 10 million, the gain for the activist with a 10% ownership stake is only € 1 million. This € 1 million is too low to cover the costs of the proxy fight if we continue to assume that the proxy fight will cost € 10 million. It seems reasonable to assume that the costs of a proxy fight are somewhat lower for a small corporation than for a large corporation, but they are probably not 100 times lower (in which case the return on investment would be the same as for the large corporation) and maybe not even 10 times lower (in which case the activist would break even, which is not an attractive investment opportunity).

This example illustrates that smaller corporations could be less attractive for hedge fund activists with a similar ownership stake – a point already made by earlier commentators.[144] This could explain why countries with smaller listed

---

[143] J. Gordon, 'Why the SEC's Proposal for "Modernization of Beneficial Ownership Reporting" Is Flawed' (28 June 2022), *CLS Blue Sky Blog* <https://clsbluesky.law.columbia.edu/2022/06/28/why-the-secs-proposal-for-modernization-of-beneficial-ownership-reporting-is-flawed/> (*"the costs of an activist contest are relatively fixed"*).

[144] J. Gordon, 'Why the SEC's Proposal for "Modernization of Beneficial Ownership Reporting" Is Flawed' (28 June 2022), *CLS Blue Sky Blog* <https://clsbluesky.law.columbia.

corporations have lower levels of shareholder activism, even if the number of listed corporations is taken into account. For example, the median market capitalization of a corporation listed on Euronext Brussels in Belgium is around € 800 million[145], while the median corporation in the Russel 3000 in the US is around € 3.3 billion.[146] It is possible that in Belgium (and in continental Europe in general), there are fewer target corporations for which shareholder activism would be worth the costs.

However, the empirical evidence for this hypothesis is shaky: in its study of determinants of shareholder activism, the paper by Maffett controls for (the natural logarithm of) the aggregated market capitalization of listed corporations in a country. It finds a positive effect of this variable on the number of activist campaigns, but the effect is not statistically significant in most specifications of the model.[147] In addition, some studies even find that large corporations are less likely to be targeted than small corporations, contrary to what the hypothesis developed above would suggest.[148]

The latter finding can be explained by an alternative hypothesis: hedge fund activists may be more willing to target smaller corporations, because less capital is needed to acquire a larger stake in those corporations. This larger stake gives the activist more voting rights and therefore a higher likelihood of being successful in their goals. This hypothesis may be more consistent with some of the empirical evidence. However, it cannot explain why the US, which has many large cap corporations, has higher levels of shareholder activism than other countries in the world. It is also possible that both hypotheses are to some extent true, but that the effect is non-linear: very small and very large corporations may be less likely to be targeted, respectively because it is not economically interesting because the chance of success is lower, while corporations of an average size are the ideal candidate for activist campaigns.

---

edu/2022/06/28/why-the-secs-proposal-for-modernization-of-beneficial-ownership-reporting-is-flawed/> ("*for a mid-cap or small-cap firm, a larger percentage of ownership is required to cover those costs as part of the activist's economic return*").

[145] F. Lecoutre, V. Burki and A. Depoortere, 'State of the Belgian Listed Companies' [2022] *Tijdschrift voor Belgisch Handelsrecht* 561, 564.

[146] Data from FTSE Russel: <www.ftserussell.com/research-insights/russell-reconstitution/market-capitalization-ranges> (last checked 11 October 2022).

[147] M. Maffett, A. Nakhmurina and D. Skinner, 'Importing Activists: Determinants and Consequences of Increased Cross-border Shareholder Activism' [2022] *Journal of Accounting and Economics*, 11.

[148] M. Becht, J. Franks, J. Grant and H. Wagner, 'Returns to Hedge Fund Activism: An International Study' [2017] *Review of Financial Studies* 2933, 2947; A. Brav, W. Jiang and R. Li, 'Governance by Persuasion: Hedge Fund Activism and the Market for Corporate Influence' (November 2021) *ECGI Working Paper Series in Finance* <https://papers.ssrn.com/sol3/papers.cfm?abstract_id=3955116>, 114.

4.6. DIFFERENCES IN STOCK MARKET LIQUIDITY

Another factor that impacts the activists' ability to build up a stake in the corporation is the liquidity of the shares. If the shares of a corporation are more liquid, it will be easier for an activist to acquire shares without the market noticing abnormal volumes and without impacting the price.[149] In addition, a higher liquidity allows the activist to buy more shares in the few days before the deadline for disclosure after the activist has crossed the ownership threshold.[150] In other words, liquidity facilitates the acquisition of a higher stake, which makes shareholder activism more profitable and more influential. The empirical evidence confirms that share liquidity is positively associated with the likelihood of being targeted by a hedge fund activist.[151] Empirical evidence also shows that activists acquire a large fraction of their stake shortly before announcing their campaign, and that this fraction increases if liquidity is higher.[152]

The liquidity hypothesis could also explain to some extent the difference across countries in the level of shareholder activism: because the US is probably the country with the most liquid stock market in the world[153], it makes sense that it has high levels of shareholder activism.

4.7. DIFFERENCES IN CULTURE

A final explanation for the difference in the level of hedge fund activism across countries concerns the differences in culture. It has been suggested that different cultural norms across countries could cause activism to be perceived differently,

---

[149] Ø. Norli, C. Ostergaard and I. Schindele, 'Liquidity and shareholder activism' [2015] *Review of Financial Studies* 486, 488; D. Katelouzou, 'Myths and realities of hedge fund activism: some empirical evidence' [2013] *Virginia Law & Business Review* 459, 794.

[150] J. Gordon, 'Why the SEC's Proposal for "Modernization of Beneficial Ownership Reporting" Is Flawed' (28 June 2022), *CLS Blue Sky Blog* <https://clsbluesky.law.columbia.edu/2022/06/28/why-the-secs-proposal-for-modernization-of-beneficial-ownership-reporting-is-flawed/> ("*For all but the largest firms, however, liquidity for significant stock purchases is somewhat limited. This means a party that seeks to accumulate a meaningful block without significantly affecting the market price needs a longer trading period*").

[151] A. Brav, W. Jiang and R. Li, 'Governance by Persuasion: Hedge Fund Activism and the Market for Corporate Influence' (November 2021) *ECGI Working Paper Series in Finance* <https://papers.ssrn.com/sol3/papers.cfm?abstract_id=3955116>, 34 and 112 (US sample);
Ø. Norli, C. Ostergaard and I. Schindele, 'Liquidity and shareholder activism' [2015] *Review of Financial Studies* 486 (US sample); M. Becht, J. Franks, J. Grant and H. Wagner, 'Returns to Hedge Fund Activism: An International Study' [2017] *Review of Financial Studies* 2933, 2947 (international sample).

[152] Ø. Norli, C. Ostergaard and I. Schindele, 'Liquidity and shareholder activism' [2015] *Review of Financial Studies* 486, 515.

[153] X. Ding, Y. Ni and L. Zhong, 'Free float and market liquidity around the world' [2016] *Journal of Empirical Finance* 236, 238.

influencing the attractiveness of shareholder activism.[154] For example, in some countries, shareholder activists may be perceived positively, as bringing useful outside perspectives to the corporation's strategy. In other countries, shareholder activists may be vilified by the media and painted as "locusts"[155], making it less attractive to be an activist and less likely that activists will find support in the media and among local investors.

Another hypothesis relating to culture could be that activists, who predominantly come from the US[156], are less likely to (successfully) engage in activism in other countries than their "home" countries, because they have a worse understanding of the local culture. Especially in small countries, such as Belgium, the investment in understanding local culture and market practices may not be worth the potential benefits of shareholder activism. This could explain why hedge fund activism is more common in the US than in Belgium, for example.

To my knowledge, none of these "cultural" hypotheses has already been tested empirically.

4.8. DIFFERENCES IN THE NUMBER OF SHAREHOLDER PROPOSALS

So far, I have focused on trying to explain the difference in the levels of hedge fund activism. However, other types of shareholder activism also differ substantially between countries. For example, the number of shareholder proposals is also larger in the US than in the UK and continental Europe, even when taking into account the difference in the size of the stock market.[157]

---

[154] M. Lowry, 'Discussion of "Importing Activists: Determinants and Consequences of Increased Cross- border shareholder activism"' [2022] *Journal of Accounting and Economics*, 5.
[155] See the following quote by Franz Müntefering in 2005, then German Social Democratic Party chairman: *"We support those companies, who act in interest of their future and in interest of their employees against irresponsible locust swarms, who measure success in quarterly intervals, suck off substance and let companies die once they have eaten them away"*, as cited by: J. Bena, M. Ferreira, P. Matos and P. Pires, 'Are foreign investors locusts? The long-term effects of foreign institutional ownership' [2017] *Journal of Financial Economics* 122.
[156] M. Becht, J. Franks, J. Grant and H. Wagner, 'Returns to Hedge Fund Activism: An International Study' [2017] *Review of Financial Studies* 2933, 2938.
[157] P. Cziraki, L. Renneboog and P. Szilagyi, 'Shareholder Activism through Proxy Proposals: The European Perspective' [2010] *European Financial Management* 738, 750; C. Van Der Elst, 'Shareholder Engagement and Corporate Voting in Action: The Comparative Perspective' in H. Kaur, C. Xi, C. Van der Elst and A. Lafarre (eds.), *The Cambridge Handbook of Shareholder Engagement and Voting*, Cambridge University Press, Cambridge 2022, (501) 526–527 (noting, however, that shareholder proposals are more common in Germany and Denmark, but that they are concentrated in only a few corporations).

Some of the explanations discussed in the previous parts could also explain this difference, such as the difference in shareholder structure or cultural differences.[158] However, some potential explanations are typical to shareholder proposals, mainly relating to differences in corporate law.

One potential explanation for the higher level of shareholder proposals in the US is that the ownership thresholds for submission are generally lower in the US. For example, to bring a proposal in the US, shareholders need to hold only $2,000 in securities with voting rights for three years, $15,000 for two years or $25,000 for one year.[159] In Europe, the threshold is typically higher, typically several percentage points of the total number of shares.[160] However, the higher number of shareholder proposals in the US does not necessarily mean that shareholder rights are stronger, as US shareholder proposals cannot be used to elect or remove directors[161], whereas shareholder proposals in European jurisdictions generally can be used to elect or remove directors.[162]

Another potential explanation for the higher number of shareholder proposals is that corporate governance in the US is much more flexible, and that shareholder proposals are used in the US to close the corporate governance gap with European countries, which typically have mandatory corporate laws that are more shareholder-friendly.[163] For example, many shareholder proposals in

---

[158] Suggesting differences in shareholder structure and in culture as the explanations for the difference in shareholder proposals: L. Strine, 'The Soviet Constitution Problem in Comparative Corporate Law: Testing the Proposition That European Corporate Law Is More Stockholder Focused than U.S. Corporate Law' [2016] *Southern California Law Review* 1239, 1264–1265.

[159] 17 CFR §240.14a-8(b)(i).

[160] P. Cziraki, L. Renneboog and P. Szilagyi, 'Shareholder Activism through Proxy Proposals: The European Perspective' [2010] *European Financial Management* 738, 746; S. Cools, 'Shareholder proposals shaking up shareholder say: a critical comparison of the United States and Europe' in A. Afsharipour and M. Gelter (eds.), *Comparative Corporate Governance*, Edward Elgar, Cheltenham 2021, pp. 308–309; A. Lafarre, 'Shareholder Engagement and Corporate Voting in a Comparative Perspective' in H. Kaur, C. Xi, C. Van der Elst and A. Lafarre (eds.), *The Cambridge Handbook of Shareholder Engagement and Voting*, Cambridge University Press, Cambridge 2022, (461) 493.

[161] 17 CFR §240.14a-8(i)(8).

[162] P. Cziraki, L. Renneboog and P. Szilagyi, 'Shareholder Activism through Proxy Proposals: The European Perspective' [2010] *European Financial Management* 738, 744 and 750–751; S. Cools, 'Shareholder proposals shaking up shareholder say: a critical comparison of the United States and Europe' in A. Afsharipour and M. Gelter (eds.), *Comparative Corporate Governance*, Edward Elgar, Cheltenham 2021, pp. 308; B. Buchanan, J. Netter, A. Poulsen and T. Yang, 'Shareholder Proposal Rules and Practice: Evidence from a Comparison of the United States and United Kingdom' [2012] *American Business Law Journal* 739 (regarding the UK).

[163] S. Cools, 'Shareholder proposals shaking up shareholder say: a critical comparison of the United States and Europe' in A. Afsharipour and M. Gelter (eds.), *Comparative Corporate Governance*, Edward Elgar, Cheltenham 2021, pp. 322.

the US relate to destaggering boards, majority (instead of plurality) voting in director elections, the right to request special meetings, and proxy access for director elections, all of which are part of mandatory corporate law in most European countries.[164]

Finally, the relatively low number of ESG-related shareholder proposals in Europe may be explained by the rule in many European jurisdictions that shareholder proposals are not admissible if the general meeting is not competent for the matter, with many ESG-related matters falling under the board's competence for setting the strategy of the corporation.[165] Indeed, in the Netherlands and Germany, even non-binding shareholder proposals are not allowed if they relate to a matter falling under the competence of the board (such as most ESG-related matters), whereas France and Belgium (arguably) allow such non-binding shareholder proposals.[166] In the US, shareholder proposals on ESG-related matters generally also need to be non-binding, in order to comply with state law.[167] In addition, shareholder proposals may be excluded in the US if they do not relate to the corporation's ordinary business.[168] This means that the shareholder proposals must relate to significant policy issues and cannot be overly prescriptive.[169] In conclusion, ESG-related shareholder proposals are generally easier to bring in the US than in the Netherlands and Germany, which could explain the different levels of shareholder proposals in those countries. However, such differences in the law cannot explain the difference with Belgium and France, where non-binding shareholder proposals relating to ESG are also generally possible – even without the possibility for the corporation to preclude overly prescriptive shareholder proposals. However, as noted above, the ownership threshold for bringing shareholder proposals is higher in France and Belgium than in the US. This is especially relevant for ESG shareholder proposals, which are typically brought by smaller shareholders.[170]

---

[164] S. Cools, 'Shareholder proposals shaking up shareholder say: a critical comparison of the United States and Europe' in A. Afsharipour and M. Gelter (eds.), *Comparative Corporate Governance*, Edward Elgar, Cheltenham 2021, pp. 322.

[165] See for this argument: S. Cools, 'Climate Proposals: ESG Shareholder Activism Sidestepping Board Authority' in T. Kuntz (ed.), Research Handbook on Environment, Social, and Corporate Governance, Edward Elgar, Cheltenham (forthcoming), <https://papers.ssrn.com/sol3/papers.cfm?abstract_id=4377030>.

[166] S. Cools, 'Climate Proposals: ESG Shareholder Activism Sidestepping Board Authority' in T. Kuntz (ed.), Research Handbook on Environment, Social, and Corporate Governance, Edward Elgar, Cheltenham (forthcoming), <https://papers.ssrn.com/sol3/papers.cfm?abstract_id=4377030>, 14–15.

[167] R. Tallarita, 'Stockholder politics' [2022] *Hastings Law Journal* 1697, 1716.

[168] 17 C.F.R. §240.14a-8(i)(7).

[169] B. McDonnell, H.M. Osofsky, J. Peel, A. Foerster, 'Green boardrooms?' [2021] *Connecticut Law Review* 335, 376.

[170] T. Barko, M. Cremers and L. Renneboog, 'Shareholder Engagement on Environmental, Social, and Governance Performance' [2021] *Journal of Business Ethics* 777.

5. THE ECONOMIC CONSEQUENCES OF SHAREHOLDER ACTIVISM

The previous parts discussed the characteristics and causes of shareholder activism. I now discuss the economic consequences of shareholder activism. In part 5.1, I first discuss the impact of hedge fund activism on shareholder value. Afterwards, part 5.2 analyzes the impact of hedge fund activism on other stakeholders than shareholders. Finally, part 5.3 discusses the economic consequences of other types of shareholder activism.

5.1. THE ECONOMIC CONSEQUENCES OF HEDGE FUND ACTIVISM FOR SHAREHOLDER VALUE

What happens to firms that are targeted by hedge fund activists? One uncontroversial consequence is that the stock price typically goes up after the activist campaign is announced: average abnormal returns in the days around the announcement are 7% in the US and 4.8% in Europe.[171] In addition, the stock price in general also reacts positively to the announcement of a settlement agreement between the corporation and the hedge fund.[172] If we assume that markets are efficient, these findings imply that the market believes that shareholder value will increase in the corporations that are targeted by activists.

However, some commentators have questioned whether this positive short-term stock price reaction means that hedge fund activism creates long-term shareholder value.[173] Implicitly, such criticism assumes that the market is inefficient and overreacts on average to shareholder activism.[174] In response to this criticism, Bebchuk and co-authors have provided empirical evidence for

---

[171] M. Becht, J. Franks, J. Grant and H. Wagner, 'Returns to Hedge Fund Activism: An International Study' [2017] *Review of Financial Studies* 2933, 2934. These results are relatively similar to the 4.8% average abnormal returns found for the US by: A. Brav, W. Jiang and R. Li, 'Governance by Persuasion: Hedge Fund Activism and the Market for Corporate Influence' (November 2021) ECGI Working Paper Series in Finance <https://papers.ssrn.com/sol3/papers.cfm?abstract_id=3955116>, 37.

[172] L. Bebchuk, A. Brav, W. Jiang and T. Keusch, 'Dancing with activists' [2020] *Journal of Financial Economics* 1, 24–25.

[173] M. Lipton, 'Bite the Apple; Poison the Apple; Paralyze the Company; Wreck the Economy' (26 February 2013) *Harvard Law School Forum on Corporate Governance* <https://corpgov.law.harvard.edu/2013/02/26/bite-the-apple-poison-the-apple-paralyze-the-company-wreck-the-economy/> ("[f]or companies that are the subject of hedge fund activism and remain independent, what is the impact on their operational performance and stock price performance relative to the benchmark, not just in the short period after announcement of the activist interest, but after a 24-month period[?]").

[174] See for this point: A. Brav, W. Jiang and R. Li, 'Governance by Persuasion: Hedge Fund Activism and the Market for Corporate Influence' (November 2021) ECGI Working Paper Series in Finance <https://papers.ssrn.com/sol3/papers.cfm?abstract_id=3955116>, 42; D.

the US that the abnormal shareholder returns do not reverse in the long term (starting in the month after the activist campaign and running over a period of three to five years).[175] More recent empirical evidence confirms that hedge fund activist campaigns in the US are followed by long-term returns that are insignificantly different from zero, which suggests that the initial positive stock price reaction is no over- or underreaction.[176] The stock price also does not decrease after the hedge fund has exited its position.[177] Similarly, the empirical study by Becht and co-authors finds in an international sample of activist campaigns that the long-term abnormal shareholder returns following the campaign until exit of the activist are not significantly different from zero.[178] However, this obscures the fact that successful activist campaigns are associated with positive abnormal returns, while activist campaigns where activists do not achieve their stated objective are associated with negative or zero abnormal returns.[179]

Several papers have also studied how hedge fund activists could increase shareholder returns. Bebchuk and co-authors found evidence that the operational performance (as measured by return on assets) and firm value (as measured by Tobin's Q) increased in the five years after a hedge fund activist's intervention in the US.[180] However, another paper finds that the positive effect of activists on operational performance (return on assets) disappears when the control group is matched on the pre-activism trend in operating performance.[181] This is important, because activist targets typically underperform their peers in the years before the activist intervention.

  Katelouzou, 'Myths and realities of hedge fund activism: some empirical evidence' [2013] *Virginia Law & Business Review* 459, 481.
[175] L. Bebchuk, A. Brav and W. Jiang, 'The long-term effects of hedge fund activism' [2015] *Columbia Law Review* 1085, 1126–1130.
[176] A. Brav, W. Jiang and R. Li, 'Governance by Persuasion: Hedge Fund Activism and the Market for Corporate Influence' (November 2021) *ECGI Working Paper Series in Finance* <https://papers.ssrn.com/sol3/papers.cfm?abstract_id=3955116>, 43; E. deHaan, D. Larcker and C. McClure, 'Long-term economic consequences of hedge fund activist interventions' [2019] *Review of Accounting Studies* 536.
[177] A. Brav, W. Jiang and R. Li, 'Governance by Persuasion: Hedge Fund Activism and the Market for Corporate Influence' (November 2021) *ECGI Working Paper Series in Finance* <https://papers.ssrn.com/sol3/papers.cfm?abstract_id=3955116>, 44 (US sample).
[178] M. Becht, J. Franks, J. Grant and H. Wagner, 'Returns to Hedge Fund Activism: An International Study' [2017] *Review of Financial Studies* 2933, 2962. This is true for both equal-weighted and value-weighted abnormal returns.
[179] M. Becht, J. Franks, J. Grant and H. Wagner, 'Returns to Hedge Fund Activism: An International Study' [2017] *Review of Financial Studies* 2933, 2962. This is true for both equal-weighted and value-weighted abnormal returns.
[180] L. Bebchuk, A. Brav and W. Jiang, 'The long-term effects of hedge fund activism' [2015] *Columbia Law Review* 1085, 1103–1117.
[181] E. deHaan, D. Larcker and C. McClure, 'Long-term economic consequences of hedge fund activist interventions' [2019] *Review of Accounting Studies* 536.

Other studies take an even more granular approach and look at the productivity and investment decisions in firms targeted by activists. For example, one paper finds that US firms targeted by hedge fund activists on average increase the productivity of their plants and their investments in IT in the following three years.[182] The study also finds that plants that are sold by the targeted firms increase their productivity under new ownership. This suggests that hedge fund activists improve the efficient allocation of capital. Another study finds that US corporations targeted by hedge fund activists reduce their investment in R&D, which seems consistent with the short-termism hypothesis.[183] However, the study finds that despite the lower investment, the innovation output (as measured by the number of patents and the number of patent citations) increases. The study concludes that activists focus on increasing innovation efficiency by cutting inefficient investments and selling non-core patents, allowing the firms to focus on core innovation expertise. Finally, empirical evidence finds that US corporations targeted by hedge fund activists engage in fewer acquisitions, especially those acquisitions that are often considered inefficient (large acquisitions, diversifying acquisitions and acquisitions during industry merger waves).[184] The acquisitions that these firms do engage in obtain higher shareholder returns. Firms targeted by hedge fund activists also divest more of their assets and these divestitures are associated with higher shareholder returns.[185] This evidence suggests that hedge fund activists help to curb CEO empire building.

Another strand of literature examines not the direct effect of activism on targeted firms, but the effect of the threat of hedge fund activists on firms that have not (yet) been targeted. One study on the US finds that non-targeted firms with a higher perception of the threat of shareholder activism (as measured by directors having educational connections to directors of past targets of shareholder activism) on average increase leverage and shareholder pay-out, while decreasing capital expenditures and cash holdings.[186] These firms also improve their operating performance (as measured by return on assets). This results in these firms becoming less likely to be targeted by hedge fund activists

---

[182] A. Brav, W. Jiang and H. Kim, 'The Real Effects of Hedge Fund Activism: Productivity, Asset Allocation, and Labor Outcomes' [2015] *Review of Financial Studies* 2723.

[183] A. Brav, W. Jiang, S. Ma, X. Tian, 'How does hedge fund activism reshape corporate innovation?' [2018] *Journal of Financial Economics* 237. See for a study with similar results: Y. Wang and J. Zhao, 'Hedge Funds and Corporate Innovation' [2015] *Financial Management* 353.

[184] N. Gantchev, M. Sevilir and A. Shivdasani, 'Activism and empire building' [2020] *Journal of Financial Economics* 526; S. WHU and K. CHUNG, 'Hedge Fund Activism and Corporate M&A Decisions' [2021] *Management Science* 809.

[185] N. Gantchev, M. Sevilir and A. Shivdasani, 'Activism and empire building' [2020] *Journal of Financial Economics* 526.

[186] N. Gantchev, O. Gredil, and C. Jotikasthira, 'Governance under the Gun: Spillover Effects of Hedge Fund Activism' [2019] *Review of Finance* 1031.

in the future. Another study, by Maffett and co-authors, finds that if a legislative change makes corporate law more activist-friendly, corporations with a high level of activism threat increase their profitability and shareholder pay-outs and reduce their investment in capital expenditures and R&D, in comparison to a control group with firms with a lower threat of shareholder activism.[187]

One recent literature review concludes from all the evidence discussed above that *"hedge fund activists bring about an overall improvement in the target firms' performance"*.[188] Other scholars are less optimistic in their interpretation of the evidence on hedge fund activism, pointing out that the long-term abnormal returns and increases in operating performance are neither significantly positive or negative, and that therefore shareholder activism may neither be particularly harmful or useful.[189] Another criticism is that hedge fund activists may simply be good stock pickers that invest in undervalued shares but do not create any value themselves, as the evidence does not necessarily prove a causal link between activism and stock returns.[190] However, such arguments are hardly a good reason to criticize shareholder activism or call for legislative interventions, as the empirical evidence does not point to a clear harm for shareholders. In addition, a recent paper used more advanced econometrical techniques to estimate that approximately 74.8% of abnormal shareholder returns were caused by activist value creation, rather than by stock picking or sample selection effects.[191] Nevertheless, the empirical evidence that shareholder activism is on average neutral or even positive, of course does not mean that each shareholder activist campaign will increase the value of the targeted corporation. A (substantial) minority of the firms may still be harmed by (the threat of) shareholder activism. This suggests that the optimal openness to shareholder activism may not be the same for all corporations and that corporations should be able to customize their governance structure.[192] However, such freedom also

---

[187] M. Maffett, A. Nakhmurina and D. Skinner, 'Importing Activists: Determinants and Consequences of Increased Cross-border Shareholder Activism' [2022] *Journal of Accounting and Economics*, 3 and 18–26. A firm was considered to have a high threat of shareholder activism if it was *"either 1) a target of a post-law-change activist campaign, or 2) had non-zero independent institutional ownership"*.

[188] A. Brav, W. Jiang and R. Li, 'Governance by Persuasion: Hedge Fund Activism and the Market for Corporate Influence' (November 2021) *ECGI Working Paper Series in Finance* <https://papers.ssrn.com/sol3/papers.cfm?abstract_id=3955116>, 63.

[189] E. deHaan, D. Larcker and C. McClure, 'Long-term economic consequences of hedge fund activist interventions' [2019] *Review of Accounting Studies* 536, 542.

[190] See for this criticism: M. Cremers, E. Giambona, S. Sepe and Y. Wang, 'Hedge fund activists: value creators or stock pickers?' (January 2021) <https://papers.ssrn.com/sol3/papers.cfm?abstract_id=3614029>, 3–4.

[191] R. Albuquerque, V. Fos and E. Schroth, 'Value creation in shareholder activism' [2022] *Journal of Financial Economics* 153 (developing a structural model that estimates both the decision to become an activist and the announcement returns).

[192] See for such an argument: Z. Goshen and R. Squire, 'Principal costs: a new theory for corporate law and governance' [2017] *Columbia Law Review* 767.

comes with a risk of opportunistic behavior, especially if corporations decide to restrict the possibility of shareholder activism in the midstream phase.[193]

5.2. THE ECONOMIC CONSEQUENCES OF HEDGE FUND ACTIVISM FOR OTHER STAKEHOLDERS

Another criticism against shareholder activists is that even if they increase shareholder value, this may simply be a transfer of value from other stakeholders. The empirical evidence supporting this hypothesis is mixed. For example, some studies find that (the threat of) shareholder activism in the US has a negative impact on creditors of the targeted corporations.[194] However, other studies are more nuanced. One study finds that activist campaigns in the US demanding a takeover or a financial restructuring have a negative impact on creditors, while governance-focused campaigns have a positive impact.[195]

Shareholder activism may also harm the interests of employees. One study of US firms finds that worker productivity increases in firms targeted by hedge fund activism, but that wages remain the same.[196] Employees therefore do not profit from the increase in shareholder value. The study also finds a decrease in employment in firms with stronger unionization. This suggests that firms with unions have more labor surplus that can be cut to increase shareholder value and that managers are less willing to take on labor unions in the absence of shareholder activism. However, this effect is offset to some extent by an increase in wages in firms with high unionization that are targeted by hedge fund activists. All in all, the evidence suggests that shareholder activists facilitate a transfer of wealth from employees to shareholders.[197] This transfer of wealth also

---

[193] See about the risks for shareholders associated with midstream changes: L. Bebchuk, 'Foreword: The Debate on Contractual Freedom in Corporate Law' [1989] *Columbia Law Review* 1395, 1399–1404.

[194] A. Klein and E. Zur, 'The Impact of Hedge Fund Activism on the Target Firm's Existing Bondholder' [2011] *Review of Financial Studies* 1735 (finding negative abnormal returns for bondholders after the announcement of the activist campaign); F. Feng, Q. Xu and C. Zhu, 'Caught in the crossfire: How the threat of hedge fund activism affects creditors' [2021] *Journal of Empirical Finance* 128 (firms with a higher level of shareholder activism threat face declines in bond prices and credit ratings, because these firms increase leverage).

[195] J. Sunder, S. Sunder and W. Wongsunwai, 'Debtholder Responses to Shareholder Activism: Evidence from Hedge Fund Interventions' [2014] *Review of Financial Studies* 3318 (analyzing bank loan spreads). See for similar results: H. Aslan and H. Maraachlian, 'Wealth Effects of Hedge Fund Activism' (August 2018) <https://papers.ssrn.com/sol3/papers.cfm?abstract_id=993170>.

[196] A. Brav, W. Jiang and H. Kim, 'The Real Effects of Hedge Fund Activism: Productivity, Asset Allocation, and Labor Outcomes' [2015] *Review of Financial Studies* 2723.

[197] A. Brav, W. Jiang and H. Kim, 'The Real Effects of Hedge Fund Activism: Productivity, Asset Allocation, and Labor Outcomes' [2015] *Review of Financial Studies* 2723, 2753 (*"hedge fund activism facilitates a transfer of "labor rents" to shareholders"*).

occurs through the funding of employee pension plans: another study finds that firms targeted by hedge fund activists decrease funding for employee pension plans by lowering employer contributions.[198] Firms justify this by increasing the assumed rates of returns on plan investments, but the evidence does not show an increased return after the activist intervention.

The more general society may also suffer as a result from hedge fund activist campaigns, through negative effect on government budgets or the environment. Cheng and co-authors find that (legal) tax avoidance increases after corporations are targeted by hedge fund activists, in comparison to a control group.[199] This suggests that activists pressure managers to take more aggressive tax policies. Another study, by DesJardine and Durand, finds that a corporation's social and environmental performance, as measured by ESG rating agencies, decreases after a hedge fund activist campaign.[200] On the other hand, two other studies find that corporations decrease their emissions of harmful chemicals after being targeted by a hedge fund activist, relative to control groups.[201] One of these studies also finds that this reduction in emissions is associated with higher long-term returns for shareholders.[202] This suggests that shareholder activists may be motivated in increasing environmental performance to the extent that this is good for shareholders.

The overall picture that emerges from a review of the evidence on the impact on stakeholders is one of hedge fund activists as opportunists. Their goal is in general to increase shareholder value, and in some cases, they pursue this goal at the expense of other stakeholders, such as creditors, employees or taxpayers. However, in other circumstances, the interests of shareholders and other stakeholders seem to be aligned, and hedge fund activists can increase a corporation's creditworthiness or environmental performance. This suggests that regulation that internalizes externalities in firms may be necessary to ensure that shareholder activism not only benefits shareholders, but also society as a whole. Finally, nearly all of the studies on the impact of shareholder activism on external stakeholders were conducted on a sample of US corporations. If we assume that regulation in European countries provides stronger protection

---

[198] A. Agrawal and Y. Lim, 'Where Do Shareholder Gains in Hedge Fund Activism Come From? Evidence from Employee Pension Plans' [2022] *Journal of Financial and Quantitative Analysis* 2140.

[199] C. Cheng, H. Huang, Y. Li and J. Stanfield, 'The Effect of Hedge Fund Activism on Corporate Tax Avoidance' [2012] *Accounting Review* 1493.

[200] M. DesJardine and R. Durand, 'Disentangling the effects of hedge fund activism on firm financial and social performance' [2018] *Strategic Management Journal* 1.

[201] P. Akey and I. Appel, 'Environmental Externalities of Activism' (January 2020) <https://papers.ssrn.com/sol3/papers.cfm?abstract_id=3508808>; Y. Chu and D. Zhao, 'Green Hedge Fund Activists' (December 2019) <https://ssrn.com/abstract=3499373>.

[202] Y. Chu and D. Zhao, 'Green Hedge Fund Activists' (December 2019) <https://ssrn.com/abstract=3499373>.

for external stakeholders than the US (which seems plausible), shareholder activism may help to monitor compliance with regulation, to the benefit of both shareholders and other stakeholders.

5.3. THE ECONOMIC CONSEQUENCES OF OTHER TYPES OF SHAREHOLDER ACTIVISM

So far, I have analyzed only the evidence on hedge fund activism, not on the other types of shareholder activism. A 2007 paper reviewing the literature concluded that empirical studies generally did not find a significant positive or negative effect of shareholder proposals in the US (which are typically not filed by hedge funds – see above in part 3.2) on the stock price and on firm performance.[203] However, more recent studies have found that shareholder activism through shareholder proposals does have a positive effect on firm performance, although the impact is generally smaller than for hedge fund activism. For example, Renneboog and Szilagyi find statistically significant, but economically small, positive effects on the announcement of shareholder proposals in the US.[204] Buchanan and co-authors finds that US firms targeted by shareholder proposals increase their market-to-book ratio and their stock returns, in comparison to a control group.[205] They find that the positive effect is concentrated in those shareholder proposals that received a majority of the votes. The positive effect also increases when the shareholder proposals are filed by larger shareholders (1% or 5% of shares). Similarly, Gantchev and Gianetti also find that the type of activist matters. Shareholder proposals filed by "gadflies" (retail investors with small stakes who repeatedly file shareholder proposals in many different corporations) are associated with negative abnormal shareholder returns when they pass in the general meeting and with negative long-term performance, suggesting that such proposals may actually destroy value.[206] Finally, in contrast

---

[203] S. Gillan and L. Starks, 'The Evolution of Shareholder Activism in the United States' [2007] Journal of Applied Corporate Finance 55, 65 ("*In general, for the overall samples of shareholder proposals, the studies have found no significant abnormal returns around the assumed date of information release*") and 67 ("*Virtually all studies of long-term operating performance have reported no statistically significant changes in the operating performance of targeted companies*").

[204] L. Renneboog and P. Szilagyi, 'The role of shareholder proposals in corporate governance' [2011] Journal of Corporate Finance 167, 173–177.

[205] B. Buchanan, J. Netter, A. Poulsen and T. Yang, 'Shareholder Proposal Rules and Practice: Evidence from a Comparison of the United States and United Kingdom' [2012] American Business Law Journal 739, 786–791.

[206] N. Gantchev and M. Gianetti, 'The Costs and Benefits of Shareholder Democracy: Gadflies and Low-Cost Activism' [2021] *Review of Financial Studies* 5629, 5644–5652. The authors also not that this negative effect is concentrated among shareholder proposals filed by individuals who file many generic shareholder proposals, while more focused shareholder proposals by others are associated with positive results.

to the US, studies on shareholder proposals in the UK and in Europe generally do not find positive effects for shareholders.[207]

Part 3.2 above discussed how other investors, like index funds, often use less confrontational tactics than shareholder proposals and proxy contests. They also tend to focus on "systemic issues", such as ESG issues. Such "behind-the-scenes" engagements with corporations can nevertheless be effective. For example, a study by Azar and co-authors finds that the big three index funds (BlackRock, Vanguard and State Street Global Advisers) focus their engagements on large firms with high carbon emissions and that big three ownership is negatively associated with carbon emissions.[208] This suggests that the engagement efforts of the big three are effective. This is consistent with other evidence that institutional ownership is positively associated with environmental and social performance.[209] Some of these studies also suggest that the effect may be concentrated among investors from countries with a strong ESG culture[210], or among investors with a long-term horizon.[211]

That ESG shareholder activism can be effective is also confirmed by other studies. For example, one study analyzed activist campaigns launched by the New York City Pension Systems in the framework of the "Boardroom Accountability Project".[212] The study finds that the firms targeted by campaigns related to climate risk reduced their toxic chemical releases and greenhouse gas emissions, in comparison to a control group. In addition, Barko and co-authors analyze engagements by an anonymous socially responsible activist fund and find that targeted firms with low ESG ratings see their ratings improve on average.[213] The study also finds that this

---

[207] B. Buchanan, J. Netter, A. Poulsen and T. Yang, 'Shareholder Proposal Rules and Practice: Evidence from a Comparison of the United States and United Kingdom' [2012] *American Business Law Journal* 739, 792 (finding no increase in firm performance and a negative effect on stock returns for shareholder proposals in the UK); P. Cziraki, L. Renneboog and P. Szilagyi, 'Shareholder Activism through Proxy Proposals: The European Perspective' [2010] *European Financial Management* 738 (finding negative stock price reactions to votes in the general meeting on shareholder proposals in several European countries and the UK).

[208] J. Azar, M. Duro, I. Kadach and G. Ormazabal, 'The Big Three and corporate carbon emissions around the world' [2021] *Journal of Financial Economics* 674.

[209] A. Dyck, K. Lins, L. Roth, H. Wagner, 'Do institutional investors drive corporate social responsibility? International evidence' [2019] *Journal of Financial Economics* 692 (analyzing a sample of non-US firms in 41 countries); T. Chen, H. Dong and C. Lin, 'Institutional shareholders and corporate social responsibility' [2020] *Journal of Financial Economics* 483.

[210] A. Dyck, K. Lins, L. Roth, H. Wagner, 'Do institutional investors drive corporate social responsibility? International evidence' [2019] *Journal of Financial Economics* 692, 705–708.

[211] I. Oikonomou, C. Yin and L. Zhao, 'Investment horizon and corporate social performance: the virtuous circle of long-term institutional ownership and responsible firm conduct' [2020] *European Journal of Finance* 14.

[212] S. Naaraayanan, K. Sachdeva and V. Sharma, 'The Real Effects of Environmental Activist Investing' (March 2021) <https://ssrn.com/abstract=3483692>.

[213] T. Barko, M. Cremers and L. Renneboog, 'Shareholder Engagement on Environmental, Social, and Governance Performance' [2021] *Journal of Business Ethics* 777.

is associated with higher abnormal returns for shareholders. A final study analyzes ESG engagements by investors with firms located in 63 different countries through the Principles of Responsible Investment (PRI) Collaboration Platform.[214] The study finds that such engagements are often successful and that firms targeted by the engagements increase their shareholder returns and operational performance (as measured by return on assets) in the years following the engagement, but only in case the engagement is led by a "lead investor".

In conclusion, other types of shareholder activism than hedge fund activism, such as activism through shareholder proposals and ESG shareholder activism can be effective in increasing firm performance, both from a traditional share value perspective as well as from an ESG perspective. An exception is gadfly activism in the US, which on average seems to destroy shareholder value. It is noteworthy, however, that the increase in performance is often not as large as for hedge fund activism, consistent with hedge fund's superior incentives (see above in part 2.2) and willingness to employ more aggressive tactics (see above in part 3.1).

6. CONCLUSION

In this chapter, I have given an overview of the characteristics, causes and consequences of shareholder activism. I have distinguished traditional shareholder activism, which focuses on shareholder value, from the more recent trend of ESG shareholder activism. I have also discussed the different types of shareholder activists, including hedge funds, index funds, pension funds, NGOs and retail investors. These activists tend to use different tactics (with hedge funds generally being most aggressive) and often have different objectives (exclusively focused on financial performance versus also on ESG performance). I have also provided evidence that many of these types of shareholder activism can play a beneficial role, both with regards to financial performance and with regards to ESG performance. The evidence that shareholder activism increases financial performance is the strongest for hedge fund activism. However, the evidence also suggests that this may sometimes come at the expense of ESG performance. Nevertheless, some studies also find a positive effect of hedge fund activism on ESG performance, in particular when the two are aligned. Some studies find that activism (or "engagement") by other institutional investors has a positive effect on financial performance, although the effect is typically smaller than for hedge fund activism. The evidence also suggests that activism by certain types of institutional investors, such as index funds and socially responsible investment funds, also increases the ESG performance of firms, often together with firms' financial performance.

---

[214] E. Dimson, O. Karakaş and X. Li, 'Coordinated Engagements' (January 2021) <https://ssrn.com/abstract=3209072>.

The overall story that emerges is that the different types of shareholder activism (perhaps with the exception of gadfly activism) each have a positive and complementary role to play in the corporate governance landscape. This raises the question whether the current levels of shareholder activism, which are much lower in Europe and especially Belgium than in the US (see above in part 4), are optimal. Opinions on the desirability of more shareholder activism differ widely, and resolving this debate falls outside the scope of this chapter.

The analysis in this chapter of the potential explanations for the different levels of shareholder activism (see above in part 4) does offer some options for encouraging or discouraging shareholder activism – depending on where one stands in the debate. For example, the analysis shows that if the legislator would want to increase the number of activist campaigns, it could make corporate laws and securities laws more activist-friendly. Nevertheless, the analysis also shows the limits of such policy interventions: differences in market factors, such as the shareholder structure, the market capitalization, and the stock market liquidity, would likely continue to hinder shareholder activists in Belgium and the rest of continental Europe, especially in comparison to the US.

In any case, shareholder activism looks like it is here to stay, and the recent trend of ESG shareholder activism makes an uptick in the number of activist campaigns even more likely. This is even true in Belgium, as several recent (ESG) activist campaigns make clear. The evidence in this chapter suggests that such an increase in shareholder activism may be a boon rather than a curse for sustainable value creation, especially when financial performance and ESG performance are aligned. That last condition should be interpreted as an invitation to the legislator to align financial and ESG performance as much as possible, by internalizing externalities imposed on external stakeholders. This would ensure that activists cannot opportunistically pursue financial performance at the expense of ESG performance. In any case, even if shareholder activists can be part of the solution toward sustainable value creation, they can only play a small part.

ESG-FOCUSED HEDGE FUND ACTIVISM

Anna CHRISTIE[*]

*University of Oxford, Faculty of Law; Newnham College,
University of Cambridge*

1. INTRODUCTION

In 2020, the Belgian multinational chemicals company Solvay became the target of an ESG-focused hedge fund activism campaign conducted by the activist hedge fund Bluebell Capital Partners. The hedge fund, which was launched in London in 2019, focused its attention on Solvay's chemical plant in Rosignano, Tuscany, a tourist destination with white sand beaches that have been described as "the Italian Maldives".[1] At first glance, the beaches of Rosignano Solvay[2] look idyllic and even featured on the cover of Vogue Italia due to the unique colouring of the sand and sea.[3] However, the beaches owe their distinctive appearance to the chemical waste that is discharged untreated into the Mediterranean sea from the factory owned by Solvay. The environmental impact of Solvay's plant on the beaches has long been a source of controversy and conflict with local environmental activists. Although Solvay has consistently argued that the production materials it releases into the sea are all inert, natural materials,[4] the World Health Organization described the area as a *"priority*

---

[*] The author is very grateful to the joint editors and organisers of the "Shareholder Activism in Belgium" conference, Tom Vos (University of Antwerp, Jean-Pierre Blumberg Chair) and Arie Van Hoe (the Federation of Belgian Enterprises), and to the participants in the conference for their helpful comments.

[1] S. Sciorilli Borrelli and A. Mooney, 'The factory by a Tuscan beach and the future of ESG investing', *Financial Times* (22 December 2020) <www.ft.com/content/fb129666-dc85–48ff-a9c8–3bfa87a715ca>.

[2] The town is also named after the Belgian corporate entity that built it.

[3] Following complaints about the feature, Vogue Italia noted that *"Using fashion to pose questions on the role and nature of beauty in today's society, on its ethical ramifications, on its ever so deceptive quality and its uncanny complexity, is part of the mission of Vogue Italia".*

[4] See, for example Solvay, 'Solvay's Soda Ash Production in Rosignano' <www.solvay.com/sites/g/files/srpend221/files/2022–01/Solvay%20Rosignano%20-%20Factsheet.pdf> and Solvay, 'Solvay Board Issues Open Letter Regarding Soda Ash Operation in Rosignano' (10 February 2022) <www.solvay.com/en/news/solvay-board-issues-open-letter-regarding-soda-ash-operations-rosignano> (arguing that Bluebell's campaign conveyed "misleading information").

pollution hotspot in the Mediterranean".[5] In its activist campaign, Bluebell Capital Partners labelled the beaches *"an open landfill"*, in stark contrast to the *"captivating (and misleading) appearance of an idyllic Caribbean beach"*.[6]

This activist hedge fund campaign is unusual in many respects. First, activist hedge fund campaigns are less prevalent in Europe[7] compared to the United States where the phenomenon is widespread. Second, activist hedge fund campaigns that focus solely or primarily on ESG issues, rather than on financial gain, are even more atypical. Indeed, activist hedge funds are typically seen much more as exclusively profit-oriented investors. Third, the campaign stood out as Bluebell Capital Partners effectively had no economic interest in its target company, Solvay. The campaign formed part of Bluebell's "One-Share" movement which is a *pro bono* initiative aimed at creating change at companies that are falling short on ESG issues.[8]

This chapter discusses ESG-focused hedge fund activism. Part 2 begins by introducing the concept of ESG hedge fund activism, a recent trend that originated with ESG-focused activist campaigns in the United States. Part 3 then proposes a framework for ESG hedge fund activism that categorises the various types of ESG hedge fund campaigns and describes the different activist hedge fund players who are instigating these campaigns. This part also considers the motivations and incentives for ESG activist hedge fund campaigns and the promise and limitations of this type of activism. Part 4 then considers other influential actors in the ESG investor ecosystem, focusing on the role of global asset managers and other institutional investors in ESG activist campaigns.

2. ESG HEDGE FUND ACTIVISM

2.1. ORIGINS OF ESG HEDGE FUND ACTIVISM

Activist hedge funds – typically portrayed as short-termist actors who are only concerned with financial gains – may at first sight seem unlikely proponents of environmental and social activism. On both sides of the Atlantic, activist hedge funds have been routinely criticised by politicians, with Hillary Clinton labelling

---

[5] Sciorilli and Mooney, *supra* note 1.
[6] Bluebell Capital Partners, 'Bluebell Capital Partners – Response to Solvay Board Open Letter Regarding Soda Ash Operations in Rosignano' (17 February 2022) <www.globenewswire.com/en/news-release/2022/02/17/2387310/0/en/Bluebell-Capital-Partners-Response-to-Solvay-Board-Open-Letter-Regarding-Soda-Ash-Operations-in-Rosignano.html>.
[7] Although rare, campaigns in Europe – and in Belgium specifically – are becoming increasingly common. This is discussed in the chapter by Tom Vos in this book.
[8] V. Zia and S. Jessop, 'Activist Bluebell calls for Solvay board to oust CEO – letter', *Reuters* (15 September 2021) <www.reuters.com/article/solvay-activist-letter-idCNL8N2QH2CX>. Bluebell's campaign at Solvay is discussed further in Part 3 below.

them "hit-and-run activists" and a German politician calling them "swarms of locusts".[9] Indeed, the business model of activist hedge funds specifically involves investing in target companies to agitate for change with the goal of unlocking shareholder value.[10] Therefore, it is unsurprising that activist hedge funds tend to focus on share price increases rather than broader environmental or social issues.

It is only very recently that activist hedge funds have begun to launch ESG-focused campaigns, and this still remains a niche strategy. The growing trend of ESG activist hedge fund campaigns first captured attention in January 2018 when two well-known, formidable, activist hedge funds – Jana Partners and ValueAct Capital – announced the creation of specialist ESG-focused funds. First, Jana Partners enlisted the input of social activists, rock star Sting and a former fund manager of BlackRock to be involved in its new impact fund, Jana Impact Capital, which was described in the press as *"a convergence of Wall Street's roughest fighters and its do-gooders"*.[11] The impact fund's first activist campaign was a well-publicised social campaign targeting Apple, which was the world's most valuable publicly traded company at that time. Here, Jana Impact Capital collaborated with the California Teachers' Retirement System ("CalSTRS") pension fund to raise concerns regarding the psychological damage to young people of too much "screen time" on Apple devices.[12] The activist fund and CalSTRS jointly issued a public letter demanding that Apple implement stronger parental controls on devices such as the iPhone.[13] It proved relatively straightforward for the activists to succeed in their campaign, with Apple responding quickly by unveiling its new "screen time" feature on its devices less than six months later.[14]

Second, ValueAct Capital announced its new Spring Fund around the same time.[15] The Spring Fund's first campaign target was the international power producer

---

[9] A. L. Christie, 'The new hedge fund activism: activist directors and the market for corporate quasi-control' [2019] 19 *Journal of Corporate Law Studies* 1, 1 (citing D. A. Katz and L.A. McIntosh, 'Corporate Governance; News; Advice on Coping With Hedge Fund Activism' [2006] 235 *New York Law Journal* 5, and B. Kochkodin and C. Melby, 'Hillary Clinton Faults "Hit-and-Run" Activist Investors', *Bloomberg* (New York, 24 July 2015) <www.bloomberg.com/news/articles/2015-07-24/hillary-clinton-faults-activist-investors-hit-and-run-tactics>).

[10] B. R. Cheffins and J. Armour, 'The Past, Present, and Future of Shareholder Activism by Hedge funds' [2011] 37 *The Journal of Corporation Law* 51, 56.

[11] D. Benoit, 'Wall Street Fighters, Do-Gooders – And Sting – Converge in New Jana Fund', *Wall Street Journal* (7 January 2018) <www.wsj.com/articles/wall-street-fighters-do-goodersand-stingconverge-in-new-jana-fund-1515358929>.

[12] A. Mooney, '*Activists Don Sustainability Cloak to Whip up Support*', *Financial Times* (13 May 2018), <www.ft.com/content/b74d2adc-2b8e-11e8-97ec-4bd3494d5f14>.

[13] A. Sheehan, 'Letter from JANA Partners & CalSTRS to Apple, Inc.', *Harvard Law School Forum on Corporate Governance* (19 January 2018) <https://corpgov.law.harvard.edu/2018/01/19/joint-shareholder-letter-to-apple-inc/>.

[14] S. Perez, 'Apple Unveils New Screen Time Controls for Children', *TechCrunch* (4 June 2018), <https://techcrunch.com/2018/06/04/apple-unveils-new-screen-time-controls-for-children/>.

[15] D. Faber, 'Jeff Ubben's ValueAct Launching Fund with Social Goals, Following Similar Moves by Jana, BlackRock', *CNBC* (19 January 2018) <www.cnbc.com/2018/01/19/jeff-ubbens-

AES. ValueAct's founder, Jeffrey Ubben, joined the board of AES in order to provide support to the company with its transition to renewable energy and the sale of its legacy coal assets.[16] In contrast to Jana's campaign at Apple, ValueAct's involvement in AES was more substantive and long-term. By the time that Jeffrey Ubben stood down from the AES board in 2021, AES had become a leading developer of renewable energy and its share price had increased by 134%.[17] The Spring Fund continued to invest in targets with the joint purpose of advancing environmental and social goals as well as generating financial returns for investors. In June 2020, Jeffrey Ubben announced that he would leave ValueAct to launch a new $1 billion ESG-focused activist hedge fund, Inclusive Capital Partners.[18]

2.2. A PIVOTAL MOMENT FOR ESG HEDGE FUND ACTIVISM

The initial ESG campaigns by well-known activist hedge funds in 2018 generated publicity for ESG hedge fund activism. However, the real tipping point which was heralded as marking a new era of ESG hedge fund activism was Engine No. 1's successful proxy contest at ExxonMobil in 2021.[19] Engine No. 1 is an impact hedge fund that was launched in December 2020.[20] The founders of the fund included former executives from the ESG-fund Jana Impact Capital and from

---

[16] valueact-launching-fund-with-social-goal.html> (describing ValueAct Capital's launch of a fund "*focused on providing environmental and social goals for the companies it invests in*").

[16] M. Chediak & S. Deveau, 'This Activist Is Taking a Stake in a Power Generator to Push for Clean Energy', *Bloomberg* (17 January 2018), <www.bloomberg.com/news/articles/2018-01-17/activist-valueact-takes-aes-stake-in-push-for-cleaner-energy> (noting that Ubben would work with AES on the company's plan to sell coal assets, reduce debt and develop more solar power and battery storage).

[17] P. Temple-West and O. Aliaj, 'Investor Jeff Ubben questions ESG funds in second act as activist', *Financial Times* (20 January 2023), <www.ft.com/content/33bf3388-2e3d-49f6-bc61-a7a063ec9f0e >.

[18] B. Nauman, 'Jeff Ubben Quits ValueAct for Social Investing', *Financial Times* (23 June 2020), <www.ft.com/content/eaa28471-e295-44a9-a138-dda047db6d1c>. Jeffrey Ubben had noted that having an impact fund and a traditional fund under the same roof at ValueAct was "confusing" for investors, as the two strategies could not peacefully coexist – those who opted for the impact vehicle worried they were leaving returns on the table, and those who opted for the flagship fund worried about being portrayed as environmentally or socially "unconscious". The separation of the Spring Fund from ValueAct also provides some evidence of ESG hedge fund activism becoming a more mainstream phenomenon. *See also* S. Herbst-Bayliss, 'ValueAct's founder Ubben retires from firm, starts new venture', *Reuters* (23 June 2020) <www.reuters.com/article/hedgefunds-valueact/valueacts-founder-ubben-retires-from-firm-starts-new-venture-idUKL1N2E01Z3>.

[19] A. Christie, 'The Agency Costs of Sustainable Capitalism' [2021] 55(2) *UC Davis Law Review* 875, 920.

[20] S. Herbst-Bayliss, 'Hedge Fund Veteran Launches Impact Firm with Former Jana, BlackRock Executives', *Reuters* (1 December 2020), <https://uk.reuters.com/article/ us-investment-funds-james/hedge-fund-veteran-launches-impact-firm-with-former-jana-blackrock-executives-idUSKBN28B6AO>.

BlackRock. The fund's inaugural activist campaign made history as the first boardroom battle to focus on the issue of climate change when Engine No. 1 undertook a proxy contest to nominate four independent director candidates to the board of the energy giant ExxonMobil.[21]

Engine No. 1's campaign at Exxon was remarkable particularly because the fund was not a well-established activist hedge fund with a reputation for activism or proxy contests. Rather, it conducted its bold campaign with only $250 million in capital, and as a result, it only held a very small proportion, 0.02%, of Exxon's shares.[22] Despite its small shareholding, three out of the four Engine No. 1 director nominees were ultimately elected to Exxon's board in June 2021.[23]

How did a fledgling activist hedge fund with only 0.02% of Exxon's shares succeed in replacing one quarter of Exxon's board? At the time of the campaign, Exxon had long underperformed its peers financially. In 2021, Exxon recorded a $22 billion loss[24] and was removed from the S&P Dow Jones Industrial Average for the first time in almost a century.[25] Shareholder discontent at Exxon was deeply rooted due to the company's financial underperformance and its refusal to engage even with its largest and most prominent investors.[26] Investors had also grown uneasy about Exxon's status as an industry laggard due to its failure to take meaningful steps towards energy transition. At the time, global asset managers had made vocal public commitments to sustainable capitalism.[27] For example, BlackRock's CEO, Larry Fink, had repeatedly emphasised that *"climate risk is investment risk"* and had warned companies that BlackRock would be increasingly disposed to vote against directors who failed to make sufficient progress on climate change.[28]

---

[21] A. Christie, 'Battle for the Board: Climate Rebellion at Exxon marks a New Era of Shareholder Activism' (12 July 2021) *Oxford Business Law Blog* <https://blogs.law.ox.ac.uk/business-law-blog/blog/2021/07/battle-board-climate-rebellion-exxon-marks-new-era-shareholder>.
[22] D. Brower and O. Aliaj, 'Engine No. 1, the giant-killing hedge fund, has big plans', *Financial Times* (3 June 2021), <www.ft.com/content/ebfdf67d-cbce-40a5-bb29-d361377dea7a>.
[23] J. Hiller and S. Herbst-Bayliss, 'Engine No.1 Extends Gains with a Third Seat on Exxon Board', *Reuters* (3 June 2021), <www.reuters.com/business/energy/engine-no-1-win-third-seat-exxon-board-based-preliminary-results-2021-06-02/>.
[24] J. Hiller, 'Pandemic Pushes Exxon to Historic Annual Loss, $20 Billion Cut in Shale Value', *Reuters* (1 February 2021), <www.reuters.com/article/us-exxon-mobil-results-idUSKBN2A21LN>.
[25] E. Platt, 'ExxonMobil Booted from the Dow After Close to a Century', *Financial Times* (25 August 2020), <www.ft.com/content/76ecd406-b08e-4c2c-8643-cd23acb7cf2c>.
[26] J. Baer, D. Lim and C. Lombardo, 'Investors Give Exxon Payback for Frustrations on Strategy and Climate', *Wall Street Journal* (28 May 2021), <www.wsj.com/articles/investors-give-exxon-payback-for-frustrations-on-strategy-and-climate-11622227480>.
[27] A. Christie, *supra* note 19, at 926.
[28] Larry Fink's letter 2020 to CEOs, 'A Fundamental Reshaping of Finance' <www.blackrock.com/americas-offshore/en/larry-fink-ceo-letter>. Since then, asset managers such as BlackRock have backtracked somewhat on their public commitments to sustainability. For example, BlackRock announced in May 2022 that they expected to back fewer shareholder

In terms of its substantive campaign, Engine No. 1 primarily focused on capital allocation, urging Exxon to cut investment in projects based on unrealistic oil and gas prices and to focus on growth areas such as renewable energy. As well as the environmental goals of climate change mitigation, Engine No.1 clearly emphasised that its proposals were designed to help Exxon secure its dividend for shareholders.[29]

Engine No. 1's campaign at Exxon illustrated how an activist with an extremely modest stake in a target company could campaign on a platform of climate issues to secure support from a wide range of institutional investors, including the Big Three asset managers, to make significant board changes. The dual platform of financial underperformance combined with ESG issues undoubtedly helped Engine No. 1 succeed in generating widespread investor support. Therefore, how Engine No. 1 ultimately succeeded in its ambitious campaign at ExxonMobil is relatively clear. What is, however, open to considerable debate is what motivated the activist hedge fund to pursue this campaign in the first place. Running a proxy contest to secure board representation is incredibly expensive. It has been estimated to cost on average $10 million.[30] Engine No. 1 was reported to have spent approximately $30 million on the ExxonMobil campaign, which is significant for a fund that only had $250 million in capital.[31] This led some commentators to argue that Engine No. 1's true motives could not be financial. For example, it was noted that the purpose of the campaign *"was not to make money for its primary investor…from an expected rise in the price of ExxonMobil's stock"*.[32] It is likely that a major motivation for Engine No.1's campaign was also to promote the launch of its new Exchange Traded Fund, the 'Transform 500 ETF'.[33]

---

      resolutions on issues such as climate change in 2022 as they believed that many of the proposals were too prescriptive. See S. Jessop, 'BlackRock to back fewer shareholder resolutions in this AGM season', *Reuters* (10 May 2022), <www.reuters.com/business/blackrock-back-fewer-shareholder-resolutions-this-agm-season-2022-05-10/>. In an interview in June 2022, Larry Fink went further and said that *"I don't want to be the environmental police"*. See S. Brush & A. Massa, 'Fink Says BlackRock Doesn't Want to Be 'Environmental Police', *Bloomberg* (2 June 2022), <www.bloomberg.com/news/articles/2022-06-02/fink-says-blackrock-doesn-t-want-to-be-environmental-police?leadSource=uverify%20wall>.

[29] O. Aliaj, D. Brower and M. McCormick, 'ExxonMobil Under Pressure as Church of England Joins Investor Campaign', *Financial Times* (10 December 2020), <www.ft.com/content/c0639fb0-d81f-4ee9-8d58-d8e8da05c454>.

[30] N. Gantchev, 'The Costs of Shareholder Activism: Evidence From a Sequential Decision Model', [2012] 107 *Journal of Financial Economics*, 610, 611.

[31] J. Hiller and S. Herbst-Bayliss, 'Exxon, Activist Spend Over $65 Mln in Battle for Oil Giant's Future', *Reuters* (15 April 2021) <www.reuters.com/business/energy/exxon-activist-spend-over-65-mln-battle-oil-giants-future-2021-04-15/>.

[32] B. S. Sharfman, 'The Illusion of Success: A Critique of Engine No. 1's Proxy Fight at ExxonMobil', [2021] 12 *Harvard Business Law Review Online*, 1, 9 <www.hblr.org/wp-content/uploads/sites/18/2022/02/Sharfman-The-Illusion-of-Success.pdf>.

[33] A. Christie, *supra* note 21.

Part 3 outlines a framework of ESG hedge fund activism, discussing the types of ESG hedge fund campaigns, and the different activist hedge fund players, in order to further analyse the incentives of ESG hedge fund activists.

3. A FRAMEWORK OF ESG HEDGE FUND ACTIVISM

3.1. TYPES OF ESG HEDGE FUND CAMPAIGNS

Activist hedge fund campaigns exist on a spectrum in terms of the motivations underlying such campaigns. At one extreme, there are "pure" ESG campaigns that focus solely on environmental or social issues, such as the campaigns initiated by Bluebell Capital Partners at Solvay and by Carl Icahn at McDonald's and Kroger.[34] At the other extreme, there are campaigns which more closely embody the traditional perception of activist hedge fund behaviour in terms of such campaigns being entirely profit-orientated and pursued purely for financial gain, potentially at the expense of other stakeholders. Somewhere in the middle of these two extremes is where most ESG-oriented campaigns can be appropriately categorised. The majority of ESG campaigns will have mixed motives where the campaign is conducted to further both a profit-oriented purpose *and* an environmental or social purpose. Engine No. 1's campaign at Exxon and ValueAct's campaign at AES are good examples of campaigns with such mixed motives, as in each case the activist hedge fund highlighted both the climate related (ESG) goal and the potential financial gain associated with transitioning to renewable energy.[35] These campaigns can generally be categorised as potential "win-win" campaigns, reflecting the fact that the campaign is designed both to increase the financial value of the target company *and* advance environmental or social goals. Within this category, the balance of the focus on profit versus purpose can also vary quite significantly.

"Pure" ESG Campaigns

The two primary examples of what might be termed "pure" ESG campaigns by activist hedge funds are Bluebell Capital Partner's campaign at the Belgian

---

[34] In his chapter in this book, Hans De Wulf calls this "halo activism", while Tom Vos refers to this as "ESG activism with a non-profit goal" in his chapter.

[35] Ultimately, however, Exxon's financial performance in 2022 was boosted by the fact that it was a laggard in terms of renewable energy, as this enabled the company to capitalise on surging fossil fuel prices following Russia's invasion of Ukraine. See J. JACOBS, 'Exxon and Chevron share $100bn in profit after surge in oil prices', *Financial Times* (1 January 2023) <www.ft.com/content/2bfced8a-f221-4100-a0b1-f18ec230bc21> (noting that Exxon was expected to record more than $56bn in profits in 2022, a record high for the company).

company Solvay, and Carl Icahn's campaigns at the US companies McDonald's and Kroger.

In order to pursue its ESG-focused campaign, Bluebell Capital Partners bought one share in Solvay (worth approximately 100 euros), to qualify as a shareholder. This intervention was the first campaign by Bluebell pursuant to its not-for-profit initiative (or "One Share ESG Campaign"). Here, the activist fund, without any material economic interest, *"deploys [its] expertise as a financial activist investor to support environmental organizations, local communities and policy makers"*. The fund stresses that the *"sole objective is to address on a pro bono basis, significant environmental or social issues, as part of [its] broader ESG commitment"*.[36] Therefore, Bluebell is not seeking any direct financial gain from its activist intervention – the stated purpose is purely to advance ESG goals.

In terms of campaign strategies, Bluebell's campaign did resemble some more traditional activist hedge fund campaigns, as the hedge fund called for the replacement of the CEO, Ilham Kadri, because she failed to put an end to the discharge of untreated chemical waste into the sea at Rosignano.[37] It is very common for activist hedge funds to request a change of management, and particularly a replacement CEO.

Part 2 explored how an activist hedge fund with an extremely small shareholding in Exxon succeeded in its campaign, by securing the support of a range of institutional investors. Similarly, Bluebell Capital Partners needed to generate support from other investors. However, in the campaign at Solvay, institutional investors and proxy advisors were more divided in supporting Bluebell than was the case with Engine No. 1's campaign at Exxon.

At Solvay's May 2022 shareholder meeting, there was 92% shareholder support to ratify the board's acts over the previous year. That level of support was down from 99% at the previous year's shareholder meeting.[38] This figure does obscure the support given by independent shareholders to the campaign. As approximately 30% of Solvay is owned by a controlling shareholder,[39] the

---

[36] Bluebell Capital Partners, 'Bluebell Capital Partners – Response to Solvay Board Open Letter Regarding Soda Ash Operations in Rosignano' (17 February 2022) <www.globenewswire.com/en/news-release/2022/02/17/2387310/0/en/Bluebell-Capital-Partners-Response-to-Solvay-Board-Open-Letter-Regarding-Soda-Ash-Operations-in-Rosignano.html>.
[37] V. Zia and S. Jessop, *supra* note 8.
[38] V. Silver, 'Solvay Board Sees Investor Support Slip Over Coastal Waste', *Bloomberg Law* (10 May 2022) <https://news.bloomberglaw.com/esg/solvay-board-sees-investor-support-slip-over-coastal-waste-dump>.
[39] Solvay, 'Major Shareholders' <www.solvay.com/en/investors/share-information/major-shareholders> (noting that in March 2021, Solvac SA held 30.81% of Solvay's share capital and therefore 30.81% of voting rights).

proportion of independent shareholders withholding support was close to 18%.[40] However, that was still far short of the level of support that was required for Bluebell to succeed. The shareholders similarly voted to reappoint the CEO whose departure Bluebell had called for.

Despite Bluebell's lack of success at the shareholding meeting, a few months later a settlement was announced between the activist and Solvay. On 6 September 2022, Solvay and Bluebell issued a joint statement with Solvay pledging to *"significantly reduce the release of limestone residues directly into the sea from its facility in Rosignano, Italy as well as a long-term objective to invest in a new soda ash production process intended to be adopted globally"*.[41] The company also highlighted that this new process should enable Solvay to reduce discharge of limestone residues to zero by 2050. This brought an end to Bluebell's One-Share ESG campaign at Solvay.[42] It seems that although Bluebell was originally unsuccessful in its campaign to replace the CEO of Solvay, the reputational impact of the public campaign may have contributed significantly to Solvay settling with the activist. For example, at Solvay's shareholders meeting in May 2022, the company faced concerns or criticisms from a wide range of stakeholders including the UN Special Rapporteur on toxic and human rights, the EC Commissioner for Environment, Oceans and Fisheries, various political bodies, other investors, proxy advisors, the ESG rating agency MSCI, environmental organisations, the local community, financial news providers, public broadcasters and social media.[43]

Bluebell Capital Partners is a relatively new activist hedge fund that was ultimately successful in its ESG-focused campaign at the Belgian company. Another "pure" ESG campaign was, however, recently conducted by a much more well-known activist hedge fund manager, Carl Icahn. In this campaign, Icahn targeted two S&P 500 companies – McDonald's and Kroger – on the social issue of animal welfare. Icahn initially purchased 200 McDonald's shares, worth around $50,000, which was an extremely modest holding for Icahn, who manages one of the biggest activist hedge funds in the US.[44] Icahn later

---

[40] V. Silver, *supra* note 38.
[41] Solvay Press Release, 'Solvay and Bluebell Capital Partners reach a settlement and issue joint statement', (6 September 2022) <www.solvay.com/sites/g/files/srpend221/files/Solvay%20 and%20Bluebell%20Capital%20Partners%20reach%20a%20settlement%20and%20issue%20 joint%20statement_0.pdf>; P. Hollinger, 'European chemicals group Solvay declares truce with activist Bluebell', *Financial Times* (Milan and London, 22 December 2020) <www.ft.co m/content/fb129666-dc85–48ff-a9c8–3bfa87a715ca>.
[42] Solvay Press Release, *supra* note 41.
[43] Solvay, 2022 Shareholders' meeting, 'Annex to the Minutes of the Ordinary Shareholders Meeting Held on May 10, 2022', 43–44 <www.solvay.com/sites/g/files/srpend221/files/2022-05/Solvay-AGM-2022-QA.pdf>.
[44] 'What is Carl Icahn's beef with McDonald's?', *The Economist* (26 February 2022) <www. economist.com/business/2022/02/26/what-is-carl-icahns-beef-with-mcdonalds>.

expanded his animal welfare campaign to Kroger, the largest supermarket chain in the US. Here, he bought only 100 shares in the company. As well as raising the issue of animal welfare, Ichan criticised the compensation disparities between Kroger's CEO and the grocer's median worker.[45]

Similar to Bluebell's campaign at Solvay, Carl Icahn's campaigns at these two S&P 500 companies involved no real economic interest. Rather, the focus of Icahn's campaign was on a specific ESG issue, animal welfare. Icahn launched a proxy contest to nominate two director candidates to McDonald's board, in order to push the company to stop buying pork from suppliers that house pigs in inhumane gestation crates. He argued in an open letter that the board of McDonald's was failing shareholders by presiding over animal welfare violations and "obscene cruelty" in its pig supply chains.[46] Icahn similarly submitted a plan to nominate two director candidates to Kroger's board.[47]

Ultimately, Carl Icahn lost his proxy contest at McDonald's in May 2022 after only about 1% of the company's shareholders voted for his two board nominees.[48] The company responded to his campaign with financial arguments that likely would appeal to many shareholders, highlighting that Icahn's proposal would result in an "untenable financial burden" for McDonald's and its shareholders.[49] The prevailing negative rhetoric surrounding activist hedge fund managers also enabled McDonald's to effectively criticise and mock "Mr Icahn's newfound focus on ESG" which they labelled as a *"thinly veiled, opportunistic attempt to gain relevancy and media exposure in the current environment"*.[50] This criticism of Icahn was misleading, as Icahn had in fact worked with the Humane Society of the United States as far back as 2011 to engage behind the scenes with McDonald's to put an end to the use of gestation crates.[51] At that time, in order

---

[45] K. Stankiewicz, 'Carl Icahn is expanding his animal-welfare campaign to Kroger, after first targeting McDonald's', *CNBC* (29 March 2022) <www.cnbc.com/2022/03/29/carl-icahn-is-expanding-his-animal-welfare-campaign-to-kroger.html>.

[46] McDonald's Corporation, Schedule14A Information (Form DFAN14A) (21 April 2022) <www.sec.gov/Archives/edgar/data/63908/000119312522112310/d322980ddfan14a.htm>;
J. Ponciano, 'Legendary Investor Carl Icahn Slams McDonald's For 'Glaring Cruelty' In Pig Supply Chain As Proxy Fight Intensifies', *Forbes* (21 April 2022) <www.forbes.com/sites/jonathanponciano/2022/04/21/legendary-investor-carl-icahn-slams-mcdonalds-for-glaring-cruelty-in-pig-supply-chain-proxy-fight/?sh=7b912d551111>.

[47] K. Stankiewicz, *supra* note 45.

[48] P. Temple-West, 'Carl Icahn loses proxy fight with McDonald's over pig welfare', *Financial Times* (New York, 26 May 2022) <www.ft.com/content/850c5d7c-3303-4a69-9944-077b8990394a>.

[49] S. Herbst-Bayliss, 'McDonald's calls Icahn demands on sourcing pigs unfeasible, expensive', *Reuters* (21 April 2022) <www.reuters.com/business/mcdonalds-calls-icahn-demands-sourcing-pigs-unfeasible-expensive-2022-04-21/>.

[50] McDonald's Corporation Form DEFA14A, Securities and Exchange Commission, <https://sec.report/Document/0001104659-22-055954/>.

[51] Icahn's work with the Humane Society of the United States to campaign to McDonald's was first revealed five years later in a book written by the CEO of the Humane Society. See W.

to fend off an activist campaign, McDonald's pledged to Icahn and the Humane Society that it would put an end to the use of such crates in their supply chain within a decade. Therefore, Icahn's approach actually epitomised "patient capital", where the hedge fund manager waited for a decade in order to attempt to hold management accountable to its earlier pledge.[52]

These rare examples of "pure" ESG hedge fund activism – conducted for purpose, rather than for profit – illustrate that it can be very difficult for activists to succeed in such campaigns. In situations where the company allows the issue to proceed to a shareholder vote, both examples serve to demonstrate that it will be difficult to achieve sufficient shareholder votes on a "pure" ESG issue. This is the case both for newer activist hedge fund managers (such as Bluebell) and seasoned activist hedge fund managers (such as Carl Icahn). Carl Icahn has decades of experience conducting effective proxy contests and negotiating settlements with target companies for board representation. However, his campaign at McDonald's generated very little shareholder support, and he also withdrew his campaign at Kroger following the McDonald's loss.[53] Icahn attributed his loss at McDonald's, and his withdrawal of the proxy contest at Kroger, to the fact that these campaigns were very different to his traditional activist campaigns, as both companies were performing well financially.[54] As noted above, Icahn only won about 1% of the shareholder vote for his McDonald's campaign. The major proxy advisors ISS and Glass Lewis also both recommended that shareholders vote with management.[55] The Big Three global asset managers BlackRock (McDonald's third-largest shareholder), Vanguard (McDonald's largest shareholder) and State Street reportedly all voted with McDonald's management.[56] BlackRock was the only asset manager to issue a

---

Pacelle, *The Humane Economy*, 38 (2016). Icahn's daughter also previously worked for the Humane Society and prompted her father to become involved in the issue. *See* P. Temple-West, *supra* note 48. Icahn also stated: *"Animals are one of the things I feel really emotional about"*. *See* 'The Economist', *supra* note 44.

[52] *Id.* (noting that McDonald's made an announcement in 2011 that they had agreed to eliminate crates from their supply chain but that they would need a phase-in period of around a decade to completely eliminate the crates; the company also did not want the public to know of Icahn's involvement).

[53] D. Sophia and D. Syamnath, 'Carl Icahn drops proxy fight against Kroger after McDonald's defeat', *Reuters* (6 June 2022) <www.reuters.com/business/retail-consumer/carl-icahn-drops-proxy-fight-against-kroger-withdraws-nominees-2022–06–06/>.

[54] L. Baertlein, 'Activist investor Carl Icahn drops proxy fight over Kroger's pig policy, WSJ reports', *Reuters* (5 June 2022) <www.reuters.com/business/retail-consumer/activist-investor-carl-icahn-drops-proxy-fight-over-krogers-pig-policy-wsj-2022–06–05/>.

[55] S. Herbst-Bayliss, 'Glass Lewis backs McDonald's directors in boardroom fight with Carl Icahn', *Reuters* (17 May 2022) <www.reuters.com/business/retail-consumer/glass-lewis-backs-mcdonalds-directors-boardroom-fight-with-carl-icahn-2022–05–17/>.

[56] S. Herbst-Bayliss, 'BlackRock, other major McDonald's shareholders side with company in fight with Icahn', *Reuters* (25 May 2022) <www.reuters.com/business/blackrock-other-major-mcdonalds-shareholders-side-with-company-fight-with-icahn-2022–05–25/>.

voting bulleting explaining its vote, where it emphasised that it always acts in the long-term financial interests of its ultimate investors.[57] This illustrates that as many shareholders prioritise financial returns, it can be exceptionally difficult for activist hedge funds to succeed in a "pure" ESG activist campaign.

As a result, most ESG-focused hedge fund activist campaigns will focus primarily on "win-win" situations (discussed below), where the ESG goals advanced can also demonstrably boost profit and thus financial returns for shareholders. Although there are limited examples of "pure" environmental and social campaigns, as highlighted above, these campaigns do not generally form part of activist hedge funds' investment strategies or core business models. The noticeable divergence from activist hedge funds' normal investment model to conduct these types of "pro bono" campaigns could perhaps be seen as an implicit admission that activists do not always expect higher ESG standards to increase profits – "doing well" does not always align with "doing good". Despite the lack of a profit motive, there are various reasons why an activist hedge fund might choose to engage in these types of pro bono campaigns. It could, for example, help with visibility and credibility when the fund pursues a for-profit ESG campaign. Or the campaigns may reflect the personal values of the activist hedge fund managers or their investors. In their core business, however, activist hedge funds tend to focus on ESG campaigns that can contribute to the "double bottom-line" – where the intervention generates a significant profit as well as being environmentally or socially beneficial.[58] Given the difficulties in succeeding, and the lack of financial incentives to pursue these campaigns, "pure" pro bono campaigns are likely to remain a minority of the overall ecosystem of ESG activist campaigns.

"Win-Win" Campaigns

As noted above, the majority of ESG activist hedge fund campaigns involve some element of a "win-win" philosophy. Activist hedge funds engaging in such campaigns will outwardly portray a dual profit and purpose motive. The actual underlying preferences of the specific activist hedge fund managers and the ultimate investors could, however, vary quite significantly. Again, there is a spectrum of the possible range of motivations. Taking the most cynical approach, the activist hedge fund manager or the ultimate investors may in reality be entirely "climate-indifferent" but are simply using an ESG platform to generate crucial support for their campaign from other "climate-conscious"

---

[57] BlackRock Investment Stewardship, 'Vote Bulletin: McDonald's Corporation', 2, (26 May 2022), <www.blackrock.com/corporate/literature/press-release/vote-bulletin-mcdonalds-may-2022.pdf>.
[58] A. Christie, 'Shareholder Activism for Profit and Purpose' [Summer 2022] Volume 03, Issue 04, *Revue Européenne du Droit* 29, 34.

investors.[59] In this sense, ESG issues could be used as a "Trojan horse" to secure the backing of other ESG-oriented investors, whereas in reality the activist hedge fund may be focused on boosting financial returns without genuine regard for environmental or social goals.[60]

On the other hand, it may be that the activist hedge fund manager or the ultimate investors in the activist fund have some non-financial preferences and can in fact be regarded as "climate-conscious" to varying extents. Again, there could be a range of reasons why investors might be climate conscious. Investor preferences are generally evolving to focus more on ESG goals, as the increasing popularity of ESG funds shows. It has been argued that younger generations of investors are much more focused on ESG goals.[61] Investors may also believe that pursuing ESG-oriented goals is a value-enhancing strategy in the long-term. This is in line with the enlightened shareholder value version of stakeholder theory, namely that corporate leaders should pursue environmental and social goals as a means of maximising long-term shareholder value (rather than as an end in itself).[62] Moreover, some investors may be willing to trade-off some financial returns in order to promote environmental or social goals. The extent to which investors are willing to forgo financial returns for social purposes also varies considerably.[63]

This win-win approach to ESG investing and activism is reflected in the evolution of the concept of corporate social responsibility to the modern-day ESG movement. While corporate social responsibility *"was once framed in moral terms as a goal for management irrespective of profit"*, ESG as a concept is generally argued *"to provide sustainable long-term value or higher risk-adjusted returns for shareholders"*.[64]

---

[59] *See generally*, J. Armour, L. Enriques and T. Wetzer, 'Green Pills: Making Corporate Climate Commitments Credible', [2023] 65 *Arizona Law Review* 285 (describing "climate indifferent" and "climate-conscious" investors).
[60] A. Christie, *supra* note 58, at 31–33.
[61] *See generally* M. Barzuza, Q. Curtis and D. H. Webber, 'Shareholder Value(s): Index Fund ESG Activism and the New Millennial Corporate Governance' [2020] 93 *Southern California Law Review* 1243 (arguing that index funds are competing to accumulate the assets of the millennial generation who place a significant premium on social issues).
[62] L. A. Bebchuk and R. Tallarita, 'The Illusory Promise of Stakeholder Governance' [2020] 106 *Cornell Law Review* 91, 108–110.
[63] *See generally* S. Hirst, K. Kastiel and T. Kricheli-Katz, 'How Much Do Investors Care About Social Responsibility', ECGI Law Working Paper No 674/2023 (January 2023) <www.ecgi.global/sites/default/files/working_papers/documents/howmuchdoinvestorscareaboutsocialresponsibilityecgi_0.pdf> (discussing the extent to which investors themselves are willing to forgo financial returns for social purposes).
[64] D. S. Lund and E. Pollman, 'The Corporate Governance Machine' [2021] 121 *Columbia Law Review* 2563, 2566.

3.2. ESG ACTIVIST HEDGE FUND PLAYERS

There are two main categories of activist hedge funds that are engaging in ESG activism. First, there are traditional, well-established hedge funds with formidable reputations for financially oriented activist campaigns that have recently extended their repertoire to include ESG campaigns. Second, there are new bespoke funds that have been specifically established to engage in ESG activism and more exclusively focus on this subset of activist campaigns. The latter types of funds can be described as "ESG-first" or "ESG-focused" funds.

Traditional activist hedge funds that have conducted ESG activist campaigns in recent years include Carl Icahn (McDonald's, Kroger), Elliott Management (Suncor Energy, SSE, Evergy), ValueAct Capital (Hawaiian Electric, AES), Starboard Value (Huntsman), Jana Partners (Apple) and Third Point Partners (Shell, Prudential). New bespoke ESG-first funds that have launched include Impactive Capital in 2018 (KBR, Avid Technology), Inclusive Capital Partners in 2020 (Bayer, AppHarvest, Nikola), Engine No. 1 in 2020 (General Motors, ExxonMobil), and Clearway Capital in 2021 (TotalEnergies). Clearway Capital is Europe's first dedicated ESG activist fund. Its first campaign was to urge the French oil and gas company TotalEnergies to exit its Russian operations in light of the Russian invasion of Ukraine or face a vote on the issue at its next shareholder meeting.[65] Bluebell Capital also launched in 2019 but it is not solely ESG-focused. It has, however, conducted ESG campaigns – both for a profit motive (for example, at Glencore), and as part of its One-Share ESG campaign discussed earlier.

Despite generally having an ESG-focused investment approach, most of the new bespoke ESG funds specifically advertise a win-win approach. Therefore, they do not profess to be established solely or even mainly to pursue social or environmental goals, and instead very vividly highlight the financial case for ESG. For example, when launching the Spring Fund, Jeffrey Ubben noted that it was built on the premise that *"there is not just societal good to be done, but excess return to be captured in identifying and investing in businesses that are emphasizing and addressing environmental and societal problems"*.[66] Similarly, Engine No. 1 stressed that it is *"a capitalist group, definitely not a non-profit"* with a mission to *"invest in companies that make money while also investing in jobs, workers, communities, and the environment"*.[67] Inclusive Capital Partners also

---

[65] S. Jessop and B. Mallet, 'Activist Clearway urges TotalEnergies to exit Russia or face vote', *Reuters* (11 March 2022) <www.reuters.com/business/sustainable-business/exclusive-activist-clearway-urges-totalenergies-exit-russia-or-face-vote-2022-03-11/>.
[66] D. Faber, *supra* note 15 (citing a letter from Ubben to ValueAct's limited partners).
[67] S. Herbst-Bayliss, *supra* note 20.

communicates its philosophy that *"investing in companies that offer compelling value propositions and generate measurable positive impact on the environment and society...drives superior long-term financial returns"*.[68] This approach adopted by the ESG activist funds aligns with the position taken by many other investors, including large asset managers (discussed in Part 4 below).

3.3. THE PROMISE AND LIMITATIONS OF ESG HEDGE FUND ACTIVISM

The discussion of the activist hedge fund players involved in ESG activism in Part 3.2 above highlights that since 2018 there have essentially been two major developments. First, traditional activist hedge funds have increasingly engaged in ESG activism. Second, a number of bespoke ESG activist hedge funds have launched. Although ESG hedge fund activism still represents a small proportion of the overall number of activist hedge fund campaigns, the trend is clearly moving towards more ESG activism.

Hedge fund activists engaging in ESG activism tend to use tried and tested campaign strategies that have been successfully utilised by established hedge fund activists. For example, Inclusive Capital Partners, the bespoke ESG fund that was launched by Jeffrey Ubben of ValueAct in 2020, has consistently gained board representation at the US companies in which it invests.[69] This mirrors the approach that had traditionally been taken in financial campaigns by ValueAct. The board seats gained by Inclusive Capital Partners have been secured in a more collaborative manner compared to Engine No. 1's contested director election at ExxonMobil, which also reflects a general trend of activist board representation increasingly being achieved through settlement agreements rather than through proxy contests.[70] However, it is also notable that in the two ESG activist campaigns that Inclusive Capital Partners has conducted in Europe, the hedge fund has not sought or secured board representation. This is in stark contrast to the US campaigns, which each involved board representation. The first European target was Countryside Partnerships, where

---

[68] Council for Inclusive Capitalism, Inclusive Capital Partners, <www.inclusivecapitalism.com/organization/inclusive-capital-partners/>.
[69] These target companies include AES Inc, Hawaiian Electric Industries Inc, Nikola Inc, Unifi Inc, App Harvest Inc, Strategic Education Inc, ExxonMobil Corporation, Verra Mobility Corporation and Enviva Inc.
[70] A. Christie, *supra* note 19, at 931 (noting that from 2010 to 2019, there were only seven proxy contests at S&P 500 companies in the US that actually culminated in a shareholder vote). *See generally also* L. Bebchuk, A. Brav, W. Jiang and T. Keusch, 'Dancing with activists' [2020] 137 *Journal of Financial Economics* 1 (discussing settlement agreements between hedge fund activists and target boards).

the ESG hedge fund launched a hostile takeover for the UK housebuilder.[71] The second target was the German industrial group, Bayer, which is the hedge fund's only campaign in the EU. Here, Jeffrey Ubben of Inclusive Capital Partners joined Bayer's sustainability council – an independent, external group of experts that advises the company's management on sustainability – rather than the board.[72] Under Germany's two-tier board system, the sustainability council does not have formal decision-making power nor oversight rights. Bayer highlighted that the position on the sustainability council would afford the activist hedge fund manager *"access to relevant documents and experts within the company"*.[73] However, the lack of a board seat illustrates that some classic activist hedge fund strategies that are consistently effective in the US can in fact be more difficult to implement in Europe, even in the context of ESG campaigns.

Sceptics of activist hedge funds engaging in ESG activism sometimes raise concerns that environmental and social issues are being used simply to gain investor support but may actually obscure the true financial motives driving the hedge funds' campaigns. Here, a parallel could potentially be drawn with the manner in which activist hedge funds sometimes also include governance issues alongside their core campaign tactics as a tactical means of securing support from institutional investors.[74] As noted in the preceding discussion on Trojan horse campaigns, activist hedge funds could similarly use ESG platforms to increase the appeal of their overall campaign to a wider range of climate-conscious investors. However, particularly in the case of the new bespoke ESG activist funds, this does not appear to be the primary motivation. These funds are generally upfront about their business models and motivations, and most of these funds are grounded in the philosophy that sustainability drives superior long-term financial returns. Overall, it seems likely that ESG hedge fund activism will continue to grow – both in the US and in Europe – especially if activist funds can identify "win-win" targets where ESG goals nicely align with financial gains.

---

[71] G. Hammond, 'US investor launches £1.5bn bid for Countryside', *Financial Times* (30 May 2022) <www.ft.com/content/953f1564-c79c-43c7-9fab-c46e14f97827>. Countryside was ultimately acquired by the FTSE 250 developer Vistry Group instead in September 2022. See G. Hammond, 'Housebuilder Vistry agrees £1.25bn deal to buy rival Countryside', *Financial Times* (5 September 2022) <www.ft.com/content/70e4cd68-aeb4-40ba-ac8c-5892f330e978>.

[72] H. Kuchler and O. Storbeck, 'Bayer embraces activist Ubben with place on its sustainability council', *Financial Times* (26 February 2023) <www.ft.com/content/0b4b2908-3f19-46d4-8574-c3d831ad3868>.

[73] H. Kuchler and O. Storbeck, *supra* note 72.

[74] W. Bratton, 'Hedge Funds and Governance Targets' [2007] 95 *Georgetown Law Journal* 1377, 1397.

4. THE ROLE OF GLOBAL ASSET MANAGERS AND OTHER INSTITUTIONAL INVESTORS IN ESG-FOCUSED ACTIVISM

4.1. COLLABORATION AND VOTING

It was noted in Part 2.2 above that Engine No. 1 only held 0.02% of ExxonMobil's shares. Therefore, clearly Engine No. 1 could not have succeeded in its boardroom battle without the support of some powerful allies in Exxon's institutional investor base. Indeed, Engine No. 1 was strategic in launching its campaign with the support of CalSTRS and other large US pension funds.[75] Collaboration with other investors can be seen as fundamental to the success of some ESG activist hedge fund campaigns.[76] ESG activist hedge funds are increasingly partnering with other types of shareholders, including pension funds and non-governmental organisations. During Bluebell's campaign at Solvay, the activist hedge fund even joined forces with local and international environmental activists. For example, Bluebell and the World Wildlife Fund challenged the Italian government's decision to renew a permit allowing Solvay to pump up to 250,000 tons of soda ash waste onto Rosignano beach each year.[77]

In Engine No. 1's campaign at Exxon it was crucial for the activist hedge fund to secure the pivotal votes of global asset managers such as the Big Three (BlackRock, Vanguard, and State Street) to successfully elect its dissident slate of nominees. The Big Three's voting reports revealed that BlackRock ultimately voted in favour of three of Engine No. 1's director nominees,[78] with Vanguard[79] and State Street[80] each supporting two of the four candidates. One early signal

---

[75] *See, for example,* CalSTRS, 'Statement on alternate board members for ExxonMobil' (7 December 2020) <www.calstrs.com/statement-on-alternate-board-members-for-exxonmobil> and S. Herbst-Bayliss and J. Hiller, 'Tiny Activist Investor's Arguments Against Exxon Draw Crowd to Its Side', *Reuters*, (11 December 2020) <https://uk.reuters.com/article/exxon-activist/tiny-activist-investors-arguments-against-exxon-draw-crowd-to-its-side-idUKKBN28L27G>.

[76] *See generally* P. O. Mülbert and A. Sajnovits, 'Emerging ESG-Driven Models of Shareholder Collaborative Engagement', ECGI Law Working Paper No 668/2022 (December 2022) <https://papers.ssrn.com/sol3/papers.cfm?abstract_id=4297434> (discussing new forms of collaboration in ESG campaigns).

[77] N. Kumar, 'Solvay to Cut Beach Waste as It Settles with Activist Bluebell', *Bloomberg* (6 September 2022) <www.bloomberg.com/news/articles/2022-09-06/solvay-to-cut-beach-waste-as-it-settles-with-activist-bluebell>.

[78] BlackRock, Vote Bulletin: ExxonMobil Corporation 1 (26 May 2021), <www.blackrock.com/corporate/literature/press-release/blk-vote-bulletin-exxon-may-2021.pdf>.

[79] Vanguard, Voting Insights: A Proxy Contest and Shareholder Proposals Related to Material Risk Oversight at ExxonMobil 1 (2021), <https://static.vgcontent.info/crp/intl/avw/mexico/documents/inv-stew-voting-insights-exxonmobil.pdf>.

[80] R. Kerber, 'Top Exxon Investors State Street, Vanguard Backed Activist Nominees', *Reuters* (27 May 2021), <www.reuters.com/business/energy/state-street-backed-two-activist-hedge-fund-nominees-exxon-board-2021-05-27/>.

that institutional investors such as the Big Three may potentially support Engine No. 1's campaign was that they had expressed considerable frustration with Exxon in the past. For example, in 2016 BlackRock had voted against key directors on Exxon's board due to a policy that prohibited direct engagement with shareholders.[81] Therefore, identifying institutional investor discontent can be a clever strategy for ESG hedge fund activists who wish to generate support for their proposed campaigns. Many asset managers have committed to voting against directors who fail to make meaningful progress on ESG issues such as climate change mitigation. For example, BlackRock reiterated in 2021 that it would vote against the re-election of directors where their companies fail to move with sufficient speed and urgency with respect to the climate crisis.[82]

At the time of Engine No. 1's campaign at Exxon, the Big Three asset managers had also recently and very publicly strengthened their commitment to mitigating climate change.[83] Therefore, the campaign was well-timed and well-publicised to test the Big Three asset managers' outward commitments in the context of a public campaign. Aligning goals with the positions of pivotal voters such as large asset managers can also result in much higher levels of support for activist hedge funds' ESG campaigns. Most recently, in Larry Fink's 2022 letter to CEOs, he stressed *"We focus on sustainability not because we're environmentalists, but because we are capitalists and fiduciaries to our clients"* and that *"stakeholder capitalism is all about delivering long-term, durable returns for shareholders"*.[84] Engine No. 1 certainly emphasised the financial case as much as the climate case during its campaign. This approach aligns more closely with the win-win philosophy outlined in Part 3 above, as opposed to the "pure" ESG campaigns where environmental and social goals may take precedence over shareholder returns.

Engine No. 1's campaign at Exxon was obviously an American shareholder activism campaign, where the holdings of the Big Three and other asset managers tend to be much greater than they are in European companies. The voting support of asset managers such as the Big Three is especially important in US proxy contests because of the very high levels of institutional ownership. The Big Three asset managers control more than 20% of shares in the average S&P 500 company, which translates into more than 25% of the shares actually voted.[85]

---

[81] R. Kerber, 'BlackRock Withheld Support from Two Key Exxon Directors: Filings', *Reuters* (29 August 2016), <www.reuters.com/article/us-exxon-directors-blackrock-idUSKCN11417F>.
[82] Blackrock, 'Our 2021 Stewardship Expectations: Global Principles and Market-level Voting Guidelines' 4 [2021], <www.blackrock.com/corporate/literature/publication/our-2021-stewardship-expectations.pdf>.
[83] A. Christie, *supra* note 19 at 885, 921, 926.
[84] 2022 Letter from Larry Fink, Chairman and Chief Exec. Officer, BlackRock, to CEOs, 'The Power of Capitalism' <www.blackrock.com/corporate/investor-relations/larry-fink-ceo-letter>.
[85] L. Bebchuk and S. Hirst, 'The Specter of the Giant Three' [2019] 99 *Boston University Law Review* 721 at 724.

By contrast, in Europe, institutional investor ownership tends to be significantly lower. In Belgium, the average percentage of shares in public companies that are held by institutional investors is around 35%.[86] In the case of Solvay, BlackRock was the only one of the Big Three asset managers that had crossed the reporting threshold of a 3% shareholding.[87] This is still a significant shareholding, but it renders the Big Three's voting support less crucial in European campaigns compared with campaigns at equivalent US companies.

In the "pure" ESG campaigns discussed earlier, asset managers and other institutional investors have been more divided on supporting activists. In the Solvay campaign, CalSTRS and another US pension fund in Florida supported Bluebell on the ground that Solvay must do more to mitigate the adverse climate impacts of its Italian soda ash facility. Many other institutional shareholders, however, supported management. The proxy advisor Glass Lewis originally recommended that shareholders vote against the board's proposal, before changing its recommendation to abstaining.[88] ISS endorsed Solvay's management. Unlike the Engine No. 1 campaign, no public statements were made by the Big Three asset managers regarding Bluebell's campaign at Solvay.

Overall, collaboration with institutional investors can contribute significantly to the success of ESG activists hedge fund campaigns, even in the European context. If a campaign includes a proxy contest in the US, the voting support of global asset managers is likely to be fundamental. In Europe, despite the comparatively lower concentration of institutional investor holdings, asset manager and institutional investor voting support will still contribute positively to the likely success of a campaign.

4.2. PORTFOLIO-WIDE CAMPAIGNS AND ENGAGEMENT

Separate to the support that they may give to ESG hedge fund activist campaigns, global asset managers and institutional investors play an important role in terms of their own stewardship and engagement.[89] This can include portfolio-wide initiatives that have an impact across a range of companies. One prominent example of portfolio-wide activism is campaigns asset managers initiated on the issue of gender diversity on boards in the US. The most visible and successful

---

[86] P. O. Mülbert and A. Sajnovits, *supra* note 67, at 4 (citing the OECD Corporate Governance Factbook 2021, at 21).
[87] Solvay, 'Participation notification by BlackRock Inc.' <www.solvay.com/en/press-release/participation-notification-blackrock-inc-21> (notifying that in January 2022, BlackRock had crossed the 3% voting threshold that requires notification under Belgian transparency legislation).
[88] Solvay, 2022 Shareholders' meeting, *supra* note 43, at 42.
[89] Shareholder stewardship with regards to ESG matters is also discussed in more depth in the chapter by Marleen Och in this book.

campaign was State Street's "Fearless Girl" initiative that was launched on International Women's Day in 2017.[90] Here, State Street's marketing campaign for its new bespoke ESG index fund was accompanied by a pledge to vote against the chair of the nominating committee of boards that lacked any female board representation.[91] In 2018, BlackRock went further by announcing it would vote against the entire nominating committee if companies did not demonstrate sufficient progress on gender diversity, adding that it expected companies to have at least two female board directors.[92] In a 2022 study, it was estimated that the campaigns of the Big Three on gender diversity on boards led US companies to add at least 2.5 times as many female directors in 2019 as they had in 2016.[93]

There has been increasing demand for ESG investment products, especially in Europe.[94] As well as being driven by market forces, this is also driven by EU initiatives such as the Sustainable Finance Disclosure Regulation (SFDR),[95] which imposes ESG disclosure obligations on asset managers, and the Taxonomy Regulation,[96] which sets out the overarching conditions that an economic activity has to meet in order to qualify as environmentally sustainable. The focus on ESG has widened the scope of institutional investors' engagement activities, with investor stewardship not only concentrating on financial and governance issues but also on environmental and social factors.[97]

---

[90] See A. L. Christie, 'A COVID-19 Index Fund – The New Fearless Girl?' in COVID-19 and Business Law (H. Eidenmüller, L. Enriques, G. Helleringer and K. van Zwieten (eds.)) 2020, at 33; and J. Rooney, '"Fearless Girl": State Street Global Advisors' CMO on the Rationale, the Controversy and What's Next', Forbes (21 April 2017) <www.forbes.com/sites/jenniferrooney/2017/04/21/fearless-girl-state-street-global-advisors-cmo-on-the-rationale-the-controversy-and-whats-next/>.

[91] M. Barzuza, Q. Curtis and D. H. Webber, supra note 61, at 1266–68.

[92] M. Barzuza, Q. Curtis and D. H. Webber, supra note 61, at 1269 (citing S. Krouse, 'BlackRock: Companies Should Have at Least Two Female Directors', Wall Street Journal (2 February 2018) <www.wsj.com/articles/blackrock-companies-should-have-at-least-two-female-directors-1517598407>.

[93] R. Wigglesworth, 'An actual ESG success story', Financial Times (21 November 2022) <www.ft.com/content/02744717-6d46-4aa6-8ad5-33799331c0d2> (citing T. A. Gormley, V. K. Gupta, D. A. Matsa, S. C. Mortal and L. Yang, 'The Big Three and Board Gender Diversity: The Effectiveness of Shareholder Voice', NBER Working Paper 30657 (November 2022) <www.nber.org/papers/w30657>.

[94] R. Henderson, 'Europe leads the $31tn charge on sustainable investing', Financial Times (1 June 2019) <www.ft.com/content/fef1a4fc-8354-11e9-b592-5fe435b57a3b>; E. Boyde, 'ESG accounts for 65% of all flows into European ETFs in 2022', Financial Times (13 January 2023) <www.ft.com/content/a3e9d87f-fa6f-4e5e-be6e-e95b42af2fec>.

[95] Regulation (EU) 2019/2088 on sustainability-related disclosures in the financial services sector.

[96] Regulation (EU) 2020/852 on the establishment of a framework to facilitate sustainable investment.

[97] G. Balp and G. Strampelli, 'Institutional Investor ESG Engagement: The European Experience' [2022] 23 European Business Organization Law Review 869, 878.

5. CONCLUSION

ESG hedge fund activism is still in the relatively early stages of development, but there are indications that most campaigns will focus both on ESG goals and on financial results. Both well-established activist hedge funds and newly launched bespoke ESG activist funds are increasingly pursuing ESG-oriented activist campaigns. Although this would have once been inconceivable behaviour on the part of activist hedge funds, these campaigns are now becoming more prevalent. Russia's invasion of Ukraine may have temporarily disrupted the growth of ESG hedge fund activist campaigns, as companies such as Exxon ultimately benefited from a focus on traditional fossil fuels rather than renewable energy. Nevertheless, in the long run it is expected that ESG activist campaigns will continue to grow both in number and in prominence. The early case studies that do exist demonstrate that it is more likely that ESG hedge fund activists succeed in their campaigns when they emphasise dual motives of profit and purpose. If promoting ESG goals can simultaneously further long-term shareholder returns, ESG activist funds tend to be more successful in generating the requisite levels of support from a broad range of other investors.

The Belgian case involving Bluebell Capital Partners and Solvay provides a different perspective involving a "pure" ESG campaign, where the activist was primarily focused on ESG goals without an obvious profit motive. Such cases are likely to remain exceptional cases of ESG hedge fund activism, rather than the predominant form. They resemble more closely the activities of other socially responsible investors as opposed to forming part of the key business model of activist hedge funds.

As well as analysing ESG hedge fund activism in depth, this chapter also discussed the role of global asset managers and other institutional investors in ESG-focused shareholder activism. Institutional investors play a number of different and important roles, including collaborating with ESG hedge fund activists and supporting their campaigns through their voting. More independently, they have also implemented their own portfolio-wide campaigns in the past, and they play a key role in stewardship through their engagements with corporate leaders.

SHAREHOLDER STEWARDSHIP AND SUSTAINABILITY – THE CURRENT EUROPEAN LEGAL FRAMEWORK AND POSSIBLE WAYS AHEAD

Marleen Och
Phd researcher at KU Leuven

1. INTRODUCTION

Shareholder stewardship is a prominent topic in the field of corporate governance that has been high on the agenda of academics and policymakers for about a decade now.[1] Like shareholder activism, stewardship concerns the link between companies, their shareholders and the use of shareholder rights. It is generally seen as a softer, less aggressive form of exchange than activism, whereby often passive institutional investors are encouraged to engage and interact with companies they have already invested in.

In fact, shareholder stewardship is viewed by many[2] as a necessary component to robust corporate governance and as a tool for long-term profitability. It is therefore encouraged, either in the form of stewardship codes or, in the case of the EU, by the Shareholder Rights Directive II (SRD II).[3] Institutional investors and asset managers, the addressees of most stewardship provisions, hold a large and growing part of equity worldwide.[4] This concentration of power makes stewardship appealing, as a change of course by a few large players with the necessary expertise and resources could have a far-reaching and positive effect

---

[1] The first stewardship code was introduced in the UK in 2010, see: Financial Reporting Council, The UK Stewardship Code (2010), <www.frc.org.uk/getattachment/e223e152–5515–4cdc-a951-da33e093eb28/UK-Stewardship-Code-July-2010.pdf>.

[2] For an overview of supporters and opponents, see: J. Hill, 'Good Activist/Bad Activist: The Rise of International Stewardship Codes' (2018) 41 *Seattle University Law Review* 497.

[3] Directive (EU) 2017/828 of the European Parliament and of the Council of 17 May 2017 amending Directive 2007/36/EC as regards the encouragement of long-term shareholder engagement (2017) OJ L 132.

[4] A. De La Cruz, A. Medina and Y. Tang, 'Owners of the World's Listed Companies' (2019) *OECD Capital Market Series*; G. Aminadav and E. Papaioannou, 'Corporate Control around the World' (2020) *Journal of Finance* 1191, 1205.

on the overall economy.[5] While stewardship rules started out in order to mitigate the perceived flaw of overly passive investors, there is now an increased focus on the role investors can play in the transition towards a sustainable economy. In order to meet the EU's ambitious climate goals, many companies will have to adapt their business models to be part of a net-zero economy.[6] The investors in those companies, who want to ensure the value of their investments for the future, have incentives to monitor their investee companies and assist them with the adaptation process. In fact, large asset managers have been very outspoken in past years on requiring higher sustainability standards from their investee companies.[7] BlackRock, the world's largest asset manager has over $8 trillion in assets under management and investments in virtually all industries globally.[8] The influence these types of investors can have on the sustainable transition could indeed be tremendous.

As promising as this idea of investors as stewards for sustainability sounds, there are also a number of flaws. Firstly, the predicted influence of institutional investors and asset managers may be overstated in continental Europe, where controlling shareholders are more dominant. Furthermore, institutional investors have only limited incentives to genuinely engage with their investee companies. Engagement may be more successful when investors cooperate with each other. Finally, while SRD II requires investors to publish their investment and engagement policies, the provisions are vague, leading to strong variations in disclosure and monitoring.

This chapter is structured as follows. First, I will first explain the concept of stewardship (2.). This will be followed by an overview of the legal framework surrounding stewardship (3.). Afterwards, I will discuss some flaws of the current legal framework, raise a number of questions and suggest pathways for further research (4.) which I summarize in my conclusion (5.). This chapter therefore adds to the picture of the relation and interaction between shareholders and companies that this book provides by adding the perspective of shareholder stewardship and sustainability.

---

[5] I. Chiu and D. Katelouzou, 'From Shareholder Stewardship to Shareholder Duties: Is the Time Ripe?' in H. Birkmose (ed) *Shareholder Duties*, Kluwer Law International 2017, p. 131–152.
[6] European Commission 'The European Green Deal' COM(2019) 640 final, <https://eur-lex.europa.eu/legal-content/EN/TXT/HTML/?uri=CELEX:52019DC0640&from=EN>.
[7] See for example BlackRock's CEO Larry Fink's annual letter to CEOs: <www.blackrock.com/corporate/investor-relations/larry-fink-ceo-letter>, accessed 15.11.2022.
[8] <www.statista.com/statistics/891292/assets-under-management-blackrock/>, accessed 15.11.2022.

2. CONCEPTUALISING STEWARDSHIP

2.1. SHAREHOLDER STEWARDSHIP IN CONTRAST TO SHAREHOLDER ACTIVISM

Shareholder activism, as extensively illustrated by the other chapters in this book, focuses on the way in which shareholders exert pressure on a company's board and management and achieve particular changes for the company. Activists do so through communication strategies and by using the tools available to shareholders, such as the right to table shareholder resolutions or the right to vote. They may do so with different goals in mind, such as increasing shareholder value or enhancing the company's environmental, social or governance (ESG) performance.

Shareholder stewardship equally concerns the link between companies, their shareholders and the use of shareholder rights, but the notion differs from that of shareholder activism.[9] Shareholder activism is typically defined as the 'shareholders' attempt to pressure management for changes in corporate policies and governance with the aim to improve firm performance.'[10] Shareholder stewardship, on the other hand, focuses on the 'engagement between institutional investors and companies to help improve long-term returns to shareholders and the efficient exercise of governance responsibilities'.[11] EU legislation makes use of the term shareholder engagement instead of stewardship and defines it as 'actively monitoring companies, engaging in a dialogue with the company's board, and using shareholder rights, including voting and cooperation with other shareholders, if need be to improve the governance of the investee company in the interest of long-term value creation.'[12]

These definitions have many aspects in common, such as the use of communication and shareholder rights to improve certain things about the company. One noticeable difference is that activism entails 'pressuring' management, while stewardship focuses on 'monitoring' and 'engagement'. This choice of wording illustrates the difference in perception, whereby activists are often seen as aggressive 'outsiders', who only recently acquired shares, while stewards are viewed as more collegial and 'insiders' to the company, already holding shares for

---

[9] For an overview of this difference in perception, see J. Hill, 'Good Activist/Bad Activist: The Rise of International Stewardship Codes' (2018) 41 *Seattle University Law Review* 497.

[10] A. Brav, W. Jiang and R. Li, 'Governance by Persuasion: Hedge Fund Activism and Market-based Shareholder Influence' (2021) *ECGI Finance Working Paper* No. 797/2021, <https://papers.ssrn.com/sol3/papers.cfm?abstract_id=3955116>, 7.

[11] This is the definition found in the first ever stewardship code issued, see: Financial Reporting Council, The UK Stewardship Code (July 2010), Preface.

[12] European Commission, 'Green Paper: The EU corporate governance framework' COM(2011) 164 final' (2011) p. 11.

a longer period of time. A number of other criteria can be employed to distinguish stewardship from activism, namely the actor in question, the common strategy by which they interact with the company and the underlying incentives.

A typical case of shareholder activism would be a classic hedge fund activist starting with a buy-in, followed by an 'aggressive' strategy to achieve significant changes in the company, with the goal of selling the shares after for a profit.[13] This more active approach is linked to the incentives that underline the fund's business model. Hedge funds typically have less diversified portfolios and select target companies which they believe to be underperforming.[14] Through engagement they aim to increase the company's profitability. This increase translates to a benefit for their clients and for the fund management itself, as their fees are typically closely linked to performance.

A classic case of stewardship on the other hand would center around an investor that holds shares for long periods of time and in a variety of companies, such as pension funds or insurance companies.[15] Starting off with pre-existing investments, the investor may want to address issues in their investee companies, if they arise.[16] To address these issues they would often rely on the private exchange of views with the management.[17] If the management remains reluctant to address the issues raised by the investors, they might in response address the company more publicly, ask questions at the general meeting or even vote for proposals that object to the management's position. Institutional investors launching their own proxy fights or shareholder proposals remain rare. On average they have less incentives to engage in such an active manner.[18] An activist campaign can be very costly for the shareholder taking such action, but the potential positive outcome would be shared with all other shareholders, leading to a free-rider problem. This is particularly true for index-tracking investment funds, as they compete with funds tracking the same indexes, on

---

[13] For a more detailed overview of a typical activist campaign see chapter 1 by Tom Vos.
[14] A. Brav, W. Jiang and R. Li, 'Governance by Persuasion: Hedge Fund Activism and the Market for Corporate Influence' (2021) *ECGI Working Paper Series in Finance*, <https://papers.ssrn.com/sol3/papers.cfm?abstract_id=3955116>, 9; M. Kahan and E. Rock, 'Hedge funds in corporate governance and corporate control' (2007) *University of Pennsylvania Law Review* 1021, 1069.
[15] S. Alvaro, M. Maugeri and G. Strampelli, 'Institutional investors, corporate governance and stewardship codes – Problems and perspectives' (2019) *CONSOB Legal Papers*.
[16] This type of engagement can also be categorized as defensive shareholder activism, see: B. Cheffins and J. Armour, 'The Past, Present, and Future of Shareholder Activism by Hedge Funds' (2011) *Journal of Corporation Law* 51, 56.
[17] L.A. Bebchuk, A. Cohen and S. Hirst, 'The Agency Problems of Institutional Investors' (2017) *JEP* 89, 105.
[18] L.A. Bebchuk, A. Cohen and S. Hirst, 'The Agency Problems of Institutional Investors' (2017) *JEP* 89, 98–99.

the basis of low fees.[19] The increased profitability of one specific company in a diversified portfolio may not be proportionate to the campaigning cost, leading to an overall loss for the investors.[20]

While these two models aim to illustrate the concept of stewardship on the one hand and activism on the other, in reality there is no clear-cut line. There are institutional investors that engage more intensely. Their hands-on approach may be viewed as activist. Hedge funds on the other hand may hardly engage or only rely on private engagement as a tool, thereby not being perceived as 'aggressive' activists. Next to classic hedge fund activists there is also a number of other actors practicing shareholder activism, particularly in the field of ESG.[21]

In conclusion, shareholder activism and shareholder stewardship display several similarities, as they both concern the shareholder-company relationship and the use of communication tools and shareholder rights to improve the company, whether regarding its value or sustainability performance. Differences may concern the strategy employed and the actor in question, as well as the perception of them. While there is no clear-cut line, this chapter will focus on what would typically be viewed as stewardship, how it is encouraged by the law and whether those legal provisions, which focus on institutional investors, are suitable in relation to the goals they aim for.

2.2. ORIGINS AND VARIETIES

After the 2008 financial crisis, European policymakers considered a lack of oversight by shareholders to be one of the flaws in the corporate governance system.[22] They identified an oversight gap between companies, institutional investors and their end beneficiaries. Considering their voting power and expertise, institutional investors and asset managers were deemed to be in a suitable position to mitigate these corporate governance problems. Apart from their shareholder rights, they were therefore given certain responsibilities or duties within the governance framework of a company. This includes the duty to actively monitor companies, to engage in a dialogue with the management,

---

[19] L.A. Bebchuk, A. Cohen and S. Hirst, 'The Agency Problems of Institutional Investors' (2017) 31 *JEP*, 89–102; S. Alvaro, M. Maugeri and G. Strampelli, 'Institutional investors, corporate governance and stewardship codes – Problems and perspectives' (2019) *CONSOB Legal Papers*.

[20] There are however also benefits to these highly diversified portfolios. As 'common owners', some large funds may have incentives to engage on a portfolio-wide level. See a more detailed discussion under 4.2.

[21] For an overview of the different actors in the field of ESG see the chapter by Tom Vos.

[22] European Commission, 'Action Plan: European company law and corporate governance – a modern legal framework for more engaged shareholders and sustainable companies' (2012) p. 3.

the board and other shareholders, and to utilize their shareholder rights to the benefit of the company.[23] The 2010 UK Stewardship Code was the first of its kind to specify these requirements in a policy document.[24] It focuses on incentivizing passive investors to monitor their investee companies and engage with them.[25] This idea of stewardship found its way into twenty jurisdictions worldwide.[26]

In addition to this first and most prominent type, Katelouzou and Puchniak identify a number of other theoretical conceptions of stewardship.[27] The second type of stewardship equally concerns the relationship between institutional investors and their investee companies but focuses on the way in which institutional investors engage with a controlling shareholder in the investee company, rather than the board or management. In light of the many companies that have a controlling shareholder and institutional investors, this type of stewardship code could play an interesting role. So far, however, no organization or jurisdiction has issued such a code.[28]

The third conception focuses on controlling shareholders as the stewards themselves and explores how they can use their controlling power to steer the company in a certain direction. In many companies, particularly in continental Europe, this is the most common ownership structure.[29] Yet, the only stewardship code of such kind exists in Singapore.[30] Whether it would be advisable to also include controlling shareholders in a European stewardship context will be discussed in section 4.1.

---

[23] These shareholder duties were developed in a 2011 Green Paper and later included in the Articles 3g and 3h SRD II. European Commission, 'Green Paper: The EU corporate governance framework' COM(2011) 164 final' (2011) p. 11.
[24] Financial Reporting Council, The UK Stewardship Code 2010. An overview of all stewardship codes including their date of issuance can be on the website of the European Corporate Governance Institute: <https://ecgi.global/content/codes-stewardship>, accessed 15.11.2022.
[25] Financial Reporting Council, The UK Stewardship Code 2010.
[26] All stewardship codes can be found on the website of the European Corporate Governance Institute: https://ecgi.global/content/codes-stewardship, accessed 01.10.2022; see further: D. Katelouzou and M. Siems, 'The Global Diffusion of Stewardship Codes' (2020) *ECGI Law Working Paper* N° 526/2020, <https://papers.ssrn.com/sol3/papers.cfm?abstract_id=3616798>.
[27] D. Katelouzou and D. Puchniak, 'Global Shareholder Stewardship: Complexities, Challenges and Possibilities' in D. Katelouzou and D. Puchniak, (eds), *Global Shareholder Stewardship*, Cambridge University Press 2022, pp. 5–9.
[28] The questions as to why controlling shareholders are so underrepresented in stewardship codes is likely due to a number of social, political and legal reasons. I discuss these more in my PhD thesis on shareholder engagement and sustainability in the EU.
[29] A. De La Cruz, A. Medina and Y. Tang, 'Owners of the World's Listed Companies' (2019) *OECD Capital Market Series*; G. Aminadav and E. Papaioannou, 'Corporate Control around the World' (2020) *Journal of Finance* 1191, 1205.
[30] Stewardship Asia Centre, Stewardship Principles for Family Businesses, (2018) <www.stewardshipasia.com.sg/sites/default/files/2020-09/SPFB-brochure-0913.pdf>, accessed 15.11.2022.

A fourth conception of stewardship again concerns institutional investors, but instead of looking at the relationship between investor and investee company, the focus lies on the relationship between the institutional investor and its client or beneficiary. It concerns the investment management side and the institutional investor's business model. One way in which investors can act as good stewards in that regard is to manage conflict of interests arising between the fund and its managers, between different funds and between the managers and end-investors. Another aspect concerns the transparency both in the fund internally as well as along the entire investment chain. The investment management side of stewardship is covered by the UK Stewardship Code[31] and also in the SRD II[32], but plays a minor role in the academic debate around stewardship.[33]

The notion of stewardship changed over the years, with the 2020 UK Stewardship code now defining it as 'the responsible allocation, management and oversight of capital to create long-term value for clients and beneficiaries leading to sustainable benefits for the economy, the environment and society.'[34] This shifted focus on sustainability can be conceptualized as a fifth type of stewardship. While the 2010 UK Stewardship Code was drafted as a response to the global financial crisis, the EU's SRD II from 2017 and the 2020 UK Stewardship Code clearly illustrate the increasing policy focus on ESG.[35] The goal behind these stewardship norms is to incentivize institutional investors to engage with companies on their ESG performance and make them become more sustainable. At the same time, it captures the growing demand for ESG investments from end-investors and beneficiaries, who may want to invest their money with an asset manager that engages on ESG topics on their behalf.

Stewardship rules within the EU, as discussed in the following section, mainly concern the first, and to some extent the fourth and the fifth conception of stewardship. They are therefore aligned with the UK's Stewardship Codes. Neither SRD II nor any of the national stewardship codes consider the role of the controlling shareholder, whether in relation to the company, or in relation to other groups of shareholders, such as institutional investors. Whether this

---

[31] For example: 'Principle 3: Signatories manage conflicts of interest to put the best interests of clients and beneficiaries first', Financial Reporting Council, UK Stewardship Code 2020, p. 10.
[32] For example, when addressing conflict of interests in Art. 3g SRD II and communication with end-investors in Art. 3a-3c SRD II.
[33] D. Katelouzou and D. Puchniak, 'Global Shareholder Stewardship: Complexities, Challenges and Possibilities' in D. Katelouzou and D. Puchniak, (eds), *Global Shareholder Stewardship*, Cambridge University Press 2022, p. 9.
[34] Financial Reporting Council, UK Stewardship Code 2020, p. 4.
[35] On the increased focus on ESG in the UK 2020 Stewardship Code, see: P. Davies, 'The UK Stewardship Code 2010–2020 From Saving the Company to Saving the Planet?' (2020) *ECGI Law Working Paper* N° 506/2020.

approach to shareholder stewardship is suitable in a continental European context will be further analyzed in section 4.1.

3. LEGAL FRAMEWORK

In this part, I describe the shareholder engagement provisions applicable in the EU, covering the scope, the engagement policies and their enforcement. Furthermore, I highlight some national stewardship codes and explain their intended function.

3.1. SRD II

3.1.1. Overview

At the EU level, stewardship is mainly regulated in the 2017 Shareholder Rights Directive. Its objective is to encourage long-term shareholder engagement and it considers 'greater involvement of shareholders in corporate governance' as 'one of the levers that can help improve the financial and non-financial performance of companies, including as regards environmental, social and governance factors'.[36] Shareholders enjoy a number of rights, such as the right to information prior to the general meeting[37], the right to add items on the agenda of the meeting and to draft resolutions[38], to participate in those general meetings[39], to ask questions[40] and to vote.[41] Certain shareholders are furthermore expected to utilize those rights by actively monitoring companies, voting and engaging in dialogue with the company's board, with the objective of improving the company's long-term value creation.[42] These additional duties, though not explicitly called that way, are very similar to requirements found in stewardship codes, as they include the requirement to adopt an engagement policy and to integrate it into the overall investment strategy.[43] SRD II has

---

[36] Recital 14 SRD II.
[37] Article 5 SRD II.
[38] Article 6 SRD II.
[39] Article 7 SRD II.
[40] Article 9 SRD II.
[41] Article 7 and 8 SRD II.
[42] Article 3g and Article 3h SRD II.
[43] The UK Stewardship Code 2020 defines stewardship as *"the responsible allocation, management and oversight of capital to create long-term value for clients and beneficiaries leading to sustainable benefits for the economy, the environment and society"*, p. 4. SRD II equally contains requirements on an engagement policy (Article 3g), but also a wider investment strategy (Article 3h SRD II) and investment management requirements (Art. 3g, Art. 3a-c).

been implemented by most Member States, including Belgium, in a rather minimalistic manner. Given that it is a minimum harmonization Directive, there was room to add or broaden the engagement requirements, but Member States largely refrained from doing so.[44] The following provisions can therefore be found more or less directly transposed into Member States' law. Next to the implemented SRD II, some Member States have a stewardship code in place, which will be discussed in section 3.2.

3.1.2. Scope and objective

The stewardship provisions cover institutional investors and asset managers that hold shares of companies incorporated and listed in the EU.[45] Institutional investors are large asset owners that invest on behalf of their beneficiaries or clients, such as pension funds and insurance companies.[46] Asset managers can be investment firms providing portfolio management services to investors[47], managers of alternative investment funds[48] (AIFMs) and self-managed UCITS funds. In addition to institutional investors and asset managers, intermediaries[49] and proxy advisors play a role in facilitating this shareholder engagement.[50] Intermediaries may administrate and maintain shares on behalf of shareholders, while proxy advisors analyze relevant information about companies and provide advice and voting recommendations to shareholders.[51]

Globally speaking, institutional investors and asset managers are the largest investors in listed companies nowadays.[52] They can therefore have a large influence on those companies but were often perceived as passive and disengaged. In order to control excessive managerial risk taking and to improve a company's long-term growth, SRD II encourages institutional investors and

---

[44] D. Katelouzou and K. Sergakis, 'When Harmonization is not Enough: Shareholder Stewardship in the European Union' (2020), *European Business Organization Law Review (EBOR)* 1.
[45] Article 2, Article 3g and Article 3h SRD II.
[46] Institutional investors are defined as either undertakings carrying out life assurance or reinsurance activities which cover life-insurance obligations or institutions for occupational retirement, though these definitions are subject to a few limitations (Art. 2(e) SRD II).
[47] Article 2(f) SRD II, referring to the definition under Article 4(1) 1 MiFID II.
[48] Article 4(1) (b) Directive 2011/61/EU (AIFMD). Provided they do not fall under the intra-group or *de minimis* exemption of Article 3 AIFMD.
[49] Intermediaries can be investment firms, credit institutions or central securities depositories, which provide services such as safekeeping, administration or maintenance of shares on behalf of shareholders, Article 2(d) SRD II.
[50] Article 2(d) SRD II.
[51] Article 2(g) SRD II.
[52] A. De La Cruz, A. Medina and Y. Tang, 'Owners of the World's Listed Companies' (2019) *OECD Capital Market Series*; G. Aminadav and E. Papaioannou, 'Corporate Control around the World' (2020) *Journal of Finance* 1191, 1205.

asset managers to actively engage and use their expertise to help improve the financial and non-financial performance of companies.[53]

Hedge fund activists are often alternative investment fund managers and therefore asset managers that have to comply with the engagement requirements. Not included in the engagement requirement are other groups of shareholders, such as controlling or retail shareholders. These groups may of course exercise their shareholder rights as well but are not specifically required or encouraged to do so.

3.1.3. Engagement and Investment Policy

The central stewardship provision is Article 3g SRD II, which requires institutional investors and asset managers to develop an engagement policy and disclose it to the public on a comply-or-explain basis.[54] This engagement policy must include how they (1) integrate engagement in the overall investment strategy; (2) monitor their investee companies on important topics, such as capital structure, strategy, financial and non-financial risks and performance, including their environmental and social impact and corporate governance; (3) communicate with these companies; (4) exercise their voting rights; (5) cooperate with other shareholders; (6) communicate with other relevant stakeholders; and (7) aim to manage actual and potential conflicts of interest.

Once such a policy is adopted, institutional investors and asset managers must annually and publicly disclose its implementation, including an explanation of the general voting strategy and the most significant votes, as well as the use of proxy advisors.[55] The disclosure of votes may be limited to those of relevance due to subject matter or size of the holding.

Both the engagement policy as well as the annual reports on its implementation must be published free of charge on the institutional investor's or asset manager's website.[56]

Article 3h SRD II further requires the annual disclosure of the broader investment strategy and how that strategy aligns with the medium to long-term liabilities and objectives of the institutional investor or asset manager. If asset managers invest on behalf of institutional investors, they have to disclose how their decisions are aligned with the investment strategy of the institutional investors.

---

[53] Recital 2 and 14 SRD II.
[54] For a more detailed discussion of this requirement see below in section 3.1.4.
[55] Article 3g (1) SRD II.
[56] Article 3g (2) SRD II.

3.1.4. Enforcement and Application in Practice

Unlike many stewardship codes, which only apply to the voluntary signatories of the code, SRD II defines a scope of mandatory applicants. Institutional investors and asset managers that fall under it must in principle apply the stewardship provisions. These principles themselves employ a comply-or-explain mechanism.[57] They can therefore either disclose their engagement policy or explain why they chose not to disclose it.

The choices regarding supervision and enforcement of these requirements lies with the national legislators, which can choose their own enforcement model and authority.[58] In implementing SRD II, many Member States have not provided any additional clarification as to how they will enforce the requirements.[59] In Belgium, the FSMA is responsible for the supervision and enforcement.[60] It has issued some guidance for institutional investors, which briefly clarifies the engagement and investment requirements found in the law[61] and states that the FSMA is prepared to show flexibility when monitoring those requirements.[62]

3.2. STEWARDSHIP CODES

Before the adoption of SRD II in 2017 there were already a number of national and international stewardship codes and guidelines. The first ever stewardship code was issued by the UK's Financial Reporting Council in 2010 and was slightly updated in 2012.[63] It contained seven principles and employed a comply-or-explain mechanism. It applied to the UK's domestic institutional investors[64] and could be voluntarily signed up for by international investors.

---

[57] Article 3g (1) SRD II.
[58] Article 14b SRD II.
[59] A. Bartolacelli et al., 'Chapter 13: Article 14a and 14b: Enforcement of SRD II Provisions', in H. Birkmose and K. Sergakis, (eds), *The Shareholder Rights Directive II*, Edward Elgar Publishing, Cheltenham 2021, p. 337.
[60] FSMA, 'Omzetting Shareholder Rights Directive FSMA_2020_07 dd. 30/06/2020' <www.fsma.be/en/news/transposition-shareholders-rights-directive>, accessed 15.11.2022.
[61] SRD II has been transposed into Belgian law by the following law: Loi transposant la directive 2017/828 du Parlement européen et du Conseil du 17 mai 2017 modifiant la directive 2007/36/CE en vue de promouvoir l'engagement à long terme des actionnaires, et portant des dispositions diverses en matière de sociétés et d'associations, Official Gazette 6 May 2020, 304880.
[62] FSMA, 'Omzetting Shareholder Rights Directive FSMA_2020_07 dd. 30/06/2020' <www.fsma.be/en/news/transposition-shareholders-rights-directive>, accessed 15.11.2022.
[63] Financial Reporting Council, UK Stewardship Code 2010; for a discussion see: P. Davies 'The UK Stewardship Code 2010–2020 From Saving the Company to Saving the Planet?' (2020) *ECGI Law Working Paper* N° 506/2020.
[64] Specifically, it covers (1) asset owners such as pension schemes, insurers, foundations, endowments, local government pension pools and sovereign wealth funds, (2) asset managers

Marleen Och

In practice, it was not very effective in making passive investors active and therefore largely deemed a failure.[65] In 2020, the new UK Stewardship Code was issued, which includes 12 principles on engagement, monitoring, voting policies and cooperation with other investors.[66] It employs a stricter apply-and-explain mechanism, thereby eliminating the option for its users to simply explain why they chose not to follow the requirements. Most noticeably, it places a much stronger focus on ESG topics. Many stewardship codes globally have followed this approach and now equally refer to ESG factors in their texts.[67] It remains to be seen whether this ESG focus will lead to a change in the way institutional investors engage and whether a stricter compliance regime will lead to a more successful application.

Within the EU, Italy, Denmark and the Netherlands are the only Member States that adopted Stewardship Codes.[68] They are inspired by the UK's Stewardship Codes and therefore have a strong focus on institutional investors and asset managers, and less on other types of investors.[69] There can be added value to such codes, as they may expand the understanding and requirements for engagement.

The Dutch Stewardship Code, for example, encourages cooperation with other shareholders[70] and communication with other relevant stakeholders.[71] It requires a more detailed disclosure of the engagement and voting strategy than SRD II, with detailed voting records and explanations, including negative or withheld votes.[72] The Code was issued by the institutional investor interest

---

who manage assets on behalf of UK clients or invest in UK assets and (3) service providers such as investment consultants, proxy advisors, data and research providers that support asset owners and asset managers to exercise their stewardship responsibilities, see: Financial Reporting Council, UK Stewardship Code 2010.

[65] B. Cheffins, 'The Stewardship Code's Achilles' Heel' (2010) 73 *Modern Law Review* 1004; E. Rock, 'Institutional Investors in Corporate Governance' in J. Gordon and W.-G. Ringe (eds), *The Oxford Handbook of Corporate Governance*, Oxford University Press, Oxford 2018, p. 16–28.

[66] Financial Reporting Council, UK Stewardship Code 2020.

[67] D. Katelouzou and D. Puchniak, 'Global Shareholder Stewardship: Complexities, Challenges and Possibilities' in D. Katelouzou and D. Puchniak, (eds), *Global Shareholder Stewardship*, Cambridge University Press 2022, p. 8.

[68] All stewardship codes can be found on the website of the European Corporate Governance Institute: <https://ecgi.global/content/codes-stewardship>, accessed 15.11.2022.

[69] D. Puchniak, 'The False Hope of Stewardship in the Context of Controlling Shareholders: Making Sense Out of a Global Transplant of a Legal Misfit' (2021) *EGCI Law Working Paper* N° 589/2021, *American Journal of Comparative Law* (Forthcoming).

[70] Eumedion, Dutch Stewardship Code (2018) Article 4, <www.eumedion.nl/en/public/knowledgenetwork/best-practices/2018-07-dutch-stewardship-code-final-version.pdf>.

[71] Eumedion, Dutch Stewardship Code (2018) Article 5, <www.eumedion.nl/en/public/knowledgenetwork/best-practices/2018-07-dutch-stewardship-code-final-version.pdf>.

[72] Eumedion, Dutch Stewardship Code (2018) Article 7, <www.eumedion.nl/en/public/knowledgenetwork/best-practices/2018-07-dutch-stewardship-code-final-version.pdf>.

group Eumedion and applies with a comply-or-explain mechanism to its members.[73]

The Danish Stewardship Code was adopted in 2016 and was heavily inspired by the original UK Stewardship Code. It equally established seven principles and employed a comply-or-explain mechanism.[74] Following the transposition of SRD II in 2020, the Danish Committee on Corporate Governance decided to phase out the Danish Stewardship Code.[75]

The Italian Stewardship Principles were first published in 2013 by the investment management association Assogestioni and revised in 2015 and 2016.[76] The six principles are similar to those found in other codes, albeit with some modifications relating to special characteristics of Italian corporate governance, which cannot be found in SRD II.[77] The principles apply on a comply-or-explain basis, and like most stewardship rules they encounter an enforcement problem, as the investor association behind the principles has no legal power to enforce compliance.[78] The principles currently undergo another review and an increased focus on ESG can be expected.

In addition to national stewardship codes or principles, a number of international codes and guidelines can be found. The European Fund and Asset Management Association (EFAMA) published a stewardship code in 2018 which acts as an additional guidance document for the SRD II's requirements and can be voluntarily applied by asset managers.[79] The International Corporate Governance Network (ICGN) also published Global Stewardship Principles in 2020.[80] The document includes seven principles and some additional guidance

---

[73] C. Van der Elst and A. Lafarre, 'Shareholder Stewardship in the Netherlands: The Role of Institutional Investors in a Stakeholder-Oriented Jurisdiction', in D. Katelouzou and D. Puchniak, (eds), *Global Shareholder Stewardship*, Cambridge University Press 2022, p. 97.

[74] The Committee on Corporate Governance, Danish Stewardship Code, November 2016. <https://corporategovernance.dk/sites/default/files/180116_stewardship_code.pdf>, accessed 15.11.2022.

[75] The Committee on Corporate Governance, 'Udfasning af Anbefalinger for aktivt Ejerskab', 28.01.2020, <https://corporategovernance.dk/udfasning-af-anbefalinger-aktivt-ejerskab>, accessed 15.11.2022.

[76] Assogestioni, 'Italian Stewardship Principles for the exercise of administrative and voting rights in listed companies', 2016.

[77] G. Strampelli, 'Institutional Investor Stewardship in Italy' in D. Katelouzou and D. Puchniak, (eds), *Global Shareholder Stewardship*, Cambridge University Press, 2022, pp. 136–147.

[78] G. Strampelli, 'Institutional Investor Stewardship in Italy' in D. Katelouzou and D. Puchniak, (eds), *Global Shareholder Stewardship*, Cambridge University Press, 2022, p. 147.

[79] European Fund and Asset Management Association, 'EFAMA Stewardship Code Principles for asset managers' monitoring of, voting in, engagement with investee companies' (2018) <www.efama.org/sites/default/files/files/EFAMA%20Stewardship%20Code_FINAL.pdf.

[80] International Corporate Governance Network, 'ICGN Global Stewardship Principles' (2020) <www.icgn.org/sites/default/files/2021-06/ICGN%20Global%20Stewardship%20Principles%202020_1.pdf>.

on them. The Principles for Responsible Investment (PRI), established under a UN initiative, set up six principles that focus on incorporating ESG issues into the signatories investment practices.[81] Signatories are strongly encouraged to work together in their engagement efforts.[82] Furthermore, the OECD principles from 2013 provide guidance for governments which want to regulate stewardship.[83] All of these codes are similar in scope, content and their limited enforcement possibilities. They may aid as additional guidance or explanatory documents but do not reach beyond the established legal provisions of SRD II.

4. ANALYSIS

The previous section has shown that a number of rules exist on shareholder stewardship, whether it be in the form of the implemented SRD II or additional stewardship codes. The question remains, however, whether those rules are effective in fostering the type of interaction between shareholders and companies that stewardship codes and other legislation in the EU aim for. In this next section, I analyze certain aspects of stewardship in more detail and point to some of the flaws within the concept of stewardship in the EU.

4.1. CONTROLLING SHAREHOLDERS

SRD II takes inspiration from the 2010 UK Stewardship Code, which focuses on institutional investors and asset managers as the most 'influential' shareholders.[84] While institutional investors may be the most influential shareholders in the Anglo-Saxon world, ownership structures in EU Member States are usually much more concentrated than those in the US and the UK.[85] In the EU, institutional investors and asset managers combined on average do not hold a controlling majority of shares. They therefore have much less direct influence on the company when voting power is measured. Instead, controlling

---

[81] <www.unpri.org/about-us/about-the-pri>, accessed 15.11.2022.
[82] For more on this cooperation and its effects, see section 4.3.
[83] G20/OECD, High-Level Principles on Long-Term Investment Financing by Institutional Investors (2013), <www.oecd.org/daf/fin/private-pensions/G20-OECD-High-Level-Principles-Long-Term-Investment-Financing-By-Institutional-Investors.pdf>.
[84] Puchniak explains how the UK Stewardship Code became the inspiration for many stewardship codes worldwide and why these codes are largely a misfit in those jurisdictions, as this paragraph summarizes.
D. Puchniak, 'The False Hope of Stewardship in the Context of Controlling Shareholders: Making Sense Out of a Global Transplant of a Legal Misfit' (2021) *EGCI Law Working Paper* No.589/2021, *American Journal of Comparative Law* (Forthcoming).
[85] A. De La Cruz, A. Medina and Y. Tang, 'Owners of the World's Listed Companies' (2019) *OECD Capital Market Series*; G. Aminadav and E. Papaioannou, 'Corporate Control around the World' (2020) *Journal of Finance* 1191, 1205.

shareholders, such as the founder or founding family, as well as other (holding) companies or the government play a larger role. In Belgium for example 63.4% of listed corporations have a controlling shareholder, and the largest shareholder on average holds 38.6% of the votes.[86] Yet, none of these groups are covered by SRD II's shareholder engagement provision or any other national stewardship code.[87] The exact influence of those shareholders further depends on the share structure. In some Member States, dual-class or loyalty shares can be issued, leading to a divergence between shares held and the voting power of that shareholder.[88] Loyalty shares, which aim to award long-time holding periods, often de facto lead to an even stronger concentration of power with the already powerful founder or early investor in a company.[89]

The question is therefore which incentives these powerful shareholders have and whether they fit the ideal of actively engaged, long-term-focused and sustainable shareholders that SRD II envisions. Controlling shareholders indeed have some incentives to focus on the long-term success of their companies.[90] They often care about the company's reputation and long-term performance and therefore want to invest into its long-term value. Whether they also follow explicit sustainability objectives can, however, not be deducted from that.

If we assume that pricing in negative externalities will increasingly be required due to changing legislation[91], it might be beneficial for the company's long-term value to invest in ESG transformation now and sacrifice some shorter-term profits for it. This approach allows companies to utilize first-mover benefits and enhance their reputation. The reality for a company's transition may however not be as clear cut. Sacrifices to the short- and long-term shareholder value might be necessary to achieve sustainability goals and the question arises

---

[86] G. Aminadav and E. Papaioannou, 'Corporate Control around the World' (2020) *Journal of Finance* 1205–1208.
[87] The questions as to why controlling shareholders are so underrepresented in stewardship codes is likely due to a number of social, political and legal reasons. I discuss these more in my PhD thesis on shareholder engagement and sustainability in the EU.
[88] C. Mosca, 'Should shareholders be rewarded for loyalty? European experiments on the wedge between tenured voting and takeover law' (2019) *Michigan Business & Entrepreneurial Law Review* 245.
[89] M. Roe and F. Venezze, 'Will Loyalty Shares Do Much for Corporate Short-Termism?' (2021) *Business Lawyer* 467, 487–496.
[90] A. Choi, 'Concentrated Ownership and Long-Term Shareholder Value' (2018) *Harvard Business Law Review* 53.
[91] See for example the proposed Corporate Sustainability Due Diligence Directive, 'Proposal for a Directive on Corporate Sustainability Due Diligence and amending Directive (EU) 2019/1937' COM(2022) 71 final 2022/0051(COD). The Directive foresees that certain companies integrate due diligence and identify and address adverse human rights and environmental impacts in their value chains. Certain companies will furthermore be required to draft a plan to ensure their businesses compatibility with limiting global warming to 1.5 °C.

whether controlling shareholders would be willing to make these sacrifices for the sake of 'the benefits of wider society' and the reputational benefits that come along with it.

Though many controlling shareholders are generally long-term focused, there are also risks associated with them, such as the private benefits of control and abuse of their controlling position.[92] Some controlling shareholders may request for the company to pay out excessive dividends to fund their private lifestyle instead of investing in the costly transformation of a company. Such transformation efforts may further be blocked by controlling shareholders if they are perceived as too costly and would harm the dividend income of a shareholder that lacks diversification. Controlling shareholders may object to new share issuances that could finance the transformation of a company if they do not want their influence on the company to be diluted and lack the financial means to purchase new shares.[93]

Not only controlling shareholders' incentives differ from that of other shareholders, but also their means of engagement.[94] As controlling shareholders usually have a direct link to the management or board, they can exert influence without making their engagement public. This makes their engagement more difficult to study and regulate. One stewardship code, albeit not in the EU, nonetheless attempts to foster a specific type of engagement by controlling shareholders. The Singapore Family Stewardship Code focuses on families as controlling shareholders and advocates for them to act as good stewards to their companies.[95] According to the Code, this includes a strong commitment to purpose and values, taking on an ownership mentality, integrating long-term perspectives and striving for ESG impact. The focus is therefore less on incentivizing otherwise passive shareholders to engage, as with other stewardship codes, but rather to commit to an 'ownership mentality' rooted in purpose and values. As with many other stewardship codes, this code only has voluntary signatories and there is no real monitoring of compliance. It is

---

[92] T. Vos, 'Controlling shareholders in corporate governance: cure or cause for short-termism?' (2022) <https://papers.ssrn.com/sol3/papers.cfm?abstract_id=4221137>, 14.

[93] D. Dhammika and V. Khanna, 'Controlling Externalities: Ownership Structure and Cross-Firm Externalities' (2021) European Corporate Governance Institute – Law Working Paper No. 603/2021, University of Chicago Coase-Sandor Institute for Law & Economics Research Paper No. 932, U of Michigan Law & Econ Research Paper No. 21–022, <https://ssrn.com/abstract=3904316 or http://dx.doi.org/10.2139/ssrn.3904316>.

[94] Albeit focusing on privately-held companies, Gözlügöl and Ringe discuss the differences in incentives and strategies in relation to controlling shareholders, see: A. Gözlügöl and W.-G. Ringe, 'Private Companies: The Missing Link on The Path to Net Zero' (2022) ECGI Law Working Paper No. 635/2022, SAFE Working Paper No. 342, LawFin Working Paper No. 38, <https://ssrn.com/abstract=4065115> or <http://dx.doi.org/10.2139/ssrn.4065115>.

[95] Stewardship Asia Centre, Stewardship Principles for Family Businesses (2018) <www.stewardshipasia.com.sg/sites/default/files/2020–09/SPFB-brochure-0913.pdf>, accessed 15.11.2022.

therefore questionable whether its usefulness goes beyond the positive signaling effect for the families that signed up for the code.

The complexity of the variety of company structures in the EU, which may include several holding companies or state-controlled companies makes it challenging to envision a type of stewardship code for controlling shareholders that would be suitable for all of them. Other questions arise about the legal possibilities and limits when requiring disclosure or engagement by a selected group of shareholders, which may just be private individuals.

Another approach could be 'relationship agreements' concluded between the controlling shareholder and the company.[96] With such a voluntary agreement the controlling shareholder can manifest certain commitments or intentions, for example relating to the long-term interest of the company or its corporate purpose. By making these agreements public and subject to internal control procedures the controlling shareholder can demonstrate their commitment to the company.

While neither of these approaches creates powerful legal requirements for controlling shareholders, there is merit in examining them further, given how much voting power in the EU lies with controlling shareholders.

4.2. INCENTIVES FOR INSTITUTIONAL INVESTORS

Not only does SRD II disregard an important group of shareholders, but the focus on engagement by institutional investors and asset managers does not fully align with their incentives either.

In particular, passive or index-tracking funds, which are rapidly growing types of investment funds, are held back by several incentives not to engage.[97] While an active investment fund sets itself apart from its competitors by choosing to invest in specific companies and therefore has an interest in those companies doing particularly well, index-tracking funds compete on the basis of low costs and track the same or similar combination of companies than their competitors They cannot enhance their portfolio's performance by selling specific shares as they need to follow the index they track. If they want to strengthen their

---

[96] The Belgian Code on Corporate Governance for example introduced such an option under provision 8.7, <https://corporategovernancecommittee.be/assets/pagedoc/2003973319-16510 62453_1651062453-2020-belgian-code-on-corporate-governance.pdf>.

[97] L.A. Bebchuk, A. Cohen and S. Hirst, 'The Agency Problems of Institutional Investors' (2017) 31 *JEP*, 89–102.; S. Alvaro, M. Maugeri and G. Strampelli, 'Institutional investors, corporate governance and stewardship codes – Problems and perspectives' (2019) *CONSOB Legal Papers*.

portfolio, they would need to engage with the companies in it.[98] Yet, this directly and equally benefits the funds' competitors, who hold the same index of companies. As shareholder engagement bears a cost and index-tracking funds typically compete for their customers on the basis of low fees, passive funds seem to lack incentives to engage with their investee companies.[99]

While some actively managed funds, such as hedge funds, have strong incentives to engage actively, as discussed in section 2.1, many of the institutional investors and large asset managers have quite diversified investment strategies. They therefore also encounter some of the incentive problems that passive funds have. Weighing the cost of engagement and research, especially when there is poor disclosure by companies, against their benefits, there are limits to the profitability of engagement for them.[100] Additionally, there are legal risks associated with collective engagement, such as possible breaches of take-over or market abuse laws, for example if shareholders are considered to act in concert or to share inside information.[101]

Despite those apparent counterincentives, institutional investors and asset managers have nonetheless actively and successfully engaged in the past. In particular, an increase in ESG engagement is noticeable. One prominent example of successful stewardship in that regard is the push for more board diversity. Starting in 2017, the three largest passive investment funds in the US publicly challenged boards to increase their gender diversity and attached numerical minimum criteria to their votes. This led to a 75% increase in female directors over the next three years and clearly demonstrates the impact these investors can have.[102] This trend of passive investment funds supporting social and environmental shareholder demands continues. BlackRock's support for environmental shareholder proposals for example rose from 6% in 2020 to 29.8% globally in 2021.[103]

---

[98] J. Fisch, A. Hamdani, S. Solomon, 'The New Titans of Wall Street: A Theoretical Framework for Passive Investors' (2019) 168 *University of Pennsylvania Law Review* 17, 17–72.

[99] L.A. Bebchuk, A. Cohen and S. Hirst, 'The Agency Problems of Institutional Investors' (2017) 31 *JEP*, 89–102; M. Barzuza, Q. Curtis, D. Webber, 'Shareholder Value(s): Index Fund ESG Activism and the New Millennial Corporate Governance' (2020) *Southern California Law Review* 93.

[100] For a more detailed overview of the costs of activist campaigns see the chapter of Tom Vos.

[101] ESMA, 'Report – Undue short-term pressure on corporations' (2019) <www.esma.europa.eu/sites/default/files/library/esma30-22-762_report_on_undue_short-term_pressure_on_corporations_from_the_financial_sector.pdf>. See also for a discussion on how securities laws could impede activism and engagement the book chapter by Marijke Spooren, Ruben Foriers and Jean-Sébastien Rombouts.

[102] M. Barzuza, Q. Curtis, D. Webber, 'Shareholder Value(s): Index Fund ESG Activism and the New Millennial Corporate Governance' (2020) *Southern California Law Review* 93.

[103] Insightia, 'The Proxy Voting Annual Review 2021, (2021) p. 6. This rise in ESG votes might partially be due to 'strategic voting', see section 4.4.

Not only passive investment funds have stepped up their engagement. More generally, the support for environmental shareholder proposals globally by all shareholders increased from 16.6% in 2019 to 18.7% in 2020 and 27.2% in 2021.[104] Noticeably, large European asset managers vote more often in favor of ESG proposals than their US counterparts.[105]

It is conceivable that the requirements of SRD II, and more generally the enhanced reporting requirements on companies and financial market participants due to the sustainable finance legislation in the EU, have contributed to the rising levels of ESG engagement by European institutional investors and asset managers.[106] The more favorable stance on ESG may also reflect client preference or changes in corporate culture in Europe.

A number of other reasons may further explain why ESG stewardship is generally on the rise.[107] There is increased demand for ESG investing, driven to some extent by the Millennial generation.[108] End investors are increasingly more interested in the sustainability of the companies they invest in and expect their asset managers to become active and work towards changes in those companies. Increased demand for ESG investment products allows the asset managers to charge higher fees and justify this with more costly research and engagement. Investment funds can attract more clients with those specialized funds. At the same time competition for those new clients drives them to compete with their stewardship efforts. They have to increase their engagement or be the first to address a new ESG problem in order to distinguish themselves from other funds.[109]

Another argument that suggests that institutional investors and asset managers can be effective stewards is that of 'common ownership'.[110] While they may have

---

[104] Insightia, 'The Proxy Voting Annual Review 2021, (2021) p. 9.
[105] A. Lafarre, 'Do Institutional Investors Vote Responsibly?' (2022) TILEC Discussion Paper No. DP2022–001, *Tilburg Law School Research Paper*; Morningstar Report, 'Proxy Voting: Managers Focus on Environmental and Social Themes' (2022) <www.morningstar.com/lp/managers-focus-on-environmental-and-social-themes>, accessed 15.11.2022.
[106] A. Pacces, 'Sustainable Corporate Governance: The Role of the Law' (2020) *ECGI Law Working Paper* N° 550/2020.
[107] W-G. Ringe, 'Investor-led Sustainability in Corporate Governance' (2021) *ECGI Working Paper* N° 615/2021.
[108] For a review of the empirical evidence in support of these claims, see: M. Barzuza, Q. Curtis, D. Webber, 'Shareholder Value(s): Index Fund ESG Activism and the New Millennial Corporate Governance' (2020) *Southern California Law Review 93*.
[109] An example of a newly introduced feature to offer more stewardship choices to end-investors is BlackRocks 'Voting Choice', whereby end-investors can choose to vote their shares directly or select between a number of voting and engagement preferences, <www.blackrock.com/corporate/about-us/investment-stewardship/blackrock-voting-choice>, accessed 15.11.2022.
[110] J. Azar, M. Duro, I. Kadach and G. Ormazabal, 'The Big Three and Corporate Carbon Emissions Around the World' (2020), *Journal of Financial Economics 2021* vol. 142, issue 2,

fewer incentives to engage on a company level, their small holdings in almost all listed European companies make them ideal candidates for indirectly influencing the entire market. Given their common or universal ownership, they have incentives to reduce climate-change related or systemic financial risks that would affect the entire economy. To that end, it can be more profitable for them to cut profits in some companies by internalizing negative externalities, than to suffer the overall negative effects of those externalities on the whole economy. Instead of engaging with each investee company individually they can send similar and overarching messages to all their investee companies, reducing their cost of engagement.[111]

Unfortunately, it is difficult for clients to distinguish between institutional investors only appearing to be sustainable stewards compared to those delivering on that promise.[112] Most of the incentives driving funds to engage are equally present when they only greenwash their commitments, allowing them to counter some of that pressure of ESG without actually adapting their engagement or voting practices. Institutional investors are regularly being criticized for a mismatch between their public statements and actual voting.[113] The popularity of ESG can be a strong incentive for investors to improve the perception of their stewardship efforts. However, as long as they can simply greenwash their stewardship policies, these additional incentives will not necessarily translate to actual improvements in the investee companies' sustainability performance.

To conclude, institutional investors and asset managers appear to have less incentives to engage than SRD II seems to assume and in the presence of a controlling shareholder, engagement becomes more difficult. While the overall benefits might be overstated, there are promising trends for engagement when looking at ESG topics and the question of common ownership. They add new value to regulating and encouraging stewardship. Stewardship codes can reduce greenwashing possibilities if they include a high level of disclosure and monitoring that require investors to draw up effective engagement policies

---

674–696. On the other hand not finding evidence that common ownership as an effect on E and S scores: K. Khoo, 'Common Ownership and Corporate Social Responsibility: Evidence from the Blackrock-BGI Merger' (2022), <https://papers.ssrn.com/sol3/papers.cfm?abstract_id=4061939>.

[111] See for example Larry Fink's Annual Letters to CEOs: <www.blackrock.com/corporate/investor-relations/larry-fink-ceo-letter>, accessed 15.11.2022.

[112] A. Christie, 'The Agency Cost of Sustainable Capitalism' (2021) *Legal Studies Research Paper Series University of Cambridge*; A. Lafarre, 'Do Institutional Investors Vote Responsibly?' (2022). *TILEC Discussion Paper* No. DP2022-001.

[113] For examples of criticism, see: <www.economist.com/special-report/2022/07/21/the-saviour-complex>, accessed 15.11.2022; <www.economist.com/by-invitation/2021/11/04/tariq-fancy-on-the-failure-of-green-investing-and-the-need-for-state-action>, accessed 15.11.2022; Showing such a mismatch between statements and votes: A. Lafarre, 'Do Institutional Investors Vote Responsibly?', (2022) *TILEC Discussion Paper* No. DP2022-001.

and see them through. SRD II is an important first step in that direction, but disclosure rules and monitoring of them is still lacking, as discussed in more detail in section 4.4. Investor cooperation, which will be discussed in more detail in the next section, can further play a part in gathering the necessary majorities and grouping shareholders with different engagement incentives.

4.3. INVESTOR COOPERATION

The previous sections have shown that the incentives for engagement by large institutional investors are limited. In the presence of a controlling shareholder the potential effects of such an engagement may become less fruitful. In the next section I move from looking at these groups separately to focusing on how engagement efforts can be coordinated and which roles different investors can play.

In recent years, numerous investor initiatives have emerged which coordinate ESG investment and engagement efforts. Among them are initiatives such as Climate Action 100+[114], the Coalition for Inclusive Capitalism[115], the Institutional Investors Group on Climate Change[116] or the Global Sustainable Investment Alliance.[117]

Climate Action 100+ for example unites 700 investors globally that combined represent over $68 trillion in assets under management.[118] They specifically aim to target the largest corporate greenhouse gas emitters. Such strong commitments combined with the sheer market power they represent paint a very promising picture for investor cooperation on ESG. However, critics point to a lack of transparency and ambition[119] and inadequate commitments and strategy on emission reduction by the target companies.[120]

The UN's Principles for Responsible Investment, which promote the integration of ESG factors into investment decisions, likewise include a commitment to 'work together to enhance the effectiveness in implementing the principles'.[121]

---

[114] <www.climateaction100.org/>, accessed 15.11.2022.
[115] <www.coalitionforinclusivecapitalism.com/>, accessed 15.11.2022.
[116] <www.iigcc.org/>, accessed 15.11.2022.
[117] <www.gsi-alliance.org/>, accessed 15.11.2022.
[118] <www.climateaction100.org/about/>, accessed 15.11.2022.
[119] <https://shareaction.org/news/greater-ambition-and-transparency-needed-to-revive-climate-action-100-initiative-ahead-of-relaunch>, accessed 15.11.2022.
[120] <www.bloomberg.com/news/articles/2022-03-30/most-climate-action-100-companies-are-failing-on-emissions?leadSource=uverify%20wall>, accessed 15.11.2022.
[121] Principles for Responsible Investment, Principle 5, <www.unpri.org/about-us/what-are-the-principles-for-responsible-investment>, accessed 15.11.2022.

Dimson, Karakas and Li have shown that collaborative campaigns coordinated through the PRI are in fact beneficial.[122] They improve target companies' performance and meet the set engagement goals. Engagement efforts led by a domestic lead investor and supported by a number of supporting investors have shown to be the most successful. By grouping expertise, resources and influence, investor groups can amplify their voices and overcome some of the disincentives institutional investors usually face with engagement.[123] While the lead investors in the campaigns need to dedicate more resources, they also benefit from enhanced reputation and may attract further clients that way.[124] Coordination through a 'neutral' party, such as the PRI, furthermore reduces the challenges arising through collaboration, such as free-rider problems and differing objectives and interests. The PRI's ESG campaigns are mainly joined by mid-sized investors, possibly because small investors may lack the resources and influence to join, and large investors have sufficient resources and influence to campaign on their own.[125]

Further models of investor cooperation can be observed between activist hedge funds and large institutional investors. While large institutional investors may have limited incentives to monitor each investee company and propose detailed shareholder proposals, activist hedge funds are specialized in it. Successful stewardship can therefore lie in the combination of these groups.[126] To enhance their chances of getting their shareholder proposals adapted, activists often cooperate with other investors and build coalitions to succeed with their proposals. Reticent institutional investors with larger voting power and activist shareholders with resources to thoroughly monitor the individual companies appear to complement each other well and their cooperation holds the promise of successful micro-level engagement.[127]

Large asset managers increasingly team up with smaller activist funds or even NGOs to engage on ESG topics, tabling shareholder proposals to introduce say-on-climate votes, emission reduction targets or demand more employee diversity.[128] While these proposals are more prominent in the US, they are

---

[122] E. Dimson, O. Karakas, X. Li, 'Coordinated Engagements' (2021) *ECGI Finance Working Paper* No. 721/2021, <https://papers.ssrn.com/sol3/papers.cfm?abstract_id=3209072>, 1.
[123] *Ibid.*, 2.
[124] *Ibid.*, 6.
[125] *Ibid.*, 4.
[126] A. Christie, 'The Agency Cost of Sustainable Capitalism' (2021) *Legal Studies Research Paper Series University of Cambridge*; R. Gilson and J. Gordon, 'The Agency Costs of Agency Capitalism: Activist Investors and the Revaluation of Governance Rights' (2013) 113 *Colum. L. Rev.* 863, 898.
[127] R. Gilson and J. Gordon, 'The Agency Costs of Agency Capitalism: Activist Investors and the Revaluation of Governance Rights' (2013) 113 *Colum. L. Rev.* 863, 898.
[128] A. Christie, 'The Agency Cost of Sustainable Capitalism' (2021) *Legal Studies Research Paper Series University of Cambridge*.

becoming increasingly popular in Europe as well.[129] Genuine ESG activists could play a key role in bridging the incentive gap present with rationally reticent and hypocritical institutional investors.[130] With activists and institutional investors joining forces behind an ESG cause, there might be a higher chance of building sufficient support.

The success of activist campaigns in controlled European companies is, however, more dependent on the controlling shareholder, rather than just on the institutional investors. In some companies the controlling power with one shareholder can be so strong that there is no realistic chance to gather the necessary votes against this shareholder, forcing activists to rely on informal mechanisms. This makes activism more challenging, but not entirely futile.[131] As discussed above, one motivating factor for controlling shareholders to become active on ESG themselves and to strengthen their engagement is reputation. This reputational factor becomes even stronger when other shareholders openly start to question the company's sustainability performance. If the controlling shareholder is perceived to be hindering the company's progress it could lead to reputational damage both for the company, expressed in the share price, as well as for its controlling shareholders personally. Investors and the wider public may have a clearer image of a company's controlling shareholder than its current management. An activist campaign that directly or indirectly targets the controlling shareholder may therefore amplify the effect on the general public's impression.

A Belgian example for a company the perception of which is closely intertwined with that of its controlling shareholder is the chemical group Solvay. The controlling shareholder of Solvay is the holding company Solvac[132], which in turn is largely held by members of the Solvay family. In 2021 Bluebell Capital Partners launched an activist campaign against Solvay, criticizing its waste discharge at the industrial facility in Rosignano in Italy and urging the group to replace its CEO. Solvay and Bluebell came to an agreement whereby Solvay committed to improve its waste management at the facility and the activist in

---

[129] E&S shareholder proposals are increasingly filed by European asset managers and coalitions of shareholders, such as e.g. LGIM, BNP Paribas Asset Management or Amundi. For a more detailed discussion see the chapter by Anna Christie.

[130] A. Christie, 'The Agency Cost of Sustainable Capitalism' (2021) *Legal Studies Research Paper Series University of Cambridge*.

[131] On the ideas of activism in a controlled company and the incentives for controlling shareholders, see: K. Kastiel, 'Against All Odds: Hedge Fund Activism in Controlled Companies' (2015) *Columbia Business Law Review*, 104–116.

[132] In March 2021, Solvac SA held 30.81% of Solvay's share capital and therefore 30.81% of voting rights, <www.solvay.com/en/investors/share-information/major-shareholders>, accessed 15.11.2022.

return would not pursue the campaign any further.[133] To launch its campaign Bluebell had only purchased one share in the company, showing that successful engagement and activism does not have to rely on majorities, but can also go through indirect channels. It furthermore emphasizes the power of reputational incentives, especially in the presence of a well-known controlling shareholder.

This example illustrates that activism and investor cooperation can be successful, even when the possibilities to formally influence the decision-making are limited due to a controlling shareholder. Investor cooperation, in its different shapes and including various types and sizes of investors, therefore holds a promise to make engagement efforts more fruitful for everyone involved.

4.4. DISCLOSURE AND MONITORING

SRD II places a strong focus on the disclosure requirements applicable to institutional investors and asset managers, asking them to publish their engagement and investment strategy. However, the Directive falls short of explaining what exactly a 'good' engagement strategy is. Too detailed requirements could interfere with the variety of engagement styles and corporate governance structures found in the EU. However, in trying to accommodate these varieties, the Directive remains more vague than the average stewardship codes. Furthermore, most Member States chose to transpose the Directive in a minimalist manner and did not alter it to accompany national specificities. This leaves the addressees of the legislation with very little guidance.[134]

SRD II has only been in force for a short period of time. The engagement policies disclosed so far vary in length, detail and focus, which makes it difficult to compare them.[135] Given that disclosure of engagement and investment strategies was previously uncommon, there is no experience or supervisory

---

[133] <www.solvay.com/en/press-release/solvay-and-bluebell-capital-partners-reach-settlement-and-issue-joint-statement>, accessed 15.11.2022.

[134] The Commission did adopt an implementing regulation with templates, but these do not focus on the engagement and investment disclosure requirements, see: Commission Implementing Regulation (EU) 2018/1212 of 3 September 2018 laying down minimum requirements implementing the provisions of Directive 2007/36/EC of the European Parliament and of the Council as regards shareholder identification, the transmission of information and the facilitation of the exercise of shareholders rights.

[135] Based on a cursory search on the web, see for example the engagement policy by Belfius Insurance <www.belfius.be/about-us/dam/corporate/corporate-social-responsibility/documents/policies-and-charters/en/Engagement_Report_2021-Belins-EN.pdf>, by BNP Paribas Asset Management <https://docfinder.bnpparibas-am.com/api/files/3B205D07-DFD8-4EBF-9BAB-1CA5EA4ACE4F> or by Lazard Asset Management <www.lazardassetmanagement.com/docs/-m0-/88455/srdiiengagementpolicy_en.pdf>, all accessed 15.11.2022.

toolbox to fall back onto.[136] Vague requirements in SRD II allow applicants to highlight those parts of their engagement they want to be public and hide other aspects, as the only have to disclose the votes that they deem relevant based on the subject matter or size of the holding.[137] I therefore believe that there should be a standardized summary of the most important votes and engagements, with an explanation. This should be followed by a comprehensive overview of all the engagement efforts undertaken by the investor in question.

The disclosure requirements furthermore do not capture every type of engagement. Non-public communication with the management, for example, is often an important part of engagement, but there is no requirement for institutional investors or asset managers to disclose which companies they had private conversations with. Disclosure of the voting strategy itself furthermore does not automatically lead to full transparency. Through 'strategic voting', institutional investors can vote for shareholder proposals on ESG topics which have no prospect to succeed, as the votes in favor of the proposal are far from a majority.[138] In their voting statistics the investor can afterwards claim that their pro-ESG votes reached a certain percentage. Through this method, they can appear more ESG-minded to their beneficiaries and the general public. On the other hand, they do not risk possible profitability losses in the short run which could for example arise when a company actually has to implement a new ambitious and costly climate policy.

Additional guidance and stricter requirements are therefore needed. These could take the form of explanatory documents elaborating on the objectives and disclosure requirements and templates that allow comparison of engagement and voting behavior.[139] Monitoring and enforcement would equally be facilitated if the disclosed information is more comparable. In the UK, a tiering system was introduced, which divides investors into different tiers depending on the level of their disclosure.[140] Some investors in the lowest group were successfully encouraged to step up their engagement efforts, while others decided to remove

---

[136] A. Bartolacelli et al, 'Chapter 13: Article 14a and 14b: Enforcement Of Srd II Provisions' in H. Birkmose and K. Sergakis, (eds), (2021). *The Shareholder Rights Directive II*, Cheltenham, UK: Edward Elgar Publishing 2022, p. 337.

[137] Article 3g (1) SRD II.

[138] R. Michaely, G. Ordonez-Calafi and S. Rubio, 'Mutual funds' strategic voting on environmental and social issues' (2022), *ECGI Finance Working Paper* No. 774/2021.

[139] The additional explanatory document issued by the Belgian FSMA for example does not go much beyond the initial text of SRD II, see: FSMA, 'Omzetting Shareholder Rights Directive FSMA_2020_07 dd. 30/06/2020' <www.fsma.be/en/news/transposition-shareholders-rights-directive>, accessed 15.12.2022.

[140] Financial Reporting Council, 'Tiering of signatories to the Stewardship Code', 14 November 2016, <www.frc.org.uk/news/november-2016/tiering-of-signatories-to-the-stewardship-code>, accessed 15.11.2022.

themselves from the list of signatories instead, which led to the abolishment of the lowest tier.[141]

In the EU, where investors must either comply or explain and cannot escape by un-signing, such an element of additional public pressure to not just disclose but disclose on a high level could be more successful. However, given that SRD II's requirements are being supervised on a Member-State level there's a risk that the application of those tiers could differ significantly in practice. Guidelines by ESMA and EIOPA for national supervisors on how to interpret these requirements could mitigate a divergence in supervisory practices.

As discussed above, a newfound meaning to stewardship can be seen in the increased ESG engagement. To utilize this movement to its full benefits and prevent that investors simply greenwash their engagement strategies, strong disclosure and monitoring of the commitments is crucial.

5. CONCLUSION

Since the rise of stewardship legislation in the beginning of the last decade many things have been set in motion. Codes issued all over the world introduced the notion that investors have a responsibility to engage with their investee companies. With SRD II this concept turned from a voluntary suggestion into a more binding requirement, which now applies to institutional investors and asset managers all over Europe. Simultaneously we can observe a rise in engagement and activism, which in the last year increasingly focused on ESG topics.

Nonetheless, shareholder stewardship legislation as it currently exists in the EU contains several flaws. The sole focus on institutional investors and asset managers does not reflect the multi-faceted reality of shareholder-company relationships. The disclosure and enforcement requirements also fall short of encouraging real ESG engagement and do not sufficiently prevent greenwashing. If legislators want to embrace the role of shareholders in a corporate governance context and particularly when looking at sustainability, a more comprehensive approach is needed.

There are a few steps that can be taken immediately. Better guidance for already applicable disclosure requirements on engagement and investment strategies could be issued. This guidance should focus on increasing comparability

---

[141] <www.frc.org.uk/news/august-2017/frc-removes-tier-3-categorisation-for-stewardship>, accessed 15.11.2022.

and preventing greenwashing of engagement policies. Better monitoring and enforcement of these requirements would be another crucial step.

In terms of more far-reaching options, the idea of additional requirements for controlling shareholders could be explored. To that end a number of open questions would need to be addressed. What are the incentives for controlling shareholders to engage, in particularly on ESG topics, and can legislation enhance them? If so, is it more beneficial to adopt one piece of legislation with a wider scope of shareholder-company relations, which may include institutional investor stewardship, shareholder activism, the role of controlling shareholders, but also smaller retail shareholders, or keep them separate? To what extent is investor cooperation hampered by legal limits often created as a protection against hostile takeovers?[142] Should those rules be re-evaluated in light of the possible benefits of cooperation between different shareholder groups?

Should stewardship rules take the form of a flexible soft-law code, possibly issued by the industry itself, hard law adopted by the legislator or a combination of the two? If hard law is adopted, what are the legal limits when imposing certain duties on specific shareholder groups and how are these competences divided between the EU and its Member States? While institutional investors and asset managers can be subject to some legal requirements as they have to act in their beneficiaries' best interest, controlling shareholders are responsible to themselves and linking certain requirements to their ownership rights would raise fundamental legal questions.

This brief chapter on shareholder stewardship is neither the place to provide answers to all these questions, nor the moment to draw a final conclusion.[143] It seems, however, that shareholder engagement can play an important role in making corporations more sustainable. Whether they hold a small or large stake, encouraging active ownership by shareholders and thereby applying a more comprehensive approach to shareholder – company relations could have a number of benefits. In light of the discrepancy between the active and sustainably-minded shareholders the EU legislator envisions and the rather superficial legal framework in place, it seems advisable to further explore the role of controlling shareholders, the benefits of shareholder platforms and cooperation in relation to ESG goals and how legislation can encourage beneficial active ownership. One conceivable outcome could be the adoption of national stewardship codes, which clarify the requirements for institutional investors

---

[142] See also for a discussion on how securities laws could impede activism and engagement the book chapter by Marijke Spooren, Ruben Foriers and Jean-Sébastien Rombouts.
[143] I address those topics in more detail and aim to answer these questions in my PhD thesis on shareholder engagement and sustainability in the EU.

and furthermore focuses on controlling shareholders, similarly to the Singapore Family Stewardship Code, and ESG topics, as the UK 2020 Stewardship Code does. Another, more far-reaching approach would be to amend SRD II and establish such requirements on an EU level.

Whichever way forward, legislators are well advised to acknowledge the importance shareholders can play in the transition to a sustainable economy and should address the arising problems in that regard accordingly.

TOWARDS A POLITICAL CORPORATION? NGOS AS ESG SHAREHOLDER ACTIVISTS AND LITIGATORS INFLUENCING CORPORATE STRATEGIES IN CONTINENTAL EUROPE

Hans De Wulf[*]

Professor of company law, Ghent University, Financial Law Institute

I.   INTRODUCING THE MAIN THEMES OF THIS CHAPTER: THERE IS A TENSION RESULTING FROM CONTRADICTORY REGULATORY CHOICES IN COMPANY LAW IN THE EU

This chapter focuses on the use of shareholder activism tactics and strategic litigation by NGOs that represent the interest of external stakeholders in order to try and influence corporate ESG policies. Belgium has seen little shareholder activism and even less ESG activism, with a few notable exceptions discussed below and in other chapters of this book. For that reason, this chapter focuses on developments in France, Germany, the Netherlands and at the EU level. But the increased activity and leverage over corporate policies of organisations acting in the interest of external stakeholders rather than (current) shareholders is a phenomenon that surely will also affect Belgian listed companies, at the latest

---

[*] The complete article was written by Hans De Wulf, but the empirical data discussed in section IV.2 were provided by Michael Bakker, Ph.D. candidate and lecturer at the University of Amsterdam (UvA). Bakker's empirical study of shareholder proposals is also discussed in his research article "Shareholder Proposals and Sustainability: An Empirically-based Critical Reflection" (accepted by ECFR and on file with author) as well as in the already published article on shareholder proposals in the 2021 AGM season: M.H.C. Bakker, "Aandeelhoudersvoorstellen en duurzaamheid: een verkenning", Ondernemingsrecht 2022, 241-255. The empirical data input of Michael Bakker provides important insights for this chapter's research but all interpretations and therefore also all mistakes in the article are my own, for which I bear sole responsibility. All internet sources in this article were last consulted on April 19 2023 unless otherwise mentioned.

when Belgian companies will become subject to sustainability due diligence legislation.

Shareholder activism is a prominent feature of the European corporate landscape[1] and will not go away anytime soon. It takes many forms[2] and uses a variety of tactics. In Europe, private activism and engagement probably play a more significant role, whereas public activism is more common in the US.[3] At the level of tactics, it is clear a that shareholder proposals play a more limited role in Europe than in the US.[4] Over the past few years – essentially since about 2016 – ESG considerations have become prominent in corporate life, also with regards to strategy development, disclosure practices, and funding as part of the sustainable finance movement that has had a huge impact on the investment fund and asset management industry, and on bank lending.[5] This is also reflected

---

[1] Just consult the annual Lazard reports, e.g. *Lazard's Review of shareholder activism 2022* at <www.lazard.com/research-insights/lazard-s-review-of-shareholder-activism-2022/>. The Lazard report on the first quarter of 2023 saw more new activist campaigns than ever in Europe (21), but with a heavy concentration on the UK and Germany, and a slight decline of activism in the US, see <www.lazard.com/research-insights/shareholder-activism-update-early-look-at-2023-trends/>.

[2] E.g. defensive versus offensive, private versus public. The distinction between defensive and offensive activism is taken from J. Armour and B. Cheffins, "The rise and fall(?) of shareholder activism by hedge funds", *Journal of Alternative Investments*, 14(3), 2012, 27.

[3] On private activism in Europe, *see e.g.* M. Becht, J. Franks and C. Mayer, "Returns to shareholder activism: evidence from a clinical study of the Hermes UK Focus Fund", *Review of Financial Studies*, 22(8), 2009, 3093–3219; G. Strampelli, "Private Meetings Between Firm Managers and Outside Investors: The European Paradigm", *Hastings Business Law Journal* 2022, 242; M. Becht, J. Franks and H. Wagner, "The Benefits of Access: Evidence from Private Meetings with Portfolio Firms", ECGI Working Papers Series in Finance No. 2021/751, available at <https://papers.ssrn.com/sol3/papers.cfm?abstract_id=3813948>. See also J. McCahery, Z. Sautner and L. T. Starks, "Behind the Scenes: The Corporate Governance Preferences of Institutional Investors", *The Journal of Finance* 2016, 71(6), 2906.

[4] This is discussed *infra*, in section IV. See already A. Taleska, *Hedge Fund Activism in Europe*, (Ghent University Law School Ph.D. thesis) 2020, at 26 and 38 and A. Taleska, "Shareholder proponents as control acquirers: a British, German and Italian perspective on the regulation of collective shareholder activism via takeover rules" *EBOR*, 19(4), 2018, 797–851.

[5] It would be futile to try and cite the enormous literature at the intersection of ESG and corporate law. I presented a broad introductory overview of ESG policy developments and developments in corporate and disclosure regulation and corporate governance practices in the EU in H. De Wulf, "ESG en vennootschapsrecht: innig verbonden maar ook duurzaam?" in H. J. de Kluiver (ed.) *Duurzaam Ondernemen en sustainable transport. Preadviezen van de Koninklijke Vereeniging Handelsrecht* 2021, Zuthpen, Paris, 2021, 29–103. For a brief but good introduction to the fundamentals of sustainable finance (not to related regulatory initiatives), see E. Bueren, 'Sustainable Finance', *ZGR* 2019, 813–875. D. Busch, G. Ferrarini and S. Grünewald, *Sustainable Finance in Europe*, Palgrave Macmillan 2021 presented the state of the art in 2020 for European regulation and policy. Important collections of essays published as books include L. Enneking et al. (eds.), *Accountability, International Business Operations, and the Law*, Routledge 2020, 301 p; B. Sjåfjell & C. Bruner, *The Cambridge Handbook of Corporate Law, Corporate Governance and Sustainability*, Cambridge University Press, 2020, 737 p.; Th. Kuntz (ed.), *Research Handbook on Environmental, Social, and Corporate Governance*, Edward Elgar, forthcoming 2023, and in Dutch and French and focusing on European, Dutch and Belgian developments H. J. de Kluiver (ed.) *Duurzaam Ondernemen*

in the rise of ESG shareholder activism.[6] The new aspect of this type of activism is not governance activism (focusing on such things as board composition, executive pay, payout policy and M&A transactions) but "E&S" (environmental and social) activism. E&S activism focuses, for example, on the impact firms have on global warming, their environmental track record, and their respect for the human rights of their workers and of local communities in developing countries affected by the activities of multinational corporations throughout their value chain.[7] In France (2017) and Germany (2023) global supply chain due diligence legislation[8] is already effective, and this will be supplemented by the EU's Corporate Sustainability Due Diligence Directive (CSDDD).[9] Such due

---

en sustainable transport. Preadviezen van de Koninklijke Vereeniging Handelsrecht 2021, Zuthpen, Paris, 2021, 287 p. and A. van Hoe and G. Croisant, *Recht en Duurzaamheid/Droit et durabilité*, Brussels, Larcier-Intersentia, 2022.

[6] See, e.g. as a general introduction W.-G. Ringe, "Investor-led Sustainability in Corporate Governance", *Annals of Corporate Governance* 2022, 93–151 or H. De Wulf and L. Van Marcke, "Duurzaamheid en vennootschapsrecht : ESG-aansprakelijkheid en de invloed van institutionele aandeelhouders" in A. van Hoe and G. Croisant (eds.) *Droit et Durabilité/ Recht en Duurzaamheid*, Antwerp, Larcier-Intersentia, 2022, 349–431; focusing on the European regulatory framework: G. Balp and G. Strampelli, "Institutional investor ESG engagement: the European experience", *EBOR*, 23, 2022, 869–904; Describing the global stewardship ecosystem: T. Bowley and J. Hill, "The global stewardship ecosystem", 7 October 2022, available at <https://papers.ssrn.com/sol3/papers.cfm?abstract_id=4240129>; focusing on the forms of collaboration between ESG shareholder activists: P. Mülbert, A. Sajnovits, "Emerging ESG-Driven Models of Shareholder Collaborative Engagement", ECGI Working Paper Series in Law No. 668/2022, available at <https://papers.ssrn.com/sol3/papers.cfm?abstract_id=4297434>. See also A. Christie, "The Agency Costs of Sustainable Capitalism" *UC Davis Law Review,* 55, 2021, 875–954 on different actors in ESG activism and how they "support" each other.

[7] For instance, farmers who are expropriated to make room for palm oil or soybean plantations or whose crops are damaged by oil leak pollution.

[8] Loi n° 2017-399 du 27 mars 2017 relative au devoir de vigilance des sociétés mères et des entreprises donneuses d'ordre, inserted into Art. L225-102-4 Code de commerce; Gesetz über die unternehmerischen Sorgfaltspflichten in Lieferketten, *Bundesgesetzblatt* Jahrgang 2021 Teil I Nr. 46, 22 July 2021, 2959.

[9] The officially published EU Commission proposal of 23 February 2022 is Proposal for a Directive of the European Parliament and of the Council on Corporate Sustainability Due Diligence and amending Directive (EU) 2019/1937, COM/2022/71 final, available at <www.ec.europa.eu/info/publications/proposal-directive-corporate-sustainable-due-diligence-and-annex_en>. My analysis of the draft in this chapter is based on later versions, namely a comparison of the "general approach" text adopted by the European Council on December 1, 2022 and the text voted by the JURI committee of the European Parliament on April 24 2023 (documents on file with Ghent University law school). After this text had been written, the plenary session of the European Parliament adopted what is in effect its final negotiation version ("first reading" text) on June 1, 2023, see <www.europarl.europa.eu/doceo/document/TA-9-2023-0209_EN.html>. These texts will be the basis for further negotiations (*trilogue*) between Commission, Parliament and Council, with a view to the final adoption of the Directive, probably in the first half of 2024.

There is a wealth of blogposts (see especially the series on the Oxford Business Law blog) on the draft CSDDD; from the article-length literature, I want to draw special attention to the special issue (exceptionally in English) of Dutch law review *Ondernemingsrecht*, 2023/5, completely devoted to the draft CSDDD, with excellent contributions by Hijink, Lambooy, Robé, Garcia Nelen, Lafarre, Lieverse, Lokin, Lennarts, Pacces, Olaerts and Dumoulin.

diligence legislation will – and in the case of the French legislation, already has[10] – created leverage for non-shareholder stakeholders, mostly climate and human rights NGOs, to influence corporate strategy, a major theme of this chapter.

But while shareholder activism is here to stay, it has never been loved by policymakers at the level of the EU. Influential voices within the European Parliament and the European Commission at least until recently seemed to believe that most activism is marred by short-termism.[11] While it is more likely that any form of short-term pressure European companies might be under is caused by leveraged private equity acquisitions – a topic that after 2000 has remained under-researched by economists[12] – EU policy-makers preferred to try and create a counterbalance against activism by exhorting, through SRDII[13], longer-term shareholders including index and pension funds to increase their shareholder engagement[14], understood as major longer term investors talking

---

See also H.-J. de Kluiver, "Towards a framework for effective regulatory supervision of sustainability governance in accordance with the EU CSDD Directive. A comparative Study", forthcoming *ECFR* 2023 (on file with the author).

[10] See *infra*, section VI.2.b., where I discuss the 10 court cases and 5 additional "notices of breach" that have been launched by NGOs against French corporations, based on the "Vigilance Act".

[11] See considerations 2 and 15 of SRD II, where combating short-termism is explicitly mentioned as a goal of the shareholder engagement rules in SRD II. See also C. Van der Elst, "Shareholder engagement duties: the European move beyond stewardship" in H. Birkmose en K. Sergakis (eds.), *Enforcing shareholders' duties*, Cheltenham, Edward Elgar, 2019, 7. The excessive fear of the EU Commission about alleged shareholder short termism was also apparent from, among many other documents, its April 2011 *Green paper: The EU corporate governance framework*, COM(2011) 164, at 13, and from its commissioning of and its first reactions to the notorious report by EY, *Study on Directors' Duties and Sustainable Corporate Governance. Final Report*, July 2020, available at <https://op.europa.eu/en/publication-detail/-/publication/e47928a2-d20b-11ea-adf7-01aa75ed71a1/language-en>. For criticism of the EY report that was as convincing as it was scathing, see M. Roe, H. Spamann, J. Fried & Ch. Wang, 'The European Commission's Sustainable Corporate Governance Report: A Critique', 14 October 2020, available at <https://ssrn.com/abstract=3711652> and ECLE (European Company Law Experts) available at <https://europeancompanylawexperts.wordpress.com/publications/european-commission-study-on-directors-duties-and-sustainable-corporate-governance/>.

[12] An overview of research mainly from the 1980s and 1990s some of which focused on whether private equity gains are made at the expense of other stakeholders is S. Kaplan and P. Strömberg, "Leveraged Buyouts and Private Equity" Journal of Economic Perspectives, 2009, 121–14, but after 2000 – in general, a boom era for private equity- economists seem to have focused on studying e.g. the question whether PE generates acceptable returns for other investors than general partners (for whom PE is a "billionaire factory", see L. Phalippou, "An Inconvenient Fact: Private Equity Returns & The Billionaire Factory" (June 10, 2020). available at: <https://ssrn.com/abstract=3623820>), as well as the contracting practices of private equity investors, but I can find very little empirical research on the impact of private equity M&A on other stakeholders than shareholders.

[13] The second, amended version of the Shareholder Rights Directive: Directive 2017/828 of the European Parliament and of the Council of 17 May 2017 amending Directive 2007/36/EC as regards the encouragement of long-term shareholder engagement [2017] *OJ* L132/1–25.

[14] See esp. art. 3g of SRD II (previous footnote). It is true that the Directive contained no incentives for institutional investors or asset managers to actively engage with investee companies, nor

to corporate leadership (top management and the board) about the long-term strategy of companies. Shareholder engagement is also encouraged by the current versions of European corporate governance codes, which have moved from promoting a shareholder value model to encouraging a stakeholder orientation for companies and their boards.[15] This came on top of stewardship codes[16], which have been prominent in some – but by no means all – European countries[17] like the Netherlands[18] (with its huge pension funds industry) and

---

did it change their business model in order to encourage shareholder engagement. But one can hardly doubt that shareholder engagement by institutional investors other than activist hedge funds has increased over the past ten years or so. On shareholder engagement and the policy considerations behind SRD II in this regard, see L. Van Marcke, "Shareholder engagement (SRD II) : zin en onzin : aandeelhoudersbetrokkenheid als regelgevend antwoord op bekommernissen van short-termism", *TRV/RPS*, 2021, 829–856. On engagement generally see the country and comparative reports in H. Kaur, Ch. Xi, C. Van der Elst and A. Lafarre (eds.), *Shareholder Engagement and Voting*, Cambridge University Press, 2022, 559 p.

[15] For the stakeholderist and sustainability flavor of the new, December 2022 version of the Dutch Corporate Governance Code, see e.g. M. van Olffen, "De corporate governance code 2022: een duurzame actualisatie?", *Ondernemingsrecht*, 2023, 319 ff. For the stakeholderist evolution in the UK corporate governance code, see B. Cheffins and B. Reddy, "Thirty Years and Done – Time to Abolish the UK Corporate Governance Code (June 9, 2022). European Corporate Governance Institute – Law Working Paper No. 654/2022, available at <https://ssrn.com/abstract=4132617>. For the sustainability-orientation in the 2022 version of the German Corporate Governance Kodex, see S. Mock and P. Velte, "Nachhaltigkeit im (neuen) Deutschen Corporate Governance Kodex", *Die Aktiengesellschaft*, 2022, 885. For France, see the 2022 *Code de gouvernement d'entreprise des sociétés cotées*; section 1.1 states that the board should promote long term value creation, taking into account the social and environmental impact of the company. This is in fact a mere copy of article 1833 of the Civil Code as amended by the 2019 "Loi Pacte" (Loi nr. 2019–486 du 22 mai 2019 relative à la croissance et la transformation des entreprises), containing the definition of the company's interest under French law.

[16] For an analysis of shareholder stewardship, see D. Katelouzou and D. W. Puchniak (eds.), *Global Shareholder Stewardship*, Cambridge University Press, 2022, 520 p. For a typology of stewardship codes worldwide (differentiating between different types of stewardship that are stressed in different codes), see A. Klettner, "Stewardship codes and the role of institutional investors in corporate governance: An international comparison and typology" *British Journal of Management*, 32, 2021, 988–1006.

[17] The stewardship code developed in 2011 and revised in 2018 by EFAMA, the European Federation of Asset Managers, served as a model for several national asset management organisations in Europe, see https://www.efama.org/sites/default/files/files/EFAMA%20Stewardship%20Code_FINAL.pdf. See on why stewardship codes may be less important or even be a "legal transplant misfit" in jurisdictions outside the US and UK where controlling shareholders are prevalent and institutional investors own a smaller percentage of shares in listed companies, E. Lim, and D.W. Puchniak, "Can a Global Legal Misfit be Fixed? Shareholder Stewardship in a Controlling Shareholder and ESG World" in D. Katelouzou and D. W. Puchniak (eds.), *Global Shareholder Stewardship*, Cambridge University Press, 2022.

[18] The first Dutch Stewardship Code – the official title is "Responsible and Engaged Shareholdership"– was adopted in 2018 by Eumedion, a private organization *"that represents the interests of institutional investors in the field of corporate governance and sustainability. All institutional investors that hold shares in Dutch listed companies can become a member of Eumedion"* (https://en.eumedion.nl/About-Eumedion.html). The Dutch pension funds, some of the largest in the world, are important and influential members of Eumedion. For the text of the stewardship code, see https://www.eumedion.nl/nl/public/kennisbank/best-

the UK.[19] These stewardship codes encouraged investment funds to act as investment stewards, which essentially means they try to take into account the preferences of their investors and transmit these to the companies they invest in through shareholder engagement practices.

I believe two forms of shareholder activism that are important in Europe have not received enough scholarly attention: shareholder activism by NGOs[20]; and the usually discreet, private (behind closed doors) defensive activism – in fact: engagement – by shareholder and retail investor advocacy groups such as Dutch VEB, French ADAM or Belgian Deminor. These are not advocacy or industry groups of the asset management industry, such as Italian Assogestioni or indeed Dutch Eumedion, but organisations that try to defend the interests of retail and minority investors in listed companies, for profit (as in the case of Deminor) or not for profit. They do so through engagement with company management, but if they feel it is necessary in the interest of their members, also through more public shareholder activism and litigation. However, I keep a closer look at these organisations for future research and in this article I focus on NGOs' ESG activism.

Indeed, NGOs that represent non-shareholder stakeholders or even non-stakeholders ("society at large"), but that have acquired a symbolic number of shares in listed companies, increasingly use shareholder activism tactics to influence corporate ESG policies. At the same time, some investment funds and asset managers engage in forms of shareholder activism that cannot readily be explained by the pursuit of financial returns, but only by a desire to do good, i.e. by a desire to influence corporate ESG policies to make them more ethical or climate-friendly, which (following Armour/Enriques/Wetzer)[21] I will call "halo activism".[22]

---

practices/2018-12-servicedocument-nederlandse-stewardship-code.pdf and see a brief discussion in D.A.M. Melis, "De Nederlandse stewardship code", *Maandblad voor Ondernemingsrecht*, 2019, 128–135.

[19] See P. Davies, "The UK Stewardship Code 2010–2020. From Saving the Company to Saving the Planet?", in: S. Grundmann/H. Merkt/P.Mülbert (eds.), *Festschrift für Klaus J. Hopt zum 80. Geburtstag*, 2020, 131–150, also available at https://papers.ssrn.com/sol3/papers.cfm?abstract_id=3553493.

[20] Non-governmental non-profit groups. Some of these NGOs buy a few shares in the companies they target in their campaigns, or transform themselves into "shareholder advocacy groups", but that should not distract from the fact that they remain e.g. climate or social activists, whose primary goals have nothing to do with defending shareholder interests. Organisations like As You Sow or Follow This only acquire shares for instrumental reasons, i.e. in order to be able to use shareholder activism tactics to pursue their campaigns, not as an investment.

[21] I believe the term "halo activism" was coined by these authors in a presentation they gave about their paper J. Armour, L. Enriques, and T. Wetzer, "Green Pills: Making Corporate Climate Commitments Credible" (December 1, 2022). European Corporate Governance Institute - Law Working Paper No. 657/2022, available at: <https://ssrn.com/abstract=4190268> even though the paper itself does not use the expression, it was featured in their presentation.

[22] For the US, R. Tallarita, "Stockholder Politics", *Hastings Law Journal*, 73, 2022, 1697–1760 has produced an important empirical study on shareholder proposals on ESG matters that cannot readily be explained by the pursuit of an investment return. In the Article, Tallarita states

In continental Europe, this NGO and halo activism clashes with corporate law rules that squarely put the competence to determine corporate strategy with the board.[23] This is especially the case in the Netherlands and Germany, two stakeholder-oriented company law jurisdictions with a dual board system[24], where this exclusive *executive* board competence for strategy is interpreted radically, and in the case of the Netherlands is also protected by court decisions (in Germany, a first case is pending at the time of writing).[25] This means it is difficult for shareholders, including NGOs and halo activists, to submit (ESG) shareholder proposals, even for non-binding votes or even mere discussion.

This in turn drives NGOs representing stakeholders to strategic litigation about corporate ESG policies. This is and will be stimulated by French, German and the future EU human rights/corporate sustainability due diligence legislation. This forces companies to enter into a dialogue with stakeholders – which in practice mainly means NGOs – when developing and implementing their ESG strategy and policies. French experiences in the 10 court cases that so far have been launched on the basis of the French supply chain due diligence Act (hereafter: "Vigilance Act") are illustrative of the potential leverage this due diligence legislation can create for NGOs and non-shareholder stakeholders.[26]

---

one of the points that I will also make here, namely that boards subject to such "stockholder politics" are in a difficult spot, as they do not get any guidance on how to rationally rank the conflicting preferences of various stakeholders.

[23] On the limits of the general meeting's powers concerning corporate strategy in various Western-European jurisdictions, and the implications this has for shareholder proposals, see also S. Cools, "Climate Proposals: ESG Shareholder Activism Sidestepping Board Authority" (March 2, 2023), forthcoming in Thilo Kuntz (ed.), *Research Handbook on Environmental, Social, and Corporate Governance*, Edward Elgar, 2023, available at https://ssrn.com/abstract=4377030. But I believe Cools attaches too much importance to the legal rule (common to most European jurisdictions) that boards have all decision-making powers that are not expressly assigned by statute to other corporate bodies, especially the general meeting of shareholders. Deducing from this uncontested rule that the general meeting should not try to influence corporate strategy (since statute does not allocate that power to the general meeting, and it should consequently be deemed a competence of the board) is in my view both wrong from a technical-legal perspective and blind to the realities of corporate life and the role that shareholders (especially blockholders and controlling shareholders) play in it in Europe.

[24] In the Netherlands, the one tier board has been regulated in public companies (*NV*) as of January 1 2013, as a result of the "Wet bestuur en toezicht", *Stb.*, 2011, 275, thus confirming its legitimacy, even though it had always been used at a limited number of public companies. But two tier boards still dominate at large Dutch firms, certainly at listed ones and are as a rule mandatory at some of the large firms (about 500) who are subject to the *structuurregime*, where the composition of supervisory boards is influenced by the works council, which of course also has employee representatives as members. In Germany a two tier board is mandatory in all public (*AG*) companies. I have to thank Harm-Jan de Kluiver and Joti Roest (both University of Amsterdam) for their insights into Dutch corporate governance, certainly not only on this point of board structure, but the usual disclaimers most emphatically apply.

[25] Discussed *infra*, section V.

[26] French scholar T. Sachs has written that the French Vigilance Act indicates a move away from self-regulation of companies as far as their corporate social responsibility is concerned, to a system of "co-regulation by stakeholders", see T. Sachs, "Loi sur le devoir de vigilance des

Strategic litigation by NGOs is also enabled by the separate trend of changes to civil procedure legislation in some western European jurisdictions that enable general interest litigation by NGOs, originally mainly to allow for the private enforcement of human rights and environmental rules and concerns.[27]

Taken together, these trends make life more difficult for boards at listed or large companies. In the recent past in Europe, they were left relatively free to approve or determine corporate strategy at the suggestion of the top executives who had initially developed that strategy (though clashes about strategy sometimes occurred between non-executive board chairs and the CEO); or at least boards could implement a strategy, the major lines of which were to a large extent designed by one coherent stakeholder group only, namely controlling shareholders. These days, boards are increasingly under pressure from various sides when determining corporate strategy, also from NGO shareholder activism and strategic litigation. Sometimes this – in particular when activists try to influence a company's climate strategy – puts boards in the same spot as politicians who have to balance incommensurable competing interests and values and cut to a decision, unguided by any framework that would allow a rational ranking or balancing of these competing interests.[28]

On top of this potential "politicization" of boards, comes their increasing transformation from potentially decisive strategy-decisionmakers and setters of firm culture into oversight bureaucracies. The monitoring function of the board these days entails at least three rather different types of activity, namely *selecting* and remunerating *top executives* and setting budgets for their departments; offering *strategy* advice and in the end actually deciding on the major lines of the company's strategy; and finally *oversight* of top management,

---

sociétés-mères et donneuses d'ordres,: les ingrédients d'une corégulation" *Revue du Droit de Travail*, 2017, 380.

[27] See M. Kruithof, "Privaatrechtelijke facetten van algemeenbelangacties bij de justitiële rechter" *Tijdschrift voor privaatrecht*, 59(1–2), 2022, 21–129. In addition to a technical description of general interest litigation in Belgium, this article also contains an analysis of the appropriateness and suitability of tort-based general interest claims that has general validity. See also the other reports of the annual meeting of the Association for the Comparative Study of Dutch and Belgian Law published in the same volume of *TPR*, namely A. Wirtgen on the compatibility of general interest litigation for injunctive relief with the constitutional balance of powers (*trias politica*), and and R. Schutgens/ J. Sillen on general interest litigation in the Netherlands. On Germany, see from a normative perspective e.g. B. Hess "'private law enforcement' und Kollektivklagen. Regelungsbedarf für das deutsche Zivilprozessrecht?" *JZ*, 2011, 66–74 and H. Roth, "Private Rechtsdurchsetzung im Zivilprozess", *JZ*, 2016, 1134–1140. An excellent comparative law introduction to the large literature on the constitutionality (mainly from a *trias politica*-perspective) of climate litigation is F. Lange and M. Lippold, "Höchstrichterliche Klimaentscheidungen und Demokratieprinzip -eine rechtsvergleichende Betrachtung", *JZ*, 2022, 685–694.

[28] A point also stressed by R. Tallarita, "Stockholder Politics", *Hastings Law Journal*, 2022, at 1733–34.

with the aim of developing a sound internal control, risk management and corporate compliance system. I argue that the increasing importance that has been attached to the board's oversight function since the 1990s, as reflected in board composition (more independent directors) and structure (more committees, including these days sustainability or ESG committees) has led to a balkanization of one tier boards, making a mockery of the idea that this is a coherent small body that takes collegial consensus decisions and where everybody has the same responsibilities and represents only the corporate interest, not the interests of a specific stakeholder group. I venture to suggest that these developments – where the board's oversight duties threaten to overwhelm or at least decrease the efficiency of its other monitoring functions and in particular its role in strategy-setting- are perhaps better handled by dual board systems than by one tier boards. Dual board systems allow for a relatively clear separation between the "political" supervisory board where oversight functions are concentrated and an executive board that is left relatively free to determine corporate strategy, taking into account but not being bound by the preferences expressed by the supervisory board that is in turn exposed to shareholder but also other stakeholder pressures. The supervisory board thus somewhat insulates top executives from stakeholder pressures while leaving the executives, as a coherent small group, to get on with strategy development and only intervening when things go seriously wrong.

An increased attention at board level for ESG concerns and increased shareholder and stakeholder engagement of boards are in my opinion both inevitable and are as such desirable evolutions. The leverage of stakeholder NGOs over corporate ESG strategies has been and is increasing. This does not only follow from increased shareholder activism. The regulatory framework (hostility in some major jurisdictions to shareholder proposals, while legislation on sustainability due diligence and on general interest litigation facilitates stakeholder litigation) is leading to ESG litigation against listed companies. But courts, and boards acting under pressure from litigation that is aiming to change corporate strategies, are not suitable to help companies develop a coherent ESG strategy. Therefore, in my view, continental European policymakers should consider enabling shareholder resolutions as a channel for dialogue between stakeholders and companies. Even though this will indeed lead to an increase of "political" shareholder proposals, it is a better way of involving stakeholders than driving them to litigation. Admittedly it is highly uncertain that such a regulatory strategy would stop undesirable ESG strategy litigation in its tracks. My final recommendation or rather hope therefore is that the CSDD Directive that will probably be adopted shortly after the publication of this book, will not copy the French enforcement model that encourages NGOs to litigate against companies about their ESG strategies.

The rest of this chapter is organized as follows. Section II discusses three court cases that neatly illustrate the trends and topics of this chapter. Section III explains how as part of the surge in ESG shareholder activism, some NGOs have turned themselves into shareholder activists, while some investment funds, mostly pension funds, engage in "halo activism", namely activism that is inspired by E&S considerations but cannot be explained by the pursuit of a financial return. Section IV, based on Michael Bakker's research, offers empirical data on the use of E&S shareholder proposals in Europe (as well as in the US, where Roberto Tallarita has done important research on this[29]). Section V explains that in the Netherlands and Germany, and to a lesser extent France, the dominant opinion is that shareholder proposals that touch upon a corporation's strategy cannot be put on the general meeting's agenda, because that would violate the executive board's exclusive competence to determine corporate strategy. Section VI explains how sustainability due diligence legislations has created leverage for NGOs that represent stakeholder interests to influence corporate strategies and how some of these NGOs engage in strategic litigation, especially on climate issues. Section VII argues that the combination of NGO shareholder activism, litigation about corporate climate strategies and enforced stakeholder dialogue as a result of due diligence legislation, threatens to politicize boards in Europe, and that that is undesirable. At the same time, however, it argues that German and Dutch law should evolve to allow shareholder proposals that touch upon strategy, as long as they are not too prescriptive. Section VIII argues that installing an extra ESG committee within one tier boards, and/or designating a lead ESG director, could be detrimental to the effectiveness of the board's role in offering strategic advice. Section IX concludes.

II. THREE COURT CASES TO ILLUSTRATE CURRENT TRENDS

1. CLIENTEARTH V. SHELL DIRECTORS

Around 9 February 2023 ClientEarth, an NGO, filed a derivative action under Part 11 of the UK Companies Act with the English High Court against eleven directors of Shell plc.[30] Substantively, the plaintiffs claim that the Shell directors breached their fiduciary duties to the company because, allegedly, the

---

[29] R. Tallarita, "Stockholder Politics", *Hastings Law Journal*, 2022, 1697–1760.
[30] Information on the case is available at ClientEarth's website, esp. the FAQ on the case, see https://www.clientearth.org/media/lf4mcv3v/shell-directors-case-faq-2023.pdf. For a good introduction to the case, see Shearman & Sterling, "Personal liability of directors for climate strategy: landmark case against energy company board", 27 February 2023, available at https://www.shearman.com/en/perspectives/2023/02/personal-liability-of-directors-for-climate-strategy--landmark-case-against-energy-company-board.

energy transition strategy that the directors developed and approved for Shell is "fundamentally flawed". ClientEarth was supported by several investment funds[31] who did not, however, become joint plaintiffs. Collectively, ClientEarth and the funds hold about 12 million shares in Shell, amounting to 0.17% of the total number of Shell shares. Under English law, there is no ownership threshold for bringing a derivative claim, contrary to what is the case in many continental European jurisdictions.[32] But a UK court must give permission for the case to proceed.[33] In the Netherlands, to which Shell also has important links and where it indeed had its head office until December 2021, derivative shareholder suits against directors are next to impossible and in any case not enabled or regulated in statute, which remains completely silent on them.[34] The filing of a derivative claim in London had been preceded, about a year earlier (March 2022) by a so-called pre-action letter by ClientEarth to Shell. It cannot be seriously argued that plaintiffs in this case were pursuing damages from the defendant directors (or their insurers). The clear goal of the suit was to put pressure on Shell's directors to change Shell's corporate strategy, namely speeding up the transition into renewables and the exit from fossil fuel products.

---

[31] These funds included the British governmental pension fund Nest UK, Swedish state pension fund AP3 (also one of the plaintiffs in the litigation against Volkswagen discussed elsewhere in this chapter), Danske Bank Asset Management and Danica Pension. See B. van Dijk, "Shell bestuurders voor rechter gesleept om klimaatbeleid", *Financieel Dagblad*, 10, February 2023.

[32] On the derivative action in the UK, see P. Davies, S. Worthington, E. Micheler, *Gower's Principles of Modern Company Law*, Londen, Thomson Reuters, 2016, 591–613. On the ownership thresholds as one of the reasons for the rareness of derivative actions in Europe, see the still valid analysis in M. Gelter, " Why do Shareholder Derivative Suits Remain Rare in Continental Europe?", *Brooklyn Journal of International Law*, 37, 2012, 843–892.

[33] See s. 260 (3) CA 2006. The judge in ClientEarth v Shell Plc & Ors (Re *Prima Facie* Case) [2023] EWHC 1137 (Ch) (12 May 2023) case (see next footnote), indicated that the substantive analysis of whether to allow the case to proceed should be based on, among other things, the following considerations: *"s.263(2) provides that an application for permission must be refused if the court is satisfied (a) that a person acting in accordance with his duty to promote the success of the company would not seek to continue the claim (…) s.263(3) makes provisions for a number of discretionary factors which the court must take into account in reaching its decision – they are (a) whether the member concerned is acting in good faith in seeking to continue the claim (b)(…) the court is also required by section 263(4) of CA 2006 to have particular regard to any evidence before it as to the views of members of the company who have no personal interest, direct or indirect, in the matter."*

[34] See the policy-oriented analysis in M. J. Kroeze, *Afgeleide schade en afgeleide actie*, Deventer, Kluwer, 2004, 430 p; for the state of the law on derivative actions in the Netherlands, see Asser/Maeijer, Van Solinge & Nieuwe Weme 2-II* 2009, nr. 451 and nr. 216 (on the question when negligence towards the company can be regarded as negligence specifically towards shareholders, so that these could claim damages from the director). The *Hoge Raad* has developed a jurisprudence about the limited cases where third parties including potentially individual shareholders can claim "reflective damages" from the corporation or sometimes its directors (the leading case is Poot/ABP from 1994). The most recent important case is HR 20 June 2008, NJ, *21*, 2009 (Willemsen/NOM). But these cases have not created a functional equivalent of the derivative shareholder action as developed in Delaware or in legislation in the UK and (for instance) Belgium.

On May 12 2023[35] The High Court of England and Wales ruled that permission to proceed with the derivative claim could not be granted. We cannot summarize and discuss the fine and fine-grained analysis of the judge in the case here. But it is clear that a central part of the judge's reasoning was based on the thought expressed by Lord Wilberforce in another case, namely, *"There is no appeal on merits from management decisions to courts of law: nor will courts of law assume to act as a kind of supervisory board over decisions within the powers of management honestly arrived at"*[36] and that *"the evidence (presented by ClientEarth – hdw) does not engage with the issue of how the Directors are said to have gone so wrong in their balancing and weighing of the many factors which should go into their consideration of how to deal with climate risk, amongst the many other risks to which Shell's business will inevitable be exposed, that no reasonable director could properly have adopted the approach that they have. This is a fundamental defect in ClientEarth's case because it completely ignores the fact that the management of a business of the size and complexity of that of Shell will require the Directors to take into account a range of competing considerations, the proper balancing of which is classic management decision with which the court is ill-equipped to interfere"*. In other words, as the judgement further explains, it is up to the board to weigh competing interests to determine what the best interest of the company requires, and as long as it acts in good faith in doing so, little judicial review is possible; ClientEarth wanted to replace the board's judgement with its own, but that is not something that a derivative action should enable.[37] The court also attached importance to the fact that ClientEarth and its supporters represented a very small part of the members (ClientEarth itself owned 27 shares in Shell) and that voting records seemed to support that a majority of members did not share the views of ClientEarth on climate policy.

2. NGO DUE DILIGENCE LITIGATION AGAINST TOTALENERGIES

In the same month that the derivative suit against the Shell directors was filed, on February 28 2023, the civil court of first instance in Paris ruled that a claim

---

[35] ClientEarth v Shell Plc & Ors (Re *Prima Facie* Case) [2023] EWHC 1137 (Ch) (12 May 2023), available at https://www.bailii.org/ew/cases/EWHC/Ch/2023/1137.html.
[36] Lord Wilberforce in *Howard Smith Ltd v Ampol Ltd* [1974] AC 821 at 832E/F.
[37] See also the judgement (fn. 35) at para 65: "In short, there is substance in Shell's submission that ClientEarth's motivation is driven by something quite different from a balanced consideration as to how best to enforce the multifarious factors which the Directors are bound to take into account when assessing what is in the best interests of Shell. It seems to me that ClientEarth has adopted a single-minded focus on the imposition of its views and those of its supporters as to the right strategy for dealing with climate change risk, which points strongly towards a conclusion that its motivation in bringing the claim is ulterior to the purpose for which a claim could properly be continued."

launched against the French energy company TotalEnergies SE ("Total"), brought on the basis of the *Loi sur le devoir de vigilance* ("Vigilance Act")[38] was inadmissible.[39] Three NGOs had sued Total in relation to a large oil exploration project in Uganda and Tanzania called "Eacop/Tilenga" that, according to the NGOs, created unacceptable environmental risks, had led to the allegedly unlawful expropriation of more than 100.000 people and contributed to the suppression of freedom of speech in the two African countries. Under the applicable French legislation, large French companies have to draft and disclose a *plan de vigilance* or supply chain due diligence plan, i.e. a kind of supply chain risk management plan identifying the ESG risks they and their subsidiaries and "established business partners" create, worldwide. The plan must include structural measures to mitigate those risks and the adverse impacts the company or parts of its supply chain might create. The law gives standing to certain NGOs to first send a "notice of breach" (*mise en demeure*) to companies if the company's due diligence plan does not, in the view of the NGO, meet the requirements of the Vigilance Act. If the company does not react in a satisfactory way within three months, the NGO has standing to sue the company both for an injunction but

---

[38] "Loi n°2017–399 du 27 mars 2017 relative au devoir de vigilance des sociétés mères et des entreprises donneuses d'ordre", integrated into the French *Code de commerce* as articles L. 225–102-4 and-5. For information in English on the Act, including a summary of the 10 pending cases, see A. Pietrancosta, "Codification in Company Law of General CSR Requirements: Pioneering Recent French Reforms and EU Perspectives", July 20, 2022, European Corporate Governance Institute – Law Working Paper No. 639/2022, available at https://ssrn.com/abstract=4083398. For some of the first articles in French literature discussing the final version of the Act, see Ch. Hannoun, "Le devoir de vigilance des sociétés mères et entreprises donneuses d'ordre après la loi du 27 mars 2017", *Dr. soc.*, 2017. 806; J. Heinich, "Devoir de vigilance des sociétés mères et des entreprises donneuses d'ordre: une loi finalement adoptée, mais amputée," *Dr. Sociétés*, 2017, Comm. 78; B. Parance, "La consécration législative du devoir de vigilance des sociétés mères et des entreprises donneuses d'ordre", *Gaz. Pal.* 18 April 2017, n° 15, 16: S. Schiller, "Exégèse de la loi relative au devoir de vigilance des sociétés mères et entreprises donneuses d'ordre", *JCP*, 2017. Doctr. 622; J.-B. Tap, "La vigilance, un nouvel horizon", *RJ com.*, 2018, n° 1.; G. Viney et A. Danis-Fatôme, "La responsabilité civile dans la loi relative au devoir de vigilance des sociétés mères et des entreprises donneuses d'ordre", *D.*, 2017, 1610; M. Lafargue, "Loi relative au devoir de vigilance des sociétés mères et des entreprises donneuses d'ordre: l'entrée dans une nouvelle ère?": *JCP*, 2017, n° 1169. For an early analysis of the Vigilance Act by a prominent French collective of activist lawyers and attorneys, Sherpa, who work together with NGOs "to combat new forms of impunity" of corporations, see M.-C. Caillet, M.-L. Guislain, and T. Malbrand, *La vigilance sociétale en droit français*, Paris, December 2016, 105 p. available at https://www.asso-sherpa.org/vigilance-societale-droit-francais. In January 2020, a government-commissioned report on the evaluation of the new legislation was published: A. Duthilleul & M. de Jouvinel, *Evaluation de la mise en oeuvre de la loi n°2017–399 du 27 mars 2017 relative au devoir de vigilance des sociétés mères et des entreprises donneuses d'ordre*, available at vie-publique.fr/sites/default/files/rapport/pdf/275689.pdf.

[39] Tribunal judiciaire de Paris, 28 February 2023, no. 22/53942. The case has already been commented upon in French scholarship, see e. g. A.M. Ilcheva,"Quelle application du devoir de vigilance après les jugements du 28 février 2023?", *Dalloz*, 13, April 2023 (also available at https://www.dalloz-actualite.fr/flash/quelle-application-du-devoir-de-vigilance-apres-jugements-du-28-fevrier-2023#.ZGIsFqXP2Uk).

possibly also for damages based on tort. The Vigilance Act provides that plaintiffs can choose between "regular" court proceedings or summary proceedings. The case against Total had been launched in 2018, based on its due diligence plan for 2018, but after a long fight before four courts on jurisdiction[40] and a 2021 Act that changed the rules by giving exclusive competence (for the whole of France) to a Paris court for claims based on the Vigilance Act[41], the case morphed into a claim about deficiencies in the 2021 due diligence plan of Total. This claim was thrown out as inadmissible by the Paris court on procedural grounds (Plaintiffs had brought the case in summary proceedings but had failed to show the conditions for such proceedings had been met; and their complaints pertained to the 2021 *plan de vigilance* of Total, but they had not sent a notice of breach concerning that plan, only about Total's 2018 plan).

The ruling most certainly did not mean Total was immediately freed from pressure to change its climate transition strategy. At the beginning of April 2023, Dutch climate NGO Follow This announced it intended to submit a shareholder proposal to the May 26 annual general meeting of Total, calling on the company to do more to cut back its CO2 emissions by 2030 by rolling back some gas projects and moving more quickly into renewable energies.[42] The NGO in particular wanted Total to increase its efforts to cut back its scope 3 emissions, namely those caused by its clients when using Total products.[43] The shareholder proposal was said to be supported by investors holding about 1% of Total.[44] The vote on the proposal would not be binding. Interestingly, the founder of Follow This declared: *"The strategy is totally up to the board"*, continuing *"We're dealing with companies[45] that don't want to change. Of course, they want to invest a bit*

---

[40] The main question was whether a regular civil court or rather a commercial court was competent to hear cases based on the Vigilance Act. After the court of cassation had decided that plaintiffs suing a commercial company like Total could choose whether to bring such a claim before a commercial or a civil court (see Cass. (fr.) Com. 15 December 2021, n° 21-11.882, D., 2022, 826), the French legislator intervened with a 2021 act giving exclusive competence to hear such cases to the Paris civil court of first instance.

[41] See Loi n°2021-1729 22 December 2021 "pour la confiance dans l'institution judiciaire" codified in Code Judiciaire art. L. 211-21.

[42] Follow This had submitted such shareholder proposals at TotalEnergies in the two preceding years as well. The first time Total refused to put the proposal on the AGMs agenda, arguing it encroached on the board's competence to determine corporate strategy, see the discussion below at V.3.

[43] S. White "Investors to pressure TotalEnergies over climate goals", *Financial Times*, April 6 2023.

[44] That is, they issued statement of support before the proposal was officially launched. In an important development, ISS declared it would support the Follow This proposal around May 12 2023, see S. White "Proxy adviser backs climate activist shareholder proposal at Total", *FT*, 15 May 2023.

[45] Follow This would launch similar campaigns at BP, Shell, Chevron and ExxonMobil in the 2023 AGM season, the shareholder proposals to be submitted by Follow This can be consulted at www.follow-this.org/resolutions-2023/ (last consulted on April 6 2023).

in renewable energy but the bulk is in fossil fuels and they want to remain oil and gas companies as long as possible".[46] This statement takes away any doubt that the aim of Follow This was to influence Total's strategy. Would the Dutch founder of Follow This have been familiar with the ruling from the Dutch Hoge Raad ruling that corporate strategy is the exclusive competence of the executive board, and not of the general meeting?

3. BOSKALIS/FUGRO: THE DUTCH DON'T LIKE SHAREHOLDER PROPOSALS

Indeed, several years earlier, on April 20 2018, the Dutch *Hoge Raad*[47] had issued a ruling ("Boskalis/Fugro") that is of great importance for shareholder activism and engagement at Dutch companies.[48] The court ruled that since Dutch law vests the exclusive competence to decide on "strategy and corporate policy" in the executive board[49], the general meeting of shareholders cannot be forced to organize a vote, not even a non-binding vote[50], on matters of corporate strategy. The case arose as a result of the attempt of Boskalis to acquire Fugro through a public takeover bid. As is not uncommon in Dutch companies, the Fugro group of companies had three types of take-over defenses in place, one including the award of call-options to a Curaçao-based foundation (*stichting*) that gave that foundation a conditional claim to "anti-takeover preference shares".[51] Boskalis wanted the Fugro boards (executive and supervisory) to dismantle this anti-takeover mechanism. In order to put pressure on the boards to do so, Boskalis (which at one stage owned 28% of Fugro) wanted to submit a shareholder resolution to Fugro's general meeting calling on the boards to do away with the mechanism. Boskalis desired a vote on that resolution, as a way of "sounding out" the other shareholders. Since Boskalis was aware that under Dutch law installing or removing such a poison pill-like mechanism was a competence of the board, not of the general meeting, it "merely" asked for a non-binding vote. Fugro refused to organize any form of vote on the resolution,

---

[46] *Ibidem*.
[47] Highest court in the Netherlands, court of cassation; the Netherlands do not have a constitutional court.
[48] I must thank the various speakers at the conference on "Shareholder activism in the Netherlands" on 9 February 2023 jointly organized by Clifford Chance Amsterdam and Radboud (Nijmegen) University's Van der Heijden Institute. Without this conference, my insight into Dutch law and attitudes among the Dutch legal and investor community about the role of shareholder proposals in Dutch governance would be far smaller.
[49] Although this is no longer mandatory – as it was until 2001– most large or listed Dutch companies operate with a dual board system, with an executive board (*raad van bestuur*) and a supervisory board (*raad van commissarissen*).
[50] US corporate law lawyers would call this a "precatory" vote.
[51] In Dutch: *preferente beschermingsaandelen*.

indeed refused to add the resolution to the general meeting's agenda. Before the courts, Boskalis argued that its proposed shareholder resolution concerned the structure and governance of the company, and not its strategy or corporate policy. It also argued that Dutch legislation had wanted to correctly implement the EU's Shareholder Rights Directive, which in the reading of Boskalis allowed 3% shareholders in listed companies to put a resolution on the agenda and to the vote, even in cases where the general meeting was not competent to take a binding decision on the matter broached in the resolution.

The Hoge Raad ruled that insofar as a resolution pertains to matters of governance and company structure on which the board has legal competence to decide, these are matters of strategy and corporate policy. Unless the companies act or the articles provide otherwise for specific such matters, the general meeting is free to discuss such matters, but the company (board) cannot be forced, if it does not want to, to submit such matters to a vote at the general meeting, even if this vote is presented as non-binding or as a mere poll of shareholder opinion. All the more so since on matters of strategy and policy, the board has no duty to consult shareholders or the general meeting before deciding on these matters and thus deciding what is *"in the interest of the company and the firm connected to it"*[52] (as is the standard expression under Dutch law of what should guide the board in all its decisions). The board has to justify its corporate strategy to the shareholders at the annual general meeting, and strategic matters may be discussed at the general meeting, including by allowing shareholders to pose questions to the board about strategy, but that does not entitle 3% (or more) shareholders to demand a vote at the general meeting on a strategic matter like dismantling anti-takeover defenses, not even a non-binding vote.

These three anecdotes and court cases illustrate at least three points: NGOs are litigating against companies and even their directors in order to influence corporate strategies, especially related to corporate climate policies. Such litigation is enabled by the French sustainability due diligence legislation. Some NGOs also buy a few shares in order to enable them to use shareholder rights to pursue their campaigns against companies, including shareholder activist tactics such as harassing the board with questions during the AGM or tabling

---

52 In Dutch: "De vennootschap en de met haar verbonden onderneming"; standard formula, used among other instances in the leading "Cancun" ruling of the Hoge Raad (HR 4 April 2014, *NJ,* 2014/286, ann. P. van Schilfgaarde, *Ondernemingsrecht* 2014/101, ann A.F.J.A. Leijten) on the meaning of the duty to act in the corporate interest. Dutch legal professionals see the reference to the "company" as a reference to (the interests of) the whole body of shareholders, whereas the reference to "the firm" is to be read as a reference to (the interests of) all stakeholders, including esp. employees; there can therefore be no doubt that under Dutch law, the interest of the company that the board should serve is broadly construed or, in American parlance, the Netherlands have a stakeholder conception of the board's fiduciary duties.

shareholder proposals. In some jurisdictions like the Netherlands the latter tactic (shareholder proposals) is almost completely unavailable because courts have ruled it is incompatible with the exclusive right of the executive board to determine a company's strategy. Oddly, this argument is not invoked against climate litigation that is as much about corporate strategy as shareholder proposals.

III. FROM SHAREHOLDERS PURSUING ESG GOALS TO NGOS BECOMING SHAREHOLDER ACTIVISTS

1. TRADITIONAL AND ESG SHAREHOLDER ACTIVISM

Shareholder activism and shareholder engagement come in many shapes and sizes. The chapter by Tom Vos in this book provides a taxonomy of the major types of activism, while Anna Christie's chapter analyzes the ESG shareholder activism landscape. While it is debatable whether index funds and other passive investors get involved in shareholder engagement to a sufficient level[53] in view of the interests of their own investors and their fiduciary duties towards them[54], it cannot be doubted that engagement by these investors has increased over the past few years, especially on E&S matters rather than on traditional governance matters. Pension funds seem to play a bigger role than other passive funds, and based on anecdotal press reports, one gets the impression that pension funds of religious orders play an outsize role.[55] The NGOs and halo activism campaigns discussed in this chapter are part of a diverse ESG stewardship ecosystem, as beautifully described by Bowley and Hill.[56] It is also important to realize that

---

[53] For the sceptical view, see L. Bebchuk and S. Hirst, "Index Funds and the Future of Corporate Governance: Theory, Evidence, and Policy", *Columbia Law Review* 2019, 2029-2146. The case for the defense is made in E. Rock & M. Kahan, 'Index Funds and Corporate Governance: Let Shareholders be Shareholders', *Boston University Law Review*, 100, 2019, 1771. (arguing that index funds are active enough as engaged shareholders).

[54] On these fiduciary duties, see the references *infra* in footnote 83. Note that in the EU, art. 3h SRD II requires institutional investors to make sure that the asset manager they choose applies policies that are aligned with their own. This says nothing directly about a duty of the investment funds themselves to take the preferences of their own clients into account, but it does encourage the transmission of such preferences to the asset manager.

[55] For a more systematic confirmation of this impression at least for the US, see P. Tkac, "One proxy at a time: pursuing social change through shareholder proposals", *Federal Reserve Bank of Atlanta Economic Review*, third quarter 2006, 1-20, available at https://www.atlantafed.org/ who at p. 6 discusses the role of the Interfaith Center on Corporate Responsibility (ICCR) which at the time brought together 275 "faith-based" institutional investors, often pension funds of Christian churches, and identified those as repeat players in tabling socially responsible shareholder proposals.

[56] T. Bowley and J. Hill, "The global stewardship ecosystem", 7 October 2022, available at https://papers.ssrn.com/sol3/papers.cfm?abstract_id=4240129.

much of it is part of a collaborative effort that is not coordinated but is stimulated by various global or Europe-wide advocacy organisations that represent institutional investor networks. These networks and collaborative efforts have been most systematically described by Mülbert/Sajnovits.[57] Of course, traditional activists, such as hedge funds, also often act in wolf packs[58] and rely on support by more passive investors, such as index funds.[59] But E&S activism often seems to be stimulated by all kinds of more or less permanent global or regional (e.g. EU) network organisations of institutional investors. Examples include Climate Action 100+[60], or the "Find it, Fix it, Prevent it" coalition of asset managers that have worked together to draw attention to "modern slavery" in certain branches of economic activity.[61] Non-profit advocacy groups such as British ShareAction[62] and Shareholder Commons draw attention to ESG issues at corporations, lobby regulators, try to interest investors in the topics they are concerned about and support certain forms of shareholder activism, for example by co-filing shareholder proposals. Ringe[63] points to the importance of what he

---

[57] P. Mülbert and A. Sajnovits, "Emerging ESG-Driven Models of Shareholder Collaborative Engagement" (fn. 6).

[58] E.g. J. Coffee and D. Palia, "The wolf at the door: the impact of hedge fund activism on corporate governance", *The Journal of Corporation Law*, 43(547) at 561 and L. Strine "Who bleeds when the wolf bites? A flesh-and-blood perspective on hedge fund activism and our strange corporate governance system", *Yale law Journal*, (126), 2017, 1871.

[59] R.J. Gilson & J.N. Gordon, 'The Agency Costs of Agency Capitalism: Activist Investors and the Revaluation of Governance Rights', *Columbia Law Review*, (113) 2013, 863–928.

[60] Www.climateaction100.org. An initiative of about 700 investors collectively managing about $ 68 trillion worth of assets and targeting the largest greenhouse gas emitters worldwide through engagement (about 166 companies that according to Climate Action 100+ are responsible for about 80% of worldwide greenhouse gas emissions.)

[61] See e.g. the 'Find It, Fix It, Prevent It' campaign (begun at the end of 2019) that brought together 56 large asset managers (with about 7 trillion assets under management) who wage campaigns against modern slavery and focused their attention in 2020 on the hospitality sector and in 2021 on the construction industry, see 'Investors urge UK building sector to check for modern slavery in supply chain', *FT*, 12 April 2021. Another coalition of 22 investors led by Rathbones, a British asset manager, each year (at least in 2020, 2021 and 2022) sought out and contacted British companies who according to this coalition did not meet the requirements of the UK's (disclosure-focused and as such rather toothless) Modern Slavery Act (see *FT* Moral Money newsletter, 31 March 2021).

[62] ShareAction is a British organization registered as a UK charity and company limited by guarantee that began in 2005 as an effort to support the largest British pension scheme (the Universities Superannuation Scheme) to develop a "responsible investment policy", but then became permanent and expanded to encourage a broad range of investors to engage companies on ESG issues, and also lobbies policymakers on such issues. Its members are mainly NGOs like Oxfam, Amnesty International, the WWF, Greenpeace and some labour union organisations. On its shareholder activism support, see https://shareaction.org/unlocking-the-power/shareholder-resolutions. At https://shareaction.org/resolutions-to-watch2023 readers can find a list of ESG shareholder resolutions (not submitted by ShareAction) from the 2023 AGM season that ShareAction encourages asset managers to vote on, either for or, in case of climate and sustainability resolutions at UBS and Credit Suisse, against.

[63] W.-G. Ringe, "Investor-led Sustainability in Corporate Governance", *Annals of Corporate Governance* 2022, 93–151.

labels international governance networks, including (and to name only a few of the most important ones) the Carbon Disclosure Project (CDP), the Interfaith Center for Corporate Responsibility (ICCR), and the Institutional Investors Group on Climate Change (IIGCC).[64]

The activities of these networks are no doubt partly animated by the insight that ESG and especially climate risks are systemic and cannot be diversified away. One may therefore credibly surmise that when asset managers are invested in companies throughout the whole economy[65], they will not focus on individual companies in their shareholder engagement, but rather engage in portfolio-wide efforts.[66]

2. NGOS USING SHAREHOLDER ACTIVISM TACTICS TO PRESS FOR ESG CHANGE AT CORPORATIONS

NGOs, which operate on a non-profit basis and are the proverbial civil society organisations, have become important voices in policy debates in Europe and the US since the 1980s, also through activist campaigns, including campaigns against corporations and their policies.[67] NGOs were important actors in the

---

[64] See https://www.iigcc.org/our-work/. This important network in early 2023 had more than 400 institutional investors as members, managing more than $ 60 trillion of assets. The organization tries to influence policymakers, foremost at the level of the EU, on climate policy and sustainable finance, and tries to inspire members on how to be active owners, but also tries to act as an intermediary in organizing climate campaigns of groups of asset managers at portfolio companies.

[65] Much has, rightly, been made, of the impact of the Big Three, i.e. BlackRock, State Street and Vanguard, the largest US asset managers (see e.g. L.A. Bebchuk and S. Hirst, "Big Three Power, and Why it Matters" *Boston University Law Review*, 102, 2022, 1547–1600). While the concentration of the asset management industry is less pronounced in Europe and the US Big Three have smaller collective positions in European companies than they have in the US (see the figures in Mülbert/Sajnovits, fn. 6, indicating that institutional ownership is significantly lower in Europe than in the US), the collective stakes of the Big Three in European companies are still very substantial: according to data in J. Fichtner & E.M. Heemskerk, 'The New Permanent Universal Owners: Index Funds, (Im)patient Capital, and the Claim of Long-termism', 2018, https://ssrn.com/abstract=2988937, at p. 18. The Big Three were the largest or 2nd shareholder in 70% of the European Stoxx50, an index of 50 listed large European companies.

[66] See for this line of analysis, M. Condon, "Externalities and the Common Owner", *Washington law Review*, 95, 2020, 1–80; J. Coffee, Jr., "The Future of Disclosure: ESG, Common Ownership, and Systematic Risk", *Columbia Business Law Review*, 2021, 602; J. N. Gordon, "Systematic Stewardship", *The Journal of Corporation Law, 47,* 2022, 627–654; L. Enriques and A. Romano, "Rewiring Corporate Law in an Interconnected World", *Arizona Law Review, 64,* 2022, 51–87.

[67] See J.P. Doh and T.R. Guay, "Corporate social responsibility, public policy, and NGO activism in Europe and the United Sates: an institutional-stakeholder perspective", *Journal of Management Studies,* 43(1), 2006, 47–73 (arguing that NGOs became influential in international affairs, including in campaigns about the corporate sector, from the 1980s

CSR movement, which has now morphed into the ESG movement. But these NGO campaigns did not initially take the form of shareholder activism. That has changed over the past few years, perhaps already earlier. Already in 2008, Sjöström's review article identified four scholarly articles, but none of them empirical, on NGOs turning themselves into shareholder activists.[68]

The NGOs that we have in mind in this article as actors that try to influence corporate policies and strategies, come in many varieties, but a primary distinction is between general purpose NGOs and shareholder advocacy NGOs. Oxfam or Amnesty international are examples of general purpose NGOs, but so are many organisations that focus on typical ESG topics such as climate change or workers' treatment. Shareholder advocacy NGOs by contrast have as a central goal to protect shareholder interests, usually by exercising shareholder rights, such as attending the general meeting. However, some of them, such as As You Sow, primarily use shareholder techniques, based on the ownership of a limited number of shares, to pursue goals like a reduction of CO_2 emissions at corporations that have little to do with the defense of the immediate financial interests of the shareholders in a company. They pursue social goals and they acquired shares not to become a permanent stakeholder in companies, but for the purely instrumental reason that this allows them to use shareholder rights in their campaigns against companies. For that reason, it is potentially misleading to call organizations like As You Sow or Follow This "shareholder advocacy groups". Alternatively, in a way they can be seen as exponents of the shareholder welfare (as opposed to shareholder wealth)idea[69], i.e. the idea that some shareholders do not want companies to pursue the creation of shareholder value at the expense of negative externalities that damage the other interest that the person who is a shareholder has, outside the company, e.g. her interest in unpolluted air and water.

---

onwards); the same argument (1980s as a turning point concerning NGO activism against corporations) was made in *The Economist*, "Non-governmental organizations and business: living with the enemy", 9 August 2003, 49–50. F. Briscoe and A. Gupta, "Social activism in and around organizations", *Academy of Management Annals*, 10(1), 2016, 671–727 is a detailed literature review of social NGO activism. The Doh and Guay article illustrates the trend with three case studies about NGO campaigns: disputes over trade in genetically modified organisms; relaxation of intellectual property protection for HIV/AIDS medications; and activism around the Kyoto Agreement on Climate Change. They cite the 1995 activist campaigns against Shell because of its sinking of the Brent Spar oil rig and because of Shell's "neutrality" when the Nigerian government executed or jailed social activists who had campaigned against Shell, as harbingers of what was then to come in the CSR area.

[68] E. Sjöström, "Shareholder activism for corporate social responsibility: what do we know?" *Sustainable Development*, 2008, 16(3), (141), 150. See also S. Waygood and W. Wehrmeyer "A critical assessment of how non-governmental organizations use the capital markets to achieve their aims: a UK study" *Business Strategy and the Environment*, 2003, 12(6), 372–385.

[69] See O. Hart & L. Zingales, 'Companies should maximize shareholder welfare not market value', *Journal of Law, Finance, and Accounting*, (2), 2017, 247–274.

As documented below in section IV, in some countries, especially in the US and in Scandinavia, these NGOs do use shareholder proposals to pressure companies on E&S topics. As is apparent from Bakker's empirical research for Europe and Tallarita's for the US, the tactic is used by a limited number of repeat players. 70% of the NGO-sponsored E&S shareholder proposals in Bakker's study was sponsored by just three organisations, namely As You Sow, Follow This and Médac.[70]

Although we have no empirical data on this, it appears a broader group of NGOs use other shareholder activism techniques than shareholder proposals, but we are still dealing with repeat players such as, prominently, the Dutch NGO Milieudefensie, which became famous for its litigation against Shell about climate issues.[71] The main tactic is asking questions to the board during the annual general meeting of shareholders (AGM)[72], which in many European countries attracts a substantial number of in-person attendees. The right to ask questions in most jurisdictions also entails the right for shareholders to give speeches about the topic they want to ask a question about.[73] Indeed, it seems obvious that in Europe, including Belgium and the Netherlands, shareholder questions are far more often used as an activist technique than shareholder proposals. One of the few (and earliest) examples of public shareholder activism in Belgium was the "Barco case".[74] This involved NGO-linked activists who had bought a few shares in this listed Belgian company and on that basis attended the AGM in order to question the board on the potential "dual use" of some Barco

---

[70] *As You Sow* (https://www.asyousow.org/) is a US-based shareholder advocacy group founded in 1992, whose *"mission is to promote environmental and social corporate responsibility through shareholder advocacy, coalition building, and innovative legal strategies"*. *Follow This* is a Dutch NGO that focuses on the oil and gas industries and is a platform for "green shareholders" that mainly wants to submit shareholder proposals on climate and environmental matters at the oil majors. The organization wants members to buy one or a few shares in the companies it targets. See https://www.follow-this.org/. In the "about us" section, the organization says "We have the power to change oil companies from within -as shareholders". *Médac* (https://medac.qc.ca/) is a Canadian shareholder advocacy organization founded in 1995 to defend the interests of minority shareholders and make shareholder democracy work, but today engages in a broad array of ESG shareholder activism, as well as lobbying activities and awareness campaigns.

[71] Https://milieudefensie.nl/aanmoediging/oproep, announced that for 2023, it would target the CEOs of 29 large polluters, including Dutch companies Ahold (supermarkets), ING (bank), Rabobank (cooperative bank, well-known as an important funder of Dutch farmers including agroindustry) and Schiphol airport, by attending the AGMs of these companies and ask the CEO about changes to the company's climate (e.g. emissions reduction) policies. The organization frequently engages in climate litigation.

[72] For the Netherlands, see A. Lafarre and C. Van der Elst, "Corporate Sustainability and Shareholder Activism in the Netherlands", in *Cambridge Handbook of Corporate Law, Corporate Governance and Sustainability*, B. Sjåfjell and C. Bruner (eds.), CUP, 2019, 260–275.

[73] For example for Germany, see §131 Aktiengesetz.

[74] See P. Baert, "En hoe gaat het met uw wapenproductie? Bedenkingen bij het vraagrecht van de aandeelhouder, naar aanleiding van de Barco-zaak", *TRV*, 2002, 397–403.

products. According to the activists, some Barco products could be used for military purposes and were sold to authoritarian regimes. The activists presented this as "arms production" and wanted the board to divulge more details about these "weapons exports". After a while, the chair of the general meeting shut the activists down, and refused to give detailed answers. This led to litigation in which the activists claimed their right to ask questions to the board had been illegally curtailed and sued to have all the decisions of the general meeting annulled. The judgement clarified that shareholders can only ask questions related to items on the agenda of the general meeting, but that since at the AGM the mandatory management report to shareholders is discussed, there is room for questions about any general policy issue concerning the company; and that while the chair of the meeting has the power to maintain orderly proceedings, this does not entail the power to decide that shareholders who have not yet asked a question, should not be allowed to pose one. The affair contributed to the decision of the government to amend the then Companies Act in order to clarify that boards may refuse to answer shareholder questions when answering them would be incompatible with the company's best interests, in that it would potentially seriously harm the interests of shareholders or employees.

The use of such tactics is certainly stimulated by the lack of ownership thresholds for taking part in the AGM and asking questions. But another factor is that in some jurisdictions, shareholder proposals that touch upon a corporation's strategy are inadmissible (see section V), and it would be hard to deny that many and probably most shareholder proposals about corporate climate policies touch upon strategic matters (unless they are not about substance, but only about disclosure).

One of the best-known examples of ESG shareholder activism in Belgium concerns supermarket chain AholdDelhaize, and this was a typical example of NGOs exercising the shareholder right to question the board to pursue E&S goals at a company. Delhaize is a Belgian-American supermarket chain which was merged into the Dutch supermarket and retail group Ahold in 2015. The Delhaize campaign was waged by at least two NGOs using the right of every shareholder to ask questions during the AGM. In March 2022, Dutch environmental and climate NGO Milieudefensie published a list of 29 companies that it wanted to pressure to increase their climate efforts that year. This included AholdDelhaize[75],[76] By the 2022 general meeting, Milieudefensie had bought a

---

[75] See W. Schramade, "Ahold Delhaize terecht onder druk wegens geringe milieutransparantie" *De Tijd*, 17 May 2021. This opinion piece reported that Delhaize had contacted its 200 largest suppliers, asking them to detail, per product, the CO2 emissions caused by the production of each product they supplied to Delhaize, in order for Delhaize to assess its own CO2 impact.

[76] The same tactic was used at the 2023 general meeting of Dutch banking group ING. Dozens of representatives of NGO Milieudefensie repeatedly asked the same question as at AholdDelhaize (whether the company would reduce its CO2 emissions with 45% by 2030)

few shares and used these to attend the meeting; it did not submit a shareholder proposal, but used the right that any shareholder holding a single share has to ask questions to the board, in this case whether the board wanted to commit to a 45% reduction of CO_2 emissions compared to 2019 by 2030. At the April 12 2023 AGM unions protested outside the meeting room against what they perceived as "social dumping" (namely the decision by Delhaize Belgium to sell all shops and their staff to independent operators) whereas inside the room, climate activists FNV and Milieudefensie repeated the 2022 initiative. The environmental groups sent 30 members as shareholders to the AGM who posed the same question to the CEO 30 times: would AholdDelhaize reduce the CO_2 emissions of itself and its suppliers by 45% compared to 2019, whereas Ahold itself had promised a reduction of "only" 37%, and the CEO did not want to make another commitment during the AGM. In spite of a call by the chair of the meeting not to keep repeating the question, the question was (after that call) repeated more than 20 times, and the CEO kept answering it, each time with a slightly different wording. This ritual caused the meeting to last for 4.5 hours.[77]

It is likely that it was this kind of – annually recurring – ritual that the chairs of 35 British firms (including 26 from the FTSE 100) had in mind when they produced a document warning about their deteriorating relationship with institutional investors.[78] The document makes the point that too much "interference" by shareholder activists with board strategy can distract the board with issues that do not materially affect the companies' performance. No doubt this report was self-serving, but it does indicate that directors do indeed genuinely feel distracted by a large number of "engagements" with shareholders – who themselves are egged on by stewardship codes[79] – that they do not always find useful and which in the chairs' view lead to a blurring of responsibilities for corporate strategy between boards and institutional investors. At least one interviewed director pointed out that the UK Corporate Governance Code does after all assign

---

and after the meeting's chair had put a stop to the same question being repeated, members of the Extinction Rebellion group took over and began to sing protest songs and shouted various climate slogans. One person who had announced he would sit on the ground and keep interrupting proceedings until ING stopped financing fossil fuel projects, was forcibly removed by the police. See e.g. the report in *Algemeen Dagblad*, 24 April 2023, https://www.ad.nl/economie/extinction-rebellion-verstoort-vergadering-ing-met-protest-activist-gearresteerd~a5a9a4a9/. VEB, the most important association for the defense of shareholder interests in the Netherlands, complained that Milieudefensie's tactics of repeating the same question dozens of times at various AGMs gave shareholder activism a bad name and condemned this.

[77] See J. Braaksma and J. Cornelissen, "Activisten en bonden kapen vergadering van Ahold Delhaize" ('activists and unions hijack the meeting of Ahold Delhaize'), *Financieel Dagblad*, 13 April 2023 at 13.

[78] See D. Thomas, "FTSE chairs warn of declining relations with institutional investors", *FT*, 7 November 2022.

[79] For the UK, see P. Davies "The UK Stewardship Code 2010–2020 from Saving the Company to Saving the Planet?" (March 12, 2020). European Corporate Governance Institute – Law Working Paper No. 506/2020, available at https://ssrn.com/abstract=3553493.

responsibility for corporate strategy to the board, not investors, who in his view could always dismiss a board that failed in strategy development.[80]

3. HALO ACTIVISM

By halo activism[81], we refer to (ESG) shareholder activism undertaken by investment funds/asset managers, not NGOs, but that cannot be explained by the pursuit of a financial return.[82] The institutional investors, whose primary purpose and fiduciary duty is to generate a return on investment for its clients[83], are often spending resources on perhaps relatively cheap but in absolute figures still costly activist campaigns, in pursuit of social and environmental goals. Especially in the case of pension funds, I believe sometimes a desire to do good is the simple explanation for this type of activism, also because the fund is a tool of its principals, whose preferences it expresses.[84] "Halo activism" will by definition never be the only or even main activity of investment funds and asset managers, since in the aggregate these always pursue financial returns. It will always be limited to either occasional campaigns or to more systematic, portfolio-wide efforts of shareholder engagement that are not detrimental to the financial bottom line.

A good example of the latter type of halo activism, that also nicely illustrates how these efforts are often collaborative, was the campaign against Amazon to force that company to disclose more of its tax data, so that the outside world could observe how much taxes the company paid in which jurisdiction, a sensitive topic in times of global tax reform and efforts to

---

[80] See D. Thomas, fn. 78.
[81] A term coined by J. Armour, L. Enriques and T. Wetzer in presentations about their "green pills"-paper, see Fn.21.
[82] In interesting research, S. Hirst, K. Kastiel, and T. Kricheli Katz, "How Much Do Investors Care About Social Responsibility?" (August 9, 2021), available at https://ssrn.com/abstract=4115854 or http://dx.doi.org/10.2139/ssrn.4115854 conducted an experiment involving real monetary rewards with 279 participants that found that many of them were prepared to forgo some investment returns in exchange for pursuing E&S-like goals (though 32% were not prepared to forgo financial returns). It is debatable how much one can deduce from such "laboratory" experiments about the potential behaviour of professional asset managers/institutional investors.
[83] On the fiduciary duties of fund managers as an impediment to ESG activism, see (with a focus on Europe) M. Lieberknecht, "Institutional Investors as Climate Activists – Curb Your Enthusiasm", 2022, available at https://papers.ssrn.com/sol3/papers.cfm?abstract_id=4198042; for the US, M. Schanzenbach and R. Sitkoff, "Reconciling Fiduciary Duty and Social Conscience: The Law and Economics of ESG Investing by a Trustee" 72 *Stanford Law Review*, 23020, 381 and also R. Tallarita, "Fiduciary Deadlock" 171 University of Pennsylvania Law Review, forthcoming 2023, available at https://ssrn.com/abstract=4197225.
[84] And for millennial investors who put money into these funds, their preferences are increasingly sustainability-focused, see the literature referenced in e.g. G. Ringe, "Investor-led Sustainability in Corporate Governance", *Annals of Corporate Governance*, 2022, his section 3.2.

make sure companies pay a minimum tax in countries where they conduct a serious amount of business. The campaign was launched by a Catholic investment fund, Missionary Oblates of Mary Immaculate, in cooperation with the Greater Manchester Pension Fund[85], who submitted a shareholder proposal to Amazon's AGM. But the campaign gradually gained support from at least 24 institutional investors, mainly pension funds but also asset management groups. Their actions were coordinated by PIRC[86], a governance and shareholder services group, which had helped to organize campaigns on tax transparency at thirty companies, including Cisco and Microsoft.[87] It is noteworthy that Amazon had tried to prevent a vote on the shareholder proposal by invoking the ordinary business exception, but had been rebuked by the SEC, which addressed a letter to Amazon stating that in its view the proposal transcended matters of ordinary business.

Tallarita has shown that such halo activism is not uncommon in the US[88], but it also occurs in Europe. Shareholder activism in Belgium is very limited, but one of the best-known campaigns was an example of halo activism, namely the campaign of Bluebell Capital partners against Solvay.[89] Bluebell Capital bought only one share in Solvay and started a campaign accusing Solvay of environmental pollution through limestone residue that was discharged into the sea at its soda plant on the Tuscan coast. Under Belgian law, any shareholder, even one holding only one share, can ask questions to the board at the general meeting, as long as they pertain to items on the agenda, but since the management report and annual accounts are discussed at the AGM, most company-related topics can be discussed through questions at the AGM.[90] At Solvay's 2021 AGM, Bluebell – which had only been set up three years earlier – asked 52 questions, during the May 2022 meeting 106, generating a lot of negative press for Solvay and putting pressure on its relatively new CEO to deal with the issue. In September 2022 Bluebell entered a settlement with Solvay, after the company had announced that a technological breakthrough it had made in soda ash production would allow it to end the controversial discharges into the sea (and reduce the CO2 emissions of soda production with 50%).[91]

---

[85] Also a repeat player in such campaigns.
[86] See https://www.pirc.co.uk/#. "PIRC" stands for Pensions & investment Research Consultants ltd. and presents itself as Europe's largest independent corporate governance and shareholder advisory consultancy, providing stewardship and proxy research services with a focus on ESG.
[87] M. McDougall, "Cisco urges shareholders to reject tax transparency proposal", *FT*, 22 September 2022.
[88] R. Tallarita, "stockholder politics" (fn. 22), at 1729–32.
[89] See also the chapter by A. Christie in this book.
[90] Art. 7:139 Belgian Companies Code.
[91] See P. Hollinger, "European chemicals group Solvay declares truce with Activist Bluebell", *FT*, 6 September 2022.

Bluebell presents itself as an activist investor concentrating on European large caps and with an ESG focus.[92] While several of its campaigns do indeed have an ESG aspect to them[93], this is not always the case.[94] The firm almost always focuses on financial returns. This was for example the case in its first well-publicised campaign, when it was part of a coalition of investors who successfully tried to oust the CEO-chairman of Danone.[95] Here, Bluebell was clearly driven by the underperformance of Danone on financial metrics compared with its peers, which the activist coalition partly blamed on too much focus by its chairman on ESG matters – the CEO who was known in France as "Mr. ESG" – and went on to become chair of the International Sustainability Standards Board. The Bluebell campaign against Danone highlights how shareholder activists with an ESG profile will often pursue financial returns through governance change that is intended to improve ESG features of the target company. This is the opposite of ESG goals getting in the way of financial returns. This was also the case for the spectacular and well- known campaign of Engine No1, which, as a small hedge fund owning 0.02% of Exxon, succeeded in getting two of its candidates appointed to the board of Exxon, in a campaign intended, among other things, to force Exxon to accelerate its move into renewable energies. But it was clear the main driver behind the campaign was the conviction that Exxon was faltering or at least falling behind peers because of a lousy strategy.[96]

So while for most or probably all halo activists, pursuing a financial return is their usual *modus operandi* and main activity, also when engaging in activism, halo activism is a genuine phenomenon. Two other examples are the campaign coordinated by ShareAction against Unilever (Europe)[97], and the Green

---

[92] Https://www.bluebellcp.com/. For press reports on 10 activist campaigns of Bluebell, see the "press" section of its website.

[93] For instance, in its campaign against Glencore it tried to move Glencore to divest its coal-related assets.

[94] For instance, its 2020 campaign against Mediobanca in any case, had nothing to do with environmental or social concerns.

[95] About this campaign, see L. Abboud, 'Danone Board ousts Emmanuel Faber as Chair and Chief executive', *FT*, 15 March 2021.

[96] See e.g. "ExxonMobil faces "winds of change" as climate battle reaches boardroom', *FT*, 24 May 2021 and 'Defeats for big oil mark "sea change" in climate battle', *FT*, 27 May 2021.

[97] ShareAction regulary submits shareholder proposals as the head of investor coalitions – those coalitions always seem to count pension funds as members, but in addition to other types of investment funds. It scored a success with its campaigns first at Unilever and then other food giants such as Nestlé, Kraft Foods, Danone and Kellogs to offer more healthy foods and increase disclosure on the health&nutrition aspects of their food products (see J. Evans, "Unilever to set new healthy food targets after investor pressure" *FT*, 7 March 2022 and J. Evans, "Investors push Nestlé and KraftHeinz to set new health targets", *FT*, April 26 2022). Arguably, the campaign it coordinated at Glencore about its coal activities is another example of activism that cannot really be explained by return on investment motives. It is true that in the near future, coal may become an uninteresting investment because using coal for energy generation might become unacceptable because of its impact on global warming. But at the time of this campaign, Glencore's profits from coal-related activities were booming. See about this campaign L. Hook, "Glencore shareholders demand more clarity about coal plans",

Century Capital Management campaign against Procter&Gamble (US), about deforestation.[98] This last campaign is a good illustration of how a "halo investor" can take the lead, but must be supported by other investors. The deforestation proposal was approved by a large majority of P&G shareholders.[99]

IV. EMPIRICAL RESEARCH ON NGO-SPONSORED ESG SHAREHOLDER PROPOSALS IN EUROPE, 2020–2022

Are the phenomena described in section III, shareholder activism by NGOs pursuing ESG goals, and halo activism, real? Until now we've only mentioned a few anecdotes, and this reflects the fact that while there is quite a bit of data on shareholder activism in Europe in general, and a burgeoning literature on ESG activism, there is very little systematic empirical research on ESG activism in Europe.[100] A recent exception is the work of Michael Bakker of the University of Amsterdam (UvA). Bakker published research on ESG activism that took the form of shareholder proposals in Europe and North-America in the 2021 AGM season. In 2023, his follow-up research covering the 2020–2022 season will be published in *ECFR* (with the title "Shareholder Proposals and Sustainability: An Empirically-based Critical Reflection"). I asked Bakker to analyse his dataset to isolate the data concerning shareholder proposals at European companies (excluding the rest of the world), and he provided the three tables presented below. If one compares his findings with the important research by Roberto Tallarita about "political" ESG activism in the US, the conclusion is warranted that NGO and halo activism are indeed real phenomena in Europe, but that shareholder proposals are far more often used by this type of activist in the US than in Europe. This is because, as I will explain in section V, it is more difficult to submit shareholder proposals in some major European jurisdictions, such as the Netherlands, Germany and to a certain extent also France. Such shareholder proposals are deemed inadmissible if they impinge on corporate strategy, which is a broader concept than the "ordinary business" concept used in the US to ban

---

FT, 5 January 2023. The article reported that shareholders including the bank HSBC, asset managers LGIM, Vision Super, and the Ethos Foundation (representing two Swiss pension funds) backed the ShareAction proposal.

[98] See https://www.greencentury.com/green-century-presses-procter-gamble-to-end-deforestation-and-forest-degradation-in-its-supply-chain/. Green Century regularly files shareholder proposals with no or no obvious financial importance, but inspired by its desire to do good, see for instance S. Murray, "Investors push food companies to go greener", *FT*, 20 October 2020 about its campaign at ConAgro, also about deforestation, or, P. McGee and P. Temple-West, "Apple fights shareholder call for more transparency on forced labour", *FT*, October 27 2021, about its support for the campaign for a consumer "right to repair" at Apple.

[99] Https://www.greencentury.com/pg-shareholders-resoundingly-support-deforestation-proposal/

[100] There is quite a bit more empirical research on environmental and climate *disclosures*, just one example being S.F.W. Van den Bosch, *Business at Risk: the Governance and Disclosure of Sustainability Risks*, 2022 (Ph.D. thesis, Tilburg University law school).

proposals that would encroach too much on the board's prerogative to run the company.

1. TALLARITA'S STUDY ON US E&S SHAREHOLDER PROPOSALS

For the US, Roberto Tallarita in a very interesting contribution, has produced a comprehensive overview of precisely the kind of social and environmental shareholder activism studied in this chapter, at least to the extent it is performed through shareholder proposals.[101] He analyzed 2933 shareholder proposals at US companies from the 2010–2021 period. He reported that 399 companies received S&E proposals, but predictably spread out unequally over industries and individual companies, with the twenty most targeted companies receiving 28.9% of all proposals and the six most frequently targeted industries being Retail, Oil & Gas, Utilities, Banks, Business Services, and Pharmaceuticals.[102] He identified only four proposals that were supported by management, and of the 1851 proposals in his sample on which shareholders voted, only 61 (3.3%) obtained a majority[103], but with (greatly) increased approval rates in 2020 (12.4%) and 2021 (19.2%).[104] The vast majority of the votes were precatory (non-binding). This is standard in the US, as opposed to Europe, where non-binding votes were until recently virtually unknown, but are now clearly being proposed more often, precisely because of the rise of shareholder activism. Tallarita convincingly argues that when a proposal is not majority-approved, that does not necessarily indicate that most shareholders are opposed to them[105] (much less that shareholders do not care about the issue). 30.7% of the sample pertained to political activity proposals (such as lobbying efforts or political spending by corporations), 28.1% was about environmental issues (including climate change – 11.4% of the proposals) and 40.3% about social issues[106],[107] One of the most interesting findings of Tallarita is that over half (53.4%) of the proposals in his sample were submitted by only 25 organizations. He labels these repeat players "stockholder politics specialists". They include investment advisers, public pension funds (some of them linked to unions), religious organisations and NGOs.

---

[101] In addition to the R. Tallarita research discussed in this section, other research with an empirical component on ESG shareholder proposals in the US includes S. Hirst, "Social Responsibility Resolutions", *Journal of Corporation Law*, 2017, 218 and J. Fisch, "Purpose Proposals", *University of Chicago Business Law Review*, 2022, 126.
[102] R. Tallarita (fn. 22) at 1712–1713.
[103] R. Tallarita (fn. 22) at 1719.
[104] R. Tallarita (fn. 22) at 1727.
[105] R. Tallarita (fn. 22) at 1726.
[106] Only 2.6% pertained to employee rights whereas 12.5% of the total number of proposals in the sample were about sex, gender and race.
[107] See R. Tallarita, (fn. 22) table 3 at p. 1714.

2. MICHAEL BAKKER'S RESEARCH ON E&S SHAREHOLDER PROPOSALS IN EUROPE BETWEEN 2020 AND 2022

As mentioned, there is very little empirical research on shareholder proposals in Europe[108] – where far fewer proposals are launched than in the US – and this is even more true of research on ESG proposals. Even empirical research on ESG activism (irrespective of whether it takes the form of shareholder proposals or even shareholder activism) is usually either anecdotal or consist of case studies, not systematic descriptive statistics.

a. Bakker's research on worldwide activity in the 2021 AGM season

Michael Bakker has produced an excellent descriptive overview of shareholder resolutions concerning environmental (including climate) and social matters in the 2021 AGM season, mainly in North-America and Europe.[109] Looking at 3580 listed companies from 40 countries, Bakker identified 589 ESG-related shareholder resolutions at 333 companies. He only included resolutions on which an actual vote had been organized, thus for example excluding cases where a submitted resolution had resulted in a settlement between the activist and the target company. 425 of the proposals were submitted in the US, the vast majority of them non-binding. Japan (44), Sweden, Canada, Australia and Norway were the other countries where more than 10 ESG resolutions were tabled. The relatively high number of resolutions in Sweden and Norway is probably influenced by the extremely flexible rule in those countries that anyone holding at least one share can submit a shareholder proposal.[110] Conversely, not a single shareholder resolution was put to the vote in 2021 in the Netherlands, which is likely influenced by the Boskalis/Fugro judgement that we discussed above. Of those 589 proposals, 72 related to climate (64) and environmental (8) matters, 112 were classified as "social" by Bakker (relating to stakeholder relations, workplace conditions, diversity in the workforce, product safety and quality) and the rest was governance-related. He also identified six resolutions urging companies not to get distracted by climate concerns, all submitted in the US by Steven Milloy of the *Burn More Coal*[111] shareholder activist organization, garnering very low levels of support.

---

[108] But see V. Verheyden, "When shareholders use their right to convene meetings and submit proposals: a comparative and empirical analysis in four European Member States", *TRV-RPS*, 2020, 975–995, which deals with shareholder proposals in France, Germany, the Netherlands and Belgium, but not with an ESG focus (and before the current wave of ESG proposals).

[109] M.H.C. Bakker, "Aandeelhoudersvoorstellen en duurzaamheid: een verkenning", *Ondernemingsrecht*, 2022, 241–255.

[110] See *infra* fn. 122.

[111] On its website, the organisation says: *"Burn More Coal (BMC) is a pro-coal electric utility shareholder activist group dedicated to promoting the increased use of coal as a fuel for*

Interestingly, Bakker distinguished the proposals by type of shareholder that submitted them, and found 85 proposals by NGOs, 30 by religious organisations, 17 by unions, two by a thinktank and six by a shareholder association. The NGO category contained "traditional" NGOs like Oxfam as well as NGOs that have specifically been set up to influence corporate ESG policies, like "Follow This"[112] and "As You sow".[113] Of the 132 proposals submitted by NGOs, religious organisations[114] and unions, 16% were majority-approved (18% of those of "dedicated" NGOs like Follow This).[115] Bakker found only two hedge funds – the traditional shareholder activists *par excellence* – that submitted ESG-related proposals, namely TCI (three say on climate proposals) and Bluebell Capital (4 proposals, at two Italian companies, all related to a possible suit against the former CEO of the bank Monte dei Paschi).

b.   *Bakker's research on E&S shareholder proposals in Europe in 2020–22*

Michael Bakker has repeated his research for 2020 and 2022.[116] Based on the database on which his research is based[117], at my request he prepared the following tables, specifically on E&S activism in Europe in the three years from 2020 through 2022.

Table 1 indicates that in Europe, too, governance issues get more attention from shareholder proposals than environmental and social issues: 158 proposals were about governance issues, whereas 61 proposals concerned climate and the environment and 55 dealt with social matters including 5 on affected communities. This is a total of 116 E&S proposals. Of those 116, only 7

---

electricity generation", see https://burnmorecoal.com/about/. The group does invest in shares of companies that generate electricity, the portfolio is described on the website.
[112]   See https://www.follow-this.org/. In the "about us" section, the organization says "We have the power to change oil companies from within -as shareholders".
[113]   Https://www.asyousow.org/resolutions-tracker listed (as of April 6 2023) 677 shareholder resolutions submitted by As You Sow between 2010 and 2023, including exactly 100 from 2023, a dozen or so of those 2023 resolutions having already been withdrawn after an agreement with the target company had been reached.
[114]   A recent example of ESG activism by a religious organization concerns Citigroup. In this case, an order of nuns that owns a small stake in Citi filed, in coalition with three other religious organisations, a shareholder resolution to Citi's 2023 AGM, calling on the board of Citi to report on the effects of its financing decisions on indigenous people and the environment. Specifically, the nuns reproached Citi to have provided important funding (about 5 billion US dollar) to a pipeline project that transports oil from the US to Canada, while the project is allegedly linked to oil spills and is opposed by indigenous people through whose living area the pipeline runs. See A. Mooney and A. Williams, "Nuns urge Citigroup to rethink financing of fossil fuel projects", *FT*, April 10 2023.
[115]   M.H.C. Bakker 2022 (fn. 109), 247 and his footnote 59.
[116]   Part of it will be presented in an article that has been accepted by ECFR, M. H.C. Bakker "Shareholder Proposals and Sustainability: An Empirically-based Critical Reflection" (on file with the author).
[117]   FactSet data for the US and Canada and hand-collected data on shareholder proposals in European companies, collected from corporate websites.

resolutions, all on climate change, were passed, i.e. received majority support at the vote during the general meeting.

Table 1. Shareholder proposals voted upon between 2020 and 2022 in Europe, organized per topic

Pillar	Topic	Proposals voted on (passed)
Environmental	Climate change	54 (5)
	Pollution	1 (0)
	Water and marine resources	–
	Biodiversity and ecosystems	2 (0)
	Resource use and circular economy	2 (0)
Social	Own workforce	14 (0)
	Workers in the value chain	3 (0)
	Affected communities	5 (0)
	Consumers and end-users	33 (0)
Governance	Corporate governance	130 (31)
	Sustainable corporate governance	2 (0)
	Business conduct	10 (0)
	Leadership (ex-board elections)	15 (2)
Other	Shareholder value	36 (12)
Total		307 (50)

Note to Table 1: This table – prepared by Michael Bakker – reports the number of shareholder proposals per category that have been put to a vote (in parentheses the number of proposals that have received a passing vote) between 2020 and 2022 at publicly traded companies that are incorporated in France, the United Kingdom, Germany, Switzerland, the Netherlands, Sweden, Spain, Italy, Denmark, Belgium, Norway, Finland, Poland, Ireland, Austria, Portugal, Luxembourg, Greece, Hungary, and the Czech Republic. The sample consist of companies that are constituents of a stock market indices that represents at least 50% of the respective capital markets of the selected jurisdictions; it includes 985 publicly traded companies. Proposals that concern director nominations or the removal of directors, proposals that have been withdrawn (e.g. after a settlement) and items submitted to the agenda for discussion only are not included. The topics have been based on the draft version of the European Sustainability Reporting Standards, available at <https://www.efrag.org/lab6> (last accessed 19 April 2023). The data was gathered through desk research, by examining the documentation pertaining to general meetings of the relevant companies.

Table 2 (below) indicates which type of organization submitted these European shareholder proposals. By far the largest individual group are individual investors, lending some support to what Americans sometimes call the "gadfly hypothesis"[118], namely that many shareholder proposals are submitted by individual shareholders who are pursuing their own hobby horses or very

---

[118] See e.g. K Kastiel and Y. Nili, "The Giant Shadow of Corporate Gadflies", *Southern California Law Review*, 2021, 569–636 who argue (and show), however, that the vast majority of proposals by individual investors in the US are not about trivial or cranky hobby horses, but relate to core governance matters. R. Tallarita, "Stockholder politics" (fn. v22) has, however, shown that in the US at least, individual shareholders play an unimportant role in E&S proposals.

idiosyncratic issues they have with the company, without giving any thought to collective shareholder interests. But more research on the nature and content of these proposals would be needed, and that is not the topic of this article. Parent and holding companies are another important group – they mostly tabled proposals on changing the governance structure of the company. Strikingly, institutional investors such as hedge funds, mutual funds, pension funds and asset managers launch few proposals, namely only 26, i.e. 8.5% of the total number of ESG proposals in Europe. By contrast, as I expected, a relatively speaking substantial number of proposals is submitted by NGOs: Bakker found 24 proposals sponsored by what in his table he calls shareholder advocacy groups and NGOs, but these advocacy groups are NGOs that only become shareholders in order to be able to use shareholder activism tactics, like As You Sow and Follow This.

Table 2. Types of shareholder who have submitted shareholder proposals to European publicly traded companies between 2020 and 2022

Types of shareholders (lead filer)	Proposals voted on (passed)	Environmental proposals voted on (passed)	Social proposals voted on (passed)	Governance proposals voted on (passed)	Other proposals voted on (passed)
Asset managers & investment advisors (non-SRI)	2 (0)	1 (0)	–	–	1 (0)
Asset managers & investment advisors (SRI)	2 (0)	2 (0)	–	–	–
Employee stock ownership funds	12 (0)	–	5 (0)	1 (0)	6 (0)
Foundations & charities	7 (0)	3 (0)	2 (0)	2 (0)	–
Governments (state)	7 (7)	–	–	3 (3)	4 (4)
Hedge funds	10 (4)	3 (3)	–	7 (1)	–
Individual investors interest groups	6 (0)	–	–	3 (0)	3 (0)
Individuals	175 (2)	22 (0)	42 (0)	102 (2)	9 (0)
Mutual funds	4 (0)	–	–	1 (0)	3 (0)
Other non-profit organizations	4 (0)	–	3 (0)	1 (0)	–
Parent companies & other holding structures	27 (22)	–	–	20 (15)	7 (7)
Pension funds (private)	1 (1)	–	–	1 (1)	–
Pension funds (public)	7 (6)	2 (1)	–	4 (4)	1 (1)

Types of shareholders (lead filer)	Proposals voted on (passed)	Environmental proposals voted on (passed)	Social proposals voted on (passed)	Governance proposals voted on (passed)	Other proposals voted on (passed)
Public development funds	2 (2)	–	–	2 (2)	–
Shareholder advocacy organizations	20 (1)	15 (1)	2 (0)	3 (0)	–
Identity of filer unknown	21 (5)	11 (0)	1 (0)	7 (5)	2 (0)
Total	307 (50)	59 (5)	55 (0)	157 (33)	36 (12)

Note to Table 2: This table presents an overview of the types of shareholders who have submitted shareholder proposals, that have been voted upon (in parentheses the number of passed proposals), to the European publicly traded companies that are included in the sample. The classification has been based on the lead filer of the shareholder proposals and the table, therefore, does not account for collaborations. Furthermore, in 21 cases the identity of the proponent was not disclosed and could not be traced through public records.

Table 3 documents that there are big differences between countries when it comes to the number of ESG shareholder proposals.

Strikingly, not a single proposal was submitted in the Netherlands. The Netherlands are no stranger to shareholder activism, but the Boskalis/Fugro court ruling has no doubt had a very chilling effect. In addition, it is not uncommon at Dutch listed companies to find a clause in the articles of association saying that only the board can take the initiative to add (certain) topics to the general meetings agenda.[119] I am convinced such clauses, when construed to mean not simply that organizationally only the board can put a shareholder proposal on the meeting agenda (including at the request of shareholders), but also that the board may ignore requests of 5% shareholders to add topics to the agenda, are a gross violation of article 6 SRD, which allows any shareholder holding 5%[120] to demand that the board puts its shareholder proposal on the agenda, irrespective of the topic. If Dutch legislation allows such oligarchic clauses, it should not be applied as it violates a higher-ranking EU norm, but my opinion is no doubt not shared by all legal advisors in the Netherlands.[121]

---

[119] See G. Van Solinge and M. Nieuwe Weme *NV en BV. Corporate governance*, Asser series, 2-IIb, 2019, at nr. 59 (*agenderingsrecht en oligargische besluitvormingsclausules*), with a fine-grained analysis of different varieties of such clauses.

[120] More precisely, the threshold is to be determined in national law, but may not be higher than 5%. In Belgium for instance, it is 3% (art. 7: 130 §1 Belgian Companies Code). The Directive does not contain any distinctions depending on the nature of the shareholder proposal.

[121] See however the leading textbook G. Van Solinge and M. Nieuwe Weme *NV en BV. Corporate governance*, 2019 Asser series, 2-IIb, (2019) at nr. 92 and especially nr. 59 where the same doubts as here are expressed, but with reference to five contributions in Dutch legal literature where the view is defended that such clauses are compatible with EU law.

Equally obvious from table 3 is that three Scandinavian countries, namely Sweden, Denmark and Norway, attract far more (ESG) shareholder proposals than other European jurisdictions. A likely explanation for this is that in those three countries, everyone holding just a single share can put a proposal on the AGM's agenda.[122]

Table 3. Shareholder proposals voted upon between 2020 and 2022 in Europe, by jurisdiction of incorporation of the companies

Jurisdiction (incorporation)	Proposals voted on (passed)	Environmental proposals voted on (passed)	Social proposals voted on (passed)	Governance proposals voted on (passed)	Other proposals voted on (passed)
Austria	8 (7)	–	–	6 (5)	2 (2)
Croatia	1 (1)	–	–	–	1 (1)
Czech Republic	4 (0)	1 (0)	–	1 (0)	2 (0)
Denmark	75 (5)	11 (1)	29 (0)	35 (4)	–
Finland	6 (3)	1 (0)	–	4 (3)	1 (0)
France	14 (0)	1 (0)	5 (0)	2 (0)	6 (0)
Germany	6 (0)	1 (0)	–	5 (0)	–
Greece	3 (3)	–	–	3 (3)	–
Hungary	4 (0)	–	–	1 (0)	3 (0)
Ireland	1 (1)	–	–	1 (1)	–
Italy	7 (2)	–	–	5 (1)	2 (1)
Norway	28 (2)	20 (0)	3 (0)	3 (2)	2 (0)
Poland	16 (12)	–	–	13 (9)	3 (3)
Portugal	1 (1)	–	–	1 (1)	–
Romania	4 (4)	–	–	–	4 (4)
Spain	6 (6)	3 (3)	–	3 (3)	–
Sweden	104 (1)	10 (0)	15 (0)	70 (1)	9 (0)
Switzerland	6 (1)	3 (1)	–	3 (0)	–
United Kingdom	13 (1)	8 (0)	3 (0)	1 (0)	1 (1)
Total	307 (50)	59 (5)	55 (0)	157 (33)	36 (12)

Note to Table 3: The table – provided by Michael Bakker – provides an overview of the number of shareholder proposals that have been put to a vote between 2020 and 2022 at publicly traded companies within the selected 20 European countries organized by jurisdiction of incorporation of the respective companies (in parentheses the number of proposals that have passed). A caveat is that it is not necessarily the case that the right to submit a shareholder proposals has been exercised on the basis of the laws of the country of incorporation of a company. In cases where the shares in a company are listed on an exchange in a foreign jurisdiction, it may be the case that shareholders have a right to submit shareholder proposals on the basis of the securities laws of that other jurisdiction. The data concerning the jurisdiction of incorporation of the companies was obtained from Compustat.

---

[122] Chap. 7, §16 of the Swedish Companies Act 2005 (*Aktiebolagslagen*); chap. 5, §11 of the Norwegian Public Limited Liability Companies Act (*allmennaksjeloven*); §11 of the Danish Companies Act 2009 (*selskabsloven*). These references were provided to me by Michael Bakker.

V. THE NETHERLANDS AND GERMANY (AND FRANCE?): NO SHAREHOLDER PROPOSALS CONCERNING THE BOARD'S STRATEGY DEVELOPMENT

1. THE NETHERLANDS: A BOARD-CENTRIC STAKEHOLDER SYSTEM

One of the striking findings from table 3 in the previous section is that not a single shareholder proposal on ESG matters was tabled in the Netherlands during the three years of 2020–2022.[123] The Netherlands gets its fair share of shareholder activism[124], but not through shareholder proposals.[125] We explained earlier that in the Netherlands, shareholder proposals concerning strategic matters may not be put to the vote at the general meeting, not even when a non-binding vote is demanded, because courts regard this as incompatible with the executive board's exclusive competence to determine the company's strategy.[126] This hostility among the Dutch corporate law community towards shareholder involvement in corporate strategy is also reflected in several cases where the Enterprise Chamber, the main corporate law court in the Netherlands[127], ruled that it constituted an abuse of shareholder power[128] when shareholders dismissed

---

[123] Though as pointed out by Bakker in his article in *Ondernemingsrecht* (fn. 109) an item was added to the agenda two times at LyondellBasell, based on a shareholder proposal, but for discussion only, see also R. Abma, 'Kroniek van het seizoen van jaarlijkse algemene vergaderingen 2021', *Ondernemingsrecht*, 2021/95. I would call LyondellBasell a *de facto* US corporation that is however registered in the Netherlands.

[124] For a general discussion, A. Lafarre and C. Van der Elst, "Corporate Sustainability and Shareholder Activism in the Netherlands", in *Cambridge Handbook of Corporate Law, Corporate Governance and Sustainability*, B. Sjäfjell and C. Bruner (eds.), CUP, 2019, 260–275.

[125] On this topic, see also S. Cools, *supra* fn. 23.

[126] Before the 2018 Boskalis/Fugro ruling applied that principle in order to exclude shareholder proposals that touch upon strategy, the *Hoge Raad* had already confirmed the executive board's primacy concerning strategy in HR 13 July 2007, ECLI:NL:HR:2007:BA7972, *NJ*, 2007/434, ann. J.M.M. Maeijer (*ABN AMRO*) and HR 9 July 2010, ECLI:NL:HR:2010:BM0976, *NJ*, 2010/544, ann. P. van Schilfgaarde (*ASMI*), par. 4.4.1. As of January 1 2022, art. 2:129 BW (Civil Code, Book 2 dealing with company law) explicitly determines that "policy and strategy" are determined by the board. As explained by C.J.C. De Brauw, "Strategiebepaling bij beursvennootschappen, activistische aandeelhouders en bescherming in het Nederlandse stakeholdermodel", *Ondernemingsrecht* 2022, 141, the Dutch governance model is resolutely different from Delaware's and is stakeholder-oriented and not necessarily shareholder-friendly.

[127] This *Ondernemingskamer* is a specialist division of the Amsterdam court of appeal.

[128] More precisely, behaviour incompatible with "reasonableness and fairness" (*redelijkheid en billijkheid*), a fundamental overarching concept in Dutch corporate law as enshrined in art. 2:8 BW and in the light of which basically all corporate law must be construed. The principle is regularly invoked by courts to intervene in company affairs, a prime example being Hoge Raad 14 September 2007, ECLI:NL:HR:2007:BA4888 ("Versatel") which ruled that fact-finding judges may invoke "reasonableness and fairness" to shove aside – in provisional measures taken in summary proceedings about a company's affairs – mandatory

directors with the clear goal of bringing about a change of strategy, so that the Enterprise Chamber could block such a director election.[129] As a non-Dutch outsider I may be permitted to vent the opinion that this type of reasoning of the Enterprise Chamber is undesirable, because if one does not want to totally rob shareholders of meaningful influence on a company's governance, they should have the right to appoint and dismiss (supervisory, non-executive) board members, precisely also if they do not like the strategy of the current board. But the case law is clear and an illustration of how legal culture in the Netherlands is still somewhat hostile to too large a role for shareholders in running a company. The Netherlands has always had, at the level of large or listed firms, a stakeholder approach to corporate governance. During the 1990s, the system was exposed to pressure from investors to become somewhat more shareholder-centric, and at the end of the 1990s and early 2000s, this led to some shareholder-friendly-reforms.[130] In general, however, the Dutch corporate law system still allows for what Dutch lawyers love to call "oligarchic" governance arrangements.[131]

---

provisions from the Dutch companies act. One of several applications by fact-finding courts is Ondernemingskamer Hof Amsterdam, 22 December 2022, ECLI:NL:GHAMS:2022:3706 in which judges ruled that, in view of "reasonableness and fairness", a major shareholder could not invoke the protection offered to its position by both mandatory statutory rules on preemption rights and a shareholder agreement, and that statutory anti-money-laundering provisions did not have to be applied in this case.

[129] See C.J.C. De Brauw, "Strategiebepaling bij beursvennootschappen, activistische aandeelhouders en bescherming in het Nederlandse stakeholdermodel", *Ondernemingsrecht*, 2022, 141 and C.J.C. de Brauw, 'De centrale rol van bestuur en RvC bij besluitvorming over strategie, openbare biedingen en bescherming tegen vijandige biedingen en aandeelhoudersactivisme' in: M. Lückerath-Rovers, B. Bier, H. van Ees en M. Kaptein (eds.), *Jaarboek Corporate Governance 2018–2019*, Kluwer, Deventer, 2020. The most notorious decision by the enterprise chamber was its Akzo/Nobel ruling, Court of Amsterdam (Enterprise Chamber), 29 May 2017, Elliott International, L.P. v. Akzo Nobel N.V., ECLI:NL:GHAMS:2017:1965. This was about a hostile bid by a US bidder for Dutch company Akzo/Nobel. An activist hedge fund that supported the bid wanted to oust the chair of the supervisory board and wanted to add this as an item to the agenda of an extraordinary general meeting. This was blocked by the Enterprise Chamber because the court was convinced that the attempt to oust the chair was also an attempt to change the corporate strategy of Akzo, which ought to be determined by the board, and that board had refused any type of negotiation with the bidder. For an English discussion of the case, see T. Vos, "The AkzoNobel Case: An Activist Shareholder's Battle Against the Backdrop of the Shareholder Rights Directive" *European Company Law*, 14(1), 2017, 238–243. From among the many discussions in Dutch literature, see F.G.K. Overkleeft, "AkzoNobel, PPG en de Ondernemingskamer", *Ondernemingsrecht*, 2017, 135.

[130] The story and intellectual history has been beautifully documented and analysed by F.G.K Overkleeft, *De positie van aandeelhouders in beursvennootschappen*, Kluwer, Deventer, 2017, 681 p.

[131] For instance, it is not uncommon to award preference shares and share subscription rights (allowing to subscribe to shares at a discount e.g. when the company becomes the target of a hostile bid) to foundations (the famous *stichtingen*) – the mechanism is clearly functionally equivalent to a Delaware poison pill, though the technicalities differ. See also the "waiting period" or, in Orwellian newspeak, "time for reflection" granted to boards of Dutch companies that become the target of a hostile takeover bid or a shareholder proposal to dismiss directors. This means boards who think more reflection time is in the interest of the company, get 250 days "to consult stakeholders" and "reflect" if a shareholder wants to change the composition of the board. The rules became effective on May 1 2021. The Dutch

2. GERMANY: DOUBTS ABOUT SHAREHOLDER PROPOSALS ON CLIMATE STRATEGY

The situation concerning shareholder proposals on strategic matters like a company's climate policy in Germany is similar to the approach in the Netherlands. §76 AktG states that the executive board (*Vorstand*) "leads [i.e. manages] *the company under its own responsibility*", which has traditionally been construed as meaning that the board may not act under the instruction of anybody, and must independently determine what it thinks is in the best interest of the company. At least one German author has written that changing the companies act to the effect that the general meeting could take binding votes on ESG issues, would be incompatible with the idea behind §76 AktG, which means that in his opinion at least it would be even more incompatible with the law as it is today.[132] The drafters of the German *Aktiengesetz* (law on public companies) took the conscious decision to emasculate the general meeting when it comes to managing the company, so that shareholders or the general meeting are not allowed to have a direct influence on the management of the company (*Geschäftführung*).[133]

Consequently, in Germany, legal obstacles to submitting ESG-related shareholder proposals to the general meeting exist.[134] As in all EU jurisdictions, as a result of SRD II, a (group of) shareholder(s) holding 5% of all shares can force the board to add an item to the agenda of the general meeting of listed companies.[135] But though this has not, to the best of our knowledge, been tested in a leading court case in Germany, German corporate law specialists assume that this does not allow such 5% shareholders to submit proposals concerning ESG-related issues unless the general meeting is competent to decide, i.e. vote in a binding way, on

---

Minister of Justice at the time declared upon approval in parliament of the new rules: "*What makes the Netherlands so special is that we have a very competitive economy with a lot of competition (sic), but within this (system) we also have regard for other interests than merely those of shareholders.*", see https://www.rijksoverheid.nl/actueel/nieuws/2021/03/23/eerste-kamer-stemt-in-met-bedenktijd-voor-beursvennootschappen-bij-vijandig-overnamebod-of-dreigend-ontslag. Elsewhere (see text at fn. 122) I briefly mention the clauses in articles of association that only allow boards to put items on the agenda of the general meeting.

[132] Ph. Jaspers "Sustainable Shareholder Activism", *Die Aktiengesellschaft*, 2022, (145), 151, nr. 24.

[133] Jaspers (previous footnote), 156, nr. 52.

[134] For a thorough analysis, see R. Harnos and Ph. M. Holle, "Say on climate", *Die Aktiengesellschaft*, 2021, 853–866. See also the analyses of German law in M-Ph. Weller and V. Hoppmann "Environment Social Governance (ESG). Neue Kompetenzen der Hauptversammlung?", *Die Aktiengesellschaft* 2022, 640; M-Ph. Weller and N. Benz, "Klimaschutz und corporate Governance", *ZGR* 2022, 563–601. A nuanced approach is taken in H. Fleischer and Ph. Hülse, "Klimaschutz und aktienrechtliche Kompetenzverteilung: zum Für und Wider eines 'Say on Climate'", *Der Betrieb*, 2023, 41 (evaluating pros and cons of a say on climate within the German governance framework).

[135] See §122 AktG.

such issues.[136] A case on the issue is now pending before the district court of Braunschweig.[137] As in other European jurisdictions, German general meetings are only competent to decide on those issues enumerated in the companies act, all other matters are the competence of the board. Corporate strategy as such, or ESG-related issues as such are not competences of the general meeting. German authors deduce from this that even a non-binding vote may not be organized about such matters, let alone that 5% shareholders would have the right to *demand* such a vote.[138] Harnos/Holle convincingly add that there are fewer objections to shareholders demanding a mere debate on e.g. corporate climate policy at the general meeting, since it is undisputed that shareholders can use their right to address the general meeting and ask questions of the board to talk about e.g. the corporation's climate policy. However, German authors are even reluctant to accept the right to demand a mere discussion (*beschlussloser Meinungsaustausch*), again based on the exclusive competence of the board to determine corporate strategy. Theoretically, the executive board is competent to – at its own initiative – submit any issue for which itself is competent to a vote of the general meeting.[139] The literature assumes such a vote may be binding or non-binding. The board may do so to get its back covered by shareholder approval of a certain decision. Nevertheless, as Jaspers point out, this almost never happens[140] and it is unlikely that a board would voluntarily seek a debate at the general meeting of sensitive ESG issues.[141] The decisive point (from a technical-legal perspective) is that neither shareholders nor anyone else can *force* the board to go down this route. In addition – precisely in order to avoid abuse of the possibility by boards that want to escape liability – the general meeting cannot be forced to take the request of the board into consideration for discussion, let alone for a vote.[142] According to the majority opinion, these rules apply not only to the possibility of the board to demand a binding decision of the general meeting, but also to the hypothesis where the board pursued a non-binding vote, the taking of a "position" by the general meeting without taking a formal decision or the organisation by the board of a mere debate at the general meeting.[143]

---

136 See Ph. Jaspers "Sustainable Shareholder Activism", *Die Aktiengesellschaft* 2022, (145), 150–51 and R. Harnos and Ph. M. Holle, "Say on climate", *Die Aktiengesellschaft*, 2021, (853), 862–64.
137 See *infra*, this section.
138 See esp. R. Harnos and Ph. M. Holle, previous footnote, with references in their footnote 104 to the general opinion but also to the dissenting opinion of two law professors (M. Roth and J. Ekkenga).
139 So-called *Vorstandsvorlage* on the basis of §119 abs. 2 AktG.
140 A recent example of a company whose board nevertheless voluntarily submitted the company's emissions reduction plan to a non-binding vote at its AGM is Alzchem Group AG, see R. Harnos, "Vorreiter bei Say on Climate: die Alzchem Group AG" *Gesellschafstrechtsblog 2023* (available at https://online.otto-schmidt.de/db/dokument?id=y-wpgesr.1428&q=say%20on%20climate).
141 Jaspers, fn. 136, p. 150 *in fine*.
142 R. Harnos and Ph. M. Holle, "Say on climate", *Die Aktiengesellschaft*, 2021, (853), 857, nr. 19.
143 For a detailed analysis of the different hypotheses, see Harnos/Holle, previous footnote, at 857–862.

At the time of writing, the issues are being tested before a court in Braunschweig, as a result of the refusal of Volkswagen to discuss at its 2022 AGM a shareholder proposal suggesting Volkswagen should change its articles of incorporation to force itself to extensively disclose its lobbying efforts concerning climate regulation.[144] It seems likely that the proposal's sponsors were well-informed about the German law on shareholder proposals and that this explains why they suggested an amendment to VW's articles: changing the articles is a competence of the general meeting, as opposed to determining a company's climate strategy. The proposal had been submitted by a group of Swedish and Danish Pension funds as well as the Church of England Pensions Board, but Volkswagen refused to accept it for the AGM because it allegedly infringed the competence of the executive board to determine VWs climate policies. This moved the investors to sue Volkswagen[145] (at the time of writing, the case is still pending). Also in 2022, the board of energy firm RWE did accept to organize a vote at its AGM on whether it should divest its lignite (*Braunkohl*) activities branch. The item was based on a shareholder proposal submitted by the investment fund Enkraft Capital, owner of 0.03% of RWE and a repeat activist at energy companies, though usually it does not focus on environmental issues.[146] In the end, 97.5% of votes rejected the proposal.[147]

The conclusion must be that shareholders who want to influence a German company's executive board and pressure it to devote more attention to ESG themes, will have to rely on shareholder engagement in the sense of talking to

---

[144] For a discussion of the case, see B. Fuhrmann and S. Röseler, "VW und die Leitungsautonomie – legitime Schranke für ESG-Aktivismus in Deutschland?", *Die Aktiengesellschaft*, 2022, 153.

[145] See https://www.clientearth.org/latest/press-office/press/investors-turn-to-courts-after-vw-withholds-climate-lobbying-details.

[146] About this campaign, see B. Fuhrmann and K. Döding, "Enkraft Capital vs RWE AG-misslungener Auftakt des ESG-Aktivismus in Deutschland?" *Die Aktiengesellschaft* 2022, p. R168. The authors mention some interesting details. Approximately 14% of RWE is owned by German cities and communities from the Ruhr region. In order to manage their shareholdings, these have contributed their shares to a GmbH (private company) called VkA (translatable as Union of Communal Shareholders). It was apparently well-known before the AGM that these cities were opposed to Enkraft's "brownspinning" campaign, because they feared for loss of employment in the region. As a reaction, Enkraft tried to neutralize KvA's voting power at the AGM, arguing that the KvA constituted a form of acting in concert and should therefore have been notified to RWE and market authorities (BaFin, which was seized about the matter by Enkraft; I have no knowledge of Bafin's reaction); since this had not happened, Enkraft argued that the voting rights of KvA were suspended, but apparently its complaint came too late to prevent KvA from voting at the AGM. What is striking is that an ESG shareholder activist here aggressively tried to exclude a "dissenting" important long-term shareholder from the vote, invoking legal rules (on the notification of stakes exceeding 3%) that are quite regularly invoked by corporate boards *against* shareholder activists (Enkraft also opposed the re-appointment of a local mayor, member of KvA, to RWE's supervisory board, but the mayor was reappointed with approximately 98% of votes in favour).

[147] H. Fleischer and Ph. Hülse, "Klimaschutz und aktienrechtliche Kompetenzverteilung: Zum Für und Wider eines 'Say on Climate'", *Der Betrieb*, 2023, 46, text accompanying their footnote 48.

directors, and the very indirect route of trying to influence the profile of those who get elected by shareholders[148] at the general meeting to the supervisory (i.e. non-executive) board that will in turn appoint the executive board that manages the company, including determining its climate and environmental policies. The German corporate Governance Code now – and this is somewhat controversial within Germany – encourages chairs of the supervisory board to sound out investors on topics relevant for the supervisory boards activities.[149] The legal situation in Germany is very similar to that in the Netherlands, with the important difference that the BGH has not explicitly ruled on the matter whereas the Dutch have the Boskalis/Fugro ruling from their highest court.

3. FRANCE: GREATER LEGAL UNCERTAINTY, BUT A CONSERVATIVE APPROACH DOMINATES

In France, the legal situation concerning shareholder proposals that touch upon corporate strategy was less clear[150], but companies also invoked the allocation of powers between boards and shareholder meetings to refuse to organize a vote on shareholder resolutions relating to corporate climate policies. Again it was TotalEnergies who did this in its 2020 shareholder meeting, but in 2021 it allowed a vote, not, however, without explaining in a written note to shareholders why it thought such a proposal was unlawful.[151] Total's stance was supported by a position paper issued by ANSA – an interest group of French public companies – which also warned that proposals that are too prescriptive about a company's sustainability strategy are incompatible with the division of powers between board and shareholders.[152] In the end, the *Haut comité juridique de la place*

---

[148] In companies employing more than 2000 people this is only 50% of supervisory board members, in companies with more than 500 but fewer than 2000 employees, it's 66% of board members who are elected by shareholders. The other board members are elected by employees.

[149] Recommendation A.6 of the Deutscher Corporate Governance Kodex 2022: *"The Supervisory Board Chair should be available – within reasonable limits – to discuss Supervisory Board-related issues with investors"*.

[150] For legal analysis also based on the division of powers between general meeting and boards, see C. Baldon, "Les résolutions climatiques au prisme du principe de séparation des pouvoirs au sein de la société anonyme", *JCP E* (= *La Semaine Juridique- Entreprises et Affaires*), 36, 2021, 24–30.

[151] See about the "resistance" by Total (and also by another French company, Vinci), https://reclaimfinance.org/site/2021/12/02/resolutions-climatiques-dinitiative-actionnariale-la-france-a-la-traine/.

[152] See https://www.ansa.fr/rappel-des-regles-applicables-pour-linscription-a-lordre-du-jour-de-points-ou-de-projets-de-resolution/ (3 March 2021). In the statement, ANSA refers to a leading French decision of the cour de cassation, *Motte* (Cass. civ. 4 June 1946, *Sirey* 1947, 1, 153 ann. Barbry; *J.C.P.*, 1947. II. 3518, ann. Bastian; *Gaz. pal.* 1946, 2, 136; *J. sociétés* 1946, 374; *Grands arrêts de la jurisprudence commerciale*, 297, n° 69, ann. Jean Noirel) but while that ruling made clear that company bodies derive their competences from the law (statute), and that in a public company statute has organized their competences in a hierarchical way so that the general meeting may not encroach on competences of the board, and while it is reasonable to deduce

financière de Paris[153] tried to arbitrate in the matter by issuing a report[154] that on the one hand opined that determining the company's climate strategy is indeed a board competence and responsibility, and that therefore prescriptive resolutions containing specific emission reduction targets or requiring the board to organize an annual vote on climate matters can be excluded from the general meeting's agenda because they relate to the boards competences[155], but on the other hand, in its conclusions[156], the report only states that there are no legal objections against non-binding ("consultative") votes on climate policy organized at the initiative of either the board or the shareholders.

As I will argue in section VII.2, the Dutch and German approaches to shareholder proposals are too restrictive to the extent they are based on a blanket ban for the general meeting to discuss or at least vote on proposals that impinge on corporate strategy. Nor should French or Belgian law be construed as if it contains a ban on such proposals. I will argue that only overly prescriptive shareholder proposals – that would have the general meeting decide on the details of corporate strategy – should be banned. But first I discuss another development contributing to more stakeholderist, politicized corporations and boards, namely sustainability due diligence legislation and NGO sponsored climate litigation. The problems caused by these developments are the same as those caused by overly prescriptive shareholder proposals, namely that they are undue influences on the board's strategy-setting role, which is why I discuss these issues first.

---

from the ruling that the board cannot receive binding instructions from the general meeting, in my view it contains nothing that would lend authority to the opinion that shareholder proposals may not touch upon matters for which the board also has (final decision-making) competences, such as, typically strategy (The case was about a company where the general meeting had decided to transfer all powers of the board to the PDG, i.e. the equivalent of the combined CEO-chair; cassation ruled that such a decision was indeed unlawful). ANSA also referred to Tribunal de commerce de Marseille, 7 November 2001, *CE Gemplus / SA Gemplus, Rev. soc.,* 2002, 57, ann R. Vatinet, to underpin its opinion that shareholder resolutions may not touch upon the *gestion* of the company, but in my reading the only thing that court ruling said was that the general meeting may not give binding instructions to the board on the management of the company, nor may itself take management decisions (*actes de gestion*).

[153] Https://hcjp.fr/. This is a committee of lawyers set up at the initiative of the French financial markets supervisor and the French National Bank in order to promote the success of Paris as a financial center by contributing to legal certainty, among other things by issuing reports on disputed legal questions.

[154] *Rapport sur les resolutions climatiques.* 'Say on climate', 15 December 2022, 52 p. https://www.banque-france.fr/sites/default/files/rapport_54_f.pdf I have to thank Sofie Cools for drawing my attention to this report which I had not seen before, by sending me her paper "Climate Proposals: ESG Shareholder Activism Sidestepping Board Authority" (March 2, 2023), forthcoming in Th. Kuntz ed., *Research Handbook on Environmental, Social, and Corporate Governance*, Edward Elgar, 2023, available at https://ssrn.com/abstract=4377030.

[155] *Rapport sur les resolutions climatiques* (fn. 155) p. 24.

[156] *Rapport sur les resolutions climatiques* (fn. 155) p. 29.

VI. ENFORCED STAKEHOLDER DIALOGUE AND STRATEGIC STAKEHOLDER LITIGATION[157]

1. SUSTAINABILITY DUE DILIGENCE LEGISLATION CREATES LEVERAGE FOR STAKEHOLDERS

a.   European law: from internal to external stakeholders

For many decades, European corporate law has been stakeholder-oriented. Admittedly "shareholder value creation" was the dominant governance tune in listed companies between approximately 1992 and 2010, but that should not distract from the fact that companies acts throughout western Europe from at least the turn of the 20th century onwards contained a host of provisions aimed at protecting creditors (many of them built around the legal capital concept[158]). Especially after the second world war, protection of employee interests also became a goal not just – obviously – of the legal system, but of corporate governance legislation in several European countries, perhaps most prominently in Germany and the Netherlands.[159] This stakeholderist approach was reflected in so-called broad definitions of "the corporate interest" – a concept which theoretically should have guided boards in all their decisions.[160]

---

[157]   M. Rajavuori, A. Savaresi and H. van Asselt "Mandatory due diligence laws and climate change litigation: Bridging the corporate climate accountability gap?" https://doi.org/10.1111/rego.12518 May 2 2023, make a point similar to mine in this section, namely that the European due diligence legislation is creating an additional avenue for stakeholders to influence (climate) policies of firms, including by enabling litigation.

[158]   The fact that these rules were largely ineffective in protecting creditors' interests, should not obscure the undeniable fact that legislators from an early date wanted to protect those interest not just through all kinds of legal rules (contract law by definition is, of course, to a large extent about protection of contractual creditors), but also specifically through mandatory rules in companies acts (and those rules were completely alien to contract law).

[159]   Prime examples are of course the German employee co-determination system (*Mitbestimmung*), but also the extensive co-decision rights granted to work councils in the Netherlands, a country where in addition in about 500 of the largest corporations, subject to the *structuurregime* ("structure regime"), 1/3 of supervisory board members need to be elected at the proposal of employee representatives; in the 1970s through the mid-90s, such "structure companies" were regularly sued by unions or other employee representatives because their supervisory boards allegedly did not have a "balanced composition" as mandated by statute (read: contained too many shareholder-oriented directors). About the role of the works council in Dutch corporate governance, see chapter 9 of J. Winter, J. Wezeman, J. Schoonbrood, *P. van Schilfegaarde's Van de BV en de NV*, Deventer, Kluwer, 18th. Ed. 2022 – tellingly, this is a chapter in a corporate law handbook.

[160]   Readers from outside continental Europe should be aware that in (western) continental jurisdictions, the rule that directors always have to be guided by "the company's interest", and the "broad" or narrow" interpretation of this "company's interest" (*Gesellschaftsinteresse, vennootschapsbelang, intérêt social*, …), serve a function similar to UK-US doctrines about to whom directors owe their fiduciary duties. In continental Europe, the concept of a duty of loyalty was developed very late (not before the 1990s). When writing in English, continental lawyers will also talk about fiduciary duties when they talk about directors'

Prime examples are, again, the Dutch and German conceptions of "the corporate interest".[161]

However, until recently, corporate law in Europe (including Belgium) did not care about wider societal interests or mitigating negative externalities. To be sure, negative externalities had to be addressed by regulation, but according to the dominant conviction among policymakers, business leaders and corporate law academics alike, things like the impact of firms on the environment or climate, had to be tackled through all kinds of mandatory regulation[162] – perhaps aided by tort law as a private enforcement mechanism – *outside* of company law, not through company law or other legislation with an impact on corporate governance structures, board composition or board duties. From the late 1970s onwards, NGOs and some academics launched a discourse about Corporate Social Responsibility (CSR), but these debates had very little impact on the way large firms operated or on their governance structure; neither were

---

duties in their jurisdictions, but in fact fiduciary thinking was (and to a large extent still is) alien to continental European law – certainly in French-inspired civil law systems – until court cases in countries like France and Germany began to mention a *devoir de loyauté/Treuepflicht* for directors (and sometimes controlling shareholders) in the 1990s. Even today, there is nothing like a statutory or court-developed general "no profit" or "no conflict" rule with the same sweeping ambit of the UK or even Delaware rules in continental European jurisdictions. Rather, companies operate(d) under a system where directors and boards had to always "respect the corporate interest" and in addition were subject to a set of specific rules on conflicts of interest applicable to board decisions (often not to decisions of individual directors outside board meetings). The latter are often statutory rules with a limited scope; in countries where courts had developed conflicts of interest rules, these were originally even (far) weaker than in countries that had statutory rules (e.g. until the 1990s the Dutch rules were virtually non-existent compared with the Belgian statutory rules, which had been in place since 1870). Today, in many jurisdictions the courts have developed loyalty doctrines to fill the gaps left by specific conflicts of interest rules and the general instruction for boards always to serve the interest of the company, but it would be seriously misleading to present these rules as having the same meaning in practice as the English duty of loyalty. On the limited role of the duty of loyalty in continental Europe, see H. De Wulf, "What is a duty of loyalty for directors or shareholders and does it exit under Belgian law," in *Liber amicorum Didier Willermain*, Brussels, Larcier, 2023.

161 For Germany, see H. Fleischer, "Unternehmensinteresse und intérêt social: Schlüsselfiguren aktienrechtlichen Denkens in Deutschland und Frankreich", *ZGR*, 2018, 703–734 (in a comparison with France where, outside academia and certainly from the 1980s onwards, a shareholder-focused, "narrow" conception of the corporate interest prevailed until the 2019 Loi Pacte defined *l'intérêt social* in art. 1833 Code civil in a stakeholderist way, in the sense that it states that companies should take into account the social and environmental stakes of their activities). The Dutch leading case (*Cancun*, Hoge Raad 4 April 2014, *NJ* 2014/286, ann. P. van Schilfgaarde, *Ondernemingsrecht*, 2014/101, ann. A.F.J.A. Leijten) states that boards should act in accordance with *"the interest of the company and the firm connected to it"*; this wording assumes that the company should be seen as "the whole body of shareholders" (read: not just controlling shareholders) and the reference to the firm is meant as a reference to other stakeholder interests. Thus, Dutch law undoubtedly has a "broad", "stakeholderist" conception of "the corporate interest".

162 Environmental regulation, health&safety rules for the workplace, product safety regulation, ...

they reflected in companies acts and related governance legislation, contrary to what was the case for creditor and employee protection.

This is now changing, as NGOs representing truly external stakeholders (i.e. others than equity or debt investors or even employees) gain influence over corporate boards and the company's polices and strategies determined by those boards. Human rights/sustainability due diligence legislation now recognizes NGOs as important corporate stakeholders, and creates leverage for them to influence corporate E&S policies. The "hard law" due diligence legislation in France, Germany and the EU will increase the leverage of NGOs to enforce such a stakeholder dialogue with firms. The French law on sustainability due diligence ("Vigilance Law") became effective in 2017 and Germany followed suit with its *Lieferkettengesetz* (effective on 1 January 2023).[163] Large firms from France and Germany have lobbied their governments to create a level playing field, at least within the EU, through the adoption of a EU Sustainability Due Diligence Directive (CSDDD, colloquially known as "triple D", still being negotiated at the time of writing). Due diligence in this context means[164] integrating due diligence concerning ESG issues in corporations' policies and risk management systems; identifying potential "adverse impacts"[165] that a company, its subsidiaries and relevant business partners may create (especially at the level of outsiders' human (and social) rights, the environment or climate); preventing and mitigating such adverse impacts and, where they materialize after all, trying to end or minimize their impact and then compensate victims; establishing a complaints procedure; periodically monitoring the effectiveness of their DD policies and measures; and reporting on DD practices on the company website and through management reports.

The non-binding international (UN, OECD) due diligence guidelines that preceded the mandatory European legislation, already offered a platform for stakeholder NGOs to enter into a dialogue with firms. Spurred on by the UN's Ruggie Principles[166] and the OECD guidelines[167], many OECD member states

---

[163] For company groups with more than 3000 employees; it will become applicable to groups with at least 1000 employees from January 1 2024 onwards.

[164] A brief summary is in fact given in article 4 (1) of the draft CSDDD (fn. 11).

[165] In effect, this concept is more or less synonymous with "negative externality" rather than with the traditional legal concept of (negligently caused) damage.

[166] UN Human Rights Office, *Guiding Principles on Business and Human Rights. Implementing the United Nations 'Protect, Respect and Remedy' Framework*, 2011, 42p., available at https://scholar.harvard.edu/files/john-ruggie/files/guidingprinciplesbusinesshr_en.pdf.

[167] The latest version of the general *OECD Guidelines for Multinational Enterprises*, 2011 edition, 95 p., available at http://mneguidelines.oecd.org/guidelines/ incorporates the Ruggie Principles. The OECD then developed more specific due diligence guidelines, the *OECD Due Diligence Guidance for Responsible Business Conduct*, 2018, 100 p., available at http://mneguidelines.oecd.org/due-diligence-guidance-for-responsible-business-conduct.htm, as well as sector-specific guidelines, all available at the "mneguidelines.oecd.org" website.

established so-called National Contact Points (NCP), which are government-sponsored organisations that can help firms understand due diligence best practices but that can also act as mediators when someone has a complaint about the due diligence policies (or the lack thereof) of a company. An example of how this creates leverage for NGO's was the 2017 complaint by Oxfam Novib, Greenpeace Netherlands, Backtrack and Milieudefensie to the Dutch NCP, asking the NCP to investigate the climate policies of ING (an international bank with Dutch roots), in order to enjoin ING to change its due diligence policies so that they would conform to the OECD guidelines.[168] The Dutch NCP was of the opinion that the request did indeed warrant a dialogue, facilitated by the NCP between the four NGOs and ING. This resulted in a so-called "final statement" in April 2019[169] which inter alia contained a commitment of ING to try and develop an emissions policy in line with the Paris Climate Agreement while at the same time pointing out that several methodological issues first had to be clarified before ING could realistically develop such a policy. The Statement explicitly stated that it would not have been useful to issue a judgement on whether ING had complied with the OECD due diligence Guidelines, as this would have complicated further dialogue between ING and the NGOs. This all confirms that the procedure based on a complaint to an NCP will usually not result in hard, enforceable commitments by the "defendant" corporation. But it did lead to a type of mediated dialogue which the NGOs would not necessarily have had with ING if the procedure had not been available.

b.   *The draft CSDDD imposes stakeholder dialogue*

In the draft CSDDD, "Stakeholders" are defined in a very broad way.[170] Not just the employees, trade unions and workers representatives of a company and its subsidiaries, but also consumers and *"other individuals, groups communities or entities whose rights or interests are or could be affected by the products, services and operations"* of the company, its subsidiaries and business partners. The definition concludes with an explicit reference to *"civil society organisations, national human rights and environmental institutions and human rights and environmental defenders"*. This means, for instance, that a Belgian multinational with an important Indonesian supplier of palm oil, will have to count not only a Belgian NGO that defends human rights world-wide as one of its stakeholders, but also an Indonesian NGO defending the interests of local farmers that have to make room for palm oil plantations.

---

[168] See for a description of this "event", the website of the Dutch NCP at https://www.oesorichtlijnen.nl/actueel/nieuws/2017/11/14/publicatie-eerste-evaluatie-melding-oxfam-novib-greenpeace-banktrack-en-milieudefensie-vs.-ing.

[169] Available for download at https://www.oecdguidelines.nl/notifications/documents/publication/2019/04/19/ncp-final-statement-4-ngos-vs-ing.

[170] In art. 3 (n) of the November 30 2023 (Council's General Approach text) draft of the CSDDD (fn. 11).

Article 6 (4) of the draft states that companies should, where relevant, consult with potentially affected groups – including stakeholders – to gather information on actual or potential adverse impacts. In case complex measures are required to prevent adverse impacts, companies should develop a "prevention action plan" and this has to be developed *"in consultation with potentially affected stakeholders"*.[171] If an adverse impact is unfortunately created and cannot be brought immediately to an end, a "corrective action plan" must be developed in consultation with stakeholders.[172] The complaints procedure that companies must organize must not only be open to persons who are affected by adverse impacts, but also to trade unions and employee representatives from throughout the value chain, and to civil society organisations active in the areas of human rights or environmental adverse impacts.[173] The draft Directive also refers to the possibility of organizing *"collaborative complaints procedures"* in which firms work together with *"multi-stakeholder initiatives"*.[174] At least every 24 months, companies must assess the effectiveness of their due diligence policies and again the draft Directive explicitly mentions that as a result due diligence policies will be updated *"with due consideration of relevant information from stakeholders"*.[175] Article 19 provides that *"natural and legal persons"* must be allowed to share substantiated concerns about CSDD with the national supervisory authorities; although stakeholders are not explicitly mentioned, no doubt they are among the eligible "natural or legal persons".

c.   *Stakeholders in the French due diligence legislation*

Under French due diligence legislation, the risk management plan that the company needs to draft, must be developed together with (*en association avec*) the company's stakeholders[176] – a concept which is not defined in the French legislation. The stakeholders can issue a formal warning to a company that its due diligence plan does not meet the demands of the legislation. If the company does not remedy the situation within three months *"any party who has an interest in the matter"* can sue the company to ask for an injunction ordering the company to take measures necessary to respect its due diligence duties.[177] It has never been doubted that NGOs should be considered such "interested parties" and therefore have standing to sue, indeed every case so far has been brought by (a coalition of) NGOs and in the TotalEnergies case, their standing was never in doubt.

---

[171]   Art. 7 (2) draft CSDDD.
[172]   Art. 8 (3) (b) draft CSDDD.
[173]   Art. 9 (2) draft CSDDD.
[174]   Art. 9 (5) draft CSDDD.
[175]   Art. 10 (1) draft CSDDD.
[176]   Art. L. 225–102–4.-I. (3rd indent) Code de Commerce.
[177]   Art. L. 225–102–4.-II.

The TotalEnergies judgement of the Paris court of first instance (28 February 2023)[178] stresses that one of the few things that are clear about the Vigilance Act – which the judgement criticizes because of the vagueness of its central concepts and of the duties it introduces – is that companies should elaborate their *plan de vigilance* in consultation with NGOs.[179] According to the court, since the Act does not indicate which NGOs could be relevant, companies could usefully enlist the input of a wide array of NGOs to help them define the desirable perimeter of their due diligence action while simultaneously reducing the risk of litigation which questions the relevance of the due diligence plan. The court then adds that such an inclusive approach can help to achieve the "monumental goals"[180] of the due diligence legislation *which are essentially political* to the extent they pertain to the protection of the environment and human rights (emphasis added – hdw). The court continues by saying that the procedure of *mise en demeure* (put on notice) is essentially part of this dialogue between NGOs and companies. This is one reason why the court action against TotalEnergies was inadmissible: the NGOs had only dialogued with Total about its 2018 due diligence plan, not about the more recent 2021 plan, even though in the end they mainly had complaints about that 2021 plan.

d. The more reluctant German attitude

The German Supply Chain Due Diligence Act is far more detailed than its French equivalent (and from a technical-legal perspective the drafting is far superior). But it envisions a far more limited role than the French Act for stakeholders. §4 (4) states that when companies design their supply chain risk management system, they should take the interests of the stakeholders who are directly affected by the activities of the company's supply chain into account, but that is obvious. There is no rule, as there is in the French act, that companies need to actively consult stakeholders in developing their risk management system. The only provision in the German Act that explicitly provides for a special role for external stakeholders and especially NGOs is §11. This allows victims of serious violations of the Act to delegate the enforcement of their rights before German courts to a domestic union or non-governmental organization. The NGO is only eligible if it can show it is a long-standing organization whose articles of association show it is not commercially active (is a non-profit, in other words)

---

[178] Tribunal judiciaire de Paris, 28 February 2023, no. 22/53942.
[179] P. 19, top, of the judgement.
[180] No doubt the court was inspired here by the work of M-A. Frison-Roche, a French compliance specialist who submitted an amicus curiae brief to the court and who is the editor of book called *Les buts monumentaux de la compliance*, Paris, Dalloz, 2022, 520 p. In an approach which is highly unusual for French courts at least until today, the Paris court encouraged several external experts to enlighten the court on how to deal with the Vigilance Act by submitting amicus briefs.

and has a more than ephemeral track record in the defense of human rights or related rights under the law of a specific national state.[181]

e. *External stakeholders are not investors*

When policymakers evaluate the desirability of and limits to stakeholder activism using shareholder activism tools, I would argue they can legitimately take into account that other stakeholders than shareholders, large creditors (mainly banks and bondholders) and employees, such as typically environmental NGOs, have indeed invested less or nothing in the companies they are trying to influence. They have no financial incentives to care about the company. They are really representatives of society, or at least of E&S activists within society. Of course, such truly external stakeholders may be exposed to the negative externalities created by companies (called "adverse impacts" in the draft CSDDD), and the NGOs may represent the interest of such victims and may engage in all kinds of efforts to force companies to internalize the cost of those externalities. If the negative externality takes the form of damage caused by negligence, the victim may of course sue the company, based on tort law. But, again, they should not try to internalize the externalities cost by directly prescribing corporate strategy in shareholder proposals or in claims for injunctions before courts. The NGOs or the external stakeholders they represent do not bear the consequences of decisions of the board or the general meeting to the same extent as long-term shareholders, employees or creditors. A classic well-founded claim of agency theory is that a divergence among shareholders between financial investment and governance power (e.g. voting power), makes agency problems worse.[182] For instance, investors who vote with borrowed shares do not bear the full (financial) consequences of their voting (governance) behavior or those enjoying multiple voting rights per share have a power disproportionate to their investment. It seems to me that the same problem arises about NGOs who have only a symbolic investment (of one share or a few 1000 euros worth of shares) but use certain shareholder rights, such as the right to ask questions to the board at the AGM, as a megaphone, sometimes (increasingly) backed up with the threat of stakeholder/general litigation.

---

[181] The wording makes one wonder whether the German Act wants to allow representative litigation by globally active human rights organisations like Amnesty International, but I assume it would suffice for, say, Amnesty, to show it has been active in the specific country where the human rights violation arose that gives rise to a potential claim under the German Act.

[182] See e.g. many of the papers discussed in R. Adams and D. Ferreira, "One Share-One Vote: The Empirical Evidence", *Review of Finance* Vol. 12, 2008, 51–91 (discussing the governance problems caused or exacerbated by discrepancies between voting power and cash flow rights); or L.A. Bebchuk and K. Kastiel, "The Perils of Small-Minority Controllers", *Georgetown Law Journal*, 107, 2019, 1453.

2. NGO LITIGATION IN ORDER TO CHANGE CORPORATE (CLIMATE) STRATEGIES

a. Strategic litigation in general, or why climate litigation is different

Activists in Europe regularly launch litigation that is intended to change both government and corporate policies. These days, this is often climate litigation intended to increase the efforts companies make to reduce their greenhouse gas emissions, or, relatedly, divest activities in the fossil fuel sector. Repeat players in climate litigation in Europe include the NGOs ClientEarth[183] and Milieudefensie. The case brought by Milieudefensie against Shell in The Hague, in order to force Shell to reduce its CO2 emissions quicker than Shell allegedly intended to do, goes to the core of Shell's corporate strategy. The court of first instance in The Hague ordered the Shell holding company to reduce the emissions of the Shell group and its clients at a specific rate[184], thus forcing Shell (which has appealed the decision) to move into renewable energy at a quicker rate than the board and shareholders had wanted to. The plaintiffs were NGOs, who successfully claimed standing on the basis of Dutch legislation that facilitates general interest litigation.[185] They sued for an injunction to reduce emissions on the basis of the Dutch statutory rules on tort law.[186] The court fleshed out the meaning of Shell's duty of care by invoking a societal consensus on the need for companies to contribute to a reduction in CO2 emissions and the human right to private life as protected in articles 2 and 8 of the European convention on Human Rights, which according to the court also encompasses a right to an environment that does not become unsupportable as a result of global warming. The court explicitly pointed out that since the inhabitants of the Netherlands represented by the NGO plaintiffs can invoke such a *right*, it did not have to balance that right against other interests or considerations.

That this litigation is an attempt to have judges impose strategic policies on companies is made even clearer by the stress both the NGO plaintiffs and the court itself put on the responsibility of Shell to also make an effort to reduce the

---

[183] Https://www.clientearth.org/ is an NGO, active world-wide, that calls itself "the world's most ambitious environmental organization" and that focuses on using the law to bring about change, also at companies, in environmental and climate policies. It frequently litigates about environmental matters. As of May 2 2023, its website said it had 168 court cases pending.

[184] See Rb. Den Haag 26 May 2021, ECLI:NL:RBDHA:2021:5337, available at https://uitspraken.rechtspraak.nl/inziendocument?id=ECLI:NL:RBDHA:2021:5337.

[185] Art. 3: 305a Dutch Civil Code. This essentially states that a non-profit organization can launch court proceedings in defense of similar interests of a group of persons other than itself. Such general interest litigation (*algemeenbelangactie*) pursues general interests (plural) that cannot be individualized because they are linked to a very large group of persons that is diffuse and indeterminate.

[186] Art. 6:162 BW (Dutch Civil Code).

emissions of its customers (scope 3 emissions). The recently launched derivative claim against Shell directors, discussed above at II.1, is also clearly intended to force the directors' and through them the company's hand concerning climate policy. It would be extremely naïve to think that receiving damages from the defendant directors is a major aim of this litigation.

I argue that this is an inconsistency within a legal system like the Dutch legal system: it bans shareholder proposals that touch upon a company's strategy (because determining that strategy is the board's exclusive prerogative), but at the same time admits climate litigation against companies at the initiative of NGOs representing external stakeholders when such litigation touches upon corporate strategies at least as much as the typical climate shareholder proposal.

This type of litigation is enabled by the trend in many European jurisdictions to facilitate general interest litigation. In another internal contradiction, class actions are still regarded unfavorably by European policymakers, at least outside the realm of consumer protection, even though they are not – contrary to climate litigation – geared towards the enforcement of the general interest, but aim to enforce individual interests that are common to a class of plaintiffs. All EU member states had to implement the Aarhus Convention, which entailed a duty for signatories to give standing to NGOs to enforce environmental regulation.[187] In Belgium, the Constitutional Court ruled that it was incompatible with the equal treatment clause in the constitution that the Aarhus rules only applied to environmental claims. Belgian Parliament reacted with the introduction of a rule essentially creating standing for NGOs to sue (before civil courts) when any human right protected by the Constitution or international treaties (when they have been ratified by Belgium) is violated.[188]

Climate litigation against corporations is different in nature than the general interest litigation that NGOs bring against companies based on more traditional human rights violations. This latter type of litigation is also, like climate litigation, often sponsored by NGOs, not primarily because they would want to obtain damages or even injunctive relief against a single company or corporate group. Rather, it often has in common with climate litigation that it is part of a wider campaign to attract attention to deplorable situations and to change policies. This type of litigation can be strategic in the double sense of being aimed at influencing corporate strategies and having aims that go beyond the

---

[187] See https://environment.ec.europa.eu/law-and-governance/aarhus_en. Art. 9(2) of the Aarhus Convention is the basis for (forcing signatories to recognize the right of) NGOs to engage in general interest litigation concerning the topics covered by the Convention.
[188] See the second paragraph of art. 17 Belgian Code of Civil Procedure, as introduced in 2018. For a description of the evolution of the rules in Belgium, see Kruithof, *supra* fn. 27.

individual case being litigated. An article on the German KiK case[189] rightly calls the KiK litigation an example of such "strategic litigation".[190] The authors, one of whom assisted some Pakistani families to build their legal case in Germany, state that *"Jabir and Others v Kik is not a regular court case"* but that it was part of a broader campaign *"to make visible the workers hidden in global chains of production by enabling their testimony in Germany. The lawsuit therefore also aims at facilitating a protest against the global economic system in a German court as a public forum in the country where KiK is headquartered and its products are bought and worn."* In other words, strategic litigation is the continuation of war on the excesses of "the global economic system" by other means. However, contrary to climate litigation, at least one of the aims of most such tort-based human rights litigation is to actually receive damages for victims.[191] Also, the litigation may be intended to change company policies on say, health & safety and he amount of investment the company devotes to combating negative externalities – "adverse impacts" in the new legal parlance – but contrary to climate litigation, it does not go the core of determining a company's strategy. The alleged tort or human rights violation (usually one and the same thing) that is at the basis of such suits is usually quite specific (e.g. causing an oil spill). As a result, courts who have to deal with such cases are not being asked to determine or review a company's strategy (but simply to help enforce respect for quite clear rules of behaviour), contrary to what is the case in climate litigation cases.

By contrast, litigation is singularly unsuitable to help determine corporate strategies concerning climate policy. In adversarial systems, parties will only present the angles to an issue that are beneficial to themselves. Plaintiffs will be focused on a single issue – e.g. CO2 reduction – without due consideration for other interests or values that are affected. As decided in the Shell climate case

---

[189] "KiK" is a German retail clothing chain. In 2012, 259 workers died, and at least 32 were injured, in a fire in the Ali Enterprises (AE) factory in Karachi, Pakistan. Ali Enterprises was a supplier (but not a subsidiary) of KiK Textilien und Non-food GmbH, which bought 70% of the output of the Karachi factory. KiK Germany was sued in 2015 by some of the (surviving family members of) victims of the fire, who alleged that KiK had been fully aware of the dire and dangerous working conditions at the AE factory, and should have done more to improve the situation or else should have terminated its business relationship with AE. In the end, a German court ruled that under applicable Pakistani tort law, the claim was time-barred when it was brought before the German courts (District court Dortmund, 10 January 2019, judgement Az: 7 O 95/15, available at https://www.lg-dortmund.nrw.de/behoerde/presse/Pressemitteilungen/PM-Urteil-KIK.pdf).

[190] M. Bader, M. Saage-Maass, C. Terwindt, "Strategic Litigation against the Misconduct of Multinational Enterprises: an Anatomy of Jabir and Others v KiK", *Verfassung und Recht in Übersee*, 52, 2019, 156–171. On this "model" of strategic litigation, see already J. Lobel, "Courts as Forums for Protest", UCLA Law Review, 52, 2004, 477.

[191] See as illustrations the "modern classics" cases of *Chandler v. Cape plc* (2012) EWCA (civ) 525, 80; *Vedanta resources plc v. Lungowe* (2019) UKSC 20; *Okpabi & Others v. Royal Dutch Shell Plc & Another* (2021) UKSC 3; Begum v Maran (UK) Ltd (Rev1) [2021] EWCA Civ 326, 10 March 2021, and several similar cases.

in the Hague, the claim will often be presented as an attempt to enforce a *right* (of plaintiff) or a corresponding duty (of the corporation). The enforcement of existing rights – which, as Dworkin taught us, are trumps[192] – leaves no room for the balancing of interests against each other, but only for the enforced application of the right or the rejection of its application. The same goes for duties. Just like the corporate boards or strategy-setters whose policies gave rise to the litigation, the court will not only be presented by the parties with distorted information, it has no meaningful guidelines on how to balance the various stakeholder interests and values at play.[193] Experts would be confronted with the same difficulty, meaning that invoking their help would be a waste of time.

b.   *French due diligence litigation*

The French vigilance act empowers NGOs to enforce the Act, by suing companies that, according to the NGO, have not complied with their duties to draft and implement a suitable *plan de vigilance*. As will become apparent from our discussion, this litigation sometimes opens the door to attempts to change a company's strategy rather than simply remedying the company's risk management concerning the adverse impacts it could create.

A French website keeps track of the court cases against companies based on the Vigilance Act, and as of April 2023, 6 years after the French Vigilance Act had been enacted, listed 10 cases where an NGO had subpoenaed a company for violation of its duties under the Act.[194] In an additional 5 cases, an NGO had sent out a *mise en demeure*, that is an official notice of breach, but had not (yet) gone to court.[195] Only one case, namely that against Total Energies, had resulted in a final judgement, with (as discussed above) the claim being ruled inadmissible for procedural reasons. This means six years after the Act came into effect, not a single judgement on the merits of a claim has been reached. Matters were

---

[192] R. Dworkin, *Taking Rights Seriously*, Harvard University Press, 1977.
[193] Lest a law and economics adept suggest that the guideline should be "efficiency", I have to point out that when incommensurable values clash, efficiency is a meaningless concept that cannot be operationalized (e.g. the "least cost avoider" principle is of no use when a judge has to decide whether to impose certain CO2 reduction duties on a company).
[194] Https://plan-vigilance.org/ The website (which calls itself a "radar for vigilance") also contains a list of companies that according to the website are subject to the Vigilance Act as well as a handy database with links to the actual *plans de vigilance* drafted by French companies and published in their management reports (accompanying the annual report). As far as we could ascertain, the website is maintained by two NGOs, Sherpa and CCFD-Terre Solidaire. According to the 2022 report on this website, in 2021 44 French companies subject to the Act would simply not (yet) have drafted a "due diligence plan" at all.
[195] See also M. Fabre Soundron, "Devoir de vigilance, six ans après: "une loi aussi ambitieuse qui tient sur une page A4 ne peut pas être révolutionnaire" at www.novethic.fr/actualite/social/droits-humains/isr-rse/devoir-de-vigilance-six-ans-apres-une-loi-qui-tient-sur-une-page-a4-ne-peut-pas-etre-revolutionnaire-151430.html (last consulted April 9 2023).

not helped by the initial uncertainty about which court (the regular court of first instance or the commercial court) was competent to deal with claims. It's also striking that the implementing regulations to be adopted by the French government, have not yet been issued.

According to a contribution on the website Novethic[196], the complaints based on the Vigilance Act so far concerned the French headquarters of 16 corporate groups but also three foreign companies with a French subsidiary subject to the Act; some of these companies faced more than one complaint. The alleged violations of substantive rules would have taken place in France in five cases and abroad in fifteen cases. Eight cases concerned climate and the environment, five concerned workers' rights and four concerned the human rights of local people (e.g. illegal taking of farm land). Eleven complaints had been directed against firms from the distribution sector (like supermarkets), Nine against energy companies and two against a bank (in addition to complaints against firms from various other sectors). Usually a coalition of several NGOs – in addition to directly affected people – filed the complaint. In addition to French or "local" NGOs (e.g. a Brazilian organization in cases about Amazon deforestation), US NGOs were coalition partners in several cases based on the French Act.

After the litigation against TotalEnergies, the second court case that was launched seems to be the suit commenced in 2019 by two NGOs, Sherpa and Uni Global Union, against a leading French call center organizer (*Teleperformance*) that in 2019 employed about 300.000 people in call centers globally. Plaintiffs argued that Teleperformance had not enacted a due diligence plan concerning the people working for it outside of France, whereas there were signs, according to plaintiffs, that working conditions in many foreign call centers of the group did not meet minimum standards.[197] Another case that drew some attention concerned French supermarket chain Casino. It was accused by several French and US NGOs as well as by a group of inhabitants of the Amazon forest that over long periods of time it had bought large amounts of beef from three suppliers who knew or should have known that their own suppliers, certain cattle ranches and beef producers in Brazil and Colombia, allegedly were responsible for illegal deforestation in the Amazon forest with negative impacts on local populations, allegedly constituting a violation of human rights of those local people.

The two campaigns just mentioned are examples of cases about environmental or human rights violations, not about corporate strategies. That is different for the recent high profile case launched against BNP Paribas, a major French

---

[196] Which tracks news about sustainability in economics and finance.
[197] Https://www.asso-sherpa.org/sherpa-and-uni-global-union-send-formal-notice-to-teleperformance-calling-on-the-world-leader-in-call-centers-to-strengthen-workers-rights.

bank[198], which stands accused of not doing enough to cut back funding to fossil fuel firms. The detailed 15-page complaint[199], filed by a coalition of NGOs at the initiative of Oxfam France and Amis de la Terre France, starts with a reminder addressed to BNP Paribas that it is under a duty to align its business with the goal of the Paris Climate Agreement to keep global warming below the 1.5°C limit, and that for a bank this entails that it should not fund any new fossil fuel projects – whereas according to the complaint, BNP Paribas is not only one of the most important funders of the oil industry, both through its lending and bond underwriting activities and because it offers a whole range of investment funds that invest in fossil fuel industries, but is also (according to the complaint) the most important financier world-wide of the "expansion of fossil energies".[200] The *plan de vigilance* of the bank is far too vague, according to the complaint, and while the bank had announced in 2017 but mainly in 2022 a whole range of "exclusions", meaning certain types of activities or clients it would no longer fund, these were, according to the plaintiffs, wholly insufficient to prevent serious harms to the planet's climate. The banking group ought to completely stop funding new fossil fuel projects but had explicitly refused to do so. A diligent *plan de vigilance* would contain a list with the names of the companies the bank had decided to defund, and a list of the fossil fuel companies it was still funding.

A case like the one against BNP Paribas illustrates that while formally, judicial proceedings against companies based on the Vigilance Act should be about deficiencies in the sustainability due diligence performed, in the accompanying risk management plan or in its implementation, in fact the "put on notice-procedure" provides NGOs with a channel through which to put pressure on companies to change their business model and which allows them to grab attention for their actions. This creates reputational pressure for the targeted companies (and even for their clients to the extent plaintiffs want BNP Paribas to publish the names of the "bad polluters" it had decided to stop funding). That such pressure can have at least an appearance of effect became clear at the 2023 AGM of BNP Paribas, where the group announced it would stop funding new gasfield projects.[201]

---

[198] The Brazilian subsidiary of BNP Paribas has been sued separately, in another case, because it allegedly funded the activities of one of the Brazilian beef producers that also supplies beef to supermarket chain Casino and that allegedly would be responsible for illegal deforestation.

[199] On file with Ghent law school.

[200] The complaint here relies on a report by several NGOs, *Banking on Climate Chaos -Fossil Fuel Finance Report 2022*, see https://www.ran.org/wp-content/uploads/2022/03/BOCC_2022_vSPREAD-1.pdf.

[201] S. White and K. Bryan, "BNP Paribas to stop funding gas projects as litigation risks mount", *FT,* 11 May 2023. The article reports that several NGOs said the move was a step in the right direction, but would only apply to direct loans and would leave room – to the dissatisfaction of the campaigners – for BNP to underwrite bonds used to finance gas projects.

I would argue that European policymakers, when finalizing the CSDD Directive, should see the French example as a warning and should not copy the French enforcement approach, relying on private enforcement through litigation by NGOs. Since, as we argued, litigation is singularly unsuitable to determine a company's strategy, it should not be encouraged.

VII. THE POLITICIZED CORPORATION – OR WHY EUROPE IS TOO RESTRICTIVE FOR SHAREHOLDER PROPOSALS AND TOO ACCOMMODATING FOR STAKEHOLDER LITIGATION

1. BOARDS ARE UNDER PRESSURE TO WEIGH INCOMMENSURABLE CONFLICTING STAKEHOLDER INTERESTS AND VALUES

I contend that the new NGO ESG activism, in its triple form of shareholder activism, strategic litigation, and mandatory dialogue with a broad array of stakeholders as part of a company's due diligence obligations, are making life more difficult for boards. It threatens to turn boards into unfocused decisionmakers that have to take the types of decisions that are normally the preserve of politicians, namely to decide what is in the general interest by balancing incommensurable values and interests of different stakeholder groups, including society at large without any guidance on how to rationally order these conflicting interests and values.[202] Roberto Tallarita has made a similar point for the US.[203] This threatens to undermine the effectiveness of the role of the board in determining corporate strategy and in the next section (VIII) I will argue this is probably made worse when companies install sustainability or ESG committees and/or lead directors in one tier boards.

I need to point out immediately that, by arguing that European boards are being politicized, I do not mean to say that the situation in Europe is (already) becoming similar to the one in the US, where in some states there is backlash against anything ESG, as part of the broader culture wars, and where boards have to make truly political decisions, like whether to protect their employees

---

[202] That that is the essence of political decision-making has been beautifully explained by Ch. Mouffe, *On the Political*, London, Routledge, 2005, 144 p. She coins the term "agonism" to refer to a "we/they relation where the conflicting parties, *although acknowledging that there is no rational solution to their conflict,* nevertheless recognize the legitimacy of their opponents" as the essence of the political (Mouffe, p. 20).

[203] R. Tallarita, "Stockholder politics" (fn. 22) at 1733.

from the consequences of the Supreme Court's abortion ruling (see below, VII.3). I only mean that boards are increasingly being buffeted from all sides by stakeholder demands, because stakeholders are turning themselves into small shareholders in order to be able to use the shareholder activist toolkit, and because due diligence legislation is increasing their leverage and possibilities to litigate.

As mentioned before, company law in Europe has been stakeholder-oriented for a long time, in the sense that it has always contained more statutory rules than Delaware law to protect the interest of creditors, and in certain countries has also given a voice to employees at the level of governance bodies, including the codetermination rules which allow employees to appoint up to half of the non-executive board members. But since the rise of the ESG movement, for the first time boards have been forced to take the interest of society at large into account when helping to set the company's strategy. The interests in large corporations of other stakeholders than shareholders, creditors and employees are now being defended more vigorously than ever by NGOs/civil society organisations, including shareholder advocacy groups that do not necessarily focus on shareholder interest, but rather focus on climate lobbying against companies, thereby defending the interest society at large has in combatting climate change.

Arguably, when shareholder advocacy groups battle climate change, they can be regarded as implementing the insight formalized by Hart and Zingales that when a firm's activities are inextricably linked with the creation of negative externalities, the firm should not maximize shareholder *value* (market value and profitability) but should pursue shareholder *welfare*[204]: a retail shareholder who has some limited investments through several funds in such a corporate sector, does not want such firms to pursue shareholder value at the expense of a polluted environment in which her children will grow up, or an economy where workers like herself are systematically exploited. I feel the Hart/Zingales framework is probably less convincing in companies with "old-style" controlling shareholders[205], who probably see and treat the company purely as a wealth-maximisation machine and are opposed to any measures that would deflect management's focus from the creation of shareholder value. In other words, such controlling shareholders are probably not interested in shareholder welfare: insofar as their investments contribute to their welfare, they have decided it will be through generating financial returns (often including private benefits of

---

[204] O. Hart & L. Zingales, 'Companies should maximize shareholder welfare not market value', *Journal of Law, Finance, and Accounting,* (2), 2017, 247–274.
[205] By which I mean not companies with important and perhaps influential but still minority blockholders, nor companies where three or four asset managers exercise a majority of votes, but companies where one or a concerted coalition of shareholders hold a majority, or at least more than 30% of voting rights.

control). But for non-controlling shareholders, or at least for retail investors and the index funds and pension funds that "represent" them, the Hart-Zingales way of thinking is indeed apposite.

My argument in the next section is that shareholder proposals that basically take away the interest-balancing act that boards have to perform and allow shareholders to instruct the board on how to balance conflicting stakeholder interests, are an unwarranted encroachment on the board's powers.

2. THE DISTINCTION BETWEEN DESIRABLE AND UNDESIRABLE SHAREHOLDER PROPOSALS – AND WHY GERMANY AND THE NETHERLANDS SHOULD BECOME MORE TOLERANT OF PROPOSALS THAT TOUCH UPON CORPORATE STRATEGY

a. Shareholder proposals should be allowed to touch upon corporate strategy

As indicated in section V, in major continental European economies like Germany and the Netherlands, and perhaps also in France, corporate law specialists (and in the Netherlands: courts and even statute) assume that the board should set strategy without the intervention of the general meeting. Therefore, in those countries, shareholder proposals that impinge on strategy are considered undesirable and the board cannot be forced to put them on the agenda of the general meeting. I think this approach is too restrictive and is undesirable. It should be refined.[206]

First, most shareholder activism, whatever the tactics used and whether they involve shareholder proposals or not, concerns strategic matters. That in itself cannot be a valid objection against shareholder proposals being discussed or voted on at the general meeting. When activists try to bring about or block a merger or encourage divestments, these transactions can have long-term impacts and can certainly be considered strategic.[207] Proxy fights intended to have board members proposed by activists appointed to the board are strategic as well, even though only indirectly: they are intended to influence the composition of the corporate body that will determine strategy.

---

[206] It seems Australian case law on shareholder proposals that touch on corporate strategy is also very restrictive about them, similar to the situation in the Netherlands, see S. Bottomley, "Rethinking the law on shareholder-initiated resolutions at company general meetings", *Melbourne University Law Review*, 43(1), 2019, 94–132 who analyses this case law and then pleads for a legislative intervention to facilitate more shareholder proposals.

[207] This is not the case for activism that is only intended to influence the price offered to shareholders in M&A transactions.

On the other hand, many shareholder proposals do not interfere with strategy development. An example are disclosure proposals. These demand, for example, that firms offer more transparency about their policies concerning such issues as workforce or top management diversity, or about a firm's lobbying efforts concerning climate change regulation. Many "social" proposals, e.g. about minimum pay or allowing unionization of the workforce, will be either about respecting workers' legal rights, or about applying "best practices", and likewise cannot really be said to encroach on corporate strategy. Somewhat more intrusive are proposals that want the company to develop explicit policies concerning a certain area of concern, for instance policies about diversity, or emissions reduction policies. Asking the board to develop a policy and disclose it in the form of a written plan will almost always entail that the proposal's sponsor suggests the policy goes in a certain direction, e.g. increasing diversity at top management level, or reducing emissions faster than until now. But as long as the proposal does not contain prescriptive elements about how the policy should be developed, and simply boils down to an exhortation that the board should devote attention to a certain issue, I believe the proposal does not really limit the freedom of the board to develop corporate strategies. I believe legal systems like the Dutch and the German legal system should be more accommodating to such proposals. If NGOs acting as shareholders are prevented from using the shareholder proposal tool to vent their opinion, they will more easily switch to litigation, which is always undesirable.

b.   But prescriptive divestment and climate proposals are unwarranted

There is, however, a category of shareholder proposals that is undesirable. These are proposals that prescribe a certain strategy or already fill it out. A typical example are the proposals that want to instruct the board to divest a certain branch of activity (e.g. proposals to spin-off all fossil fuel activities and completely, within a certain time-path designed in the proposal, transform the company into a renewable energy company). The fact that there is probably no European or North-American legal system where the general meeting of a public company can issue a binding instruction to the board for such matters, does not diminish the fact that votes on them at the general meeting directly encroach on the board's strategy-setting powers. This is even more the case for the not uncommon proposals, or demands formulated as a shareholder question at the AGM, that companies reduce their CO_2 emissions by a certain quantity towards a specific date (e.g. proposals saying that an oil major, or a supermarket chain, should by 2030 reduce its emissions by 45% compared to their 2019 levels).

Such specific climate action plan proposals ask of companies, that is their boards, to develop policies the way politicians have to do this. By this I mean that these forms of activism ask the board to weigh against each other various stakeholder interests that are incompatible, in that a corporate decision or policy cannot serve the interests of one stakeholder group without hurting the interests of another one. These conflicting interests are associated with incommensurable values, and neither economics, ethics, management science, political science nor any other set of rules or methodologies to guide decision-making can help to order these values, interests and preferences in a rational or even well-considered way. Decision-makers – in our context: boards – often have to cut a Gordian knot and do what they think is best, provided they have no conflict of interest and provided they have decided on an informed basis, taking into account all relevant interests. Take a European oil major that in the spring of 2022, shortly after the outbreak of the Ukraine war and with Europe in the midst of an energy crisis, needs to consider its corporate strategy with attention for climate issues. In the interest of society at large and because it knows it will be expected to contribute to the pursuit of the goals of the Paris Climate Agreement and of the European Commission's Green Deal, the company wants to reduce its CO_2 emissions. In its own interest and especially that of its shareholders, it wants to develop a long term strategy that will generate nice financial returns and it realizes that someday, it will need to transform itself into a renewable energy company. But at present and in the next few years, it is clear that investments in oil will generate nice returns that at least in 2022 will very much exceed the returns of investments in renewables. The country where the company is headquartered wants the company to contribute to energy security by providing sufficient amounts of oil in the near future, especially now that Russian gas is no longer available. The government of that country tries to keep energy affordable for middle class and low-income consumers during the Ukraine war, and expects or hopes companies will cooperate with that goal, in the case of oil majors by supplying sufficient oil to the country's economy. Such a European oil major in 2022 had to develop a policy concerning a gradual switch to renewable energy and reduction of climate impact by balancing conflicting interests and values in exactly the same way as European governments had to develop a climate and energy security policy in that same year. Just like even the constitutional and administrative courts are not allowed to second-guess government policy by themselves developing, through judicial review, their own version of a national climate policy, developing such a corporate climate policy is something that should be left to the board, free from specific instructions from shareholders, even through precatory shareholder proposals on which the general meeting votes.[208]

---

[208] It is clear that such thinking rightfully also inspired the judge in the ClientEarth v. Shell derivative action discussed in section II.1 *supra* fn. 37 to refuse to grant permission for this derivative claim to proceed.

c. *The link with the debate on stakeholderist directors' duties*

The criticism of such prescriptive shareholder proposals that encroach too far on the board's strategy-setting competence, is very much related to one of the convincing criticisms against a stakeholderist approach to directors' duties. During the debates that raged among European corporate law scholars (and attorneys) especially during the 1980s and 1990s[209] about whether boards should be guided by a "broad" (stakeholderist) or narrow (shareholder-focused) interpretation of "the corporate interest", many scholars convincingly pointed out that imposing a broad conception of the corporate interest on boards made no sense because nobody could provide boards with criteria on how to weigh conflicting stakeholder interests against each other, or in other words how to rank those conflicting stakeholder preferences.[210] In other words, nobody could offer an algorithm, or even vague guidelines that could help the board to operationalize the (possible) instruction to pursue the interests of all stakeholders. In the recent debates about corporate purpose and stakeholderism[211], this convincing argument has resurfaced, most elaborately and cogently in the criticism levied by Lucian Bebchuk and Roberto Tallarita against stakeholderism.[212] Bebchuk and co-authors have added to the existing arguments by showing in empirical research that at least in the US, boards and executives do not act in accordance with stakeholderist rhetoric: they

---

[209] In France, the debate started earlier under the influence of the "institutional theory" of the corporation as propagated by J. Pailluseau in his influential (among scholars) *La société anonyme. Technique d'organisation d'entreprise*, Paris, Sirey, 1967, 259 p.

[210] The European literature is enormous. One of the best analyses was J.E. Parkinson, *Corporate Power and Responsibility. Issues in the Theory of Company Law*, Oxford: Clarendon Press 1993, e.g. at p. 82 ff. See also H. De Wulf *Taak en loyauteitsplicht van het bestuur in de naamloze vennootschap*,(Ph.D. thesis) Antwerp, Intersentia, 2002, 521–529 (where I argued "the corporate interest" broadly construed was a concept that cannot be falsified or operationalized, that it is therefore useless in guiding directors in their decisions, let alone courts in their review of such decisions, and that generally, the concept however construed serves no useful purpose in judicial review of board decisions, e.g. with a view to their annulment by courts on the basis of art. 2:42 Belgian Companies Code). For a summary of the views on the meaning of "the corporate interest" in continental European legal scholarship (Belgium, France, Germany, the Netherlands) in the 1950–1999 period, see A. François, *Het vennootschapsbelang in het Belgisch vennootschapsrecht. Inhoud en grondslagen*, Antwerp, Intersentia, 1999, 401 ff. and the cornucopia of references therein.

[211] A rich summary of the original phases (2018–2020) of the purpose debate, with references to all the major contributions (in English) at the time, is G. Ferrarini, "Redefining corporate purpose: sustainability as a game changer" in D. Busch, G. Ferrarini & S. Grünewald (eds.), *Sustainable Finance in Europe*, Palgrave Macmillan, 2021, 85–150. A recent important contribution from a mainly American perspective on how corporate law is becoming "welfarist" and therefore to a certain extent stakeholderist (though the authors suggest the "movement" may have a bigger impact on politics than on private enterprise) is M. Kahan and E. Rock, "Governance Welfarism" (December 22, 2022), European Corporate Governance Institute – Law Working Paper No. 683/2023, available at https://ssrn.com/abstract=4328626.

[212] L.A. Bebchuk & R. Tallarita, 'The Illusory Promise of Stakeholder Governance', *Cornell Law Review*, 106, 2020, 91–178.

negotiate and take decisions in the interest of those who appoint and dismiss them (shareholders) and in the interest of management, but not in the interest of other stakeholders.[213] It would be interesting to do similar research in European jurisdictions where employees have serious governance powers. One thinks of the anecdote where the CEO of Volkswagen was forced out mainly under the influence of employee representatives in the non-executive supervisory board[214] – an example of non-executive directors clearly "bargaining" in favor of others than shareholders. But the point that nobody can guide directors in how to balance the conflicting interests of stakeholders, holds in a system where non-shareholders have serious governance powers. It is far *easier* (although not necessarily more desirable) for boards to serve the interest of only one stakeholder group, such as shareholders, whose interest are relatively uniform – the classic justification for only allowing shareholders to vote.[215] The irrationalities of decision-making known from social choice theory[216] are less likely in "coherent" groups with one overriding common interest – firm value – and hence more or less uniform values.[217]

The impossibility of finding objective criteria for deciding between incommensurable conflicting interests and values is an important justification for not allowing courts to second-guess a board's strategic decisions. Such business judgements are protected by the business judgement rule in Delaware, and in Europe by various doctrines that require judges to show restraint in reviewing the decisions of corporate bodies, such as in Belgium the doctrine of *marginale toetsing* (marginal review only) or in Germany doctrines about limits to *materielle Inhaltskontrolle* (material judicial review of the content of corporate decisions). If *ex post* review of such decisions is to be limited to egregious cases of mismanagement ("waste", "intent to defraud minority interests", …), the case for limiting *ex ante* instructions on strategy to the board issued either in the form of shareholder proposal instructions from the general meeting or injunctions ordered by a court, is all the more convincing.

---

[213] See L.A. Bebchuk, K. Kastiel, and A. Toniolo, "How Twitter Pushed Stakeholders Under The Bus" (January 19, 2023), forthcoming, *Stanford Journal of Law, Business, and Finance*, 28, 2023, available at https://ssrn.com/abstract=4330393 and references therein to earlier work of Bebchuk and co-authors proving the same point, such as L.A. Bebchuk, K. Kastiel, and R. Tallarita, "For Whom Corporate Leaders Bargain" *Southern California Law Review*, 94, 2021, 1467–1560.

[214] See J. Miller, "Herbert Diess ousted as Volkswagen boss", *FT*, July 22, 2022.

[215] H. Hansmann, *The Ownership of Enterprise*, Cambridge Mass., Harvard University Press, 1996.

[216] As expressed, for instance, in the Condorcet voting paradox or in Arrow's impossibility theorem; see for a formal and informal advanced introduction to social choice theory A. Sen *Collective Choice and Social Welfare* (expanded edition), Penguin, 2017, 640 p.

[217] Even though such matters as time horizons may differ and even though many investors do not care very much about the firm value of individual firms, as long as their whole portfolio generates a good return.

Therefore, the same criteria that I proposed to judge the admissibility of shareholder proposals, can also be used to help courts determine whether they can accept stakeholder litigation aimed at influencing corporate strategy. If an NGO sues a company for damages because it has treated employees in a (foreign) mine almost like slaves, or has illegally expropriated local farmers in order to clear land for a palm oil plantation, then the NGO is simply trying to get the company civilly punished for violating clear mandatory rules. Such claims should be admissible and the judge can not only award damages but also issue cease and desist orders (which are a form of injunction). But if Milieudefensie sues Shell in order to obtain a court order for Shell to reduce its CO2 emissions with 45% by 2030 compared to 2019 levels, then such claims should at least be found unfounded – if they are admissible – because they are asking the court both to replace politically elected or appointed state regulators and to determine the strategy of a corporation in a detailed, prescriptive way. This is not just undesirable, it is illegal.[218] I think a similar attitude is warranted towards the efforts by a coalition of NGOs who are threatening to sue BNP Paribas, a major French bank, in order to stop it from funding fossil fuel companies like the oil majors. Shareholder proposals to that effect should, in my view, not be taken into consideration by the general meeting for the same reason, whereas shareholder proposals that enjoin the board of a bank to take a stance and develop and announce a policy about funding of the fossil fuel industry, should be considered legitimate and can be put to a vote.

d. *Illustrations of the right approach*

The right attitude was recently taken by a court in Braunschweig in a suit against Volkswagen. NGOs including Milieudefensie sued the three major German carmakers (Volkswagen, BMW, Mercedes-Benz) to demand an injunction ordering them to stop the production of fossil fuel cars by 2030 (this was before the EU had decided to phase out most of that production in the non-truck sector by 2035). The district court in Braunschweig rightfully rejected such a claim against Volkswagen, not based on the argument that courts cannot be used to determine a company's strategy, but on the – in this case even better (and related) – ground that private companies like Volkswagen, that are not directly subject to treaties like the Paris Climate Agreement and that by definition are not legally bound by soft law, aspirational environmental and climate goals, cannot be held, on the basis of tort law, to a higher standard than governments

---

[218] I tried to explain in e.g. H. De Wulf, "Some thoughts on the regulatory use of tort law in a corporate context" in F. Mourlon Beernaert, G. Collard, D. Szafran, & D. Willermain (eds.), *Liber Amicorum Xavier Dieux : hommage d'exception à un esprit libre*, Brussels, Larcier, 2022, Vol. 1, 731–770 why I think the the Hague ruling in the Shell climate case would at least in France and Belgium have to be regarded as incompatible with tort law, and as a violation of the constitutional principle of separation of powers.

and than the standard imposed by mandatory regulation in implementing a climate strategy.[219]

I think the attitude BlackRock took in 2022 towards climate shareholder proposals is also about the right one, and one that could inspire European rulemakers about shareholder proposals. 2022 saw shareholders in US companies offering less support for climate-related shareholder proposals. According to an analysis by The Conference Board, investors submitted more environmental and social proposals than ever before in 2022 – namely 389 – but support dropped from 37 to 33 percent.[220] Investors cited as reasons that the board should direct corporate strategy[221] and that some proposals were too prescriptive, e.g. when they prescribed specific emission reduction targets or when the proposals to demand banks to stop financing fossil fuel industries, only gained 10% of the vote support. BlackRock had indeed announced before the start of the proxy season that it would not support proposals that were too prescriptive.[222] It was perhaps telling that at ExxonMobil, where the previous year they had supported the nomination of two directors by Bluebell, they now voted against a proposal that asked ExxonMobil to set specific targets for greenhouse gas emissions, whereas they did approve of a proposal asking the company to engage in scenario planning for a range of energy transition pathways.[223] I think the attitude of BlackRock is commendable: it points towards the right approach for European regulators to take to shareholder proposals that allegedly encroach on the board's power to determine corporate strategy.

The approach I favour is probably similar to the SEC's former policy about the "ordinary business exception" to shareholder proposals[224] as explained in its now rescinded 2019 Staff legal Bulletin no 14 K (CF), and thus before the 2021 changes to that policy with its 14L Bulletin.[225] Rule 14a-8 of the Securities Exchange Act

---

[219] See Landgericht Braunschweig ruling 6 O 3931/21 of 24 February 2023, as discussed in "Zivilklage gegen Volkswagen AG wegen Verringerung der CO2-Emissionen erfolglos", https://www.die-aktiengesellschaft.de/82788.htm (last consulted on April 30 2023).

[220] B. Masters, "Shareholders back away from green petitions in US proxy voting season", *FT*, July 1 2022. Analysis by Blackrock of data provided by ISS said there was a drop from 36% of the vote-support in 2021 to 27% in 2022, see B. Masters, "Blackrock pulls back support for climate and social resolutions", *FT*, July 26 2022. The same article mentions that BlackRock supported 43% of environmental and social proposals in 2021 but that this dropped to 24% of the total number of proposals in 2022.

[221] See the quote in the FT "green petitions" article (previous footnote) from the head of stewardship of stewardship for State street Global Advisers.

[222] See the statement in BlackRock Investment Stewardship, *2022 climate-related shareholder proposals more prescriptive than 2021*, available at https://www.blackrock.com/corporate/literature/publication/commentary-bis-approach-shareholder-proposals.pdf.

[223] B. Masters, "Shareholders back away from green petitions in US proxy voting season", *FT*, July 1 2022.

[224] See Rule 17 C.F.R. §240.14a-8 on shareholder proposals.

[225] For the latter, see https://www.sec.gov/corpfin/staff-legal-bulletin-14l-shareholder-proposals.

1934 contains the US federal rules on shareholder proposals and establishes that a company must as a rule include a shareholder proposal (submitted by an eligible shareholder) in its proxy materials, unless the company can invoke one of the 13 exclusion grounds listed in the Rule. Companies that want to exclude certain proposals will typically try to obtain a so-called "no-action letter" from the SEC.[226] Rule 14a-8(i)(7) is the exclusion ground for a shareholder proposal that *"deals with a matter relating to the company's ordinary business operations."* It has never been very clear what the contours are of the "ordinary business" concept[227], but it does seem clear that the fact that a shareholder proposal touches upon corporate policies or strategies is not in itself sufficient grounds for a shareholder proposal to be disqualified. However, when a proposal becomes too prescriptive, it could be blocked as being an attempt at forbidden micromanagement. According to the SEC's policy guidance – which is not binding legal guidance – in its now rescinded 2019 Bulletin 14K:

> *"In considering arguments for exclusion based on micromanagement, and consistent with the Commission's views, we look to whether the proposal seeks intricate detail or imposes a specific strategy, method, action, outcome or timeline for addressing an issue, thereby supplanting the judgment of management and the board. Thus, a proposal framed as a request that the company consider, discuss the feasibility of, or evaluate the potential for a particular issue generally would not be viewed as micromanaging matters of a complex nature. However, a proposal, regardless of its precatory nature, that prescribes specific timeframes or methods for implementing complex policies,*

---

[226] J. Cox and R. Thomas, "The SEC's Shareholder Proposal Rule: Creating A Corporate Public Square", *Columbia Business Law Review*, 2021, 3, 1147–1198 provide a history of the evolution of Rule 14a-8 and make the interesting suggestion that, since boards tend to be insulated and lack information, shareholder proposals can function like a "town square", allowing a broad range of shareholders to canvass opinions that, even if such proposals are not supported by a large number of shareholders, may provide the board with useful information. This raises the question whether shareholder proposals are not a very expensive and procedurally complicated way of allowing shareholders to voice their opinions. In Europe, the potentially disruptive but far cheaper method of allowing shareholders to ask questions and give speeches at the general meeting, seem more suitable to provide such a townhall square function. But this admittedly only works because – and as long – as meetings are held physically, in relatively small countries where shareholders travel to meetings, as until today they still often do in continental Europe. Experiences with online meetings during the COVID19 epidemic showed that online meetings do not lend themselves very well to critical questioning of the board by participating shareholders.

[227] It appears from SEC policy announcements made in various so-called "Staff Legal Bulletins" (it seems esp. SLB 14 E, K and L are relevant for this matter, though E and K have now been rescinded) that the ordinary business exception permits exclusion of proposals that are *"fundamental to management's ability to run the company on a day-to-day basis"*. Proposals that focus on policy issues that are deemed to be so significant that they transcend ordinary business cannot be excluded. Shareholder proposals that engage in micromanagement, *"by probing too deeply into matters of a complex nature upon which shareholders, as a group, would not be in a position to make an informed judgment"*, can be excluded. In 2021, the SEC's Staff Legal Bulletin No. 14L announced changes in the no-action letter policy, including about the ordinary business exception, in general making it more difficult for companies to invoke the exception. The details do not need to detain us here.

consistent with the Commission's guidance, may run afoul of micromanagement. In our view, the precatory nature of a proposal does not bear on the degree to which a proposal micromanages."[228]

I think those views were commendable and could guide policy changes in European countries that are too restrictive for shareholder proposals. However, in 2021 (when the ownership thresholds for introducing shareholder proposals were also lowered) the SEC changed its guidance with its 14L Bulletin, making clear it wanted to facilitate shareholder proposals on ESG matters by reintroducing its 1976 exception to the ordinary business exclusion rule for proposals about significant social policy issues, and by "clarifying" that the "micromanagement"-possibility to bar proposals should not necessarily exclude proposals that contain specific timelines or methods to achieve a desired goal, such as emission reductions. But it gives as an example that illustrates its new guidance, its refusal in 2021 to grant a no-action letter in a case where a shareholder proposal wanted to impose specific greenhouse gas emission reductions on a company and its products, but without imposing a specific method for doing so – which creates unclarity about whether suggesting specific methods is acceptable or not.

In any case, I think the newest SEC guidance would be hard to swallow for policymakers in European countries such as Germany and the Netherlands, and as explained above, I personally also think that shareholder proposals that impose specific quantified targets with a timeline, are too intrusive concerning strategy to be desirable.

To conclude, my recommendation to courts and policymakers in the Netherlands and Germany would therefore be to take a more nuanced approach to shareholder proposals that impinge on board competences. That a proposal

---

[228] Excerpt from SLB 14K (CF) (October 16 2019, now rescinded and replaced by SBL14L) (internal footnotes omitted) where it was added: *"For example, this past season we agreed that a proposal seeking annual reporting on "short-, medium- and long-term greenhouse gas targets aligned with the greenhouse gas reduction goals established by the Paris Climate Agreement to keep the increase in global average temperature to well below 2 degrees Celsius and to pursue efforts to limit the increase to 1.5 degrees Celsius" was excludable on the basis of micromanagement. In our view, the proposal micromanaged the company by prescribing the method for addressing reduction of greenhouse gas emissions. We viewed the proposal as effectively requiring the adoption of time-bound targets (short, medium and long) that the company would measure itself against and changes in operations to meet those goals, thereby imposing a specific method for implementing a complex policy. In contrast, we did not concur with the excludability of a proposal seeking a report "describing if, and how, [a company] plans to reduce its total contribution to climate change and align its operations and investments with the Paris [Climate] Agreement's goal of maintaining global temperatures well below 2 degrees Celsius." The proposal was not excludable because the proposal transcended ordinary business matters and did not seek to micromanage the company to such a degree that exclusion would be appropriate."*

touches upon matters on which only the board can take a binding decision, should not be sufficient ground for the board/the company to refuse to put such a proposal on the agenda of a general meeting. Only proposals that are too prescriptive, in that they impose a specific strategy on the board, should be refused. Although it would be naïve to assume that shareholder proposals and litigation about corporate, e.g. climate strategy are communicating vessels, and that if shareholder proposals are admitted more easily, such litigation will diminish, I do think the pressure to litigate will at least be alleviated. Perhaps more importantly, the legitimacy of such litigation – which is always the worst solution to stakeholder conflict – will be diminished. Dutch policymakers and Dutch and German attorneys and scholars who defend the current very restrictive approach to shareholder proposals in those two countries, also seem to me to have an unrealistic image of the way corporate strategy is determined. It is fine to write into statute that the (executive) board has exclusive competence to determine the strategy of the corporation, but this will not prevent non-executive supervisory boards and controlling shareholders or blockholders to work with the board to help it develop a strategy. Nor should it. A supervisory board that totally neglects to talk about strategy with the executive board, fails in part of its monitoring duty and does not play the corporate governance role that it should play. At the same time, in companies with a controlling shareholder, it is unrealistic to expect that that shareholder will not try to influence strategy setting. Indeed when SRD II, national corporate governance codes and stewardship codes encourage shareholder engagement, such engagement can only be meaningful if it also pertains to strategy, as long as nobody gets it into their heads that they can *dictate* a specific strategy to the board.

3. ESG IS EVEN MORE POLITICIZED IN THE US

While in Europe boards, under pressure from external stakeholders, increasingly have to take the *type* of decision that politicians have to take (namely cutting Gordian knots in situations where incommensurable stakeholder values and interests clash), the situation is still largely different from that in the US, where boards take decisions that are viewed as political.[229] The debate about

---

[229] Just one example are shareholder proposals (at least 22 were identified by the FT) that demand that companies produce more detailed disclosure of their "abortion policies", and about how their workforce is affected by the reversal of *Roe v. Wade* by the US supreme Court in *Dobbs v. Jackson Women's Health Organization*, see P. Temple-West, "Shareholders bring US abortion battle to the boardroom", *FT,* January 10 2023. See more generally L. Stewart (Morningstar Inc.), "Proxy-voting insights: voting on politics", April 2 2032, https://corpgov.law.harvard.edu/2023/04/02/proxy-voting-insights-voting-on-politics/ (full Morningstar report available at https://www.morningstar.com/lp/esg-proxy-voting-on-politics), focusing on how many shareholder proposals concerning political lobbying disclosures and about climate change were launched in the US in 2020–2022 and how the 10 largest US asset managers voted on them.

the involvement of corporations and their investors in ESG issues is very much alive in the US, and in certain states (where Republicans are in control of state political bodies) there is a clear backlash against ESG. Some states like Texas and West Virginia have prepared bills that would ban state agencies from doing business with asset managers and investment funds that are too ESG-focused. Texas seems to have instructed state pension funds to divest themselves from funds that exclude fossil fuel companies from their portfolio, whereas Florida has banned its state pension funds from considering ESG factors in their investments. BlackRock has been a prominent target of such state divestment efforts, because of the relatively vocal stance of its CEO, Larry Fink, on ESG and corporate purpose[230], and no doubt also simply because it is the largest asset manager in the US, and thus potentially influential. But attorney-generals from 21 states also targeted leading proxy advisors ISS and Glass Lewis in a letter accusing them of failing their fiduciary duties because of their support for climate proposals.[231] In 2022, "conservative" shareholder activists, like the National Legal and Policy Centre and the National Center for Public Policy Research's Free enterprise Project, allegedly submitted a record number of shareholder proposals, though this still only amounted to 5% of all shareholder proposals.[232] A recent iteration of the debate is the saga around the Department

---

[230] See B. Masters, "BlackRock denies Republican claims of climate 'activism'", *FT*, September 7 2022, mentioning 19 Republican attorneys-general writing a letter to BlackRock in August 2022 accusing the firm of prioritising activism over its fiduciary duty towards state pension funds. At the same time, BlackRock, which in 2022 shied away from supporting shareholder proposals on climate that it found "too prescriptive", e.g. because they wanted to set specific emission reduction targets for individual companies, found itself under attack from the (UK-based) Bluebell Capital Partners activist fund for "ESG hypocrisy", i.e. not doing enough on ESG issues, see B. Masters, "Blackrock chief Larry Fink pressured to resign over 'ESG hypocrisy'", *FT*, 6 December 2022. Remarkably, Bluebell objected in particular to BlackRock's new (2022) "Voting Choice Program", which is a platform that allows some of BlackRocks largest institutional investor clients to vote directly at AGMs, without using the voting services of Blackrock, enabling these investors to directly express their own preferences through a vote (see https://www.blackrock.com/corporate/about-us/investment-stewardship/2021-blackrock-voting-choice). In other words, Bluebell did not want these pension funds and other investors to express their own preferences on ESG, but wanted BlackRock to use its substantial power at AGMs (based on its asset management services) to systematically support ESG proposals at AGMs. Bluebell lamented that its own ESG proposals at Glencore and Solvay had not been supported by BlackRock.

[231] P. Temple-West, "Republicans target proxy advisors ISS and Glass Lewis in ESG backlash", *FT*, 17 January 2023.

[232] See A. Edgecliff-Johnson and B. Masters, "Political proxies: conservative activists file record shareholder proposals", *FT*, March 28 2022. From the examples given, it seems many of the 'conservative' proposals are about the same topics as 'liberal' proposals (e.g. about board diversity, or a proposal criticizing Disney for using a subcontractor from China that was active in Xinjiang province, where according to US Congress China is committing genocide), but they regularly have a different intent: the article cites a 'conservative'-backed proposal demanding a racial equity audit at Johnson & Johnson, but because the sponsor (NCPPR) was concerned that anti-racist training at companies was itself "deeply racist" and that employees deemed "non-diverse" could be discriminated against.

of Labour rules. In November 2022, the DOL had revoked Trump-era rules that banned retirement fund managers to consider ESG factors in their investments. But in early 2023, US Congress overturned the more lenient new rules, which led president Biden to exercise the first veto of his presidency, in order to block the anti-ESG rules.[233]

Strikingly, shareholder proposals on ESG topics are far more widespread in the US than in Europe, as is clear from the empirical research of Tallarita and Bakker in particular.[234] It is unlikely that this is because US investors are more ESG focused than investors (many of them US asset managers) in European companies or than European investors. A far likelier explanation is that it has become far easier in the US than in most continental European jurisdictions to submit shareholder proposals, not only because the ownership thresholds in the US[235] are lower than in many European countries, but also because the US federal "ordinary business"-exception – barring shareholders from submitting proposals that would interfere with the daily management of companies, thus attempting to micromanage them[236] – is far less restrictive than the prohibition for general meetings in Germany or the Netherlands and possibly France to interfere with corporate strategy.

VIII. BOARD EFFECTIVENESS AND BOARD STRUCTURE: SUSTAINABILITY COMMITTEES AND ESG LEAD DIRECTORS

When companies, under pressure from ESG activists, adapt the structure of their boards by introducing a sustainability committee (or committee with a different name but similar functions) and/or nominate a "lead director" for ESG matters[237], this may be good for their "ESG performance" and oversight of such

---

[233] See for this story about the DOL's rules e.g. S. Rajgopal, A. Srivastava and R. Zhao, "Do political anti-ESG sanctions have any economic substance?", available at clsbluesky.law.columbia.edu/2023/04/04/do-political-anti-esg-sanctions-have-any-economic-substance/ (April 4 2023).

[234] *Supra* section IV.

[235] The ownership threshold in Rule 14a-8 was amended in 2020, see e.g. https://www.sec.gov/news/press-release/2020–220.

[236] See discussion at section VII.2.d.

[237] See, for example, the 2021 campaign of IICCG (Institutional investors climate change group) to have companies not only organize an annual vote on the follow-up of their climate transition plans, but also appoint a lead director responsible for these climate plans, as reported in A. Mooney, 'Big investors demand vote on companies' net zero plans', *FT,* 30 July 2021. See also the plea by a group of leading Dutch corporate law scholars for the installation by listed companies of a separate "societal advisory board", in addition to the supervisory and executive boards and with whom the official two boards would meet regularly: J.W. Winter, J.M. De Jongh, J.B.S. Hijink, L. Timmerman, and G. van Solinge, "Naar een zorgplicht voor

matters, but could be detrimental to the strategic role of the board. Perhaps a "solution" to this trade-off[238] could be found in switching to a dual, two tier board structure, with the supervisory board concentrating on oversight and the executive board on strategy. But while the ideas put forward in this section are based on research by economists, I want to stress that I'm fully aware that my conclusions here are far more tentative than in the rest of the article, and that far more research on these issues is needed. This section is therefore more about the development of a research hypothesis than about drawing firm conclusions or making sound policy recommendations.

1. SUSTAINABILITY COMMITTEES AND ESG LEAD DIRECTORS

As part of societal and investor pressure on firms to devote more attention to stakeholder and ESG issues, it is sometimes suggested companies should install a sustainability committee, or appoint a "lead director" who's the target person within the board for ESG matters. Once CSDD legislation will apply throughout the EU instead of only in France and Germany, pressure to bolster the board's oversight function concerning ESG matters (which are at the heart of CSDD legislation) will likely increase.

Many companies already have a sustainability committee (which goes by various names; in the early days "environmental committee" was sometimes used and today they are also often called "ESG committees")[239] within the board[240], and

---

bestuurders en commissarissen tot verantwoordelijke deelname aan het maatschappelijk verkeer. Een antwoord op reacties". *Ondernemingsrecht*, (1), 2021, 31–39, section 5 of this article.

[238] Two articles studying trade-offs between different expected roles of boards are J. Winter and E. Van Looy, "Boards on task: developing a comprehensive understanding of the performance of boards", in M. Belcredi and G. Ferrarini (eds.,) *Boards and shareholders in listed European companies*, Cambridge, Cambridge university Press, 2013, 225–250 and J. A. Mccahery, E. P.M. Vermeulen, M Histake, "Understanding the role of the board of directors: what is the right balance between managerial oversight and value creation" in H. Birkmose, M. Neville and K.E. Sörsensen, *Boards of directors in European companies*, Wolters Kluwer, 2013, 301–325.

[239] On such committees, see International Finance Corporation (part of the World Bank Group), *Sustainability committees: structure and practices*, 2021, 80 p.; D. Salvioni, and F. Gennari, "Stakeholder Perspective of Corporate Governance and CSR Committees" (December 1, 2019) available at https://ssrn.com/abstract=3523684. For Japan, see S. Kozuka, "Introducing Sustainability into the Japanese Corporate Governance: The Shift to the "New Capitalism" or the Continued Gradual Transformation?", May 14, 2022, available at https://ssrn.com/abstract=4109982.

[240] For instance, J. Burke, R. Hotaish and U Hotaish "The Heterogeneity of Board-Level Sustainability Committees and Corporate Social Performance", *Journal of Business Ethics* 154(4), 1–26 report that *in the US* in 2010, 65% of S&P 100 and 20% of Russell 1000 companies had such a committee, and that, predictably, their prevalence was greater in environmentally sensitive industries. In 2020, 73 of 151 *Italian companies* that produced a non-financial

this development predates the increased attention to ESG matters from about 2016 onwards. Usually such a committee is not exclusively composed of board members, but also contains several officers. It seems certain that the adoption of such committees is on the rise, but that far fewer companies have one, compared to an audit committee or a remuneration committee. Empirical data is patchy, but makes sufficiently clear that they are not adopted at the same rate in every west-European country. There is not enough empirical research yet to say anything reliable about their effectiveness, but there is no research showing an effect of sustainability committees on firm (financial) performance, whereas there is some research showing higher quality disclosure on some ESG topics in firms with a sustainability committee.[241]

In the US, Strine and co-authors[242] rightfully argue that companies should be wary of adding too many committees to the board, because this could prevent an integrated approach to ESG matters, which they see as part of or at least closely linked to the board's compliance oversight function under *Caremark*.[243] At the same time these authors contest the view that, because ESG oversight should be a matter for the whole board, therefore no separate committee should be set up. They assert that some level of specialization is required for effective oversight of these matters. We disagree with the latter contention. Of course explicitly

---

management statement on the basis of the European Non-Financial Reporting Directive had a sustainability committee, up from 54 in 2019: N. Linciano, A. Ciavarella, G. Di Stefano, L. Pierantoni, and L Piermattei, *Rapporto 2020 sulla rendicontazione non finanziaria delle società quotate italiane*, June 23, 2021, CONSOB Statistics and Analyses 2020, available at https://ssrn.com/abstract=3872828. *For Germany*, Ph. Jaspers, "Nachhaltigkeit-und ESG-Ausschüsse des Aufsichtsrat" *Die Aktiengesellschaft*, 2022, 310 lists 10 companies in the Dax40 that have such a committee, and cites a report based on a poll in which "many more" German listed firms indicated they intended to set up such a committee. *For France*, research by the AMF (financial markets supervisor that also plays a role in monitoring the implementation of the French corporate governance code) found that in 2021, almost two-thirds of SBF 120 companies had a committee in charge of CSR matters, compared with 25% in 2015, see the report on French governance arrangements at https://thelawreviews.co.uk/title/the-corporate-governance-review/france. *For Australia*, L. Law Chapple, Z. Chen and Y. Zhang, "Sustainability Committee Effectiveness and CSR Assurance", March 10, 2017, available at https://ssrn.com/abstract=2967165 report that 26% of the ASX 200 companies (200 of the largest Australian companies) in their sample had a sustainability committee in the 2010–2014 period and that during that period, that percentage was stable.

[241] See J. Burke, R. Hotaish and U. Hotaish, (fn. 242). Like earlier research, the article – which deals with US companies in the 2003–2013 period – found no link between sustainability committees and firm performance, but did find a positive influence of these committees on sustainability disclosure by companies. The same finding (but for a more recent period) was reported for a sample of US and non-US firms by H. Driss, W. Drobetz, S. El Ghoul and O. Guedhami, "The Sustainability Committee and Environmental Disclosure: International Evidence", November 6, 2022, available at: https://ssrn.com/abstract=4226967.

[242] L. Strine, Jr., K. Smith, and R. Steel, "Caremark and ESG, Perfect Together: A Practical Approach to Implementing an Integrated, Efficient, and Effective Caremark and ESG Strategy", *Iowa Law Review*, 106, 2021, 1885–1922, esp. at 1919–20.

[243] In re Caremark International Inc. Derivative Litigation, 698 A.2d 959 (Del. Ch. 1996).This the fundamental case about the board's oversight duties under US law.

making attention to ESG matters part of the remit of a board committee[244] or creating a specific sustainability committee will allow directors to devote more attention to the topics, but ESG topics are so core to a company's strategy and its culture, that in our view the whole board needs to deal with these issues; delegating important work to a separate committee tends to disenfranchise the directors who are not part of the committee, while at the same time some directors will feel they don't need to be very involved concerning those topics, precisely because the specialist committee is dealing with ESG and can be relied upon. As we'll detail in the next section, a surfeit of oversight committees may be detrimental to the board's strategy-setting role.

2. BALKANIZED ONE-TIER BOARDS STRUGGLE WITH STRATEGY-MAKING

a. Boards as oversight bureaucracies

In Europe, there have always been, at least since the early 20th century, two competing board models, one tier and two tier.[245] These models operate in a way that makes them more alike than could be thought by someone who is only familiar with the relevant statutory rules, for instance in that most large companies in one tier systems have always had an executive committee consisting of top executives some (but not all) of whom are also board members, whereas in both the German and the Dutch two tier system, it is standard for the supervisory board to hold joint sessions with the executive board, indeed at many companies the supervisory board only seems to meet separately when it discusses sensitive staff issues concerning the executive board, or to discuss its own functioning. Still, differences between the two systems remain substantial, also at the level of board dynamics.[246] As is well-known, there are no indications

---

[244] Apparently, in the US such matters are often (30% of cases) assigned to nominating and remuneration committees, see L. Strine, Jr., K. Smith, and R. Steel, "Caremark and ESG, Perfect Together: A Practical Approach to Implementing an Integrated, Efficient, and Effective Caremark and ESG Strategy ", *Iowa Law Review*, *106*, 2021, 2019.

[245] See e.g. K. Hopt and P. Leyens, "Board Models in Europe – Recent Developments of Internal Corporate Governance Structures in Germany, the United Kingdom, France, and Italy, *European Company and Financial Law Review*, 2004, 135–168. On boards in Europe generally, 2013 saw the publication of three "legal aspects of corporate governance"-oriented collective volumes that are still worth consulting: P. Davies, K. Hopt, R. Nowak and G. van Solinge, *Corporate boards in practice- a comparative analysis in Europe*, Oxford University Press, 2013, 880 p.; M. Belcredi and G. Ferrarini *Boards and shareholders in listed European companies*, Cambridge, Cambridge university Press, 2013, 437 p. and H. Birkmose, M. Neville and K.E. Sörsensen, *Boards of directors in European companies*, Wolters Kluwer, 2013, 399 p. The overview article by Davies/Hopt, "Boards in Europe -accountability and governance" in the first volume presented the state of the art at the time.

[246] For a brief introduction to the scholarly discipline, see Ph. Stiles, *Board Dynamics*, Cambridge University Press, 2021; See also e.g. J.D. Westphal, and E.J. Zajac, "A behavioural

that one system is superior as a governance system to the other.[247] Dual board systems seem better suited to deal with conflicts of interest of executives in a clear-cut way, but seem to suffer from less information flow from executives to non-executives than in a one tier system, and their decision-making seems to be slower.[248]

Beginning in the 1990s, the one tier board was transformed in Europe. In the wake of the 1992 Cadbury Code in the UK, all western European countries adopted corporate governance codes that stressed the monitoring and oversight function of the board.[249] In order to effectively fulfill that role, it was recommended to split the roles of chair and CEO (which until then had been combined in many, probably a majority of cases, even mandatorily so under the French companies act at that time); to appoint a sufficient number of non-executives to balance the role and influence of the executives in the board; and to appoint a sufficient number – read: more – independent directors. Also, it was recommended to install an audit committee and a remuneration committee, which often doubled as the third classic committee, the nomination committee. Today, audit committees are mandatory for listed companies in the EU[250] and few listed companies would dare to operate without a remuneration committee in view of corporate governance code recommendations and other pressures.

---

theory of corporate governance: Explicating the mechanisms of socially situated and socially constituted agency", *Academy of Management Annals*, 2013, 607–661.

[247] See from among many authors e.g. C. Jungmann, "The effectiveness of corporate governance in one-tier and two-tier board systems", *ECFR* 2006, 426–474; K.J. Hopt, "The German two-tier board: experience, theories, reforms" in K. Hopt, E. Wymeersch et al. (eds.) *Comparative Corporate Governance. The State of the Art and Emerging Research*, Oxford, OUP, 1998, 227.

[248] This seems to have been if not the consensus then at least the dominant opinion among those with a knowledge of two tier systems for a long time, see already M. Lutter, "Defizite für eine effiziente Aufsichtsratstätigkeit und gesetzliche Möglichkeiten der Verbesserung", *ZHR*, 1995, at 287.

[249] For a comparative analysis of what that monitoring and oversight role entailed in some major European jurisdictions (Belgium, Netherlands, France, Germany) around the year 2000, after the heady developments of the 1990s, see H. De Wulf, *Taak en loyauteitsplicht van het bestuur in de naamloze vennootschap*, Antwerp, Intersentia, 2002, 235–297. For a more detailed and more recent comparative analysis, see S. De Geyter, *Organisatieaansprakelijkheid*, Antwerp, Intersentia, 2012. For an up-to date overview of the state of the art in the US, see J. Arlen, "Evolution of Director Oversight Duties and Liability under Caremark: Using Enhanced Information-Acquisition Duties in the Public Interest" (August 28, 2022), available at https://ssrn.com/abstract=4202830. See also the "macro view" expressed by a US law firm in https://corpgov.law.harvard.edu/2021/05/10/directors-oversight-role-today-increased-expectations-responsibility-and-accountability-a-macro-view/.

[250] See Directive 2006/43/EC of the European Parliament and of the Council of 17 May 2006 on statutory audits of annual accounts and consolidated accounts, amending Council Directives 78/660/EEC and 83/349/EEC and repealing Council Directive 84/253/EEC, *OJ* L 157, 9.6.2006, 87–107.

The increased importance attached to board composition and governance has resulted today in what I would call one tier boards as oversight bureaucracies. Within the suite of the board's monitoring tasks, its oversight function, in the sense that it has to oversee that the company installs state of the art internal controls, risk management and compliance systems, has vastly gained in importance. For companies that will become subject to the CSDDD (or are already subject to equivalent French or German legislation), the oversight function will now gain a new add-on, namely at least an increased focus on oversight of the supply chain due diligence system. This oversight function centers around risk management, regulatory compliance, and keeping top executives in check by making sure they do not shirk but above all, that they act in the best interest of the company rather than in their own interest, including trying to prevent self-dealing in such matters as the determination of executive remuneration. The oversight function should be distinguished from, and is of a different nature than the broader monitoring role of the board. As part of that monitoring role, the board will approve (and sometimes choose between) strategic options presented by the CEO and his top executive team. Adams and Ferreira reflect this in what is perhaps a terminologically clearer distinction, namely between the oversight and strategic advice functions of the board.[251]

In the (in the low countries) famous words of 1960s Dutch corporate law professor Löwensteyn[252], boards have always been a *"nexus of conflicting interests"*, irrespective of whether a legal system officially honors a shareholder value or a stakeholder orientation. But the post-Cadbury evolutions have led to an ever-increasing differentiation between directors: the separation between chairman and CEO stresses that one is the representative of non-executives and the other is management's top dog; the explicit distinction in corporate governance reports in the annual report between executive and non-executive directors has of course had the same effect. Legally, directors are supposed to represent the interests of "the whole company", meaning all shareholders or all stakeholders depending on the legal system, but the explicit designation of some directors as independent and others as "mere" non-executives, has driven home the point, and the feeling among directors, that some of them are *de facto* representatives of controlling shareholders, whereas the job description of the independent directors is explicitly to be a counterweight to both executives and controlling shareholders and their representatives in the board. The installation of board committees – in addition to the executive committee than many if not most large companies with a one tier board had voluntarily organized for decades – is now

---

[251] R.B. Adams and F. Ferreira, "A Theory of Friendly Boards", *Journal of Finance*, 62, 2007, 217.
[252] See F.J.W. Löwensteyn, "De naamloze vennootschap als raakpunt van contraire belangen" in *Honderd jaar rechtsleven*, Zwolle, Tjeenk Willink, 1970, 85 and *Wezen en bevoegdheid van het bestuur van de vereniging en de naamloze vennootschap*, Zwolle, Tjeenk Willink, 1959.

in the EU mandatorily supplemented by an audit committee and a remuneration committee (that usually doubles as the nomination committee, although some companies split the roles). This has led to a clearly more differentiated role for directors, leading also to *de facto* (but usually not legal) differences in the exposure to liability risk.[253] There are of course still plenary sessions of the board where real work is done, especially when the board wants to involve itself in discussions about strategy, and in meetings about budget allocation. But my contention is that the evolutions I just sketched have led to an increasing balkanization of one tier boards[254], where directors increasingly have different roles and probably also feel that they are not equal and not all representing the same "support base", and non-executives are busier exercising oversight functions than being able to deal with strategy. Non-executive directors – the recruitment of whom has also been made subject to diversity requirements[255] that were virtually non-existent twenty years ago – also serve as an important link to stakeholders, in that one of their roles is supposed to be to make sure that, through their intermediary role, the company internalizes important evolutions in societal convictions about how companies should behave responsibly.

b.   *The oversight-strategy trade-off*

Theoretical models devised not by social psychologists or organization specialists but by economists, suggest the functioning of groups is affected by the existence of subgroups, and in particular, the model of Aghion/Tirole

---

[253] For instance, cases from Australia to Belgium (AWA-case, AWA Ltd v Daniels (formerly practising as Deloitte Haskins & Sells), New South Wales Court of Appeal, 15 May 1995, see G.P. Stapledon, "The AWA-case: non-executive directors, auditors and corporate governance issues in court" in D. Prentice and PRJ Holland (eds.) *Contemporary issues in Corporate Governance*, Oxford, Clarendon Press, 1993, 187–219; Lernout&Hauspie (criminal case), Court of Appeal Ghent, 20 September 2010, not officially reported, on file with Ghent law School) indicate that audit committee members are expected to have their nose closer to possible accounting irregularities or other forms of fraud than other directors, i.e. they seem more likely to be sued for negligence when things go wrong. An early illustration from Germany was the wide-ranging ARAG-Garmenbeck case (OLG Düsseldorf, *ZIP*, 1997, 27 and see J. Grooterhorst, "Die ARAG/Garmenbeck-prozesse -eine Gesamtschau im Rückblick", *ZIP*, 1999, 1118).

[254] On this phenomenon see also, with a special focus on bank boards in Belgium as influenced by the 2014 Banking Act, J. Cerfontaine, *Corporate Governance in Banken*, VUB Press, 2015, 146 ff.

[255] At the level of the EU, the most important legislative initiative is probably Directive (EU) 2022/2381 on improving the gender balance among directors of listed companies and related measures *OJ* L315, 44-29, 7 December 2022 which came quite late compared to the mandatory legislation on gender balance in national legislations, such as the 2011 Belgian law (Norway were the pioneers with a mandatory law from 2003, after a 1988 Equal Opportunities Act had already introduced gender quota, but that latter law was hard to enforce and therefore had limited effect, see e.g. M. Huse, "The Norwegian gender balance law- a benchmark?" in M. De Vos and Ph. Culliford (eds.), *Gender Quotas for Corporate Boards*, Antwerp, Intersentia, 2014, 173–187).

(1997) plausibly suggests that communication within the group – e.g. the board – can be negatively affected by the existence of subgroups such as board committees.[256] One of the contentions of that article was that members of committees that lack formal decision-making power, strategically withhold and manipulate information from group members (of the group where formal power resides) outside the committee in order to gain influence, and the reverse is also true (e.g. executive board members withholding information from a non-executive committee). Inspired by empirical research on the effects of board composition and monitoring on various governance outcomes, Adams and Ferreira (2007) developed their "friendly boards" theoretical model about the trade-off between the board's role as a monitor and its role as an advisor to top management.[257] They start from the finding that independent boards are tougher monitors of CEOs. This may lead the CEO to share less information with such an "unfriendly" board than he would with a manager-friendly board, which in turn would have a negative effect on the quality of the advice the independent board is able to provide, for instance on strategy. The authors stress, as we do, that information flows in a dual board system are often limited. This could be explained by the Adams/Ferreira theory, namely that since a separate supervisory board, containing only non-executives who are all independent from management, is considered an "unfriendly board" by top management. I hypothesize that this effect may be worse if the supervisory board contains representatives of various stakeholders and indeed others than shareholder representatives, because I assume the typical corporate executive feels aligned more closely with shareholders than with labour or other stakeholder groups, even in companies where the supervisory board, containing 50 or 33% employee representatives has appointed the executives, and not the general meeting of shareholders.

Adams, Ragunathan and Tumarkin (2021) report that in the US in 1996, 25% of all director meetings took place in board committees composed exclusively of non-executive directors, while that percentage of meetings had increased to 45% by 2010. Based on empirical research, namely looking at the correlation of such matters as the prevalence of committee meetings consisting of only "outside directors" and firm financial performance indicators such as cumulative abnormal returns of acquisitions, they found that formally delegating authority to board committees can have a negative effect on the board's efforts to maximize firm value. They also found that the existence of committees of non-executives ("outside directors") can indeed have a negative effect on the

---

[256] See P. Aghion and J. Tirole "Formal and real authority in organizations", *Journal of Political Economy*, 107, 1997, 1–29. For a somewhat comparable model, see H. Li and W. Suen, "Delegating decisions to experts", *Journal of Political Economy 112*(S1), 2004, S311–S335.
[257] R. B. Adams and F. Ferreira, "A Theory of Friendly Boards", *Journal of Finance*, 62, 2007, 217–250.

flow of information between directors – especially between non-executives on committees and executive directors who remain outside the committee – and on decision-making.[258] Research based on interviews with (the admittedly limited number of) 32 directors reported that in the US, directors themselves believed the Sarbanes-Oxley Act, by demanding an increased reliance on board committees composed of non-executive directors, had a very negative impact on both the amount and the quality of decision-making by the full board on corporate strategy[259] and J. Lorsch also argued that there is a trade-off between board oversight and attendant interventions on the board's composition and structure, and the board's effectiveness in strategy development.[260] There is more systematic empirical research that supports the existence of such a trade-off. O. Faleye, R. Hoitash, and U. Hoitash report *"greater sensitivity of CEO turn-over to firm performance, lower excess executive compensation, and reduced earnings management"* when board committees contain a majority of independent directors. But *"The improvement in monitoring quality comes at the significant cost of weaker strategic advising and greater managerial myopia. Firms with boards that monitor intensely exhibit worse acquisition performance and diminished corporate innovation."*[261] Because of the methodological challenges of such correlational research, the evidence should be overwhelming before one draws any firm policy conclusions from it. As yet we do not have nearly enough robust empirical research on this topic. But what we have is consistent with the suggested strategy-oversight trade-off.

3. A SWITCH TO A DUAL BOARD STRUCTURE AS PART OF THE SOLUTION?

In many continental European jurisdictions where the one tier board is dominant, legislation provides the option for companies to switch, through a change to their articles of association, to a dual board model[262], with a supervisory board chosen by the shareholders at the general meeting, and an

---

[258] R. Adams, V. Ragunatham and R. Tumarkin, "Death by committee? An analysis of corporate board (sub)committees, *Journal of Financial Economics*, 141, 2021, 119–146.
[259] J.R. Cohen, C. Hayes, G. Krishnamoorthy, G. S. Monroe, and A. M. Wright, "The Effectiveness of SOX Regulation: An Interview Study of Corporate Directors" *Behavioral Research in Accounting*, 25, 2013, 61–87.
[260] J. Lorsch, "Boardroom challenges, lessons from the financial crisis and beyond" in J. Lorsch (ed.) *The future of boards: meeting the governance challenges of the Twenty-First Century*, Harvard Business Review Press 2012, 13.
[261] O. Faleye, R. Hoitash, and U. Hoitash, "The costs of intense board monitoring" *Journal of Financial Economics*, 101(1), 2011, 160–181.
[262] E.g. Belgium and France, art. 7: 104 Belgian Companies Code and art. L225–57 French Code de Commerce, offering the possibility (in both countries) for every public company (*société anonyme*) to opt into the dual board system through an amendment to its articles of association.

executive board appointed by the supervisory board. Members of one board cannot also be members of the other board at the same company.

My feeling is that a dual board system may be more effective in allowing boards to deal with their two roles of oversight and strategy-setting. In such a system, the supervisory board can concentrate on oversight, and the executive board on strategy. By separating the two functions and allocating to two bodies that would have no members in common, group coherence between the team members of each board could be cemented[263] while at the same time, each group could focus on its core task without being distracted by conflicting roles. Within each board, members would all have a very similar role. The small executive team could gain in decision-making efficiency when determining the corporate strategy. It would be relatively insulated from conflicting stakeholder demands about the company's strategy, since the stakeholders would not be directly represented in the executive board. The influence of stakeholders would be mediated by the supervisory board. The latter would in certain jurisdictions contain members directly chosen by certain non-shareholder stakeholders, such as under worker codetermination systems.[264] This type of direct representation is without a doubt a more effective way of giving a voice to non-shareholder stakeholders than instructing directors who are appointed, dismissed and remunerated by shareholders to take the interests of other stakeholders into account or to (only) rhetorically subjugate them to a broad corporate purpose declaration.[265] The supervisory board could then concentrate on oversight (meaning with a compliance and risk management mindset) and on selecting executives with the desired profile to determine corporate strategy with, if such an executive profile is desirable in the supervisory board, also with the interests of various

---

[263] Some will object that this will contribute to undesirable groupthink, but I don't think this would outweigh the advantages of coherence. This is however one of the many questions of board dynamics in this section that would need further research by a wide body of scholars and scientists.

[264] On the German worker codetermination system, its pros and cons and empirical research on its effects, see now J. Daman and H. Eidenmüller, "Co-determination: a poor fit for US corporations" *Columbia Business Law Review*, 2020, 870–941 with references to most of the relevant literature in English.

[265] L.A. Bebchuk & R. Tallarita, 'The Illusory Promise of Stakeholder Governance', *Cornell Law Review*, (106), 2020, 91–178, see also the overview of arguments from European literature in H. De Wulf, *Taak en loyateitsplicht*, 2002, 525–531 with also my argument, at p. 542, about German *Mitbestimmung* as a system that, whatever one might think of it in general, and contrary to a stakeholderist interpretation of directors' duties, is effective in giving non-shareholder stakeholders, namely employees, a voice in corporate governance by giving employees the right to appoint, dismiss and remunerate a certain number of (non-executive) directors; see also the different but related (and convincing) views on how a purpose statement and purpose-orientation of directors duties will either be ineffective because unenforceable, or unnecessary, in P. Davies, "Shareholder Voice and Corporate Purpose: The Purposeless of Mandatory Corporate Purpose Statements" (November 1, 2022), available at https://ssrn.com/abstract=4285770.

stakeholders in mind. The supervisory board would however not directly interfere with the determination of corporate strategy, limiting itself to replacing executives who have proven to be ineffective in their role as strategy-setters. Even under such a system it would be naïve to think that the supervisory board would not involve itself at all in corporate strategy. Indeed, in spite of the law assigning the power to set corporate strategy to the executive board in both Germany and the Netherlands, it is widely accepted that the supervisory board has to play an advisory/supervisory role in this respect and this is one explanation of why in those jurisdictions, supervisory boards rarely meet without the executive board joining the meeting. Still, my feeling is that board members would have a less muddled, conflicted view of their respective roles under a dual board system with a clear separation of powers and membership than in one tier systems with a board and an executive committee. Perhaps I'm too optimistic about the possibility to make a clear-cut distinction between the oversight responsibilities of a supervisory board and the strategy decision-making role of the executive board. Perhaps this impossibility is the reason for the (probably purposeful) ambiguity in European banking regulation[266] about where strategy determination should be located.[267]

Also, it could be objected that in dual board systems, information flows from executives to non-executives in the supervisory board are even more restricted than in a one tier board. But as we argued above, the situation may be equally bad in one tier boards with several strong committees. Also, precisely because the supervisory board would have only very limited involvement in strategy, the kind of information it needs would be different. It would need sufficient and timely information to exercise its oversight function, but that type of information is more easily provided in the form of formal reports and through the internal control systems of the company. Finally – and to repeat – the information flow disadvantage of a dual board system would likely be off-set by an increased group coherence within each board[268], with an exclusive focus on their respective core tasks, and without

---

[266] Which is "board model neutral".
[267] I thank Jan Cerfontaine (UGent and director in financial sector companies) for pointing this out to me. Documenting this ambiguity would require another page of text at least, please read paragraphs 22 and 28 through 34 of EBA *Guidelines on Internal governance under Directive 2013, 16/EU*, 2021 edition, available at https://www.eba.europa.eu/eba-publishes-its-final-guidelines-internal-governance.
[268] That is not to deny that even within relatively small executive boards, one may be confronted with a CEO acting as an *Einzelgänger* rather than with the backing of a tight team. One thinks here, e.g., of the role Paul Polman played as CEO of Unilever. Polman wanted Unilever to focus on sustainability, but the strategy he developed in that regard seemed not to be backed by the whole executive board, nor by the supervisory board and, importantly, shareholders also had their doubts. Some quipped (grossly exaggerating, but still driving home a point about how he was perceived) that the first time Polman cared about shareholders was when HeinzKraft launched a hostile bid for Unilever. For a very instructive interview with Paul

executives being buffeted by conflicting stakeholder demands and conflicting strategy and oversight roles.

IX. CONCLUSION

The life of boards at listed companies is not getting any easier. Evolutions in society and in financial markets mean that, at the same time when their compliance and risk management oversight function is stressed more and more, at least in Europe, boards can no longer focus exclusively on the creation of shareholder value. This is even true in systems where, contrary to what is the case in systems like Germany with its worker codetermination regime, directors are exclusively appointed, remunerated and dismissed by shareholders. Boards are increasingly exposed to ESG shareholder activism that forces them to take more account of stakeholder interests and, especially as a result of recent due diligence legislation, the negative externalities ("adverse impacts") companies create. This article focused on NGOs using shareholder activism tactics to exert pressure on boards to take negative externalities and the interest of other stakeholders than shareholders seriously. These NGOs often want to influence a company's strategy, especially when they "lobby" companies about their climate strategy. Certain economically important jurisdictions like Germany and the Netherlands take a radical view on the exclusive competence of the executive board to determine a company's strategy. The shareholder activism by NGOs (and their climate litigation) is hard to reconcile with the board's exclusive competence. That is also why in those jurisdictions, the activism does not take the form of shareholder proposals, as opposed to what we see in the US. The influence of these non-governmental non-profits organisations will, and already is, leveraged by recent due diligence legislation that forces companies into a dialogue with these civil society organisations. That dialogue is sometimes and with increasing frequency continued in the form of litigation launched by those same NGOs. The climate litigation against companies brought by these NGOs goes to the heart of corporate strategies. I argued that it would be deplorable if the EU were to copy the French litigation-focused enforcement model in its soon-to be adopted CSDD Directive. Litigation is singularly unsuitable as a mechanism to help form a company's strategy. In any case, the result of these developments is that the strategy setting role of boards is being made more difficult, buffeted as boards are by conflicting stakeholder demands while at the same time group coherence and therefore decisiveness within the board is being undermined by the increased use of specialist board committees and

---

Polman while he was CEO of Unilever, see "Captain Planet", *Harvard Business Review*, June 2012 issue.

distinctions between directors with different roles. In this climate, I argued, tentatively, that boards may perhaps fulfill their conflicting oversight and strategy roles more effectively in a dual board system, where the supervisory board can concentrate on oversight, and the executive board on strategy. But more research on this last issue is surely needed.

SECURITIES LENDING AS A BARRIER TO (OR AN INSTRUMENT FOR) SHAREHOLDER ACTIVISM AND THE ROLE OF INTERMEDIARIES AS LENDING AGENTS

Louise VAN MARCKE
Doctoral Researcher, Financial Law Institute, Ghent University

ABSTRACT

This chapter discusses the corporate governance implications of securities lending transactions in the European Union, in particular with regard to the exercise of voting rights by activist shareholders. When shares are on loan, both sides of the lending equation (i.e. that of the lender and the borrower) affect the exercise of voting rights: lenders must recall lent out shares in a timely manner if they do not want to lose the voting rights attached to them, and borrowers may employ stock borrowing practices to increase their voting power and manipulate voting outcomes. By analysing legal doctrine, consulting with practitioners and examining recent securities lending cases (such as Mediobanca/Generali), this chapter highlights the ongoing risks that stock lending poses to corporate governance. Techniques such as negative risk-decoupling, record date capture and empty voting are analysed from the perspective of stock lending. It is found that securities lending can be as much a barrier to activism as it can be used to the advantage of activists. As a conclusion, some recommendations and guidelines for future regulation are included.

1. INTRODUCTION[1, 2]

1. Chains of Intermediaries. In today's markets, one of the requirements for admission to most trading venues is that shares are traded electronically rather than on paper and are therefore held in book-entry form (i.e. dematerialised or immobilised[3]) on securities accounts. The relationship between listed companies and their shareholders is also generally characterised by the presence of intermediaries (such as (custodian) banks, brokers, central securities depositaries (hereafter: "CSD's") etc.) who offer a wide range of services related to holding their clients' securities in book-entry form.[4] In most cases, shares are therefore held in an intermediated way (referred to as 'indirect holding'), although (often impractical) exceptions apply.[5]

---

[1] The practical approach of this chapter was enabled by discussions with practitioners, for which my utmost gratitude goes to Andrew Dyson and Adrian Dale (International Securities Lending Association), James Cunningham (Bank of New York Mellon) and Marije Verhelst (Euroclear Bank). These exploratory discussions had the form of semi-structured interviews, that took place through videoconference during spring 2022. The idea was to gain additional insights from three perspectives: an industry association representing market participants (the ISLA), a major custodian bank (or 'intermediary', BNYM) and an International Central Securities Depository (Euroclear Bank). While processing these data, it was taken into account that these individuals could be biased, and results were always cross-checked with the existing literature. At no point were these discussions considered as a sole source for the findings of this chapter.

[2] This research was made possible by the support of the Research Foundation Flanders (FWO. OPR.2020.0064.01). All interpretations, conclusions and errors are my own. I furthermore wish to thank prof. dr. Hans De Wulf and em. prof. dr. Eddy Wymeersch for their valuable feedback to the initial working paper of this book chapter.

[3] Dematerialization refers to the fact that financial instruments exist (have been issued) *ab initio* as book entry records, while immobilization assumes the securities being deposited for safekeeping with a CSD, who then books them onto securities accounts. The book-entry form has become mandatory in the EU/EEA from 1 January 2023 for new securities, and from 1 January 2025 for all existing securities. See art. 3 j. 76 Regulation (EU) No 909/2014 of the European Parliament and of the Council of 23 July 2014 on improving securities settlement in the European Union and on central securities depositories and amending Directives 98/26/EC and 2014/65/EU and Regulation (EU) No 236/2012, *Oj.L.* 28 August 2014, ep. 257, 1–72 (hereafter: "CSDR").

[4] See annex 1, Section B (1) Directive 2014/65/EU of the European Parliament and of the Council of 15 May 2014 on markets in financial instruments and amending Directive 2002/92/EC and Directive 2011/61/EU Text with EEA relevance, *Oj.L.* 12 June 2014, ep. 173,349–496 (hereafter: "MiFID II") and Annex, Section A (for core services of central securities depositories) CSDR. For an interesting overview of the roles of different intermediaries in the chain, see EUROPEAN POST-TRADE FORUM, "EPTF Report: Annex 3", 15 May 2017, https://finance.ec.europa.eu/publications/report-european-post-trade-forum-eptf_en, 26–30 (3.1.3).

[5] "It is debatable whether subscribers of publicly traded securities have a choice as many stock exchanges today make the holding of securities on an intermediated system a condition of listing.", M. Ooi, "Re-enfranchising the investor of intermediated securities", *Journal of Private International Law*, 16(1), 2020, 69, 86. "Equity investors in European companies often have no practical alternative to being part of a custody chain because of the way that trading, clearing and settlement is organized", E. Ferran, "Shareholder Engagement and Custody Chains", University of Cambridge Faculty of Law Research Paper No. 1/2022, 6 January

The phenomenon of a complex network of securities accounts (with corresponding cash accounts for the purpose of settlement of transactions and, for example, dividend payouts) held in different layers is commonly referred to as a 'chain of intermediaries'. In a typical chain, an upper-tier intermediary (usually, the CSD) holds the total amount of issued securities directly from the issuer on behalf of other institutions (CSD-participants), who in turn hold securities for others and so on. Intermediaries in the holding chain can hold securities for their own account but can also, and will more generally, hold securities in their own name but *on behalf* of other natural or legal persons, i.e. their clients. For efficiency reasons, the upstream accounts intermediaries hold with a higher-tier intermediary on behalf of their combined clients will often pool clients' securities in one and the same account. These accounts are then referred to as 'omnibus accounts' (as opposed to individually segregated client accounts).[6]

At the intersection of chains of intermediaries and corporate law, several issues and questions arise (some of which have been addressed elsewhere[7]) that are the subject of a growing body of literature.[8] One of these issues, explored in this book chapter, are shareholders engaging in 'securities financing transactions'. According to DONALD, at least in the US, *"the anonymity, complexity, and uncertainty created by the indirect holding system is aggravated by share lending and the related practice of short selling"*.[9] The relationship between securities financing transactions and corporate governance has been much less explored in the EU.

2022, https://papers.ssrn.com/sol3/papers.cfm?abstract_id=4001702, 9 (accessed 21.09.2022). For example, in the UK, 'direct membership' in Crest (allowing the investor to appear as the registered company member vis-à-vis the issuer) is somewhat bothersome since only few brokers in the UK offer it, and those that do charge very high fees for it. Consequently, its popularity has declined. See Law Commission, "Intermediated securities: who owns your shares? A Scoping Paper", 11 November 2020, https://www.lawcom.gov.uk/project/intermediated-securities/, 29 (accessed 21.09.2022).

[6] See L. Gullifer, *Goode and Gullifer on Legal Problems of Credit and Security*, Oxford, Sweet & Maxwell, 2017, 243; P. De Gioia-Carabellese and M. Haentjens, *European Banking and Financial Law*, New York, Routledge, 2020, 176.

[7] One of the most insightful recent papers on this topic that summarises several problems to a great extent, is E. Ferran, "Shareholder Engagement and Custody Chains", University of Cambridge Faculty of Law Research Paper No. 1/2022, 6 January 2022, https://papers.ssrn.com/sol3/papers.cfm?abstract_id=4001702, 30 p. (accessed 21.09.2022). See also E. Micheler, "Transfer of Intermediated Securities and Legal Certainty" in T. Keijser (ed.), *Transnational Securities Law*, Oxford, Oxford University Press, 2014, 117–43; C. van der Elst and A. Lafarre, "Blockchain and Smart Contracting for the Shareholder Community", *EBOR*, 20(1), 2019, 111–37.

[8] The author's doctoral research is focusing on a comparative legal analysis of the corporate law problems caused by chains of intermediaries in the holding of shares in listed companies and their possible solutions.

[9] D.C. Donald, "Heart of Darkness: The Problem at the Core of the U.S. Proxy System and its Solution", *Virginia Law & Business Review*, 6(1), 2011, 41, 77.

2. **Securities Financing Transactions.** While shares[10] may be held on a securities account until their owner (i.e. an investor) decides to dispose of them, investors may engage in some transactions during the time the shares are held in their portfolio. The underlying idea is that the portfolio may be used to realise an additional source of income by allowing shares to be 'used' by market actors in need. This kind of efficient resource management on the market takes the form of securities financing transactions (SFT's)[11], which include inter alia securities lending agreements and repurchase transactions (hereafter: "repos").[12] This book chapter focuses on the first of these transactions, i.e. stock (share) lending. The general ideas and conclusions of this book chapter may, however, also be applied to repo's: while the initiating party, the intent and/or the maturity of a repo may be different, both transactions have the same outcome in terms of transfer of title and can therefore have the same consequences for corporate governance and the exercise of voting rights.

There are many reasons why shareholders would engage in stock lending transactions, including the facilitation of the settlement process (in the case of automated lending programs[13]) which leads to reduced trading costs, the

---

[10] This book chapter is concerned with shares of publicly listed companies. Any reference to 'securities', should be interpreted as referring to shares only.

[11] For a definition, see art. 3 (11) of Regulation (EU) 2015/2365 Of The European Parliament And Of The Council of 25 November 2015 on transparency of securities financing transactions and of reuse and amending Regulation (EU) No 648/2012, *Oj. L.* 23 December 2015, ep. 337, 1–34 (hereafter: "SFTR").

[12] In a repurchase agreement, the investor (in need of cash (short-term capital)) sells its securities to another investor (buyer) and buys them back after a short period of time (often, the following day) at a slightly higher purchase price. As explained by Haentjens, "*the main difference between the two types of standardised financial collateral transactions is that in securities lending transactions it is the transferee of securities, that is the borrower, who initiates the transaction as she is in need of securities, whilst in repos, it is the transferor of the securities, that is the seller, who initiates the transaction as she is in need of cash. This difference is reflected in the fee: in securities lending transactions, it is paid by the transferee of securities, that is the borrower, whilst in repos, it is paid by the transferor of the securities, that is the seller*", M. Haentjens, *Financial Collateral: Law and Practice*, Oxford, Oxford University Press, 2020, 115. "The main differences are that: securities lending does not necessarily involve cash (it can be security against security); is generally driven by the demand to borrow specific securities (rather than cash); and tends to be transacted on an open basis", see European Post-Trade Forum, "ETPF Report: Annex 3", 15 May 2017, https://finance.ec.europa.eu/publications/report-european-post-trade-forum-eptf_en, 184–89 (accessed 21.09.2022).

[13] As a CSD, Euroclear operates an automated lending programme that many intermediaries (including Bank of New York Mellon) use. The programme essentially detects settlement fails due to a shortage in securities supply, and automatically provides securities from a large lending pool to allow the settlement of the transaction to proceed. Once lenders and borrowers join the pool, Euroclear can use it automatically to cover settlement positions. The main difference between this type of securities lending and 'negotiated securities lending' is that the loans are concluded for a much shorter period and securities are usually returned at the end of the trading day, or 1 or 2 days later. For shares, recalls and other corporate governance problems are therefore much less likely to occur. In automated lending programs, borrowers pay a significantly higher fixed lending fee than in negotiated securities lending transactions.

facilitation of the market pricing mechanism (by allowing for short selling to correct overvaluations[14]), enhanced liquidity and efficiency in the market (due to effective resource management) and – on an individual level, often the most important reason – increased revenue by having an additional source of income stemming from lending fees (and investing provided collateral).[15]

3. To illustrate the significance of today's[16] securities lending markets, the International Securities Lending Association (hereafter: "ISLA"[17]) asserted that 'the size of the global securities lending industry (securities available for loan) [was] estimated to be in the region of € 24 trillion as at the end of 2020. Over 90% of this supply is attributable to lendable assets of beneficial owners, in the form of Pension Plans, Insurance Companies, Mutual and Retail Funds, Sovereign Entities and Government offices, Foundations and Endowments, and Corporations (both LLC and LLP)'.[18] More recent figures estimate the size of the global securities borrowing market at € 32.4 trillion.[19] In terms of loaned securities, roughly half of today's market are government bonds but there is

---

"Euroclear's (...) automated securities lending and borrowing programme (...) targets borrowing demand to avoid settlement fails and counterparty claims", see Euroclear, "Securities Lending and Borrowing", https://www.euroclear.com/services/en/securities-lending-and-borrowing.html#:~:text=An%20automated%20fail%2Dcuring%20solution,confidential%2C%20secure%20and%20flexible%20solution (accessed 21.09.2022); Euroclear Bank, "The Operating Procedures of the Euroclear System", October 2020, https://investor.ryanair.com/wp-content/uploads/2020/11/The-Operating-Procedures-of-the-Euroclear-System-October-2020-Circular-reference-s.6f-of-Part-1B.pdf, 147–150 (Part V: Section 5 – Securities Lending and Borrowing Program).

[14] See below, fn. 89.
[15] For a more elaborate discussion, see G. Raaijmakers, "Securities Lending and Corporate Governance", Maastricht University Faculty of Law Working Paper, 2006, https://papers.ssrn.com/sol3/papers.cfm?abstract_id=928312, 5 (2.2 Reasons for securities lending) (accessed 21.09.2022). See also the preamble of International Corporate Governance Network, "ICGN Guidance on Securities Lending", 2016, https://www.icgn.org/sites/default/files/2021-06/ICGN068_Guidance_On_Securities_Lending_24pp_AUG16-v3_0.pdf, 5 (accessed 21.09.2022).
[16] From a historical perspective, according to Ringe "the volume of 'borrowed' securities rose sharply in global markets in the years just before the financial crisis (...). In the years following 2008, however, we saw a significant decrease in such transactions. (...) More recently, the industry appears to have revived", see W. Ringe, *The Deconstruction of Equity: Activist Shareholders, Decoupled Risk, and Corporate Governance*, Oxford, Oxford University Press, 2016, 36–37.
[17] The ISLA is the leading non-profit industry association representing the interests of participants in the securities lending and financing market in Europe, the Middle East and Africa. The ISLA has developed the "Global Master Securities Lending Agreement" which functions as the widely used, global standard master agreement in securities lending.
[18] ISLA, "Institutional Investors & Securities Lending", December 2020, https://www.islaemea.org/institutional-investors-and-securities-lending/ (accessed 21.09.2022).
[19] ISLA, "Securities Lending Market Report" (16th edition), March 2022, https://www.islaemea.org/assets/smart-pdfs/isla-securities-lending-market-report-march-2022/files/downloads/2516_21_June_ISLA_Market_Report_-_March_2022_final.pdf, 6–7 (accessed 21.09.2022).

also a big equity component – according to the European Post-Trade Forum, over 50% of securities on loan are equities (shares).[20]

4. Goal of this chapter. Activist shareholders can engage in stock lending transactions both on the side of the lender, as well as on the side of the borrower. It should be clarified that aggressive and 'offensive' activists, such as hedge funds, are more likely to be on the borrowing side and large institutional investors (i.e. traditional activists making use of defensive activist techniques) on the lending side.[21]

The starting point of this chapter is that lending agreements affect an activist's ability to exercise voting rights (as a lender), and (the expansion of) an activist's voting power (as a borrower). While more ink has flowed on (short seller) activists in their capacity of share borrowers and empty voting practices, especially in the US, less attention has been paid to the angle of shareholders as stock lenders. This chapter aims to make a contribution in both respects.

The first part of this chapter discusses stock lending from the perspective of stock lenders (i.e. transferors of securities) and the corporate governance implications of lending transactions, especially with regards to voting rights. In particular, this chapter analyses the (in)ability for institutional shareholders, such as activists, to exercise voting rights when large share portfolios appear to be out on loan in the run-up to the annual general meeting. By analysing the implications of lending practices in company law (including, inter alia, the exercise of voting rights as a shareholder (lender) and the right to 'recall' loaned shares), this chapter sheds light on the potential risks posed by securities lending practices for activist shareholders who cannot afford to 'lose' voting rights when launching an activist intervention in a target company. On the other hand, the second part of this chapter explores the position of activists as stock borrowers and explains the phenomena of 'vote decoupling' and 'empty voting'. This way, it is examined whether activists can increase their voting power by deliberately borrowing shares in the run-up to the general meeting, and the risks such practices may cause with respect to corporate governance.

---

[20] European Post-Trade Forum, "ETPF Report: Annex 3 Detailed analysis of the European Post Trade Landscape", 15 May 2017, https://finance.ec.europa.eu/publications/report-european-post-trade-forum-eptf_en, 195 (accessed 21.09.2022).

[21] This common distinction between activists was also highlighted in e.g. A. Brav, W. Jiang and R. Li, "Governance by Persuasion: Hedge Fund Activism and Market-based Shareholder Influence", European Corporate Governance Institute – Finance Working Paper No. 797/2021, 10 December 2021, https://ssrn.com/abstract=3955116, 9–10 (accessed 21.09.2022).

2. SECURITIES LENDING AGREEMENTS AND THE ROLE OF INTERMEDIARIES

5. A securities lending agreement is generally defined as a transaction where an investor (the lender) lends securities to a borrower (often with cash or securities being provided as collateral[22]), with the borrower returning to the seller equivalent securities and a fee at the date of maturity (and the seller subsequently returning the provided collateral). Essentially, the lender is sacrificing liquidity in a security for a given period of time, in return for a (at times, quite substantial[23]) lending fee.

The term 'loan', however, does not accurately reflect what is happening from a legal perspective. In fact, the lender transfers the ownership of its securities fully and unconditionally to another party (the borrower), against the obligation for the borrower to return equivalent securities.[24] Importantly, from the moment the securities have been transferred to the borrower, the latter obtains ownership thereof, accompanied by all the rights and entitlements attached to

---

[22] As a principle, the value of the provided collateral will be greater than that of the lent securities. After all, when securities are lent, the lender runs a counterparty risk, i.e., the risk that the borrower cannot return the shares at the end of the loan, in which case the collateral provided by the borrower will be sold and from those proceeds the securities can be bought back in the market. See R. Aggarwal, P.A.C. Saffi and J. Sturgess, "The Role of Institutional Investors in Voting: Evidence from the Securities Lending Market", *The Journal of Finance*, 70(5), 2015, 2309, 2314. Collateral can also be delivered by a pledge, so that the borrower retains ownership of the pledged assets. According to the ISLA, in the European model almost 100% of all loaned securities are collateralised by non-cash assets, while the North American model primarily relies on cash collateral.

[23] For a study estimating securities lending revenue in exchange traded funds (ETF's) and index mutual funds (IMFs), see J. Blocher and R.E. Whaley, "Passive Investing: The Role of Securities Lending", working paper 6 November 2014, https://acfr.aut.ac.nz/__data/assets/pdf_file/0010/29917/WhaleyPassive-Investing.pdf, 40 p. (accessed 21.09.2022).

[24] G. Raaijmakers, "Securities Lending and Corporate Governance", *Maastricht University Faculty of Law Working Paper*, 2006, https://papers.ssrn.com/sol3/papers.cfm?abstract_id=928312, 4 (accessed 21.09.2022); M.C. Faulkner, *An Introduction to Securities Lending* (4th edition), London, Spitalfields Advisors Limited, 2007, 15-22; W. Ringe, "Hedge Funds and Risk Decoupling: The Empty Voting Problem in the European Union", *Seattle University Law review*, 36, 2013, 1027, 1039; P. Ali, I. Ramsay and B. Saunders, "Securities lending, empty voting and corporate governance", *Law and Financial Markets Review*, 8(4), 2014, 326, 327; D. Marais, "Decoupling Voting Rights from Economic Interest: The Case of Empty and Negative Voting", *Trinity College Law review*, 18, 2015, 180, 186; R. Aggarwal, P.A.C. Saffi and J. Sturgess, "The Role of Institutional Investors in Voting: Evidence from the Securities Lending Market", *The Journal of Finance*, 70(5), 2015, 2309, 2313-314; W. Ringe, *The Deconstruction of Equity: Activist Shareholders, Decoupled Risk, and Corporate Governance*, Oxford, Oxford University Press, 2016, 36; European Post-Trade Forum, "ETPF Report: Annex 3", 15 May 2017, https://finance.ec.europa.eu/publications/report-european-post-trade-forum-eptf_en, 193 (accessed 21.09.2022); J. Benjamin and L. Gullifer, "Stewardship and Collateral: The Advantages and Disadvantages of the No Look Through System", in L. Gullifer and J. Payne (eds.), *Intermediation and Beyond*, Oxford, Hart Publishing, 2018, 218; M. Haentjens, *Financial Collateral: Law and Practice*, Oxford, Oxford University Press, 2020, 114-15.

those securities. Correctly put, the lender remains the owner of the securities only in an economic sense, since *"the lender and not the borrower is [ultimately] exposed to any change in the value of the securities"*.[25] For this particular reason, the practice of short selling[26] is at times criticised because the original owner (lender) may end up with less valuable shares and, by lending out its shares, may have contributed to its own worsened position (as discussed below, fn. 92–93). This situation illustrates that from a short selling perspective, stock lending often comes down to a 'bet' by long-term investors who believe their shares have long-term intrinsic value that will remain unaffected by short selling – in return for a lending fee to offset that risk.

6. In terms of contract drafting, two agreements govern the lending relationship. In practice, the overwhelming majority of cross-border securities lending agreements (concluded between the lender (or its agent), and the borrower (or its agent)) are drafted on the basis of the ISLA's Global Master Securities Lending Agreement (hereafter: "GMSLA").[27] Alternatively, securities lending transactions may take the form of *ad hoc* lending agreements: these are customised, tailor-made agreements that are not standardised within the industry. The lending agreements of Euroclear, for example, are drawn up solely on an *ad hoc* basis for both the negotiated securities lending programme and the automated securities lending programme (a policy-based, historical choice that has been adhered to for the time being).[28] Even though great value emanates from the GMSLA, in principle securities lending agreements may be freely drafted by the parties involved and, in reality, may vary in terms of the extent to which the lender's shareholder rights are protected. Here, the bargaining power of the lender (or its agent) inevitably plays a major role.

---

[25] P. Ali, I. Ramsay and B. Saunders, "Securities lending, empty voting and corporate governance", *Law and Financial Markets Review*, 8(4), 2014, 326, 327.

[26] Short sellers ('going short') speculate on a possible drop in the share price. A short seller borrows a certain number of securities and sells them at the market price (X). Once the share price has dropped, the seller buys the securities back at the lower price (X – 20), in order to return them to the lender. The difference between the higher sale price (X) and the lower purchase price (X – 20) constitutes the net profit (20). As opposed to short shareholders, long shareholders benefit from an increase in the stock price.

[27] The GMSLA was originally published in 2000. The current version is that of 2010, with minor amendments made in 2012. For the full text, see ISLA, "Global Master Securities Lending Agreement", 2010, https://www.fixedincome.global/uploaded_files/privacy_sercurity/GlobalMasterSecuritiesLendingAgreement(GMSLA).pdf (accessed 21.09.2022). One of the main reasons for the success of the GMSLA is the fact that the ISLA maintains the GMSLA from a legal enforceability perspective. Since the lending arrangement is a collateralised transaction, the ISLA collects enforceability opinions from counsel in over 60 jurisdictions on an annual basis, to ensure that, in an event of default on the part of the borrower, the received collateral can effectively be used to net out the position. See ISLA, "GMSLA Netting Opinions", https://www.islaemea.org/gmsla-title-transfer/gmsla-netting-opinions/ (accessed 21.09.2022).

[28] Although it should be noted that both of Euroclear's lending programmes are mainly oriented towards fixed income securities such as bonds. These findings became evident after discussions with practitioners, see fn. 1.

The second agreement governing the lending relationship is the 'securities lending authorisation agreement' concluded between the lender and its agent – often its direct intermediary. These non-standardised agreements set the terms on which the intermediary, as a lending agent, will lend securities from its clients.[29]

7. Investors may manage their lending activities themselves, but more commonly intermediaries are placed in between lenders and borrowers as 'lending agents' (be it an intermediary with whom an existing custody relationship exists, or a specialist third-party agent), 'to whom lenders[30] delegate lending power'[31] by means of the securities lending authorisation agreement. Although relatively little attention is paid to it in the literature, intermediaries play an important role in securities lending transactions. Securities lending is mainly offered by intermediaries to clients as an ancillary service, allowing them to earn a return on the portfolio that can offset the cost they charge for their services (at least to some extent, since revenue from securities lending will be shared between the intermediary and the investor[32]). Working with

---

[29] SFT's in respect of financial instruments that are held by an investment firm on behalf of a client, may only take place on the double condition of (a) prior express consent to the use of the instruments on specified terms and (b) restricted to the specified terms to which the client consented. See art. 5, par. 1 of Commission Delegated Directive (EU) 2017/593 of 7 April 2016 supplementing Directive 2014/65/EU of the European Parliament and of the Council with regard to safeguarding of financial instruments and funds belonging to clients, product governance obligations and the rules applicable to the provision or reception of fees, commissions or any monetary or non-monetary benefits, Oj. L 31 March 2017, ep. 87, 500–517.

[30] Both lenders and borrowers can make use of intermediaries as agents, so that additional layers of intermediaries become involved in lending transactions, J. Benjamin and L. Gullifer, Stewardship and Collateral: The Advantages and Disadvantages of the No Look Through System, in L. Gullifer and J. Payne (eds.), *Intermediation and Beyond*, Oxford, Hart Publishing, 2018, 217. For example, most securities are borrowed by prime brokers on behalf of underlying clients, such as hedge funds.

[31] S. Hirst and A.Z. Robertson, "Hidden Agendas in Shareholder Voting", *Yale Journal on Regulation*, 39(3), 2022, 1225. See also for agency lending, D. Turing, *Clearing and Settlement in Europe*, Haywards Heath, Bloomsbury Professional, 2012, 484–85.

[32] Revenue not only consists of the borrowing fee. In addition, "the lender earns a spread by investing the collateral in low-risk short-term securities", see R. Aggarwal, P.A.C. Saffi and J. Sturgess, "The Role of Institutional Investors in Voting: Evidence from the Securities Lending Market", *The Journal of Finance*, 70(5), 2015, 2309, 2314. While intermediaries, acting as lending agents, can receive a part of lending revenue, the European Union prohibits fund managers from profiting from securities lending. To this extent, ESMA has clarified that "all the revenues arising from efficient portfolio management techniques, net of direct and indirect operational costs, should be returned to the UCITS". See ESMA, "Guidelines for competent authorities and UCITS management companies", 18 December 2012, https://www.esma.europa.eu/sites/default/files/library/2015/11/2012-832en_guidelines_on_etfs_and_other_ucits_issues.pdf, 7 (Guideline 29) (accessed 21.09.2022). Fund managers can only deduct from the gross revenue stemming from securities lending a fee, payable to the securities lending agent, that is considered a 'normal' compensation for the agent's services. Nevertheless, in recent years, questions have arisen as to whether asset managers actually follow this rule and pass on all income derived from securities lending to their clients (institutional investors), or rather pocket revenue they

intermediaries for lending purposes generates a number of advantages: for example, the portfolios of several smaller investors can be pooled and both lenders and borrowers can benefit from the intermediary's established customer base and, accordingly, can be matched more efficiently.[33] For this reason, omnibus accounts prove to be very effective. Omnibus accounts also allow for the reallocation of loans (as discussed below, fn. 54–55) as opposed to segregated accounts, which are less commonly used when it comes to securities lending.

8. Lending authorisation agreements are often part of an existing custody arrangement with the intermediary.[34] The authorisation agreement will allow the intermediary, when the opportunity presents itself, to lend the client's securities without prior authorisation and within the limitations that have been set by the client in advance.[35] At the client's discretion, the authorisation agreement thus specifies certain parameters or criteria between which the agent is allowed to engage in securities lending (e.g., an exclusion of certain borrowers, a limitation of only lending particular types of assets to particular borrowers, restrictions in terms of accepted collateral, the maturity (term or open term) of the transactions etc.).

Over time, some concerns have risen on the awareness of investors that (some of) their shares have been lent out and the consequences for voting entitlements, especially in the US and the UK.[36] Similar concerns have arisen in the

---

are not entitled to. See S. Riding, "Fund groups challenged over securities lending practices", *Financial Times* 11 May 2019, and the report drawn up by consumer group BetterFinance, BetterFinance, "Efficient Portfolio Management Techniques: Attribution of Profits Derived from Securities Lending by UCITS and Exchange-traded Funds", 13 May 2019, https://betterfinance.eu/wp-content/uploads/BETTER-FINANCE-Research-Paper-Securities-Lending-11062019.pdf, 24 p. (accessed 21.09.2022).

[33] M.C. Faulkner, *An Introduction to Securities Lending* (4th edition), London, Spitalfields Advisors Limited, 2007, 23; M. Haentjens, *Financial Collateral: Law and Practice*, Oxford, Oxford University Press, 2020, 119–20.

[34] Discussed more deeply in J. Benjamin and L. Gullifer, "Stewardship and Collateral: The Advantages and Disadvantages of the No Look Through System", in L. Gullifer and J. Payne (eds.), *Intermediation and Beyond*, Oxford, Hart Publishing, 2018, 217–18.

[35] Also referred to as a 'general authority' from clients to use their shares for lending purposes, see Shareholder Voting Working Group, "Shareholder Proxy Voting: Discussion Paper on Potential Progress in Transparency", July 2015, https://uk.practicallaw.thomsonreuters.com/9-616-7485?transitionType=Default&contextData=(sc.Default)&firstPage=true, 35 (accessed 21.09.2022).

[36] "Typically, large institutional investors will either have the custodian bank handle the securities lending or will put the business out to bid to a third-party specialist. As a result, the personnel in the institutional investor with responsibility for voting the shares may not even be aware that the shares are out on loan", M. Kahan and E.B. Rock, "The Hanging Chads of Corporate Voting", *The Georgetown Law Journal*, 96, 2008, 1227, 1256; In 2009, the International Corporate Governance Network spoke of a 'loss of control' depending on the breadth of the lending agent's mandate, see ICGN, Response to the Panel on Securities Lending and Investor Protection Concerns, File No. 4-590, 24 September 2009, https://www.sec.gov/comments/4-590/4590-10.pdf, 5 (accessed 21.09.2022); *"Investment managers often do not know that stock they are managing has been lent out, if being lent out by custodians"*, Shareholder Voting Working Group,

EU[37], although these are generally older and, as became clear from discussions with practitioners[38], are not reflected by current market practices. In any case, a securities lending authorisation agreement that forms part of a wider custody relationship with an intermediary, who acts as a lending agent on the basis of a general mandate and only informs the investor (its client) retrospectively, in principle places the investor at greater risk of not knowing if and/or when shares have been lent and how this affects the exercise of its voting rights. For example in the UK, it was argued 'the involvement of two other parties [i.e. intermediaries] in the chain increases the risk of missed votes and indeed this is compounded by the fact that the beneficial owner may not know whether the securities are out on loan'.[39] Timely awareness about the number of shares that have been lent out is nevertheless a crucial first step would the investor be willing to recall the loaned shares for voting purposes.

"Shareholder Proxy Voting: Discussion Paper on Potential Progress in Transparency", July 2015, https://uk.practicallaw.thomsonreuters.com/9-616-7485?transitionType=Default&contextData=(sc.Default)&firstPage=true, 64 (accessed 21.09.2022); *"Broker-dealers do not always inform their customers about the fact of specific share loans, or their effect on vote entitlements"*, A. Sheehan and J. C. Coates, "Proxy Plumbing Recommendation", Harvard Law School Corporate Governance Forum, 10 September 2019, https://corpgov.law.harvard.edu/2019/09/10/proxy-plumbing-recommendation/#53b, (annex) (accessed 21.09.2022). See also P. MYNERS, "Review of the impediments to voting UK shares", Report by Paul Myners to the Shareholder Voting Working Group, January 2004, 20; G. Raaijmakers, "Securities Lending and Corporate Governance", *Maastricht University Faculty of Law Working Paper*, 2006, https://papers.ssrn.com/sol3/papers.cfm?abstract_id=928312, 8 (accessed 21.09.2022).

[37] *"In some cases, the lender does not know that securities are being borrowed from his securities account. He is only informed after the event. (…) It also occurs that securities lending is based on specific agreements, whereby the lender is aware of the actual lending"*, The Expert Group On Cross Border Voting In Europe, "Cross-border Voting in Europe: Final Report", August 2002 https://repository.wodc.nl/bitstream/handle/20.500.12832/1326/on2002-6-full-text_tcm28-67161.pdf?sequence=2&isAllowed=y, 47 (accessed 21.09.2022); *"Where a custody lending agent manages the lending, the investor has to await activity reports from the custodian. Where no activity report has been established or reached, (…) [and] an investor wants to vote his shares between two activity reports, he might discover at that moment that his shares are lent and that he therefore is prevented from doing so. An additional problem arises where the investor has outsourced also the voting process: here the voting agency may not even be informed about the stock lending where the information does indeed reach the investor"*, P. Santella, E. Baffi, C. Drago and D. Lattuca, "Legal Obstacles to Institutional Investor Activism in the EU and in the US", *European Business Law Review*, 23(2), 2012, 257, 287. It has been noted by the European Commission that *"it happens that stock held for the account of investors can in some instances be lent without informing investors"*. This statement in itself, however, need not necessarily express an underlying problem, as it merely reflects standard market practices where, indeed, investors are not notified by their agent until after shares have been lent and there is no prior authorisation of loans. European Commission, "Fostering an Appropriate Regime for Shareholders' Rights: Third consultation document of the Services of the Directorate General Internal Market and Services", 30 April 2007, https://www.treasurers.org/ACTmedia/consultation3_en.pdf, 4 (accessed 21.09.2022).

[38] See above, fn. 1.

[39] Shareholder Voting Working Group, "Shareholder Proxy Voting: Discussion Paper on Potential Progress in Transparency", July 2015, https://uk.practicallaw.thomsonreuters.com/9-616-7485?transitionType=Default&contextData=(sc.Default)&firstPage=true, 36 (accessed 21.09.2022).

Louise Van Marcke

3. THE EFFECT OF SECURITIES LENDING AGREEMENTS ON THE EXERCISE OF SHAREHOLDERS' VOTING RIGHTS

4. THE ENTITLEMENT TO VOTE

9.   As explained above (see fn. 24–25), a lending transaction fundamentally alters ownership status, at least from a legal perspective.[40] The transfer of title to the shares is accompanied by a transfer of shareholder rights (except for the right to dividends[41]), including voting rights. The legal position is therefore, as a principle, that the borrower becomes entitled to vote. In some jurisdictions, like the UK, the borrower will even appear on the register as the registered holder.[42] Moreover, the lender in principle has no say in how voting rights are exercised by the borrower. This principle is also part of the GMSLA (*"where any voting rights fall to be exercised in relation to any Loaned Securities or Collateral, [no] Borrower (…), shall have any obligation to arrange for voting rights of that kind to be exercised in accordance with the instructions of the other Party in relation to the Securities borrowed by it (…), unless otherwise agreed between the Parties"*[43]).

In theory, the parties to a lending agreement are therefore free to stipulate a right of instruction on the part of the lender, vis-à-vis the borrower.[44] It is extremely doubtful, however, to what extent such a clause would be enforceable

---

[40]   Above, at fn. 25, it was argued that the lender remains the owner in an economic sense since he ultimately bears the investment risk related to the shares (that will, eventually, have to be returned to him).

[41]   It is generally contractually provided *"the dividend and other distributions in respect of the shares must be paid or forwarded by the borrower to the lender"* since the lender remains the owner of the shares from an 'economic' perspective. See G. Raaijmakers, "Securities Lending and Corporate Governance", *Maastricht University Faculty of Law Working Paper*, 2006, https://papers.ssrn.com/sol3/papers.cfm?abstract_id=928312, 4 and 7–8 (accessed 21.09.2022). See also ISLA, Guidance Notes to the Global Master Securities Lending Agreement (2010 Version), 18 April 2010, https://www.islaemea.org/wp-content/uploads/2019/03/GMSLA_2010_Guidance_Notes_Freshfields.pdf, 7 (Principle 2.5) (accessed 21.09.2022).

[42]   Shareholder Voting Working Group, "Shareholder Proxy Voting: Discussion Paper on Potential Progress in Transparency", July 2015, https://uk.practicallaw.thomsonreuters.com/9-616-7485?transitionType=Default&contextData=(sc.Default)&firstPage=true, 35 (accessed 21.09.2022).

[43]   Art. 6.6 GMSLA.

[44]   The Expert Group On Cross Border Voting In Europe, "Cross-border Voting in Europe: Final Report", August 2002 https://repository.wodc.nl/bitstream/handle/20.500.12832/1326/on2002-6-full-text_tcm28-67161.pdf?sequence=2&isAllowed=y, 47 (accessed 21.09.2022); G. Raaijmakers, "Securities Lending and Corporate Governance", Maastricht University Faculty of Law Working Paper, 2006, https://papers.ssrn.com/sol3/papers.cfm?abstract_id=928312, 8 (accessed 21.09.2022).

on the market and would lead to the desired result in practice. Since the borrower becomes the legal owner of the shares on loan, he is free to sell them on the market to any third purchasing party (and it is for this purpose that some borrowers, such as short sellers, borrow shares in the first place). The anonymity surrounding stock exchange trading prevents buyer and seller from being linked to each other for the purpose of passing on voting instructions. The increasing volatility of share ownership in listed companies only exacerbates this.[45] Requiring a third-party purchaser to vote according to the (original) lender's instructions or requiring him to execute a proxy to the (original) lender's benefit, is downright impracticable (if not impossible) in today's market.[46]

It has been argued in the US that intermediaries often do not provide enough transparency about the person entitled to vote on shares on loan, resulting in a risk of 'overvoting' (because both the lender and the borrower exercise the voting right attached to the shares).[47]

5. THE RIGHT TO RECALL SHARES ON LOAN

10. The most common way to address the voting issue is the inclusion of a "recall clause" in the securities lending agreement that allows the investor to instruct the borrower to return equivalent securities for voting purposes. Par. 8.1 of the GMSLA contains a clause stating that *"subject to (...) the terms of the relevant Loan, [the] Lender shall be entitled to terminate a Loan and to call for the delivery of all or any Equivalent Securities at any time by giving notice on any Business Day of not less than the standard settlement time for such Equivalent Securities on the exchange or in the clearing organization through which the Loaned Securities were originally delivered."* In practice, most stock loan agreements are 'open term', that is, with no set maturity date, so the loan will continue until one of the two parties decides to terminate it and the securities are returned. Open term agreements include a right of recall that can accommodate, for example, a lender's voting wishes. If, on the other hand, the maturity period is "fixed" (i.e. a 'term' agreement), the shares on loan are only returned at the end of the term without a right to recall on the part of the lender. In a term contract, 'the lender is not obliged to accept the earlier return of the securities; nor does

---

[45] C. Clottens, *Proportionaliteit van stemrecht en risico in kapitaalvennootschappen*, Antwerpen, Biblo, 2012, 401.
[46] M. Kahan and E.B. Rock, "The Hanging Chads of Corporate Voting", *The Georgetown Law Journal*, 96, 2008, 1227, 1257.
[47] *Ibid*, 1258–263; A. Sheehan and J. C. Coates, "Proxy Plumbing Recommendation", Harvard Law School Forum on Corporate Governance, 10 September 2019, https://corpgov.law.harvard.edu/2019/09/10/proxy-plumbing-recommendation/#47b, (last par.) (accessed 21.09.2022).

the borrower need to return the securities early if the lender requests it'.[48] While borrowers may prefer term agreements (in order to gain certainty about how long they can hold the shares), these come at the price of higher lending fees for the benefit of the lender. It must also be noted that for some programmes, such as Euroclear's automatic lending programme, term agreements are not an option since in any case, reimbursement of the shares takes place in the short to very short term (usually one day, or the next day).

11. Before entering in securities lending agreements, it is considered good practice for lenders to develop and communicate some kind of 'voting policy' that makes the exercise of the right to recall more predictable. To avoid confusion, this voting policy is actually a kind of 'recall policy', and it has nothing to do with voting instructions as discussed above, fn. 44–46.[49]

12. Voting policies may range from (i) not voting (and thus not recalling) the shares at all, (ii) only voting (and thus recalling) the shares for important matters (possibly with an indicative, but not exhaustive, list of subjects to be voted on), (iii) voting (and thus recalling) all shares at every voting opportunity.[50] The decision to recall lent shares for voting purposes ultimately rests on a cost-benefit consideration of the benefits of voting, *versus* the (forfeited) lending fees. In general, there is no obligation to recall shares for voting purposes as a shareholder, but some regulators are being advised to introduce such a principle. In the Netherlands, in its 2022 proposal for updating the 2016 Dutch Corporate Governance Code, the Monitoring Commission introduced article 4.3.8 stipulating *"shareholders should recall their lent shares for voting before the record date of a general meeting of the company if the agenda for that meeting contains one or more significant matters"*.[51] According to the proposal, shareholders may determine for themselves what is considered a 'significant matter', but

---

[48] M.C. Faulkner, *An Introduction to Securities Lending* (4th edition), London, Spitalfields Advisors Limited, 2007, 36. See also T. Adrian, B. Begalle, A. Copeland and A. Martin, "Repo and Securities Lending", National Bureau of Economic Research Working Paper 18549, 2012, www.nber.org/papers/w18549, 4 (accessed 21.09.2022); M. Haentjens, *Financial Collateral: Law and Practice*, Oxford, Oxford University Press, 2020, 115.

[49] See, for example, the 'best practice recommendations' set out by the Global Alliance of Securities Lending Associations ("GASLA"), a collaboration of leading global securities lending industry associations, GASLA, "Voting Practices and Shareholder Engagement", November 2021, https://www.paslaonline.com/downloads/esgresources/GASLA-Voting-Guide-202111-FINAL.pdf, 7 (accessed 21.09.2022).

[50] Based on M.C. Faulkner, *An Introduction to Securities Lending* (4th edition), London, Spitalfields Advisors Limited, 2007, 49.

[51] The Dutch Corporate Governance Code applies to (*inter alia*) all companies with registered offices in the Netherlands whose shares (or depositary receipts for shares) are admitted to trading on a regulated market or a comparable system. See Monitoring Commissie Corporate Governance Code, "Consultatiedocument: voorstel voor actualisering", https://www.mccg.nl/publicaties/codes/2022/2/21/voorstel-voor-actualisering (accessed 24.10.2022).

this includes at least a proposal on the agenda of a general meeting (1) that is of economic or strategic importance; (2) where the outcome of the vote is expected to be uncertain or controversial; (3) in respect of which the shareholder disagrees with the opinion of the company's board.[52]

It is also advised the lender maintains at least one share of a portfolio company as a 'buffer' (i.e. *not* on loan) to ensure that he is directly – as a shareholder for voting purposes – and timely informed by the company of information leading up to the AGM (such as the notice of the general meeting and/or the record date).[53]

13. An alternative to ending the loan agreement upon a recall, whereby the borrower would be forced to return the shares on loan, is the reallocation of the outstanding loan to another lender. This is common practice in the industry.[54] A reallocation, initiated by the intermediary (i.e. the lending agent) changes the loan position from one lender to another, without any effect on the outstanding loan vis-à-vis the borrower. *"The outright ownership position is never impacted, as custody position must [remain in place] in order to execute the change on loan position."*[55] This is another advantage for big custodian banks with large client portfolios held in omnibus accounts since it is unlikely all clients would want to recall their shares at the same time.

6. OBSTACLES FOR SHAREHOLDERS TO RECALLING SHARES ON LOAN IN THE US COMPARED TO THE EU

14. Overall, securities lending transactions are generally presented as a low-risk, revenue generating activity. Despite its obvious benefits (not only to shareholders, but also to the market as a whole), shareholders should approach stock lending with some precaution, not least because of the common presence of intermediaries acting as lending agents and the ambiguity, and, at times,

---

[52] *Ibid*, 27.
[53] *Ibid*. Some intermediaries, like Euroclear, voluntarily inform their clients on the announcement of general meetings for outstanding loans (so that the lender is informed and can send a recall instruction if it wishes to exercise the voting rights), but this seems to be more of a favour to the benefit of the lender (i.e., a kind of market practice), rather than an enforceable right. For this reason, it is highly advisable to keep at least one share in the custody account, in order to receive company information directly from the issuer (instead of waiting for the intermediary to pass it along in a timely manner).
[54] A finding that became evident after discussions with practitioners, see fn. 1.
[55] Securities Market Practice Group, "Securities Lending/Borrowing Settlement Market Practice", October 2016, https://www.smpg.info/fileadmin/documents/3_Settlement%20and%20Reconciliation%20WG/A_Final%20Global%20Market%20Practices/SMPG_MP_SR_Securities_Lending_and_Borrowing.pdf, 4 (accessed 21.09.2022).

uncertainty stock lending creates for voting entitlements. Some areas of concern with respect to voting rights are highlighted here.[56]

15. First, some institutional investors, by virtue of their fiduciary duties to their ultimate beneficiaries, will be pressured to reduce the costs of intermediation, for which stock lending fees are an obvious method.[57] In practice, the decision to recall shares on loan (and the expected benefits resulting from the exercise of voting rights) will always be weighed against the benefits resulting from an ongoing loan (i.e. the lending fee).

In addition, index funds (and their fund managers) are particularly exposed to governance risks when shares are being lent out. In practice, it has been observed that lending index fund portfolio shares often happens *"without the option of retransferring for the general meeting"*.[58] The fee structure of fund managers also incentivises the decision not to recall the shares on loan for voting purposes, since the fund manager is sometimes remunerated by fees solely stemming from securities lending without any additional salary.[59]

16. Next, even when a securities lending agreement contains a recall clause – which is indeed almost always the case and considered good market practice[60] – it is argued by some that the actual exercise of the right to recall may not be as straightforward in practice as it is on paper and recalls are therefore met with a certain scepticism, even in the EU.[61] According to RINGE, three problems

---

[56] Advocates of securities lending have argued that corporate governance complications arising from securities lending are a result of the investor's free choice to engage in such practices: *"Investors who agree to lend their shares to their securities intermediaries cannot have their cake and eat it"*, see The Expert Group On Cross Border Voting In Europe, "Cross-border Voting in Europe: Final Report", August 2002 https://repository.wodc.nl/bitstream/handle/20.500.12832/1326/on2002-6-full-text_tcm28-67161.pdf?sequence=2&isAllowed=y, 47 (accessed 21.09.2022).

[57] E. Hu, J. Mitts and H. Sylvester, "The Index-Fund Dilemma: An Empirical Study of the Lending-Voting Tradeoff", The Center for Law and Economic Studies Columbia University School of Law, Working Paper No. 647, https://papers.ssrn.com/sol3/papers.cfm?abstract_id=3673531, December 2020, 9 (accessed 21.09.2022).

[58] W. Ringe, *The Deconstruction of Equity: Activist Shareholders, Decoupled Risk, and Corporate Governance*, Oxford, Oxford University Press, 2016, 50.

[59] *Ibid*, 47.

[60] *"The ability for a lender to recall securities is a standard feature of industry securities lending contractual documentation"*, Global Alliance Of Securities Lending Associations, "Voting Practices and Shareholder Engagement", November 2021, https://www.paslaonline.com/downloads/esgresources/GASLA-Voting-Guide-202111-FINAL.pdf, 3 (accessed 21.09.2022).

[61] W. Ringe, *The Deconstruction of Equity: Activist Shareholders, Decoupled Risk, and Corporate Governance*, Oxford, Oxford University Press, 2016, 45–47; J. Benjamin and L. Gullifer, Stewardship and Collateral: The Advantages and Disadvantages of the No Look Through System, in L. Gullifer and J. Payne (eds.), *Intermediation and Beyond*, Oxford, Hart Publishing, 2018, 230.

can arise in this respect.[62] Each of these should be nuanced, however, especially within the EU (when compared to the US).

First, exercising the recall clause does not necessarily mean that the lender will timely recover the shares, taking into account standard settlement cycles (T+2). It may also take some time for the borrower to have the securities available to redeliver them. Intermediaries generally counter this by pointing out that, while it is the lending agent's duty to inform its clients of the date at which the right to recall can be exercised at the latest, lenders bear the risk of failing to inform their agents of their wishes in this regard in good time.[63] Another sore point related to this timetable, especially in the US, is that recalling shares may conflict with the proxy voting timeline. In the US, the agendas of AGM's (i.e. the matters to be voted upon), which are part of companies' proxy statements, are generally not distributed to investors *before* the record date.[64] This is because there is currently no obligation for public companies to file proxy statements *before* the record date. This leaves lenders in the US at the real risk of not knowing if a recall for voting purposes is useful – a problem referred to as 'hidden agendas'.[65] A recent empirical analysis in the US found that 'for 88% of shareholder votes, investors are unable to find out what questions they will be voting on in time to decide whether they wish to vote on them'.[66] This sharply contradicts with most European jurisdictions, where the convocation of the annual general meeting generally includes the agenda (for example in Belgium, France and Germany[67]). It can be concluded, hence, that shares on loan from European listed companies would be recalled by investors in a more informed way, and in this respect EU national company laws are more suited to shareholders in their capacity of stock lenders.

---

[62] Based on W. Ringe, *The Deconstruction of Equity: Activist Shareholders, Decoupled Risk, and Corporate Governance*, Oxford, Oxford University Press, 2016, 45–7.

[63] According to the industry, these processes are nowadays highly automated and reduce any risks for lenders in this respect, provided that they exercise their right to recall in a timely manner.

[64] This is the result of the complex interplay between state corporate law rules (governing the record date) and federal securities laws (governing the filing of proxy statements). For a detailed explanation of how both timelines overlap in practice, see S. Hirst and A.Z. Robertson, "Hidden Agendas in Shareholder Voting", *Yale Journal on Regulation, 39*(3), 2022, 1230–1232.

[65] C. Clottens, "Empty Voting: A European Perspective", *ECFR*, 2012, n°4, 477–478; S. Hirst and A.Z. Robertson, "Hidden Agendas in Shareholder Voting", *Yale Journal on Regulation*, 2022, *39*(3), 1218–1273. See also the 'securities lending surprise' in relation to agenda-setting after the record date as described in M. Kahan and E.B. Rock, "The Hanging Chads of Corporate Voting", *The Georgetown Law Journal, 96*, 2008, 1227, 1257.

[66] S. Hirst and A.Z. Robertson, "Hidden Agendas in Shareholder Voting", *Yale Journal on Regulation*, 39(3), 2022, 1220.

[67] Respectively, art. 7:129, §2 *Wetboek Vennootschappen en Verenigingen* (Belgium); Art. R225-66 Code de Commerce (France); §121(2) *Aktien Gesetz* (Germany). Also in the UK, Sec. 311(2) Companies Act 2006 stipulates the notice of a general meeting must state the general nature of the business to be dealt with at the meeting, and in practice, notices will accurately set out the actual resolutions to be considered at the AGM, accompanied by explanations, see L. Kosmin Qc and C. Roberts, *Company Meetings and Resolutions: Law, Practice, and Procedure* (third edition), Oxford, Oxford University press, 2020, 21.

Second, it is warned borrowers could be actively looking out for lending arrangements where the right to recall is *not* included (i.e. term agreements)[68], which has the potential of steering financial markets in a direction where the borrower is disadvantaged from a governance perspective. However, it should be noted that today, most lending agreements are still concluded on an open term basis, and there may be different reasons to opt for a term or open term contract on both sides (as discussed above, fn. 48). What is more, lenders remain free to exclude term agreements from the authorisation agreement with their lending agent.

Lastly, it has been suggested that actual exercise of the right to recall would damage the lender's reputation towards the borrower, which could impede future lending transactions and the resulting fees.[69] This may be true to some extent: indeed, from the borrowers' point of view, lenders may differ in attractiveness depending on the limits they set in the authorisation agreement with their lending agent. The impact of this finding may, however, be mitigated by the mere fact that securities lending remains an ancillary service to investors (and is not their main source of income). Over the years, borrowers have furthermore become aware of the increasing trend in shareholder engagement and activism and consequent recalls for these purposes – it could even be argued the borrower's image would be damaged to a much greater extent by a failure to return recalled shares in a timely manner. In practice, both in the US and in the EU, share recalls have become standard market practice and large intermediaries holding omnibus accounts prove useful in this respect, for example by providing reallocation of outstanding loans to other lenders (as discussed above, fn. 54–55).

It is true, however, that most shares are only recalled in exceptional circumstances when voting stakes are particularly high.[70] In absolute terms, therefore, it is not surprising that in practice the recall rate of all outstanding lent shares remains relatively low.[71]

---

[68] W. Ringe, The Deconstruction of Equity: Activist Shareholders, Decoupled Risk, and Corporate Governance, Oxford, Oxford University Press, 2016, 45.

[69] *"Funds' recall of securities might also reduce their potential securities lending income in the future because borrowers tend to borrow from lenders with a lower likelihood of recalling stocks"*, see J. Xie, "Are passive investors also passive voters? Evidence from securities lending by mutual funds", 28 February 2022, https://papers.ssrn.com/sol3/papers.cfm?abstract_id=3754346, 16 (accessed 21.09.2022); Ringe speaks of a reputation as *an "unreliable business partner"*, W. Ringe, *The Deconstruction of Equity: Activist Shareholders, Decoupled Risk, and Corporate Governance*, Oxford, Oxford University Press, 2016, 46–7.

[70] W. Ringe, *The Deconstruction of Equity: Activist Shareholders, Decoupled Risk, and Corporate Governance*, Oxford, Oxford University Press, 2016, 45. A finding confirmed by G. Raaijmakers, "Securities Lending and Corporate Governance", *Maastricht University Faculty of Law Working Paper*, 2006, https://papers.ssrn.com/sol3/papers.cfm?abstract_id=928312, p. 11 (accessed 21.09.2022); P. Santella, E. Baffi, C. Drago and D. Lattuca, "Legal Obstacles to Institutional Investor Activism in the EU and in the US", *European Business Law Review*, 23(2), 2012, 257, 260; D. Marais, "Decoupling Voting Rights from Economic Interest: The Case of Empty and Negative Voting", *Trinity College Law review*, 18, 2015, 180, 188.

[71] W. Ringe, *The Deconstruction of Equity: Activist Shareholders, Decoupled Risk, and Corporate Governance*, Oxford, Oxford University Press, 2016, 47. To the best of the author's knowledge,

7. EMPIRICAL FINDINGS AND INPUT FROM THE INDUSTRY

17. Recent empirical research has also revealed a number of sore points on the voting activity of investors that engage in securities lending. According to a study from 2022 analysing the securities lending and voting data for actively managed mutual funds in the US from 2005 to 2011, active mutual funds are more inclined to forego lending fees and recall their shares for voting purposes when their ownership stake in the stock is larger and thus, the potential to gain greater benefit from governance improvements increases.[72] This finding is in line with traditional free-riding theory about shareholder participation.[73] Adding to the free-riding problem, it has been argued that while the benefits of shareholder intervention are shared between all shareholders, the lending fee is foregone only by the intervening shareholder which in itself incentivises lending over voting.[74]

A slightly older study from 2015, using lending and voting data from 2007 to 2009 (on aggregate blockholders, mutual funds, banks and insurance companies, pensions and endowments, and long-term investors), furthermore found that recall is associated with more voting support for shareholder proposals and less for management proposals (e.g., those related to corporate control and compensation).[75] This finding confirms that shares on loan are recalled mainly in cases that are critical to activist shareholders, e.g., because

---

there is no recent publicly available data on the exact number of recalls.

[72] J. Xie, "Are passive investors also passive voters? Evidence from securities lending by mutual funds", 28 February 2022, https://papers.ssrn.com/sol3/papers.cfm?abstract_id=3754346, 53 (accessed 21.09.2022).

[73] Traditionally, it has been held that the willingness of a shareholder to intervene in a company increases with the holding stake, see A. Shleifer and R.W. Vishny, "Large shareholders and corporate control", *Journal of Political Economy*, 94, 1986, 461–88. There is nevertheless a debate as to whether shareholding size is a determinant of shareholder engagement. McCahery, Sautner and Starks, for example, hypothesised in their research that *"larger investors are more likely to have larger holdings in their portfolio firms, and larger holdings provide stronger engagement incentives because they allow an investor to keep a larger share of the benefits if engagement is successful."* However, their qualitative (survey) research could not confirm this hypothesis and the size of an institutional investor was therefore not retained by the authors as a determinant for shareholder engagement. See J.A. McCahery, Z. Sautner and L.T. Starks, "Behind the Scenes: The Corporate Governance Preferences of Institutional Investors", *The Journal of Finance*, 71(6), 2016, 2483, 2905–932.

[74] E. Hu, J. Mitts and H. Sylvester, "The Index-Fund Dilemma: An Empirical Study of the Lending-Voting Tradeoff", The Center for Law and Economic Studies Columbia University School of Law, Working Paper No. 647, https://papers.ssrn.com/sol3/papers.cfm?abstract_id=3673531, December 2020, 4 (accessed 21.09.2022); J. Mitts, "The Price of Your Vote: Proxy Choice and Securities Lending", 11 October 2021, The CLS Blue Sky Blog, https://clsbluesky.law.columbia.edu/2021/10/11/the-price-of-your-vote-proxy-choice-and-securities-lending/ (accessed 21.09.2022).

[75] R. Aggarwal, P.A.C. Saffi and J. Sturgess, "The Role of Institutional Investors in Voting: Evidence from the Securities Lending Market", *The Journal of Finance*, 70(5), 2015, 2309, 2309–346.

the voting outcome may have a positive impact on the stock price that is greater than the lending fee (earned if the shares were not recalled). On the other hand, this study also shows that in the period prior to the record date, the lending supply is significantly lower.[76] A recent study from 2022, using securities lending data from 2014 to 2020, has also found that 'the number of shares available to lend falls sharply a week or two before record dates before jumping back up the day after the record date'.[77] The ISLA, too has confirmed that a lot of shares are increasingly being recalled in the period leading up to the record date.

Based on these findings, it thus seems justified to conclude that investors – regardless of any agreements with lending agents – nowadays have sufficient control over the outstanding number of shares on loan and seem to be (more) aware of the loss of voting rights that such lending causes, and – at least in the EU – are able to make informed decisions on the "dilemma" between maintaining the loan and the resulting fees, or voting (and thus recalling shares for that purpose). The Dutch Monitoring Committee's proposal to require shareholders in Dutch listed companies to recall lent shares for the purpose of exercising voting rights in certain cases (see above, fn. 97) may be too far-reaching. After all, such a rule brings the significant disadvantage that it distorts free (securities lending) market mechanisms. It also ignores the undeniable reality that some long-term institutional shareholders (lenders) have no interest in exercising voting rights themselves but instead wish to remain passive, and it might be useful to let activist borrowers exercise the voting rights in such a case.

8. ACTIVISTS AS STOCK BORROWERS: STOCK LENDING AS AN INSTRUMENT FOR SHAREHOLDER ACTIVISM

18. On the other side of the lending equation are borrowers, i.e. those institutions that wish to acquire shares *temporarily* with the view to returning them in a later stage – a practice viewed as cheaper, quicker and less risky than the alternative of buying and re-selling shares. Several reasons may explain borrowers' interest in the stock lending supply, including settlement facilitation (for example, in automatic lending programs), short selling and risk-decoupling (i.e. separating or decoupling the economic exposure of shares from formal legal ownership and subsequent voting rights). Risk-decoupling related to stock lending will generally take the 'negative' form: the shareholder *"seeks to keep*

---

[76] *Ibid.*
[77] S. Hirst and A.Z. Robertson, "Hidden Agendas in Shareholder Voting", *Yale Journal on Regulation*, 39(3), 2022, 1221.

their entitlement to all formal shareholder rights (…), but attempts to exclude (or to limit) bearing the economic consequences".[78]

Since the (first) settlement motive is self-evident and does not present any corporate governance problems in practice, this section of the paper focuses on the latter two techniques. Borrowers are often hedge funds looking to reduce the economic risk associated with their equity portfolio[79] (as also recently confirmed by M. Lipton with regard to the US markets[80]), although borrowers may also include other types of (long or short) shareholders.[81] In any case, as mentioned in the introduction of this chapter, it is more likely that borrowing demand comes to the lending market from aggressive and offensive activist shareholders while large institutional investors (i.e. traditional activists making use of defensive activist techniques) may make part of their portfolio available to meet this demand (for other reasons of their own). The existence and frequent use of the stock lending market, and the shift in voting entitlements that accompanies it, thus raises a number of corporate governance risks that require closer consideration.

19. The borrowing side (as well as some of the concepts used in this section) can be summarised by the following scheme.

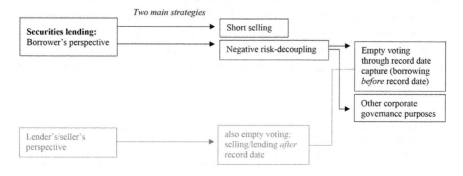

Figure 1. Strategies of activists as stock borrowers.

---

[78] As opposed to 'positive risk-decoupling', where there is a greater economic exposure than the formal shareholder position, a strategy often used in takeover attempts but not discussed here, see W. Ringe, *The Deconstruction of Equity: Activist Shareholders, Decoupled Risk, and Corporate Governance*, Oxford, Oxford University Press, 2016, 27.

[79] W. Ringe, *The Deconstruction of Equity: Activist Shareholders, Decoupled Risk, and Corporate Governance*, Oxford, Oxford University Press, 2016, 23.

[80] In a recent update of the Wachtell Lipton memorandum on shareholder activism techniques, one of the attack devices of (hedge fund) activists mentioned is 'using stock loans, options, derivatives and other devices to accumulate positions secretly, announce surprisingly large, leveraged economic stakes or increase voting power beyond the activist's economic equity investment', see M. Lipton, "Wachtell Lipton on Dealing with Activist Hedge Funds and Other Activist Investors", The CLS Blue Sky Blog, 7 September 2022, https://clsbluesky.law. columbia.edu/2022/09/07/wachtell-lipton-on-dealing-with-activist-hedge-funds-and-other-activist-investors-3/ (accessed 21.09.2022).

[81] C. Clottens, "Empty Voting: A European Perspective", *ECFR*, 2012, n°4, 446, 452.

'Negative risk-decoupling', 'empty voting' and 'record date capture' (see above, 4.2–4.3) are concepts that have been established in the US and that have been widely researched and described in US literature.[82] One of the reasons for this is without a doubt the particularly large time span, in the US, between the record date (i.e. the date (and sometimes more specifically, the moment in time) at which it is established who are the eligible shareholders for the purposes of attendance to and voting at the general meeting) and the date of the general meeting. This timespan usually being between 30 and 60 days.[83] In the US, this creates a significant risk that economic ownership and voting power of shares will have become disconnected by the time of the general meeting.[84] For several reasons, however, it is worth contemplating the potential of these phenomena in European jurisdictions. Before doing so, another common strategy among activist borrowers, i.e. that of short selling, will be examined.

9. SHORT SELLING AND NEGATIVE VOTING BY SHORT SHAREHOLDER ACTIVISTS

20. Short selling is one of the primary purposes of securities lending transactions.[85] As discussed before (see above, fn. 26), in neutral terms short selling can be defined as the financial technique of *"1) borrowing shares of a company owned by a long investor (...), 2) selling those shares in the market, and 3) repaying later the share loan by buying back the shares in the market"*.[86, 87] Short activism has the goal of profiting from a downward movement of the share

---

[82] For prominent treatment of these issues, see H.T.C. Hu and B. Black, "The New Vote Buying: Empty Voting and Hidden (Morphable) Ownership", *Southern California Law Review*, 79, 2006, 811–908; A. Brav and R.D. Mathews, "Empty Voting and the Efficiency of Corporate Governance", *Journal of Financial Economics*, 99(2), 2011, 235, 289–307; S. Christoffersen, C.C. Geczy, D.K. Musto, and A.V. Reed, "Vote Trading and Information Aggregation", *The Journal of Finance*, 62(2), 2007, 2557, 2897–2929; M. Kahan and E.B. Rock, "The Hanging Chads of Corporate Voting", *The Georgetown Law Journal*, 96, 2008, 1227, 1227–281.

[83] According to DGCL §213(a), the record date shall not be more than 60 nor less than 10 days before the date of the general meeting, but some exchanges like the NYSE recommend *"that a minimum of 30 days be allowed between the record and meeting dates so as to give ample time for the solicitation of proxies"*, see Rule 401.03 NYSE Listed Company Manual.

[84] See R.F. Balotti, J.A. Finkelstein, *Delaware Law of Corporations and Business Organizations* (4th edition), s.l., Wolters Kluwer, 2022–1 Supplement (§7.8 Voting).

[85] S. Hirst and A.Z. Robertson, "Hidden Agendas in Shareholder Voting", *Yale Journal on Regulation*, 39(3), 2022, 1226.

[86] C. Block, "Muddy Waters Capital LLC's observations on the parliamentary mission report on activism submitted by the Finance, General Economy Control Commission of the French Parliament ("Assemblée Nationale") on October 2, 2019", 3 December 2019, https://papers.ssrn.com/sol3/papers.cfm?abstract_id=3499127, 4 (accessed 21.09.2022).

[87] 'Naked' or 'uncovered' short selling involves selling shares (short) that were *not* rightfully borrowed at the time of the short sale and has now been prohibited in the EU, see art. 12 (*"Restrictions on uncovered short sales in shares"*) Regulation (Eu) No 236/2012 of the European Parliament and of The Council of 14 March 2012 on short selling and certain aspects of credit default swaps, *Oj.L.* 24 March 2012, ep. 86, 1–24.

price, by returning to the lender shares that the investor has bought back in the market at a lower price than he had first sold them.

Even though short activism has a predominantly negative connotation (in part, due to its frequent use during the 2008–2009 global financial crisis which had the potential of aggravating the downward spiral in stock prices[88]), the phenomenon in itself need not necessarily be viewed unfavourably in all cases. This is especially true in a situation where a company's share price is overvalued (i.e. deviates significantly from the company's fundamental value) and is in need of a downward correction to the benefit of all stakeholders.[89] Short sellers equally contribute to more information about companies in the market ('informational efficiency')[90] and short selling is even a technique to protect investors from risk (for example by holding part of a predominantly "long" portfolio 'short').[91]

21. Short selling bears the risk, on the other hand, of becoming problematic when shares are borrowed *before* the record date, voting rights are exercised with the aim to effectively reduce the company's value, and the shares are subsequently shorted (i.e. sold on the market and bought back at a reduced price once the share price has dropped, to return them to the lender). This phenomenon is labelled as 'negative voting', referring to the negative interest (opposite to that of long investors) of the shareholder exercising the voting

---

[88] See consideration (1) Regulation (Eu) No 236/2012 of the European Parliament and of The Council of 14 March 2012 on short selling and certain aspects of credit default swaps, *Oj.L.* 24 March 2012, ep. 86, 1–24.

[89] In his study on the agency costs of overvalued equity, Jensen recommends that companies consult with short sellers on a frequent basis on potential overvaluations, admitting that "establishing such practices would require abandoning the generally held belief that short sellers are evil and damaging to the firm", see M.C. Jensen, "Agency Costs of Overvalued Equity", *Financial Management*, 34(1), 2005, 5, 16. According to some short sellers, such as Muddy Waters, bankrupt companies often point the finger to short sellers as the cause of their declining stock price, when in fact such declines are primarily due to the loss of long-term investors' confidence in the company and the sale of their holdings for this reason. While this may be true, high volumes of short sales may effectively exacerbate a company's financial distress, see C. Block, "Muddy Waters Capital LLC's observations on the parliamentary mission report on activism submitted by the Finance, General Economy Control Commission of the French Parliament ("Assemblée Nationale") on October 2, 2019", 3 December 2019, https://papers.ssrn.com/sol3/papers.cfm?abstract_id=3499127, 9 (accessed 21.09.2022).

[90] Research has found that short sellers can detect fraud in the market *before* the public revelation of a firms' financial misconduct (and the amount of short selling increases with the severity of the misconduct). The same study found that 'short selling not only anticipates financial misconduct; it also helps expose it since a firm at the 75th percentile of abnormal short interest will be publicly revealed 8 months sooner than a firm at the 25th percentile'. This way, short selling provides external benefits to uninformed investors, see J. M. Karpoff and X. Lou, "Short Sellers and Financial Misconduct", *Journal of Finance*, 65(5), 2010, 1879, 1911.

[91] C. Block, "Muddy Waters Capital LLC's observations on the parliamentary mission report on activism submitted by the Finance, General Economy Control Commission of the French Parliament ("Assemblée Nationale") on October 2, 2019", 3 December 2019, https://papers.ssrn.com/sol3/papers.cfm?abstract_id=3499127, 7–8 (accessed 21.09.2022).

right.[92] An example of such negative voting was described by BLACK and HU in 2006, when a couple of hedge funds borrowed Henderson Investment shares before the record date and voted against a buy-out at the general meeting. This way, they effectively blocked the buy-out, contrary to the expectations of the other shareholders and the market. Anticipating on the share price drop the outcome of the general meeting would cause, they then sold the shares short and profited from the share price drop caused by the buy-out they defeated themselves.[93]

22. According to Clottens, *"negative voting (…) presents by far the greatest potential for inefficiency and welfare destruction"*[94], a view shared by ESMA in its latest 2012 feedback statement in response to a call for evidence on empty voting in the EU.[95] Unfortunately, it remains difficult, and often impossible, for lenders to assess borrowers' intentions (other than based on the borrower's historical voting behaviour) before lending out their shares to them.[96] For this reason, the lending decision remains a weighing of interests and is estimated by lenders according to their 'belief' in the long-term value of the shares.

23. In the Netherlands, regulatory efforts have recently (2022) been made by to overcome negative voting by short activists. In its proposal for updating the 2016 Dutch Corporate Governance Code, the Monitoring Commission introduced article 4.3.7 prohibiting shareholders from voting *"if their short position in the company is larger than their long position".*[97] No such principle was present in the 2016 Code: at the very least, this seems to be an indication of an increased awareness and changing mindset in this area.

---

[92] J. Cohen, "Negative Voting: Why It Destroys Shareholder Value and a Proposal to Prevent It", *Harvard Journal on Legislation, 45,* 2008, 237, 245; D. Marais, "Decoupling Voting Rights from Economic Interest: The Case of Empty and Negative Voting", *Trinity College Law Review, 18,* 2015, 180, 188.

[93] H.T.C. Hu and B. Black, "The New Vote Buying: Empty Voting and Hidden (Morphable) Ownership", *Southern California Law Review,* 79, 2006, 811, 834–35.

[94] C. Clottens, "Empty Voting: A European Perspective", *ECFR,* 2012, n°4, 446, 451–52.

[95] *"ESMA tends to agree (…) that the most risky practice related to empty voting is when an investor borrows shares (…) in order to vote in a way that is perceived to be against the long-term interest of the company and which may be with the objective of pursuing a personal gain from the trading position built up (often taking advantage from the share's price falling)",* ESMA, "Feedback Statement: Call for Evidence on Empty Voting", 29 June 2012, https://www.esma.europa.eu/system/files_force/library/2015/11/2012-415.pdf, 6–7 (accessed 21.09.2022).

[96] For this reason, restricting the lending agent in the securities lending authorisation agreement to only lend shares to borrowers who disclose their intentions for borrowing shares *prior* to taking out the loan, does not seem very workable in practice.

[97] Monitoring Commissie Corporate Governance Code, "Consultatiedocument: voorstel voor actualisering", https://www.mccg.nl/publicaties/codes/2022/2/21/voorstel-voor-actualisering (accessed 24.10.2022).

10. NEGATIVE RISK-DECOUPLING

24. A second, common strategy to engage in stock lending as a borrower (both a long or short activist) is negative risk-decoupling, i.e. making the formal shareholder position greater than the underlying economic exposure.[98] Negative risk-decoupling can be brought about by different financial techniques (such as the use of derivatives)[99], but for reasons of relevance only the risk-decoupling that is the result of borrowing shares is analysed here.

11. FORMAL SHAREHOLDER FOR GOVERNANCE PURPOSES (OTHER THAN VOTING ENTITLEMENT)

25. One of the reasons to borrow shares for the purpose of negative risk-decoupling is to meet minimum participation thresholds (in the company's capital) for bringing certain claims as a shareholder. These include thresholds for corporate internal remedies (e.g., the right to put items on the agenda of the general meeting and to table draft resolutions[100] or the right to call a general meeting[101]) and thresholds for remedies that require judicial intervention (e.g., bringing liability claims against directors[102]). Some of these remedies are especially relevant to minority shareholders – including activists who, more often than not, hold relatively small stakes in target companies.

---

[98] W. Ringe, *The Deconstruction of Equity: Activist Shareholders, Decoupled Risk, and Corporate Governance*, Oxford, Oxford University Press, 2016, 28–36; H.T.C. Hu and B. Black, "The New Vote Buying: Empty Voting and Hidden (Morphable) Ownership", *Southern California Law Review*, 79, 2006, 811–908.

[99] For a discussion, see W. Ringe, *The Deconstruction of Equity: Activist Shareholders, Decoupled Risk, and Corporate Governance*, Oxford, Oxford University Press, 2016, 28–36; H.T.C. Hu and B. Black, "The New Vote Buying: Empty Voting and Hidden (Morphable) Ownership", *Southern California Law Review*, 79, 2006, 811–908.

[100] See art. 6 SRD I (EU) and art. 7:130 WVV (for the Belgian Public Limited Company (NV), requiring shareholders who together hold at least 3% of the capital of a listed company). See Directive 2007/36/Ec Of The European Parliament And Of The Council of 11 July 2007 on the exercise of certain rights of shareholders in listed companies, *Oj. L* 184, 14 July 2007, 17–24 (hereafter: "SRD I").

[101] Art. 7:126 WVV (for the Belgian Public Limited Company (NV), including an obligation for the board of directors to convene the general meeting and set its agenda within three weeks when shareholders representing one-tenth of the capital request it, with at least the agenda items proposed by the shareholders concerned.).

[102] See for the Belgian Public Limited Company (NV) art. 7:156 WVV (the *actio mandati* or *vennootschapsvordering* – requiring a simple majority at the general meeting) or art. 7:157 WVV (the 'minority shareholders' claim – *minderheidsvordering* – requiring, on the day the general meeting decides on the discharge to be granted to the directors, shareholders to hold securities representing at least 1% of the votes attached to all the securities existing on that day, or hold on the same day securities representing a portion of the capital worth at least EUR 1 250 000).

The possibility of exercising certain information rights as a shareholder seems a less relevant motive for stock borrowing, since in the EU, thresholds are not always set for these. For example, the right to ask questions on the general meeting is vested in 'any' shareholder, regardless of the size of their holding.[103]

An illustration of stake-building through stock lending for the purpose of meeting thresholds as a shareholder is the *Lindner* case, decided before the German Federal Supreme Court in 2009.[104] In this case, a shareholder (initially holding about 62% of the share capital) borrowed shares from his fellow shareholders to acquire a holding of 95% of the company's capital, which was the threshold for initiation of a squeeze-out procedure in accordance with §327a *Aktiengesetz*. Although the squeeze-out was challenged by some minority shareholders, it was ultimately upheld by the *Bundesgerichtshof*.[105]

26. Admittedly, stakes in a target company can also be expanded by borrowing shares for the purpose of informal, 'behind-the-scenes' engagements with members of the board or management.[106] As a shareholder expands its voting power through borrowed shares, it increases its bargaining power. In practice, the threat of casting a public, negative vote at the general meeting has proved an effective pressure tool to push through significant changes in target companies (even before the general meeting).[107]

---

[103] See art. 9 SRD I and art. 7:139 WVV (for Belgium). Other, more far-reaching inspection rights that require judicial interference generally do come with a threshold (and can therefore give rise to share borrowing). For example, in Belgium article 7:160 WVV (NV) stipulates that the request for an expert investigation of a company's books and accounts (*vennootschapsrechtelijk deskundigenonderzoek*) must be made by one or more shareholders who hold at least 1% of the entire number of votes, or who hold securities representing a portion of the capital worth at least EUR 1.250.000.

[104] Bundesgerichtshof, judgment of 16 March 2009 (II ZR 302/06), *Entscheidungen des Bundesgerichtshofes in Zivilsachen* 180, 154.

[105] See also E. Čulinović-Herc, A. Zubović, "Tackling Empty Voting in the EU: The Shareholders' Rights Directive and the Revised Transparency Directive", *Croatian Yearbook of European Law and Policy*, 11(1), 2015, 133, 141; W. Ringe, *The Deconstruction of Equity: Activist Shareholders, Decoupled Risk, and Corporate Governance*, Oxford, Oxford University Press, 2016, 39.

[106] J.A. Mccahery, Z. Sautner and L.T. Starks, "Behind the Scenes: The Corporate Governance Preferences of Institutional Investors", *The Journal of Finance*, 71(6), 2016, 2905–932. This bargaining power is also recognised by W. Ringe, *The Deconstruction of Equity: Activist Shareholders, Decoupled Risk, and Corporate Governance*, Oxford, Oxford University Press, 2016, 38–9.

[107] L. Van Marcke, "Shareholder engagement (SRD II): zin en onzin: aandeelhoudersbetrokkenheid als regelgevend antwoord op bekommernissen van short-termism", *TRV/RPS*, 2021, n° 8, 829, 841.

12. FORMAL SHAREHOLDER TO EXERCISE VOTING RIGHTS: 'EMPTY VOTING'

27. As indicated by HU and BLACK, *"omit the short sale, and share borrowing becomes an easy route to empty voting"*.[108] 'Empty voting' refers to the most extreme form of negative risk-decoupling, i.e. that of *full* depletion of risk – in such a case, the shareholder is completely 'emptied', so to speak, from any economic consequences related to the shares while retaining the voting rights.[109] Borrowers may find themselves in (or actively steer themselves towards) a situation of empty voting when they borrow shares shortly *before* the record date, so that they become the shareholder entitled to exercise the voting rights (by holding title to the shares on the decisive record date). After the record date, the borrowed shares can be returned to the lender without affecting the voting entitlement at the AGM in any way. A similar, yet slightly riskier position can be brought about by buying (instead of borrowing) the shares before the record date, and subsequently selling them shortly after.[110] This strategy is also referred to as 'record date capturing'[111]: on the record date, the shareholder 'seizes' the voting rights of shares he will dispose of prior to the meeting (by returning them to the lender or selling them on the market), allowing them to vote at the general meeting without any economic exposure (i.e. empty voting).

---

[108] H.T.C. Hu and B. Black, "The New Vote Buying: Empty Voting and Hidden (Morphable) Ownership", *Southern California Law Review, 79*, 2006, 811, 833.

[109] E. Čulinović-Herc, A. Zubović, "Tackling Empty Voting in the EU: The Shareholders' Rights Directive and the Revised Transparency Directive", *Croatian Yearbook of European Law and Policy, 11*(1), 2015, 133, 135; D. Marais, "Decoupling Voting Rights from Economic Interest: The Case of Empty and Negative Voting", *Trinity College Law Review, 18*, 2015, 180, 183; W. Ringe, *The Deconstruction of Equity: Activist Shareholders, Decoupled Risk, and Corporate Governance*, Oxford, Oxford University Press, 2016, 27–8. Empty voting can also have another, less common meaning: for example (according to Fisch, an analogy with empty voting by hedge funds), it can refer to the voting behaviour of mutual funds (or their management) that are formally entitled to exercising voting rights of portfolio shares, but that do not themselves hold the underlying beneficial ownership (which lies with the underlying investors of the fund). For such 'mutual fund empty voting' which essentially amounts to the broader principal-agent problem of institutional investors, see J.E. FISCH, "Mutual Fund Stewardship and the Empty Voting Problem", *Brooklyn Journal of Corporate, Financial & Commercial Law, 16*(1), 2021, 1, 71–96.

[110] H.T.C. Hu and B. Black, "The New Vote Buying: Empty Voting and Hidden (Morphable) Ownership", *Southern California Law Review, 79*, 2006, 811, 835.

[111] E. Čulinović-Herc, A. Zubović, "Tackling Empty Voting in the EU: The Shareholders' Rights Directive and the Revised Transparency Directive", *Croatian Yearbook of European Law and Policy, 11*(1), 2015, 133, 136; W. Ringe, *The Deconstruction of Equity: Activist Shareholders, Decoupled Risk, and Corporate Governance*, Oxford, Oxford University Press, 2016, 52–8; D. Marais, "Decoupling Voting Rights from Economic Interest: The Case of Empty and Negative Voting", *Trinity College Law Review, 18*, 2015, 180, 189–90; H.T.C. Hu and B. Black, "The New Vote Buying: Empty Voting and Hidden (Morphable) Ownership", *Southern California Law Review, 79*, 2006, 811, 832–35.

28. It should be noted, however, that record date capture does not necessarily have to be accompanied by empty voting at the general meeting. Should the shareholder still hold a block of his own shares, on top of which he has increased his voting power through record date capture, he will be voting at the general meeting in a negative risk-decoupled way, but not completely 'empty'.[112] For example, both in the *Mediobanca* and *Laxey/British Land* cases (discussed below, fn. 124-135), the borrower already held shares in the company *prior* to increasing its voting power through a stock lending transaction. Since there was still some economic exposure in both cases, albeit less than the formal voting position, the vote cannot be considered 'empty' but merely reflects a situation of negative risk-decoupling in combination with a record capture strategy.[113]

29. A situation of empty voting may, on the other hand, also occur in a more incidental and unintentional way as a logical and inevitable consequence of the record date system. This is the case where a shareholder sells or lends out its shares *after* the record date (i.e. in the period between the record date and the general meeting) (see **Figure 1**).[114] The prevailing view in the literature[115], among market authorities (such as ESMA[116]) and practitioners[117] is that such cases of empty voting are inevitable, but much less harmful. Many cases of empty voting

---

[112] Despite the confusion in this regard in some literature (with a different use of the term 'empty voting'), see for example J.M. Barry, J.W. Hatfield and C.D. Kominers, "On Derivatives Markets and Social Welfare: a Theory of Empty Voting and Hidden Ownership", *Virginia Law Review*, 99(6), 2013, 1103, 1127.

[113] Admittedly, some of the confusion comes from different definitions adopted in literature. Hu and Black define empty voters as *"persons whose voting rights substantially exceed their net economic ownership"*, thus referring to full *or* partial decoupling. In the author's view, it seems more advisable to make a clear distinction between empty voting as (according to Ringe) "complete risk depletion" (i.e., full decoupling from economic interests) and other negative risk-decoupling situations that reflect *reduced* risk. This approach is also taken by E. Čulinović-Herc, A. Zubović, "Tackling Empty Voting in the EU: The Shareholders' Rights Directive and the Revised Transparency Directive", Croatian Yearbook of European Law and Policy, 11(1), 2015, 133, 135; W. Ringe, *The Deconstruction of Equity: Activist Shareholders, Decoupled Risk, and Corporate Governance*, Oxford, Oxford University Press, 2016, 27-28. See for their definition also H.T.C. Hu and B. Black, "The New Vote Buying: Empty Voting and Hidden (Morphable) Ownership", *Southern California Law Review*, 79, 2006, 811, 825.

[114] "Between the record date and actual voting date, securities may be sold or lent, but the right to exercise the attached voting rights is retained by the seller or lender", N. Rachman and M. Vernaas, "Corporate Actions in the Intermediated System: Bridging the Gap between Issuer and Investor", in T. Keijser (ed.), *Transnational Securities Law*, Oxford, Oxford University Press, 2013, 153.

[115] E.g., W. Ringe, The Deconstruction of Equity: Activist Shareholders, Decoupled Risk, and Corporate Governance, Oxford, Oxford University Press, 2016, 52.

[116] ESMA, "Feedback Statement: Call for Evidence on Empty Voting", 29 June 2012, https://www.esma.europa.eu/system/files_force/library/2015/11/2012-415.pdf, 9 (accessed on 21.09.2022).

[117] *Cf.* interviews with practitioners, fn. 1.

take this (less harmful) form. For this reason, prohibiting empty voting would not be desirable.[118]

30. In spite of the development of some arguments to defend empty voting by borrowers (e.g., that it has the potential to overcome shareholder passivity on the lending side[119]), the overall consensus by scholars is that empty voting by stock borrowers is, more often than not, a harmful practice.[120] The main reason for this is that the exercise of voting rights without any underlying economic exposure may prove harmful to other shareholders and stakeholders. Indeed, the shareholder passivity argument presupposes that voting rights are exercised in a manner that benefits all shareholders as a group, which is not necessarily the case.[121] Empty voting further touches on a fundamental concept inherent to company law that voting power is principally attributed on the basis of financial risk taking, and for this reason also raises reluctance from a 'moral' point of view. Many industry groups and codes of conduct in securities lending have explicitly stated that shares should not be borrowed for the sole purpose of exercising voting rights.[122] The UK has even banned this practice (see below, fn. 155–156). Interviews with practitioners equally confirmed that such borrowing intentions are strongly frowned upon. The GMSLA even includes a representation and warranty on the part of the borrower that *"it is not entering into a Loan for the primary purpose of obtaining or exercising voting rights in respect of the Loaned Securities"* (art. 14, (e) GMSLA). Still, in terms of enforceability it should be stressed these are *"only (…) best-endeavor obligation[s], and one should not be overly optimistic about the result"*[123] To date, there is no European legislation that prohibits such practices.

---

[118] Whereas the borrower would normally become entitled to exercise the voting rights of the borrowed shares, in this case the voting rights remain with the lender (who was, after all, the voting shareholder on the record date and remains untouched by subsequent transfers of the shares). As explained above, at fn. 44–46, voting instructions are not a viable solution here.

[119] D. Marais, "Decoupling Voting Rights from Economic Interest: The Case of Empty and Negative Voting", *Trinity College Law Review*, 18, 2015, 180, 190-91. For other potential benefits of risk-decoupling, see J.M. Barry, J.W. Hatfield and C.D. Kominers, "On Derivatives Markets and Social Welfare: a Theory of Empty Voting and Hidden Ownership", *Virginia Law Review* 2013, 99(6), 1103, 1124–129.

[120] D. Marais, "Decoupling Voting Rights from Economic Interest: The Case of Empty and Negative Voting", *Trinity College Law Review*, 18, 2015, 180, 192-193; W. Ringe, *The Deconstruction of Equity: Activist Shareholders, Decoupled Risk, and Corporate Governance*, Oxford, Oxford University Press, 2016, 41–3.

[121] Ibid.

[122] Gasla, "Voting Practices and Shareholder Engagement", November 2021, https://www.paslaonline.com/downloads/esgresources/GASLA-Voting-Guide-202111-FINAL.pdf, 7 (accessed 21.09.2022); International Corporate Governance Network, "ICGN Guidance on Securities Lending", 2016, https://www.icgn.org/sites/default/files/2021–06/ICGN068_Guidance_On_Securities_Lending_24pp_AUG16-v3_0.pdf, 16 ("Improper borrowing and lending practices") (accessed on 21.09.2022).

[123] G. Raaijmakers, "Securities Lending and Corporate Governance", *Maastricht University Faculty of Law Working Paper*, 2006, https://papers.ssrn.com/sol3/papers.cfm?abstract_id=928312, 8 (accessed 21.09.2022).

In practice it does happen that shares are borrowed with the main or sole aim of increasing the shareholder's voting power at the AGM and deliberately engaging in empty voting. Such an act occurred in the EU, for instance, in the recent Mediobanca/Generali case, which received a lot of media attention but has (to the author's best knowledge) not yet been discussed in the context of securities lending and the resulting corporate governance concerns. This case is discussed next.

13. EMPTY VOTING AND RECORD DATE CAPTURE IN PRACTICE

14. MEDIOBANCA/GENERALI

31. A recent case that caused a great deal of controversy was the increase of voting power of shareholder Mediobanca, a Milanese investment bank, in Assicurazioni Generali, a leading Italian insurance company (hereafter: "Generali"). On 23 September 2021, Mediobanca, which held just under 13% of Generali's capital, announced it had engaged in a securities lending transaction for 4.42% of Generali's shares, with the goal of increasing its voting power for the next general meeting. To this end, Mediobanca announced the transaction would have a duration of *"approximately eight months, or, without prejudice to the foregoing, until at least the Annual General Meeting of Assicurazioni Generali called to reappoint the company's Board of Directors"*.[124] Responding to rising criticism, Mediobanca published a second press release in April 2022 to defend its position, arguing *"the aim of the (…) securities lending transaction is to protect its proprietary investment'* and *'it is fully legitimate to exercise at the Annual General Meeting of Assicurazioni Generali to be held shortly the voting rights in respect of the shares borrowed"*.[125] On 29 April 2022, Generali's AGM took place and it appeared Mediobanca had effectively increased its voting rights to a total of 17.2%, despite heavy criticism during the run-up to the AGM.[126]

The goal of the increase in voting power through stock lending was the re-election of Generali's CEO Philippe Donnet at the general meeting, 'whose leadership was under challenge from a number of shareholders that opposed

---

[124] Mediobanca, "Press Release", 23 September 2021, https://www.mediobanca.com/en/media-relations/press-releases/press-release.html (accessed 21.09.2022).
[125] Mediobanca, "Press Release", 11 April 2022, https://www.mediobanca.com/en/media-relations/press-releases/comunicato-stampa-11-aprile.html (accessed 21.09.2022).
[126] See S.S. Borrelli and I. Smith, "Insurer Generali faces new test as bitter battle for control nears climax", *Financial Times*, 26 April 2022.

Donnet's re-election for a third term'.[127] The counterparty of the loan (i.e. the lender) was, amongst others, the French bank BNP Paribas. The loan agreement was covered by a strict confidentiality agreement, but later on, word came out in the Italian financial press that 'the securities loan [had relieved] the French bank, and some transalpine institutions, of the embarrassment of having to vote for (or even worse, *against*) Philippe Donnet, a manager who began his career at Axa and for years at the head of a rival like Generali'.[128] At the general meeting, Mediobanca ensured Donnet's re-election. In May 2022, Mediobanca's stake decreased below 13% after returning the borowed shares.[129]

32. Mediobanca's actions as a borrower were heavily condemned by the industry, including the ISLA[130], emphasizing the reputational damage this type of activity may have on the securities lending industry. Institutional Shareholder Services added that Mediobanca's *"questionable practice of borrowing shares… brings back memories of high-profile "empty voting" cases from the 2000s"*.[131] On the occasion, the industry reminded borrowers that bolstering voting power through securities lending violates many securities lending conduct rules (see above, fn. 122), but otherwise stood by helplessly in the absence of regulation (see below, fn. 155).

33. From a legal perspective, a situation comparable to the *Mediobanca* case could also occur in Belgium. In European jurisdictions, it would generally be expected there is less opportunity for abusive record date capture than in the US since there is a shorter time span between the record date and the date of the general meeting (according to article 7(3) SRD I, not more than 30 days). Italian companies, such as Generali, face a comparatively 'late' record date of 7 trading days before the AGM (art. 83*sexies*(2) Italian Securities Act). While one would theoretically expect this to deter empty voting, the *Mediobanca* case exposes an ongoing risk of record day capture and subsequent empty voting. Since Belgium has installed an even longer time span between the record day and the AGM,

---

[127] Securitiesfinancetimes, "Empty voting: back in the spotlight?", 5 July 2022, https://www.securitiesfinancetimes.com/specialistfeatures/specialistfeature.php?specialist_id=560&navigationaction=features&page=&newssection=features (accessed 21.09.2022).

[128] S. Bennewitz, "Mediobanca, assist francese. E' Bnp Paribas a prestare il 4,3% di Generali a Nagel", 29 September 2021, https://www.repubblica.it/economia/2021/09/29/news/generali-320019933/ (accessed 21.09.2022).

[129] Reuters, "Mediobanca's stake in Generali drops back to just under 13% after AGM win", 18 May 2022, https://www.reuters.com/markets/europe/mediobancas-stake-generali-drops-back-just-under-13-after-agm-win-2022-05-18/#:~:text=MILAN%2C%20May%2018%20 (Reuters),regulatory%20filing%20showed%20on%20Wednesday (accessed 21.09.2022).

[130] *"[It is] disappointing to recently see the open use of securities lending to gather votes ahead of a public AGM"*, see A. Dyson, "Reflections of the CEO", 26 May 2022, https://www.islaemea.org/blog/reflections-of-the-ceo-16/ (accessed 21.09.2022).

[131] See S.S. Borrelli and I. Smith, "Insurer Generali faces new test as bitter battle for control nears climax", *Financial Times*, 26 April 2022.

namely 14 days (art. 7:134, §2 WVV), the same risk prevails and may be even greater than in Italy.[132]

What is more, both in the EU and the US, lenders generally lack insight into the identity, intentions and reputation of borrowers because lending occurs automatically within set parameters, meaning individual loans are not checked *ex ante* for manipulations.[133] Lenders may not become aware of voting manipulations until *after* the voting has taken place and are thus at risk of not recalling shares in manipulative situations.

15. LAXEY PARTNERS/BRITISH LAND

34. As the ISS mentioned, record date capture situations have occurred before. The first notorious case is definitely the 2002 *Laxey Partners/British Land* case, in which the hedge fund Laxey Partners (holding 1% in British Land) increased its voting power to nine times its economic exposure (i.e. to 9%) by borrowing almost 42 million shares.[134] In this way, Laxey Partners tried to put a hold on the re-election of the British Land chairman at the general meeting (though Laxey failed to do so). According to HU and BLACK, this case was 'the first publicly reported instance' of record date capture.[135]

16. OTHER EMPIRICAL FINDINGS RELATED TO ACTIVISM: THE EMERGENCE OF A TREND?

35. In addition to these incidents (and others, not discussed here[136]), the question can rightly be asked whether record date capture and empty voting

---

[132] Although to the author's best knowledge, this has not yet materialised in a publicly available case in Belgium.

[133] D. Marais, "Decoupling Voting Rights from Economic Interest: The Case of Empty and Negative Voting", *Trinity College Law Review*, 18, 2015, 180, 188.

[134] H.T.C. Hu and B. Black, "The New Vote Buying: Empty Voting and Hidden (Morphable) Ownership", *Southern California Law Review*, 79, 2006, 811, 817; J.M. Barry, J.W. Hatfield and C.D. Kominers, "On Derivatives Markets and Social Welfare: a Theory of Empty Voting and Hidden Ownership", *Virginia Law Review*, 99(6), 2013, 1103, 1127; W. Ringe, *The Deconstruction of Equity: Activist Shareholders, Decoupled Risk, and Corporate Governance*, Oxford, Oxford University Press, 2016, 40.

[135] H.T.C. Hu and B. Black, "The New Vote Buying: Empty Voting and Hidden (Morphable) Ownership", *Southern California Law Review*, 79, 2006, 811, 817.

[136] For example, see *P&O Princess Cruises plc and Carnival Corporation* as discussed by W. Ringe, *The Deconstruction of Equity: Activist Shareholders, Decoupled Risk, and Corporate Governance*, Oxford, Oxford University Press, 2016, 40; see *Henderson Land* as discussed by H.T.C. Hu and B. Black, "The New Vote Buying: Empty Voting and Hidden (Morphable) Ownership", *Southern California Law Review*, 79, 2006, 811, 834; see *Mylan Pharmaceuticals*, as discussed by P. Ali, I. Ramsay and B. Saunders, "Securities lending, empty voting and

are widespread phenomena, particularly in the EU. Empirical studies that conclude record-date capture and empty voting are common occurrences, are relatively old and primarily US-focused.[137] By sharp contrast, practitioners in the EU (both those from the 2011 ESMA's call for evidence, as those from recent interviews) are convinced that both phenomena are less common in the EU, especially the more harmful practice of purposely borrowing shares to increase voting power and manipulate voting outcomes.[138] Recent, conclusive data demonstrating the occurrence of record date capture and/or empty voting in the EU is unfortunately lacking because these strategies, if they occur, would often remain under the radar.

36. Even when it is difficult (in the absence of conclusive empirical evidence) to observe a shift towards fewer cases in the EU, such a conclusion would be consistent with the rise in shareholder engagement and shareholder activism over the last years. In effect, recalling shares for the purpose of exercising voting rights is now a widespread practice in securities lending markets. It can be assumed that 'active' shareholders will increasingly strive to exercise voting rights themselves, and, hence, recall their shares before the record date or make their shares unavailable around that period – especially with the *Mediobanca* case in mind. Where lenders may have been less vigilant in the past[139], they can be expected to be more so today. It is the author's prediction that, in line with growing shareholder activism which is now also increasingly focused on sustainability and ESG, fewer and fewer securities will become available to lend around registration dates. Nevertheless, it is vital that the link between securities lending markets and voting rights continues to receive attention, and the ISLA's efforts in this area should be encouraged. After all, the *Mediobanca*

---

corporate governance", *Law and Financial Markets Review*, 8(4), 2014, 326, 337 (fn. 8); S.M. Haas, "SEC Resolves Empty Voting Action Involving King-Mylan Merger", Harvard Law School Forum on Corporate Governance, 19 August 2009, https://corpgov.law.harvard.edu/2009/08/19/sec-resolves-empty-voting-action-involving-king-mylan-merger/ (accessed 21.09.2022).

[137] For example, a study from Christoffersen et al. analyses US data from November 1998 until October 1999 and found that securities lending (borrowing) significantly increases around the record date, see S. Christoffersen, C.C. Geczy, D.K. Musto, and A.V. Reed, "Vote Trading and Information Aggregation", *The Journal of Finance*, 62(2), 2007, 2897–929; T.C. Hu and B.S. Black, "Equity and Debt Decoupling and Empty Voting II: Importance And Extentions", *University of Pennsylvania Law Review*, 156(3), 2008, 625–739. For an overview of empirical evidence, see P. Ali, I. Ramsay and B. Saunders, "Securities lending, empty voting and corporate governance", *Law and Financial Markets Review*, 8(4), 2014, 326, 329; W. Ringe, *The Deconstruction of Equity: Activist Shareholders, Decoupled Risk, and Corporate Governance*, Oxford, Oxford University Press, 2016, 70–4.

[138] ESMA, "Feedback Statement: Call for Evidence on Empty Voting", 29 June 2012, https://www.esma.europa.eu/system/files_force/library/2015/11/2012-415.pdf, 9 (accessed 21.09.2022).

[139] *Cf.* The *Laxey Partners/British Land* case, where the lenders (long-term institutional investors) were totally in the dark on Laxey's borrowing and voting intentions and later on apologised to British Land.

story demonstrates a continuing risk to shareholders. Abuse is never far away. While for the time being, the *Mediobanca* case may not illustrate a 'trend' in the EU, it cannot be considered an isolated case either. Rather than a theoretical hypothesis, it is realistic to presume that such practices can *and will* occur in the future and raise significant ethical and corporate governance concerns within listed companies.

17. REGULATORY CONCERNS

37. Over the past few years, securities lending transactions have increasingly become included in the (European) legislator's transparency framework – first more ambiguous, later more pronounced. For some time, art. 10 (b) of the Transparency Directive[140] has mandated a transparency notification of the acquisition or disposal of voting rights (in accordance with the thresholds of art. 9) when *"voting rights [are] held (...) under an agreement (...) providing for the temporary transfer for consideration of voting rights"*. According to the European Commission as well as the industry, art. 9 and 10 (b) together implicitly included stock lending agreements and, hence, triggered a notification duty on the part of the lender and the borrower.[141] Most European member states – like Germany[142], the UK[143] and Belgium[144] – adopted this approach in

---

[140] Directive 2004/109/EC of the European Parliament and of the Council of 15 December 2004 on the harmonisation of transparency requirements in relation to information about issuers whose securities are admitted to trading on a regulated market and amending Directive 2001/34/EC, *Oj. L.* 31 December 2004, ep. 390, 38–57.

[141] European Commission, "Commission Staff Working Document The review of the operation of Directive 2004/109/EC: emerging issues", COM(2010)243, 27 May 2010, https://www.europarl.europa.eu/registre/docs_autres_institutions/commission_europeenne/sec/2010/06 11/COM_SEC(2010)0611_EN.pdf, 81 (accessed 21.09.2022); Mazars, "Transparency Directive Assessment Report", https://www.mazars.be/content/download/40806/998379/version/3/file/Transparency_Directive_Assessment_Report.pdf, 123–25 (accessed 21.09.2022).

[142] See art. 21 and 25 a *Wertpapierhandelsgesetz*; E. Čulinović-Herc, A. Zubović, "Tackling Empty Voting in the EU: The Shareholders' Rights Directive and the Revised Transparency Directive", Croatian Yearbook of European Law and Policy, *11*(1), 2015, 133, 154–55.

[143] This was not always the case. In the initial transposition of the Transparency Directive, the UK exempted lenders from the requirement to disclose stock lending transactions (DTR5.1.1R(5)), but this provision (together with DTR5.1.3R(6)) was deleted in 2015. See for the changed policy, https://www.fca.org.uk/publication/consultation/cp15-11.pdf, p. 21–3 (accessed 21.09.2022); see for the amendments, FCA, "Disclosure and Transparency Rules Sourcebook (Transparency Directive Amending Directive) Instrument 2015", 5 November 2015, https://www.handbook.fca.org.uk/instrument/2015/FCA_2015_54.pdf, 9–11 (accessed 21.09.2022).

[144] Belgium opted for a directive-compliant transposition. In the explanatory memorandum for the conversion of art. 10 (b) of the Transparency Directive, the legislator describes the case where the voting rights of shares are transferred, without the securities themselves being transferred. In such a case, both the transferor and the acquirer are under a notification obligation. If we may follow the intention of the European regulator, art. 10 (b) is not limited to such a situation only, but also covers stock lending agreements where both the shares,

their implementation of the Transparency Directive. Some member states, like France, took a different view. In 2010, France explicitly installed a mandatory regime for shareholders temporarily holding shares amounting to 0.5% of the voting rights (which includes borrowers), to notify the issuing listed company and the French supervisor (AFM), with the sanction of losing the right to vote in the absence of such notification (art. L22-10-48 of the *Code de Commerce*[145]).

What is remarkable about the transparency regulatory framework is that a notification by a shareholder (even when that shareholder is a borrower) of its acquisition of a certain percentage of a listed company's voting rights (according to the thresholds of art. 9), says nothing about that shareholder's (borrower's) underlying economic exposure – which could effectively be decoupled, for example by means of securities lending.[146] The French system seems to differ from this in that the issuer itself must become informed that the borrower is holding the shares only 'temporarily', so that a situation of negative risk-decoupling may well be suspected by the market.

Another sore point is that the borrower does not have to disclose to the market its intentions for borrowing shares. While there are legitimate reasons to borrow shares, other strategies are arguably less desirable (e.g., to engage in negative voting as a short-seller, or record date capture for the purpose of empty voting). These uses of securities lending cannot be detected by the existing regulatory framework.[147]

38. A relatively new and far-reaching EU transparency mechanism related to inter alia securities lending was installed in 2015 by the Securities Financing Transactions Regulation (SFTR)[148], whose disclosure obligations only entered into force on 13 July 2020[149], 12 October 2020 and 11 January 2021. SFTR now

---

and the voting rights, are transferred to the acquirer. By analogy, it can then be concluded that, also in the case of stock lending agreements, Belgium has opted for a notification obligation for both parties. See *Parl.St.* Kamer 2007, nr. 51 2963/001 (Wetsontwerp op de openbaarmaking van belangrijke deelnemingen in emittenten waarvan aandelen zijn toegelaten tot de verhandeling op een gereglementeerde markt en houdende diverse bepalingen), 26–7.

[145] Previously art. L225-126 of the *Code de Commerce*.
[146] For this reason, Ringe proposes an attractive amendment to the Transparency Directive in the form of a 'notification of risk-modifying agreements', see for his proposal W. Ringe, *The Deconstruction of Equity: Activist Shareholders, Decoupled Risk, and Corporate Governance*, Oxford, Oxford University Press, 2016, 193.
[147] The lack in transparency *"in terms of who is the ultimate borrower and for what purpose they are borrowing the stock"* was also condemned in P. Madigan (BNY Mellon), "Stock Lending: Dispelling the Myths", January 2020, https://www.bnymellon.com/us/en/insights/aerial-view-magazine/stock-lending-dispelling-the-myths.html (accessed 21.09.22).
[148] See Regulation (EU) 2015/2365 (SFTR), above fn. 11.
[149] The first phase of the reporting obligation was to become applicable on 11 April 2020, but was postponed by ESMA due to the COVID-19 crisis.

requires counterparties[150] to a SFT to report the conclusion, modification or termination of a SFT to a trade repository within one day (T+1).[151] Whereas the Transparency Directive left room for doubt as to the person who should report a lending transaction, SFTR installs the principle of 'dual-sided reporting', meaning both lenders and borrowers must now disclose their side of the lending transaction to a trade repository who matches them according to the 'unique transaction identifiers' (UTI's) that are included in their submissions. Reporting obligations are generally delegated to lenders' and borrowers' lending agents.[152] SFTR has had a huge impact on the industry[153], especially in terms of standardization.[154] These transparency reports do not address the motivations of borrowers either, and the securities lending data is not shared with the market. The SFTR disclosures to trade repositories, however, facilitate large-scale data collection on SFTs, which can be shared with (national) market authorities (e.g. ESMA) (art. 12 SFTR). The main purpose of SFTR was thus to provide regulators with a clear view of the current risk exposures that remain in the market and to use the collected data to identify major shifts and trends in SFT's.

39. Increased transparency, however, is not a cure-all. The Mediobanca story illustrates that, even when a shareholder goes beyond its transparency obligations and voluntarily notifies the public that it is expanding its stake by borrowing additional shares (and voting rights), it can often not be prevented from doing so. This is because in most jurisdictions, as well as at the European level, there is currently no prohibition on borrowing shares in order to exercise voting rights. The UK forms an exception in this respect. The UK Money Markets Code proclaims that *"it is accepted good practice in the market that securities should not be borrowed solely for the purpose of exercising the voting rights at, for example, an AGM or EGM. Lenders should also consider their corporate governance responsibilities before lending stock over a period in which an AGM or an EGM is expected to be held"*.[155] This rule is enforced on individuals subject to the Senior

---

[150] A counterparty to a SFT is subject to SFTR-reporting when it is established in the EU, *"including all its branches irrespective of where they are located"*, or if it is established in a third country, when *"the SFT is concluded in the course of the operations of a branch in the Union of that counterparty"* (art. 2 SFTR). The latter implies SFTR has a huge global reach, since also third-country counterparties that engage in SFT's through European branches are captured within its scope.

[151] Art. 4 (1) SFTR.

[152] Art. 4 (2) SFTR.

[153] Refinitiv , "Solving the SFTR Data Challenge", s.d., https://www.refinitiv.com/content/dam/marketing/en_us/documents/reports/solving-the-sftr-data-challenge.pdf, 5 p. (accessed 21.09.2022).

[154] Standardization of terms and by the use of SFT reports in common electronic and machine-readable form, which include Legal Entity Identifier (LEI) codes for issuers, ISIN-codes, and UTI's (art. 4 (10) SFTR).

[155] Chapter 4, article 6.3 UK Money Markets Code, https://www.bankofengland.co.uk/-/media/boe/files/markets/money-markets-committee/uk-money-markets-code.pdf (accessed

Managers and Certification Regime (SM&CR), who must adhere to the FCA's 'recognised codes', which include the UK Money Markets Code.[156] The European legislator and European member states have not jumped on the bandwagon (despite the ISLA's encouragements to do so), possibly because 'active' record date capturing and empty voting with great impact (and great media coverage) only occur occasionally.[157] For the time being, monitoring the transparency notifications can be a useful instrument, but arguably *only* to assemble market information to provide a better empirical view of securities lending (and the various strategies that are maintained as a result) in the long-term. If at some point, a trend would be noticed, a ban such as that in the UK could be the legislator's next move. In any case, the market should not expect too much from transparency obligations since they will not solve problems like vote manipulation on an individual basis – as the *Mediobanca* story painfully demonstrates.

40. It can rightly be noted that empty voting and record date capture (as negative risk-decoupling strategies by means of securities lending) can also be used by long activist shareholders for positive, value-creating purposes that benefit the company, its shareholders and stakeholders. Examples include ESG activism and sustainability oriented activist campaigns in listed companies.[158] From this angle, borrowing shares for the primary purpose of exercising voting rights arguably also has the potential of *benefitting* listed companies (and by extension, the market and even society) in the long run. This is yet another factor that regulators should take into account when regulating securities lending practices.

18. CONCLUSION

41. The relationship between securities financing transactions such as stock lending and corporate governance concerns has remained relatively unexplored in recent years. Activist shareholders may borrow shares for various reasons,

---

21.09.2022).
[156] The Money Markets Code is a recognized code of conduct that institutions subject to the SM&CR must adhere to. These institutions include all banking-sector firms regulated by the FCA (i.e. banks, UK branches of foreign banks, large investment firms…). Consequently, all financial institutions that are active in securities lending (e.g. as lending agents) have to adhere to the Money Markets Code, see FCA, "Senior Managers and Certification Regime: dual-regulated firms", https://www.fca.org.uk/firms/senior-managers-certification-regime/dual-regulated-firms (accessed 24.10.2022); FCA, "FCA confirms recognition of the FX Global and UK Money Markets Codes", 26 June 2019, https://www.fca.org.uk/news/statements/fca-confirms-recognition-fx-global-uk-money-markets-codes (accessed 21.09.2022).
[157] For example, the Mediobanca case took place in Italy, and the market authority *Commissione Nazionale per la Società e la Borsa* did not object to the transaction in any way.
[158] H. De Wulf and L. Van Marcke, "Duurzaamheid En Vennootschapsrecht: ESG-Aansprakelijkheid En de Invloed van Institutionele Aandeelhouders", in A. Van Hoe and G. Croisant (eds.), *Droit et Durabilité / Recht en Duurzaamheid*, Brussel, Larcier, 2022, 349–431.

but can also lend out (part of) their share portfolio. Both sides of the lending equation have an impact on the exercise of voting rights related to the shares: lenders must recall shares on loan to exercise voting rights and borrowers may employ stock borrowing practices to increase their voting power. The implications of lending transactions for voting rights were analysed more deeply in this chapter.

While some argue that *"securities lending impedes fund voting participation"*[159] and *"securities finance can be seen as a structural barrier to activism"*[160], I would not go this far in my conclusions. Not only can activists extract additional revenue by lending out part of their share portfolio, empirical research and the findings of practitioners show that recalls have become common practice and that fewer and fewer shares are lent out over the record date. Moreover, in the European Union, lenders have the advantage of exercising recalls in an informed manner at the time of announcement of the AGM (and are not confronted with so-called 'hidden agendas' as in the US). On the other hand, stock lending techniques effectively prove to be a tool for shareholder activism, as the recent *Mediobanca* case illustrates. Although extending voting power by means of stock lending may be contrary to market best practices, it generally remains unprohibited.

In sum, this chapter therefore finds that securities lending can be as much a barrier to activism as it can be used to the advantage of activists.

42. As a final note, some recommendations and guidelines for future regulation of securities lending (from a corporate governance perspective) are included. First, it seems appropriate to discourage investors from lending out *all* their shares in a company and to mandate the retention of at least one share, so that information about the AGM reaches investors promptly and allows for timely recall of the remainder of its (lent out) shares. In this way, lenders will be less dependent on the cooperation of intermediaries (lending agents). Second, the current MiFID II framework would perhaps benefit from being supplemented by more concrete risks to be pointed out to clients; including 1) the consequences of lending shares for the exercise of voting rights, 2) the distribution of lending fees between the intermediary and the investor and 3) the risks posed by certain stock borrowing strategies, as addressed in this chapter.[161] An additional mandatory

---

[159] J. Xie, "Are passive investors also passive voters? Evidence from securities lending by mutual funds", 28 February 2022, https://papers.ssrn.com/sol3/papers.cfm?abstract_id=3754346, 33 (accessed 21.09.2022).

[160] J. Benjamin and L. Gullifer, "Stewardship and Collateral: The Advantages and Disadvantages of the No Look Through System", in L. Gullifer and J. Payne (eds.), *Intermediation and Beyond*, Oxford, Hart Publishing, 2018, 230.

[161] See the disclosure requirement of art. 49, par. 7 Commission Delegated Regulation (EU) 2017/565 of 25 April 2016 supplementing Directive 2014/65/EU of the European Parliament and of the Council as regards organisational requirements and operating conditions for

acceptance of these consequences on the part of the lender may further eliminate any doubt about voting entitlements, as well as some of the risks highlighted in this chapter. Furthermore, the European legislator could consider adding to SRD I (as amended by SRD II[162]) a sufficiently long minimum period between the announcement of the AGM and the record date (for example, 10 days) to facilitate timely and duly informed recalls.

On the borrower side, it was pointed out that – from the perspective of corporate governance – transparency notifications of increased voting rights and SFTR-reporting by counterparties can be expected to have little to no effect on an individual basis. This is because transparency does not prevent activists from deliberately borrowing shares for the primary purpose of exercising the voting rights. Transparency can, however, prove useful to monitor how often vote borrowing occurs, so that future consideration can be given to a ban (to borrow shares for the primary purpose of exercising voting rights) such as it already exists in the UK today. The collection of data under, for example, the SFTR framework should be used for such an evaluative purpose.

Lastly, it was noted in this chapter that not all securities lending for the (primary) purpose of exercising voting rights is value-destructive in nature. ESG and sustainability oriented activist campaigns where long activists increase their voting power by means of borrowing shares may actually *increase* value in listed companies in the long-term; and may just be desirable from that perspective. This makes securities lending also a useful tool for activists (borrowers), especially in light of the increased focus on sustainability many financial markets have seen in recent years. Policymakers should not lose sight of this advantage when mitigating other corporate governance risks caused by securities lending.

---

investment firms and defined terms for the purposes of that Directive Oj. L 31 March 2017, ep. 87, 1–83.

[162] Directive (EU) 2017/828 of the European Parliament and of the Council of 17 May 2017 amending Directive 2007/36/EC as regards the encouragement of long-term shareholder engagement, *Oj. L* 20 May 2017, ep. 132, 1–25.

THE COMPANY'S RIGHTS, CHALLENGES AND OBLIGATIONS WHEN FACED WITH SHAREHOLDER ACTIVISM

Deborah JANSSENS
Partner at Freshfields Bruckhaus Deringer LLP

Sigrid VERVERKEN
Counsel at Freshfields Bruckhaus Deringer LLP

1. *Introduction*. An activist campaign often tests not only the energy levels of a company's senior leadership team, but also raises delicate and untested questions under Belgian company law and MAR.[1] This contribution looks at activism from the (practical) point of view of the companies faced with it, with a focus on Belgian companies the shares of which are listed on the regulated market of Euronext Brussels.[2] We focus on the impact of different activist fund approach scenarios on such listed companies, and discuss the potential challenges these scenarios hold for such companies under Belgian company law and MAR. Our contribution includes guidance both on how to prepare for shareholder activism *before any approach is made* and on how to deal with activist funds *in case of an actual approach*. We also describe the at times unequal playing field in which companies and activist funds operate during the campaign. It should be clear from the outset that there is no 'one-size-fits-all' approach: judgement calls need to be made in each case, often with little time at hand, and any response needs to be tailored to each specific situation.

---

[1] Regulation (EU) 596/2014 of the European Parliament and of the Council of 16 April 2014 on market abuse (market abuse regulation) and repealing Directive 2003/6/EC of the European Parliament and of the Council and Commission Directives 2003/124/EC, 2003/125/EC and 2004/72/EC [2014] OJ L173/1 (*Market Abuse Regulation* or *MAR*).

[2] *Genoteerde vennootschappen / sociétés cotées* as defined in article 1:11 of the Belgian Code of Companies and Associations (*BCCA*).

1. ACTIVIST FUNDS AND RECURRING THEMES

2. ***Defining shareholder activism.*** There is no single prevailing definition of shareholder activism in view of the broad variety of actors, campaigns, themes and goals as well as national and international doctrine having differing views. Defined broadly, 'shareholder activism' describes an approach by a shareholder or group of shareholders to a company's board of directors[3] seeking a change in the company's behaviour.[4] Activist(s) are positioned on a spectrum, ranging from the more aggressive activist investors or funds, which consistently pursue activist investment and agitation strategies as an asset class, to smaller, often private, investors who tend to be more issue-focused and, while possibly holding fewer shares individually, can potentially attract significant attention.

3. ***Actors.*** Shareholder activism dates from the 1980s and coincided with the wave of takeovers by corporate "raiders". Where raiders aimed at taking (or threatened to take) control over companies to impose discipline on boards of directors and management, institutional investors looked for other ways to exert this pressure.[5] Activism has been, overall, an increasing trend since then and, in recent years, institutional investors which traditionally played a more passive role towards listed companies, have taken, and have been encouraged to take, a more active, engaged role, including as a result of SRD II[6] and the UK Stewardship

---

[3] In this contribution, we use the term board of directors to refer to a Belgian company's governing body (*bestuursorgaan / organe d'administration*), whether such body constitutes a board of directors (*raad van bestuur / conseil d'administration*) or supervisory board (*raad van toezicht / conseil de surveillance*).

[4] See i.a. the contribution of T. Vos in this book; E. Hellebuyck, *Hedge funds. Instituut Financieel Recht.*, vol. 16, 1st ed., Intersentia, Cambridge 2014, 159; A. Brav, W. Jiang and R. Li, "Governance by Persuasion: Hedge Fund Activism and Market-based Shareholder Influence" (2022) *European Corporate Governance Institute – Finance Working Paper* No. 797/2021 <https://ssrn.com/abstract=3955116> or <http://dx.doi.org/10.2139/ssrn.3955116> accessed 02.03.2023; D. Schmidt, "Quatre questions sur l'activisme actionnarial en droit français", *RISF/IJFS*, 2021/4, 61–67; L. Van Marcke, "Shareholder engagement (SRD II): zin en onzin. Aandeelhoudersbetrokkenheid als regelgevend antwoord op bekommernissen van short-termism", *TRV-RPS*, 2021, 829–856.

[5] A. Brav, W. Jiang and R. Li, 'Governance by Persuasion: Hedge Fund Activism and Market-based Shareholder Influence' (2022) *European Corporate Governance Institute – Finance Working Paper* No. 797/2021 <https://ssrn.com/abstract=3955116> or <http://dx.doi.org/10.2139/ssrn.3955116> accessed 02.03.2023.

[6] Directive (EU) 2017/828 of the European Parliament and of the Council of 17 May 2017 amending directive 2007/36/EC as regards the encouragement of long-term shareholder engagement [2017] OJ L132/1 (*SRD II*), as implemented into Belgian law by *Wet van 28 april 2020 tot omzetting van richtlijn (EU) 2017/828 van het Europees Parlement en de Raad van 17 mei 2017 tot wijziging van richtlijn 2007/36/EG wat het bevorderen van de langetermijnbetrokkenheid van aandeelhouders betreft, en houdende diverse bepalingen inzake vennootschappen en verenigingen / Loi du 28 avril 2020 transposant la directive (UE) 2017/828 du Parlement européen et du Conseil du 17 mai 2017 modifiant la directive 2007/36/CE en vue de promouvoir l'engagement à long terme des actionnaires, et portant des dispositions diverses en matière de sociétés et d'associations*, BS/MB 06.05.2020, 30488. SRD II contains various disclosure requirements applicable to institutional investors (life insurance and reinsurance undertakings and institutions for

Code.[7] In addition, non-governmental organisations (*NGOs*) have in recent years found their way to the company law toolbox available to shareholders to build and/or aid their case, as have done plaintiffs in a variety of litigations. The recent focus on sustainability, including environmental, social and governance

---

occupational retirement), their asset managers (credit institutions, investment firms providing portfolio management, AIFMs and UCITS managers), including:
- institutional investors and their asset managers are required to prepare and disclose their shareholders' engagement policy publicly in their written statement (for institutional investors) or on their website (for (re)insurance undertakings and asset managers). This engagement policy must describe how they integrate shareholder engagement in their investment strategy, how they supervise and interact with the listed companies in which they invest, how they exercise their voting rights, how they cooperate with other shareholders, how they communicate with stakeholders and how they manage factual and potential conflicts of interest.
- they also have to publicly report annually (together with the publication of their annual report) on the implementation of their engagement policy, on how they have exercised their voting rights and whether they made use of the services of proxy advisors. In this respect, institutional investors should also refer to the reports of their asset managers and where these can be found, if the implementation of their engagement policy is taken care of by the asset managers on their behalf.

Institutional investors and their asset managers may opt not to comply with the obligations described above (i.e. preparing and publishing an engagement policy and reporting on the implementation thereof) if they are able to provide clear and motivated reasons not to do so ('comply or explain').

Institutional investors are also required to disclose the key elements of their arrangements with asset managers, such as (i) how it incentivises the asset manager to align its investment strategy and decisions with the profile and duration of the liabilities of the institutional investor, (ii) how it incentivises the asset manager to make investment decisions based on assessments about medium- to long-term performance and to engage with investee companies to improve their performance, (iii) how the method and time horizon of the evaluation of the asset manager's performance and its remuneration are in line with the profile and duration of the liabilities of the institutional investor, (iv) how the institutional investor monitors portfolio turnover costs and how it defines and monitors a targeted portfolio turnover or turnover range and (v) the duration of the arrangement. In case the publication does not contain one of the key elements, the institutional investors must set out the reasons therefor.

Finally, asset managers need to provide information to the institutional investors on an annual basis allowing them to assess how the asset manager acts in their best interests. The information should also set out the medium- and long-term risks, the portfolio composition, turnover and turnover costs of the investment portfolio, the use of proxy advisors and the use of securities lending (and how this corresponds with the engagement policy). In addition, information on how investment decisions are made based on medium- and long-term performance criteria and whether any conflicts of interest occurred, needs to be disclosed.

[7] The UK Stewardship Code 2010 has made the concept of "stewardship" a common term in the investment environment. The current UK Stewardship Code 2020 defines "stewardship" as *"the responsible allocation, management and oversight of capital to create long-term value for clients and beneficiaries leading to sustainable benefits for the economy, the environment and society"*, and applies, generally speaking, to institutional investors which invest with funds of other persons (and those that provide services to these investors). Legal doctrine defines the term "stewardship" as *"the relationship between shareholders (asset managers and investors) and a company. Stewardship reflects a commitment on the part of asset managers and investors to be accountable to the beneficial owners whose money they invest, and to use their power as shareholders to foster sustainable, long-term value creation."* M. Lipton, "It's Time to Adopt the New Paradigm" (2019) *Harvard Law School Forum on Corporate Governance* <www.wlrk.com/webdocs/wlrknew/AttorneyPubs/WLRK.26358.19.pdf> accessed 02.03.2023.

(*ESG*) matters, has further encouraged certain institutional investors and NGOs to take a more active role, and at the same time there is a growing universe of activist funds dedicated solely to sustainability improvements to drive value.[8] Adding to those trends is that traditionally passive funds and institutional investors are, if not activist themselves, increasingly willing to support other activist funds where their interests are aligned. Such institutional backing has caused some activist funds to strike a more constructive tone such that institutional investors are less shy of rallying behind them, keen to be seen as demonstrating their own stewardship credentials (particularly on sustainability matters). Finally, proxy advisors have also in Belgium gained significant influence on the discussions at, and the outcome of, general shareholders' meetings of Belgian listed companies.[9] All these developments have further blurred the lines between actively engaged shareholders and activist funds, and in some cases, plaintiffs in litigation.[10] In this contribution, we focus on traditional activist

---

[8] See e.g. Lazard's Capital Markets Advisory Group, "2021 Review Of Shareholder Activism" (2021); Insightia, "The Shareholder Activism Annual Review", *The tenth annual review of trends in shareholder activism* (2023); Insightia, "The Activist Investing Annual Review 2022", *The Ninth Annual Review of Trends In Shareholder Activism* (2022); Insightia, "Shareholder activism in 2021 overview" (2022).

[9] Article 1(2)(g) of the SRD II defines "proxy advisors" as legal persons who *"analyse, on a professional and commercial basis, the corporate disclosure and, where relevant, other information of listed companies with a view to informing investors' voting decisions by providing research, advice or voting recommendations that relate to the exercise of voting rights"*. In view of their potentially important role, SRD II also imposes disclosure requirements on proxy advisors. Proxy advisors must publicly disclose a reference to a code of conduct and how they apply it (or explain why they do not) on their website. In order to inform their clients of the accuracy and reliability of their services, proxy advisors are required to disclose on their website certain key information relating to the preparation of their research, advice and voting recommendations, including the information sources, the procedures, the voting policies, the communication policy with listed companies and the conflicts of interest policy. In addition, any actual or potential conflict of interest or business relationship that may influence the preparation of the research, advice and voting recommendation must be reported to their clients, including the measures taken to resolve, limit or manage these conflicts of interest. (See also recital 25 of SRD II.) The scope of the Belgian implementing rules applicable to proxy advisors is broad. They apply to proxy advisors with registered seat in Belgium, proxy advisors without a registered seat in the EU if they have their head office in Belgium and proxy advisors without a registered seat or head office in the EU that are located in Belgium or conduct their activities through a branch in the EU for their services in relation to listed companies in the EU.

[10] See for example Harlan Zimmerman, Senior Partner at Cevian Capital, comment in the Sunday Times of 21 June 2021: *"The spectrum of activist funds has never been wider and more blurred. From short-term focused "attackavist" hedge funds, to institutional investors engaging with companies, to big index managers whose stewardship teams look after thousands of companies, to environmental, social and corporate governance groups advancing specific agendas – they are all "activist funds" today."* See also Freshfields, "On the frontline of the war against shareholder activism with Harlan Zimmerman" <https://www.freshfields.com/en-gb/our-thinking/campaigns/beyond-the-pandemic/on-the-frontline-of-the-war-against-shareholder-activism/> accessed 02.03.2023.

funds which hold shares in a company and which allocate most, if not all, of their assets to activist strategies.[11]

4. *Campaign themes*. The campaign of an activist fund can focus on one or a combination of perceived vulnerability or underperformance areas such as overall slow growth, flawed strategy, share price underperformance, lower total shareholder returns relative to peers and/or weaknesses in governance. To prepare and articulate the campaign, activist funds often engage in extensive due diligence, based on publicly available information[12], in a preparatory phase before first engaging with the listed company. During such preparatory phase, the activist fund will deploy its own specialist teams, leverage industry experts and consultants, and sometimes seek to contact former employees and/or executives of listed companies (see also below). Schematically, the customary range of vulnerability areas and resulting activist fund demands can be presented as follows:

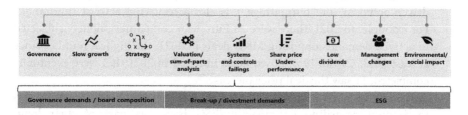

The primary categories of activist fund demands resulting from such (perceived) underperformance or vulnerability have in the past years been the following[13]:

– *Capital allocation/return*: A first recurring demand of activist funds is to increase a company's returns to its shareholders, by e.g. a revised dividend policy, *ad hoc* dividends and/or share buy-backs. As indicated by Insightia[14], a somewhat surprising trend in 2022 was the surge of demands to return cash to shareholders, given the economic uncertainty. It appears that companies increased their cash reserves during the COVID-19 pandemic, so that cash

---

[11] See also the definition of "Primary focus activist" in Insightia, "Shareholder activism in 2021 overview" (2022).
[12] See item 5.3 for a summary of the information Belgian listed companies are required to make public.
[13] See also Lazard's Capital Markets Advisory Group, "2021 Review Of Shareholder Activism" (2021); Insightia, 'The Shareholder Activism Annual Review', *The tenth annual review of trends in shareholder activism* (2023); Insightia, "The Activist Investing Annual Review 2022" *The Ninth Annual Review of Trends In Shareholder Activism* (2022); Insightia, "Shareholder activism in 2021 overview" (2022).
[14] *Insightia Monthly*, October 2022.

held by companies in the United States was estimated to have increased from $1.6 trillion in 2000 to approximately $5.8 trillion as at October 2022. With growth slowing and interest rates rising, many activist funds appear to believe that they are in a better position to invest these funds compared to management.
- *Break-up / divestments / M&A*: A recurring demand of activist funds is to request improvements to companies' portfolios (*i.e.* disposing or carving out non-core assets or non-ESG assets), a strategic review of the business and/or a plain sale of the entire company. Such a demand can also underpin an activist fund's demand for increased shareholder returns, as the break-up, divestment or sale would result in cash becoming available for distribution to the company's shareholders. In some cases, this goal was already recognised by the market or even the company, but activist funds may seek to claim credit for the company's initiatives or accelerate them. Agitating for better terms on announced transactions ("sweeten campaigns") or sometimes seeking to block them entirely ("scuttle campaigns" and, together "event-driven activism" or "bumpitrage"), is also a recurring activist fund angle. For example, in 2021, there were 28 European companies publicly subjected to activist demands opposing M&A deals in 2021, the highest number since at least 2013. Of the 19 opposed deals initiated in 2021 that were eventually completed, 11 saw the deal price increase.[15]
- *Sustainability/ESG*: Activist funds are increasingly holding companies to account regarding sustainability/ESG issues as part of their long-term strategy and/or the manner in which the company reports such sustainability/ESG matters to shareholders. There is increased pressure on investors for financial returns not to be their sole objective now the world has broader environmental and societal goals, many of which (such as tackling climate change) have an impact on asset values.[16] Such type of action will likely only increase in future times as a result of the increased sustainability/ESG focus of regulators worldwide, such as the European Union (*EU*) with the Corporate Sustainability Reporting Directive[17] and the proposal for the Corporate Sustainability Due Diligence Directive[18],

---

[15] Insightia, "Shareholder activism in Europe 2022, definitive analysis on activist investing, investor voting, and short selling in the region" (2022). In 'The Shareholder Activism Annual Review' *The tenth annual review of trends in shareholder activism* (2023), Insightia reported 29 European companies subject to activist demands opposing M&A deals in 2021 (compared to 15 in 2022).

[16] See also H. Daems, "Nieuwe corporate governance is onvermijdelijk", *De Tijd* (2022), <https://www.tijd.be/opinie/algemeen/nieuwe-corporate-governance-is-onvermijdelijk/10421935.html> accessed 02.03.2023.

[17] Directive of the European Parliament and of the Council amending Regulation (EU) No 537/2014, Directive 2004/109/EC, Directive 2006/43/EC and Directive 2013/34/EU, as regards corporate sustainability reporting (*CSRD*).

[18] Proposal for a directive of the European Parliament and of the Council on Corporate Sustainability Due Diligence and amending Directive (EU) 2019/1937, COM/2022/71 final.

as well as the United States and its Securities and Exchange Commission's planned legislation on sustainability reporting. Sustainability/ESG activism knows many forms, from using sustainability as a "wedge" issue to find support with index funds, institutional investors and other sustainability-focused investors for other more financial themes, or requisitioning specific sustainability-related resolutions at general shareholders' meetings, to fundamental strategic attacks.[19] However, it has been noted at the occasion of recent activist campaigns with a sustainability aspect that *"ESG can't just be sprinkled on top of a campaign as an artificial additive"*, but that instead *"if activist funds are to pursue successful ESG strategies, they will have to tie ESG issues to long-term shareholder value."*[20] More specifically, in early 2023, it has been reported that, *"following the success of Engine No. 1's sustainability-fueled campaign at ExxonMobil in 2021, a surge of budding ESG activists emerged last year, conscious that implementing environmental and social considerations into their campaigns would help drive support from institutional investors. However, despite activists' best efforts, 2022 proved to be a challenging year for ESG activism, with green stocks underperforming as oil and gas prices soared. Despite the number of environmental demands publicly made at companies globally in 2022 increasing by 81%, only 11.5% of demands were at least partially successful, down from 25.8% a year prior. Amid fears of a recession and rising interest rates, ESG activist campaigns that failed to make a compelling link between a company's ESG credentials and a company's financial performance were largely doomed to fail. <<It may be easier to support ESG activism when the market is flying, but it becomes tougher to do so when companies have to make difficult decisions about where to focus resources,>> Gabrielle Wolf, director at Innisfree M&A, told Insightia."* In addition, a reverse tendency of anti-ESG activism, nascent in the United States, has recently also made its way into Europe (see Unilever[21]). Listed companies are accordingly possibly facing an ESG and anti-ESG activism campaign on the same theme or – given the broad scope and many aspects of "sustainability" and "ESG" – on conflicting themes. Blackrock is for example facing such conflicting criticism since end of 2022.[22]

- *Governance*: Board composition is scrutinised by activist funds from multiple angles, such as diversity, tenure, over-boarding, dominance of a large shareholder, industry experience and international background, typically

---

[19] Lazard's Capital Markets Advisory Group, "2021 Review Of Shareholder Activism" (2021).
[20] See Insightia, "ESG Activism 2022 overview" (2022).
[21] R. Naidu and R. Kerber, "Unilever under pressure to show sustainability focus is good for business" (2022) Reuters <https://www.reuters.com/business/retail-consumer/unilever-under-pressure-show-sustainability-focus-is-good-business-2022-02-09/> accessed 02.03.2023.
[22] K. Griffith, "Texas subpoenas BlackRock to discover how much taxpayer money has been 'wasted in woke ESG funds' – as activist investor calls for CEO to resign over 'greenwashing'" (2022) *Daily Mail Online* <https://www.dailymail.co.uk/news/article-11513409/Texas-subpoenas-BlackRock-documents-ESG-strategy.html> accessed 02.03.2023.

with the intention to alter management policies or business strategies and thereby present a solution for the (perceived) underperformance. In making demands on governance, an activist fund will not only use the BCCA and Belgian Corporate Governance Code[23] in its support (where useful) but it will use all types of (near) "soft law" relevant for Belgium (or the EU), such as national and international guidance or recommendations, position papers, doctrine or case law that may be helpful to press its points (and convey (a perception of) non-compliance). Like sustainability/ESG, governance demands can be deployed in support of more financially driven themes. Demands can include the activist fund seeking to secure a board seat or replacing board members – whether for its representatives or for additional or alternative independent directors. As certain activist funds are growing in credibility and repute, they are often able to tap on a broad network of industry experts and other credible individuals to propose as new or alternate board members.

5. *Value accretive or destructive?* Substantial research has been done on whether activism is generally creating or destroying value, and there is no consensus on the outcome of such research.[24] Any company that is or may become the target of an activist approach, should therefore on a case-by-case basis consider the merits of the approach and the appropriate response thereto (see also item 5).

2. TOOLS OF ACTIVIST CAMPAIGNS

6. *Mounting pressure.* Activist funds will not always be visible or known, or be immediately visible or known. They can employ a combination of different strategies, with varying levels of publicity and pressure to achieve one or more of the goals that we have outlined under item 1 above. There can be stages in a *crescendo* process, or an activist fund can just keep to one of such stages or strategies and not pursue any next steps. An activist fund may also unilaterally impose deadlines to each of the stages, threatening to move to a next stage if the company does not comply with such deadlines. A company will need to assess whether it is possible and in its corporate interest (as we will describe further below under item 5.1) to comply with such deadlines, as there is *a priori* no reason for a company to dance by that imposed tune and, if and when

---

[23] 2020 Belgian Code on Corporate Governance as implemented by the Royal Decree of 12 May 2019 laying down the corporate governance code (*Koninklijk besluit houdende aanduiding van de na te leven code inzake deugdelijk bestuur door genoteerde vennootschappen / Arrêté royal portant désignation du code de gouvernement d'entreprise à respecter par les sociétés cotées*, BS/MB 17.05.2019, 47344).

[24] See i.a. the contribution of T. Vos in this book.

The Company's Rights, Challenges and Obligations
when Faced with Shareholder Activism

engaging with the activist fund, the company will have to seek to (re)introduce reasonableness in the pace of the exchanges and interactions. The chart below outlines each of the traditional steps of such (pressure) tactics in summary form. Below the chart, we provide additional information per step:

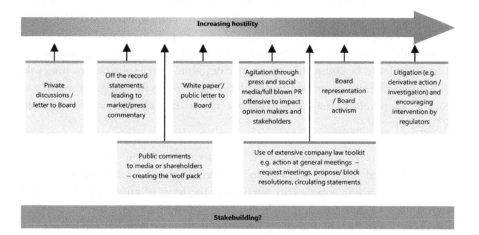

7. *Private engagement.* An activist fund would usually first pursue its objectives through private engagement with the company and its board of directors or senior management (telephone calls or meetings, or letters or emails). Such initial engagement can be immediately clear as to the activist fund's intentions. However, initial engagement may not always be recognisable or labelled as "activist" and can even take the form of a(n innocent) question at an earnings call or a simple email to the investor relations team. Those under-the-radar contacts can be genuine, so as to understand an issue better, or can be disingenuous, simply serving to extract commentary or information from the company to further build or feed the activist fund's thesis. It is therefore advisable to inform and train all investor-facing teams within the company that such contacts may take place, when to pay more-than-customary attention and when such contacts, however loose and small and whatever the media, should be flagged or escalated to other colleagues.

8. *Seeking allies/building credibility.* When an activist fund believes that its objectives will not be met through private engagement and/or believes that it may have insufficient credibility or power acting alone, it may seek to influence, or gain support from, other shareholders or stakeholders privately or publicly, and thereby create a so-called "wolf pack" of supportive stakeholders. To rally support, activist funds will combine multiple sources to retrieve names and contact details of potential allies as there is no legislation imposing to make public lists of shareholders per company under Belgian or EU law (such lists would in any event change all the time due to continuous trading): activist funds

will therefore consult the information made public by the listed company (see item 3.3.2 below) or institutional investors (see footnote 6), they may take note of other attendants at earnings calls or general shareholders' meetings and they may scout internet fora. At the same time, they may also leak ideas or rumours to the research analyst community or engage with journalists on or off record, issue public announcements or open letters, or launch website and/or social media campaigns to voice concerns and obtain support for proposals from other shareholders, stakeholders and representative bodies (see however below in item 4 on the rules to be complied with in case of public proxy solicitations under the BCCA and the risk of market manipulation under MAR). (At times, such 'wolf pack' of shareholders may constitute concert parties under Belgian law (see item 3.3.2.2 below).)

9. *"White papers".* In some cases, an activist fund will prepare a detailed operational and strategic analysis to support its theses and demands, known as a so-called 'white paper'. This often takes the form of an extended slide deck and, similar to the campaign itself, the activist fund may have spent months on the preparation thereof, including by in-depth public record due diligence and leveraging of industry experts, consultants, and sometimes former employees and/or executives of listed companies, before approaching the company. Certain activist funds will use the "white paper" only to form the basis for their private approach to the company. In other cases, white papers are also published in full (typically on the activist fund's website) to further its public relations' and rallying goals, sometimes in an attempt to make the board of directors or management look inept to other shareholders and wider stakeholders. While white papers may of course bring valid points, a classic example to make a company's performance look underwhelming is by comparing it to flawed peer groups in non-relevant time periods.

10. *Exercising shareholder rights.* Depending on the activist fund's percentage shareholding (as the case may be increased by that of the allies that is has found), it has an extensive toolkit available under Belgian company law to further its goals. Activist shareholders may for example ask written or oral questions before or during general shareholders' meetings, be able (either alone or with other shareholders) to propose agenda items or resolutions to the general shareholders' meeting or request to convene a general shareholders' meeting to consider resolutions to effect changes (see item 4.1 below for more information on the company law toolbox).

11. *Litigation.* While legal action remains uncommon in Belgium, certain activist funds may (threaten to) bring claims against the board of directors for breach of duty as part of maintaining the pressure or may initiate proceedings to request the appointment of an expert (panel) (see also item 4.1 below). In Europe, there are two recent ESG activism related court cases.

- First, Volkswagen is facing legal action by institutional shareholders concerning information on its corporate climate lobbying. Shareholders (different European pension funds) sought to place an agenda item in respect of climate lobbying at Volkswagen's 2022 annual general shareholders' meeting. These shareholders requested Volkswagen to give information on its corporate climate lobbying at the 2022 annual general shareholders' meeting. Volkswagen rejected this agenda item. In October 2022, the shareholders brought legal action against Volkswagen before Braunschweig local court (*Amtsgericht*). They want to test whether Volkswagen has the right to refuse to include the agenda item. The shareholders are assisted by environmental law charity and NGO ClientEarth. Their aim is to achieve that Volkswagen reveals "direct or indirect lobbying activities" of group companies which are "directed at the climate change" at the annual general shareholders' meeting. The shareholders are claiming that while Volkswagen is publicly presenting the green transition, it may be undertaking lobbying activities that run counter to its stated climate ambitions via its membership to a number of automotive and business associations. This potential contradiction, the investors say, exposes the company to reputational and operational damage and puts the security of their investments in question. Volkswagen on the other hand argues that the claimant's motion is inadmissible. It encroached on the powers of the executive board. According to Volkswagen, its articles of association should not force its board of directors to do something it is free to decide by law – for example, how it fulfils its reporting obligations on non-financial issues.[25]
- Second, on 9 February 2023, ClientEarth itself, as minority shareholder in Shell, with the support from institutional investors, filed a shareholder derivative action against the board of directors of Shell in the English High Court in London. In a first for statutory derivative actions under the UK Companies Act 2006, ClientEarth alleges that Shell's directors have breached their duties to the company by mismanaging the risks related to climate change and failing to adequately prepare the company for the transition to net zero.[26]

---

[25] See e.g. "Investors file lawsuit against Volkswagen over climate-change related lobbying disclosures" (2022) <https://www.euronews.com/next/2022/10/21/volkswagen-court> accessed 02.03.2023.

[26] See press release ClientEarth "ClientEarth files climate risk lawsuit against Shell's Board with support from institutional investors" (9 February 20223) < https://www.clientearth.org/latest/press-office/press/clientearth-files-climate-risk-lawsuit-against-shell-s-board-with-support-from-institutional-investors/> accessed 02.03.2023; Since writing this, the High Court has rendered two judgements dismissing ClientEarth's derivative action, see: *ClientEarth v Shell Plc & Ors* [2023] EWHC 1137 and *Clientearth v Shell Plc & Ors* [2023] EWHC 1897; See also further H. De Wulf, "The failed derivative action by ClientEarth against Shell's directors: minority shareholders should not try to determine a corporation's climate change strategy through the courts" (2023), *ECCL*, 2023/2, forthcoming.

12. *Stakebuilding*. To support all of this, the activist fund may be stakebuilding publicly or non-publicly, i.e. increasing its shareholding in the company – even before any approach is made – to provide itself with greater influence and to potentially allow it to use some of the tools offered by Belgian company law as described in item 4.1 below. As set out in item 4.2 below, activist funds should in any stakebuilding attempts comply with MAR and the law of 2 May 2007 on the disclosure of significant shareholdings in issuers the securities of which are admitted to trading on a regulated market and containing various provisions[27] (the *Transparency Law*).

13. *Activist fund track record*. As set out above, an activist fund can go through a *crescendo* process in approaching a company, or may keep to just one of these tactics. When being so approached by an activist fund, it is important for the listed company to understand the track record of the fund and its patterns in precedent approaches, so as to assess how it commonly acts and how its behaviour towards the company and the public may evolve.

3. HOW TO ANTICIPATE AND PREPARE FOR ACTIVISM

3.1. INTRODUCTION: WHAT TO EXPECT IF AN ACTIVIST FUND EMERGES

14. *Impact of activist approach*. As shown above, an activist approach may be designed to surprise the company, and may be accompanied with certain pressure in terms of timing or threatened disclosure (or may be public from the outset). An activist approach – whether private or public – can therefore have an important impact on the company, its board of directors and its senior management, which may result in a (serious) distraction from the company's ongoing business. Companies can be impacted as follows:

- *Time investment*: An activist approach will require time investment from the board of directors, management and the legal and investor relations (IR) teams, as a result of an increased number and frequency of meetings of the board of directors and management/advisor meetings to prepare for interactions with the activist fund, discuss options for response, re-evaluate

---

[27] *Wet van 2 mei 2007 op de openbaarmaking van belangrijke deelnemingen in emittenten waarvan aandelen zijn toegelaten tot de verhandeling op een gereglementeerde markt en houdende diverse bepalingen / Loi du 2 mai 2007 relative à la publicité des participations importantes dans des émetteurs dont les actions sont admises à la négociation sur un marché réglementé et portant des dispositions diverses*, BS/MB 12.06.2007, 31588.

certain aspects of the company's strategy that are being challenged, consider engagement with other stakeholders, consider announcement obligations, etc. Depending on the nature of the activist fund's thesis, other teams will also need to be involved (finance, R&D, corporate development, etc.). Such time investment will sometimes result in other projects receiving less attention in a resources-constrained environment and/or may lead the company to attract interim human resources.

- *Meetings and correspondence with the activist fund:* Activist funds will often reach out to meet with company representatives with a view to understanding certain decisions by, or policies from, the company. Similarly, as we will set out in item 5.4 below, the company will often also wish to engage in a dialogue with the activist fund to have a better understanding of certain of the elements brought forward.

   At the same time as engaging through live meetings, activist funds also often 'build a written file' for the event they would later go public, to feed press leakages or sometimes as litigation record. Sufficient time will therefore have to be dedicated to the careful review of and response to correspondence from the activist fund and its representatives. The activist fund will seek to adopt tone, content, timing and method of delivery that is designed to persuade and pressure the board of directors and management to agree with the activist fund's goals, either privately or publicly. Often, the activist fund will use a harsher tone in written correspondence than it does in live meetings.

- *Increased concern within, or scrutiny by, other stakeholder groups:* The fact that an activist campaign is ongoing, may trigger, certainly at the public stage of the campaign, questions from or concerns with other shareholders. This may result in increased enquiries with the *IR* team and, as the case may be, impact the stock price.

   Not only shareholders, but also other stakeholder groups, such as employees, the regulators, the press, analysts will generally be more attentive and may similarly ask an increased number of questions to test the activist thesis (critical of the company's performance relative to its business plan, stated goals, peer group(s) and the capital markets generally).

   More generally, an activist campaign can result in increased scrutiny and critical analysis of the company's corporate governance practices, as well as the company's executive and director compensation arrangements, backgrounds and tenure of, and inter-relationships among, directors and officers, and external affiliations of directors and officers. The company will therefore, as the case may be, also have to engage with other stakeholders to explain or even defend itself against such enhanced scrutiny, even in respect of matters that have been unchanged for many years.

   Such scrutiny may also be exacerbated by changes in the broader shareholder basis of a company as a result of the activist campaign, as additional activist funds and event-driven hedge funds may follow the original activist fund.

There could also be increased trading activity in the shares, options or derivatives from short-term and event-driven investors. (The company will be generally able to track this through the investor identification tools outlined in item 3.3.2.)

15. *Prevent surprise as much as possible.* In view of such potential impact of an activist campaign on a company – possibly from the outset of the campaign – it is important for companies to identify an activist fund approach as soon as possible and to be well-prepared for activism, even if there is no actual sign of an activist fund preparing to launch a campaign. A number of steps can be taken in "peacetime" which require limited effort, but aim at allowing companies to react in an efficient manner, which are set out in the next item.

3.2. STAKEHOLDER ENGAGEMENT PLAN

16. *Proactive and transparent communication.* A first step is that companies can prepare and update shareholder and stakeholder engagement plans so that the market understands well the reasons for which a company has taken a certain decision or announced a certain change in policy or strategy. Transparent and consistent communication should contribute to avoiding investor frustration and action. For example, in its 2021 activism overview, Lazard has found that in the course of 2021, shareholders have appeared to be increasingly willing to overrule the leadership of the company when it comes to transactions, suggesting that every M&A deal should have an activism/enhanced communication plan.[28]

17. *Monitoring and building relationship with company supporters and proxy advisors.* Companies should, in any preparedness steps they undertake prior to, and during the initial stages of, an activist approach, not only focus on potential activist funds and their potential themes, but also on (minority) shareholders and proxy advisors that would support the company's strategy in case of an actual approach.

As detailed above, institutional investors and their assets managers are required by SRD II to prepare and disclose their shareholders' engagement policy publicly, including how they integrate shareholder engagement in their investment strategy, how they supervise and interact with the listed companies in which they invest, how they exercise their voting rights, how they cooperate with other shareholders and how they communicate with stakeholders. They also have to publicly report annually (together with the publication of their annual report) on the implementation of their engagement policy, on how they have exercised their voting rights and whether they made use of the services of

---

[28] Lazard's Capital Markets Advisory Group, "2021 Review Of Shareholder Activism" (2021).

proxy advisors. Further, institutional investors are required to disclose the key elements of their arrangements with asset managers.

In addition, as detailed above, proxy advisors must publicly disclose a reference to a code of conduct and how they apply it (or explain why they do not) on their website. In order to inform their clients of the accuracy and reliability of their services, proxy advisors are also required to disclose on their website certain key information relating voting policies, conflict of interests, etc.

These disclosure requirements – as well as listed companies' continuous engagement with institutional investors and proxy advisors – may assist listed companies in monitoring and building their relationship with company supporters and proxy advisors.

3.3. EARLY SIGNALS MONITORING

3.3.1. Signals during Shareholder Engagement

18. *Spotting an activist fund as soon as possible.* Activist funds may build shareholdings (often referred to as "toeholds") and remain under the radar because they are below the mandatory disclosure thresholds set out in the Transparency Law that we will describe below or similar applicable legislation waiting for the right time, if ever[29], to emerge.

In such time period, the presence of activist funds is hard to spot, but the company's IR team should remain alert on (challenging) questions or out-of-the-blue positions which may be asked or taken by or on behalf of activist funds or following discussions with activist funds (e.g. by institutional investors, analysts or journalists with whom the activist fund may have had contact), at the occasion of any engagement with shareholders and stakeholders, such as general shareholders' meetings, earnings calls or capital markets days.[30] Such questions could give an indication of the presence of an activist fund and should be closely monitored and communicated internally.

3.3.2. Legal levers for identifying activist funds

3.3.2.1. Mandatory disclosure by activist fund of significant shareholding

19. *Belgian Transparency Law requirements.* In addition, Belgian and EU law provides companies with legal levers that can be used to help analyse and

---

[29] Some activist funds take positions that they then later decide not to act on.
[30] In this respect, the Belgian Corporate Governance Committee and the FSMA have for example, in their explanatory note and press release, respectively, described in footnote 61, given guidance on shareholder engagement tools which would, if implemented, also allow companies to spot early activist signals.

understand their investor base and identify potential activist funds. Pursuant to the Transparency Law, holders of securities giving access to voting rights of listed companies are generally required to disclose the percentage of voting rights they hold as a security holder once they reach 5% of the total number of outstanding voting rights, and any subsequent incremental holding of 5%. Article 18 of the Transparency Law permits companies to set additional transparency thresholds at 1%, 2%, 3%, 4% and/or 7.5%. Such additional transparency thresholds must be included in a company's articles of association and disclosed publicly. The Belgian Financial Services and Market Authority (*Autoriteit voor Financiële Diensten en Markten /Autorité des Services et Marchés Financiers*) (FSMA) discloses on its website[31] an overview of Belgian listed companies the articles of association of which contain additional notification thresholds, which indicates that an additional 3% transparency threshold is relatively common.

Any reaching of a transparency threshold needs to be notified to the FSMA and the company as soon as possible and in any event within four trading days of reaching such threshold (article 12 of the Transparency Law). Within three trading days of receipt of such notification, the company needs to make public the information received (article 14 of the Transparency Law), and on the basis of such publications, the FSMA publishes a summary overview of the shareholding of each Belgian listed company on its website.[32]

The securities giving access to voting rights of which their holding gives rise to the notification obligation is broadly defined and includes voting rights attached to shares, entitlements to acquire shares and instruments with similar economic effect to holding shares and entitlements to acquire shares (including cash settled instruments) (article 6, §6 of the Transparency Law[33] and guidance of the European

---

[31] Https://www.fsma.be/nl/thresholds.
[32] *Https://www.fsma.be/nl/aandeelhouderschap-0.*
[33] "... *are equivalent to voting securities:*
 1° *financial instruments that, on maturity, give the holder, under a formal agreement, either the unconditional right to acquire or the discretion as to his right to acquire, shares to which voting rights are attached, already issued, of an issuer whose shares are admitted to trading on a regulated market;*
 2° *financial instruments which are not included in point 1° but which are referenced to shares referred to in that point and with economic effect similar to that of the financial instruments referred to in that point, whether or not they confer a right to a physical settlement.*
 For the purposes of the first paragraph, the following financial instruments shall be considered equivalent financial instruments provided they meet the conditions referred to in the first paragraph, 1° or 2°:
 (a) *transferable securities;*
 (b) *options;*
 (c) *futures;*
 (d) *swaps;*
 (e) *forward rate agreements;*
 (f) *contracts for differences; and*

Securities and Markets Authority (*ESMA*)[34]. This includes share loans, as well as most share swaps. Accordingly, any attempt at stakebuilding would typically be notifiable under the Transparency Law as soon as the total number of voting rights acquired in any manner reaches the applicable transparency threshold.

20. *Sanctions for breach of Transparency Law.* The following sanctions apply in case of non-compliance with the requirements of the Transparency Law:

- A shareholder who has not declared possession of its securities in accordance with the requirements of the Transparency Law, at least twenty days before the date of a general shareholders' meeting of a company (regardless of whether it is an ordinary, special or extraordinary general shareholders' meeting[35]), may not take part in the vote at such general shareholders' meeting and the voting rights attached to these securities are suspended (article 25/1 of the Transparency Law). In case such transparency declaration has or should have been made in the period between the twentieth day before the date of a general shareholders' meeting and the date of the meeting itself, the board of directors is entitled to adjourn the meeting with up to five weeks (article 7:131 of the BCCA).
- If the declarations required under the Transparency Law have not been made in the prescribed manner and within the prescribed time limits, the president of the enterprise court[36], acting as if in summary proceedings[37], may: (1) order the suspension of the exercise of all or part of the rights attaching to the securities concerned for a period of not more than one year (this request must, if a notification had been made, be made, on penalty of inadmissibility, not more than fifteen days after the notification); (2) suspend the holding of a general shareholders' meeting which has already been convened for such period as the president may determine; or (3) order, under the supervision of the president, the sale of the securities concerned to a third party which is not related to the current shareholder, within a period which it shall determine and which is renewable (article 25/2 of the Transparency Law).
- Criminal and administrative sanctions are also provided (article 23 of the Transparency Law).

(g) *any other contracts or agreements with similar economic effects which may be settled physically or in cash.*
This equivalence shall also apply to certificates not admitted to trading on a regulated market relating to voting securities if they give the holder the unconditional right or decision on that right to acquire the, already issued, voting securities to which they relate.
If the holder's right to acquire the underlying voting securities depends only on an event that the holder is able to trigger or prevent, such right shall be regarded as unconditional."

34   ESMA, "Indicative list of financial instruments that are subject to notification requirements according to article 13(1b) of the revised Transparency Directive" (2015), *ESMA/2015/1598*.
35   Gewone, bijzondere of buitengewone algemene aandeelhoudersvergadering / Assemblée générale ordinaire, spéciale ou extraordinaire.
36   Voorzitter van de ondernemingsrechtbank / président du tribunal de l'entreprise.
37   Recht doende als in kort geding / statuant comme en référé.

– The FSMA may require a shareholder, its directors or persons who control it or whom it controls, to provide the information required to be communicated or made public under the Transparency Law and, if necessary, to require the communication of additional information and documents, as well as to make such information public in the manner and within the time limits it determines. A penalty payment may be imposed in the event of non-compliance with the imposed deadlines (article 26 and 27 of the Transparency Law).

21. *Other transparency legislation*. Companies which have a dual or secondary listing on other stock exchanges, may also be subject to additional transparency legislation (e.g. in case of a dual or secondary listing on the New York Stock Exchange or Nasdaq).[38, 39]

3.3.2.2. Mandatory disclosure by certain "wolf packs"

22. *Qualification of wolf pack as concert*. As mentioned above, activist funds will be focused on identifying other shareholders (including institutional investors) to support their position, i.e. on creating a wolf pack, often quite early on in their campaign (see item 2 above). Such support may result in these shareholders acting in concert[40], which is defined in article 3, §1, 13° of the Transparency Law (including by reference to the law of April 2007 on takeover bids (the *Takeover Law*)[41]) as natural or legal persons who:

(a) *"cooperate with the offeror, the target company or other persons, on the basis of an agreement, whether or not tacit, oral or written, with a view to obtain control of the target company, to frustrate an offer, or to maintain control of the target company;"*[42] or

---

[38] The Transparency Law is an implementation of Directive 2004/109/EC of the European Parliament and of the Council of 15 December 2004 on the harmonisation of transparency requirements in relation to information about issuers whose securities are admitted to trading on a regulated market and amending Directive 2001/34/EC [2004] OJ L390/38. The effectiveness of this framework was considered in the context of a German activist approach in 2018. In February 2018, Geely was able to acquire a shareholding of nearly 10% in Daimler, seemingly overnight. However, it has been established that the transparency framework was generally complied with and that Geely did not necessarily find a loophole in the transparency framework. Rather, the exceptionally high liquidity of the Daimler stock allowed Geely to effectively acquire (with the involvement of investment banks) a notifiable percentage overnight. Shares of Belgian companies (and the great majority of other listed companies) would generally not be as liquid, and would therefore not allow activist funds to build such a significant shareholding in such a short timeframe, even taking into account the period of four trading days during which the notification can be made.

[39] For further details, see contribution of M. Spooren in this book.

[40] *In onderling overleg handelen / agir de concert*.

[41] Wet van 1 april 2007 op de openbare overnamebiedingen / Loi du 1 avril 2007 relative aux offres publiques d'acquisition, BS/MB 26.04.2007, 22378.

[42] "Die met de bieder, met de doelvennootschap of met andere personen samenwerken op grond van een uitdrukkelijk of stilzwijgend, mondeling of schriftelijk akkoord dat ertoe strekt de controle over de doelvennootschap te verkrijgen, het welslagen van een bod te dwarsbomen

(b) *"have concluded an agreement on the concerted exercise of their voting rights, with a view to pursuing a durable common policy towards the company in question"*[43]

A notification under the Transparency Law is required if shareholders agree to act in concert and the voting rights attached to their respective above-mentioned instruments together reach the thresholds set out in the previous item (article 6, §4 of the Transparency Law). To this end, it suffices that the shareholders enter into the concert relationship, it is not needed that such concert party arrangement is accompanied by a simultaneous or subsequent acquisition of securities.

Such concert party arrangement does not need to exist in writing, and can appear from a variety of behaviours.[44] The FSMA has even indicated that an agreement to act in concert does not need to result in the same voting behaviour by all concert parties, as the definition in the Transparency Law does not refer to the fact that the agreement must oblige the concert parties, through the concerted exercise of their voting rights, to pursue a durable common policy towards the company.[45] An agreement whereby parties agreed to consult each other prior to the general shareholders' meeting and on a potential takeover bid, without an obligation to act in the same manner following such consultation, was in this manner considered by the FSMA to constitute concert.[46] Of course, not every group of shareholders acting together will form a "concert" under the above-mentioned definition and each group will have to be analysed under such guidance on concert relationships.

---

dan wel de controle over de doelvennootschap te handhaven / qui coopèrent avec l'offrant, avec la société visée ou avec d'autres personnes, sur la base d'un accord, formel ou tacite, oral ou écrit, visant à obtenir le contrôle de la société visée, à faire échouer une offre ou à maintenir le contrôle de la société visée."

[43] *"Die een akkoord hebben gesloten aangaande de onderling afgestemde uitoefening van hun stemrechten, om een duurzaam gemeenschappelijk beleid ten aanzien van de betrokken emittent te voeren / qui ont conclu un accord portant sur l'exercice concerté de leurs droits de vote, en vue de mener une politique commune durable vis-à-vis de l'émetteur concerné."*

[44] See e.g. G. Callens, A. Cautaerts, H. Culot, Y. De Cordt, G. De Pierpont, T. Flament, E. Fosséprez, J.M. Gollier, A. Hannouille, and N. Tissot, "Chapitre 4 – Publicité des participations importantes" (2021) Société anonyme, 2nd ed., Larcier, Brussels 2021, 137–167; X. Dieux and L. Legein, "Questions relatives à la notion de concert en droit financier belge" (2012) *DBF-BFR*, 2012/3–4, 143–157; P.A. Foriers, S. Hirsch and V. Marquette, "Item I. – Champ d'application et définitions principales", *Les offres publiques d'acquisition*, 2nd ed., Larcier, Brussels 2018, 11–28. See also Wagons-Lits case: Cass. 10 March 1994, Pas. 1994, I, 237; Arr.Cass. 1994, 236; *JT*, 1994, 419; *Bank Fin.*, 1994, 528, Note A. Bruyneel; R.Cass. 1994, 278, Note T. Denys and D. Meulemans; *RW*, 1994–95, 431; *TBH*, 1995, 15, Note F. Glansdorff.

[45] Praktijkgids FSMA_2011_08 dd. 10 november 2011 (update 11 februari 2020) – Transparantieregelgeving, p. 12 <https://www.fsma.be/sites/default/files/legacy/sitecore/media%20library/Files/fsmafiles/circ/nl/2011/fsma_2011_08.pdf> accessed 02.03.2023.

[46] Verslag van het directiecomité CBFA 2007, 58.

23. *To be monitored by companies.* The duty for activist funds and shareholders acting in concert to publicly notify the concert to both the FSMA and the company should be closely monitored by the company as it could be an important tool to challenge an activist fund intervening at a general shareholders' meeting, in view of the sanctions that may apply to the absence of a notification as set out in the previous item.[47]

3.3.2.3. SRD II

24. *Right for companies to identify shareholders.* Under SRD II, companies have obtained the right (not the obligation) to identify their shareholders. As explained above, SRD II was implemented in Belgian law pursuant to the Law of 28 April 2020, which introduced the provisions relating to the right of listed companies to identify their shareholders in a new Title II/I in the Transparency Law, which entered into force on 3 September 2020.

Shares in listed companies are often held through chains of intermediaries, be it investment firms, credit institutions or the central securities depository, which provide services of safekeeping or administration of shares or maintenance of securities accounts. Any such intermediary in the holding chain, whether or not it is situated in the European Economic Area (*EEA*), will, upon first request of the listed company (or a third party designated by it), have to communicate certain information with respect to the relevant shareholders to the listed company without delay. Such information includes certain personal or company details as well as contact details of the relevant shareholder, the number of shares held, and (if specifically requested) the category of shares and date of acquisition. If more than one intermediary is included in a holding chain, then the company's request must be passed on by one intermediary to the other, without delay and no later than during the business day immediately following the date of receipt of the request by the responding intermediary. In case of a holding chain of intermediaries, the request will flow through the chain and back, subject to longer deadlines (see Commission Implementing Regulation (EU) 2018/1212). In its implementation in Belgian law of SRD II, the Belgian legislator has not set any minimum threshold and listed companies are therefore able to identify their shareholders without minimum threshold.

25. *Monitoring tool for companies, but not for any purpose and not for any other person.* On this basis, SRD II can provide an effective means for companies to routinely monitor their investor base, spot changes and identify potential activist funds among its shareholders.[48] In addition, SRD II should allow companies to track when an activist fund first invested.

---

[47] For further details, see contribution of M. Spooren in this book.
[48] For further details, see contribution of M. Spooren in this book.

On the other hand, unlike transparency declarations received pursuant to the Transparency Law, the information on a company's shareholders gathered pursuant to SRD II cannot be made public by the company. Article 3a SRD II indeed provides that *"the personal data of shareholders shall be processed pursuant to this article in order to enable the company to identify its existing shareholders in order to communicate with them directly with the view to facilitating the exercise of shareholder rights and shareholder engagement with the company."* Article 29/3, §2 of the Transparency Law also provides that the personal data of shareholders are processed to enable the company to identify its existing shareholders in order to communicate directly with them, with a view to facilitating the exercise of shareholder rights and shareholder engagement with the company, without providing for other purposes. Parliamentary works confirm that this provision aims at implementing SRD II: *"De richtlijn bevat specifieke bepalingen die ertoe strekken de bescherming van de persoonsgegevens van de aandeelhouders te garanderen. Het voorstel zet de desbetreffende bepalingen van de richtlijn zonder meer in Belgisch recht om. / La directive contient des dispositions spécifiques visant à assurer la protection des données personnelles des actionnaires. La proposition transpose purement et simplement les dispositions prévues par la directive à cet égard."*[49] The Belgian legislator has thus not used the possibility provided in article 3a SRD II of providing by law that the personal data of shareholders may be processed for other purposes, e.g. to enable shareholders to cooperate with each other (see Recital (6) of SRD II).

26. *Practical limitations.* In practice, however, there are limitations on the information companies can obtain on the basis of SRD II. Firstly, the identification is done at a certain date, and upon receipt of the information, shares will by definition have been transferred since that date. Secondly, only "intermediaries" as defined in SRD II are obliged to provide the information. As a result, to the extent that the last identified holder in the chain is not the actual shareholder (e.g. the activist fund), but e.g. a nominee, and such nominee does not qualify as an "intermediary", it may not be possible to identify the underlying shareholder.[50] Finally, SRD II does have an extraterritorial application to any intermediary, whether they are located in Belgium, the EEA or outside the EEA. However, SRD II only allows the identification of holders of securities listed on

---

[49] *Wetsvoorstel tot omzetting van Richtlijn (EU) 2017/828 van het Europees Parlement en de Raad van 17 mei 2017 tot wijziging van Richtlijn 2007/36/EG wat het bevorderen van de langetermijnbetrokkenheid van aandeelhouders betreft, en houdende vennootschaps- en verenigingsbepalingen / Proposition de loi portant transposition de la directive (UE) 2017/828 du Parlement européen et du Conseil du 17 mai 2017 modifiant la directive 2007/36/CE en vue de promouvoir l'engagement à long terme des actionnaires, et portant des dispositions en matière de société et d'association*, Parl.St. 0553/001, 13.

[50] See also D. Van Gerven and P. De Pauw, "L'identification des actionnaires des sociétés cotées et le rôle des intermédiaires financiers" (2020), *RDC-TBH*, 2020/5, 591–602.

a regulated market within the EEA. Accordingly, Belgian listed companies with part of their shares or depositary receipts representing (part of) their shares (e.g. American Depositary Receipts or ADRs) listed on a market outside the EEA, will not be able to use SRD II to identify the holders of these shares or depositary receipts. Finally, practice shows that a limited number of shareholders can still not be identified, even if not falling outside of the scope of SRD II. ESMA has on 11 October 2022 launched a "call for evidence" on the implementation of SRD II i.a. aimed at assessing the effectiveness of the shareholder identification rights under SRD II.[51]

3.3.2.4. Short Positions

27. *Description of short selling and potential activist fund use.* Activist funds may also engage in short selling of a company's shares as part of their campaign. A short sale is defined in the Short Selling Regulation[52] as any sale of a share or debt instrument which the seller does not own at the time of entering into the agreement to sell including such a sale where at the time of entering into the agreement to sell the seller has borrowed or agreed to borrow the share or debt instrument for delivery at settlement. When selling short, a seller bets that the shares can at or prior to the settlement date, be bought at a lower price than the price at which it has sold these, with the difference between the two prices profiting the seller. Short seller activist funds take this practice to the next level by doing extensive research on companies they suspect of being involved in shady business tactics, opaque accounting procedures, or even illegal activities. Their targets are capital structure, corporate governance issues, incorrect accounting, and financial reporting, as well as suspected insider dealing. By publishing their findings and allegations, the activist funds bet on strong market reactions and the consequent fall of the targeted company's share price.[53] In 2022, sharp declines in company's share prices have rewarded activist short sellers betting on overvalued companies, and such sellers have now also turned their attention to companies with high share prices on the basis of such companies' claims that they are addressing environmental or social issues, which claims appeared or were alleged by activist funds to be exaggerated.[54]

---

[51] Https://www.esma.europa.eu/press-news/consultations/call-evidence-implementation-shareholders-rights-directive-2.
[52] Regulation (EU) 236/2012 of the European Parliament and of the Council of 14 March 2012 on short selling and certain aspects of credit default swaps [2012] OJ L86/1 (*Short Selling Regulation*).
[53] Z. Bach, A. Fink and R. Leithauser, "Short Selling Activism in Europe – A Strategic Communications Perspective" (2022) *Harvard Law School Forum on Corporate Governance* <https://corpgov.law.harvard.edu/2022/07/10/short-selling-activism-in-europe-a-strategic-communications-perspective/> accessed 31 May 2023.
[54] Insightia, "The Shareholder Activism Annual Review", *The tenth annual review of trends in shareholder activism* (2023).

28. *Disclosure of short positions.* Pursuant to the Short Selling Regulation, market participants – regardless of whether they are domiciled or established within the European Union or in a third country – are required to notify the FSMA of significant net short positions in issuers of shares traded on a regulated market or a multilateral trading facility, and for which Belgium is the most relevant market in terms of liquidity for the shares concerned. The Short Selling Regulation contains a series of requirements, including the following:

- all short sales of shares must be covered (i.e. naked short selling in shares where the seller does not already have an agreement in place to borrow the shares it will need to deliver, or a reasonable expectation that it will be able to deliver the shares, is banned);
- significant net short positions (*NSPs*) in shares must be reported to the FSMA (when they reach 0.2% of the issued share capital and every 0.1% above that) and disclosed to the public (when they reach 0.5% of the issued share capital and every 0.1% above that) – such disclosure is arranged for by the FSMA on its website.[55]

Accordingly, companies are able and recommended to monitor whether any material NSPs in their shares exist.

3.3.2.5. Mandatory Disclosure during Takeover Bid Period

29. *Additional disclosure requirements in case of a public takeover bid.* As set out in item 1 above, "bumpitrage" is a recurring activist theme. If the transaction an activist fund is opposing takes the form of a public takeover bid, additional trade disclosure obligations may arise for activist funds. A public announcement of a bidder's intention to launch a takeover bid in accordance with article 8 of the royal decree of 27 April 2007 on takeover bids[56] (the *Takeover Decree*) opens, on the basis of article 9 of the Takeover Decree, the so-called "bid period".[57] During such bid period, pursuant to article 12 of the Takeover Decree, the acquisition or disposal of securities of the takeover bid target and, in case of a (partial) exchange offer, the bidder, carrying voting rights (or giving access thereto such as convertible bonds or subscription rights) by certain persons must be disclosed to the FSMA, on a daily basis. The following persons are subject to these disclosure requirements:

(i) the bidder;
(ii) the target;

---

[55] Https://www.fsma.be/en/short-selling.
[56] *Koninklijk besluit van 27 april 2007 op de openbare overnamebiedingen / Arrêté royal du 27 mai 2007 relatif aux offres publiques d'acquisition*, BS/MB 23.05.2007, 27736.
[57] *Biedperiode / période d'offre.*

(iii) the members of the board of directors of the target and the bidder, as well as any other bodies to which the board of directors has delegated some of its responsibilities;
(iv) any persons owning directly or indirectly more than 1% of the shares of the target; and
(v) any persons acting in concert with the target or the bidder.

The responsibility for such disclosure to the FSMA lies with the person having carried out the trade in the relevant shares. The disclosure to the FSMA must include the name and title of the person carrying out the disclosure, the date(s) of the transaction(s), the number of shares purchased or sold, the price paid and the number of shares held following the transaction (article, 12 §3 of the Takeover Decree). The FSMA will make these transactions public on its website on a daily basis.[58]

In view of (iv), during the bid period of a takeover bid, activist funds are required to disclose, and target companies are able to identify, any of the above-mentioned transactions as soon as the activist fund holds more than 1% of the shares of the target, irrespective of the number of shares acquired by the activist fund and irrespective of the transparency thresholds mentioned in item 3.3.2.1.

30. *Sanctions.* Several sanctions are provided for in the law of 2 August 2002 on the supervision of the financial sector and the financial services[59] (the *2002 Law*) to ensure, *inter alia*, the correct application of the Takeover Law and Takeover Decree, whereby the FSMA has broad investigative and sanctioning powers. In the event of breach of the obligation of trading disclosures, the FSMA may i.a.:

(a) order any person responsible for such breach to comply with this obligation and to put an end to the irregularity (article 36, §1, 1°, Takeover Law). The FSMA may make public such decision of injunction (article 36, §1, 11°, Takeover Law);
(b) prohibit the person responsible from making use of the rights or benefiting from the advantages that he or she may derive from this omission (article 36, §1, 2°, Takeover Law) – the scope of this provision is, however, not clear and remains untested;
(c) impose an administrative fine, which may not be less than EUR 2,500 nor more than EUR 2,500,000 (article 37, Takeover Law);

---

[58] Https://www.fsma.be/nl/transactions-opa.
[59] *Wet van 2 augustus 2002 betreffende het toezicht op de financiële sector en de financiële diensten / Loi du 2 août relative à la surveillance du secteur financier et aux services financiers*, BS/MB 04.09.2002, 39121.

(d) impose a penalty payment which may not exceed EUR 50,000 per calendar day, nor exceed EUR 2,500,000 in total, on any person who fails to comply with an injunction imposed by FSMA as set out in paragraph (a) above (article 36, §4, Takeover Law).

In addition:

(e) persons who intentionally carried out a transaction, placed an order or engaged in any other conduct which gives or is likely to give false or misleading indications as to the offer, demand or price of a financial instrument, may be punished by imprisonment of between one month and four years and a fine of between EUR 300 and EUR 10,000 (with 'additional decimals' of which coefficient is currently 8), unless the person who effected the transaction, placed the order or engaged in the other conduct establishes that such transaction, order or conduct was for legitimate reasons and is in accordance with an accepted market practice on the relevant trading venue (article 39, §1, 1° a) of the 2002 Law). Although untested in practice, such sanction may possibly be imposed on activist funds if they would trade without complying with their disclosure obligations in order to influence the offer, demand or price of the takeover bid target's shares (see also item 4.2 below on market manipulation);

(f) persons who knowingly provide the FSMA with inaccurate or *incomplete information* may be punished by imprisonment of between one month and one year and a fine of between EUR 50 and EUR 10,000 (with 'additional decimals' of which coefficient is currently 8) or by one of these penalties only (article 41, 2002 Law). Such sanction may be imposed on activist funds if they would trade without complying with their disclosure obligations.

None of the BCCA, 2002 Law, the Takeover Law or the Takeover Decree, however, provides a basis for a suspension of voting or other rights attached to the shares that were acquired in violation of the trading disclosures at one or more general shareholders' meetings of the target, except potentially item (a)(ii) above which is broadly and vaguely written and remains untested so far.

3.3.3. Spotting an Activist: Impact under MAR

31. *Disclosure obligation under MAR?* Once a company has identified an activist fund in its shareholder base, such information may as described above not be (immediately) public. In such scenario, the company needs to consider if any disclosure obligations arise under MAR, i.e. whether such presence constitutes inside information which the company is required to make public. This should rarely be the case absent any known campaigns or approaches because the uncertainty about whether such activist fund will become active, will typically result in the available information not meeting the threshold of inside information as such term is defined under MAR. (See item 5.2.1 below.)

3.4. ORGANISE CORE TEAM AND ESCALATION CHART

32. *Identified and up-to-date team members.* Companies are also advised to identify a core team during so-called 'peacetime' to ensure that the company can react in an organised manner, consulting all the relevant decision-makers in the company, once an activist fund has been identified in a company's shareholder base and/or has approached a company. This core team should consist of the relevant decision-makers depending on the seriousness of the approach (and should be periodically refreshed and updated to reflect the most appropriate composition (Chair, CEO/CFO, legal, IR, employee communications, …)). The core team list can also identify an external adviser team (financial adviser, law firm, proxy consultants, PR firm) upfront, so that they can be immediately mobilised if needed.

Importantly, awareness within these core teams of indications and types of activism, as well as the usual suspects, should be created and refreshed. Each of the team members should also know whom to inform and escalate to within the organisation when there is a (credible) indication of an activist approach.

3.5. REGULARLY REVIEW VULNERABILITY FROM AN ACTIVIST FUND PERSPECTIVE

33. *Identify potential activist angles of attack and activist funds.* Identifying a company's possible areas of vulnerability and preparing potential responses is key to defining an adequate and effective activist response strategy and preparedness. Companies should therefore review, test and update their strategy, long-term business plan, M&A, governance, capital structure, leverage, capital allocation, key financial performance metrics and dividend policy to identify areas of potential weakness or vulnerability, as such matters are, as set forth under item 1 above, regular angles of attack of an activist approach. Vulnerability assessments change over time and thus need to be reassessed regularly, including on the basis of market feedback. In addition, companies should research which activist funds are most likely to approach them (activist funds may have different areas of focus and specialisms) and consider their likely agenda, for which purpose e.g. website traffic monitoring could be used (subject to compliance with applicable data protection laws).

Companies will indeed wish to be sure that the board of directors and management have already considered any topic that could be the subject of a thesis or demand from an activist fund. A useful tool for preparedness is therefore that the company itself, possibly with the help of its financial advisor, writes a so-called 'white paper' in respect of itself, to be internally reviewed by the board of directors and management, and to prepare rebuttals, explanations and/or avenues of dialogue. On the basis of such exercise, pre-emptive changes to the stakeholder engagement plan and investor relations messaging (see item 3.2 above) and/or even the strategy of a company could be considered.

34. *Test business plan and stakeholder engagement on business plan.* Ultimately, the best defence against any activist approach remains the soundness of the company's own long-term business plan and the clear explanation thereof to the shareholders and other stakeholders. Companies should therefore revisit, at least annually, the metrics used internally for understanding and evaluating their long-term plan and for explaining their long-term plan to the market. Companies should also consider whether more proactive efforts are needed to build shareholder and stakeholder support for its existing business plan (see item 3.2 above). Data suggests that companies that have appeared to be most vulnerable are those which have recognised issues internally but have not yet communicated their plan to remedy those issues. The same is suggested by Insightia: Insightia regularly identifies companies that are vulnerable to activism, and has reported that, in total, 42 companies that Insightia reporters have highlighted as vulnerable to activism in reports between 2018 and 2022 were subjected to activist demands in 2022.[60] Whether changed or not as part their vulnerability assessment or revisiting of their long-term business plan, companies should be clearly articulating to their stakeholders their strategy in a consistent and timely manner.

3.6. GOVERNANCE

35. *Governance shortcomings as activist angle of attack.* As referenced under the activism themes in item 1 above, corporate governance shortcomings provide activist funds with a relatively straightforward lever to agitate for change. Pointing at (perceived) governance failures to explain financial underperformance is a recurring argument. The fact that such topics are also

---

[60] Insightia, *Our vulnerability track record*, 22 February 2023.

generally of concern to institutional investors and proxy advisors, makes this angle of (additional) attack often used by activist funds to strengthen their thesis and/or rally support.

It is therefore crucial for companies to regularly review and update their governance profile in light of recent developments and trends and to focus, in their vulnerability assessment and in general, on governance. In their assessment, companies should not only focus on the BCCA and the Belgian Corporate Governance Code, but also review recommendations, position papers and/or benchmarking reports issued by the FSMA and other institutions, reports issued by proxy advisors such as ISS, guidance by the Belgian Corporate Governance Commission, market practice, pending EU legislation, … As mentioned under item 1 above, in any campaign, an activist fund will use any of those sources to strengthen its thesis, even if the source is not part of "soft law" and/or does not reflect current law, in Belgium.[61]

Typical areas where companies may receive criticism relate to the composition of the board of directors, including diversity and inclusion, independent directors versus directors appointed by a larger shareholder, the number, experience and skillsets of non-executive directors, over-boarding, etc. Succession planning, remuneration of board of directors and senior management and transparency in this respect are also a focus point of activist funds.

3.7. ACTIVISM MANUAL

36. *Store all activism preparedness information in one place.* Similar to a takeover defence manual, it is useful for a company to store documents in respect of preparedness for activism in one place. This could be a secured

---

[61] For example, on 21 October 2022, the Belgian Corporate Governance Committee published an explanatory note seeking to clarify the responsibilities of independent directors, and the specific cases in which independent directors play a decisive role and must show enhanced vigilance. In addition, on 4 October 2022, the FSMA issued a press release launching 20 projects for the future in its areas of supervision, which includes topics on "organising shareholders' dialogue on sustainability", "checks and balances and integrity within listed companies" and "interaction between the FSMA and the courts and tribunals". While the explanatory note of the Belgian Corporate Governance Committee seeks to clarify the Belgian Corporate Governance Code with regard to the role of independent directors and consequently may need to be taken into account in corporate governance charters and any explanation therein with respect to deviations from the Corporate Governance Code, the FSMA press release only includes proposals for change of, or additions to, the current legislative framework most of which would first need to pass through the legislative process to come into force. On EU level, there is for example draft European Commission consultation: "Guidelines on the standardised presentation of the remuneration report under Directive 2007/36/EC, as amended by Directive (EU) 2017/828, as regards the encouragement of long-term shareholder engagement".

intranet site or a manual. This can be an enormous aid in preparing for a surprise activist approach and can save crucial time when assessing a response. Typical elements included in such intranet site/ activism manual are:

- the team members, internally or externally, who can assist in preparing the response and/or who need to know of the approach (as well as their contact details);
- do's and don'ts when receiving direct phone calls or approaches (e.g. no blame games, no overoptimism, ...);
- an overview of the duties and responsibilities of the board of directors, management, etc;
- day 1 response plan to a public activist approach (if needed) and further communication steps and
- communication protocols, key response messaging, including draft press releases (which would be regularly updated to reflect performance and strategy) and communications to employees, customers, etc.

3.8. MOCK EXERCISE

37. Simulate activist approach with relevant teams. Similar to takeover mock exercises, companies may wish to simulate an activist approach focusing on one or more vulnerabilities, to test preparedness and – if appropriate – adapt a plan of response. Whether or not to organise a mock exercise, will of course depend on the company. Certain companies may, by the nature of their shareholder base and/or activity, be more vulnerable to activism than others.

4. RIGHTS AND OBLIGATIONS OF ACTIVIST FUNDS

4.1. COMPANY LAW RIGHTS AND OBLIGATIONS

4.1.1. Rights

38. Overview of shareholder rights in a Belgian listed company in function of the percentage of shares they hold. As mentioned in item 2, activist funds can use their rights as shareholders, as set forth in the BCCA, as part of their activist campaign. Shareholders' rights in a Belgian listed company generally depend on the percentage of shares a shareholder holds. In a typical activist approach, the following rights may be most relevant, in each case subject to the applicable rules:

Threshold	Obligations and Rights
>0%	Each individual shareholder may: • review the shareholders' register (7:28 BCCA), subject to GDPR; • ask questions to the board of directors and auditor(s) (i) at the general shareholders' meeting or (ii) in writing (by letter or e-mail) from the publication of the convening notice until six days prior to the general shareholders' meeting (7:139 BCCA) (see also below in this item); • solicit proxies in view of the general shareholders' meeting (7:143 BCCA, subject to compliance with 7:144 and 7:145 BCCA, to the extent applicable (see also below in this item)); • claim the nullity of decisions of the general shareholders' meeting, subject to the applicable rules (2:44, 12:19–12:20 BCCA); • file a liability claim against the company's directors in its own name and behalf (not on behalf of the company) if it evidences damages distinct to that of other shareholders (2:56–2:57 BCCA).
1%	Shareholders holding at least 1% (or shares representing at least EUR 1.25 million of the company's capital) may: • file a lawsuit on behalf of the company against the board of directors, to the extent they have not (validly) approved the discharge of directors (7:157 BCCA) • demand an expert examination of the company (i.e. an audit of certain books and accounts of the company) (7:160 BCCA)
3%	Shareholders holding at least 3% of the outstanding share capital of the company, may request items to be added to the agenda of the general shareholders' meeting and/or propose draft resolutions to be added to agenda items of the general shareholders' meeting (7:130 BCCA)
5%	Shareholders holding at least 5% of the outstanding shares of the company may: • block a squeeze out of minority shareholders in case of a public offer (95% acceptance threshold) (7:82 BCCA) • request the dismissal of the statutory auditor by the court (3:66 BCCA)
10%	Shareholders holding at least 10% of the outstanding shares of the company may request the board of directors of the company to convene a general shareholders' meeting of the company (7:126 BCCA)
20% + 1 share	Shareholders representing at least 20% + 1 of the votes cast at the general shareholders' meeting of the company may: • veto amendments to the corporate object and purpose of the company (7:154 BCCA) • block modifications to the legal form of the company (14:8 BCCA) • block decisions on cross-border reorganisation of the company (14:24 BCCA)
25% + 1 share	Shareholders can block further key corporate decisions provided they represent at least 25%+1 or more of the votes cast at the general shareholders' meeting of the company. Such key decisions include changes to the articles of association (7:153 BCCA), capital increases/decreases and granting authorised capital (7:177, 7:208 and 7:199 BCCA), (de)mergers (12:56 and 12:70 BCCA), and liquidation of the company (2:71 BCC)- as well as an authorisation for share buy-backs (7:215 BCCA) or disposals of treasury without equal treatment of shareholders (7:218, §1, 5° BCCA)

Threshold	Obligations and Rights
50% + 1 share	Shareholders representing at least 50% + 1 of the votes cast at the general shareholders' meeting of the company may approve most resolutions without support from further shareholders, except for: • changes to the articles of association, capital increases and decreases and mergers as well as an authorisation for share buy-backs or disposals of treasury without equal treatment of shareholders, which require a 75% majority vote (see above) • changes to the company's legal form and corporate object and purpose, which require an 80% majority vote (see above)

39. *Public proxy solicitation.* Article 7:145 of the BCCA contains the Belgian rules for public proxy solicitation, i.e. a public campaign aimed at obtaining shareholders' powers of attorney to vote at a certain general shareholders' meeting, in the manner as proposed by an activist fund.[62] These rules can be summarised as follows:

- a proxy can only be requested for one general shareholders' meeting (or subsequent general shareholders' meetings with the same agenda);
- the proxy should be revocable;
- proxy solicitation document shall contain at least the following information:
  - the agenda, indicating the items to be discussed and the proposed decisions;
  - the statement that the company's documents are available to the shareholder requesting them;
  - an indication as to how the proxyholder will exercise the voting rights;
  - a detailed description and justification of the objectives of the person soliciting the proxy.
- a copy of the proxy solicitation shall be communicated to the FSMA three days before publication. The FSMA reviews whether the request sufficiently informs the shareholders and does not mislead them. If its comments are not taken into account, the FSMA may publish its opinion.

Whereas proxy fights through a public proxy solicitation process are relatively common in the United States, in Europe and in particular in Belgium, these are very rare.[63] It is important to note in this respect that a public campaign recommending shareholders to vote in a certain manner, i.e. soliciting votes, be it by an activist fund or the listed company itself, without actually requesting to receive a power of attorney, does not constitute in principle a public proxy

---

[62] Article 8:1 of the RD BCCA contains the criteria pursuant to which a proxy solicitation is public.

[63] See i.a. J. Malherbe, Y. De Cordt, P. Lambrecht, P. Malherbe and H. Culot, *Droit des sociétés*, 5th ed., Brussels, Larcier, 2020, 676.

solicitation subject to these rules.[64] However, companies are advised to monitor whether any campaign of an activist fund constitutes a public proxy solicitation requiring compliance with these rules.

4.1.2. Limits to company law rights

40. Invalid / abusive exercise of shareholder rights. The company's defence against the exercise of these shareholders' rights can generally only be based on a (potentially) invalid exercise of such shareholders' rights, in addition to the general rules and principles of abuse of rights, in this context often called "abuse of minority".[65] For example:

- *Question right:* Case law and legal doctrine interpret shareholders' right to ask questions broadly, without there being a right to receive documentation.[66] The board of directors and the statutory auditor can generally refuse to respond to questions submitted by shareholders in the realm of their competences in the following circumstances only:
  • if the disclosure prejudices the corporate interest or confidentiality obligations of the company or the confidentiality obligations of the directors towards the company. On this basis, the board of directors can justify its refusal to answer a question in order not to compromise ongoing negotiations, to respect a contractual duty of confidentiality, to protect trade secrets, but also to curb abuse of the right to ask questions (see further below). When questions about company policy are asked, the board of directors is pursuant to this provision not obliged to be granular and reveal the details of the corporate strategy, let alone expose its trade secrets.[67]

---

[64] See for example the campaign of Recticel NV in preparation of its special general shareholders' meetings at the end of 2021.

[65] See i.a. J. Bossuyt, "Misbruik van minderheidspositie in de algemene vergadering: Rechtsgrond en sancties" (2012) *DAOR*, 2012/4, nr. 104, 459–469; H. Braeckmans and P. Baert, 'Vraagrecht van de aandeelhouder' in R. Houben et al. (ed), *JPB – Liber amicorum Jean-Pierre Blumberg*, 1st ed., Brussels, Intersentia, 2021, 25; S. De Rey, "Plaatsvervangende uitspraak bij misbruik van stemrecht in de algemene vergadering: mogelijkheden en grenzen" (2016) *RPS-TRV*, 2016/5, 523–554; E. Goldschmidt, "§4. – Rechtsmisbruik bij de uitoefening van aandeelhoudersrechten" (2018) *Aandeelhoudersaansprakelijkheid*, 1st ed., Brussels, Intersentia, 2018, 219–248; A. Goris, "De Wet Aandeelhoudersrechten: een praktische benadering", *TRV*, 2012/2, 81–104; R. Houben, "Grenzen aan de uitoefening van stemrecht door aandeelhouders – In essentie een afweging van belangen", *Le juge des sociétés et associations / De vennootschaps- en verenigingsrechter*, 1st ed., Brussels, Larcier, 2017, 217–241.

[66] See e.g. the Barco cases: Kh. Ieper 17 May 1999, *TRV*, 1999, 534, note, *V&F*, 1999, 247; Gent 18 April 2002, *TRV*, 2002, 255, note. See also KG Nederlandstalige Orb. Brussel 20 July 2020, *TRV-RPS*, 2021, 83; KG Orb. Antwerpen (afd. Antwerpen) 7 January 2020, *TRV-RPS*, 2020, 108; H. Braeckmans and P. Baert, above n. 59, 25.

[67] H. Braeckmans and P. Baert, "Vraagrecht van de aandeelhouder" in R. Houben (ed.), N. Goossens (ed), C. Leunen (ed), *JPB. Liber amicorum Jean-Pierre Blumberg*, 1st ed., Brussels, Intersentia, 2021, 33.

- if the disclosure would result in the director incriminating him/herself (or the company) of the violation of a criminally sanctioned rule;
- if the question does not relate to the agenda of the general shareholders' meeting. Although it is of course accepted that agenda items can give rise to a great variety of questions and that all such questions should be responded to as a rule, Belgian case law has confirmed that responses could be refused on this basis[68];
- if the question does not relate to the company;
- if the shareholder has not complied with the deadline to submit its questions, in writing or by email, at the latest the sixth day prior to the general shareholders' meeting (but such questions could still be raised orally at the meeting by a shareholder attending);
- if the shareholder has not validly registered to attend the general shareholders' meeting;
- if the modalities of the question right, such as time limits and limitations on follow-up questions by one shareholder, which legal doctrine states can be included in a company's articles of association or internal regulations, are not complied with[69];
- if the question right is abused in accordance with the Belgian principle of abuse of right, e.g. in case of repetitive questions (even if the shareholder does not agree with the responses given), questions raised for other purposes than for the exercise of a shareholder's voting right, and/or filibustering.[70]

– *Right to add items or proposed resolutions to the agenda*: A shareholder's request to add items or proposed resolutions to the agenda of a general shareholders' meeting can generally be refused in the following circumstances only:
  - if the shareholder has not complied with the deadline to submit the request to the company, in writing or by email, at the latest the 22nd day prior to the general shareholders' meeting;
  - if the shareholder has not submitted the required proof of ownership of 3% (i) at the moment submitting request, and (ii) at the registration date for the general shareholders' meeting;
  - if the shareholder has not validly registered to attend the general shareholders' meeting;

---

[68] KG Nederlandstalige Orb. Brussel 20 July 2020, *TRV-RPS*, 2021, 83.
[69] H. Braeckmans and P. Baert, "Vraagrecht van de aandeelhouder" in R. Houben (ed.), N. Goossens (ed), C. Leunen (ed), *JPB. Liber amicorum Jean-Pierre Blumberg*, 1st ed., Brussels, Intersentia, 2021, 34.
[70] H. Braeckmans and P. Baert, "Vraagrecht van de aandeelhouder" in R. Houben (ed.), N. Goossens (ed), C. Leunen (ed), *JPB. Liber amicorum Jean-Pierre Blumberg*, 1st ed., Brussels, Intersentia, 2021, 38.

- if the item requested to be added to the agenda:
  - would be prejudicial for the company or certain other persons;
  - does not relate to the company;
  - is manifestly illegal or contrary to the interest of the company;
  - is impossible to take seriously;
  - is outside of the competences of the general shareholders' meeting.[71]
- *Right to exercise voting rights attached to shares*: A shareholder can be prevented from voting at a general shareholders' meeting in the following limited circumstances:
  - if the shareholder has not validly registered (with all the shares with which it wishes to vote) to attend the general shareholders' meeting in accordance with article 7:134, §2 BCCA;
  - if voting rights that are required to be notified in accordance with the Transparency Law (see item 3.3.2.1 above) have not been notified at least 20 days before the date of the general shareholders' meeting (subject to certain exceptions) in accordance with article 25/1 Transparency Law.[72]

4.2. RIGHT TO MAKE PUBLIC STATEMENTS AND LIMITS UNDER MAR

4.2.1. Rights

41. ***Activist funds have the right to make public statements.*** As set out in item 2 above, activist funds have various channels to make public statements about a company. They can issue press statements, but they can also leak ideas or rumours to the research analyst community, engage with journalists on or off the record, issue open letters, or launch website and/or social media campaigns to express their concerns and seek support for proposals from other

---

[71] See i.a. *Parl.St.* 53 0421/001, 17; A. Dirckx, "Art. 533*ter* W.Venn" in Braeckmans, H., Geens, K., Wymeersch, E. (ed.), *Vennootschappen en verenigingen. Artikelsgewijze commentaar met overzicht van rechtspraak en rechtsleer* (2012), 24; A. Goris, "De Wet Aandeelhoudersrechten: een praktische benadering", *TRV*, 2012/2, 81–104; E. Leroux, and G. Davignon, "Art. 7:130 C.S.A" in X., *Commentaire systématique du Code des sociétés* (2021), 5; P. Vandepitte, "Het agenderingsrecht van de aandeelhouders' in Th. Tilquin and V. Simonart (ed.), *Les assemblées générales/De algemene vergaderingen*, 1st ed., Brussels, Intersentia, 2011, 85–103; V. Verheyden, "When shareholders use their rights to convene meetings and to submit proposals. A comparative and empirical analysis of activism in four EU Member States", *RPS-TRV*, 2020/8, 975–995. See also in The Netherlands: Hoge Raad 20 april 2018, ECLI:NL:HR:2018:652.

[72] See e.g. S. D'hollander, "Art. 7:131 WVV" in H. Braeckmans, K. Geens, E. Wymeersch (ed.), *Vennootschappen en verenigingen. Artikelsgewijze commentaar met overzicht van rechtspraak en rechtsleer* (2019) 5p.

shareholders, stakeholders, and representative bodies. Additionally, they may voice their opinion and ask questions during general shareholders' meetings. Indeed, activist funds have the right to make public statements. However, they are still subject to certain regulations and restrictions.

4.2.2. Limits under MAR and other Legislation

42. Activist fund publications and actions may constitute market manipulation. Activist funds are subject to limited restrictions when communicating publicly on their activist campaign. One important restriction that applies to anyone dealing with, or communicating in respect of, listed companies, *i.e.* including activist funds, is MAR. Pursuant to article 12 MAR, market manipulation comprises, among other things:

> *(a) "entering into a transaction, placing an order to trade or any other behaviour which:*
>
> *(i) gives, or is likely to give, false or misleading signals as to the supply of, demand for, or price of, a financial instrument, a related spot commodity contract or an auctioned product based on emission allowances; or*
>
> *(ii) secures, or is likely to secure, the price of one or several financial instruments, a related spot commodity contract or an auctioned product based on emission allowances at an abnormal or artificial level;*
>
> *unless the person entering into a transaction, placing an order to trade or engaging in any other behaviour establishes that such transaction, order or behaviour have been carried out for legitimate reasons, and conform with an accepted market practice as established in accordance with article 13;" …*
>
> *(c) "disseminating information through the media, including the internet, or by any other means, which gives, or is likely to give, false or misleading signals as to the supply of, demand for, or price of, a financial instrument, a related spot commodity contract or an auctioned product based on emission allowances or secures, or is likely to secure, the price of one or several financial instruments, a related spot commodity contract or an auctioned product based on emission allowances at an abnormal or artificial level, including the dissemination of rumours, where the person who made the dissemination knew, or ought to have known, that the information was false or misleading;"*

Companies may have arguments to claim that the activist fund's public campaigning in media and/or stake-building or short-selling is constitutive of market manipulation in an effort to take advantage of the resulting share price movements (see also item 3.3.2.4 above on short selling). Although claims by targets against activist funds are rare throughout the EU, there are precedents on this basis of market manipulation.[73, 74]

43. *Activist fund publications may be investment recommendations.* Depending on the circumstances, companies may also argue that certain publications made by an activist fund in the context of a public campaign qualify as an "investment recommendation" or "other information recommending or suggesting an investment strategy" (article 20 MAR). If its publications would meet this qualification, then the activist fund may be required to (i) take reasonable care to ensure that such information is objectively presented, and (ii) disclose its interests or indicate conflicts of interest concerning the financial instruments to which that information relates (the requirements to comply with (i) and (ii) are set out in Commission Delegated Regulation (EU) 2016/958).

44. *Activist fund trading may constitute insider dealing.* Pursuant to article 8 MAR, *"insider dealing arises where a person possesses inside information and uses that information by acquiring or disposing of, for its own account or for the account of a third party, directly or indirectly, financial instruments to which that information relates".* As set out below (see item 5.2.1), an activist approach may constitute inside information, i.e. it may have a significant effect on the share price of the target company. An activist fund may indeed be acquiring shares prior to its approach becoming public, intending for the share price to increase as a result of its approach, to be able to sell its shares at a higher price. Alternatively, an activist fund may be short-selling shares (see also item 3.3.2.4) prior to its public campaign, intending to drive down the share price through its public campaign by the time it needs to acquire and deliver the shares.[75] Such trading by the activist fund prior to its campaign becoming public, may constitute insider dealing.

---

[73] See e.g. A. Pietrancosta, "Brief Remarks on the Necessary Clarification of Market Abuse Prohibitions in Times of Shareholder Activism" [2019] *Revue trimestrielle de droit financier – Corporate Finance and Capital Markets Law Review* <https://ssrn.com/abstract=3476301 or http://dx.doi.org/10.2139/ssrn.3476301>; M. Celarier, "Are Activist Short Sellers Misunderstood?" [2022] *The New York Times Dealbook Newsletter* 12 February 2022 <https://www.nytimes.com/2022/02/12/business/dealbook/are-activist-short-sellers-misunderstood.html>; D. Cetemen, G. Cisternas, A. Kolb and S. Viswanathan, "Activist Manipulation Dynamics" [2022] *Federal Reserve Bank of New York staff reports* <https://www.newyorkfed.org/research/staff_reports/sr1030>; Z. Bach, A. Fink and R. Leithauser, above n. 52.

[74] The activist fund, on the other hand, may invoke market manipulation to claim that its target misled the market by over-optimistic / pessimistic communications, thereby creating wrongful expectations which exposed the activist fund and drove it to its campaign.

[75] See also the references in footnote 73.

4.3. POTENTIAL CIVIL LIABILITY OF ACTIVIST FUNDS

45. *Broad boundaries of civil liability.* As we have set out under item 3.1 above, activist campaigns can lead to enhanced costs for the company, more volatility in the stock price, reduced access to equity or debt capital markets and difficulty to retain or attract resources, leading to damage for the company, its senior leadership teams and/or other shareholders. Where certain activist campaigns have resulted in constructive dialogue, other campaigns have been (ultimately) found to be value destructive and companies sometimes query whether damage can be claimed from the activist fund. The reality is however that activist funds are generally limited – towards the target companies – only by the fairly wide boundaries of the civil and criminal liability regime (in addition to the considerations set out in item 4.2.2). Civil liability would only arise if the activist fund commits a violation of laws, an intentional fault or negligence that causes damage to the company, its board of directors and/or its shareholders whereby, importantly, damages suffered by shareholders, are distinct of those suffered the company or its board of directors and can therefore not be recovered by the latter. In accordance with article 1382 (old) Belgian Civil Code, the following evidentiary thresholds need to be met:

- companies and/or its directors would be required to demonstrate that the activist fund's actions were either wrongful (such as a violation of the law or intentional wrongdoing) or at least negligent. For instance, they could argue that the activist fund's public statements were made without proper investigation, and without allowing them adequate response and preparation time. This would indicate negligence on the part of the activist fund, as their aggressive and confrontational approach may have caused harm to the company without considering less harmful alternatives.
- companies and/or its directors must also demonstrate that they have suffered damage, such as (i) the costs of hiring advisors and litigation expenses, (ii) the costs associated with limited or more expensive access to capital markets, (iii) reputational harm, and (iv) a decrease in the stock price of treasury shares. Recovering an overall decline in the stock price can be challenging since it does not necessarily impact the company's assets and liabilities but instead affects the shareholders' interests for which the company cannot claim, except in the case of treasury shares.
- companies and/or its directors would finally also need to prove a causal link between the fault and the damage.

46. *Jurisdiction.* Moreover, if an activist fund does not have its registered office, any assets or any operations in Belgium (which is the case for most activist funds), it will need to be assessed whether companies and/or their directors can file a civil liability claim in Belgium against the fund. Belgian[76] or, as applicable, European[77] law stipulates that civil liability claims must be filed in the defendant's country of residence, with exceptions for the place where the tortious behavior has been (or may be) committed or the damage resulted from the tort has (or may be) occurred. Companies and/or their directors will therefore need to be able to locate the actions of activist funds and/or damage suffered by Belgian listed companies mentioned in the previous paragraph in Belgium to be able to file a claim in Belgium. However, if an activist fund initiates a civil liability claim against the company or its directors before a Belgian court, a counterclaim can be made before the same Belgian court.

47. *Injunctions.* If companies and/or their directors want to prevent an activist fund from making public statements, they would need to file a summary proceeding seeking an injunction. In this proceeding, they must provide the challenging evidence that, in the trial on the merits, they are likely to succeed in their civil liability claim.

48. *Conclusion: rare and potentially not desirable.* Except for securities law breaches (i.e. breaches of the rules described in items 3.3.2 and 4.2), civil liability claims against activist funds have only rarely been initiated in Belgium and the situation is similar in the United States, the United Kingdom and the EU. Threats of such claims that were made may moreover be viewed critically by other shareholders who may wonder why resources of the company would be spent on suing a shareholder who merely had openly expressed a concern. In addition to the fairly high burden of proof and other procedural hurdles mentioned above, the company will indeed need to consider the impact or perception of bringing claims against shareholders.

4.4. CRIMINAL LIABILITY UNDER BELGIAN LAW

49. *Difficult and potentially undesirable criminal liability claims.* In another unusual move, companies may attempt to (implicitly) warn that they will initiate criminal action, likely for defamation (*laster/calomnie* or *eerroof/diffamation*).[78] However, besides being challenging to substantiate and potentially creating a negative perception among other shareholders (similar to civil liability claims), companies would have no control over the criminal investigations or proceedings once they begin. These proceedings may also take years before a conclusion is

---

[76] Article 96 of the Belgian Code of Private International Law.
[77] Article 7 of Regulation (EU) No 1215/2012 of the European Parliament and of the Council of 12 December 2012 on jurisdiction and the recognition and enforcement of judgments in civil and commercial matters (recast) (Brussels I*bis*).
[78] Article 443 et seq. of the Belgian Criminal Law Code.

reached. If activist statements are blatantly not true, a company may consider bringing these claims, even if they will last years, to show to investors that the company is serious about its contention that the statements are not true and to deter others from making similar criminally sanctionable statements.

5. RIGHTS AND OBLIGATIONS OF COMPANIES

5.1. ROLE OF THE BOARD OF DIRECTORS AND CORPORATE INTEREST

50. *Responsibility of the board of directors to assess any substantive activist approach.* In accordance with article 2:49 BCCA, all legal entities, including companies, act through their corporate bodies, the powers of which are determined by the BCCA and the company's object and articles of association. Pursuant to article 7:93 BCCA, in a monist or one-tier governance structure, the board of directors is authorised to carry out all actions that are necessary or useful to achieve the company's purpose, except for those for which the general shareholders' meeting is authorised by law. Pursuant to articles 7:109 and 7:110 BCCA, in a dualist or two-tier governance structure, the supervisory board is responsible for the general policy and strategy of the company and for all actions that are specifically reserved to it pursuant to the BCCA. In addition, the supervisory board is responsible for supervising the management board. The management board on the other hand exercises all management powers as referenced in article 7:93 BCCA that are not reserved to the supervisory board.[79]

Accordingly, while not explicitly mentioned in the BCCA[80], the board of directors is responsible for the management of the company and compliance with all applicable laws and regulations. It is therefore in principle the board of directors' responsibility to assess any substantive activist approach (subject to 4.1.1) – whereby in the two-tier system, the roles of the supervisory board and the management board will need to be considered based upon the subject-matter and materiality of the approach.[81]

51. *Collegiality of the board of directors in assessing any substantive activist approach.* Pursuant to articles 7:85, 7:105 and 7:107 BCCA, the board of directors, the supervisory board and/or the management board constitute a collegial body. This implies that the powers mentioned in the previous paragraph

---

[79] See also B. Tilleman and K. Dewaele, *Bestuur van vennootschappen*, Brussels, die Keure/la Charte, 2022, 290 ff.
[80] See also S. Cools, *De bevoegdheidsverdeling tussen algemene vergadering en raad van bestuur in de NV*, Roularta (Biblo), 2015, 213.
[81] See also B. Tilleman and K. Dewaele, *Bestuur van vennootschappen*, Brussels, die Keure/la Charte, 2022, 278 ff.

do not belong to the individual members, but to the body as a whole, and that individual member have no powers to decide individually on behalf of the company.[82] In case of an activist approach, it is therefore important for the board of directors to remain collegial and respect the confidentiality of the decision-making. Activist funds often seek to drive a wedge and will gratefully use any hint of disagreement or misalignment within the board of directors in their campaign. Without prejudice to this collegial decision-making, a board of directors will often delegate interactions with the activist fund that require board involvement to the chair or another (often independent) director, who then reports back to the board.[83]

52. *Corporate interest of the company.* In taking any decision and in making any proposal to the general shareholders' meeting (or omission to decide or make a proposal to the general shareholders' meeting) on the proposals by the activist fund, the board of directors is to assess the corporate interest of the company, which is defined by the Belgian Supreme Court as *"the collective financial interest of all present and future shareholders"*. It is generally considered that all stakeholders' interests, including creditors and employees, should be taken into account when considering the corporate interest of the company, as part of a factual assessment to be made by the board of directors taking into account all relevant circumstances.[84]

This means that circumstances to be considered include not only the current shareholders financial interest, possibly including majority or reference shareholders, but also current minority (activist) shareholders' (perceived) interest, as well as the company's current and future investment opportunities, access to capital markets, risk management and leverage approach, and any other elements that are included in the broader definition, such as the interest of the company's employees, suppliers, creditors, community and any other constituency that may be relevant, all of which could impact the collective financial interest of the company's shareholders both in the short and longer term.

53. *Interest and investment horizon activist fund.* According to the majority of doctrine, shareholders are not bound by such corporate benefit. They are

---

[82] Notably, in its "20 projects for the future in its areas of supervision" published on 4 October 2022 (see footnote 61), the FSMA proposes that one director is appointed as contact person for shareholders. See also B. Tilleman and K. Dewaele, *Bestuur van vennootschappen*, Brussels, die Keure/la Charte, 2022, 380 ff.

[83] See also B. Tilleman and K. Dewaele, *Bestuur van vennootschappen*, Brussels, die Keure/la Charte, 2022, 286.

[84] Hof van Cassatie / Cour de Cassation, 28 November 2013 (*TRV*, 2014, 286, note N. Cooreman, *TBH*, 2014, 854, note D. Willermain). See e.g. R. Houben, "Vennootschapsbelang en algemeen belang" in *Liber Amicorum Xavier Dieux*, Brussels, Larcier, 2022, 225–257; D. Van Gerven, *Handboek Vennootschappen – Algemeen deel*, 2nd ed., Brussels, Intersentia, 2020, 525 ff.

entitled to act in their own corporate benefit, subject to abuse of minority.[85] Activist funds, as described in item 1, are therefore primarily bound by their own corporate interest, as may be defined in the investment contract with their ultimate investors, and have to act in their interest. Consequently, activist funds – towards their investors – are obliged to strive to maximise the shareholder value of the investee companies within the investment horizon of their fund. The fund investment horizon does not necessarily coincide with a company's long-term strategy or corporate interest (although it has been established that activist funds are not necessarily short-term investors[86]), which can come to bear in certain campaigns, e.g. activist funds pursuing short-term capital returns and the company preferring to invest in R&D pipeline.

While activist funds often argue that they are acting 'in the company's corporate benefit', it is useful to keep the above background in mind when assessing their approach as the two will not necessarily coincide.

54. *Possibility of unequal playing field.* In addition, activist funds are often privately held companies which are not subject to the same rules and regulatory constraints as listed companies.[87] Activist funds are generally limited – in particular towards the target companies – only by the fairly wide boundaries of the market abuse prohibitions under MAR and the civil and criminal liability regime (see items 4.2 and 4.3 above). As we detail below in the next items, Belgian listed companies, on the other hand, are subject to a range of obligations in respect of its disclosures and interactions with its shareholders, driven by MAR, the BCCA and all other relevant legislation. This narrows the scope for

---

[85] R. Houben, "Het verbod op rechtsmisbruik als beperking op de uitoefening van aandeelhoudersrechten" in A. Van Oevelen, S. Rutten and J. Rozie (eds.), *Rechtsmisbruik*, Antwerp, Intersentia, 2015, 152, nr. 5; Y. De Cordt, *L'égalité entre actionnaires*, Brussels, Bruylant, 2004, 654; V. Simonart, "Les conflits d'intérêts au sein de l'assemblée générale de la société anonyme en droit comparé" in *Les conflits d'intérêts – Les conférences du centre de droit privé*, Brussels, Bruylant, 1994, 217; K. Geens, "De jurisprudentiële bescherming van de minderheidsaandeelhouder tegen door de meerderheid opgezette beschermingsconstructies" *TPR*, 1989, 43, nr. 13; J. Ronse and K. Geens, "Misbruik van minderheidspositie" in *Van vennootschappelijk belang. Opstellen aangeboden aan Prof. Mr. J.M.M. Maeijer*, Zwolle, Tjeenk Willink, 1988, 235; P. Coppens, *L'abus de majorité dans les sociétés anonymes*, Gembloux, Imprimerie J. Duculot, 1947, 75–83. Contra: O. Caprasse and R. Aydogdu, *Les conflits entre actionnaires. Prévention et résolution*, Brussels, Larcier, 2010, 202–209; X. Dieux, «Nouvelles observations sur l'abus de majorité ou de minorité dans les personnes morales fonctionnant selon le principe majoritaire" in X. Dieux (ed.), *Legal tracks I – Essays on contemporary corporate and finance law*, Brussels, Bruylant, 2003, 477; W. Van Gerven, *Bewindsbevoegdheid*, Brussel, Bruylant, 1962, 153; J. Van Ryn, *Principes de droit commercial, I*, Brussels, Bruylant, 1954, 444–445; J. Dabin, *Le droit subjectif*, Paris, Dalloz, 1952, 224, footnote 5.
[86] A. Brav, W. Jiang and R. Li, above n. 4.
[87] Ibid. Activist funds may of course be subject to other legislation, such as Directive 2011/61/EU of the European Parliament and of the Council of 8 June 2011 on Alternative Investment Fund Managers and amending Directives 2003/41/EC and 2009/65/EC and Regulations (EC) 1060/2009 and (EU) 1095/2010 [2011] OJ L174/1.

reaction and communication with activist funds and may at times create an unlevel playing field.

5.2. DISCLOSURE REQUIREMENTS IN CASE OF ACTIVIST APPROACH

5.2.1. Inside Information

55. If the activist approach and the company's intended reaction constitute inside information, such information should, as a rule, be immediately disclosed. In assessing any activist approach and any reaction thereto, a company is to consider the rules set out in MAR. In accordance with article 17(1) MAR, issuers of listed securities must, as a rule, disclose to the public any "inside information" which directly concerns itself immediately.

In accordance with article 7(1) MAR, "inside information" is defined as any information:

- which is of a precise nature;
- which has not been made public;
- relating, directly or indirectly, to one or more issuers or to one or more financial instruments; and
- which, if it were made public, would be likely to have a significant effect on the prices of those financial instruments or on the price of related derivative financial instruments.

A private activist campaign or stake-building by an activist fund (which holds less than the thresholds required for disclosure under the transparency laws and is therefore not publicly known (see item 3.3.2)) can potentially qualify as inside information. Determining whether a situation constitutes inside information depends on the specific circumstances, such as the clarity and specificity of the activist fund's plans and/or requests, as well as the significance of the fund's shareholding. Simply being aware that an activist fund is acquiring shares does not necessarily qualify as inside information since it may not be clear what the fund's goals are or what strategies (if any) it will employ.

In contrast, public campaigns by activist funds typically do not constitute inside information. Since the activist fund will usually make sure that its concerns, demands and objections are widely disseminated, the information is likely to be public and, therefore, would not qualify as inside information.

The potential responses of the company to an activist approach could, moreover, in itself constitute inside information, depending on the circumstances.

5.2.2. Permitted Delay of Disclosure of Inside Information

56. Companies may choose to delay disclosure if certain conditions are met. In accordance with article 17(4) MAR, companies may, under their own responsibility[88], decide to defer immediate disclosure if all of the following conditions are met:

- they consider that such immediate disclosure is likely to prejudice their legitimate interests;
- such deferral is not likely to mislead the public; and
- the issuer is able to ensure the confidentiality of that information (through a non-disclosure agreement (*NDA*) for instance).

If a private approach or stake-building by an activist fund (or any related circumstances) constitutes inside information and a company decides to make use of the possibility to delay the disclosure thereof, the rationale behind this decision must be well-documented and regularly reviewed.

Such justification could include: (i) the lack of clarity regarding the outcome of the activist fund's approach, which means that the public would not be misled by delaying disclosure, (ii) publishing the information would be contrary to the legitimate interests of the company as such could unsettle shareholders, bankers,

---

[88] On 7 December 2022, the European Commission proposed measures to further develop the EU's Capital Markets Union (CMU) to, amongst others, alleviate – through a new listing act – the administrative burden for companies of all sizes, in particular SMEs, so that they can better access public funding by listing on stock exchanges. The package contains amendments to i.a. MAR, and includes a proposed amendment to article 17(4) to replace the general condition that the delay should not mislead the public by a list of specific conditions that the inside information that the issuer intends to delay must satisfy the following conditions:
  (i) it is not materially different from the previous public announcement of the issuer on the matter to which the inside information refers to;
  (ii) it does not regard the fact that the issuer's financial objectives are not likely to be met, where such objectives were previously publicly announced;
  (iii) it is not in contrast with the market's expectations, where such expectations are based on signals that the issuer has previously sent to the market, including interviews, roadshows or any other type of communication organised by the issuer or with its approval.
In addition, the proposal considers that issuers currently face a lack of legal clarity around the conditions that need to be met to delay disclosure when immediate disclosure would be likely to prejudice the legitimate interests of the issuers (e.g., by jeopardising the successful conclusion of ongoing negotiations). Therefore, the timing of the notification of the delay to the national competent authority is advanced to the moment immediately after the decision to delay disclosure is taken by the issuer (instead of the moment immediately after the information is disclosed to the public as currently provided by MAR). Thus, the issuer shall inform the competent authority of its intention to delay the disclosure of inside information and provide a written explanation of how the conditions set out above were met, immediately after the decision to delay is taken. In this manner, the proposal would return to the previous regime that applied under the market abuse directive (Directive 2003/6/EC of the European Parliament and of the Council).

customers, suppliers, and employees due to the uncertainty of the demands and their outcome, (iii) disclosure may attract other activist funds or short-term traders, thereby increasing the harm, and (iv) there is a risk of reputational damage resulting from unclear demands, which could put disproportionate pressure on the company's board of directors and management.

It is important to note that delay of disclosure would not be permitted if there is a market rumour that is "sufficiently accurate", containing core elements of facts that compromise the confidentiality of the inside information, for instance if certain press agencies would report on the activist fund's approach.

5.2.3. Disclosure of Activist Approach

57. Companies may decide to disclose activist approach, even if not legally required. Even if permitted under MAR not to disclose the activist approach on the basis of (i) the information not constituting inside information or (ii) the possibility to delay the disclosure of inside information, companies may still decide to disclose the approach. In the latter case, companies must immediately disclose the inside information via an ad-hoc announcement compliant with MAR, thereby making the activist approach and/or the company's reaction public. Companies could indeed decide to publish the approach by an activist fund so as to possibly gain the tactical advantage of controlling the process and reacting proactively. It is of course key, if a company decides to make an announcement to the public, not to make any false or misleading statements (see also below) and, for instance, resist the trap of defensive, overly optimistic statements.

5.2.4. Insider List and Selective Disclosure

58. Procedure to be followed and restrictions if disclosure of inside information is delayed. If the disclosure of inside information is delayed based upon the above assessment, a specific insider list containing details of all persons having access to such inside information and that act for or on behalf of the company[89] needs to be prepared and kept updated (article 18 MAR). The activist fund itself does not have to be included on the company's insider list (but it is of course otherwise bound by MAR). The company must also inform the FSMA of its decision to postpone after the information is disclosed to the public and provide a written explanation on how the conditions for deferral were met (and keep a written record for such purposes).[90] If the activist

---

[89] See article 18(1) of the MAR: all persons who have access to inside information and who are working for them [the issuer or the persons working on its behalf or for its account] under a contract of employment, or otherwise performing tasks through which they have access to inside information, such as advisers, accountants or credit rating agencies.

[90] See previous footnote on the proposed amendment to this mechanism.

disappears or sells, such that the inside information never materialises, no announcement has to be made.

Any person having inside information, including the activist fund, the company itself and all persons included on the insider list, is considered an insider. Insiders are prohibited by MAR from insider dealing, *i.e.*, acquiring or disposing of the relevant securities on their own account or on the account of or on behalf of a third party, or from recommending any such securities to a third party (articles 14(a) and 8 MAR).

59. *No selective disclosure of inside information.* Furthermore, inside information of which the disclosure has been legitimately delayed, must generally not be disclosed or made available to a third party. Inside information can only be selectively disclosed to a third party if:

- the disclosure is made in the normal course of the exercise of an employment, profession or duties; and
- the recipient owes the company a duty of confidentiality (either through an NDA or by law).

If and when an activist approach constitutes inside information, a company is typically authorised to inform the following persons in order to fulfil its professional duties, in which case such persons need to be included in the above-mentioned insider list:

- the board of directors and such members of management who, in the reasonable judgment of the board of directors, need to be informed;
- the advisors retained for such situation;
- the FSMA;
- if necessary and justified, subject to an NDA, material shareholders, in order to learn their position and to take such into account when deciding upon the potential reaction to the approach;
- a joint venture partner if the inside information is relevant for it.

Generally, it is not necessary, and therefore not justified, to inform:

- the employees or employee representatives at an early stage as no firm decision, action plan or agreement yet exists;
- politicians or lobbying groups, unless there is a specific need;
- individual analysts, because it is difficult to see how an analyst can be of help in a potential activist situation (other than by unduly influencing the markets on the basis of information not publicly available);
- journalists.

5.3. SHAREHOLDERS' INFORMATION RIGHTS AND ACTIVIST INFORMATION REQUESTS

60. *Legal information obligations of companies are very expansive.* Belgian listed companies are subject to multiple and substantial disclosure requirements:

- disclosure requirements of a financial and non-financial nature under article 34 of the Royal Decree of 14 November 2007 on the obligations of issuers of financial instruments admitted to trading on a regulated market[91], the BCCA[92], the royal decree of 29 April 2019 in execution of the BCCA[93], accounting rules and European legislation[94];
- disclosure requirements on governance and conflicts, including a corporate governance statement and remuneration report (article 3:6 and 3:32 BCCA) as well as detailed disclosures on conflicts of interest and related party transactions (articles 7:96 and 7:97 BCCA);
- ad hoc disclosure requirements under MAR (see above);
- this information is to be fair, accurate and true, and must allow shareholders and the public in general to assess its impact on the position, the business and the results of the company. In particular, the 2002 Law contains obligations regarding the publication, completeness and accuracy of all regulated information, including (but not limited to) full-year results releases, annual reports, half-year reports, and quarterly reports (if published).

These disclosure requirements are closely monitored by the FSMA, which has also issued a circular on the obligations of listed companies.[95]

---

[91] Koninklijk besluit van 14 november 2007 betreffende de verplichtingen van emittenten van financiële instrumenten die zijn toegelaten tot de verhandeling op een gereglementeerde markt / Arrêté royal du 14 novembre 2007 relatif aux obligations des émetteurs d'instruments financiers admis à la négociation sur un marché réglementé, BS/MB 03.12.2007, 59762.

[92] Including articles 3:6, §3 and 3:32, §2 of the BCCA implementing Directive 2014/95/EU of the European Parliament and of the Council of 22 October 2014 amending Directive 2013/34/EU as regards disclosure of non-financial and diversity information by certain large undertakings and groups (NFRD).

[93] Koninklijk besluit van 29 april 2019 tot uitvoering van het Wetboek van vennootschappen en verenigingen / Arrêté royal du 29 avril 2019 portant exécution du Code des sociétés et des associations, BS/MB 30.04.2019, 42246 (RD BCCA).

[94] Including Regulation (EU) 2020/852 of the European Parliament and of the Council of 18 June 2020 on the establishment of a framework to facilitate sustainable investment, and amending Regulation (EU) 2019/2088 [2020] OJ L198/13 and, upon its entry into force and implementation in Belgian law, CSRD, which will require reporting in 2025 on the financial year 2024 for companies already subject to the NFRD.

[95] FSMA_2012_01 dd. 11 januari 2012 (update 12 juli 2022) – Verplichtingen van op een gereglementeerde markt genoteerde emittenten / FSMA_2012_01 du 11 janvier 2012 (mise à jour du 12 juillet 2022) – Obligations incombant aux émetteurs cotés sur un marché réglementé.

61. Furthermore, when a public offering or listing on a regulated market of securities occurs, it is generally required to prepare a prospectus in compliance with Regulation (EU) 2017/1129 of the European Parliament and of the Council of 14 June 2017 on the prospectus to be published when securities are offered to the public or admitted to trading on a regulated market, and repealing Directive 2003/71/EC. A prospectus provides information about the securities being issued and/or admitted to trading, as well as a company's primary line of business, financial status, and shareholding structure. It must contain all pertinent information which, based on the specific nature of the issuer and securities offered to the public or admitted to trading on a regulated market, is necessary for investors to make an informed evaluation of the assets and liabilities, financial condition, profit and losses, and prospects of the issuer and any guarantor, as well as the rights attached to such securities. Information rights of shareholders are broad, but not unlimited. Activist funds sometimes demand information from the company on top of the information already published pursuant to the legal requirements described in the previous paragraph (such as information underlying a certain decision, board minutes, …). There is, however, not, under Belgian law, a right for a shareholder to freely access company information (other than the rights described in item 4.1) and allowing such access for one shareholder and not others, could create concerns for a company and be challenged.

62. *No selective disclosure of any information.* Although shareholder engagement is generally encouraged, companies must be mindful of their duties under general corporate and financial law (including MAR) and the regulatory constraints involved. There are limits on the information that a company can share with an activist fund, irrespective of the type of information that would be shared. As a general principle under Belgian corporate law, shareholders in equal circumstances are to be treated equally.[96] This principle is indeed generally accepted, even though it has not been explicitly provided for in the BCCA as a general rule – it has solely been included in the procedural provisions governing the organisation of the general shareholders' meetings (art. 7:123 BCCA). It is important to note – and activist funds tend to ignore – that activism does not grant a right to more information under company law or MAR.

If a company intends to share information with an activist fund that constitutes inside information, the general rule under MAR is that it cannot be shared until the information is publicly announced. The selective disclosure of inside information is only permitted in limited and justified circumstances under MAR (see above). These conditions are unlikely to be met in the absence of any proposed transaction or corporate action by the company that would justify selective disclosure to an activist fund. Furthermore, if a company intends to

---

[96] See principle 8 of the Corporate Governance Code.

share inside information, the activist fund would need to keep the information confidential by entering into an NDA before receiving it. The fund would also need to be comfortable with the consequences of receiving the information, *i.e.* being unable to deal in relevant securities until the information is made public and being unable to use the information received directly or indirectly in its public campaign. Consequently, an activist fund may very well choose to inform the company that it does not wish to receive inside information.

In addition, information that falls outside the scope of inside information as defined by MAR would typically also have to be disclosed to all shareholders equally, unless there are clear, objective factors that differentiate among them. Such information can otherwise not be selectively disclosed only to an activist fund requesting it. The criteria outlined above for the selective disclosure of inside information can also be used as guidance for the selective disclosure of any non-public information.

5.4. CONCLUSION: HOW TO ENGAGE WITH AN ACTIVIST FUND

63. *Calm, efficient and thoughtful process.* As is clear from the above, when a company is faced with an activist fund, it is important to take its approach seriously and consider engaging with the fund in a thoughtful, strategic, professional and respectful manner rather than ignoring it. The response to the activist fund should be controlled by the board of directors in consultation with the company's management and advisors. It is important for the board of directors to consider and decide on the plans for responding to the activist fund and to take into account the different directions that developments may take, including potential outcomes and risks.

We propose the following summary for actions to consider when an activist fund approaches the company:

1. *Brief the board*: The board of directors should be briefed on any serious activist approach and be convened to decide on the plan (and team) for responding to the activist fund.
2. *Direct inquiries to investor relations*: Directors, management and employees should be reminded to direct inquiries from the media or other interested parties to the team that has received the authority to deal with the activist approach (often, the chair, CEO and/or company's investor relations department).
3. *Stay calm and objective*: Activist funds can be very aggressive, but it is important for companies to stay calm and objective when dealing with them. Companies should assess the situation carefully and objectively, and avoid responding with anger or defensiveness.

4. *Gather information*: The company should conduct research to learn more about the activist fund. This can include looking at the fund's (team's) past actions, other holdings and public statements, as well as any regulatory filings or public disclosures to understand its goals, strategies, and track record. This will help companies to better understand the fund's motivations, intentions and next steps.
5. *Assess the activist fund's thesis*: The board of directors should assess the activist's thesis and weigh it against the corporate interest of the company for the benefit of all stakeholders. The board of directors should consider the potential benefits and risks of the proposals, as well as the impact they could have on the company's short- and long-term strategy. The board of directors may need to seek financial and/or legal advice to make an informed decision. The company should not assume that what the activist fund is saying is wrong, and the activist fund may even drive for acceleration of actions that the company is already contemplating (for which the activist fund may then wish to take credit).
6. *Establish a response plan*: The board of directors, in consultation with management and the company's advisors, should establish a plan for responding to the activist fund. This plan should include a clear understanding of the activist fund's goals, potential responses the company could take, and the risks and benefits of each response. It is also important to determine whether to defend against or engage with the activist fund, as not all activist funds are aggressive, and clear decisions must be made while assessing risks.
7. *Decide whether to engage publicly or privately*: Depending on the situation, the company may decide to engage with the activist fund publicly or privately. This may involve meeting with representatives of the fund to discuss their proposals and concerns, and working together to find a mutually beneficial solution. However, the sequence of events could take such decision out of the board's hands, as the approach may become public before the decision to engage publicly or privately (if in any manner) is made. The company should consider the potential risks and benefits of each approach.
8. *Communicate with stakeholders*: Companies should regularly communicate with their stakeholders, including shareholders, employees, customers, and suppliers, about the situation and the steps they are taking to address it and to understand any concerns they may have. This will help to maintain transparency and build trust with stakeholders.
9. *Keep a record of external advice*: The company should keep a record of all external advice received, including any financial or legal advice.
10. *Document discussions carefully*: The company should keep a careful record of all discussions, particularly board meetings where decisions are being

made on how to engage with the activist fund. Any private discussions with the activist or their representatives should also be carefully documented; it should be assumed that these discussions are being recorded by the activist fund.
11. *Think about the long game*: The company should consider the long-term implications of any decision made in response to the activist approach. Maintaining relationships with the activist fund and managing their exit where possible is important.
12. *Keep focus on valuable elements of strategy*: The board of directors should remain focused on the valuable elements of the company's current strategy and avoid being diverted in its execution by the activist fund's demands.

Overall, the key to dealing with an activist fund is to stay calm, objective, and proactive. By carefully assessing the situation, possibly engaging with the activist fund, and communicating with stakeholders, companies can navigate this challenging situation and emerge stronger and more resilient.

THE SECURITIES LAW FRAMEWORK: A FLY IN THE OINTMENT OF ACTIVISTS?[*]

Marijke Spooren, Ruben Foriers and Jean-Sébastien Rombouts
Cleary Gottlieb Steen & Hamilton

1. INTRODUCTION

The standard playbook of activists is well-known: conduct thorough research, build a position, rally support from other shareholders, engage privately with the company, go out with public statements, launch a public PR campaign, etc. What is less well-known is that all tactics which activists (wish to) employ necessarily have to be carried out within a securities law framework that subjects the timing, scope and opportunity of these tactics to certain limitations.

Activists, particularly those that are entering the (Belgian or European) field for the first time, and issuers who are faced with an activist approach, are not always aware of these limitations. Even when they are familiar with the securities law framework in general, they may not fully grasp how this could impact an activist campaign. This should not come as a surprise. The current body of securities laws is the product of decades of rulemaking seeking to protect shareholders as traders on the public markets. Such rulemaking has often been reactive to specific trends or events. Shareholder activism in that sense is a relatively "new" phenomenon. As a result, to date, securities laws have matured without much regard to shareholder activism, and are therefore not always apt to the specifics of an activist approach and strategy.

In this contribution, we discuss the securities law angle of activism. First, we focus on transparency rules that require activists to put their cards on the table about their investment in the issuer as well as on tools available to issuers to map out their shareholder base. Next, we look at the Market Abuse Regulation and the possible qualification of an activist approach as inside information and consequences thereof. In addition, we discuss how the prohibitions on insider

---

[*] The text of this contribution was updated until 5 April 2023.

dealing and market manipulation may play out in an activist context. Finally, we take a closer look at the possibility for like-minded activists to work together as a wolf pack and whether this could possibly qualify as a "concert action" with significant ripple effects.

2. TRANSPARENCY RULES

Transparency rules are rules that require investors with ownership in (or exposure to) an issuer to disclose their ownership in (or exposure to) such issuer and the market when they reach or cross (upwards or downwards) certain reporting thresholds. Such rules are directly relevant to activism.

In a typical activist campaign, the activist investor starts by acquiring a stake in the target[1] and then seeks to engage in private communications with the issuer.[2] If the issuer is unresponsive to its demands or the engagement does not produce the desired outcome, the activist may "go public", for instance through the release of a white paper or a public letter setting forth its strategy and objectives for the issuer.

Transparency rules determine the size of the initial stake that an activist can build up before being legally required to disclose its ownership to the issuer and the market.[3] From the activist's perspective, transparency rules thus limit its ability to build a stake in a target secretly, at a time when its contemplated campaign is not yet public. At the same time, they may help the activist in its initial assessment of the issuer as a "good" target, by allowing it to identify possible supporters in that issuer's shareholder base.

---

[1] Although in less common cases, activists may pursue goals without having a material economic interest. See e.g., Bluebell's "One Share ESG Campaign" against Solvay or Engine no. 1's campaign against Exxon with 0.02% of the share capital. In such campaigns, transparency rules will be of little relevance as the activist is unlikely to reach or cross ownership reporting thresholds (unless they would be acting in concert with other shareholders – see *infra*, section 6).

[2] Such "private" dialogue is generally encouraged in order to pre-empt certain campaigns, as it may allow to alleviate the activist's concerns. This is why in France, the French financial regulator, the Autorité des Marchés Financiers ("AMF") specifically recommends that *"any public campaign be preceded by an attempted dialogue between the relevant investor and the issuer"* (AMF, « Guide de l'information permanente et de la gestion de l'information privilégiée », Position–recommendation DOC-2016-08, updated 29.04.2021 1, 32, https://www.amf-france.org/sites/default/files/private/2021-09/2016-08-avril-2021.pdf accessed 19.01.2023).

[3] A. Taleska, *Hedge Fund Activism in Europe: A Perspective from a Shareholder-Centric System of Corporate Governance*, Ghent, University of Ghent (Faculty of Law and Criminology), 2020, 35.

From the perspective of the issuer and other market participants, transparency disclosures are an important source of information on potential activist activity. The crossing of the lowest reporting threshold (or, more precisely, the statutory deadline for reporting such crossing – see *infra*, section 2.2.4) constitutes the latest point in time[4] by when the issuer and the public will be informed of the acquisition of a significant stake by a shareholder and which may, in particular if the investor has an activist reputation, augur the launch of an activist campaign.

2.1. THE TRANSPARENCY DIRECTIVE

In the EU, transparency rules were harmonised through Directive (EU) 2004/109/EC.[5] Equivalent rules exist in most jurisdictions outside of the EU too.[6]

Under the Transparency Directive, the Member States must ensure that investors reaching, exceeding or falling below the thresholds of 5%, 10%, 15%, 20%, 25%, 30%, 50% and 75% of an issuer's voting rights should notify the issuer thereof.[7] The issuer, in turn, must make the notification public.[8] The purpose of this rule is to inform the public of important changes in the voting structure of issuers, which should enable investors to acquire or dispose of shares in full knowledge of such changes.[9] It is also aimed at enhancing effective control of issuers and overall market transparency of important capital movements.[10]

Importantly, the Transparency Directive is a minimum harmonisation directive, meaning that it sets a threshold that Member States' laws must meet but may exceed. The use of the minimum harmonisation technique entails that significant differences exist among Member States' transparency rules. As further discussed below, notification thresholds vary across Member States and, even among Member States that opted for the thresholds set forth in the Transparency Directive, some Member States allow issuers to provide for additional thresholds

---

[4] It will be the latest point in time because, as discussed in section 3 below, the issuer may have identified the activist earlier, for instance on the basis of its right to identify shareholders. An activist may also voluntarily decide to "go public" even though it has not yet crossed a reporting threshold or does not intend to cross such threshold.

[5] Directive 2004/109/EC of the European Parliament and of the Council of 15 December 2004 on the harmonisation of transparency requirements in relation to information about issuers whose securities are admitted to trading on a regulated market and amending Directive 2001/34/EC, as consolidated 18.03.2021, 02004L0109. Hereinafter the "Transparency Directive".

[6] See e.g., in the U.S., Exchange Act Sections 13(d) and 13(g).

[7] Article 9(1) Transparency Directive.

[8] Article 12(6) Transparency Directive, which further also provides that the publication should occur no later than three trading days after receipt by the issuer of the notification.

[9] Recital (18) Transparency Directive.

[10] Ibid.

in their articles of association. Similarly, while the Transparency Directive prescribes the minimum content of a transparency notification, Member States may require investors crossing reporting thresholds to disclose additional information in their notifications, such as their intentions with respect to the newly acquired securities.

2.2. THE TRANSPARENCY LAW

In Belgium, the Transparency Directive was implemented through the Law of 2 May 2007 on the disclosure of major holdings in issuers whose shares are admitted to trading on a regulated market[11] and the Royal Decree of 14 February 2008 on the disclosure of major holdings.[12]

In accordance with the Transparency Directive, the provisions of the Transparency Law are primarily applicable to issuers whose shares are admitted to trading on an EU regulated market[13] and who have Belgium as their "home" member state.[14] This includes issuers who have their registered seat in Belgium and those who have their registered seat in a third country but chose Belgium as their home member state. In addition, most provisions were also made applicable to issuers whose shares are admitted to trading on the multilateral trading facility Euronext Growth (ex-Alternext).[15]

The basic principle of the Transparency Law is that any person who, directly or indirectly, acquires, transfers or holds voting securities (*stemrechtverlenende effecten*), financial instruments equivalent to voting securities (*met stemrechtverlenende effecten gelijkgestelde financiële instrumenten*) or voting

---

[11] Law of 2 May 2007 on the disclosure of major holdings in issuers whose shares are admitted to trading on a regulated market, as consolidated 09.07.2021, <www.ejustice.just.fgov.be/eli/wet/2007/05/02/2007003215/justel> accessed 19.01.2023. Hereinafter the "Transparency Law". Belgium had already adopted rules on the disclosure of major holdings before the adoption of the Transparency Law, which were reflected in the Law of 2 March 1989 on the disclosure of major holdings in listed companies and regulating takeover bids and the Royal Decree of 10 May 1989 on the disclosure of major holdings in listed companies. Those were abolished with the entry into force of the Transparency Law.

[12] Royal Decree of 14 February 2008 on the disclosure of major holdings, as consolidated 27.09.2016, <www.ejustice.just.fgov.be/eli/besluit/2008/02/14/2008003071/justel> accessed 19.01.2023. Hereinafter the "Transparency RD".

[13] Or on a regulated market of a non-EU EEA Member State (Norway, Iceland or Liechtenstein).

[14] Article 5 Transparency Law. The Transparency Law also contains certain provisions applicable to issuers who do not have Belgium as their home member state but whose shares are admitted to trading on Euronext Brussels, essentially requiring publication of transparency notifications in Belgium in French, Dutch or English. See articles 19 and following of the Transparency Law.

[15] See article 5 of the Royal Decree of 21 August 2008 determining the complementary rules applicable to certain multilateral trading facilities.

rights (*stemrechten*) of an issuer, which reach or cross (upwards or downwards) 5%, 10% or any subsequent multiple of 5% of the total voting rights, is required to submit a transparency notification to the issuer and the Belgian financial regulator, the Financial Services and Markets Authority (the FSMA). The information contained in such notification will subsequently be made public.

In the next sections, we will focus on the key features of the notification obligation relevant in the context of shareholder activism. For a description of this obligation outside of the activism context, we refer to the numerous contributions and articles published on the Belgian transparency rules[16], as well as the FSMA's practical guide, which further provides guidance on notifications in practice.[17]

2.2.1. Reporting thresholds

The appropriate threshold for the first disclosure of ownership in listed companies has gained renewed attention in the context of shareholder activism.[18] On the one hand, low disclosure thresholds are said to have the potential to discourage shareholder activism – because the value of the shares that activists would acquire before revealing themselves would be key to their profitability –[19], damage private shareholder dialogue – because issuers and activists would favour private dialogue and low disclosure thresholds would thus lead to premature disclosure –[20] and result in excessive administrative burdens

---

[16]   See e.g., E. Janssens, "De omzetting van de Transparantierichtlijn in de Belgische rechtsorde" (2008) *TFR,* 210, 221; K. Maresceau, "Verplichtingen voor houders van belangrijke deelnemingen" (2020) *Financieel recht: commentaar met overzicht van rechtspraak en rechtsleer,* 43; J. Malherbe, Y. De Cordt, P. Lambrecht, P. Malherbe and H. Culot, *Droit des sociétés,* 5th ed., Brussels, Larcier, 2020, 1075.

[17]   FSMA, "Practical instructions for making transparency notifications", published on 10.11.2011, <https://www.fsma.be/sites/default/files/legacy/sitecore/media%20library/Files/fsmafiles/circ/en/2011/fsma_2011_08.pdf>, which includes extracts in English from the FSMA, «Guide pratique FSMA_2011_08 du 10 novembre 2011 (mise à jour du 11 février 2020) – La réglementation en matière de transparence», <https://www.fsma.be/sites/default/files/legacy/sitecore/media%20library/Files/fsmafiles/circ/fr/2011/fsma_2011_08.pdf> accessed 19.01.2023.

[18]   In France, for instance, the AMF recently considered the need to lower the statutory reporting thresholds further to the publication of various reports highlighting the need for increased supervision of activists. See AMF, «Communication de l'AMF sur l'activisme actionnarial» (2020), <https://www.amf-france.org/sites/default/files/2020-04/communication-amf-sur-activisme-actionnarial_avril20_2.pdf> accessed 19.01.2023.

[19]   L.A. Bebchuk and R. Jackson, JR, "The Law and Economics of Blockholder Disclosure" (2012) *Harvard Business Law Review, 39,* 47–51; G. Calafi and D. Bernhardt, "Blockholder Disclosure Thresholds and Hedge Fund Activism" (2021) *Journal of Financial and Quantitative Analysis,* <https://ssrn.com/abstract=3807293> accessed 19.01.2023.

[20]   Club des juristes, "Shareholder activism" (2022) 1, 13, <https://www.leclubdesjuristes.com/wp-content/uploads/2022/12/Activisme-actionnarial-Le-Club-des-juristes-Dec-2022_EN.pdf> accessed 19.01.2023.

and hence costs for issuers. On the other hand, the ability for investors to secretly accumulate a stake may damage market transparency and investor confidence.[21]

Belgium – like other countries such as France – established 5% as the first mandatory reporting threshold (as provided for by the Transparency Directive). By contrast, certain other Member States – such as Italy, the Netherlands, and Germany – lowered the first legal threshold to 3%.[22]

This being said, the Transparency Law also allows issuers to adopt additional notification thresholds at 1%, 2%, 3%, 4% and 7.5% in their articles of association. If an issuer decides to introduce any (or all) of these additional thresholds in its articles of association, the applicable regime is identical to that of the mandatory statutory thresholds, including the obligation to make the notification public.[23] This is important as it effectively means that providing for a lower threshold in the articles of association cannot be used as a tool for issuers to increase transparency solely for their own benefit, i.e., without the relevant investor's stake becoming public.[24]

In practice, many Belgian issuers have adopted additional notification thresholds in their articles of association, often set at 3%.[25] Activists contemplating stake-building in a Belgian target should carefully consider whether, in addition to the legal thresholds, notification is required pursuant to the issuer's articles of association. Issuers, in turn, should consider whether providing for such lower thresholds in their articles of association is desirable in a context of increased activist activity, as it could lead to bringing the dialogue with the activist into the public sphere prematurely.

2.2.2. "Equivalent" financial instruments

Activists may seek to get financial exposure to a target in various ways. Acquiring voting securities in the target may seem the most natural investment strategy, but in practice activists will often use other financial instruments, such as

---

[21] See e.g., Recital (18) Transparency Directive; petition from Wachtell, Lipton, Rosen & Katz to the U.S. Securities and Exchange Commission ("SEC") (2011), <www.sec.gov/rules/petitions/2011/petn4-624.pdf> accessed 19.01.2023.

[22] For an overview of statutory thresholds across Member States, see ESMA, "Practical Guide – National rules on notifications of major holdings under the Transparency Directive" (2022), no. ESMA31-67-535, <https://www.esma.europa.eu/document/practical-guide-notifications-major-holdings-under-transparency-directive> accessed 19.01.2023.

[23] Article 18 Transparency Law.

[24] This is different from other jurisdictions, such as France, where notifications made pursuant to thresholds foreseen in the articles of association must only be communicated to the issuer. Club des juristes, "Shareholder activism", above n. 21, 1, 28.

[25] Pursuant to article 18 Transparency Law, issuers whose articles of association provide for an obligation to notify the crossing of certain thresholds, are obliged to inform the FSMA. The FSMA publishes a list of issuers whose articles of association provide for such an obligation, see <https://www.fsma.be/fr/thresholds> accessed 19.01.2023.

derivatives, to increase their economic exposure or stake-build. Such derivatives will generally also count towards the thresholds for ownership reporting.

Under the Transparency Law, the types of financial instruments which may give rise to a notification obligation are indeed broadly defined and include financial instruments deemed "equivalent" to voting securities (*met stemrechtverlenende effecten gelijkgestelde financiële instrumenten*). Such financial instruments are those that[26]:

(i) on maturity, give their holder, under a formal agreement, either the unconditional right to acquire, or the discretion as to his or her right to acquire, voting securities already issued;
(ii) are not included in point (i) but which are referenced to voting securities referred to therein and which have an economic effect similar to that of the financial instruments referred to therein, whether or not they confer a right to physical settlement.

This notion of "equivalent" financial instruments had originally not been included in the Transparency Directive (nor in the Transparency Law): the Transparency Directive only required notification of financial instruments that entitle their holder to acquire shares to which voting rights are attached (i.e., equity-settled derivatives).[27] It was introduced by Directive 2013/50/EU amending (among others) the Transparency Directive[28], because the requirement of a legal "entitlement" to the shares led to a loophole in those instances where derivatives did not confer a direct entitlement but only put the holder in a similar economic position (i.e., cash-settled derivatives).[29] Nevertheless, such derivatives

---

[26] Article 6, §6 Transparency Law.
[27] See article 13(1) of the original version of the Transparency Directive.
[28] Directive 2013/50/EU of the European Parliament and of the Council of 22 October 2013 amending Directive 2004/109/EC of the European Parliament and of the Council on the harmonisation of transparency requirements in relation to information about issuers whose securities are admitted to trading on a regulated market, Directive 2003/71/EC of the European Parliament and of the Council on the prospectus to be published when securities are offered to the public or admitted to trading and Commission Directive 2007/14/EC laying down detailed rules for the implementation of certain provisions of Directive 2004/109/EC, as consolidated 26.11.2013, 2013L0050.
[29] M. Lehmann and C. Kumpan (eds), *European Financial Services Law: Article-by-article Commentary*, Nomos, 2019, 1165–66. See also Recital (9) of Directive 2008/22/EC of the European Parliament and of the Council of 11 March 2008 amending Directive 2004/109/EC on the harmonisation of transparency requirements in relation to information about issuers whose securities are admitted to trading on a regulated market, as regards the implementing powers conferred on the Commission (2008) OJ L76/50: *"Financial innovation has led to the creation of new types of financial instruments that give investors economic exposure to companies, the disclosure of which has not been provided for in Directive 2004/109/EC. Those instruments could be used to secretly acquire stocks in companies, which could result in market abuse and give a false and misleading picture of economic ownership of publicly listed*

– in addition to increasing economic exposure – can also be used in order to influence or control an issuer and/or to build a stake in such issuer[30], as several high-profile cases – where disclosure requirements were circumvented using cash-settled equity instruments, such as Contracts for Difference (CfD) – had shown.[31, 32]

The Transparency Law includes a list of financial instruments considered "equivalent" financial instruments if they meet the conditions set forth in (i) or (ii) above. The list includes: (a) transferable securities; (b) options; (c) futures; (d) swaps; (e) forward rate agreements; (f) contracts for differences; and (g) any other contracts or agreements with similar economic effects which may be settled physically or in cash.[33]

In addition, the European Securities and Markets Authority (ESMA) published an indicative list of financial instruments that are subject to the notification requirements, provided they satisfy the conditions, which includes: (a) irrevocable convertible and exchangeable bonds referring to already issued shares; (b) financial instruments referenced to a basket of shares or an

---

companies. In order to ensure that issuers and investors have full knowledge of the structure of corporate ownership, the definition of financial instruments in that Directive should cover all instruments with similar economic effect to holding shares and entitlements to acquire shares".

[30] It is indeed not uncommon for cash-settled derivates to be ultimately settled in kind. To illustrate, in a cash-settled equity swap, the derivatives dealer has to pay, upon maturity, the positive difference in share price (if any) to the holder of the swap. To hedge its position, the dealer often holds a matching number of underlying shares. When the swap expires and the counterparty is required to pay the difference in share price, the counterparty will typically sell the underlying shares. And although the holder of the swap has no formal right to acquire the underlying shares, it is free to acquire, in a separate transaction, and partially using the cash received upon settlement of the swap as the case may be, the block of shares to which it previously only had economic exposure.

[31] See e.g., the *Hermès/LVMH* case, where LVMH announced in October 2010 that it had acquired a 17.1% stake in Hermès International, using cash-settled equity swaps, allowing LVMH to avoid any disclosure until then; the *Wendel/Saint-Gobain* case, where Wendel used cash-settled derivatives to acquire a stake in Saint-Gobain; the *Porsche/Volkswagen* case, where Porsche announced in October 2008 that it had built up a stake of 72% in Volkswagen, almost half of which had been acquired without triggering disclosure requirements, since, in addition to 42% of Volkswagen's shares, Porsche held about 30% of the share capital through cash-settled derivatives; and the *Schaeffler/Continental* case, where Schaeffler, which had a direct share interest of just under 3% in Continental AG, entered into cash-settled derivatives for around 28% of Continental's shares before announcing a takeover bid on Continental.

[32] Although on the other side of the Atlantic, cash-settled derivatives have until now not been counted toward the reporting thresholds of Section 13(d), in February 2022, the SEC proposed new rules considering holders of cash-settled derivatives to have beneficial ownership of the reference equity securities. See SEC, "Modernization of Beneficial Ownership Reporting" (2022) 1, 49 and onwards, <https://www.sec.gov/rules/proposed/2022/33-11030.pdf> accessed 19.01.2023.

[33] Article 6, §6 Transparency Law.

index; (c) warrants; (d) repurchase agreements; (e) rights to recall lent shares; (f) contractual buying pre-emption rights; (g) other conditional contracts or agreements than options and futures; (h) hybrid financial instruments; (i) combinations of financial instruments; and (j) shareholders' agreements having financial instruments as an underlying.[34]

Activists active in Belgium, and the EU more generally, must thus cope with this broad notion of "equivalent" financial instruments when considering whether ownership reporting thresholds may be met. As a result, "covert" stake-building through derivatives has become significantly more difficult.

From the issuer's perspective, it is important to carefully review transparency notifications. Where relevant, issuers should seek to understand the – potentially complex – dynamics underlying the financial instruments used by a (potential activist) investor and what it says about its stake in, and exposure to, the issuer. This may, in turn, have other implications, including from a corporate governance perspective.[35]

2.2.3. Persons acting in concert

Importantly, the voting rights of investors acting "in concert" are aggregated for the purposes of computing whether the reporting thresholds of the Transparency Law are met, even when such investors' voting rights individually do not reach such threshold.[36] This is particularly relevant for cases where multiple activist investors are congregating around a target – the phenomenon of the so-called "wolf pack".

As discussed in further detail in section 6, the definition of acting in concert is, however, not clear-cut and its application in an activism context raises many questions that remain unanswered to date.

---

[34]   ESMA, "Indicative list of financial instruments that are subject to notification requirements according to Article 13(1b) of the revised Transparency Directive" (2015), no. ESMA/2015/1598, <https://www.esma.europa.eu/document/indicative-list-financial-instruments> accessed 19.01.2023.

[35]   E.g., when assessing the issuer's obligations under the principle of equal treatment of its "shareholders" of article 6 of the Royal Decree of 14 November 2007 on the obligations of issuers of financial instruments admitted to trading on a regulated market and article 7:123 of the Belgian Code of Companies and Associations (CCA). Holders of derivatives which do not grant their holder actual voting rights are not shareholders and should thus not be assimilated with shareholders.

[36]   Article 6, §§4 and 5 Transparency Law.

2.2.4. Filing and publication deadlines

Next, filing deadlines for notifications are also relevant for shareholder activism, as they put an outside date on the time during which activists have the ability to secretly increase their stake even though they have reached the first reportable ownership threshold.

On the one hand, shorter filing deadlines are said to have a chilling effect on activism, because they reduce the scope for secret trading by activists and hence make it more costly for activists to accumulate a sizeable stake.[37] On the other hand, longer filing deadlines allow an information asymmetry between shareholders to remain in place for a longer period, which may affect market transparency and undermine investor confidence.[38]

The Transparency Law provides, in line with the Transparency Directive, that notification to the issuer and the FSMA must take place at the latest within four trading days following the event triggering the notification obligation.[39] This is broadly in line with most other Member States.[40]

Upon receipt of a notification, the issuer is required to publish the information contained in the notification by way of a press release on its website, within three trading days.[41] Such information must be communicated to the FSMA in parallel.

2.2.5. No mandatory disclosure of intent

The required content of a transparency notification is specified in the Transparency RD and broadly reflects that of the Transparency Directive. This includes, among others, the following information: (i) the identity of the investor and the chain of controlled undertakings through which voting rights are effectively held, if applicable; (ii) the event triggering the notification obligation; (iii) the date on which the threshold was reached or crossed; and (iv) the situation resulting from the notification trigger in terms of voting rights.[42] The FSMA has

---

[37] D. Katelouzou, "Worldwide Hedge Fund Activism and Legal Determinants" (2015), *U. of Pennsylvania Journal of Business Law*, 17, 789, 813.
[38] SEC, "Modernization of Beneficial Ownership Reporting", above n. 33.
[39] Article 12 Transparency Law. By way of exception, notifications required further to the adoption of a new threshold in the articles of association of an issuer may be filed up to ten trading days following the publication of the new threshold (article 18, §2 Transparency Law).
[40] For an overview of filing and publication deadlines across EU Member States, see ESMA, "Practical Guide – National rules on notifications of major holdings under the Transparency Directive", above n. 23. For comparison purposes, the notification deadline in the U.S. is currently ten calendar days, but the recent SEC proposal referred to above n. 33 provides for the acceleration of the filing deadline for Schedule 13D reports to five calendar days.
[41] Article 14 Transparency Law.
[42] Articles 13 through 19 Transparency RD.

developed a standardised and automated form to effect the notification, which is available on its website (Form TR-1 BE).

Crucial to note in this respect, however, is that the Transparency Law does not require the person making the notification to disclose its intentions, i.e., whether it holds its stake passively or whether it intends to pursue certain objectives. Although the Transparency Directive is silent on this issue, certain other Member States have imposed a declaration of intent through their national legislation.[43]

In practice, this means that Belgian issuers (and the public) may, at the time of a notification, not be able to determine whether an investor is stake-building with a view to initiating an activist campaign. Of course, should the notifying investor have an activist reputation, this may be a strong indicator of a potential upcoming campaign. Nevertheless, market transparency would benefit from the investor clarifying its intentions publicly in such case.

2.2.6. Enforcement and sanctions

Potential civil, administrative and criminal sanctions to which breaches of the Transparency Law are subject, should lead activists to proceed with caution when considering their obligations under the Transparency Law.

First, the Transparency Law provides for the temporary suspension of voting rights attached to financial instruments which are not notified by the relevant investor at least 20 days prior to the date of a general meeting.[44] In the event of non-compliance with the Transparency Law, the President of the Enterprise Court may decide to impose a suspension of all or part of the rights attached to the relevant financial instruments for up to one year.[45] The President of the

---

[43] See e.g., in France, article L233-7, VII of the French Commercial Code which provides that *"Lorsque les actions de la société sont admises aux négociations sur un marché réglementé, la personne tenue à l'information prévue au I est tenue de déclarer, à l'occasion des franchissements de seuil du dixième, des trois vingtièmes, du cinquième ou du quart du capital ou des droits de vote, les objectifs qu'elle a l'intention de poursuivre au cours des six mois à venir"*. Similarly, in the U.S., investors acquiring more than 5% of an issuer are required to file with the SEC if they have an interest in influencing the management of the company.

[44] Article 25/1 Transparency Law. Specifically, the voting rights that are suspended are those that exceed the lowest (legal or statutory) threshold the crossing of which the investor failed to notify, or did notify but only within the 20-day window prior to the relevant general meeting. The purpose of this provision is, among others, to avoid that the board of the issuer must cope with unexpected changes in the voting power among shareholders shortly before the general meeting, although the board could – in such case – also decide to postpone the general meeting by five weeks pursuant to article 7:131 CCA.

[45] Although the threat of a suspension of voting rights may, for activists, have limited deterrent effect (as most activists need not make use of their voting rights in order to pursue their campaign), the President of the Enterprise Court's power importantly extends to suspending

Enterprise Court may also suspend a general meeting that has already been convened or order the sale of the financial instruments by the relevant investor to a third party.[46]

Moreover, the Transparency Law grants the FSMA broad administrative powers to ensure compliance with the Transparency Law. These include the power to enjoin a person to make the necessary notifications pursuant to the Transparency Law (which may be coupled with a penalty payment)[47], to publish a warning of non-compliance[48] and to impose administrative sanctions.[49]

Finally, criminal sanctions also apply to certain specific breaches of the Transparency Law, including deliberate failure to make a transparency notification and refusal to comply with the FSMA's orders under the Transparency Law.[50]

3. THE RIGHT TO IDENTIFY SHAREHOLDERS

Transparency notifications are valuable sources of information for issuers and the public alike when it comes to identifying potential activist interventions. But issuers also have other tools available to them to identify movements in their shareholder base that may augur the launch of an activist campaign.

Since the entry into force of Directive (EU) 2017/828[51], EU-based issuers have a right to identify their shareholders, and issuers may make use of such right to detect "early signs" of activism. In the context of an activist campaign, issuers may also make use of such right to engage with other shareholders and rally support from "friendly" shareholders when facing attempts from the activist to exercise pressure on the company.

---

the right to dividends, which may be more deterrent from that perspective. See Law of 2 March 1989 on the disclosure of major holdings in listed companies and regulating takeover bids, parliamentary works Chamber 1988, no. 522/1–1988 1, 11–12.

46 Article 25/2 Transparency Law.
47 Article 23, §2, 4° and §5 Transparency Law.
48 Article 24, §2 Transparency Law.
49 Article 27 Transparency Law.
50 Article 26 Transparency Law.
51 Directive (EU) 2017/828 of the European Parliament and of the Council of 17 May 2017 amending Directive 2007/36/EC as regards the encouragement of long-term shareholder engagement (2017) OJ L132/1. Hereinafter "SRD II".

3.1. SRD II

At the roots of the recognition of a right for issuers to identify their shareholders lies the fact that shares of listed companies are often held through complex chains of intermediaries and this, in turn, renders the exercise of shareholder rights more difficult and may act as an obstacle to shareholder engagement.[52] SRD II was adopted against this background and amended Directive 2007/36/EC.[53] Among others, SRD II provides that Member States must ensure that companies have the right to identify their shareholders, although they may limit it to the identification of shareholders holding more than 0.5%.[54]

Like the Transparency Directive, SRD II is a minimum harmonisation directive and thus sets a threshold that the laws of the Member States must meet but may exceed. In addition, minimum requirements as regards the request to disclose shareholder information and the response to be transmitted are foreseen in Commission Implementing Regulation (EU) 2018/1212.[55]

3.2. SRD II LAW

In Belgium, SRD II was implemented through the Law of 28 April 2020 transposing SRD II.[56] It led, among others, to the introduction of a new title II/1 in the Transparency Law, which entitles companies that have their registered seat in Belgium and whose shares are admitted to trading on an EU regulated market[57] to identify their shareholders and collect certain data to foster their engagement processes.

Specifically, listed companies have the right to "look through" the chain of intermediaries, and identify their shareholders, by directing a request for

---

[52] Recital (4) SRD II.
[53] Directive 2007/36/EC of the European Parliament and of the Council of 11 July 2007 on the exercise of certain rights of shareholders in listed companies, as consolidated 12.08.2022, 02007L0036. Hereinafter "SRD I".
[54] Article 3a(1) SRD II.
[55] Commission Implementing Regulation (EU) 2018/1212 of 3 September 2018 laying down minimum requirements implementing the provisions of Directive 2007/36/EC of the European Parliament and of the Council as regards shareholder identification, the transmission of information and the facilitation of the exercise of shareholders rights (2018) OJ L223/1.
[56] Law of 28 April 2020 transposing the Shareholder Rights Directive II (2017/828) and correcting the Code of Companies and Associations, *Belgian Official Gazette*, 06.05.2020. Hereinafter the "SRD II Law".
[57] Or on a regulated market of a non-EU EEA Member State (Norway, Iceland or Liechtenstein).

identification to the relevant intermediaries.[58] Intermediaries include investment firms, credit institutions and central securities depositories, regardless of their country of incorporation, as long as they provide custodial services with respect to shares of listed companies incorporated in Belgium.[59]

In the next sections, we discuss the key features of this right to identify shareholders in the context of activism.

3.2.1. No minimum threshold

The SRD II Law does not limit the issuer's right to request the identification of shareholders to those holding more than 0.5% of the voting rights, as permitted by SRD II.[60] This is a difference with certain other EU countries – including Italy and the Netherlands – that did introduce such minimum threshold.[61]

The absence of a minimum threshold is an important feature of the Belgian regime as it effectively enables, at least theoretically, the issuer to get a complete overview of its shareholder base. In the context of activism, it implies that the issuer may be able to identify a potential activist intervention as soon as an investor with an activist reputation would own a single share in the company.

Based on our experience, in practice, shareholder identification surveys based on SRD II have become quite efficient, particularly as the intermediaries have become more used to receiving these requests. Regular shareholder base monitoring pursuant to the SRD II Law has as such become a key component for Belgian issuers to consider within the framework of their (activism) defence preparedness.

3.2.2. Limited to "shareholders"

While a great tool, the issuer's right to identify its shareholders also has its limits, given that it is, as the name suggests, limited to "shareholders". This is

---

[58] Articles 29/1 and 29/3 Transparency Law.
[59] Article 29/2 Transparency Law.
[60] The initial draft of the SRD II Law provided that companies could only request the identification of shareholders holding more than 0.5% of the voting rights. However, during the parliamentary debate, it was acknowledged that the introduction of such threshold could give rise to a number of practical issues. For instance, a shareholder may have multiple security accounts at different financial institutions and may hold the same company's shares in several capacities. To avoid these issues, the threshold was ultimately abandoned, and has not been included in the final version of the SRD II Law.
[61] For an overview of national thresholds for shareholder identification, see ESMA, "National thresholds for shareholder identification under the Revised Shareholder Rights Directive" (2021), <https://www.esma.europa.eu/sites/default/files/library/esma32–380–143_national_thresholds_for_shareholder_identification_under_the_revised_srd.pdf> accessed 19.01.2023.

an important difference with the transparency rules which, as discussed in section 2.2.2 above, extend the notification obligation to "equivalent financial instruments", such as equity-settled and cash-settled derivatives.

In practice, this limited scope implies that issuers cannot obtain information about persons – including activists – that would be building up a stake through derivative instruments. Such persons can thus remain under the radar as long as they do not cross the relevant thresholds under the Transparency Law.

3.2.3. Type of information

The information the issuer may obtain from the intermediary includes: (i) the shareholder's name and contact details; (ii) the number of shares held; and (iii) if so requested by the issuer, the classes of shares held and the acquisition date.

Another important difference with the transparency rules is that the information obtained by the issuer pursuant to its right to identify its shareholders must not be made public. This is not necessarily surprising, as also the purposes of both regimes are fundamentally different: while the rules on the disclosure of major holdings seek to inform the markets of important changes in the voting structure of issuers, the right to identify shareholders is aimed at facilitating the exercise of shareholder rights and shareholder engagement.[62] That lack of publication may have certain benefits in the context of activism. Most importantly, the use of the issuer's right to identify its shareholders will enable the issuer to have early discussions with the activist in private, before the activist would go public and before the market is alerted of the presence of the activist.

4. DISCLOSURE OF NET SHORT POSITIONS

Sections 2 and 3 assume that the activist would take a long position by purchasing voting securities or acquiring equivalent financial instruments of the target. While that is the case in most activist campaigns, in recent years, there have been a few notorious cases of "short selling activism", a practice whereby an activist takes a short position in a target and then seeks to drive down the target's share price by alleging that the company is overvalued.[63] Rules on the disclosure of net short positions are relevant in the context of such campaigns, as they allow the issuer and the public to identify the activist's short position and

---

[62] Also, the information received from the intermediaries will often include personal data, the disclosure of which would be incompatible with EU data protection laws and, more generally, the protection of privacy.
[63] One of the most well-known recent examples being Wirecard.

hence, where its economic interests lie and how these match up with its public statements.

In the EU, the rules regarding short selling were harmonized in 2012 through Regulation (EU) 236/2012.[64] As a "regulation", the Short Selling Regulation is applicable directly in all Member States.

Pursuant to the EU Short Selling Regulation, among others:

(i) net short positions exceeding or falling below 0.1%[65] of the issued share capital of a Belgian issuer whose shares are admitted to trading on a regulated market or MTF in the EU, and each 0.1% above that, must be notified to the FSMA[66]; and

(ii) net short positions exceeding or falling below 0.5% of the issued share capital of a Belgian issuer whose shares are admitted to trading on a regulated market or MTF in the EU, and each 0.1% above that, must be publicly disclosed by the investor.[67] These are also made publicly available on a designated section of the FSMA's website.[68]

The Short Selling Regulation thus provides for a two-tier model aimed at enhancing the transparency of net short positions: at the lower threshold (0.1%), notification of a position should be made privately to the FSMA in order to enable it to monitor and, where necessary, investigate short selling that could create systemic risks, be abusive or create disorderly markets; at the higher threshold (0.5% and each 0.1% above), positions should be publicly disclosed to the market in order to provide useful information to other market participants about significant individual short positions in shares.[69]

---

[64] Regulation (EU) no 236/2012 of the European Parliament and of the Council of 14 March 2012 on short selling and certain aspects of credit default swaps, as consolidated 31.01.2022, 02012R0236. Hereinafter the "Short Selling Regulation".

[65] Article 5 Short Selling Regulation. The first reporting threshold under the Short Selling Regulation had initially been set at 0.2%. It was temporarily lowered to 0.1% in the context of the COVID-19 crisis, in order to improve both ESMA's and national regulators' monitoring ability of such positions, determine whether more stringent actions could be appropriate and be able to react quickly. Since then, the Short Selling Regulation was amended to permanently lower the reporting threshold to 0.1%. See Commission Delegated Regulation (EU) 2022/27 of 27 September 2021 amending Regulation (EU) no 236/2012 of the European Parliament and of the Council as regards the adjustment of the relevant threshold for the notification of significant net short positions in shares (2022) OJ L6/9.

[66] The notification to the FSMA occurs via a designated short selling form, available on its website in English, Dutch and French, to be confirmed by mail or fax.

[67] Article 6 Short Selling Regulation.

[68] Accessible at: <https://www.fsma.be/sites/default/files/media/files/replacement_files/Disclosure%2520net%2520short%2520positions%2520-%2520FSMA.xlsx> accessed 19.01.2023.

[69] Recital (7) Short Selling Regulation.

In the context of short selling activism, this means that issuers and the public are informed of net short positions exceeding 0.5%, but not those between 0.1% and 0.5%. However, as the FSMA is informed of such net short positions, issuers faced with activism by a party with limited to no economic interests may consider enquiring with the regulator about possible short positions that such investors would have but that do not reach the 0.5% threshold. Net short positions below 0.1% can in any event remain under the radar.

Importantly, the notification and disclosure obligations only apply to *net* short positions, that is after deducting total long exposure from total short exposure. Total long and total short exposure are defined functionally (i.e., any transaction creating a long or short position effect) but must be related to issued share capital.[70]

The increased level of short selling activism in recent years has given rise to discussions as to whether the rules of the Short Selling Regulation are sufficient to ensure the transparency of net short positions. This has led to several proposals to amend the rules on the disclosure of net short positions.[71]

5. MAR

5.1. GENERAL FRAMEWORK

5.1.1. What is MAR?

The Market Abuse Regulation[72] sets out uniform rules applicable throughout the EU aimed at certain types of unlawful behaviour in financial markets, notably insider dealing, unlawful disclosure of inside information and market manipulation (market abuse), and provides for specific and prescriptive rules of

---

[70] Article 3 Short Selling Regulation.
[71] Among others, the French AMF has proposed supplementing the declaration of net short positions on shares with information on debt instruments, and specifically bonds and credit default swaps (see AMF, «Communication de l'AMF sur l'activisme actionnarial», above n. 19, 1, 7). Further, calls have been made to aggregate net short positions held by parties acting in concert, which is currently not the case (see e.g., Club des juristes, "Shareholder activism", above n. 21, 1, 33).
[72] Regulation (EU) no 596/2014 of the European Parliament and of the Council of 16 April 2014 on market abuse (market abuse regulation) and repealing Directive 2003/6/EC of the European Parliament and of the Council and Commission Directives 2003/124/EC, 2003/125/EC and 2004/72/EC, as consolidated 01.01.2021, 02014R0596. Hereinafter "MAR".

conduct for issuers incorporated in the EU, their management and other market participants (disclosure obligations).[73, 74]

As a "regulation", MAR is applicable directly in all Member States and, as such, forms the "Single European Rulebook"[75] for market abuse in the EU. Since national securities regulators are charged with the enforcement of MAR in their respective jurisdictions, their – not always consistent – interpretation of MAR shapes national administrative practice, although the scope for national implementing standards is limited.[76]

Separately, the EU legislator has enacted a criminal sanctions directive[77] requiring the Member States to set up a framework of criminal prosecution for "serious" forms of market abuse.

MAR[78] was designed to reinforce market integrity of the EU and ensure the smooth functioning of securities markets while bolstering public confidence in such markets. It was not designed with shareholder activism in mind. However, as explained throughout this section, MAR is always just around the corner when considering an activist approach from a securities law angle.

---

[73] On 7 December 2022, the European Commission put forward a number of proposals on clearing, corporate insolvency and company listing to make EU capital markets more attractive. One key component of these proposals is the so-called "Listing Act", that has as its primary objectives to (i) achieve a better access to public funding by listing on stock exchanges and (ii) alleviate the administrative burden when listed on public markets. The Listing Act will, among others, amend MAR. At the time this contribution was submitted, the Listing Act remained a proposal to be submitted to the European Parliament and the Council. Where relevant, we will note amendments proposed by the Listing Act in footnotes throughout this section. See also Cleary Gottlieb, "The EU Listing Act: Important Proposed Changes to MAR", <https://www.clearygottlieb.com/news-and-insights/publication-listing/the-eu-listing-act-important-proposed-changes-to-mar>, accessed 05.04.2023.

[74] For a detailed overview of MAR, its application, and consequences for Belgian issuers, see L. Legein, «Le nouveau règlement Abus de Marché et ses conséquences pour les sociétés cotées belges» (2016) 5 *Revue pratique des sociétés – Tijdschrift voor Rechtspersoon en Vennootschap*, 479. For an article-by-article commentary of MAR, see S. Kalls, M. Oppitz, U. Torggler and M. Winner (eds), *EU Market Abuse Regulation: A Commentary on Regulation (EU) No 596/2014*, Edward Elgar Publishing, Massachusetts (US) 2021.

[75] See also J.L. Hansen, "Market Abuse Case Law – Where Do We Stand With MAR?" (2017) *European Company and Financial Law Review*, 367, 367–370.

[76] The EU legislator has opted for a tri-level approach to legislating for MAR: (i) MAR itself, (ii) Commission Delegated Acts, Commission Implementing Acts and ESMA Technical Standards, and (iii) ESMA Guidance and ESMA Q&A.

[77] Directive 2014/57/EU of the European Parliament and of the Council of 16 April 2014 on criminal sanctions for market abuse (2014) OJ L173/179.

[78] Including its predecessors such as Directive 2003/6/EC of the European Parliament and of the Council of 28 January 2003 on insider dealing and market manipulation (market abuse).

5.1.2. Scope of application

MAR applies to[79]:

(a) *EU regulated markets*: financial instruments admitted to trading on a regulated market or for which a request for admission on a regulated market (as defined under MiFID[80]) has been made;
(b) *EU MTFs*: financial instruments traded on a multilateral trading facility (or "MTF", as defined under MiFID), admitted to trading on an MTF or for which a request for admission on an MTF has been made;
(c) *EU OTFs*: financial instruments traded on an organised trading facility (or "OTF", as defined under MiFID); and
(d) *Other financial instruments*: financial instruments of which the price or value depends or has an effect on the price or value of the financial instruments mentioned above (mainly OTC derivatives).

The concept of "financial instruments" is defined broadly as including any transferable securities (whether equity or debt), money-market instruments, units in collective investment undertakings, certain derivatives (including security, currency or interest rate derivatives whether settled physically or in cash, (optional) cash-settled commodity derivatives, etc.), and emission allowances.[81]

With respect to these financial instruments, MAR applies to behaviour (actions and omissions) irrespective of whether such behaviour takes place in the EU or elsewhere and irrespective of whether such behaviour takes place on or outside of a trading venue.[82, 83] Therefore, also investors and activists that are not based in the EU will need to take MAR into account when preparing and executing their investment strategy to financial instruments falling within MAR's scope of application.[84]

---

[79] Article 2 MAR.
[80] Directive 2014/65/EU of the European Parliament and of the Council of 15 May 2014 on markets in financial instruments and amending Directive 2002/92/EC and Directive 2011/61/EU, as consolidated 28.02.2022, 02014L0065. Hereinafter "MiFID".
[81] Article 3(1)(1) MAR, which refers to article 4(1)(15) of Directive 2014/65/EU of the European Parliament and of the Council of 15 May 2014 on markets in financial instruments and amending Directive 2002/92/EC and Directive 2011/61/EU.
[82] Article 2(3) MAR.
[83] The application of MAR also extends to the non-EU EEA Member States (Norway, Iceland and Liechtenstein).
[84] See L. Legein, « Le nouveau règlement Abus de Marché et ses conséquences pour les sociétés cotées belges », above n. 75, 479, 483–484.

5.1.3. The four main prohibitions and obligations under MAR

As mentioned above, MAR contains four main obligations and prohibitions[85]:

(i) *Insider dealing*: a prohibition to use "inside information" to trade in financial instruments[86];
(ii) *Disclosure obligations*: an obligation for issuers of financial instruments to immediately publicly disclose "inside information" which directly concerns such issuer when it arises, with the ability to defer disclosure if certain conditions are met;
(iii) *Unlawful disclosure*: an obligation to keep inside information confidential, unless disclosure is made in the normal course of an employment, a profession, or duties; and
(iv) *Market manipulation*: a prohibition to engage in market manipulation, which consists of manipulative or misleading market behaviour (e.g., entering into transactions or conducting behaviour likely to give misleading signals as to supply, demand or price of a financial instrument, or spreading false or misleading information as to supply, demand or price of a financial instrument).

The first three obligations and prohibitions are all based on the core concept of "inside information". Therefore, we will briefly outline the key elements of "inside information", before discussing the interplay between activism and each of the four main obligations and prohibitions as such.

5.2. THE CORE CONCEPT OF "INSIDE INFORMATION"

Under MAR, information is considered to be "inside information" when it concerns information (i) of a precise nature, (ii) which, if it were made public, would be likely to have a significant effect on the prices of the financial instruments or on the price of related derivative financial instruments, (iii) which has not been made public, and (iv) relates, directly or indirectly, to one or more issuers or to one or more financial instruments. These four criteria are cumulative, and information should not be considered inside information if one of them is not satisfied.[87] Each of these conditions is discussed in the following sections.[88]

---

[85] Articles 14 and 15 MAR.
[86] In addition, MAR contains a prohibition for persons discharging managerial responsibilities to deal in the issuer's shares during so-called "negative windows" aimed at preventing any (perception of) insider dealing (article 19(11) MAR).
[87] Article 7(1) MAR.
[88] See also L. Legein, « Le nouveau règlement Abus de Marché et ses conséquences pour les sociétés cotées belges », above n. 75, 479, 484–488.

Important to note upfront is that although the determination whether a certain piece of information qualifies as inside information must in practice be done by the relevant market participants (e.g., issuers or activists), as it dictates their obligations under MAR, such determination is not binding on courts or regulators when it comes to the enforcement of MAR. In other words, courts and regulators may challenge an issuer's assessment that certain information did not qualify as inside information (prior to a certain date, as the case may be) as they seek to enforce MAR. This makes it particularly important for market participants to substantiate and record their assessment as they consider whether certain information qualifies as inside information.

5.2.1. Precise

First, the information needs to be of a "precise nature" in order to qualify as inside information. Pursuant to article 7(2) MAR, information is considered to be of a precise nature *"if it indicates a set of circumstances which exists or which may reasonably be expected to come into existence, or an event which has occurred or which may reasonably be expected to occur, where it is specific enough to enable a conclusion to be drawn as to the possible effect of that set of circumstances or event on the prices of the financial instruments ..."* (emphasis added). This definition implies two sub-criteria, each of which has been further developed through the jurisprudence of the Court of Justice of the European Union (CJEU).

First, required is *"a set of circumstances which exists or which may reasonably be expected to come into existence, or an event which has occurred or which may reasonably be expected to occur"*, which is also known as the "reality" criterion. While it is typically not difficult to assess whether a set of circumstances or an event has occurred, the scale of "reasonable expectation" prior to its occurrence is much more wide-ranging and typically comes up in multi-stage processes.

Established case law from the CJEU considers that this "reasonable expectation" refers to a *"realistic prospect"* that the set of circumstances will come into existence, or that the event will occur, based on an overall assessment of the factors existing at the relevant time (*Geltl* case).[89] There should, accordingly, be a more than fanciful chance of the set of circumstances or the event coming into

---

[89] Case C-19/11, *Markus Geltl v. Daimler AG*, ECLI:EU:C:2012:397. In its Geltl judgment, the CJEU interpreted the terms *"may reasonably be expected"* as referring to *"future circumstances or events from which it appears, on the basis of an overall assessment of the factors existing at the relevant time, that there is a realistic prospect that they will come into existence or occur"* (emphasis added).

existence or occurring, but the likelihood does not have to be "more likely than not".[90, 91]

In relation to a protracted process that consists of various intermediate steps, careful attention should be paid to each step, and not only to the outcome of the process. Indeed, each intermediate step (in addition to the final outcome) may be deemed to be precise information and could accordingly qualify as "inside information".[92]

The second criterion is the "inference" criterion, i.e., whether the information is specific enough to draw a conclusion as to the possible effect on the price of financial instruments. In this respect, in its *Lafonta* judgment[93], the CJEU held that clarity as to the likely direction of the price (i.e., up or down) of the financial instruments concerned based on such information is not a prerequisite to the existence of such inference.[94] Put differently, this means that the criterion will be met once the information is specific enough to conclude that there will be a possible effect on the price of the financial instruments, regardless of whether such price effect will be positive or negative. The inference criterion

---

[90] Case C-19/11, *Markus Geltl v. Daimler AG*, ECLI:EU:C:2012:397: "*The question whether the required probability of occurrence of a set of circumstances or an event may vary depending on the magnitude of their effect on the prices of the financial instruments concerned must be answered in the negative*".

[91] To assess the likelihood of a set of circumstances or event occurring, several considerations need to be taken into account, including, e.g., (i) what the time horizon is for the set of circumstances or event to take place; (ii) what preparatory steps still need to take place and which hurdles still need to be overcome for the set of circumstances or event to take place; (iii) whether the occurrence of the set of circumstances or event requires any internal approval (e.g., board or shareholders' approval), and whether there is certainty that such approval will be obtained; (iv) in case the likelihood is based on a set of projections, whether these are final projections or interim projections which still need to be validated; (v) whether various scenarios, each with a possible different likelihood and financial consequences, are being considered; (vi) how up to date the information is; etc.

[92] In the framework of a transaction consisting of various stages, the decisive element to assess the "realistic prospect" will be the parties' intentions, and not the label assigned to the intermediate step (e.g., "preliminary" terms). In addition, information may become "precise" again in relation to the same transaction following the initial public announcement of such transaction.
Potential future changes: The Listing Act proposes to exempt the intermediate steps in a protracted process from the immediate disclosure requirement of article 17(1) MAR: immediate disclosure would no longer be required for intermediate steps in a protracted process where those steps are connected with bringing about a set of circumstances or an event. Thus, even when the intermediate steps would be deemed to be "precise information" and would therefore qualify as inside information under article 7(3) MAR, the issuer would not be required to disclose this information before the "end result" (i.e., the event that the protracted process intends to bring about) materialises.

[93] Case C-628/13, *Jean-Bernard Lafonta v. Autorité des Marchés Financiers*, ECLI:EU:C:2015:162.

[94] "... *it need not be possible* to infer from that information, with a sufficient degree of probability, that, once it is made public, its potential *effect on the prices* of the financial instruments concerned *will be in a particular direction*" (emphasis added).

is, accordingly, a low bar and basically only excludes vague information or rumours.

In an activist situation, the eventual result of an activist campaign is not known up front.[95] However, the mere fact that an activist (intends to) acquire shares in a target or launch a public campaign may in itself satisfy the preciseness-requirement. Indeed, by now, the markets are familiar with activists' tactics and research has shown that investors often start acquiring shares in the target when an activist campaign is made public or when there are clear indications that such campaign is forthcoming.[96] This may suggest that even at early stages, an activist campaign or approach could satisfy the preciseness criteria.

5.2.2. Price sensitive

Second, article 7(4) MAR outlines that information is deemed of a price sensitive nature when *"if it were made public, [such information] would be likely to have a significant effect on the prices of financial instruments, [which] ... shall mean information a reasonable investor would be likely to use as part of the basis of his or her investment decisions"* (emphasis added).

The criterion of price sensitivity thus essentially is a "reasonable investor" test, i.e., is it information a reasonable investor would use as part of its investment decisions. As reasonable investors base their decisions on information that is already available to them, the test should be applied in light of the *ex ante* (as opposed to *ex post*) available information, meaning the information available at the time of the investment decision.[97] In the absence of an EU-wide definition of a "reasonable investor", it is, however, unclear how speculative information should be treated in this respect.

What is clear, is that there is a link with the inference criterion of the "precise" limb of the definition of inside information. The "price sensitivity" limb effectively operates as a *de minimis* filter by excluding information that would have no or minimal impact on price.[98]

---

[95] As it depends on whether the activist makes any formal demands, the nature of the demands, the issuer's reaction to such demands, the traction the campaign gets with other shareholders, etc.

[96] See A. Taleska, *Hedge Fund Activism in Europe: A Perspective from a Shareholder-Centric System of Corporate Governance*, above n. 4, 83–84.

[97] In practice, *ex post* information such as actual price movements can be used to check the presumption that the *ex ante* information was price sensitive, but not to take action against persons who drew reasonable conclusions from *ex ante* information available to them (*cf.* Recital (15) MAR).

[98] In the U.K., the Upper Tribunal has held that a price effect needs to be more than "trivial" (case of *Ian Hannam v. FCA*, 27.05.2014). As to the fact that a "significant effect" needs to be "likely", according to (still applicable) guidance given by ESMA's predecessor, the Committee

As to the price sensitive nature of the information in an activist setting, certain empirical evidence seems to suggest that an acquisition of securities in a target by an activist can be associated with an abnormal return around the date of public disclosure.[99] While a general conclusion may not necessarily be the right indicator for any particular situation (as e.g., the reputation and prior track record of the activist also play a role), depending on the circumstances, an (intended) approach of the target may be price sensitive.[100]

5.2.3. Not public

Third, the information must be non-public. The non-public nature of information needs to be assessed based on the past communications of the issuer as well as any other publicly available information.

While MAR prescribed certain technical standards for public disclosure of inside information to be deemed appropriate[101], this is not the only way through which information can be disclosed to be considered "public". However, there is no specific guidance in Belgium or at EU level as to when information is considered public.

The U.K.'s Financial Conduct Authority (FCA) has issued some (national level) guidance in this respect. The FCA lists four factors that are indicative of the fact that information has been made public and therefore does not constitute inside information. First, information that has been disclosed to regulated markets using a designated information service for disseminating regulated information (i.e., similar to the requirements of Commission Implementing Regulation (EU) 2016/1055). Second, information contained in records that are

---

of European Securities Regulators, "likely" on the one hand means that the fact that a piece of information has the mere possibility to have a significant price effect is not enough but, on the other hand, it is not necessary that there should be a degree of probability close to certainty. A plain English reading of "likely" indicates that the likelihood of the price effect should be "probable".

[99] See e.g., E. Verstraete and F. Verhelst, " 'Announcementeffect' van aandeelhoudersactivisme door hedge funds in Europese genoteerde ondernemingen" (2022) *Revue bancaire et financière / Bank- en Financiewezen*, 3, 173; N. Boyson and R. Mooradian, "Corporate Governance and Hedge Fund Activism" (2010) *Review of Derivatives Research*, 14(2), 169, 179–84; M. Becht, J. Franks, C. Mayer and S. Rossi, "Returns to Shareholder Activism: Evidence from a Clinical study of the Hermes UK Focus Fund" (2009) *Review of Financial Studies* 22(8), 3093, 3095–97; A. Brav, W. Jiang, F. Partnoy and R. Thomas, "Hedge Fund Activism, Corporate Governance, and Firm Performance" (2008), *The Journal of Finance*, 63(4), 1729, 1729–775.

[100] A. Taleska, *Hedge Fund Activism in Europe: A Perspective from a Shareholder-Centric System of Corporate Governance*, above n. 4, 85.

[101] Commission Implementing Regulation (EU) 2016/1055 of 29 June 2016, laying down implementing technical standards with regard to the technical means for appropriate public disclosure of inside information and for delaying the public disclosure of inside information in accordance with Regulation (EU) no 596/2014 of the European Parliament and of the Council (2016) OJ L173/47.

open to inspection by the public. Third, information that is otherwise generally available, including through the internet, or some other publication (including if it is only available upon payment of a fee), or is derived from information which has been made public. Fourth, information that can be obtained by observation by members of the public, without infringing rights or obligations of privacy, property, or confidentiality.[102] The FCA further also notes that it is not relevant whether the information is only generally available outside the U.K., or whether the analysis is only achievable by a person with above average financial resources, expertise, or competence.[103]

Especially in the context of private meetings between activists and management of the issuer, e.g., in regular investor meetings or as part of a roadshow, this is something activists should be mindful of. Although issuers in principle cannot engage in selective disclosure of inside information (see *infra*, section 5.3.3), it could happen that information is disclosed during private meetings that, although none of the information in itself qualifies as inside information, together with the deductions a sophisticated investor may still be able to make from such information when combined with the research it has been doing, nevertheless constitutes inside information.[104]

5.2.4. Relating to an issuer or financial instruments

The last condition, whether the information relates to an issuer or financial instruments, is typically rather straightforward to assess. Only in exceptional circumstances, such as listings of various financial instruments in a cascade of entities, the determination may be more challenging.

The relationship with financial instruments or their issuers is to be construed broadly, and an indirect relationship suffices. Information that "directly" relates to an issuer or its securities covers all types of information that specifically relate to such issuer's business. This includes e.g., operating performance, forecasts, investment policy, strategic choices, dividend policy, corporate governance and management, M&A transactions, etc. Information that "indirectly" relates to an issuer or its securities covers all types of

---

[102] FCA, "FCA Handbook – MAR 1.2.12", <https://www.handbook.fca.org.uk/handbook/MAR/1/2.html> accessed 19.01.2023. The FCA gives the following example: if a passenger on a train passing a burning factory calls his broker and tells him to sell shares in the factory's owner, the passenger will be using information which has been made public, since it is information which has been obtained by legitimate means through observation of a public event (*cf.* FCA, "FCA Handbook – MAR 1.2.14").
[103] FCA, "FCA Handbook – MAR 1.2.13", <https://www.handbook.fca.org.uk/handbook/MAR/1/2.html> accessed 19.01.2023.
[104] See e.g., B.J. Bushee, M.J. Jung and G.S. Miller, "Do Investors Benefit from Selective Access to Management" (2017), *Journal of Financial Reporting*, 2(1) 31, 35.

information that do not specifically relate to such issuer's business yet may still be relevant to assess the performance thereof, such as macro-economic, regulatory, or political developments.[105]

5.3. INTERPLAY BETWEEN MAR AND SHAREHOLDER ACTIVISM FROM THE ISSUER'S PERSPECTIVE

5.3.1. Disclosure obligations

If an issuer is in possession of "inside information" which directly concerns such issuer, as a rule, the issuer must immediately publicly disclose such inside information.[106] Only if certain conditions are met, the issuer may decide to temporarily defer disclosure, i.e., if (i) the issuer has legitimate interests that are likely to be prejudiced by immediate public disclosure, (ii) the deferral of disclosure is not likely to mislead the public, and (iii) the issuer is able to ensure confidentiality.[107] In addition, the issuer needs to notify the FMSA (or other national securities regulator) if and when the information is ultimately made public with a written explanation of how the conditions allowing deferral were met (or, in certain jurisdictions, to keep such information on file and provide it to the regulator upon request).[108] Issuers thus need to follow a formal process to adopt and

---

[105] Under MAR, there are different consequences depending on whether the information "directly" or "indirectly" relates to an issuer. While both types can give rise to the qualification as inside information, an issuer is under no obligation to disclose publicly the inside information that indirectly relates to it. Such information will, however, trigger the insider dealing and unlawful disclosure prohibitions.

[106] Article 17(1) MAR.

[107] Article 17(4) MAR.
Potential future changes: The Listing Act proposes to amend the requirements for delayed disclosure under article 17(4) MAR, essentially preventing issuers to delay disclosure of inside information if (a) there are erroneous expectations on the market as to the issuer's situation and prospects, and (b) those expectations are based on previous disclosures by the issuer. To this end, the current requirement that "*the delay of disclosure is not likely to mislead the public*" (article 17(4)(b) MAR) will be replaced by the following requirements: (i) the relevant information is not materially different from previous public announcements by the issuer on the matter; (ii) it does not contradict previously announced financial objectives of the issuer; and (iii) it generally does not contrast with the market's expectations, where such expectations are based on signals previously sent to the market by the issuer. As these requirements are already contained in the ESMA Guidelines on delayed disclosure of inside information, this is not expected to have a significant impact in practice (*cf.* ESMA, "MAR Guidelines – Delay in the disclosure of inside information" (20.10.2016), no. ESMA/2016/1478 EN, <https://www.esma.europa.eu/sites/default/files/library/2016-1478_mar_guidelines_-_legitimate_interests.pdf>. accessed 19.01.2023). However, if adopted, it will be good practice for any 17(4) MAR decision to explicitly justify compliance with these requirements.

[108] *Potential future changes*: Under the proposal in the Listing Act, the issuer should already inform the FMSA of its intention to delay immediately after the decision to delay disclosure is taken, instead of immediately after the information is disclosed to the public.

record each deferral decision. When disclosure of inside information is deferred by the issuer, the issuer must in principle refrain from "selective" disclosure (see *infra*, section 5.3.3 on the general prohibition of unlawful disclosure).

If disclosure has been deferred, MAR nonetheless obliges issuers to disclose the information as soon as possible if confidentiality has been compromised. Issuers will therefore want to have an "emergency" press release ready in situations where disclosure is deferred. Such mandatory disclosure obligation also arises in case of rumours (including from external sources), if these are sufficiently accurate to indicate that confidentiality has been breached.

In light of the above, the question arises to what extent an activist approach could qualify as inside information and therefore trigger a disclosure obligation for the issuer or, alternatively, require the issuer to defer the disclosure of such information. This question will always require an *in concreto* assessment of the prevailing facts. Nevertheless, a few general observations can be made based on the key characteristics of an activist campaign:

(i) As indicated above (see *supra*, section 2), a typical activist campaign starts with stake-building by the activist and a subsequent private approach of the issuer during which the activist shares its griefs. Other than if the stake built by the activist would trigger an obligation to file a transparency notification, the stake-building and private engagement with the activist would not be known to the public. In this context, the issuer will need to assess whether the stake-building and/or approach by the activist is such that it could qualify as inside information. The assessment will need to take into account, among other factors, the size of the stake built by the activist, the level of preciseness and materiality of the plans and/or demands of the activist, and the reputation and history of past campaigns of the activist.

(ii) In other cases, the activist may not preview its campaign with the issuer but decide to go immediately for a public offence. Similarly, if the activist at some point feels that it has exhausted its possibility to exert pressure on the issuer in private, it could make its investment thesis known to the public. At this point in time, there will typically not (or no longer) be any inside information: the activist will have taken care itself of the public dissemination of its criticism, demands and objectives.

(iii) Last, the issuer needs to be mindful of the fact that also a potential reaction contemplated by the issuer's board of directors or management could in itself, under certain circumstances, constitute inside information. Examples are negotiations with an activist regarding board representation or with respect to a fundamental change in the issuer's strategy (whether operational or financial, such as the dividend policy) which may – depending on the degree of likelihood that the issuer and the activist come to terms and the price sensitivity of the information in particular – constitute inside information. If these negotiations are private, there will, however, most likely be legitimate reasons to delay disclosure pursuant to article 17(4) MAR.

5.3.2. Insider dealing

The prohibition on insider dealing is a prohibition for a person in possession of inside information to, directly or indirectly, use that information to acquire or dispose of a financial instrument to which that information relates (or cancel or amend an earlier order). The prohibition applies irrespective of whether such transaction is done for such person's own account or for the account of third parties. While insider dealing requires the "use" of the inside information in the relevant transaction, a (rebuttable) presumption of use applies in case the person is in possession of inside information.[109] Also the use of a recommendation of, or inducement by, another person to act on the basis of inside information (i.e., upon a "tip" by such person) is covered by the prohibition where the person using the recommendation or inducement knows or ought to know that it is based upon inside information.[110]

The insider dealing prohibition applies to members of the corporate bodies of the issuer, but also to shareholders, employees and external advisors of the issuer who possess inside information. Outside of the issuer, the prohibition also applies to persons involved in criminal activities who possess inside information, and anyone else who possesses inside information if such person knows or ought to know that the information constitutes inside information. In other words, it is universally applicable, also to non-EU investors. The EU definition of the term "insider" is centered on the information that the person possesses, and not on how that person has come to possess such information (e.g., through breach of a duty) as is the case for instance in the U.S.[111]

---

[109] Recital (24) MAR.
[110] Article 8 MAR.
[111] In the U.S., the federal prohibition of insider trading under SEC Rule 10b-5 is based on the "misappropriation theory", which provides that a person commits insider trading (or rather, securities fraud in violation of Section 10b and Rule 10b-5), when he or she purchases or sells a security, "*on the basis of material nonpublic information about that security or issuer, in breach of a duty of trust or confidence owed (directly or indirectly) to the source of the information (the issuer or the tipster)*" (Rule 10b5-1). Under this theory, a fiduciary's undisclosed, self-serving use of a principal's information to purchase or sell securities, in breach of a duty of trust or confidence, defrauds the principal of the exclusive use of the information. On the other hand, a person can trade on the information without disclosing it to the market if such person does not owe a fiduciary duty to the issuer or tipster.
This approach differs sharply from the approach taken by the EU legislator, who – inspired by the principle of equality of information for all market participants – imposed a prohibition of insider trading that encompasses a general duty of abstention from use and communication imposed on any person in possession of inside information, with the aim of guaranteeing the integrity of financial markets (irrespective of whether such person owes any duty of trust or confidence to the source of the information).

MAR contains a list of presumed "legitimate behaviours", but as these are of limited relevance to the issuer itself, these will be examined in further detail when discussing the activist's perspective below (see *infra*, section 5.4.2).

In an activist context, for issuers as well as their directors, managers and employees, the insider dealing prohibition will therefore come to the forefront whenever the issuer is in possession of inside information and decides to delay disclosure thereof. In these instances, the decision to delay disclosure of inside information will trigger a corollary set of measures at the issuer's level aimed at preventing insider dealing. MAR itself mandates the drawing up of insider lists[112] and the insider dealing codes of most issuers require that a "prohibited period" be announced during which directors, managers and employees who find themselves on such insider list are prohibited from trading in financial instruments of the issuer.[113] As indicated above (see *supra*, section 5.3.1), examples of periods during which trading will be restricted could be when there are ongoing private settlement negotiations with an activist that entail significant changes to the governance set-up or strategy of the issuer, where those negotiations qualify as inside information.

5.3.3. Unlawful disclosure

The prohibition of unlawful disclosure is broad and covers any dissemination of inside information to any person. The personal scope of application is identical to that of the prohibition on insider dealing. The prohibition includes a prohibition on "tipping" (recommending or inducing another person to engage in insider dealing), as well as a prohibition of "selective" disclosure of inside information.

Accordingly, in principle, there can be no "private" communication of inside information by the issuer or its agents to any other party. Disclosure of inside information is nevertheless allowed if such disclosure is made "*in the normal exercise of an employment, a profession or duties*"[114], and provided that the recipient of such information is bound by a legal or contractual confidentiality obligation.[115] Thus, at analyst meetings, road shows, etc. issuers should exercise care not to disclose any inside information.[116]

---

[112] Article 18 MAR.
[113] Typically, as a precautionary measure, persons discharging managerial responsibilities, regardless of whether or not they have actual access to the relevant inside information, will also be covered by the trading prohibition included in the dealing code.
[114] Article 10 MAR.
[115] This follows from article 17(8) MAR. Absent a confidentiality obligation, selective disclosure of inside information by the issuer or its agents requires the issuer to make the information public simultaneously if the information was intentionally disclosed, and promptly in the case of a non-intentional disclosure.
[116] See also AMF, «Activisme actionnarial: l'AMF fait évoluer sa doctrine» (2021), < https://www.amf-france.org/fr/actualites-publications/actualites/activisme-actionnarial-lamf-fait-

One could wonder whether an issuer could strategically pre-empt an activist from taking certain actions such as stake-building, by disclosing inside information in the private dialogue or negotiations with the activist. As a result, the activist would find itself in a position where it is faced with potential legal risks as to its pre-existing trading strategy in light of the insider dealing prohibition. This strategy is also known as "insider tainting".[117] While theoretically interesting, the strategy of insider tainting will face certain practical and legal hurdles. First and foremost because at the outset of the private phase of a dialogue between an activist and an issuer, the parties will often put in place a confidentiality or non-disclosure agreement (NDA). These NDAs generally either foresee that no inside information will be disclosed[118] or that trading in the issuer's securities will be prohibited for a certain period, by way of a standstill undertaking. Even if no NDA with such restrictions would have been entered into, issuers will need to exercise great caution as they consider disclosing inside information for strategic purposes. Not only is it questionable whether such disclosure would still qualify as a disclosure "*in the normal exercise of an employment, a profession or duties*"[119], but selective disclosure of inside information without adequate protection of the confidentiality thereof would also breach the prohibition of unlawful disclosure of MAR.

5.4. INTERPLAY BETWEEN MAR AND SHAREHOLDER ACTIVISM FROM THE ACTIVIST'S PERSPECTIVE

5.4.1. *Disclosure obligations*

Investors are not subject to a disclosure obligation that is equivalent or comparable to that of an issuer when in possession of inside information. Hence, an activist has no duty to immediately publicly disclose any inside information

---

evoluer-sa-doctrine> accessed 19.01.2023, in which the AMF states, with respect to shareholder dialogue, that «*Ce dialogue ne peut, en tout état de cause, pas porter sur des informations privilégiées*».

[117] See e.g., A. Verstein, "Insider Tainting: Strategic Tipping of Material Nonpublic Information" (2018) *Northwestern University Law Review*, 112, 725.

[118] Generally combined with an obligation for the disclosing party to purge any inside information that would have been accidentally disclosed as part of the private dialogue by way of a public disclosure.

[119] Which the CJEU stressed, under the old EU Directive 89/592/EC that provided for a similar exception, should be interpreted narrowly and requires a "close link" to the duties of the disclosing party, "strict necessity" for the exercise of the employment, profession or duties and compliance with the principle of proportionality (*cf.* Case C-384/02, *Grøngaard and Bang*, ECLI:EU:C:2005:708). There is some debate today as to whether "strict necessity" is still required under MAR (see e.g., S. Kalss *et al*, "EU Market Abuse Regulation: A commentary on Regulation (EU) No 596/214" (2021) 143).

that may come in its possession.[120] As regards any campaign that the activist would pursue and that could constitute inside information, this would otherwise largely defeat the purpose: an activist would typically prefer to first contact the issuer in private and only when it does not manage to get (sufficient) traction with the issuer, launch its public campaign. In addition, the activist may first wish to rally support from other shareholders in private to assemble a "wolf pack" (see *infra*, section 6).

This being said, "*in order to foster loyal and fair debate between issuers and activist investors*", the French AMF has issued some recommendations on activists' communications. Among others, the AMF recommends each investor who initiates a public campaign to, without delay, disclose to the issuer all plans and proposals that it would address to other shareholders, together with the corresponding arguments (as set forth in a "white paper" type of document, where relevant). In addition, in the event of a public campaign, the AMF also considers it best practice for the investor to make these plans and proposals public, to ensure that the market and shareholders are informed adequately and equally.[121]

While in possession of inside information, the prohibitions on insider dealing and unlawful public disclosure in any event remain relevant for activist investors. Therefore, it is important for the activist to consider whether its activist investment strategy (including the intention to publish an activist letter or white paper or to engage in discussions with an issuer) constitutes inside information relating to the issuer. The assessment will need to be performed based on the four criteria outlined earlier (see *supra*, section 5.2).

5.4.2. Insider dealing

While in possession of inside information, the prohibition on insider dealing applies in full to activists.

As mentioned above (see *supra*, section 5.3.2), with respect to insider dealing, MAR contains a list of presumed "legitimate behaviours" in article 9, although engaging in any such behaviour for illegitimate purposes may still be considered insider

---

[120] However, activists may be subject to disclosure obligations stemming from other regulations that may be relevant to their activities and impact their campaigns. For instance, activist hedge funds that qualify as "institutional investors" or "asset managers" may, among others, be required to draw up an "engagement policy", describing how they integrate shareholder engagement in their investment strategy, in accordance with article 3(g) SRD II (as implemented in Belgium through articles 7:146/1 and 7:146/2 CCA). In this respect, see e.g., L. Van Marcke, "Shareholder engagement (SRD II): zin en onzin", *TRV-RPS* (2021) 829.

[121] AMF, « Activisme actionnarial: l'AMF fait évoluer sa doctrine », above n. 117.

dealing.[122] From that list, there are two key exceptions relevant in an activist context. First, the use of inside information obtained in the conduct of a public takeover or merger and used solely for the purposes of proceeding with that merger or public takeover can be legitimate, but such exception does not apply to stake-building.[123] Second, the mere fact that a person uses its own knowledge that it has decided to acquire or dispose of financial instruments in the acquisition or disposal of those financial instruments is not necessarily, in itself, insider dealing.[124]

Thus, it is important for an activist to determine whether its knowledge of its activist strategy (be it its contemplated actions such as stake-building or assembling of a wolfpack or any non-public information it may have obtained while conducting research on the issuer) would constitute inside information preventing the self-insider activist from building a stake in the target, or whether it would constitute permitted trading based merely on its own knowledge that it has decided to acquire or dispose of financial instruments. The distinction between both will often be difficult to make.

There are two recitals in MAR which shed some further light on the question. Recital 31 states, among others, that *"[s]ince the acquisition or disposal of financial instruments necessarily involves a prior decision to acquire or dispose taken by the person who undertakes one or other of those operations, the mere fact of making such an acquisition or disposal should not be deemed to constitute use of inside information. Acting on the basis of one's own plans and strategies for trading should not be considered as using inside information."* In line with article 9(5) MAR, this recital sets forth an exception for the use of one's "own knowledge". An activist investor will be able to develop a proprietary investment strategy, and can execute such strategy, without the need to publicly disclose it, provided that two conditions are met: (i) the transaction is not executed for an illegitimate purpose and (ii) no inside information is used in developing the investment strategy. However, the question as to whether the expected publication of the activist's campaign in itself constitutes inside information,

---

[122] Article 9(6) MAR.
[123] Article 9(4) MAR.
[124] Article 9(5) MAR. This, however, remains an exception only and not an exemption. On the basis of article 9(6) MAR, it may still be found that there was illegal use of such self-inside information. As a result, certain authors limit the exception of article 9(5) MAR to transactions that form part of one and the same decision. Different transactions, even if they all reflect the insider's own knowledge, may be executed in such a sequence that the insider nevertheless illegally takes advantage of his or her own knowledge to the detriment of third parties (see J.L. Hansen, "Article 9: Legitimate behaviour" in M. Ventoruzzo and S. Mock (eds.), *Market Abuse Regulation: Commentary and Annotated Guide (Second Edition)*, Oxford, Oxford University Press, 2022, (332) 350–351).

and therefore prohibits the activist to trade, remains unanswered by this recital.[125]

The second relevant recital is recital 28 which provides, among others, that *"[r]esearch and estimates based on publicly available data, should not per se be regarded as inside information and the mere fact that a transaction is carried out on the basis of research or estimates should not therefore be deemed to constitute use of inside information."* This recital thus formulates an exception for "own research" and recognises the socially desirable function of market professionals such as analysts and portfolio managers (whether activist investors or not). Their analysis requires resources, which they would not be willing to spend if they did not have any incentive – read: a chance of financial gain – to do so. Research and recommendations from analysts will not amount to inside information if they are merely based on information that is already public[126] and trading on that basis will therefore not constitute prohibited insider dealing. If, on the contrary, the analysis or recommendations are based on non-public information, they may qualify as inside information and lead to a prohibition to trade.[127] Nevertheless, this often remains a thin line in practice.

Furthermore, it is important to note that recital 28 also contains an express reservation for information of which *"publication or distribution … is routinely expected by the market and … contributes to the price-formation process of financial instruments, or the information provides views from a recognised market commentator or institution which may inform the prices of related financial instruments …"*. For such information, market actors need to *"consider the extent to which the information is non-public and the possible effect on financial instruments traded in advance of its publication or distribution, to establish whether they would be trading on the basis of inside information"*.

It was on the basis of that reservation that the French *Conseil d'Etat* in 2019 recognised the privileged nature of certain analysts' recommendations. In its judgment, the *Conseil d'Etat* convicted an employee of a recognised financial analyst firm who had traded securities prior to publicly distributing the recommendations.[128] Again, it remains an open question to what extent this

---

[125] A. Pietrancosta, "Brief remarks on the necessary clarification of market abuse prohibitions in times of shareholder activism" (2019) *Revue trimestrielle de droit financier – Corporate Finance and Capital Markets Law Review*, 3, 1, 16, <https://papers.ssrn.com/sol3/papers.cfm?abstract_id=3476301> accessed 19.01.2023.
[126] See *supra*, section 5.2.3 on when information can be considered public.
[127] See also A. Taleska, *Hedge Fund Activism in Europe: A Perspective from a Shareholder-Centric System of Corporate Governance*, above n. 4, 73–75.
[128] French *Conseil d'Etat* 30.01.2019, n° 412789, ECLI:FR:CECHR:2019:412789.20190130.

reservation should also be applied to the situation in which a (reputable) activist shareholder merely discloses its own intended campaign.[129]

Based on the above, an activist acquiring a toehold in an issuer through one or a series of transactions on the basis of its own knowledge of its, singular, investment/activist strategy, which is based solely on publicly available information, is unlikely to find itself in an insider dealing situation, particularly where the market is not expecting or anticipating such activist intervention. Outside of these strict boundaries, however, the water becomes much murkier.

5.4.3. Unlawful disclosure

Activists in possession of inside information are also subject to the prohibition of unlawful disclosure which, as discussed above (see *supra*, section 5.3.3), includes a prohibition on "tipping" as well as a prohibition of "selective" disclosure.

As explained in section 6 below, there are several reasons why activists often choose to work together, advance the same agenda with the issuer, and form a wolf pack. If such wolf packs are established by a lead hedge fund disclosing its activist strategy to selected other investors prior to public announcement thereof or by tipping investors of their pending campaign or share acquisitions, this may run afoul of the prohibition on unlawful disclosure under MAR.[130] As a result, the investors joining the wolf pack cannot trade in the target's shares until the inside information has become public (or has ceased to be inside information) making the potential financial benefit of participating in a wolf pack less attractive.

The prohibition on selective disclosure and tipping may therefore remove the incentives to create a wolf pack and, more generally, lead to less (effective) shareholder activism in Europe.

A partial solution can be found in the exceptions to the prohibition on unlawful disclosure, i.e., for disclosure made *"in the normal exercise of an employment, a profession or duties"*.[131] As the profession of an activist investor inherently hinges on (successful) activist campaigns, one could wonder whether seeking support for their campaign from other investors would not qualify for this exception. Nevertheless, the solution is only an imperfect one, given that even if sharing of inside information by investors were to be allowed, the impact

---

[129] A. Pietrancosta, "Brief remarks on the necessary clarification of market abuse prohibitions in times of shareholder activism", above n. 126, 1,16–17.
[130] A. Taleska, *Hedge Fund Activism in Europe: A Perspective from a Shareholder-Centric System of Corporate Governance*, above n. 4, 79–80.
[131] Article 10(1) MAR.

would be limited as the recipient would qualify as insider upon receipt of such information and therefore not be allowed to trade (while activist hedge funds are notoriously unwilling to agree to be bound by trading restrictions).

A similar reasoning applies to the (optional) safe harbour of the "market-soundings" regime set forth in article 11 MAR. The market soundings-regime, among others, allows takeover bidders and merging companies to wall-cross[132] investors to determine their interest in participating in a transaction (takeover bid or merger, respectively). In each case, the wall-crossing can only occur provided that the recipient investors agree to be wall-crossed, keep the information received confidential, and abstain from trading on the basis of the inside information received.

5.5. MARKET MANIPULATION

The fourth main prohibition under MAR is the prohibition of market manipulation. In articles 12 and 15, MAR prohibits certain manipulative or misleading market behaviours, such as (i) entering into transactions, placing orders or conducting behaviour (a) likely to give false or misleading signals as to supply, demand or price of a financial instrument or (b) likely to secure a price for a financial instrument at an abnormal or artificial level, (ii) spreading false or misleading information through the media as to supply, demand or price of a financial instrument, etc.[133]

Market manipulation is an important consideration in any activist campaign, as it is at the same time a risk as well as a means of pressure for both the issuer and the activist shareholder.

The most obvious form of market manipulation that could occur in an activism context is the dissemination of false or misleading information. For instance, an activist could spread a false rumour about its intended actions towards a target or publish a white paper with a misleading analysis of the target's (future) performance, just after having built up a (long or short) stake in the issuer and hoping for a (positive or negative) spike in the share price in order to benefit from it immediately afterwards.[134] This, of course, does not mean that any activism is abusive or manipulative. That will only be the case if it is likely to give "false or

---

[132] Wall-crossing is the act of making a person an "insider" by providing them with inside information.
[133] Articles 12 and 13 MAR set forth a list of prohibited conduct as well as acceptable market practices. See also M. Spooren, "Liquiditeitscontracten: een analyse van het toepasselijk juridisch kader" (2019), *Revue Pratique des Sociétés – Tijdschrift voor Rechtspersoon en Vennootschap*, 6, 585, 596–97.
[134] E. Hellebuyck, *Hedge funds*, Antwerpen, Intersentia, 2014, 435–437.

misleading signals" as to the evaluation of a financial instrument or secures the price of a financial instrument "at an abnormal or artificial level".[135] However, there may be circumstances in which even dissemination of an analysis or facts which, by themselves, are accurate – or at least plausible – could result in market manipulation, e.g., if it is combined with the withholding of information or other facts which are essential to accurately interpret the disseminated info (e.g., by not simultaneously disclosing that the activist has taken a (long or short) position in the securities of the targeted issuer[136]). Therefore, it is important that the information disclosed is not only accurate, but also complete.[137]

Similarly, activists may reproach the targeted issuer for having disclosed certain matters in a misleading fashion. In that respect, issuers must at all times be guided by, and ensure compliance with, the general standard of fair disclosure applicable to issuers.[138] This includes that they need to make the necessary information available to the public to ensure the transparency, integrity and proper functioning of the market, and ensure that the information provided is true, accurate and fair and enables the public to assess the impact of the information on the issuer's position, business and performance. It should be noted that this standard does not apply to activist investors, thus potentially giving rise to an unequal playing field for issuers and activists in this respect.[139, 140]

Nevertheless, it will often be difficult to prove "false or misleading signals" as to the evaluation of a financial instrument or that a certain behaviour secures the price of a financial instrument "at an abnormal or artificial level". The assessment will need to be done on a case-by-case basis and will require a balancing of what constitutes a mere expression of dissatisfaction with an issuer's existing governance practices or strategy without misrepresenting the facts and what constitutes actual false or misleading information amounting to market manipulation.[141]

In addition, in practice there is an increasing use of anonymous or pseudonymous accounts on digital media platforms by activists, especially for "short and distort"

---

[135] K.U. Schmolke, "Activist Short Sellers under EU Financial Markets Regulation" (2021) *International Journal for Financial Services*, 4, 52, 58–59.
[136] Article 12(2)(d) MAR.
[137] J.T.C. Leliveld, "Aandeelhoudersactivisme en marktmisbruik" (2007), *TFR*, 4, 104, 105; K.U. Schmolke, "Activist Short Sellers under EU Financial Markets Regulation", above n. 136, 58–59.
[138] Article 5 of Royal Decree of 14 November 2007 on the obligations of issuers of financial instruments admitted to trading on a regulated market.
[139] Which may, however, be partially mitigated if the legislative framework on investment recommendations were to apply (see *infra*, section 5.6).
[140] See also Club des juristes, "Shareholder activism", above n. 21, 1, 17.
[141] E. Hellebuyck, *Hedge funds*, above n. 135, 435–437. See also ECHR, *Petro Carbo Chem v. Romania*, no. 21768/12 (on the right of shareholders to criticize the issuer); J.T.C. Leliveld, "Aandeelhoudersactivisme en marktmisbruik", above n. 138, 105.

campaigns by which the shorting activist spreads false rumours or any other misleading information, in an attempt to shield themselves from potential claims or reputational damage. Despite the lack of legitimacy of the authors, such posts and publications regularly cause "noise" in the market that last for a sufficient time to allow the respective activists to reap a profit before the market discovers that the information is untrue.[142] The fast and widespread dissemination of information through digital media platforms only exacerbates such effect.

While such kinds of manipulative behaviour will generally breach the prohibition of market manipulation when the information is misleading, enforcement thereof is much more difficult. Issuers that are confronted with anonymous attacks are forced to fight a "shadowboxing" match against an invisible adversary, and the effects of such attacks often persist in the issuer's share price for a longer term.[143]

Another recent phenomenon is the rise of "political" activism. The most notorious example to date being the GameStop saga in January 2021, whereby activist investors acquired long positions in GameStop to trigger a short squeeze giving rise to major losses for short sellers.[144] The reverse scenario is also conceivable, whereby activists would short the shares of an issuer based on political motives. While "regular" activism is based on the fundamental value of the issuer, "political" activism is not and, from an efficient capital markets perspective, is therefore deemed undesirable as it creates "noise".[145]

Relatedly, it is also much more complex to assess whether such political activism rises to the level of market manipulation. If the underlying political rationale is publicly disclosed, political activism does not send "false or misleading signals". Nevertheless, the question whether political activism secures the price of a financial instrument "at an abnormal or artificial level" is much more convoluted. A successful political activist campaign may shift the price of the targeted instrument to a level that is no longer reflective of the underlying fundamental value of the issuer and could in that sense be considered "artificial" from a pure financial perspective. The question, however, also has a normative component, including whether – and if so, under which conditions – it would be desirable to consider political activism as illegal market manipulation.[146]

---

[142] See J. Mitts, "Short and Distort" (2020), *Journal of Legal Studies*, 49, 287.
[143] A. Pietrancosta, "Brief remarks on the necessary clarification of market abuse prohibitions in times of shareholder activism", above n. 126, 1, 13.
[144] See e.g., D.J. Lynch, "The GameStop stock craze is about a populist uprising against Wall Street. But it's more complicated than that" (02.02.2021) *The Washington Post*; J. Powell, "GameStop can't stop going up" (25.01.2021) *Financial Times*.
[145] K. Langenbucher and L. Pelizzon, "Short Selling – On Ethics, Politics, and Culture" (2021) *Zeitschrift für Bankrecht und Bankwirtschaft*, 33(5), 301, 309.
[146] K.U. Schmolke, "Activist Short Sellers under EU Financial Markets Regulation", above n. 136, 52, 56–57.

5.6. INVESTMENT RECOMMENDATIONS

Certain publications made by an activist investor in the context of a public campaign could qualify as an "investment recommendation" or "other information recommending or suggesting an investment strategy".[147] Indeed, these concepts are very broad, particularly the concept of "investment recommendation", and statements made by the activists on the value of the issuer such activist is targeting may well fall within the confines of these notions.[148]

Publications by an activist investor that can be considered investment recommendations have to abide by the regulatory framework of article 20(1) MAR as further specified by the standards set forth in Commission Delegated Regulation (EU) 2016/958.[149] These requirements include an obligation for the activist to (i) take reasonable care to ensure that such information is objectively presented and (ii) disclose its interests or indicate conflicts of interest concerning the financial instruments to which that information relates. The former includes, among others, a requirement to clearly distinguish facts from interpretations, estimates, opinions and other types of non-factual information and to cite all material sources. The latter comprises the obligation to disclose any circumstance *"that may reasonably be expected to impair the objectivity of the recommendation"* and whether the activist holds any net short or long position of 0.5% or more in the capital of the targeted issuer. Further, there also is an obligation for the person producing the recommendation to disclose its identity, which could aid in countering the occurrence of anonymous or pseudonymous activist attacks.[150]

---

[147] "Information recommending or suggesting an investment strategy" means information (i) produced by an independent analyst, an investment firm, a credit institution, any other person whose main business is to produce investment recommendations, or a natural person working for them under a contract of employment or otherwise, which, directly or indirectly, expresses a particular investment proposal in respect of a financial instrument or an issuer; or (ii) produced by persons other than those referred to in point (i), which directly proposes a particular investment decision in respect of a financial instrument (article 3(1)(34) MAR).
An "investment recommendation" means information recommending or suggesting an investment strategy, explicitly or implicitly, concerning one or several financial instruments or the issuers, including any opinion as to the present or future value or price of such instruments, intended for distribution channels or for the public (article 3(1)(35) MAR).

[148] See also Club des juristes, "Shareholder activism", above n. 21. The French AMF announced in this respect that it will approach ESMA and the European Commission to ask for (i) clarifications, through the ESMA Q&A on MAR, regarding the interpretation of the scope of application of Delegated Regulation no. 2016/958, in particular with respect to its potential application to activist shareholders and behaviours and (ii) precise details regarding the extent of the information on conflicts of interest which must be provided by the author of an investment recommendation (see AMF, «Communication de l'AMF sur l'activisme actionnarial», above n. 19).

[149] AMF, «Communication de l'AMF sur l'activisme actionnarial», above n. 19.

[150] K.U. Schmolke, "Activist Short Sellers under EU Financial Markets Regulation", above n. 136, 52, 58.

6. ACTING IN CONCERT

The notion of "acting in concert" takes a central position in securities law as well as, perhaps somewhat more unexpected, in activism. The situation in which issuers, activists and regulators alike will be confronted with difficult questions around acting in concert is one where multiple activist investors are congregating around a target. This is the phenomenon of the so-called "wolf pack".[151] In a wolf pack, several activists work together (based on a formal or informal understanding) to advance the same agenda with the issuer. Often times, one of these activists will be taking on a leading role, with the other activists being peripheral activists. There are ample reasons why activists would work together: being able to combine their respective shareholding will allow them to exert greater pressure on the issuer, activists that are new to the game will be able to piggyback on the reputation of the more established ones, traditional activists may want to cooperate with ESG-focused counterparts to legitimise their credo, etc. Wolf packs appear in many configurations. There are highly organised ones where the activists present themselves as a group in their external communications (e.g., release of joint white paper or creation of joint website) and others where they simply adopt parallel behaviour and follow suit of the ringleader.

Also outside the situation of a wolf pack, questions on the applicability of acting in concert rules can arise: what to think of the scenario where an activist tries to rally support from significant (non-activist) shareholders for its thesis? What if board representatives of an activist and those of the reference shareholder align their voting behaviour over a sustained period of time? The complexity of the acting in concert rules are clearly not only at stake during the approach phase but can continue to cast a shadow on a more permanent basis, once the activist has established itself within the company, in its interactions between other (significant) shareholders of the company.

The legislator has typically taken a protective stance on concerted action, based on the assumption that in such case, special rules are warranted to avoid circumventing an otherwise mandatory legal obligation. In essence these rules come down to attributing the behaviour of one of the concert shareholders to all of them. Take for example the rules on mandatory takeover bids based on which the legislator has sought to protect minority shareholders against the situation where control of their company has been acquired. The reality is that control could be exercised by different persons (affiliated or not) who do not breach

---

[151] 2014 being called the "year of the wolf pack" on the Harvard Law School Forum on Corporate Governance. See A. Brav, A. Dasgupta, R. Mathews, "Wolf Pack Activism" (2021), *European Corporate Governance Institute – Finance Working Paper no. 501/2017*, <https://papers.ssrn.com/sol3/papers.cfm?abstract_id=2529230> accessed 19.01.2023.

the "control"-threshold on a standalone basis. Thus, when different persons are cooperating to implement a joint strategy for the company (i.e., "acting in concert"), the rules on mandatory takeover bids may equally be triggered.

Nevertheless, a key element to keep in mind is that there are different forms of concert action, and not all of these should be labelled as "undesirable" as such. As Ghetti has argued[152], a more nuanced distinction could be made between "monitoring cooperation" and "circumventing cooperation". The former is a form of concert action carried out by two or more shareholders that are working together to keep management in check and enhance enterprise value. This kind of cooperation, Ghetti argues, should even be encouraged as (i) it is deemed to have a positive effect on the performance of the issuer and (ii) does not result in a loss of value for any shareholder.[153] Circumventing cooperation, on the other hand, occurs when shareholders attempt to evade certain rules and where their behaviour (i) benefits only the cooperating shareholders and (ii) may damage the other shareholders and hinder general investor confidence, which is why it should be efficiently detected and subjected to appropriate rules.[154]

From a theoretical perspective, this distinction between "desirable" and "undesirable" cooperation seems clear-cut but in practice, that is rarely the case. As discussed in greater detail below, the main issue is that the definition of "acting in concert" under Belgian law[155] is overly broad, leaving little room to distinguish between the different forms of cooperation. Moreover, different definitions for acting in concert have been developed by the European legislator for different purposes (transparency vs. protection of minority shareholders in a takeover bid context) whereas the Belgian legislator has chosen to cumulatively apply them throughout the securities law framework. In practice, this leaves significant uncertainty as to the scope of application of the acting in concert notion to collective shareholder action. Such uncertainty has its price considering the significant consequences that a concert relationship may have for the parties deemed to act in concert. While it is difficult to extrapolate the exact impact on the collective activism landscape in Belgium, the costs associated with the legal uncertainty arising out of the application of the European acting in concert rules to collective shareholder actions, have in the past been estimated to

---

[152] R. Ghetti, "Acting in concert in EU Company Law: How Safe Harbours Can Reduce Interference with the Exercise of Shareholder Rights" (2014), *European Company and Financial Law Review*, 11(4), 594, 598–599.
[153] R. Ghetti, above n. 153, 594, 596–597 and the sources cited there.
[154] R. Ghetti, above n. 153, 594, 597–598 and the sources cited there.
[155] Although the definitions of "acting in concert" stem from EU directives, such directives are minimum harmonisation directives such that Belgium could expand – and has indeed expanded – their already broad scope.

amount to 3 to 27% of the total cost of the activist intervention.[156] In addition, it is considered a significant legal risk to those considering commencing an activist intervention.[157]

In the next sections, we will identify the areas of law where the acting in concert rules are relevant in the context of shareholder activism and dissect the definitions from that perspective.

6.1. TRANSPARENCY RULES

6.1.1. Background

As discussed in section 2 above, the purpose of the transparency rules as regards the disclosure of major holdings (the so-called "transparency rules *sensu strictu*") is to inform the public of important changes in the voting structure of issuers, which should enable investors to acquire or dispose of shares in full knowledge of such changes.[158] In addition, these rules are also aimed at enhancing effective control of issuers and overall market transparency of important capital movements.[159] From that perspective, it makes sense, for notification purposes, to not only look at the holding of an investor on a stand-alone basis, but equally include holdings of other investors that are acting together with the former. Indeed, since long, rules on acting in concert have been present in the Belgian transparency legislation.[160]

6.1.2. Definition

Article 3, 13° of the Transparency Law sets forth the definition of "persons acting in concert" for purposes of the rules on the disclosure of major holdings:

---

[156] European Commission, Commission Staff Working Document, Annex to the Proposal of a Directive of the European Parliament and of the Council, on the exercise of voting rights by shareholders of companies having their registered office in a Member State and whose shares are admitted to trading on a regulated market and amending Directive 2004/109/EC (2006) Impact Assessment, no. SEC(2006) 181, (1) 223.

[157] A. Taleska, *Hedge Fund Activism in Europe: A Perspective from a Shareholder-Centric System of Corporate Governance*, above n. 4, 145.

[158] Recital (18) Transparency Directive.

[159] *Ibid.*

[160] See Directive 88/627/EEC of 12 December 1988 on the information to be published when a major holding in a listed company is acquired or disposed of, Law of 2 March 1989 on the disclosure of major holdings in listed companies and regulating takeover bids. To aid the assessment of the concept, a number of presumptions were put in place in the Transparency RD. See E. Janssens, "De omzetting van de Transparantierichtlijn in de Belgische rechtsorde" (2008), *TFR*, 2–3, 210, 221, for an overview.

"a) the natural persons or legal entities acting in concert within the meaning of Article 3, §1, 5°, a) of the Law of 1 April 2007 on takeover bids;

(b) the natural persons or legal entities which have concluded an agreement concerning the concerted exercise of their voting rights in order to implement a lasting common policy towards the issuer concerned;" (free translation)[161]

This definition thus has two legs: (i) paragraph a), which is a cross-reference to the definition of acting in concert under the Law of 1 April 2007 on public takeover bids[162] and is derived from Directive 2004/25/EC on takeover bids[163]; and (ii) paragraph b), which is derived from the Transparency Directive.[164] Originally, the definition also included a paragraph c), which covered *"natural or legal persons who have concluded an agreement concerning the holding, acquisition or transfer of voting securities"* (free translation).[165] This paragraph, which contrary to the other legs did not find its origin in EU law, was repealed by the Law of 27 June 2016 to align the notion of acting in concert under Belgian law with how it is being applied by other EU countries.[166] At the same time, the obligation to notify any changes to the "nature" of the concert action was abolished.[167]

---

[161] In Dutch: *"a) de natuurlijke personen of juridische entiteiten die in onderling overleg handelen in de zin van artikel 3, §1, 5°, a), van de wet van 1 april 2007 op de openbare overnamebiedingen; b) de natuurlijke personen of juridische entiteiten die een akkoord hebben gesloten aangaande de onderling afgestemde uitoefening van hun stemrechten, om een duurzaam gemeenschappelijk beleid ten aanzien van de betrokken emittent te voeren."*

[162] Law of 1 April 2007 on public takeover bids, as consolidated 06.05.2020. Hereinafter the "Takeover Bids Law".

[163] Directive 2004/25/EC of the European Parliament and of the Council of 21 April 2004 on takeover bids (2004) OJ L142. Hereinafter the "Takeover Bids Directive".

[164] Article 10 (a) Transparency Directive.

[165] In Dutch: *"de natuurlijke of rechtspersonen die een akkoord hebben gesloten aangaande het bezit, de verwerving of de overdracht van stemrechtverlenende effecten."*

[166] Government bill amending, for the purpose of transposing Directive 2013/50/EU and implementing Regulation 596/2014, the Law of 2 August 2002 on the supervision of the financial sector and financial services, the Law of 16 June 2006 on the public offering of investment instruments and the admission of investment instruments to trading on a regulated market, and the Law of 2 May 2007 on the disclosure of major holdings in issuers whose shares are admitted to trading on a regulated market and laying down miscellaneous provisions, and laying down miscellaneous provisions, parliamentary works Chamber 2015–16, no. 541835/001. The same paragraph was also included in article 513, §1 of the old Company Code, which was repealed by the Law of 31 July 2017 to align the definition of concert action for purposes of the standalone squeeze-out regime with that of the transparency rules. See Law of 31 July 2017 amending the Law of 2 August 2002 on the supervision of the financial sector and financial services, for the purpose of implementing Regulation no. 596/2014 on market abuse and transposing Directive 2014/57/EU on criminal penalties for market abuse and Implementing Directive (EU) 2015/2392 on the notification of violations, and containing various provisions, Belgian Official Gazette (11.08.2017).

[167] Former article 6, §4, second indent of the Transparency Law.

Following this amendment, the definition of acting in concert under the Transparency Law has become the same as under the Takeover Bids Law. However, as discussed in further detail below, the purpose of both frameworks is fundamentally different: the Transparency Directive is geared towards the market for corporate influence, whereas the Takeover Bids Directive is geared towards the market for corporate control, which constitutes a subset of the former.[168] By mixing up these concepts and applying the same definitions within both frameworks, the Belgian regulator may (unintentionally) dissuade activists from working together.

In this section, we will focus on paragraph b) of the definition as paragraph a) of the definition will be discussed below in section 6.2.2.

6.1.3. Analysis of the definition

Paragraph b) of article 3, 13° of the Transparency Law (*"the persons or entities who have concluded an agreement concerning the concerted exercise of their voting rights, to adopt a lasting common policy towards the issuer in question"* (free translation)), is derived from the Transparency Directive, yet the Transparency Directive does not contain a definition of concert action as such. Rather, the Transparency Directive sets forth the circumstances in which voting rights held by a person should be considered together with the voting rights held by a third person or held by the former person in a different capacity. One of these circumstances where the voting rights of a person or entity need to be aggregated with those of a third party is where the voting rights are held by a third party *"with whom that [first mentioned] person or entity has concluded an agreement which obliges them to adopt, by concerted exercise of the voting rights they hold, a lasting common policy towards the management of the issuer in question"*.[169]

Paragraph b) of the definition of persons acting in concert as contained in the Transparency Law can be broken down into three components, each of which we will analyse and compare with the description contained in the Transparency Directive.

(i) An "agreement"

First, both the Transparency Law and the Transparency Directive require that an "agreement" has been entered into. Much ink has been spilled on the exact

---

[168] R. Ghetti, "Acting in Concert in EU Company Law: How Safe Harbours Can Reduce Interference with the Exercise of Shareholder Rights", above n. 153, 594, 600; B.R. Cheffins and J. Armour, "The Past, Present and Future of Shareholder Activism by Hedge Funds" (2011) *Journal of Corporation Law*, 1, 58–59, <https://papers.ssrn.com/sol3/papers.cfm?abstract_id=1932805> accessed 19.01.2023.
[169] Article 10(a) Transparency Directive.

meaning of the word *"agreement"*, *"overeenkomst"*, *"accord"* (not: *"contrat"*) in the Transparency Directive, its imperfect transposition to *"akkoord"* and *"accord"* in the Transparency Law and the consequences for the binding nature of the agreement.[170] Taking a position on this spectrum is directly relevant to qualify the cooperation between activists: rarely will there be a formal agreement in place between them, yet sustained parallel behaviour as co-members of a wolf pack may nevertheless point to a gentlemen's agreement of some sort. What is clear is that their relationship should carry a certain weight and have a certain recurrence: occasional discussions between activists ahead of a shareholders' meeting do not suffice.[171]

In addition to the question on the binding nature of the agreement, one may wonder whether the agreement requires the shareholders to exercise their vote in a certain way or whether it suffices that they are required to consult with one another (without being required to exercise their vote in a certain way if, after such consultation, they fail to agree).[172, 173] Indeed, while the Transparency Directive refers to *"obliges to adopt"*, this has not been replicated in the Transparency Law, which has led the FSMA among others to endorse the latter view.[174] Although the activists in a wolfpack will typically not only consult with each other but are also likely to adopt the same voting behaviour, the broad interpretation given to the notion of "an agreement" by the FSMA will cast a wide net over the various forms of "agreements" between members of a wolfpack.

---

[170] See, among others, M. Wyckaert, "Zeggenschap, (gezamenlijke) controle en onderling overleg: een verhaal van schakeringen en nuances" in C. Clottens, K. Geens, H. Laga, e.a., *Openbaar bod en transparantie, 2007*, Kalmthout, Biblio, 2008, 86; X. Dieux and L. Legein, « Questions relatives à la notion de concert en droit financier belge » (2012), *Droit Bancaire et Financier 3–4*, 143, 150.

[171] R. Ghetti, "Acting in Concert in EU Company Law: How Safe Harbours Can Reduce Interference with the Exercise of Shareholder Rights", above n. 153, 594, 602.

[172] M. Wyckaert, "Zeggenschap, (gezamenlijke) controle en onderling overleg: een verhaal van schakeringen en nuances", above n. 171, p. 85. Contra: H. De Wulf, "Toepassingsgebied inclusief IPR en kernbegrippen inclusief onderling overleg" in H. De Wulf and C. Van der Elst (eds), *De Belgische overnamewetgeving na de hervorming van 2007*, Antwerpen, Intersentia, 2008, 58 and onwards.

[173] Taking it one step further, even if there would be a requirement to vote in a particular way, actual concert action should not be required. The underpinning rationale of the Transparency Directive is indeed one of *ex ante* transparency: the directive seeks to provide information on how persons are entitled to exercise their voting rights, not how they ended up exercising these rights. R. Ghetti, "Acting in Concert in EU Company Law: How Safe Harbours Can Reduce Interference with the Exercise of Shareholder Rights", above n. 153, 594, 602.

[174] See FSMA, « Guide pratique FSMA_2011_08 du 10 novembre 2011 (mise à jour du 11 février 2020) – La réglementation en matière de transparence », (1) 12, <https://www.fsma.be/sites/default/files/legacy/sitecore/media%20library/Files/fsmafiles/circ/fr/2011/fsma_2011_08.pdf> accessed 19.01.2023; and CBFA (later renamed into FSMA), "Verslag van het directiecomité 2007", (1) 58, <https://www.fsma.be/sites/default/files/legacy/sitecore/media%20library/Files/publications/ver/nl/cbfa_dc_2007.pdf> accessed 19.01.2023.

Although the text does not state this explicitly (contrary to paragraph a), which is derived from the Takeover Bids Directive), the agreement can be either express or tacit and either oral or written.[175]

(ii) Regarding a "concerted exercise of their voting rights"

Next, the agreement should concern the concerted exercise of the shareholders' voting rights. The focus on voting rights is understandable as these are a natural extension of the political rights of a shareholder. The exercise of voting rights is considered to be the most powerful legal tool that shareholders have at their disposal. However, shareholders can have an impact and exert pressure in many ways (e.g., publishing an open letter to the issuer, coordination with and giving instructions to their board representatives, etc.). Therefore, a focus on voting rights may not necessarily be the only proxy to measure shareholders' influence. Be that as it may, depending on the thesis developed by activists (campaign to scuttle/sweeten an M&A transaction, governance overhaul, ...) and the stage of their attack, their actions do not necessarily lead to or imply an exercise of voting rights.

(iii) With a view to adopting a "lasting common policy towards [the management of] the issuer"

Third, the objective of the concert action should be to adopt a lasting common policy towards the issuer. Notably, the Belgian legislator (deliberately or not) did not take into account the "management" (*beheer*) element of the Transparency Directive such that the policy is to be adopted with respect to the issuer and not necessarily the management of the issuer. From a practical perspective, and particularly since the agreement supposes the exercise of voting rights by the shareholders, this may be more a question of semantics.[176]

More interesting however, is the question of what should be considered as "lasting" – does the concert action need to occur on several occasions or during a certain time period before it could be labelled as "lasting"? Or is a one-off action by activists that has a lasting impact on the company (e.g., changes in the board composition) also captured? Notwithstanding the use of the same wording in the Transparency Law and the Takeover Bids Law, a more extensive scope under the former makes sense where it concerns the public disclosure of

---

[175] Government bill on disclosure of major holdings in issuers whose shares are admitted to trading on a regulated market and containing various provisions, *parliamentary works* Chamber 2006–07, no. 51-2963/001, (1) 16. In the same sense: X. Dieux and L. Legein, « Questions relatives à la notion de concert en droit financier belge », above n. 171, 143, 149.

[176] X. Dieux and L. Legein, « Questions relatives à la notion de concert en droit financier belge », above n. 171, 143, 155.

the balance of power within a company, whereas for the latter, considering the grave consequences and the fundamental change to the shareholder structure that a mandatory takeover bid would have, a more cautious approach would seem warranted.[177]

6.1.4. Transparency notifications

As mentioned above, the "acting in concert" notion is important for the transparency rules as the voting rights of investors acting "in concert" are aggregated for the purposes of computing whether the reporting thresholds of the Transparency Law are met, even though the shareholders' voting rights do not individually reach such threshold.[178] The mere creation of a concert relationship will already trigger the notification requirements of the Transparency Law.[179] Activists seeking to remain "under the radar" thus need to think twice before working with others (based on a formal or informal understanding) to advance the same agenda. To the extent they would, by doing so, be deemed to act in concert and cross a reporting threshold, they would indeed be required to disclose their common economic interest pursuant to the Transparency Law.

Importantly, investors can indicate which voting rights should be considered to form part of the concert action and the obligations from the Transparency Law only cover those voting rights which are subject to the concert action. This may give rise to some creative structuring for activists, in order to ensure that their cooperation goes unnoticed.

---

[177] E. Hellebuyck, *Hedge Funds*, above n. 135, p. 391 and onwards, and in particular the author's conclusions with respect to The Netherlands, Germany and the U.K. See also H. De Wulf, "Toepassingsgebied inclusief IPR en kernbegrippen inclusief onderling overleg", above n. 173, 64; M. Wyckaert, "Zeggenschap (gezamenlijke) controle en onderling overleg: een verhaal van schakeringen en nuances", above n. 171, 85; X. Diex and D. Willermain, « Les O.P.A. obligatoires en droit belge et européen après la Directive du 21 avril 2004 et la Loi du 1er avril 2007 (y compris les règles transitoires) » (2007) *Revue Pratique des Sociétés*, 6949, 7, 41.

[178] In the U.S., activists will be considered a "group" and will be required to make an aggregated filing if they have agreed to act together "*for the purposes of acquiring, holding, voting or disposing*" of shares (*cf.* 17 C.F.R §240.13d-5(b)). The SEC has recently proposed a new exemption to mitigate the risk that the "group" definition would chill otherwise appropriate and beneficial shareholder engagement. This new exemption would extend to concerted actions among shareholders that do not have the purpose or effect of changing or influencing control of the issuer. (See SEC, "Modernization of Beneficial Ownership Reporting" (2022), 49 and following, <https://www.sec.gov/rules/proposed/2022/33-11030.pdf> accessed 19.01.2022.).

[179] Even if no shares are acquired but provided of course that the notification thresholds are met (article 6, §4 of the Transparency Law).

6.2. TAKEOVER BIDS LAW

6.2.1. Background and definition

The notion of "acting in concert" plays a vital role in the takeover bid framework, particularly as regards mandatory takeover bids. In this context, any person who, acting alone or in concert, acquires voting securities and as a result holds more than 30% of the voting securities in an issuer is obliged to launch a takeover bid on all voting securities of such issuer.[180] Article 3, 5° of the Takeover Bids Law defines concert parties as follows:

> "(a) those natural or legal persons who cooperate with the bidder, with the target company or with other persons by virtue of an agreement, whether express or tacit, oral or written, aimed at acquiring control of the target company, frustrating the success of a bid or maintaining control of the target company;
>
> (b) the natural or legal persons who have concluded an agreement concerning the concerted exercise of their voting rights in order to adopt a lasting common policy towards the company in question;" (free translation)[181]

As is the case for the definition of concert parties contained in the Transparency Law, the definition of concert parties in the Takeover Bids Law comprises two legs. Paragraph a) finds its origin in the Takeover Bids Directive. Paragraph b), on the contrary, is nowhere to be found in the Takeover Bids Directive – instead, it stems from the Transparency Directive. The Belgian legislator wanted to cast a wider net than simply transposing the definition from the Takeover Bids Directive by taking into account the cooperation between persons who, although at the time of acquiring the shares could not be considered as bidders, were still acting in concert.[182]

As we already analysed paragraph b) of this definition above (see *supra*, section 6.1.3), the following section will focus on paragraph a).

---

[180] Article 50, §1 and §4 Royal Decree of 27 April 2007 on public takeovers (hereinafter the "Takeover Bids RD").

[181] In Dutch: *"a) de natuurlijke personen of rechtspersonen die met de bieder, met de doelvennootschap of met andere personen samenwerken op grond van een uitdrukkelijk of stilzwijgend, mondeling of schriftelijk akkoord dat ertoe strekt de controle over de doelvennootschap te verkrijgen, het welslagen van een bod te dwarsbomen dan wel de controle over de doelvennootschap te handhaven; b) de natuurlijke personen of rechtspersonen die een akkoord hebben gesloten aangaande de onderling afgestemde uitoefening van hun stemrechten, om een duurzaam gemeenschappelijk beleid ten aanzien van de betrokken vennootschap te voeren."*

[182] Government bill on public takeover bids, *parliamentary works* Chamber 2006–07, no. 51-2834/001 1, 13–14.

6.2.2. Analysis of the definition

Paragraph a) stems from the Takeover Bids Directive. Article (2)(1)(d) of the Takeover Bids Directive defines persons acting in concert as *"natural and legal persons who cooperate with the offeror or the offeree company on the basis of an agreement, either express or tacit, either oral or written, aimed either at acquiring control of the offeree company or at frustrating the successful outcome of a bid"*.

Paragraph a) of the definition of persons acting in concert as contained in the Takeover Bids Law can be broken down into two components, each of which we will analyse and compare with the description contained in the Takeover Bids Directive.

(i)   An "agreement"

First, the concert action needs to be formalised through an agreement. Although similar questions on the binding nature of the agreement can be raised based on an inconsistent use of terminology (*"agreement"*, *"overeenkomst"* and *"accord"* in the Takeover Bids Directive and *"akkoord"* and *"accord"* in the Takeover Bids Law), a differentiation between the two legs, which employ identical terms both at EU level (*"agreement"*, *"overeenkomst"* and *"accord"*) and Belgian level (*"akkoord"* and *"accord"*), would only be possible based on the different origin and *ratio legis* of these provisions.[183] It is not a situation that offers comfort to those who intend their "agreement" to be non-binding. In any event, this leg of the definition explicitly states that such agreement can be express or tacit, oral or written.

Interestingly, there is no need for the parties of the concert action to all be "shareholders" as the agreement can include other parties that are involved in the offer but not necessarily hold shares themselves.[184] In an activism context, this could have potential far-reaching consequences: what to think for instance of NGOs that, although not holding any shares themselves, actively support and publicly side with the activist? Since they hold no stake in the issuer, they will

---

[183]   According to certain legal scholars, this is a key difference between the two legs of the definition of "concert action" where the leg stemming from the Takeover Bids Directive would result in a binding exercise of voting rights by the concert parties which is not necessarily the case for the leg stemming from the Transparency Directive. See E. Hellebuyck, *Hedge funds*, above n. 135, 384–385. See also H. De Wulf, "Toepassingsgebied inclusief IPR en kernbegrippen onderling overleg", above n. 173, 58.

[184]   E. Hellebuyck, *Hedge funds*, above n. 135, 389–90. See also the reference in the definition of concert parties to "or with other persons".

not be contributing to (b)reaching any threshold, yet may find themselves in a very unfortunate situation by being considered a concert party of the activist.

(ii)   Aimed either at "acquiring control", "frustrating the successful outcome of a bid" or "maintaining control"

Second, the concert action needs to be aimed at one of three objectives: acquiring control, frustrating the successful outcome of a bid or keeping control. Whereas the Takeover Bids Directive focuses solely on acquiring control and frustrating the successful outcome of a bid, the Belgian legislator has added a possible third objective with reference to the U.K. model.[185] The parliamentary works also further clarify that such notion does not only capture the maintaining of control, but also includes the broadening or strengthening of an already existing control situation.[186]

For the notion of "control", the Takeover Bids Law refers to control within the meaning of the CCA. Control thus comes down to the power, in law or in fact, to exercise a decisive influence on the appointment of the majority of directors or on the orientation of "management" (i.e., policy).[187] There will rarely be any instances where control would be exercised by shareholders holding less than 30% of the voting securities (i.e., the threshold for a mandatory bid).[188] Nevertheless, in an activist context, this is not beyond the realm of possibilities: one of the most frequent attacks relates to governance, where the activists will try to replace a number of the incumbent directors and put forward their own slate of directors. Although this will rarely involve a replacement of a majority of the board[189], it is also not excluded. What's more, activists typically target an issuer because they believe the company is undervalued, either because it is not ran efficiently or because it has the wrong strategy. So effectively, the activists want to weigh in on the orientation of "management", which possibly makes them susceptible to being caught by the definition.

6.2.3.   *ESMA public statement*

By now, the reader will have realised that the definition of acting in concert is not clear-cut. At the suggestion that the concept of "acting in concert" should

---

[185]   Government bill on public takeover bids, above n. 183; M. Wyckaert, "Zeggenschap, (gezamenlijke) controle en onderling overleg: een verhaal van schakeringen en nuances", above n. 171, 82.
[186]   *Ibid.*
[187]   Article 1:14 CCA.
[188]   M. Wyckaert, "Zeggenschap, (gezamenlijke) controle en onderling overleg: een verhaal van schakeringen en nuances", above n. 171, 84.
[189]   We are unaware of any precedents in the Belgian context where an activist has succeeded (with or without the support of the company) to replace the majority of the directors.

be clarified at EU level to lessen the uncertainty for international investors wishing to cooperate with each other on corporate governance issues, ESMA, in 2014, issued a public statement on shareholder cooperation and acting in concert under the Takeover Bids Directive.[190] Although the statement was formally issued by ESMA, it is in fact a representation of the collective view of the members of the Takeover Bids Network.[191]

The public statement contains a "white list" of activities in which shareholders may engage and which engagement will not, in and of itself, lead to those shareholders being regarded as persons acting in concert within the meaning of the Takeover Bids Directive (which, in Belgium, means that it relates to the first leg of the definition of acting in concert as included in both the Takeover Bids Law and the Transparency Law). It covers matters such as entering into discussions about possible matters to be raised with the issuer's board, making representations to the issuer's board about particular actions that the issuer might consider taking and agreeing to vote the same way on a particular resolution put to a general meeting.[192] These are clearly the kind of activities that wolf pack activists would be jointly undertaking.

The white list does however not function as a true safe harbour for potential activists. First, the statement makes it clear that each engagement needs to be assessed on its own particular facts and that the national competent authorities

---

[190] ESMA, "Public statement: information on shareholder cooperation and acting in concert under the Takeover Bids Directive" (updated 08.01.2019), no. ESMA/2014/677-REV, <https://www.esma.europa.eu/sites/default/files/library/esma-2014-677-rev_public_statement_concerning_shareholder_cooperation_and_acting_in_concert.pdf> accessed 19.01.2023.

[191] The Takeover Bids Network is a permanent working group, under ESMA's auspices, that promotes the exchange of information on practices and application of the Takeover Bids Directive across the EEA, and comprises the relevant national competent authorities under the Takeover Bids Directive.

[192] The full list of activities is as follows: (a) entering into discussions with each other about possible matters to be raised with the company's board; (b) making representations to the company's board about company policies, practices or particular actions that the company might consider taking; (c) other than in relation to the appointment of board members, exercising shareholders' statutory rights to: (i) add items to the agenda of a general meeting; (ii) table draft resolutions for items included or to be included on the agenda of a general meeting; or (iii) call a general meeting other than the annual general meeting; (d) other than in relation to a resolution for the appointment of board members and insofar as such a resolution is provided for under national company law, agreeing to vote the same way on a particular resolution put to a general meeting, in order, for example: (A) to approve or reject: (i) a proposal relating to directors' remuneration; (ii) an acquisition or disposal of assets; (iii) a reduction of capital and/or share buy-back; (iv) a capital increase; (v) a dividend distribution; (vi) the appointment, removal or remuneration of auditors; (vii) the appointment of a special investigator; (viii) the company's accounts; or (ix) the company's policy in relation to the environment or any other matter relating to social responsibility or compliance with recognised standards or codes of conduct; or (B) to reject a related party transaction.

may take into account "all other relevant factors" in making their decisions.[193] Second, the guidance given in the statement does not cover the appointment of board members, which is an action on which shareholders typically will want to cooperate. Even though the fact that a certain form of cooperation is not included in the white list does not mean that the behaviour will be considered a concert action, activists (and shareholders in general) should carefully assess their cooperation against this background. According to the statement, cooperation around the appointment of board members can be particularly sensitive in a takeover bid context and national competent authorities have adopted different approaches in this respect.[194] For Belgium, it has been clarified that when shareholders are cooperating to exercise their votes together on one particular occasion to support the appointment or removal of one board member only, that cooperation is unlikely to, in and of itself, lead to a determination that those persons are acting in concert.[195] The relevant factors to take into account for purposes of the assessment include: (a) the nature of the relationship between the shareholders and the proposed board member(s); (b) the number of proposed board members being voted for pursuant to a shareholders' voting agreement; (c) whether the shareholders have cooperated in relation to the appointment of board members on more than one occasion; (d) whether the shareholders are not simply voting together but are also jointly proposing a resolution for the appointment of certain board members; and (e) whether the appointment of the proposed board member(s) will lead to a shift in the balance of power on the board.[196] Lastly, the regulators can sidestep the guidance contained in the public statement as it is not legally binding on them, thus creating significant uncertainty.

6.2.4. Mandatory takeover bid

As mentioned previously, the reason why the notion of acting in concert is so important is due to the rules on mandatory takeover bids: crossing of the 30% voting securities threshold will trigger the obligation to launch a takeover bid and for the crossing of this threshold, one should look at the voting securities held by persons acting in concert (in addition to those held by their "connected persons", etc.). In case the 30% threshold is being crossed by the concert parties in the aggregate, each party to the concert action will have the obligation to launch a takeover bid.[197] In case the 30% threshold is being crossed by one of the

---

[193] ESMA, "Public statement: information on shareholder cooperation and acting in concert under the Takeover Bids Directive", above n. 191, 1, 2.
[194] Ibid, 6.
[195] Ibid, 18–19.
[196] Ibid, 7.
[197] Pursuant to article 50, §4 Takeover Bids RD, they are severally obligated to launch a mandatory takeover bid.

concert parties, the obligation to launch a takeover bid only exists for the party that crossed the 30% threshold and not its fellow concert parties.[198] Contrary to the Transparency Law, where the shareholders can indicate which shares should be considered to form part of the concert action, there is no possibility to exclude certain voting securities from the calculation of the threshold for purposes of the takeover bid rules.

From time to time, a misconception exists that the mere entry into of a shareholders' agreement or creation of a wolf pack could give rise to the obligation to launch a mandatory takeover bid. This is incorrect. An essential feature of the mandatory takeover bid regime is that the 30% threshold is being crossed due to <u>an acquisition</u>, i.e., the mere entry into of a shareholders' agreement or creation of a wolf pack will not trigger the obligation to launch a takeover bid.[199] However, when one of the parties to the concert action acquires any voting securities within the next three years thereafter, the obligation will nevertheless be triggered.[200] If the parties manage to not cross this threshold during the first three years, they are freed from the standstill obligation.[201] A wolf pack thus requires a significant amount of trust between the concert parties, as a wrong step by one of them could have detrimental implications for all of them and require each party to the concert action to launch a takeover bid.[202]

Furthermore, the obligation is also triggered in case one of the concert parties transfers its shares to a third party, which accedes to the concert action.[203] Exemptions exist, among others, if (i) one is able to demonstrate that a third party is exercising control over the issuer[204] or (ii) in case the threshold of 30% is exceeded by maximum 2% and provided that the voting rights attached thereto are not exercised and that the excess is disposed of within twelve months.[205]

---

[198] Article 50, §5 Takeover Bids RD.
[199] M. Wyckaert, "Zeggenschap, (gezamenlijke) controle en onderling overleg: een verhaal van schakeringen en nuances", above n. 171, 68.
[200] Article 50, §7, 1° Takeover Bids RD. Or in case the 30% threshold is being crossed by one of the concert parties, the obligation to launch a takeover bid only exists for the party that crossed the 30% threshold (and this obligation exists regardless of the time when this threshold was crossed).
[201] M. Wyckaert, "Zeggenschap, (gezamenlijke) controle en onderling overleg: een verhaal van schakeringen en nuances", above n. 171, 69.
[202] The "trust" between members of the pack can be backed up by a formal standstill commitment by each member, during a certain amount of time, not to acquire any shares in the issuer. However, a breach of this standstill commitment by a party would not release the other members from the obligation to launch a mandatory takeover bid (provided the other conditions are met).
[203] Unless the parties to the original concert action (meaning a concert action that lasts for longer than three years) always maintained a shareholding of more than 30%. See Article 50, §7, 2° Takeover Bids RD.
[204] Article 52, §1, 6° Takeover Bids RD.
[205] Article 52, §1, 7° Takeover Bids RD.

6.3. GENERAL CORPORATE LAW

The CCA has introduced and streamlined a number of definitions in Book 1. Nevertheless, the CCA does not contain a general definition of "acting in concert". Presumably this is due to the fact that the acting in concert notion is of limited relevance only to the CCA given the few provisions that make use of it.

6.3.1. Standalone squeeze-outs

The first provision is article 7:82 CCA[206] in connection with the (private or public) squeeze-out (*uitkoopbod*), where acting in concert is defined as follows:

> "1° *natural persons or legal entities cooperating with the bidder, with the target company or with other persons by virtue of an agreement, either express or tacit, either oral or written, aimed at acquiring or retaining control of the target company;*
>
> 2° *natural or legal persons who have concluded an agreement relating to the concerted exercise of their voting rights with a view to pursuing a lasting common policy towards the company in question;*" (free translation)[207]

For this definition, which was first introduced in 2007 in article 513 of the former Company Code, the legislator borrowed heavily from the definitions of the Transparency Law and the Takeover Bids Law. Nevertheless, although the preparatory works of the CCA state as much[208], this definition is not exactly the same as the definition under the Takeover Bids Law. The difference can be attributed to the fact that the CCA's rules on squeeze-outs only apply outside the context of a takeover bid. Indeed, in the context of a takeover bid, a simplified

---

[206] A similar provision exists for the SRL/BV, i.e., article 5:69 CCA.
[207] In Dutch: "*1° de natuurlijke personen of rechtspersonen die met de bieder, met de doelvennootschap of met andere personen samenwerken op grond van een uitdrukkelijk of stilzwijgend, mondeling of schriftelijk akkoord dat ertoe strekt de controle over de doelvennootschap te verkrijgen dan wel de controle over de doelvennootschap te handhaven; 2° de natuurlijke personen of rechtspersonen die een akkoord hebben gesloten aangaande de onderling afgestemde uitoefening van hun stemrechten, om een duurzaam gemeenschappelijk beleid ten aanzien van de betrokken vennootschap te voeren*".
[208] Government bill introducing a Code for Companies and Associations and including various provisions, *parliamentary works* Chamber 2018, no. 54-3119/001 1, 222, "*Deze bepaling herneemt artikel 513 W.Venn., met dien verstande dat de defin[i]tie van onderling overleg uit de wet van 1 april 2007 op de openbare overnameaanbiedingen in het wetboek wordt geïntegreerd.*" In article 513 of the former Company Code, the definition was phrased slightly differently as: "*Onder personen die in onderling overleg handelen wordt verstaan: a) de natuurlijke personen of rechtspersonen die in onderling overleg handelen in de zin van artikel 3, §1, 5°, a), van de wet van ... op de openbare overnameaanbiedingen; b) de natuurlijke personen of rechtspersonen die een akkoord hebben gesloten aangaande de onderling afgestemde uitoefening van hun stemrechten, om een duurzaam gemeenschappelijk beleid ten aanzien van de betrokken vennootschap te voeren.*"

procedure is available for a follow-on squeeze-out that is governed by a separate legal framework.[209]

6.3.2. Capital increases

The second provision is article 7:193 CCA[210] in connection with the limitation or cancellation of the preferential subscription rights of existing shareholders to the benefit of certain pre-identified persons. Pursuant to this provision[211], a shareholder who, alone or together with, among others, persons with whom such shareholder is acting in concert, holds more than 10% of the voting rights and is the beneficiary of the limitation or cancellation of the existing shareholders' preferential subscription rights, cannot participate in the vote on the limitation or cancellation of the preferential subscription rights of existing shareholders.[212] For purposes of this rule, acting in concert is identical to the definitions contained in the Transparency Law and the Takeover Bids Law.

Furthermore, for purposes of calculating the 10% threshold of article 7:201, first indent, 3° CCA, which deals with the prohibition for the board to use its powers under the authorised capital to increase the share capital via a contribution in kind reserved for shareholders holding securities to which more than 10% of the voting rights are attached, the same definition as in article 7:193 CCA is applied.[213]

Given that these provisions are not likely to be at play in an activism context[214], we will not elaborate on them in further detail. For a discussion of the relevant elements of the definition, please refer to sections 6.1.3 and 6.2.2.

6.4. ASSESSMENT

Based on the above, it is clear that the notion of "acting in concert" suffers from a number of flaws. First, due to the streamlining of the definitions of "acting in concert" in the Transparency Law and the Takeover Bids Law, the legislator has failed to accurately capture the *ratio legis* of the relevant framework,

---

[209] Articles 42 and 43 of the Takeover Bids RD.
[210] A similar provision exists for the SRL/BV, i.e., article 5:131 CCA.
[211] This provision did not yet exist in the former Company Code and was introduced in the CCA.
[212] A mirroring provision applies at the level of the board where the directors that *de facto* represent any shareholder or any persons acting in concert with such shareholder holding 10% or more, cannot participate in the vote on any capital increase occurring within the authorised capital. See article 7:200 CCA.
[213] Article 7:201, last indent CCA. Article 598 former Company Code did not contain a definition of acting in concert for purposes of this provision.
[214] Other than perhaps the implausible scenario where an issuer would issue shares to a white knight in an ultimate attempt to rid itself from a wolf pack, by diluting the latter's stake.

which would otherwise contribute to providing the necessary nuance and interpretation guidance. Second, the meaning of the various elements of the definition is not always clear, which risks casting an overly broad net on acts of shareholders that are collaborating. While one can understand the desire to make the definitions broad enough to avoid the risk of under-deterrence, too broad definitions create a risk of over-deterrence.[215] Particularly when looked at from the lens of collective shareholder action such as activism, the pendulum may have swung too far, to the side of over-deterrence.

There is no other area of the law where the tension between the aspiration to encourage shareholders to actively exercise their rights versus the protection of minority shareholders against creeping control is felt more strongly than with respect to the acting in concert notion of the Takeover Bids Directive and, even more so, the Takeover Bids Law. On the one hand, the European legislator considers effective shareholder control as a pre-requisite to sound governance and wishes to encourage and facilitate such cooperation.[216] On the other hand, shareholders who wish to cooperate with each other, and jointly exercise their right with a view to effectively monitor and/or discipline management, may feel inhibited from doing so out of fear that they risk having to make a mandatory takeover bid. This is caused in part by the broad definition that was inherited from the Takeover Bids Directive but also by the Belgian legislator's approach to plug the definition from the Transparency Directive into the Takeover Bids Law. Although it might seem rather theoretical that activists would find themselves in a situation where they would be required to launch a mandatory takeover bid, it has an important deterrent effect in practice. Certain regulators have already expressed their support for further clarification, requesting ESMA to define, based on the white list contained in ESMA's public statement on shareholder cooperation and acting in concert under the Takeover Bids Directive, the activist behaviours which are not in themselves likely to be presumed to be acting in concert.[217] It remains to be seen whether and how ESMA will respond to this invitation.

7. CONCLUSION

One of the central threads to be distilled from this contribution, is that most securities laws have not been designed with activism in mind. This often leads to uncertainty in practice (e.g., with respect to the scope of the notion of "acting

---

[215] R. Ghetti, "Acting in Concert in EU Company Law: How Safe Harbours Can Reduce Interference with the Exercise of Shareholder Rights", above n. 153, 594, 610.
[216] See Recital (3) SRD II.
[217] AMF, « Communication de l'AMF sur l'activisme actionnarial », above n. 19.

in concert"). It also means that activist campaigns typically require a detailed case-by-case analysis from a securities law perspective (e.g., whether one is in possession of inside information under MAR), as part of which national specificities resulting from diverging transpositions of EU directives may need to be considered (e.g., for the thresholds at which transparency declarations need to be made). Such questions and conundrums are even more exacerbated when activists start coordinating or cooperating with each other in so-called wolf packs. Navigating the activist landscape, both as a matter of offence and defence, therefore requires close attention to the securities law framework, from activists and issuers alike.

Certain national regulators have also picked up on a number of these topics. The French AMF, for example, has issued some guidance in relation to activism, and also extended an invite to ESMA to take further action in clarifying the application of a number of points in an activism context. It will be interesting to monitor how this space further develops over the coming months and years, including in Belgium specifically, where the FSMA may be increasingly paying attention to shareholder dialogue.[218]

---

[218] See e.g., the FSMA's "20 projects for the future" announced on 4 October 2022, in which the FSMA indicates, in relation to sustainable finance, that issuers should *"organize themselves proactively to engage in a dialogue with investors and prepare the potential impact of shareholder activism."*

SHAREHOLDER ACTIVISM IN THE BELGIAN COURTROOM

Karel SCHULPEN
Arcas Law

1. INTRODUCTION

1. Minority shareholders can seek relief in court. No specific comprehensive legislation outlines the legal remedies of minority shareholders. Nor is there a specialised court dealing exclusively with such matters (unlike e.g., the Netherlands).

The activist minority shareholder who seeks to investigate or influence the decision-making process in the company or to obtain compensation for wrongdoing by directors, must use the traditional remedies of company law before the territorially competent Court of Enterprises.

This contribution[1] is essentially focused on the legal remedies that are available to minority shareholders in listed companies, in particular the appointment of a provisional administrator / ad hoc trustee / judicial sequester, the action for suspension or nullity of company decisions, the derivative action, the court expert examination, and the action for compulsory liquidation of the company.

The forced sale or purchase of shares, which is a popular remedy to settle conflicts in unlisted companies, will not be addressed here. This action is not available to shareholders of listed companies.

This contribution is based on the new legislation contained in the Belgian Code on Companies and Associations (BCCA).[2]

---

[1] I would like to thank Prof. Robbie Tas for our joint presentation at the VBO conference on 9 June 2022 that served as an inspiration for this contribution. In addition, I would also like to thank Jan-Sebastiaan Janssens (Arcas Law) and Thomas Swennen (Arcas Law) for their research assistance.

[2] Act of 23 March 2019 on the Belgian Code of Companies and Associations, *Belgian Official State Gazette*, 4 April 2019.

2. INVESTIGATIVE MEASURES: THE EXPERT REPORT

§1. INTRODUCTION AND LEGAL BASIS

2. A minority shareholder who wishes to take legal action against company decisions or against the directors has a certain burden of proof.

Seeking to have an expert report will allow a minority shareholder to have sufficient knowledge to subsequently initiate other actions (such as the derivative action).[3]

If there are sufficient indications that the company's interests are seriously jeopardised or threatened, the president of the Court of Enterprises may appoint one or more experts to examine the company's books and accounts, as well as the transactions carried out by its bodies.

3. An expert report is only possible for the BV/SRL, CV/SC, and NV/SA.[4] The legal basis is set out in the articles 5:106 (for the BV/SRL), 6:91 (for the CV/SC) and 7:160 (for the NV/SA) of the BCCA.

§2. APPLICATION CRITERIA

4. The appointment of a court expert is subject to two cumulative conditions. First, the shareholder bringing the claim must meet the statutory threshold requirements (nr. 5 *infra*), and second, the shareholder must prove that the company's interests are or are likely to be seriously compromised (nr. 6 *infra*).

5. The ownership threshold requirements differ depending on the form of the company.

In the NV/SA minority shareholders may request the appointment of an expert when they, on the day when the annual general meeting decides to grant discharge to the directors, hold securities representing at least 1% of the votes attached to all the securities existing on that day, or hold securities representing the capital of at least EUR 1.250.000 (art. 7:160 of the BCCA). However, shares without voting rights or shares with suspended voting rights are not taken into

---

[3] In addition to a court expert in corporate litigation matters, each party who has a legal interest and standing (as meant in the articles 17 and 18 of the Belgian Judicial Code) may initiate a common law claim in order to obtain the appointment of a court expert (as regulated by the articles 968 and further of the Belgian Judicial Code). This common law remedy shall not be dealt with under this chapter that is limited to the court expert examination in the framework of a corporate litigation.

[4] H. Braeckmans and R. Houben, *Handboek Vennootschapsrecht*, Antwerp, Intersentia, 2020, 756.

account for the calculation of the 1% threshold but do count for the calculation of the total votes.[5]

In the BV/SRL (Art. 5:106 of the BCCA) and CV/SC (6:91 of the BCCA), the threshold is set at minority shareholders representing at least 10% of the number of issued shares on the day when the annual general meeting decides to grant discharge (*kwijting/décharge*).

The legal wording of these articles allows that several (smaller) shareholders can cooperate to meet the threshold.[6] Since there is a minimum threshold, it is also generally accepted that majority shareholders can bring a claim for the appointment of a company law expert.[7]

The assessment of whether the thresholds are met is made at the time of filing the action.[8] Whether the shares are fully paid up or not has no relevance.[9]

If the expert report is sought in order to substantiate a subsequent derivative claim relating to historical facts, the thresholds for launching such a derivative claim relating to these facts must also be met in order to request an expert report.[10] In that scenario, minority shareholders can only request an expert report relating to facts that occurred during the financial years for which they met the thresholds for launching a subsequent derivative action (article 7:157 of the BCCA).[11]

6. The minority shareholder(s) must prove that the interests of the company are or are likely to be seriously compromised.

This material condition is open-ended and covers, among others, breaches of the law or the articles of association, wrongdoings, omissions or negligence by the directors etc.[12] The invoked grounds may relate to the policy, the operation

---

[5] D. Van Gerven, *Handboek Vennootschappen*, Brussels, Larcier, 2020, 950 H. Braeckmans, "Conflicten in vennootschappen en het wetboek van vennootschappen: de vlag dekt niet de lading", *TPR*, 2010, 1658; see further C. Piette, "Deskundigenonderzoek" in H. Braeckmans (ed.), *De NV/SA in de praktijk*, Mechelen, Wolters Kluwer Belgium, 392–393.

[6] M. Roelants, "Specifieke kwesties in het vennootschapsrecht" in D. De Buyst, P. Kortleven, T. Lysens and C. Ronse (eds.), *Bestendig Handboek Deskundigenonderzoek*, Mechelen, Wolters Kluwer Belgium, 2022, (19) 33.

[7] H. Braeckmans and R. Houben, *Handboek Vennootschapsrecht*, Antwerp, Intersentia, 2020, 757.

[8] President of the Enterprise Court of Antwerp (Antwerp Division) 2 July 2021", *TRV-RPS*, 2022, 444; C. Piette, "Deskundigenonderzoek" in H. Braeckmans (ed.), *De NV/SA in de praktijk*, Mechelen, Wolters Kluwer Belgium, 289.

[9] H. Braeckmans, "Conflicten in vennootschappen en het wetboek van vennootschappen: de vlag dekt niet de lading", *TPR*, 2010, 1658.

[10] President of the Enterprise Court of Antwerp (Antwerp Division) 23 September 2022, *TRV-RPS*, 2022, 682.

[11] Please note that this judgement is still under appeal.

[12] M. Roelants, "Specifieke kwesties in het vennootschapsrecht" in D. De Buyst, P. Kortleven, T. Lysens and C. Ronse (eds.), *Bestendig Handboek Deskundigenonderzoek*, Mechelen, Wolters Kluwer Belgium, 100.

of the bodies or the company's accounts, or consist of eroding the substance of the company for the benefit of another party.[13]

The question whether the company's interests are seriously endangered, is examined on a *prima facie* basis (i.e. at first sight), meaning that minority shareholders must present enough (although not exhaustive) evidence to support their claim.[14]

7. The published case law concerns mainly unlisted companies.[15] For example, an expert was appointed because the company's management could not offer a convincing explanation for a number of suspicious accounting transactions.[16] In another case, a company law expert was appointed in a company whose director had a significant conflict of interest and where, moreover, several necessary licences were missing.[17]

The company's interests were also endangered in the following circumstances: a black money circuit was set in motion within the company; important information was withheld from a shareholder holding 33% of the shares; a report from the company auditors indicated that the company would have to make write-downs that would trigger the alarm procedure, etc.[18]

§3. CLAIMANTS AND PROCEDURE

8. Only shareholders can claim an expert report under the applicable sections of the BCCA.[19] Other than in the Netherlands or France, this possibility is not provided for creditors and employees.[20] Certificate holders, who are only entitled to the proceeds of or income from shares[21], are also barred from bringing the claim.[22]

---

[13] President Court of Enterprises Antwerp (division Antwerp) 23 September 2022, *TRV-RPS*, 2022, 684.
[14] D. Van Gerven, *Handboek Vennootschappen*, Brussels, Larcier, 2020, 951.
[15] For caselaw concerning listed companies, see: President Enterprise Court of Antwerp (division Antwerp) 2 June 2021, *TRV-RPS*, 2022, 438 (Nyrstar case); Enterprise Court of Antwerp (division Antwerp) 9 November 2021, *TBH*, 2022, 648.
[16] Liege (7th ch.) No 2015/RG/823, 10 May 2016, *DAOR*, 2017, vol. 122, 67.
[17] Enterprise Court of Dendermonde (4th ch.) 25 February 2008, *RW*, 2011–12, no. 29, 1308.
[18] Enterprise Court of Dendermonde (4th ch.) 25 February 2008, *RW*, 2011–12, no. 29, 1308; K. Geens, M. Denef, R. Tas, F. Hellemans and J. Vananroye, "Overzicht van rechtspraak, Vennootschappen 1992–1998", *TPR*, 2000, no. 343.
[19] H. Braeckmans, "Conflicten in vennootschappen en het wetboek van vennootschappen: de vlag dekt niet de lading", *TPR*, 2010, 1658.
[20] See C. Piette, "Deskundigenonderzoek" in H. Braeckmans (ed.), *De NV/SA in de praktijk*, Mechelen, Wolters Kluwer Belgium, 290.
[21] See Article 7:61 BCCA; Article 5:160 of the BCCA (BV/SRL); and Article 6:91 of the BCCA (CV/SC).
[22] The issuer's articles of association or terms of administration may nevertheless provide for a possibility, see C. Piette, "Deskundigenonderzoek" in H. Braeckmans (ed.), *De NV/SA in de praktijk*, Mechelen, Wolters Kluwer Belgium, 290.

The trustee (*curator/syndic*) of a bankrupt company holding shares in another company, is also entitled to claim an expert report in relation to the latter company.[23]

9. Shareholders may bring their claim for an expert report in summary proceedings before the President of the Court of Enterprises.[24] The Court of Enterprises of the location where the company is registered has jurisdiction.[25]

In normal summary proceedings, a claimant must show that his/her claim is urgent (art. 584 of the Judicial Code). Although the BCCA provides that expert reports are claimed in summary proceedings, there is no need to prove urgency (other than the burden of proof that the interests of the company are or are likely to be seriously compromised).[26]

§4. THE EXPERT AND HIS MISSION

10. The expert is given an audit assignment that may cover all aspects of the company's activity.[27] The competent court may appoint one or more experts *"to examine the books and accounts of the company and also the transactions carried out by its bodies"*.[28] Case law usually orders the production of all the documents the expert deems useful to his mission.[29] Besides annual accounts and books, these may include accounts, agreements, and minutes of various meetings.[30]

The term "bodies" is also interpreted broadly and the operations of any body of the company can be examined, including general meetings, the board of directors, the managing director, the executive committee, the statutory auditor, or the liquidator.[31]

---

[23] Liege 10 May 2016, DAOR 2017, afl. 122, 64.
[24] M. Roelants, "Specifiek kwesties in het vennootschapsrecht" in D. De Buyst, P. Kortleven, T. LysenS T. and C. Ronse (eds.), *Bestendig Handboek Deskundigenonderzoek*, Mechelen, Wolters Kluwer Belgium, 102.
[25] Art. 628, 13° Belgian Judicial Code; D. Van Gerven, *Handboek Vennootschappen*, Brussels, Larcier, 2020, 955.
[26] President Court of Enterprises Antwerp (division Antwerp) 23 September 2022, *TRV-RPS*, 2022, 684.
[27] M. Roelants, "Specifieke kwesties in het Vennootschapsrecht" in D. De Buyst, P. Kortleven, T. Lysens and C. Ronse (eds.) *Bestendig Handboek Deskundigenonderzoek*, Mechelen, Wolters Kluwer Belgium, 105.
[28] Art. 7:160 of the BCCA (NV/SA).
[29] Enterprise Court of Kortrijk 10 February 1994, *DAOR*, 1996, vol. 40, 81.
[30] C. Piette, "Deskundigenonderzoek" in H. Braeckmans (ed.), *De NV/SA in de praktijk*, Mechelen, Wolters Kluwer Belgium, 319.
[31] H. Braeckmans, "Conflicten in vennootschappen en het wetboek van vennootschappen: de vlag dekt niet de lading", *TPR*, 2010,1662.

3. ACTIONS INTERFERING WITH THE MANAGEMENT OF THE COMPANY AND/OR THE ADMINISTRATION OF ITS ASSETS

§1. INTRODUCTION

11. A minority shareholder will, unless agreed otherwise, not have sufficient voting power to be able to determine the composition of the board within the general meeting and thus (directly or indirectly) company policy.

As discussed further in this contribution, company law provides for remedies that allow minority shareholders to recover (for the benefit of the company) the damages resulting for wrongdoings by the directors (i.e. the derivative action; *infra* section 5) or to have certain adopted decisions (of the board of directors or general assembly) suspended or annulled (*infra* section 6). These measures are rather curative in nature.

This chapter discusses those measures that have a more preventive nature. The first and most drastic option available for a minority shareholder to address mismanagement concerns the request for the appointment of a temporary administrator to take over the management of the company (wholly or partially). A less far-reaching option is the appointment of an *ad hoc* trustee with a well-defined mandate (e.g., the convening of a general meeting, certain veto rights, etc.). Finally, there are measures aiming solely at protecting the company's assets or documents, such as the appointment of an expert custodian (with certain controlling or custodial duties) or a sequester.

§2. PROVISIONAL ADMINISTRATOR

A. Basis and definition

12. A provisional administrator in company matters is a judicial agent appointed by a court to perform one or more acts of governance in the name and on behalf of the company to protect the interests of the company, shareholders, directors and/or creditors.[32] This appointment results in the board losing all or part of its authority to this provisional administrator.[33]

---

[32] Cass. 10 September 2015, *Arr.Cass* 2015, 1976; K. Byttebier, N. Sneyers, "Het voorlopig bewind en het vennootschaps-, respectievelijk het ondernemingsbelang", *RW*, 2020–21, (562) 562; H. Braeckmans and R. Houben, *Handboek vennootschapsrecht*, Antwerp, Intersentia, 2020, 749; H. Braeckmans, "Conflicten in vennootschappen en het wetboek van vennootschappen: de vlag dekt niet de lading", *TPR* 2010, (1603) 1634; J. Verhaert, "The provisional administrator", in X., *Bestendige Handboek Vennootschap & Aansprakelijkheid*, Mechelen, Wolters Kluwer, 2017, (II.1–35) II.1–38.

[33] K. Byttebier and N. Sneyers, " Het voorlopig bewind en het vennootschap-, respectievelijk het ondernemingsbelang", *RW*, 2020–21, (562) 562.

The corporate administrator is barely standardised in the legislation which merely provides that the appointment of a provisional administrator will be published in the relevant annexes of the *Belgian State Gazette* (art. 2:8 §1,5d of the BCCA). The concept of the provisional administrator finds its origins mainly in case law.

The scope of the administrator's mandate and powers are determined by the court.[34] These powers may be totalitarian when the provisional administrator acts alone as a substitute for the administrative body.[35] The provisional administrator may also be given a more limited remit, e.g., as an addition to the current board of directors.

A distinction must be made as to the type of provisional administrator. In wider corporate law, there are two types of administrators: one based on company law[36] and one based on insolvency law.[37] This contribution will only focus on the administrator established by company law.

B.   Conditions for the appointment

13. The minority shareholder will have to demonstrate that an extreme emergency exists, i.e., when urgent and special circumstances block or render the normal operation or management of the company (virtually) impossible, or seriously endanger the company's survival, and when other measures do not provide a solution.[38]

This legal instrument has far-reaching consequences and is hence of a subsidiary nature, i.e., the court should exercise restraint.[39] The court must therefore weigh up different interests, pondering the benefit to the claimant if the measure is granted against the disadvantage suffered by the company if a provisional administrator is appointed.[40] In doing so, the court must take into account the corporate interest and the principles of "corporate governance".[41]

---

[34]   B. Tilleman and K. Dewaele, "Acting as a legal person under the Companies and Associations BCCA" in R. Jafferali (ed.), *Entre tradition et pragmatisme*, Brussels, Larcier, 2021, (1401) 1421.

[35]   Cass. 4 November 2004, *TRV-RPS*, 1, 2005, 34; Cass. 10 September 2015, *Arr.Cass.* 2015, 1976.

[36]   Art. 2:8 §1, 5° d of the BCCA.

[37]   Art. XX. 31–32 of the Belgian Code of Economic Law.

[38]   *Infra* no. 12 and following.

[39]   I. Verougstraete, J.P. Lebeau, "Transferts de compétences: le tribunal de commerce devient le juge naturel de l'entreprise", *TBH*, 2014, 547–548; S. Raes, "The interlocutory procedure in company matters", *TRV*, 1988, 329–330; E. Pottier and M. De Roeck, "Administrateur provisoire: bilan et perspectives", *TBH*, 1997, 205; K. Byttebier and N. Sneyers, "Het voorlopig bewind en het vennootschap-, respectievelijk het ondernemingsbelang", *RW* 2020–21, (562) 566.

[40]   H. Braeckmans, "Conflicten in vennootschappen en het wetboek van vennootschappen: de vlag dekt niet de lading", *TPR*, 2010, (1603) 1641.

[41]   K. Byttebier and N. Sneyers, "Het voorlopig bewind en het vennootschap-, respectievelijk het ondernemingsbelang", *RW*, 2020–21, (562) 566–567; H. Braeckmans and R. Houben, *Handboek vennootschapsrecht*, Antwerp, Intersentia, 2020, 750; H. Braeckmans, "Conflicten

14. There is much case law in (mainly unlisted) companies relating to the appointment of a provisional administrator (claimed by minority shareholders or other stakeholders). An example is the situation where the daily management of a company had committed irregularities and wrongdoings.[42] A provisional administrator was also appointed in the cases where the board was unable to convene the general meeting or the board of directors, where there was an abuse of a majority or minority that upset the balance within the board or when it was necessary in order to avoid bankruptcy or mismanagement.[43]

C. *Claimants and procedure*

15. Any plaintiff with a sufficient interest or capacity may in theory request a provisional administrator (articles 17–18 of the Belgian Judicial Code).[44] Hence, a shareholder has the required capacity and interest. There are no thresholds in terms of share ownership.[45] This remedy is therefore also available for minority shareholders.

However, according to certain case law, a party cannot acquire a (minority) share with the intention to attack governance or acts predating its share ownership. In the well-known Fortis case, a plaintiff group sought the appointment of a provisional administrator over the bank with broad powers, including a right of veto. This claim was rejected by the court based on the reasoning that the action had a purely speculative nature ("lack of legitimate interest"). According to the court, the plaintiff could not acquire shares after the disputed acts *"with full knowledge of the facts [...] and the sole intention of participating in the proceedings: [...] that the mission of the courts is in no way to settle disputes that have been artificially created"*.[46]

16. An action for the appointment of a provisional administrator may be sought both in summary proceedings and as an interim measure in proceedings

---

[42] in vennootschappen en het wetboek van vennootschappen: de vlag dekt niet de lading", *TPR*, 2010, (1603) 1642.
Brussels 26 June 1995, *AJT*, 1995–96, 340; President of the Enterprise Court of Bruges 6 July 1981, *RW* 1982–83, 2781; President of the Enterprise Court Bruges 15 January 1982, *RW*, 1982–83, 2784; President of the Enterprise Court of. Liège 13 January 1986, *TBH*, 1987, 447; Enterprise Court of Veurne 16 October 1991, *TRV-RPS*, 1991, 532.
[43] J. Verhaert, "De voorlopige bewindvoerder" in X. (ed.), *Bestendig Handboek Vennootschap & Aansprakelijkheid*, Mechelen, Wolters Kluwer, 2017, (II.1–35) II.1–47.
[44] President of the Enterprise Court of Turnhout,16 July 2008, *RW*, 2009–10, 1266; H. Braeckmans, "Conflicten in vennootschappen en het wetboek van vennootschappen: de vlag dekt niet de lading", *TPR*, 2010, (1603) 1637; J. Verhaert, "De voorlopige bewindvoerder" in X (ed.), *Bestendig Handboek Vennootschap & Aansprakelijkheid*, Mechelen, Wolters Kluwer, 2017, (II.1–35) II.1–47.
[45] President of the Enterprise Court of Liege (Namur division) 16 October 2017, *TRV-RPS* 2018, 234; D. Van Gerven, *Handboek Vennootschappen*, Brussels, Larcier, 2020, 1137.
[46] President of the Enterprise Court of Brussels 20 November 2008, *TRV-RPS*, 2008, 686.

on the merits.[47] The claim must be brought against the company itself.[48] In exceptional cases, a provisional administrator can also be requested in summary proceedings by means of a unilateral petition (*ex parte* proceedings). A unilateral petition can only be accepted in case of absolute necessity, for example when a judgment is so urgent that an adversarial procedure, even with a shorter summons period (summary proceedings), is no longer possible[49], or when an adversarial procedure would impair the efficiency of the measure requested (in particular because of the effect of surprise).[50]

§3. AD HOC TRUSTEE

A. Basis and definition

17. The *ad hoc* trustee is a judicial agent appointed by the court to carry out a specific task within the company, e.g., convening a general shareholders meeting (with a specific agenda determined by the court), chairing a general meeting, finalising and filing the annual accounts, exercising certain veto rights, etc.[51]

The appointment of an *ad hoc* trustee is not published in the *Belgian State Gazette*.[52]

The BCCA contains no specific clauses dealing with an *ad hoc* trustee. The *ad hoc* trustee finds its origins in case law[53] and the broad powers granted to the President of the Court of Enterprises acting in summary proceedings[54] (article 584 of the Judicial Code).

---

[47] H. Braeckmans, "Conflicten in vennootschappen en het wetboek van vennootschappen: de vlag dekt niet de lading", *TPR*, 2010, Afl. 4, (1603) 1636.

[48] President of the Enterprise Court of. Brussels 31 January 2019, *TRV-RPS*, 4, 2019, 413, note A. Hanoteau, T. Sion.

[49] Cass. 8 December 2014, *RABG* 2015, 1224.

[50] President of the Enterprise Court of. Mechelen, 18 August 2000, *TRV-RPS*, 4, 2002, 317, note D. Blommaert.

[51] E. Janssens, "Maatregelen tegen het bestuur", in X. (ed.), *Bestendig Handboek Vennootschap & Aansprakelijkheid*, Mechelen, Wolters Kluwer, 2017, (II.1–52ak) II.1–52bj; D. Van Gerven, *Handboek vennootschappen*, Brussels, Larcier, 2020, 1146.

[52] H. Braeckmans and R. Houben, *Handboek vennootschapsrecht*, Antwerp, Intersentia, 2020, 752.

[53] H. Braeckmans, "Conflicten in vennootschappen en het wetboek van vennootschappen: de vlag dekt niet de lading", *TPR*, 4, 2010, (1603) 1653; T. Vandersmissen, "Het gerechtelijk sekwester en de lasthebber ad hoc" in H. Braeckmans (ed.), *De BV/SRL in de praktijk*, Mechelen, Wolters Kluwer, 2019, (WVV-I.6.2–1) WVV-I.6.2–14.

[54] H. Braeckmans and R. Houben, *Handboek vennootschapsrecht*, Antwerp, Intersentia, 2020, 751.

B. Conditions of appointment

18. The conditions under which an *ad hoc* trustee can be appointed are broadly the same as those for the appointment of a provisional administrator. Considering the less far-reaching powers of the *ad hoc* trustee, the balancing of interests will obviously be assessed less strictly. The appointment of an *ad hoc* trustee is therefore often requested in subsidiary order as a less drastic alternative to the provisional administrator.[55]

C. Claimants and procedure

19. As in the case of the provisional administrator, any claimant with sufficient interest and capacity[56] may request the appointment of an *ad hoc* trustee. This claim is therefore also open to the minority shareholder. No minimum share thresholds apply in this respect.

20. An ad hoc agent may be requested in proceedings on the merits, as well as in summary proceedings.[57] Again, it is possible to bring the action by unilateral petition if there is a situation of absolute necessity.[58]

§4. JUDICIAL SEQUESTER

A. Basis and definition

21. A sequester is entrusted with the custody of a property pending the outcome of a dispute.[59] This tool is often used in ownership disputes (to avoid selling of certain assets pending litigation). A sequester can also be useful for a minority shareholder who, for example, has serious indications that the company and its management intends to sell company assets under conditions contrary to the company's interest.

The sequester has no legal basis in the BCCA and finds its origins in case law and general principles of law.[60]

---

[55] Brussels 14 July 1995, *TRV-RPS*, 1995, 584; T. Vandersmissen, "Het gerechtelijk sekwester en de lasthebber ad hoc" in H. Braeckmans (ed.), *De BV/SRL in de praktijk*, Mechelen, Wolters Kluwer, 2019, (WVV-I.6.2–1) WVV-I.6.2–18.
[56] An interest in the sense of art. 17 and 18 Belgian Judicial Code.
[57] Art. 700 Belgian Judicial Code.
[58] Art. 584, third paragraph Belgian Judicial Code.
[59] H. Braeckmans and R. Houben, *Handboek vennootschapsrecht*, Antwerp, Intersentia, 2020, 754.
[60] E. Janssens, "Maatregelen tegen het bestuur" in X. (ed.), *Bestendig Handboek Vennootschap & Aansprakelijkheid*, Mechelen, Wolters Kluwer, 2017, (II.1–52ak) II.1–52bl; H. Braeckmans, "Conflicten in vennootschappen en het wetboek van vennootschappen: de vlag dekt niet de

Unlike the provisional administrator and the *ad hoc* trustee, the sequester has no broader powers. The sequester does not interfere with the management of the company.[61]

B. Material conditions

22. If the claim for a judicial sequester is made in summary proceedings, the conditions for summary proceedings apply, notably a situation of urgency, prima facie evidence, and a balance of interests weighing in favour of the claimant.[62]

Under these review criteria, the purely custodial nature of the measure will also be examined. A sequester may not exceed its duty as custodian to sell shares and consign the sale price. Generally speaking, the sequester should not be granted any power to dispose of assets.[63]

The sequestered property must be clearly defined. A sequester cannot be appointed to take custody of all the property of a company.[64]

C. Claimants and procedure

23. Any party with a legitimate interest can initiate a claim for the appointment of a judicial sequester.[65] There are no specific thresholds. Hence, this means of action is also available for a minority shareholder.

24. The procedure is similar to the one described above for the provisional administrator and the trustee, i.e. the procedure is contradictory. However, in the event of extreme urgency or if one seeks a specific effect of surprise (which is often necessary in the case of a sequestration to overcome the risk of removal), the action may be brought by way of a *ex parte* petition.[66]

---

lading", *TPR*, 2010, (1603) 1647; H. Braeckmans, "Conflicten in de vennootschap", *RW*, 2002-03, (1081) 1083.

[61] H. Braeckmans, "Conflicten in vennootschappen en het wetboek van vennootschappen: de vlag dekt niet de lading", *TPR*, 2010, (1603) 1648.

[62] B. Tilleman, "Bijzondere overeenkomsten C. Bruikleen, bewaargeving en sekwester" in X. (ed.), *Principles of Belgian Private Law*, Mechelen, Kluwer, 2000, 344–354.

[63] H. Braeckmans, "Conflicten in vennootschappen en het wetboek van vennootschappen: de vlag dekt niet de lading", *TPR*, 2010, (1603) 1649.

[64] Antwerp 22 June 2002, *NJW* 2003, 201; Antwerp 22 November 2001, *RW*, 2002–03, 1511; T. Vandersmissen, "Het gerechtelijk sekwester en de lasthebber ad hoc" in H. Braeckmans (ed.), *De BV/SRL in de praktijk*, Mechelen, Wolters Kluwer, 2019, (WVV-I.6.2–1) WVV-I.6.2–17.

[65] H. Braeckmans, "Conflicten in vennootschappen en het wetboek van vennootschappen: de vlag dekt niet de lading", *TPR*, 2010, (1603) 1648; T. Vandersmissen, "Het gerechtelijk sekwester en de lasthebber ad hoc" in H. Braeckmans (ed.), *De BV/SRL in de praktijk*, Mechelen, Wolters Kluwer, 2019, (WVV-I.6.2–1) WVV-I.6.2–20.

[66] Art. 584, third paragraph Belgian Judicial Code.

4. ACTIONS AGAINST MAJORITY DECISIONS OR VOTES

§1. BASIS AND DEFINITION

25. Every stakeholder may request the suspension (in summary proceedings) or nullity (in a procedure on the merits) of decisions made by the board of directors or shareholders. This is not limited to decisions of the general assembly; this action may also be directed against decisions made by other corporate bodies.

This legal instrument is also available to minority shareholders in listed companies who are aggrieved by a decision of the board or of the shareholders (controlled by the majority or reference shareholders).

26. Before the entry into force of the BCCA, only a legal framework relating to the nullity of decisions of the general meeting existed. The nullity of board decisions was not regulated.

Articles 2:42–2:48 of the BCCA provide a uniform regime concerning the nullity of decisions (*nietigheid/nullité*) of the general meeting, the company board and even individual votes. These articles stipulate, on the one hand, the grounds on which nullity can be claimed and, on the other hand, who is entitled to bring the claim. This procedure is of mandatory law, meaning that exemptions in shareholder agreements or company articles of association are not possible.[67]

§2. CONDITIONS OF IMPLEMENTATION

27. Article 2:42 BCCA stipulates the legal grounds on which a corporate resolution can be suspended or annulled.

In the same vein, article 2:43 BCCA provides for the possibility of having a vote annulled. If it is found that the votes that have been annulled influenced the decision-making process, the decision taken on the basis of these votes will also be annulled.[68]

The judge will always carry out his review with due restraint. After all, he may not substitute himself to the body that made the decision and render a judgment of expediency.[69]

---

[67] H. Braeckmans and R. Houben, *Handboek vennootschapsrecht*, Antwerp, Intersentia, 2020, 414.

[68] H. Jansen and S. Van Haute, "Nietigheid van besluiten van organen, van besluiten van de algemene vergadering van obligatiehouders en van stemmen" in H. Braeckmans (ed.), *De NV/SA in de praktijk*, Mechelen, Wolters Kluwer, 2019, (WVV-I.4.6–1) WVV-I.4.6.1–2; H. Braeckmans and R. Houben, *Handboek vennootschapsrecht*, Antwerp, Intersentia, 2020, 423.

[69] D. Van Gerven, *Handboek Vennootschappen*, Brussels, Larcier, 2020, 733; H. Braeckmans and R. Houben, *Handboek Vennootschapsrecht*, Antwerp, Intersentia, 2020, 415.

28. The first legal ground on which nullity can be claimed concerns the situation when the decision is defective in form[70], i.e., there are irregularities in the manner in which the decision was made. This may refer to how the meeting was convened, how the deliberation took place, etc.[71]

To successfully invoke this ground for nullity, the minority shareholder must show that the irregularity could have affected the deliberation or the vote.[72] For example, the minority shareholder will have to demonstrate that compliance with certain notice formalities that were ignored would have led to a different decision.[73] This is also known as the influence test. Because of this influence test, formal nullities are less likely to be a useful tool for minority shareholders in listed companies.

However, if the minority shareholder can prove that the formal irregularity was committed with fraudulent intent, it is not required that he/she proves that the formal irregularity affected the decision.[74] In that case, the decision is struck with nullity.

29. The second ground for nullity relates to decision-making that exceeds the competences of the corporate bodies or constitutes a misuse of their power.[75]

This ground for nullity involves a substantive test. The influence test does not come into play here.[76]

Among other things, there is an excess of competence if the company board of general meeting makes a decision that is not within its purview. Another example is the failure to respect legal or statutory majorities.[77]

A decision that is contrary to the corporate interest may also be annulled on this basis.[78] An exhaustive description of the notion of corporate interest is beyond the scope of this article. Importantly, however, the interests of minority shareholders can also fall under the notion of corporate interest.[79]

---

[70] Art. 2:42 1° BCCA.
[71] D. Van Gerven, *Handboek Vennootschappen*, Brussels, Larcier, 2020, 738.
[72] H. Jansen, S. Van Haute, ""Nietigheid van besluiten van organen, van besluiten van de algemene vergadering van obligatiehouders en van stemmen " in H. Braeckmans (ed.), *De NV/SA in de praktijk*, Mechelen, Wolters Kluwer, 2019, (WVV-I.4.6–1) WVV-I.4.6.1–4.
[73] Cass. 4 April 1975, *RCJB* 1977, 551; Kh. Dendermonde 24 April 2014, *JDSC.*, 2016, 77.
[74] D. Van Gerven, *Handboek Vennootschappen*, Brussels, Larcier, 2020, 742; Cass. 6 November 2002, *JT* 2003, 310.
[75] Art. 2:42 2° WVV.
[76] D. Van Gerven, *Handboek Vennootschappen*, Brussels, Larcier, 2020, 743.
[77] H. Jansen and S. Van Haute, "Nietigheid van besluiten van organen, van besluiten van de algemene vergadering van obligatiehouders en van stemmen" in H. Braeckmans (ed.), *De NV/SA in de praktijk*, Mechelen, Wolters Kluwer, 2019, (WVV-I.4.6–1) WVV-I.4.6.1–5.
[78] D. Van Gerven, *Handboek Vennootschappen*, Brussels, Larcier, 2020, 743.
[79] K. Byttebier and N. Sneyers, "Het voorlopig bewind en het vennootschap-, respectievelijk het ondernemingsbelang", *RW*, 2020–21, (562) 564; For an in-depth analysis of the notion corporate interest, see: A. François, *Het vennootschapsbelang in het Belgische vennootschapsrecht*, Antwerpen, Intersentia.

There is an abuse or diversion of power when the board or general meeting uses its competence irregularly, i.e., for a purpose other than the one for which it was granted.[80]

An abuse of law occurs if a voting right is manifestly used beyond the limits of the normal exercise of that right by a prudent and considerate or attentive shareholder or director.

The Fortis case[81] is a well-known example of a minority shareholder action against a decision of the board of a listed company. During the 2008 worldwide economic and financial crisis, the Fortis financial group was dismantled and the Belgian bank, Fortis Banque Belgique, was acquired by the Belgian state and then sold to BNP Paribas. Several minority shareholders of the Fortis group initiated summary proceedings to suspend the decision of the board of directors to transfer assets to Belgium and the Netherlands and to BNP Paribas. This case was based among others on the argument that the board of directors exceeded its competence. The court of appeal of Brussels, acting as summary judge in appeal, ruled on 12 December 2008 that the board of directors had violated the articles of association and the Fortis governance statement by not involving the general assembly despite this being required by the governance statement. In addition, the Court of Appeal considered the fact that several directors felt they had been subjected to unacceptable pressure from the government to reach a decision despite their objections. The question of whether the decisions were taken in the corporate interest was also brought up. The shareholders obtained the right to hold a general shareholders' meeting to allow them to voice their concerns about the proposed restructuring of the group, and to vote on it. Ultimately, a modified restructuring proposal was put forward and accepted by the shareholders.

30. The third ground for nullity involves the exercise of voting rights which were suspended based on provisions other than those mentioned in the BCCA.[82] This provision can only be successfully invoked if, without these votes, the attendance or majority quorum would not have been reached.[83] This nullity ground targets the shares of credit institutions whose voting rights were suspended by the supervisory authorities such as the NBB and the FSMA.[84]

---

[80] *Parl.St.* Kamer, Z. [1989/1990], No 1214/1, 34.
[81] Brussels 12 December 2008 (A. e.a. / Fortis, SFPI en BNP Paribas), *Bank Fin.R.*, 2008, 399.
[82] Art. 2:42 3° BCCA.
[83] H. Braeckmans and R. Houben, *Handboek Vennootschapsrecht*, Antwerp, Intersentia, 2020, 422; D. Van Gerven, *Handboek Vennootschappen*, Brussels, Larcier, 2020, 747; H. Jansen and S. Van Haute, ""Nietigheid van besluiten van organen, van besluiten van de algemene vergadering van obligatiehouders en van stemmen" in H. Braeckmans (ed.), *De NV/SA in de praktijk*, Mechelen, Wolters Kluwer, 2019, (WVV-I.4.6–1) WVV-I.4.6.1–5.
[84] D. Van Gerven, *Handboek Vennootschappen*, Brussels, Larcier, 2020, 747.

31. As a fourth and final ground for nullity, the minority shareholder may invoke all other grounds for nullity stipulated elsewhere in the BCCA.[85] To use this ground for nullity, the plaintiff does not have to prove that this irregularity affected the decision-making process.[86]

32. In addition to the grounds of nullity based on Article 2:42 BCCA, decisions or votes can also be declared null and void based on the general legal grounds for nullity (in particular defects in consent, violation of public order and morality, etc.).

§3. CLAIMANTS AND PROCEDURE

33. Article 2:44, §1 of the BCCA mentions two types of claimants. On the one hand, anyone who has an interest in complying with the legal rule that was violated can claim nullity (or suspension). On the other hand, the company itself can also bring the nullity claim, as it is always deemed to have an interest. The plaintiff's interest must be reasonable. In other words, the plaintiff must show that he or she suffers a disadvantage because of the decision.[87] It follows that minority shareholders have a legitimate interest in pursuing nullity or suspension. However, third parties, such as creditors or employees, are not deemed to have an interest.[88] An aggrieved creditor can only bring the nullity action by way of a collateral claim or an *actio pauliana* if the conditions for such proceedings are met.[89]

A request for the annulment of an individual vote, can only be initiated by a shareholder or the company itself.[90]

Plaintiffs who voted in favour of the contested decision persons or who have expressly or tacitly waived their right to invoke nullity thereof, cannot claim the nullity at a later stage, unless their consent was defective.[91]

It is important to note that (minority) shareholders are not in a position to claim the nullity of resolutions passed at the meeting of bondholders.[92]

---

[85] Art. 2:42 4° BCCA.
[86] H. Braeckmans and R. Houben, *Handboek Vennootschapsrecht*, Antwerp, Intersentia, 2020, 422.
[87] Brussels 8 July 1954, *TRV-RPS*, 1955, no 4514, 285; H. Jansen and S. Van Haute, "Nietigheid van besluiten van organen, van besluiten van de algemene vergadering van obligatiehouders en van stemmen" in H. Braeckmans (ed.), *De NV/SA in de praktijk*, Mechelen, Wolters Kluwer, 2019, (WVV-I.4.6-1) WVV-I.4.6.1-8.
[88] *Parl.St.* Kamer, 2017–18, no. 3119/001, 54–55.
[89] *Parl.St.* Kamer, 2017–18, no. 3119/001, 54–55.
[90] Art. 2:43 second paragraph BCCA.
[91] Art. 2:44 second paragraph BCCA; Gent 30 September 2013, *RW* 2014–15, 1629.
[92] Art. 2:44 third paragraph BCCA.

34. The action for nullity must be brought against the legal entity itself[93] before the Enterprise Court in the district where the company seat is located.[94]

In urgent cases, the minority shareholder may, in addition to the nullity claim before the judge ruling on the merits of the case, also claim the provisional suspension of the disputed decision in summary proceedings before the President of the Enterprise Court. The President of the Enterprise Court can only rule upon the case provided that the claim for suspension is urgent, the minority shareholder proves that the decision *in prima facie* in breach with above-mentioned provisions of the BCCA and the balance of interests weighs in favour of the minority shareholder.

These summary proceedings are in principle conducted on a contradictory basis. However, in cases of extreme urgency, a claimant could file an *ex parte* motion awaiting the further outcome of the contradictory summary procedure or the procedure on the merits of the case.[95]

35. Claims for nullity or suspension of corporate decisions should be brought before the competent court within six months as from the day on which the decisions are legally deemed to be opposable against the claimant (for example, the publication of the decision in the Belgian State Gazette) or from the day on which the plaintiff became aware of the decision.[96] This limitation period cannot be suspended or interrupted.[97]

Furthermore, the action for nullity is also no longer possible when a regularisation has already taken place.[98]

5. LIABILITY CLAIMS – THE DERIVATIVE ACTION

§1. BASIS AND DEFINITION

36. Shareholders can hold the directors accountable for their wrongdoings or negligence by means of a director's liability claim (or *actio mandati*). The *actio mandati* is decided upon by the general shareholders' meeting by a simple majority vote unless the company statutes provide otherwise. A director's liability claim is initiated by the company itself.

---

[93] Art. 2:45 BCCA.
[94] Art. 2:44 first paragraph of the BCCA, in conjunction with art. 628, 13° Belgian Judicial Code.
[95] D. Van Gerven, *Handboek Vennootschappen*, Brussels, Larcier, 2020, 734.
[96] Art. 2:143 §3 second paragraph BCCA.
[97] Gent 26 October 2015, *NJW*, 2017, 363; H. Braeckmans and R. Houben, *Handboek Vennootschapsrecht*, Antwerp, Intersentia, 2020, 422.
[98] H. Jansen and S. Van Haute, "Nietigheid van besluiten van organen, van besluiten van de algemene vergadering van obligatiehouders en van stemmen" in H. Braeckmans (ed.), *De NV/SA in de praktijk*, Mechelen, Wolters Kluwer, 2019, (WVV-I.4.6–1) WVV-I.4.6.1–9.

However, it is possible that a company may not litigate if a wrong has been done, for example: (i) where the directors are themselves responsible for the wrongdoing; or (ii) the minority shareholders cannot execute sufficient voting power at a general meeting to compel the directors to institute proceedings.[99]

Hence, the BCCA provides for the possibility for minority shareholder for initiating a derivative action. This is essentially the same claim as the director's liability claim but introduced by minority shareholders for the benefit of the company.[100]

As previously mentioned, there is a close link between the derivative action and the examination by a court expert (in corporate litigation matters), a procedure which is usually initiated prior to it.[101] The BCCA lists the companies in which this action is possible and the necessary thresholds to bring them.

The derivative action can only be launched against the directors of the NV/SA (Art. 7:157–159 of the BCCA), the BV/SRL (Art. 5:104–105 of the BCCA) and the CV/SC (Art. 6:89–90 of the BCCA). The derivative action is not available against executive board members in a NV/SA with a two-tier board structure.

§2. APPLICATION CRITERIA

37. A derivative claim (or derivative action) is a claim initiated by a shareholder or group of shareholders to the benefit of the company in relation to a breach of duty or wrongdoing by a director. This procedure is necessary as a director owes duties to the company and not to the shareholders.

38. Prior to the entry into force of the BCCA, there were few examples in the published case law of derivative actions.

The recent examples in case law are from a factual viewpoint comparable as those where the minority shareholders seek an expert report (see title 2). As discussed, the expert report serves as a prelude to a derivative action. The case law covers situations whereby the company's interests are at stake due to director's wrongdoings or negligence. It may cover acts or omissions relating to the policy, operation of the bodies or companies accounts, or consist of eroding the substance of the company for the benefit of another person or company.

---

[99] H. Braeckmans and R. Houben, *Handboek Vennootschapsrecht*, Antwerp, Intersentia, 2020, 336; F. Voet, "The minority claim: the sacred goal without means", *TRV-RPS*, 2019, no. 3, 257.
[100] F. Voet, "De Minderheidsvordering: het heilig doel zonder middelen," *TRV-RPS*, 2019, 256.
[101] To that effect, President of the Enterprise Court of Antwerp (Antwerp Division), sitting in summary proceedings, 2 July 2021, *TRV-RPS*, 2022, no. 5, 438–446; President of the Enterprise Court of Antwerp (Antwerp Division), sitting in summary proceedings, 9 November 2021, *TRV-RPS*, 2022, no. 5, 447–458.

§3. CLAIMANTS AND PROCEDURE

39. The initiation of a derivative action is subject to two conditions. On the one hand, several threshold requirements apply, and on the other hand, this claim is not possible for shareholders who voted in favour of a discharge for the director(s) involved.

40. The minimum thresholds for initiating a derivative action are the same ones as those required for the appointment of a court expert (in corporate litigation matters).

Minority shareholders in a BV/SRL holding at least 10 per cent of shares issued on the day when the annual general meeting decides to grant discharge (*kwijting/décharge*) to the directors may file a derivative for the benefit of the company against the directors.

Minority shareholders in an NV/SA have the same right to bring such claim if they, on the day when the annual general meeting decides to grant discharge to the directors, hold securities representing at least 1 per cent of the votes attached to all the securities existing on that day, or hold securities representing the capital of at least EUR 1.250.000.

The minority shareholders who wish to bring an action on behalf of the NV/SA must unanimously appoint a special proxyholder, who does not have to be a shareholder (art. 7:158 of the BCCA). In a BV/SRL, the minority shareholder does not need to appoint a special proxyholder to file the minority claim.

The reference date for evaluating these thresholds is the date on which the shareholders' meeting decides on the discharge from liability of the board of directors' members and the statutory auditors.[102]

If at a later stage after the valid initiation of a derivate action the threshold is no longer met (because certain shareholders withdraw their claim or have sold their shares), this does not affect the admissibility and continuation of the derivate action.[103]

41. The second condition is that no discharge should have been granted by the minority shareholders. This requires that the minority shareholders voted against, abstained, were absent or invalidly approved the discharge.[104] However, the discharge granted by the minority shareholders does not exclude a liability claim when the discharge was not granted with sufficient knowledge of affairs

---

[102] H. Braeckmans, "Conflicten in vennootschappen en het wetboek van vennootschappen: de vlag dekt niet de lading", *TPR*, 2010, 1627.
[103] Art. 7:157 §2 BCCA.
[104] Art. 7:157 §1, second paragraph WVV; S. De Geyter, "Court of Cassation, 18 June 2021, C.19.0255.N", *TRV-RPS*, 2022, no. 2, 99.

or when the discharge relates only to the closed financial year, and not to the alleged director wrongdoings thereafter.[105]

A point of attention is the issue of the proof of non-approval of the discharge.[106] Minority shareholders should always have their voting behaviour recorded in the minutes to provide evidence of this second condition.[107]

42. Since the derivative action is initiated to the benefit the company, the proceeds of the claim – the compensation obtained from the directors – accrue in full to the company.[108] The minority shareholder only benefits indirectly from a derivative action as a result of the restored value of his shares.

However, the same is not true for the costs. The applicant of a derivative action must advance the procedural costs when it files the action (art. 7:159 of the BCCA). If the derivative action is dismissed, the minority shareholders may be personally condemned to pay the procedural costs and damages to the defendants (if there are grounds for ordering it). Hence, the benefits of the derivative action are spread, but not the costs and risk.[109]

6. JUDICIAL DISSOLUTION

§1. INTRODUCTION AND LEGAL BASIS

43. Under normal circumstances a company is dissolved following a decision of the general meeting of shareholders (voluntary dissolution). However, a company can also be dissolved following a court order (judicial dissolution).

The judicial dissolution is regulated in article 2:73 of the BCCA. For companies without legal personality, article 4:17 §2 of the BCCA is also relevant.

Considering that this procedure has major consequences for the company and may result in the dissolution and liquidation of the company, it is a measure of subsidiary nature, meaning that judicial dissolution can only be granted if no less far-reaching remedies are available. Therefore, the courts handle this legal instrument with great caution.

The procedure of judicial dissolution is of mandatory law and therefore cannot be contractually restricted or excluded.

---

[105] President of the Enterprise Court of Antwerp (division Antwerp), 23 September 2022, *TPR-RPS*, 2022, 684.
[106] H. Braeckmans, "Conflicten in vennootschappen en het wetboek van vennootschappen: de vlag dekt niet de lading", TPR 2010,1628.
[107] H. Braeckmans and R. Houben, *Handboek Vennootschapsrecht*, Antwerp, Intersentia, 2020, 338.
[108] F. Voet, "De minderheidsvordering: het heilig doel zonder middelen", *TRV-RPS*, 2019, 257.
[109] F. Voet, "De minderheidsvordering: het heilig doel zonder middelen", *TRV-RPS*, 2019, 257.

§2. APPLICATION CRITERIA

44. A company may be dissolved for legitimate reasons. According to articles 2:73 and 4:17 §2 of the BCCA, legitimate reasons refer to the following situations: (i) gross breach by a shareholder of his/her obligations; (ii) illness which makes it impossible for a shareholder to fulfil his/her obligations; and also (iii) any situation which renders the normal continuation of the company impossible, such as a profound and permanent disagreement between the shareholders.

In the absence of other workable remedies, a minority shareholder could consider this procedure in case of, *inter alia*, a continuous violation of the corporate interest by the majority shareholder[110] or an abuse of majority where the minority is systematically oppressed by the majority.

45. In addition, the BCCA provides that any party (hence also a minority shareholder) may claim the dissolution of a NV/SA before court if the value of the net assets has fallen below the EUR 61.500 (i.e. the minimum amount of capital). However, the judge may grant the company an additional period to regularise its situation.

§3. CLAIMANTS AND PROCEDURE

46. Article 2:73 of the BCCA stipulates that an action for judicial dissolution can be brought by a shareholder or partner. This claim can therefore also be pursued by a minority shareholder. Of course, the court will always weigh the interests of the parties involved.

This claim is not allowed for third parties (such as employees, creditors, etc.).

The claim is brought against the company and not against the shareholders. However, it is appropriate to include the shareholders, with whom there is a conflict situation, in the proceedings.

The president of the commercial court of the territory in which the company has its registered office, acting as if it were a summary procedure. The latter means that it concerns a procedure on the merits, however, conducted in accordance with the procedural rules applicable to summary proceedings.

7. CONCLUSION

47. The BCCA provides a series of mechanisms that enable minority shareholders to enforce their rights in both listed and unlisted companies.

---

[110] J. Lievens, "De wettelijke bescherming van de minderheidsaandeelhouder", *TRV,* 1988, 52.

Nonetheless the (published) case law on shareholder activism in listed companies is rather limited. Several explanatory factors must be taken into account from a legal viewpoint.

The shareholder structure of listed companies is a first element which could help explain this phenomenon. Large Belgian companies often have large shareholders, groups of shareholders, or reference shareholders that effectively control the company on the one hand and a very fragmented minority shareholdership on the other hand. These large shareholders can strongly influence the appointment of directors and determine corporate policy. This then seems to discourage minority shareholders, who are often less organised, from seeking relief in court.

Another important factor is related to the litigation costs. As discussed under the chapters in relation to the expert report and derivative action, minority shareholders have to advance the costs of proceeding. In the best case scenario, the minority shareholders obtain a refund of the procedural costs incurred and their share value is recovered. In the worst case scenario, the minority shareholders are liable for the procedural costs and damages. The trade-off between risk and return does not always plead in favour of shareholder activism in court.

Litigation funding could be of assistance to minority shareholders seeking relief. However, minority shareholders cannot, at least according to certain case law, proceed on purely speculative motives which creates a hurdle for litigation funders. One could of course argue that this case law goes against the stock market philosophy.

The following years will demonstrate whether the modified rules in the BCCA are a game-changer in terms of minority shareholder activism in the Belgian courtroom.

SHAREHOLDER ACTIVISM IN BELGIUM: WHAT IS AWAITING US?[*]

Marieke WYCKAERT
Professor of company law, Jan Ronse Institute of Company and Financial law, University of Leuven.

1. *The traditional disclaimer* – The few thoughts below are based on the reflections I made during the closing panel debate of the Conference organized by the VBO/FBE and the Jean-Pierre Blumberg Chair (UAntwerpen) on 9 June 2022 on shareholder activism in listed companies in Belgium. While the opinions expressed here are my responsibility alone, I am very grateful to all speakers, including my two co-panelists Xavier Dieux and Thierry L'Homme: their contributions have enriched my own thoughts.

2. *Nothing new under the sun* – Shareholder activism is far from being a novelty in Belgium. It has undoubtedly been given a more fashionable name. As is the case with most phenomena, it is a not static but a dynamic phenomenon, and it has showed and still is showing different appearances. It has surely been impacted by the internationalization of the shareholding in Belgian listed companies. But it has been there since long.

To demonstrate my point: the following persons (in alphabetical order) were, only a few decades ago, the epigons of active and critical shareholders, not all of whom were necessarily very successful in achieving meaningful goals: André de Barsy (Electrabel, Punch International, Copeba, Schneider)[1], Philippe Delville (Tractebel, Electrabel)[2], Benito Francesconi[3], and Erik Geenen (NBB[4], Fortis, Dexia, KBC, Electrabel).[5] Even now, we are talking of very different profiles. All of them were (or are) natural persons, mostly owning a very limited

---
[*] Small change in the title, as it better reflects my thoughts. I have handed in this contribution on 23 December 2022, but life goes on. I have not fully updated the contents as per June 2023, as I believe the essence of what I wrote is still standing, but I have made minor amendments here and there.
[1] Https://www.standaard.be/cnt/gv5k37bf.
[2] Https://www.standaard.be/cnt/gv5k3fno.
[3] Https://www.standaard.be/cnt/gv5k3fnm.
[4] Http://nbb4ever.blogspot.com/.
[5] Https://www.standaard.be/cnt/gv5k3fnq.

shareholding; some of them sought allies, some of them acted as lone crusaders. Some of them were closer to anecdotal folklore than to the reality, others were sharp and to-the-point and asked relevant questions to directors. They often focused – and some still do – on one specific company (group), and were or are mostly personally rather heavily involved in the struggle against this company (group). Their struggles were and are financial in nature only. Some of them are almost forgotten today, other are still active.

There is another Belgian example, starting in 1990, showing that shareholder activism has been part of our culture since a while: in that year Deminor was founded by a Belgian listed private equity investor.[6] This advisory firm (not a law firm, nor a fund, nor a proxy advisor) is a good example of a totally different approach to shareholder activism: based on a commercial business model, aiming at generating financial gains for those either actively practicing it (see below, nr. 3), or for consultants assisting frustrated shareholders. It has since long expanded its activities to business of the same kind in other jurisdictions, as well as other types of similar business (sometimes using other legal entities) and seems to be faring well. Around the same period, also some law firms started to systematically focus on this business, with more, less and/or temporary success.[7]

One should also name major Belgian cases involving listed companies, where either physical or legal persons, shareholders' advisors (be it the Deminor approach or legal assistance by attorneys) and/or investment funds induced discussion, change of plans, the departure of CEOs, transactions, and sometimes litigation. Some have already been mentioned (Tractebel-Electrabel, Fortis, NBB, Arco-Dexia, Cera-KBC), but there were others (e.g., Barco[8], Picanol I[9] and Picanol II[10]).

3. *Is shareholder activism today fundamentally different?* – The individuals mentioned under nr. 2 are not those corporate lawyers may first be thinking

---

[6] Namely Deficom (then Definance), that sold its take to the Deminor partners in 2003: see https://sgs.deminor.com/en/why-deminor/history/.

[7] Well known are, arbitrarily chosen among others, Mischaël Modrikamen, Robert Wtterwulghe, Laurent Arnaults and Geert Lenssens. This does not mean that other law firms are not assisting active shareholders, but these attorneys are clearly focusing on this type of cases. In some instances, they actively seek clientele; in other cases, they are approached by shareholders.

[8] This case is particularly worth mentioning, as it concerns a case of purely moral indignation by an activist shareholder against the contribution of Barco to the weapon industry (Commercial Court Ieper 17 May 1999, *TRV*, 1999, 543, note; *V&F*, 1999, 247; Court of Appeal Ghent 18 April 2002, *TRV* 2002, 255, note; see also P. Baert, "Standpunt – 'En hoe gaat het met uw wapenproductie?' – Bedenkingen bij het vraagrecht van de aandeelhouders, naar aanleiding van de Barco-zaak".

[9] Https://www.standaard.be/cnt/gg6dcqqh.

[10] See https://www.standaard.be/cnt/dmf20160307_02168856. In this case Berkshire Hathaway was the initiator of the – financially driven – protest, supported by proxy-advisor ISS.

of when they consider shareholder activism today. Such individuals were (and a few of them still are) mostly active at a time where Belgian listed companies still largely knew their shareholders, including the then still numerous and often Belgian retail shareholders. Meanwhile, retail shareholders massively invest through funds, which drastically reduces the chances that they will militate directly against companies. Furthermore, with the professionalization and the systematic opening of European financial markets to international investors promoted by Europe, Belgian companies have seen drastic changes in their functioning and in their shareholding.[11] The Belgian listed company's annual meeting less and less became a gathering of shareholders and more and more a professional event. Shareholder activism professionalized alongside these developments, and has become a source of business itself, not only for Belgian but also for international players. While Deminor advises shareholders, certain funds seek direct gain by activating as a shareholder, and pick their investments to that end.

Of course, in Belgium, as elsewhere, it can continue to happen that shareholders, though not making it a business to seek financial gain through activism, are simply confronted with an undue attack on their rights. Evidently, they can and should take action in such a case. One may call this shareholder activism as well, but it is coincidental in nature, and not structural.

4. *After all, Belgium is a small country* – So shareholders activism is not new, but hardly big business in Belgium (yet?). It seems that Belgian listed companies have until now been relatively spared from this systematic and structural activism, at least to the extent they come in the open.[12] My best guess is that no Belgian funds focusing on shareholder activism exists, and that that is not prone to change quickly. Also, I do not think that foreign activists will flood Belgium. An explanation may lie in the small market share of Belgian listed entities in international investment possibilities, and in the still largely prevalent concentrated shareholding model in the Belgian context, as well as in the relatively substantial presence of (at least partially) Belgian anchoring shareholders. For any non-Belgian fund or proxy advisor to make the investment in launching a fight, necessitating at least a basic knowledge and understanding of local company law, culture and available tools, there must at least be sufficient potential gains to be made. The smaller the company an activist may be aiming

---

[11] Though Belgian companies, due to their relatively small size, still have a substantial Belgian (indirect) shareholding: see https://www.nbb.be/nl/blog/belgische-aandelen-minder-buitenlands-dan-het-lijkt-nl.

[12] Though again, one should mention cases such as Lucerne's attacks on Telenet (https://www.tijd.be/ondernemen/telecom/Telenet-aandeelhouder-Liberty-Global-dreigt-ons-af/10022417), or the current struggle around Nyrstar (https://www.tijd.be/dossiers/de-verdieping/stoet-rechtszaken-rond-nyrstar-bereikt-cruciaal-kruispunt/10424933.html). It may not be a coincidence that both companies have non-Belgian controlling shareholders.

at, the slimmer the chance that such investment is worth it. On top of that, controlling (or at least) reference shareholders also keep an eye on the directors and the management. The disadvantage of this is the risk of entrenchment by such shareholders, but Belgium has introduced conflict-of-interest rules for controlling shareholders dealing with listed companies and their subsidiaries since 2001, and I have had the impression since a long time that, generally speaking, these rules have functioned quite well, again to the extent visible. I refrain for the time being my judgment on the efficiency of the changes necessitated to these rules by SRD II, as it is too early to say whether they will have a substantial impact on the corporate culture in this respect.

And finally – and this is by no means positive – the slowness of the Belgian judicial system may not encourage structural activism either. Dogs can bark a couple of times, first privately and then out in the open, but if the aggressed party is not impressed, the dog will either have to withdraw, or bite. Biting usually means going to court. Going to court when it may take a very long time to obtain a judgment, is not encouraging the step from barking to biting. Nevertheless, litigation can be a weapon, and threatening with litigation an even more efficient one. Listed companies highly care about reputation and prefer to use their energy and resources for their business, not to fight. To avoid misunderstandings, we did have and still have quite a few shareholders litigation cases where the litigation came mostly after the facts, and where the plaintiffs were not in a position to exercise any pressure to change those facts. As mentioned above, they can be related, but one should not assimilate shareholder litigation with shareholder activism (nr. 3).

5. *Do advisors generate activism?* – While I do not believe that advisors to shareholders are able to massively trigger shareholders activism, they undoubtedly encourage it when being consulted, and it is fair to assume that their mere existence entails that shareholders who think they may have a case, will more easily consult them, as well that they can trigger a consultation by publicly communicating about some corporate events. In taking the decision to pursue a lead a commercial advisor is certainly prone to more own risk taking than attorneys, and therefore possibly more selective. On the other hand, attorneys often only intervene after the harm is purportedly done and need to invest time and reputation. It therefore seems likely that advisors will facilitate and support shareholders activism, but that they will rarely create it.

6. *What do activists really care about? Still "All about the money"?*[13] – Of course, shareholders activism can be caused by a very wide range of triggers, and in the current challenging times ESG-related triggers are gaining in importance. It is high time. But let us not yet fool ourselves: if shareholder activists invest in

---

[13] After Meja: https://www.youtube.com/watch?v=cXd155v8Z5U.

battles, their main triggers today are still mostly financial in nature. Undoubtedly ESG-related elements are thrown in, but there is massive greenwashing in the mainstream. It remains to be seen whether the impressive legal roll-out of the European Green Deal will lead to a rapprochement between the financial triggers and the urgently needed triggers for stopping or at least limiting climate change, increasing worldwide social justice, and better distributing the earth's wealth. The time will – too soon – come that such rapprochement will have become inevitable, but we are not there yet, and hopefully humankind will still be in a position then to keep the earth viable for as many people as possible. On a personal sidenote, current tendencies do not give reason to be very optimistic: the war in Ukraine has caused a massive switch of investors into fossil energy.[14] QED.

In his 2022 Letter to the CEO's[15], the famous Larry Fink, Chairman CEO of mastodont investment fund Blackrock, is clear about earning money as the major trigger for determining investment policies: *"Stakeholder capitalism is not about politics. It is not a social or ideological agenda. It is not "woke." It is capitalism, driven by mutually beneficial relationships between you and the employees, customers, suppliers, and communities your company relies on to prosper. This is the power of capitalism"*. But he is also touching upon the need to end the discord between money and viability of our planet: *"we focus on sustainability not because we're environmentalists, but because we are capitalists and fiduciaries to our clients"*. One cannot but help noticing that his starting point remains that in the end, investors should earn money.[16] I tend to think that this is still fully the case today for the average activist shareholder: their core business is not to make a better place of this world, so they should not pretend it is.[17] I have seen activists switching positions because more money could be made at the side it was originally fighting against. And when a professional intermediary is placed between the company and the shareholder, there is one

---

[14] Https://www.standaard.be/cnt/dmf20221027_97653715. See also the recent decision of Shell to switch to the (more profit generating fuel industries (https://www.standaard.be/cnt/dmf20230608_96544557).

[15] Https://www.blackrock.com/corporate/investor-relations/larry-fink-ceo-letter.

[16] Things may indeed start to change, see e.g. https://www.abp.nl/over-abp/duurzaam-en-verantwoord-beleggen/ons-standpunt.aspx; https://www.kbc.com/content/dam/kbccom/doc/sustainability-responsibility/PerfRep/2021/csr-sr-2021.pdf?zone=.

[17] I could not help but noticing that gender nor race diversity are at the forefront of activist Bluebell's concerns. In this respect it remains to be seen to which extent greenwashing and marketing-driven ESG will come to the surface under the new transparency rules for proxy-advisors (art. 7:146/1 CCA), pension funds (art. 95 of the Law of 6 October 2006), UCITS (art. 224 a.f. of the Act of 3 August 2012), AIFs and AIFMs (art. 72 a.f. of the Act of 19 April 2014), banks (art. 75/1 a.f. of the Bank Act), insurance companies (art. 101/1 of the Insurance Act), and the like (based on SRD II).

level more to convince that it may be wise to consider other factors than financial return, all the more since those intermediaries also have to make a living.[18]

This is not the place to open the very lively debate on shareholders' or stakeholders' rights, or on the social responsibility of – especially – listed companies, in times where, in the very first place, the legislatures should be courageous and set the rules directly. But Larry Fink is probably right: in the end, the concern for the viability of the earth and even more of the people on earth will coincide with (reasonable) profits for shareholders. Still, we have to get there.

In the meanwhile, we can be certain to expect a worldwide surge in activism for the climate, for social justice, for human rights, and large companies are coming more and more under siege by these activists. I also believe we will see a surge of (proper) NGOs pursuing this type of activism, not driven by profit but by results. Let them do their work, but it will be of a different nature and lead to different results.

7. *Keep talking* – It sounds like a platitude, but it is not: companies and shareholders should under all circumstances try to keep talking to each other, as of the moment a shareholder believes he has an important message to convey, still when they are publicly opposing one another, and even when that happens in court. Yes, there will be cases where such discussions are in vain, useless, or a loss of time. Yes, there will be cases where the activist shareholder only wants to exercise pressure, or even worse, intends to blackmail. And there will be cases where the company and the shareholder are not able to even listen to each other, or have nothing to say to each other. But I firmly believe that there are more cases where discussions will lead to a reasonable solution, albeit a compromise. Supervisory authorities, intermediaries and advisors should under all circumstance support and facilitate such discussions. This is becoming more and more difficult and at the same time important in an increasingly polemizing environment where all opinions can be uttered and shared worldwide in an instance.

8. *Benediction or curse?* – I do not think it is possible to take a general stance pro or contra shareholder activism as such. It exists, and there is no doubt that all shareholders are fully entitled to voice concerns. Also, it depends: there are surely cases where the critical voices of shareholders have avoided or reduced losses in value; likewise, there are surely cases where shareholder activism

---

[18] In this respect it remains to be seen to which extent greenwashing and marketing-driven ESG concerns will come to the surface under the new transparency rules for proxy-advisors (art. 7:146/1 CCA), pension funds (art. 95 of the Law of 6 October 2006), UCITS (art. 224 a.f. of the Act of 3 August 2012), AIFs and AIFMs (art. 72 a.f. of the Act of 19 April 2014), banks (art. 75/1 a.f. of the Banking Act), insurance companies (art. 101/1 of the Insurance Act), and the like (based on SRD II).

led to value destruction. And there may be cases where it was unfortunate that there were no activists keeping an eye on the company, its controlling or reference shareholders, its directors and its management. I am not tempted to believe that the relative absence of shareholders activism in the Belgian context makes the Brussels financial market into a better or a worse one compared to the other financial markets. I do not think the legislator and/or the market itself should proactively encourage or discourage shareholders activism as such. Instead, the focus should be on a reasonable overall balance between the rights of all stakeholders in a listed company in all circumstances, and, if need be, a correction of these rules if practice shows that the balance is lost. Rules on proxy solicitation[19] were introduced in Belgian law at the end of last century before there was one single case of such solicitation, and as far as I am aware today there still is none. The facilitation of minority shareholders' involvement in the general meeting by making it easier to ask questions or add items to the agenda of a meeting that has already been convened[20] is under all circumstances a good idea, even if the results may be rather disappointing up to now.[21]

In short: shareholders activism is a fact listed companies have to deal with, whatever form it takes. It has existed and will continue to exist, and it is not by itself good or bad. Going public in a globalized world has consequences: dealing with activist shareholders, whatever their motives and background, is one of them.

---

[19] Art. 7:145 CCA.
[20] Art. 7:139 and art. 7:130 CCA, (partially) based on SRD I.
[21] V. Verheyden, "When shareholders use their rights to convene meetings and to submit proposals – A comparative and empirical analysis of activism in four EU Member States, *TRV-RPS*, 2020, 975.